About the Author

James R. Lewis has worked as a professional astrologer for over two decades. Among astrologers, he is best known for his innovative work on Babylonian astrology and on the astrological significance of the planetary moons.

Having completed his graduate work in religious studies at the University of North Carolina, Chapel Hill, Lewis has an extensive background in history, psychology, philosophy, and comparative religion. He has contributed to the *New Age Almanac, Religious Leaders of America,* and *The Churches Speak* series.

Dr. Lewis is a world recognized authority on non-traditional religious movements. He is the editor of the only academic journal dedicated to alternative religions, and has been called in as a media consultant on such cult-related events as the 1993 crisis at the Branch Davidian community outside of Waco, Texas.

THE
ASTROLOGY
ENCYCLOPEDIA

T H E
ASTROLOGY
ENCYCLOPEDIA

JAMES R. LEWIS

VISIBLE
INK
PRESS

DETROIT   WASHINGTON, D.C.   LONDON

THE ASTROLOGY ENCYCLOPEDIA

Published by **Visible Ink Press**™
a division of Gale Research Inc.
835 Penobscot Bldg.
Detroit MI 48226-4094

Visible Ink Press is a trademark of Gale Research Inc.

ISBN 0-8103-9460-X

Cover and Page Design: Mary Krzewinski
Cover Art: Andreas Cellarius (Dutch)
From: Atlas Coelestis seu Harmonia Macrocosmica, 1660
Rare Book and Special Collections Division
Library of Congress

Printed in the United States of America

$42.95   133.503

For my partner and wife Eve who originally inspired this project, and without whose support this book might never have been completed.

The stars say you'll also find these books intriguing...

UNEXPLAINED!

347 Strange Sightings, Incredible Occurrences, and Puzzling Physical Phenomena

Unexplained! lets you investigate some of humankind's most extraordinary and baffling phenomena. You'll examine the possibilities, review existing evidence, read eyewitness accounts and draw your own conclusions. Author Jerome Clark, Vice President of the J. Allen Hynek Center for UFO Studies, provides photos, illustrations and sources for further reading.
$14.95

> "Ample fascinating reading... Buy *Unexplained!*, it's a winner!"
> — *The Gate*

NEW AGE ALMANAC

Probe the personalities and explore events that have shaped (and continue to shape) the New Age movement — from altered states to vegetarianism, astrology to yoga, the Age of Aquarius to vibrations from space. Nationally recognized author, lecturer and scholar J. Gordon Melton has compiled more than 300 in-depth definitions, descriptions and biographical sketches. Also: hundreds of addresses, phone numbers and suggestions for further reading.
$16.95

> "The most thorough coverage to date of New Age concepts and personalities."
> — *Spectrum Review*

VISIBLE INK PRESS

To order, call: 1-800-776-6265

Contents

Hekate   Heliacal   Helio   Heliocentric Astrology
Hemisphere   Hera   Herschel
Hesperus   Hestia   Hidalgo
Hindu Astrology   Hipparchus
History of Astrology in America
History of Western Astrology
Homosexuality and Astrology
Honoria   Hopi   Horary Astrology
Horary Time   Horizon
Horizon System   Horoscope   Horus   Hot
Hours   Houses   Huberta   Human Signs
Humanistic Astrology   Humors   Hurtful Signs
Hygiea   Hyleg   Hypothetical Planets

Iatromathematics   Icarus   Immersion
Impeded   Imum Coeli   Inception   Inclination
Industria   Inferior Conjunctions
Inferior Planets   Influence
Infortunes   Ingress   Intercepted
Isis

Jeff Jawer   Charles A. Jayne, Jr.
L. Edward Johndro
Marc Edmund Jones   Jones Patterns
Jubilatrix   Judicial Astrology
Julian Day   Carl Jung   Juno
Jupiter   Justitia

Kassandra   Katababazon   Katharsis
Johannes Kepler   Kite   Koch House System
Walter A. Koch   Bradley Wayne Kochunas
Kolisko Effect   Karl Ernst Krafft   Kronos

Lacrimosa   Laetitia   Lamb   Lancelot   Latitude
Law and Astrology   Leo   Alan Leo
William Grant Lewi II   Jim Lewis   Liberatrix
Libra   Lilith   William Lilly   Lion
Local Mean Time   Locational Astrology
Locomotive Pattern   Logarithms   Longitude
Lord   Lucifer   Lucina   Luminaries   Luna
Lunar Mansion   Lunar Nodes   Lunar Year
Lunation   Lysistrata

Joan McEvers   Magic and Astrology   Malefic
Manilius   A. T. Mann   Manto   Manzil
Marion D. March   Mars   Mars Effect
Masculine Signs   Mathematicians   Mathesis
Matutine   Mean Motion   Medea
Medical Astrology   Medium Coeli   Medusa
Melancholic   Melete   Melothesic Man
Mercury   Meridian   Merlin
Mesoamerican Astrology
Mesopotamian Astrology   Metals
Meteorological Astrology   Metonic Cycle
Neil Franklin Michelson   Midheaven   Midpoint
Minerva   Mithraism and Astrology
Mixed Application   Mnemosyne   Modern
Planets   Modestia   Modus Equalis   Moira
Moon   Marcia M. Moore   Jean-Baptiste Morin
Morinus System   R. J. Morrison   Movable Signs
Roxana Muise   Mundane Aspect
Mundane Astrology   Mutable Signs   Mute Signs
Mutual Application   Mutual Reception
Mystic Rectangle
Mythology and Astrology

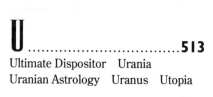

Introduction

Many great thinkers, including ancient and medieval European thinkers, and even such architects of the scientific revolution as Sir Isaac Newton, were avid students of astrology. The contents of this encyclopedia—780 entries covering all aspects and technical terms of astrology—are intended to help today's students of astrology better understand the heavenly influences.

Getting Started in Astrology

The Astrology Encyclopedia can be used as a foundation or textbook for acquiring a basic understanding of astrology.

The basic building blocks of astrology are the signs and the planets. The student should begin by reading and studying the entries for each of the signs of the Zodiac in their natural order—Aries, Taurus, Gemini, Cancer, Leo, Virgo, Libra, Scorpio, Sagittarius, Capricorn, Aquarius, and Pisces. Read the entry on Rulership, and then study the entries for the Sun, the Moon, and the planets. The planets need not be studied in any particular order. However, because the meanings of signs and planets overlap, you should refer each planet to the sign(s) that it rules. Next, read the entry on the houses, relating each of the signs to each of the houses. Finish up this course of reading with the entries on the ascendant, the aspects, the asteroids, and Chiron. When studying the aspects, it is also advisable to read the entries on the major aspects (angular positions)—conjunctions, sextiles, squares, trines, and oppositions.

To understand the basics of chart casting and chart interpretation, the student of astrology must memorize the glyphs (symbols) for the planets, the signs, and the aspects (found at the end of this introduction). Do not attempt to learn the symbols for the asteroids until *after* you've memorized the other glyphs, and, even then, focus on the most commonly utilized planetoids— Ceres, Pallas, Vesta, Juno, and Chiron. Then read the chart casting appendix. After completing this reading, you will have a basic grasp of natal astrology.

The next course of reading involves the subdivisions and branches of astrology. Begin this study with the entries on transits, electional astrology, solar returns, progressions, and directions. Then read the entries on the branches of astrology, such as mundane astrology, horary astrology, medical astrology, heliocentric astrology, astrotherapy, and so forth.

Since all of the great civilizations—from the ancient Mayans to the Chinese—developed some form of astrology, indicating that the notion of a correlation between celestial and earthly events is one of the universal constants of the human mind, the final course of reading focuses on history (Mesopotamian astrology, the history of Western astrology, and the history of astrology in America), and the astrology of other cultures (Mesoamerican astrology, Chinese astrology, and Hindu astrology.)

Understanding the Appeal of Astrology

Derided by many as medieval superstition, astrology, "the science of the stars," nevertheless continues to fascinate the human mind. Recent Gallup Polls indicate that almost one-fourth of all Americans believes in astrology. As a society we have reached a point where—rather than continuing to simply dismiss astrology as a superstitious retreat from the modern world—we should explore astrology's appeal as well as the reasons it has been so passionately criticized.

Since the Enlightenment, the Western world has been home to a vocal group of scientists and science believers who have railed against religion and anything else that dared suggest the human being is anything more than a physical-chemical organism. Astrology has been lumped into the category of irrational superstition, along with anything else that does not fall within a narrow definition of science. But just how irrational is astrology?

Anyone who has visited the seashore has noticed the ebb and flow of the water-line; the Sun and the Moon rule the tides. From this observation, how big a step is it to assert that celestial bodies influence human beings—who are composed mostly of water? We cannot touch, taste, or see astrological forces, but neither can we touch, taste, or see gravity. Gravity is perceived only indirectly—in terms of its effects. Astrological forces are also perceived indirectly—in terms of their impact on human beings and worldly events. Furthermore, astrological claims can be subjected to the methods of empirical, statistical research, as has been done most notably in the work of European statisticians and psychologists Michel and Françoise Gauquelin *(see* pages 221 and 220), which have yielded significant correlations between career choices and the prominence of certain planets in the natal chart. Another recent astrological discovery involved the correlations between certain planetary aspects and the likelihood of increased earthquake activity. NASA uses a form of heliocentric (sun-centered) astrology for predicting—and thus avoiding space missions during—periods of solar flare activity. Astrologers do not utilize illogical principles of reasoning, so astrology should not be considered irrational. Rather, astrology is labelled irrational because it has not yet been accepted into the mainstream of academic science.

In early history, human beings were not so insulated from their environment as we are today. Human life was ordered according to the seasonal migration of the Sun from north to south and south to north. The streetlights and other lights of our urban/suburban environment obstruct a view of the night sky, but it was not always so; the starry heavens used to be (barring inclement weather) a nightly experience. Aware of the relationship between Sun, Moon, and the tides, as well as the correlation between cycles such as menstruation and the lunar cycle, it is not difficult to understand why people sought out other kinds of correlations between celestial and terrestrial phenomena.

To understand the attraction of astrology for the average person in an industrialized society, one has to see that, even for people with the slightest belief in traditional religion, ordinary, everyday life seems to be void of significance. Many people feel they are at the mercy of social, economic, and political forces that they might not understand, much less predict. Astrology may be unappealing to some because of its apparent determinism, but it allows people to comprehend the events in their lives as part of a meaningful, predictive system over which they can gain some control.

What Is Astrology?

Astrology literally means the study (or science, depending on how one translates the Greek word *logos*) of the stars *(astron)*. Astrology differs from astronomy by confining its attention to the study of correlations between celestial events and human events. Most people are familiar with only a tiny portion of astrology, namely the 12 signs of the Zodiac as they relate to personality, and the use of astrology for divination.

The Zodiac (literally the "circle of animals" or, in its more primary meaning, the "circle of life" or "circle of living beings") is the belt constituted by the 12 signs— Aries, Taurus, Gemini, Cancer, Leo, Virgo, Libra, Scorpio, Sagittarius, Capricorn, Aquarius, and Pisces. This belt is said to extend 8 or 9 degrees on either side of the *ecliptic* (the imaginary line drawn against the backdrop of the stars by the orbit of the Earth). The orbits of the planets in the solar system all lie within approximately the same geometric plane, so that, from any position within the system, all the planets appear to move across the face of the same set of constellations. Several thousand years ago, these constellations gave their names to the Zodiac.

The notion of the Zodiac is very ancient, with roots in the early cited cultures of Mesopotamia. The first 12-sign zodiacs were named after the gods of these cultures. The Greeks adopted astrology from the Babylonians, and the Romans, in turn, adopted astrology from the Greeks. These peoples renamed the signs of the Mesopotamian Zodiac for their own mythologies, which is why the familiar Zodiac of the contemporary West still bears names from Mediterranean mythologies. The notion of a 12-fold division is derived from the lunar cycle (the orbital cycle of the Moon around the Earth), which the Moon completes 12 times a year.

Zodiacal symbolism can be found throughout history, and zodiacal expressions are still in use in modern English—for example, "bull-headed" is an allusion to Taurus the Bull and "crabby" is an allusion to Cancer the Crab. The popularity of "Sun sign" astrology has kept these ancient symbols alive, so that even automobiles have been named after some of the signs (the Taurus and the Scorpio, for instance).

The sign of the Zodiac that the Sun is in at the time of birth is called the Sun sign (or birth sign). The Sun, as the most important celestial body for Earth dwellers, is considered the greatest influence in a horoscope (astrological chart) and, therefore, on an individual's personality. When people say that they are such-and-such a sign, they are almost always referring to their Sun sign.

Sun sign astrology, which is the kind of astrology you find in newspapers and magazines, has the advantage of simplicity— all you need to know is your birthday to be able to figure out your sign. But this simplicity is at the expense of all other astrological influences. Other important celestial bodies were located in signs at the moment of your birth. So, if you are a Scorpio Sun sign, you might also have a Sagittarius Moon sign, a Virgo Venus sign, a Libra Mercury sign, and so forth. Each of these other signs has an influence, which is why—contrary to popular belief—everyone with the same Sun sign does *not* have the same personality. The subsidiary influences of the planets' positions in signs is further modified by the angles between them (referred to as *aspects)*, as well as by their *house* positions (another set of 12 divisions).

These other influences make Sun sign astrology a hit-or-miss system— working sometimes but failing miserably at others. Professional astrologers tend to dislike it because its inaccuracy leads non-astrologers and critics to reject astrology as untrue. Similar skepticism applies to predictions of the future *(divination)* by the 12 signs. The columns found in popular periodicals create misconceptions about the nature of astrological prediction. In particular, readers may get the impression that astrological prediction is a kind of fortune-telling that uses the stars to predict an irrevocable destiny. Modern astrologers tend to distance themselves from this tradition of predicting specific events, choosing instead to describe upcoming planetary conditions, with the understanding that people have the free will to respond to planetary influences in the way they choose. Like a meteorologist predicting the weather, an astrologer can only forecast trends and probabilities—not predict the future.

Christianity and Astrology

The church absorbed astrology along with many other aspects of Hellenic civilization. Some Christian thinkers worried about the tension between free will and the perceived determinism of astrology, but for the most part, the science of the stars occupied an honorable position in the Western tradition. Although some of the Biblical prophets disparaged star gazing, the three wise men were astrologers, and in scriptural passages it is evident that God utilized heavenly signs to instruct the faithful.

Despite tensions in the marriage, astrology and Christianity did not become divorced until the Christian fundamentalist movement emerged in the early twentieth century. For various reasons, but particularly because of astrology's association with metaphysical religion, fundamentalists, and later most other conservative Christians, rejected astrology as delusion at best and a tool of Satan at worst.

The Metaphysical Subculture and Astrology

Despite the increasing antagonism from militant secularists and conservative Christians, astrology has been growing steadily for the past hundred years. This growth may well have something to do with the decreasing power of astrology's critics. Despite the increasing number of conservative churches, the influence of traditional religion on society has been waning for more than a century. As for secular humanists, because science creates at least as many problems as it solves, the appeal of a quasi-religious secularism tied to mainstream science has also lost social influence. While both conservative Christianity and secular humanism have been losing ground, the West's metaphysical subculture—which has been friendly toward astrology—has been growing in size and influence.

The metaphysical community is a loose-knit subculture. Its most distinctive institution is the metaphysical bookstore, and there are many metaphysical organizations. The largest of these organizations, such as the various Theosophical societies and Spiritualist churches, were formed in the nineteenth century, but the community was relatively small until the late twentieth century. As the counter-culture of the 1960s faded in the next decade, many former "hippies" found themselves embarking on spiritual quests—quests that, in many cases, departed from the Judeo-Christian mainstream. These new seekers swelled the ranks of the metaphysical subculture until it became a significant social force.

One important manifestation of this subculture is the so-called "New Age movement." While segments of the metaphysical community have long referred to themselves as New Age, neither the community nor the term were familiar to the cultural mainstream until the late 1980s. In North America, the single most important event prompting general awareness of this subculture was the 1987 broadcast *Out on a Limb,* the made-for-television miniseries based on Shirley MacLaine's best-selling book about her beliefs in meditation, reincarnation, and spiritual channeling. The success of this miniseries prompted the mass media to write articles and produce programs about the New Age. The media's interest was still high at the time of the Harmonic Convergence (a powerful cosmic event that was thought to indicate a shift in human mental orientation) in August

1987, causing the convergence to attract more public attention than any New Age event before or since.

The widespread interest in the New Age led to the December 1987 *Time* feature, "New Age Harmonies," the most significant article on the movement to appear in a major news magazine. Like many previous mainstream media stories, "New Age Harmonies" focused on the flashier, less substantive aspects of the movement. This article, unlike earlier, similar pieces, influenced many of the more serious individuals within the movement to back away from the label "New Age."

In the same way that the media seized the expression "New Age" in the late 1980s and transformed it into a term of derision, an earlier wave of media interest in the early 1970s seized the word *occult* and succeeded in connecting it with such negative phenomena as black magic.

Occult comes from a root word meaning "hidden," and the original connotation of the word was that it referred to a body of esoteric beliefs and practices that were in some sense *hidden* from the average person (in other words, practices and knowledge that are accessible only after an initiation). Alternately, it is sometimes said that practices were occult if they dealt with forces that operated by means that were hidden from ordinary perception—magic, tarot cards, and astrology, for example. Modern astrology is not occult in the sense of secret initiations, but it is occult in the sense that it deals with "hidden" forces.

Under the impact of the Human Potentials movement and humanistic psychology, astrology, tarot, and so forth were no longer regarded as mere fortune-telling devices, but became tools for self-transformation. The result of this on the contemporary practice of astrology is that at least two kinds of astrologers can be distinguished: Astrologers who—like Joan Quigley, the Reagans' astrologer—primarily predict events and advise clients on when to perform certain actions, and astrologers who see themselves as quasi-therapists, leading their clients to deeper understandings of themselves. Most contemporary astrologers would fall somewhere between these two definitions.

Theories of Astrological Influence

Approaches to explaining how astrology "works" move between two poles, one that stresses the study of the stars as a natural science and another that emphasizes the spiritual (or occult) dimension of planetary influences. The natural science model tends to conceive of astrological influences in terms of forces (analogous to the forces of gravity and magnetism) that are "radiated" by the planets.

The spiritual model of astrology, while often speaking in terms of "occult forces," usually emphasizes that correlations between celestial and mundane spheres result from a kind of "pre-arranged harmony" that is built into the structure of the cosmos. This model maintains that the various correspondences between the stars and worldly events are the result of *synchronicity* (to use Carl Jung's term), rather than cause and effect. While these models seem to be in opposition to each other, many astrologers adhere simultaneously to both.

The cosmic interconnectedness of the occult model implies a kind of monistic view of the universe that is related to the world view held by most of America's metaphysical subculture. This is why astrology has been severely criticized by militant secularists and many Christians.

There are people who adhere to secular humanism as if it were a religion, regarding mainstream science as the sole arbiter of truth. Consequently, anything that falls outside science, whether it be traditional religion or an alternative healing practice, is viewed as superstition. Some secular humanists have assumed the role of skeptic, critic, or even professional debunker. The sTARBABY incident (*see* page 487) in the mid-1970s brought the conflict between mainstream science and astrology to light and has since become part of the folklore of contemporary astrology.

Branches and Traditions of Astrology

When most people think of astrology, they usually think either of natal astrology—the subdivision that deals with individual personalities—or predictive astrology. The material presented here deals almost exclusively with natal astrology, although the basic understandings acquired in the study of this branch of astrology carry over into other branches. While the beginner should not attempt to memorize these subdivisions, it is useful to have some sense of what the full science encompasses.

Traditionally, astrology's major division is between natal astrology (or genethetical astrology) and mundane astrology (or judicial astrology). Whereas natal astrology deals with individuals, mundane astrology deals with larger entities and processes, such as nations and economic cycles. A third major branch, though not traditionally regarded as such, is horary astrology—the practice of casting charts for particular questions. (For more information on mundane astrology and horary astrology, *see* pages 380 and 281.)

Electional astrology *(see* pages 184–187), regarded as a part of horary astrology, is the art of selecting ("electing") the best time to carry out a particular activity. The traditional practice of "planting by the signs," which is still used in the rural United States, is a form of electional astrology. Many other distinct subdivisions are not included in traditional classifications of astrological science, although some can be placed under the major branches. Medical astrology, for example, falls most naturally under natal astrology, and business astrology (sometimes called astroeconomics) falls under mundane astrology.

Contemporary astrology has seen the development of many new branches. Heliocentric astrology, for example, constructs charts from the point of view of the Sun, unlike traditional, geocentric astrology, which constructs charts from the perspective of the Earth. Other cultures, such as China and India, developed distinct approaches to astrology. Clearly, there are too many different types of astrology for any one person to master. Rare, indeed, is the individual who has a working knowledge of every variety.

Elements of Astrological Meaning

Because there is a certain similarity of meaning between particular planets and particular signs (each sign is said to be *ruled* by a particular planet), as well as a link between each successive sign with each successive *house,* a sound knowledge of the 12 signs of the Zodiac makes it easier to understand the astrological significance of the planets and the houses.

There are various ways of classifying the signs, some more useful than others. Of particular importance are the four elements—earth, water, air, and fire—which represent certain basic personality orientations. Earth represents practicality; water, emotional sensitivity; air, a mental orientation; and fire, activity. So for people whose charts are comprised primarily of water signs (Cancer, Scorpio, and Pisces), feelings are what are most *real* in life; for a predominance of air signs (Gemini, Libra, and Aquarius), ideas are most valued; for earth (Taurus, Virgo, and Capricorn), practical concerns; and for fire (Aries, Leo, and Sagittarius), activity.

The other primary system by which the signs are classified is the so-called qualities—cardinal, mutable, and fixed. Each of the 12 signs of the Zodiac is a unique combination of an element and a quality: Aries is a cardinal fire sign, Taurus is fixed earth, Gemini is mutable air, and so forth. The elemental nature of a sign is said to refer to its basic temperament, while quality is said to refer to its mode of expression. Cardinal signs are portrayed as outgoing signs that initiate new activities; fixed signs persist with their established activities; mutable signs adapt to changing circumstances.

These two classification systems—elements and qualities—are helpful in memorizing sign traits.

The interpretation of a horoscope is built around the influence of the planets as modified by three primary factors—signs, aspects (the angular relationships between the planets), and houses. An oversimplified but nonetheless useful rule is that planetary sign positions indicate personality tendencies, aspects between planets reflect how various components of one's personality interact, and house positions show how the personality manifests itself in the world.

Perhaps it is because of the horoscope—which is the most well-known aspect of astrology—that interest in astrology is growing: There are probably more than 10,000 professional astrologers in the United States, serving more than 20 million clients, which does not include those who read astrology magazines or those who read their horoscopes in almost every daily newspaper and in many popular magazines. Astrologers write syndicated advice columns for the national news services; among the better known of these public figures are Jeanne Dixon, "Zolar" (Bruce King), Sydney Omarr, and "Ophiel." Computers, which now are widely used to carry out the calculations needed to erect a chart, have added to the modern panache of astrology. The pages that follow will help you understand the science of the stars as well as provide you with a picture of astrology's history and future.

—James R. Lewis

Acknowledgements

M any thanks to the contributors, who trusted me with the fruits of their labor, to Alice May Kesemochen, who drew many of the illustrations for this book, and to Cosby Steuart, who typed sections of the final manuscript. At Gale Research/Visible Ink Press, I am grateful to acquisitions editor Chris Nasso, who originally took interest in this project, and to my developmental editor Becky Nelson and associate editor Kelle Sisung, who, in the final stages, labored over this volume as much as I did. I would particularly like to thank Gordon Melton—a supportive friend who also introduced me to writing reference books.

My understanding of astrology has been shaped by conversations with many people over the years. Each and all have my heartfelt gratitude. I would especially like to express thanks to the astrological community, which has generously supplied me with information and encouragement for this project.

PLANET	COMMON ABBREVIATION	GLYPH
*Sun	SUN	☉
Mercury	MER	☿
Venus	VEN	♀
Earth	EAR	⊕
*Moon	MON or MOO	☽
Mars	MAR	♂
Jupiter	JUP	♃
Saturn	SAT	♄
Uranus	URA	♅ ⚨
Neptune	NEP	♆
Pluto	PLU	♇ ♇

*Not planets, but traditionally listed

SIGN	COMMON ABBREVIATION	GLYPH
Aries	ARI	♈
Taurus	TAR or TAU	♉
Gemini	GEM	♊
Cancer	CAN	♋
Leo	LEO	♌
Virgo	VIR	♍
Libra	LIB	♎
Scorpio	SCO	♏
Sagittarius	SAG	♐
Capricorn	CAP	♑
Aquarius	AQU	♒
Pisces	PIC or PIS	♓

OTHER POINTS	COMMON ABBREVIATION	GLYPH
North Node	NN	☊
South Node	SN	☋
Galactic Center	GC	☋
Part of Fortune	P of F	⊗

Planet-signs identification.

ASTEROID	GLYPH	ASTEROID	GLYPH
Aesculapia		Hygiea	
Amor		Icarus	
Apollo		Industria	
Arachne		Isis	
Ariadne		Juno	
Astraea		Kassandra	
Atlantis		Lilith	
Bacchus		Minerva	
Ceres		Nemesis	
Chiron		Niobe	
Circe		Orpheus	
Cupido		Pallas	
Daedalus		Pandora	
Dembowska		Persephone	
Demeter		Pittsburghia	
Diana		Proserpina	
Dike		Psyche	
Dudu		Sappho	
Eros		Sisyphus	
Eurydike		Siva	
Frigga		Terpsichore	
Hebe		Themis	
Hera		Toro	
Hidalgo		Urania	
Hopi		Vesta	
Hybris			

IMAGINARY PLANET	GLYPH
Admetos	⯓
Apollon	♃♉
Coda	⯝
Cupido (also an asteroid name)	♃⚨
Dido (also an asteroid name)	
Hades	⯗
Hercules	
Hermes	⯒
Horus (also an asteroid name)	
Isis (Also an asteroid name)	⯖
Jason	
Kronos	⯛
LaCroix	
Lilith (also an asteroid name)	⦸
Lion	⬓
Loki	⊖
Melodia	
Midas (also an asteroid name)	⯚
Minos	
Moraya	
Osiris (also an asteroid name)	⯘
Pan (also an asteroid name)	
Persephone (also an asteroid name)	
Polyhymnia (also an asteroid name)	
Poseidon (also an asteroid name)	⯖
Shanti	◎
Transpluto	⯗
Vulcan	⊙
Vulcanus (Vulkanus)	⯙
Wemyss—Pluto	
Zeus	⯟

Names and glyphs of imaginary bodies.

Abundantia

Abundantia, **asteroid** 151 (the 151st asteroid to be discovered), is approximately 42 kilometers in diameter and has an **orbital** period of 4.1 years. Its name is Latin for affluence or abundance. Abundantia's location by sign and **house** in a **natal chart** may show where one experiences the most abundance or an area that can be cultivated to achieve affluence.

Sources:

Kowal, Charles T. *Asteroids: Their Nature and Utilization.* Chichester, West Sussex, England: Ellis Horwood Limited, 1988.
Room, Adrian. *Dictionary of Astronomical Names.* London: Routledge, 1988.

Accidental Ascendant

Horary astrology is the branch of astrology in which an astrological chart is cast for the moment a question is asked. The chart is then read to determine an answer to the question. The **ascendant** (**degree** of the **zodiac** on the eastern **horizon**) for a horary chart is referred to as the accidental ascendant.

Accidental Dignity

A **planet** is said to be in its dignity when it is in the sign that it **rules**. For example, because **Pluto** rules **Scorpio**, Pluto is in dignity when in the sign Scorpio. As the term implies, this is regarded as a fortunate placement; a planet in its dignity is traditionally regarded as being in harmony with the sign and consequently strengthened.

A planet's being in the sign of its rulership is sometimes referred to as **essential dignity** to distinguish it from certain other placements that tend to strengthen a planet's influence by virtue of its position in an astrological chart;

these other placements are traditionally termed "accidental" dignities. For example, the 12 signs of the **zodiac** correspond to the 12 astrological **houses** so that there is a natural affinity between successive signs and successive houses (i.e., between **Aries**, the first sign, and the first house; **Taurus**, the second sign, and the second house; **Gemini**, the third sign, and with the third house; etc.). When a planet is placed in a **natal chart** so that it falls in the house corresponding to the sign it rules, it is said to be "accidentally" dignified. Thus, **Mars** in the first house, **Venus** in the second house, and **Mercury** in the third house would be accidentally dignified because Mars rules Aries, Venus rules Taurus and Mercury rules Gemini.

Planets are also strengthened by certain other placements, such as when a planet in the first house is **conjunct** the **ascendant**, or one in the tenth house is conjunct the **midheaven**. These other placements are sometimes also referred to as accidental dignities.

Sources:

deVore, Nicholas. *Encyclopedia of Astrology.* New York: Philosophical Library, 1947.
Gettings, Fred. *Dictionary of Astrology.* London: Routledge & Kegan Paul, 1985.

Achilles

Achilles, **asteroid** 588 (the 588th asteroid to be discovered), is approximately 116 kilometers in diameter and has an **orbital** period of 11.8 years. It was named after the famous Greek hero and was the first of the so-called Trojan asteroids (asteroids that travel along the same orbital path as Jupiter) to be discovered. Achilles' location by sign and **house** in a **natal chart** shows an area of exceptional strength, but at the same time the site of an Achilles' heel.

Sources:

Kowal, Charles T. *Asteroids: Their Nature and Utilization.* Chichester, West Sussex, U.K.: Ellis Horwood Limited, 1988.
Room, Adrian. *Dictionary of Astronomical Names.* London: Routledge, 1988.

Acronycal

Acronycal (Greek for: on the edge of night) refers to a **planet** directly opposite the **Sun** that rises after sunset or sets before sunrise, which as a consequence is in a favorable location for astronomical observation. The *acronycal place* is the **degree** in the sign of the **zodiac** directly opposed to the Sun.

Adad

Adad is a term from **Mesopotamian astrology** that refers to meteorological and astrological phenomena.

Adams, Evangeline

Evangeline Adams, born February 8, 1868, in Jersey City, New Jersey, was the premier American astrologer of the early twentieth century. She was the daughter of George and Harriette E. (Smith) Adams and a descendant of John Quincy Adams, sixth president of the United States. Raised in Andover, Massachusetts, she was educated there and in Chicago. She became part of the elite metaphysical community in the larger Boston area and was introduced to astrology by J. Hebert Smith, a professor of medicine at Boston University. Adams also studied Hindu philosophy under Swami Vivekananda. She eventually became so interested in the science of the stars that she chose it as her life's work.

In 1899, Adams moved to New York City and began residing at the fashionable Windsor Hotel. Her first client was Warren F. Leland, owner of the Windsor. After casting his chart, she told him that he was under a planetary combination that threatened immediate disaster. The next afternoon, on March 17, 1899, the hotel burned to the ground. On the day following the fire, New York newspapers carried front page stories about Adams's prediction of the disaster. Overnight, this publicity transformed her into an astrological superstar, and she began her career as an astrologer to the rich and powerful. She was consulted in her Carnegie Hall headquarters by J. P. Morgan, King Edward VII, Enrico Caruso, and actress Mary Pickford, among others.

In 1914, Adams was arrested and charged with fortune-telling. Rather than paying the fine, she insisted on standing trial. She went to court armed with reference books and proceeded to systematically explain the principles of astrology. She concluded her defense by reading a chart of an individual unknown to her. The anonymous **horoscope** was that of the judge's son. Impressed with the accuracy of her reading, Judge John H. Freschi remarked that "the defendant raises astrology to the dignity of an exact science" (*The Bowl of Heaven,* p. 54). He dismissed the charge against her.

Adams continued to practice and promote the science of the stars to the general public. She wrote *Monthly Forecasts,* a publication featuring her predictions about political and economic events (including a 1931 prediction that the United States would be at war in 1942). During the last decade of her life, she wrote some of the most popular astrology books ever published: *The Bowl of Heaven* (1926), *Astrology: Your Place in the Sun* (1928), *Astrology: Your Place Among the Stars* (1930), and *Astrology for Everyone* (1931). On April 23, 1930, Adams began to broadcast on radio three times a week. As a result of this show, she received 150,000 requests for astrological charts over the course of the next three months. As much as a year later, requests and letters were still being received at the rate of 4,000 a day. She was a major contributor to the popularization of astrology. She died November 10, 1932, in New York City.

Selected Publications:

The Bowl of Heaven. 1926. Reprint. New York: Dodd, Mead & Co., 1970.
Astrology: Your Place in the Sun. New York: Dodd, Mead & Co., 1927.
Astrology: Your Place Among the Stars. New York: Dodd, Mead & Co., 1930.
Astrology for Everyone. New York: Dodd, Mead & Co., 1931.

Sources:

MacNeice, Louis. *Astrology.* Garden City, N.Y.: Doubleday, 1964.
Melton, J. Gordon. "The Revival of Astrology in the United States." In *Religious Movements: Genesis, Exodus, and Numbers,* edited by Rodney Stark, 279–299. New York: Paragon House Publishers, 1985.
Shepard, Leslie A. "Evangeline Adams." *Encyclopedia of Occultism and Parapsychology.* 2d ed. Detroit: Gale Research, 1984.

Addey, John

John Addey, a contemporary British astrologer and philosopher, was born June 15, 1920, in Barnsley, Yorkshire, England. He graduated from Saint John's College, Cambridge (M.A.). He became interested in astrology while still in school. He joined the Astrological Lodge of the Theosophical Society in 1946, served as vice-president (1951-1958), and obtained the Faculty of Astrological Studies Diploma (1951).

Addey was dissatisfied with the uncertainty of astrology, and began seeking a more scientific approach. In 1956-7, his studies of longevity and polio led him to a "wave theory" of astrology. Reflection on his own studies and the statistical work of others led him to feel that **harmonics** was the basis of astrological influence. He founded the Astrological Association in 1958 to promote serious work in astrology, and as president built it into the most prominent association of its kind. Addey also edited the *Astrological Journal,* and in 1970 set up the Urania Trust, an educational foundation devoted to the reconciliation of astronomy and astrology. Addey's principle publications are *Astrology Reborn* (1972), *Harmonics in Astrology* (1976), *Harmonics Anthology* (1976), and *Selected Writings* (1976).

Sources:

Brau, Jean-Louis, Helen Weaver, and Allan Edmands. *Larousse Encyclopedia of Astrology.* New York: New American Library, 1980.

Holden, James H., and Robert A. Hughes. *Astrological Pioneers of America.* Tempe, Ariz.: American Federation of Astrologers, 1988.

Adjusted Calculation Date

The adjusted calculation date is the date on which a **planet** in a progressed horoscope **culminates** (reaches the **midheaven**).

Admetos

Admetos is one of the eight **hypothetical planets** (sometimes referred to as the trans-Neptunian points or planets, TNPs) utilized in **Uranian astrology**. It may symbolize blockage, patience, frustration, delay, hindrances, standstill, and so forth. More positively, Admetos may represent depth, profundity, and that which is fundamental. For example, a link between the **planet Mercury** and Admetos may indicate limited thinking, or it may indicate deep thinking.

Sources:

Lang-Wescott, Martha. *Mechanics of the Future: Asteroids.* Rev. ed. Conway, Mass.: Treehouse Mountain, 1991.
Simms, Maria Kay. *Dial Detective: Investigation with the 90 Degree Dial.* San Diego, Calif.: Astro Computing Services, 1989.

Adorea

Adorea, **asteroid** 268 (the 268th asteroid to be discovered), is approximately 122 kilometers in diameter and has an **orbital** period of 5.5 years. Adorea is a "concept" asteriod; the name means glory and originally referred to the gift of corn that was given to soldiers after a victory. In a **natal chart**, Adorea's location by sign and **house** position indicates where a person gives or receives recognition. When **afflicted** by inharmonious **aspects**, Adorea may indicate negative or false recognition.

Sources:

Kowal, Charles T. *Asteroids: Their Nature and Utilization.* Chichester, West Sussex, U.K.: Ellis Horwood Limited, 1988.
Room, Adrian. *Dictionary of Astronomical Names.* London: Routledge, 1988.

Aestival Signs

The aestival signs are the summer signs, namely, **Cancer**, **Leo**, and **Virgo**.

Aeternitas

Aeternitas, **asteroid** 446 (the 446th asteroid to be discovered), is approximately 52 kilometers in diameter and has an **orbital** period of 4.7 years. Its name is Latin for eternity. When prominent in a **natal chart**, Aeternitas may indicate a person with interest in the "eternal verities" or one who can expect a long life.

Sources:

Kowal, Charles T. *Asteroids: Their Nature and Utilization.* Chichester, West Sussex, U.K.: Ellis Horwood Limited, 1988.

Room, Adrian. *Dictionary of Astronomical Names.* London: Routledge, 1988.

Affinity

Astrologers use the term affinity to refer to compatibility between certain **planets** or signs. It is also used to denote attraction between people whose charts interact harmoniously and magnetically with each other.

Affliction

An affliction is (1) any difficult **aspect**, such as a **square**, or (2) a more neutral aspect, such as a **conjunction**, in which at least one of the **planets**, is a "difficult" planet, such as **Saturn**. A planet involved in more than one such aspect, especially if there are no **benefic** aspects counterbalancing the **hard aspects**, is said to be heavily afflicted.

The term affliction is not generally used among contemporary astrologers; they are more likely to refer to such aspects as inharmonious, challenging, or difficult. More is involved in this change of terminology than the goal of making the language less dramatic: Some difficult aspects are necessary to bring challenges into one's life, and the modern terminology more accurately denotes challenge. People without at least a few such aspects in their **natal charts** usually lack character and rarely accomplish much in life.

Sources:

Bach, Eleanor. *Astrology from A to Z: An Illustrated Source Book.* New York: Philosophical Library, 1990.

deVore, Nicholas. *Encyclopedia of Astrology.* New York: Philosophical Library, 1947.

Age of Aquarius (Aquarian Age)

The Age of Aquarius is one of 12 successive 2150-year periods, each of which corresponds with one of the 12 signs of the **zodiac**. In the same manner in which individuals born at different times of the year are thought to be dominated by different astrological signs, astrologers also tend to view different historical periods as being dominated by the influence of particular signs. For the past several thousand years, Earth, according to this view, has been passing through a period dominated by the sign **Pisces** (the Age of Pisces). This succession of ages is based on a phenomenon known as the **precession of equinoxes**.

Due to the precession of equinoxes, the spring equinox moves slowly backward through the **constellations** of the Zodiac, so that approximately every 2,000 years the equinox begins taking place in an earlier constellation. Thus, the spring equinox has been occurring in Pisces for the past several thousand years and will begin to occur in the constellation **Aquarius** in the near future. This is the background for current speculations about the so-called Age of Aquarius. The phenomenon of the precession of equinoxes also means that the spring equinox occurred in the sign **Aries** during the Hellenistic period (the period of **Ptolemy**), in Taurus several thousand years prior to the Hellenistic period, and so forth backward through the zodiac.

Because of the space between different constellations, it is difficult if not impossible to determine precisely when one age ends and another one begins, although this has not prevented many practitioners of traditional astrology as well as **esoteric astrology** from asserting that the Aquarian Age has already begun. A popular date for the beginning of the Age of Aquarius is the year 2000. If, however, the Age of Pisces began with the ministry of Jesus (as many claim), and if each age is 2150 years in duration, then we clearly have a long way to go before we pass into the Age of Aquarius.

The contemporary notion of the Age of Aquarius, developed in occult and theosophical circles in the last century, was mediated to the larger society by the counterculture of the 1960s (as in the well-known song "Age of Aquarius" that was featured in the rock musical *Hair*). The metaphysical subculture that emerged as a successor to the counterculture in the early to middle 1970s eventually dropped the appellation Aquarian Age in favor of New Age. Most popular accounts of the difference between the Piscean Age and the Aquarian Age emphasize the negative traits of Pisces and the positive traits of Aquarius. Thus, attention is called to the negative Piscean tendency to adopt an attitude of blind faith, and to the positive Aquarian tendency to adopt a more empirical attitude. The limits of this approach—which often ignores positive Pisces traits as well as negative Aquarius characteristics—should be clear.

A comprehensive critique of the Aquarian Age notion can be found in Nicholas Campion's important treatment, "The Age of Aquarius: A Modern Myth." Although this work is useful, contrary to Campion's argument, the ancients did put forward a theory of successive astrological ages based on the precession of equinoxes (see **Mithraism and Astrology**).

Sources:

Bach, Eleanor. *Astrology from A to Z: An Illustrated Source Book.* New York: Philosophical Library, 1990.

Campion, Nicholas. "The Age of Aquarius: A Modern Myth." In *The Astrology of the Macrocosm,* edited by Joan McEvers, 195–231. Saint Paul, Minn.: Llewellyn Publications, 1990.

Ulansey, David. *The Origins of the Mithraic Mysteries: Cosmology and Salvation in the Ancient World.* New York: Oxford University Press, 1989.

Ages of Man

The Ages of Man refers to the ancient notion that the different stages of human life are **ruled** by different **planets** and the **luminaries** (the **Sun** and the **Moon**). The traditional schema was as follows: Moon—growth (ages 1–4); **Mercury**—education (5–14); **Venus**—emotion (15–22); Sun—virility (23–42); **Mars**—ambition (43–57); **Jupiter**—reflection (58–69); and **Saturn**—resignation (70–99).

Agricultural Astrology (Planting by the Signs)

Agricultural astrology is the practice of choosing the time to plant and harvest crops according to the phase and sign of the **Moon**. As such, agricultural astrology is a branch of **electional astrology**. Planting according to the phase of the Moon (during the waxing phase for most yearly food crops that produce their yield aboveground) may be humanity's oldest astrological practice. In the more recent history of the West, agricultural astrology has been referred to as planting by the signs—the practice of planting seeds according to the astrological sign of the Moon (which, because of the relative shortness of the Moon's **orbit,** changes every two or three days). Planting by the signs has been a regular feature of **almanacs,** such as *The Old Farmer's Almanac,* and in some agricultural regions (e.g., rural Appalachia) planting by the signs is still practiced.

Agricultural astrology is the one area of contemporary astrology in which people still rely on the traditional classification of **fruitful signs** and **barren signs**. If planted while the Moon (which **rules** the principle of **conception**) is in a fruitful sign, crops supposedly grow bigger and better; planted in a barren sign, crops are less healthy and less tasty. Periods during which the Moon is in a barren sign are good for cultivating and destroying weeds, however.

Sources:

Brau, Jean-Louis, Helen Weaver, and Allan Edmands. *Larousse Encyclopedia of Astrology.* New York: New American Library, 1980.
Riotte, Louise. *Astrological Gardening: The Ancient Wisdom of Successful Planting and Harvesting by the Stars.* Pownal, Vt.: Storey Communications, 1989.
Starck, Marcia. *Earth Mother Astrology: Ancient Healing Wisdom.* Saint Paul, Minn.: Llewellyn Publications, 1989.

Air Signs

The 12 signs of the **zodiac** are subdivided according to the 4 classical **elements**—earth, air, fire, and water. The 3 air signs (the *air triplicity* or *air trigon*) are **Gemini, Libra**, and **Aquarius**. Astrologically, air is mental. For people in whom the air element predominates, ideas and communication are the most important aspects of human life.

This mental trait shows itself somewhat differently in each of the signs of the air triplicity. Gemini's airy nature typically manifests as the ability to understand, utilize, and communicate facts; Geminis are natural teachers and

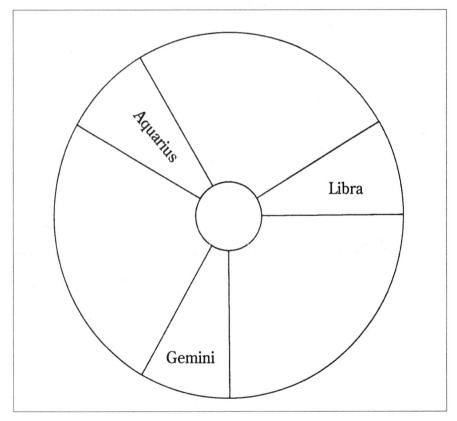

◄
Air signs.

communicators. As Libra's symbol, the Scales, suggests, Libra's airiness is expressed as the ability to make comparisons by weighing and balancing. This sign has a highly developed social nature that makes Libras talented hosts and insightful psychologists. Aquarius's airy quality appears as intuition and the ability to understand universal principles. Aquarius also has a natural inclination to work with others for the upliftment of humanity.

Negatively, air people can be too intellectual and too verbal. Unless counterbalanced by other factors, excess air in a **natal chart** indicates an individual who is stuck at the mental level, never able to manifest ideas in a practical manner. Conversely, lack of air can indicate a person who has difficulty communicating and formatting clear ideas.

Sources:

Hand, Robert. *Horoscope Symbols.* Rockport, Mass.: Para Research, 1981.
Sakoian, Frances, and Louis S. Acker. *The Astrologer's Handbook.* New York: Harper & Row, 1989.

Albedo

Albedo (literally, "*whiteness*") is a measure of the power of a **planet, moon,** or **asteroid** to reflect light.

Al-Biruni

Al-Biruni (Abu'l-Rayhan Muhammad ibn Ahmad Al-Biruni), known for his classic works on the chronology, customs, and science of Hindu astrology, was born in 973 A.D. in what is now Khiva, Uzbek (formerly part of the USSR). At the time of Al-Biruni's birth, the area was a suburb of Kath, the capital of Khwarizm (north and northeast of ancient Parthia on the lower Oxus River in the region south of the Aral Sea). Khiva was known to the classical Greeks and Romans as Chorasmia and was the homeland of a people related to the Sogdian Magi who lived to the south and southeast of Khwarizm on the Oxus in the eastern reaches of what had once been the Persian Empire. The proximity to India meant that Indian cultural and scientific traditions had certainly pervaded the region for centuries. Not far away, on the western shore of the Caspian Sea, lay the remnants of the Jewish Empire of the Khazars, which had fallen to the duke of Kiev 4 years prior to Al-Biruni's birth.

Only 23 years after Al-Biruni's birth, the last of the Khwarizmshahs, Abu Abdallah Muhammad, a direct descendant of the Khusraws (the last dynasty of Persian kings before Islam), was overthrown by the Moslem emir Ma'mun ibn Muhammad. Thus, Persian-Magian traditions lingered in and around Al-Biruni's birthplace. Indeed, despite the conversion to Islam, the whole region was steeped not only in Zoroastrianism but also in Manicheanism and astrological doctrines, as is apparent from Al-Biruni's *Chronologies of Ancient Nations, India* and *The Book of Instruction in the Elements of the Art of Astrology.* The latter work will hereafter be referred to by its Arabic short title, the *Tafhim.* The Tafhim was translated into English by R. Ramsay Wright in 1934.

Al-Biruni thus came from a highly cultured society known for its mathematical, scientific, astronomical, and astrological lore. In his various works he shows interest in and familiarity with the cultures and sciences of the peoples who surrounded him. He shows profound and advanced knowledge of scientific subjects. His mind was precise and he was a close observer of nature. He studied the Hindu numeral system and showed how to determine **latitude** and **longitude** accurately. When he visited India and viewed the Indus Valley, he concluded that it was an ancient sea basin filled with alluvium. In many ways he was ahead of his time.

He traveled widely, leaving his birthplace for the Samanid court of Nuh ibn Mansur at Ghaznah in eastern Afghanistan, the Samanid capital, sometime in the 990s. While on his travels, Al-Biruni began his *Chronologies of Ancient Nations.* In this work, completed in the year 1000, he shows advanced understanding of the comparative chronologies of the surrounding peoples. He seems to have returned to Khwarizm around age 37 and to have remained there until age 46, when his patron, Abu'l-'Abbas Ma'mun ibn Ma'mun, was murdered by rebellious subjects. As a result of the murder, Mahmud of Ghaznah invaded Khwarizm and subjugated the country, exiling its ruling class (and Al-Biruni with them) to Ghaznah in the following year. Al-Biruni served Mahmud as court astrologer, but somehow found time between 1016 and 1029 to travel to India and write his classic *India,* detailing the social, religious, and scientific characteristics of the Indians. During this period he also produced the *Tafhim,* a textbook on astrology and related subjects.

The *Tafhim* is a truly remarkable book in several respects. First of all, it is a medieval Oriental book dedicated to a woman. This by itself is remarkable. The woman, Rayhana bint al-Hasan, was a Persian noblewoman who was apparently a student of Al-Biruni's while both were semicaptive at Mahmud's court at Ghaznah. Hardly one paragraph of the *Tafhim* is without interest. Al-Biruni seems to have written both an Arabic and a Persian version. It contains 550 paragraphs plus a colophon that Al-Biruni tells us was intended as an aide-memoire for Rayhana in the form of questions and answers. The 1934 Wright translation deletes this feature and presents a text arranged in paragraphs with headings. Though Wright's translation shows signs of incompletion (it is typewritten, not typeset, with unpolished notes and comments, and clearly paraphrased in places), the overall composition and handling of the subject shows Al-Biruni to have possessed a mind of the highest quality and probity. As a teacher he must have been outstanding. He writes with clarity and conciseness uncharacteristic of medieval astrological writers. He tells us, at the very end of the book, that he has set forth what a beginner needs to know about astrology. He exceeds the modern standards in this regard and provides us with what amounts to an introduction to mathematics, geography, chronology, and **astronomy** before finally addressing **judicial astrology**.

As a textbook on astrology, the *Tafhim* is on a par with **Ptolemy**'s *Tetrabiblos*. Indeed, it is superior to it, in that it contains a good deal of material contained in Ptolemy's *Almagest* as well. Much of the *Tafhim* is clearly an attempt to epitomize the *Almagest*. Its value lies in the scope of its contents. In no other astrological work is there such a comprehensive survey of medieval astrological science and the subjects that supported it. The book reveals the many-faceted skills and duties of an eleventh-century Persian astrologer. Al-Biruni is also interested in the Hindu astrological traditions and how they differ or coincide with those he is familiar with. He also reports Magian astrological practices. The shortcoming of the book is that, written as an aide-memoire, it lacks examples showing how to apply the methods, astrological or mathematical, so thoroughly set forth. However, the book does provide a uniquely clear window into the level of knowledge attained by a Persian astrologer in 1029. By comparison, his European counterparts were deprived.

Al-Biruni's exposition of astrology places the subject squarely in the context of the mathematical disciplines. He begins by introducing the student to geometry and arithmetic to provide the would-be astrologer with the ability to calculate. The calculations are prelogarithmic, and geometrical trigonometry is used. Curiously absent is any mention of the forty-seventh proposition of Euclid, also known as the Pythagorean theorem, which Ptolemy used to such good effect in the first book of the *Almagest* to find the lengths of chords subtending arcs of the circle.

Al-Biruni's discussion of arithmetic is Pythagorean, based clearly on Nicomachus's *Introduction to Arithmetic*. Initially, this seems strange and possibly even esoteric, until it is realized that ancient calculation in the Middle East, insofar as it was based on Greek mathematics, was based on theoretical arithmetics such as Nicomachus's. As late as the thirteenth century, this was still true in Europe. For instance, Guido Bonatti in *Liber Astronomiae* asserts that the art of calculation has to do with the knowledge of numbers and tables (such as the multiplication tables and tables of roots and powers either found in Nicomachus's work or suggested by him). In practice, such tables were used in conjunction with the abacus. Throughout the geometry and arithmetic sections he emphasizes ratio and proportion. As in Ptolemy's *Almagest,* the solution of triangles relies on the application of areas and the Pythagorean theorem.

For reasons he does not make clear Al-Biruni discusses conic sections in the *Tafhim,* an example of the aide-memoire character of this text. Clearly he must have explained the relevance of conic sections to astrology to Rayhana, but he does not make it clear to the reader. Were it not known that scientists in his day (and even in Ptolemy's day) knew that light expanded in cone shapes, and that the theory was fairly widely held that astrological influence was transmitted from heaven to earth via the light of the **stars**, there would be no hint as to why he included this discussion at all.

Al-Biruni also includes a discussion of the five regular Platonic polyhedra, equating them, in good Neoplatonic fashion, with the five elements (earth, water, fire, air, and ether). Paragraph 107 treats of the powers of numbers from the first power to the fourth. Paragraph 108 gives us the eleventh–century Persian understanding of the decimal notation of the Hindus, including the use of the cipher as a placeholder. His handling of arithmetic includes an introduction to algebra. The algebra of his day was truly "occult." The laws regulating it were not yet known, and his very short exposition shows this fact by its incompleteness. He then introduces astronomy, beginning with the sphere. Step by step he explains basic geocentric astronomy, discussing the celestial circles, their subdivisions, the movements of the **luminaries** (the **Sun** and the **Moon**) and the **planets**, the **constellations**, the planetary theory of his day. He, like John Dee, brings his geocentric astronomy into his **geocentric astrology** (paragraph 387), interpreting the meaning of planets at **perigee**, **apogee**, and on different places on their **epicycles**. He discusses and voices skepticism about the trepidation theory, which held that the **precession of the equinoxes** was not constant in a **retrograde** direction but oscillated back and forth—an incorrect idea first put forth by Thabit ben Qurrah in the tenth century.

He next discusses the size and distance of the planets and elements, the distribution of the land and water masses, and terrestrial longitude and latitude. He discusses the gnomon (a kind of sundial) and its shadow (so basic for chronology) in between discussing details of the **horizon** system of **celestial coordinates** (**azimuth** and **altitude**).

Having prepared the student with the basics, he then discusses geography, including the seven climates, their extent, and their characteristics. His presentation of the various cities in the climates shows that, although he has a fairly accurate mathematical sense of the terrestrial globe, his knowledge of exact latitude and longitude on Earth is approximate. One of the surprises of this book is Al-Biruni's mention in paragraph 239 of the mythological mountain Meru (the World Axis), under which angels dwell, and the island Lanka (modern Sri Lanka), where the demons dwell. This lore is Indian, not Persian and definitely not Islamic. Could it be that the Persian Al-Biruni sought to keep ancient traditions common to both Iran and Aryan India alive? Likewise, paragraph 240 contains another surprise—red as well as white men lived in northwestern Europe. He clearly means red-skinned men, as in every one of the other cases in which he identifies the denizens of the various regions of the world by their skin color. Could it be that he was repeating reports of contact between the Viking Rus (who were in the Volga basin and Byzantium in his day) and the Amerindians?

In paragraph 242 he returns to astronomy to pin down with what degree a given star will culminate, rise, or set. In paragraphs 245–248 he addresses the **houses** of the **horoscope**, using **equal houses** from the **ascendant**. Next he discusses Astronomy of the Anniversary which is, on the macrocosmic level, called "Revolution of Years of the World" in medieval parlance (**Aries** ingress in modern). On the microcosmic level, Astronomy of the Anniversary is a **solar return** or birthdate for an individual. Paragraph 250 deals with the **Saturn–Jupiter conjunctions**. Lunar motion follows, with a discussion of the phases of the Moon followed by a presentation on **eclipses** and the problem of parallax.

Next he switches to the problems of chronology, showing that the astrologer of his day was called upon to regulate the calendar and to understand how the calendar of his nation related to those of other nations who used different systems of chronology. He discusses leap years, solar and **lunar years**, intercalation, and the religious festivals of various peoples of the Middle and Far East, including the Indians and Sogdian Magi. There follows a description of the **astrolabe** and its use in astronomy, desert navigation, and trigonometrical measurements.

After the astrolabe Al-Biruni returns to the subject of astrology, discussing the zodiacal signs and their correspondence to directions of the compass, professions, character, appearance, diseases, crops, and animals. Next he shows the relation of the signs to each other, the year, and the **triplicities**. He then expounds on the planets with their various correspondences. Some of his correspondences seem a bit beside the point or of little importance; for instance, he lists pimples as a **Cancer** "disease." Paragraph 348 presents us with a surprise, stating that the planets have a tendency to take on the gender of the sign they are in. This seems to mean that even male planets become effeminate in female signs! He discusses the Years of the Planets table found so frequently in medieval texts and consisting of Least, Mean, Great, and Greatest Years (used in predicting longevity). He confesses that he doubts that people ever lived as long as the Greatest Years (e.g., the Sun's Greatest Year is 1461 years). He clearly does not know how to use the Greatest Years of the Planets. He then launches into the **dignities** and **debilities** of the planets, their friendships and enmities, **decans**, **paranatellon**, the nine-fold division of signs (nawamsas), and the twelve-fold divisions called dwadasamsas, or more currently "dwads." He gives characteristics of individual **degrees**. Correspondences of the houses follow in natal and horary figures. The **Arabic parts** are discussed in paragraphs 475–480. The subject of application and separation is then dealt with. Next there follows more on dignities.

The vexed question of the oriental/occidental positions of the planets (i.e., whether they are in the left or right **hemisphere** of a horoscope) and the effect this has on their influences is the subject of paragraphs 481–486. The orientality or occidentality of the planets is found obscurely in Dorotheus's *Pentateuch* (first century A.D.) and gets a fuller and thoroughly problematical treatment in Ptolemy's *Tetrabiblos* (second century A.D.). Al-Biruni's treatment is based on Al-Kindi's. It is systematic, ultimately not at odds with Ptolemy's (in fact, he cites the *Almagest*), and has the advantage of being somewhat more rational than the available English versions of *Tetrabiblos.*

In the *Tafhim,* Al-Biruni begins his discussion of the oriental/occidental question with the position of the planets relative to the Sun. He then shows that the **superior planets** become occidental when 90° from the Sun (the Sun having passed them). They then go retrograde and later **direct.** Then comes the **opposition**. This divides the circle into two parts; in one the planet is oriental and in the other, occidental. Al-Biruni does not say so, but implies that the other half of the zodiac is handled in the same way. With the **inferior planets** a different situation holds. Neither **Venus** nor **Mercury** is ever 90° from the Sun, but both can be on either side of the Sun at an eastern or western elongation. The western elongation is oriental; presumably the eastern is occidental. Al-Biruni asserts that planets in **cazimi** (within 16′ of the center of the Sun) are strongest. They are weakest when **combust** (the acceptable distance for this varies from planet to planet) and are more powerful when oriental than when occidental. There are various degrees of debility when occidental. They also change their qualities of hot, cold, wet, or dry, depending on their relation to the Sun. Al-Biruni asserts that the planets change their gender depending on their relation to the horizon, though his discussion of this dimension of the problem of orientality and occidentality is less clear than Ptolemy's in *Tetrabiblos* (in Book III, chapter 3 of Robbins's translation and Book III, chapter 4 of the Ashmand translation).

The last section of the *Tafhim* gets to judicial astrology. It is here that the author's lack of examples is most disheartening. Case studies would have been helpful. He divides the subject of astrology into five categories: (1) meteorology, (2) **mundane astrology** relating to famine, plague, epidemics, etc., (3) environmental effects on the individual, (4) human activities and occupations, and (5) a division including **horary** and **electional astrology**. Al-Biruni says the foundations of this latter division are unknown: "Here astrology reaches a point which threatens to transgress its proper limits, where problems are submitted which it is impossible to solve for the most part, and where the matter leaves the solid basis of universals for particulars. Where this boundary is passed, where the astrologer is on one side and the sorcerer on the other, you enter a field of omens and divinations which has nothing to do with astrology, although the stars may be referred to in connection with them" (pp. 317–19).

What today is called **natal astrology** is subsumed under categories 3 and 4 (environmental effects and human activities and occupations). Al-Biruni considers two initial points for natal astrology: the conception and the birth. He finds the length of life through the alcocoden (which he calls by its Persian name, *kadkhuda*). He defines the alcocoden, rather than the **hyleg,** as the planet with the most dignity. The number of years attributed to the native's life is determined by whether the alcocoden is angular, succedent, or cadent. Al-Biruni is less than complete and clear here. He says "a large number" is given when the alcocoden is angular, "a mean number" when succedent, and "a small number" when cadent. The tradition is more fully expounded in other medieval works, such as Bonatti's *Liber Astronomiae* and Abu 'Ali Al-Khayyat's *The Judgements of Nativities.* From the latter two books we learn that the numbers referred to come from the Years of the Planets table. The rule varies from author to author, but is generally that Great Years are given when the alcocoden is angular, the Mean Years when it is succedent, and the Least Years when it is cadent. Yet, in addition to this, Al-Biruni, following Ptolemy, still tries to predict the exact time of death by directing the hyleg to the place of the Apheta. His complete method, therefore, is twofold and seems to be a fusion of two techniques originally used independently of each other.

He employs **solar returns** and **progressions** as well as the divisor (Ruler of the Year by profection of the ascendant) for discovering the important events in the native's life each year. He directs by profection (down to the week) and by term from year to year. He discusses **rectification** of an unknown birth time by using the animodar of Ptolemy and the trutine of Hermes. Feeling assured that he has set forth the knowledge necessary to a beginner, he warns readers not to exceed the limits of the knowable and thereby bring scorn and derision upon themselves.

Such then is Al-Biruni's *Tafhim.* It is certainly one of the classic works in astrology and should be closely studied by all interested in the history and practice of traditional astrology. It opens a window onto the astrological and mathematical expertise of one of the world's finest astrological minds. Al-biruni was highly regarded in his day, and his work was preserved and transmitted. As mentioned, it was a source for Guido Bonatti's thirteenth-century *Liber Astronomiae,* which was itself highly influential. Except for its failure to provide practical examples, it constitutes a veritable treasure trove of astrological lore.

—Robert Zoller

Selected Publications:

The Chronologies of Ancient Nations. Translated and edited by Edward Sachau. London: W. H. Allen & Co., 1879.

The Book of Instruction in the Elements of the Art of Astrology. Translated by R. Ramsay Wright. London: Luzac & Co., 1934.

Albiruni's India. Translated by Edward C. Sachau. New Delhi: S. Chand & Co., 1964.

Sources:

Al-Khayyat, Abu 'Ali. *The Judgements of Nativities.* Translated by James H. Holden. Tempe, Ariz.: American Federation of Astrologers, 1988.

Dorotheus. *Pentateuch.* (published as *Carmen Astrologicum,* Dorotheus Sidonius). Translated by Pingree. Leipzig, Germany: B. G. Teubner, 1976.

Hoyt, Edwin P. *Arab Science.* New York: Thomas Nelson, 1975.

Ptolemy, Claudius. *Almagest.* Translated by R. Catesby Taliaferro. Brittanica Great Books Series, vol. 16. Chicago: University of Chicago Press, 1938, 1952.

———. *Ptolemy's Tetrabiblos.* Translated by J. M. Ashmand. London: Foulsham & Co., 1922.

———. *Tetrabiblos.* Translated by F. E. Robbins. Cambridge, Mass.: Harvard University Press, 1964.

Shumaker, Wayne and J. L. Heilbron. *John Dee on Astronomy: Propaedeumata Aphoristica 1558 & 1568.* Berkeley, Calif.: University of California Press, 1978.

Alcoholism

Alcoholism and other forms of escapist drug addiction are associated primarily with the **planet Neptune** and, secondarily, with **Pisces,** the sign **ruled** by Neptune. Neptune is associated with sensitivity to the subtle dimensions of existence. When strong and positively situated in a **natal chart,** Neptune can manifest as musical sensitivity, mystical sensitivity, and so forth. When negatively aspected, however, Neptunian sensitivity will manifest as deceptiveness or escapism.

Charles E. O. Carter, an important astrologer of the early twentieth century, discussed alcoholism and drug addiction in An *Encyclopedia of Psychological Astrology.* Carter associated alcoholism and drug addiction with a number of different factors. In the birth chart of an alcholic, according to Carter, the **Sun** and the **Moon** are almost always weak by sign and **house** position, "or else they are badly afflicted, especially in or from Fire or Water, or both. Fire gives the convivial drunkard, Water the weak or besotted one" (p. 30). Furthermore, "The fifth house (the house of pleasure and entertainment) is nearly always afflicted by Neptune or by planets in watery signs, and Mars is very frequently afflicted by Neptune, in or from **Pisces**" (p. 30).

A more recent study, reported in Ann Parker's *Astrology and Alchoholism,* confirmed the importance of Neptune. Parker, however, also found that the planet **Uranus** was significantly represented in the **horoscopes** of alcoholics, especially Moon-Uranus **aspects**. She explains this unusual finding by pointing out that a Moon-Uranus contact, "even linked in good aspect, represents great emotional excitability and self-will, both charcteristic of the alchoholic" (p. 28). When linked by a **hard aspect,** "these planets produce states of fear and anxiety, extreme self will, a craving for sensation, restlessness, and a tendency to exaggerate and magnify things" (p. 28), all of which are associated with alcoholic personalities.

Sources:

Carter, Charles E. O. *An Encyclopedia of Psychological Astrology.* 1924. Reprint. London: Theosophical Publishing House, 1963.
Parker, Ann E. *Astrology and Alcoholism.* York Beach, Maine: Samuel Weiser, 1982.

Aletheia

Aletheia, **asteroid** 259 (the 259th asteroid to be discovered), is approximately 103 kilometers in diameter and has an **orbital** period of 5.6 years. It is named after the Greek for truth or sincerity. When prominent in a **natal chart**, Aletheia shows a sincere person. Its location by sign and **house** indicates where one is most sincere or experiences sincerity. When **afflicted**, Aletheia may signify insincerity or confrontations with unpleasant truths.

Sources:

Kowal, Charles T. *Asteroids: Their Nature and Utilization.* Chichester, West Sussex, U.K.: Ellis Horwood Limited, 1988.
Room, Adrian. *Dictionary of Astronomical Names.* London: Routledge, 1988.

Almagest

The *Almagest* is the famous astronomer–mathematician **Ptolemy's** treatise on astronomy.

Almanac

An almanac is a book or booklet containing sets of tables, particularly calendrical tables, announcing astronomical or astrological events (**Moon** phases, beginnings of seasons, **eclipses**, etc.) and carrying historical facts, information on planting by the signs, and other types of data. Older almanacs (the almanac tradition has been traced as far back as the Hellenistic period) contained prophetic announcements, a tradition carried on by modern almanacs, which usually predict the day-by-day weather on the basis of meteorological astrology. In U.S. history, the most well known almanac was *Poor Richard's Almanac* (1732–1757), which was issued by Benjamin Franklin. *The Old Farmer's Almanac* is still popular in rural areas

Sources:

deVore, Nicholas. *Encyclopedia of Astrology.* New York: Philosophical Library, 1947.
Gettings, Fred. *Dictionary of Astrology.* London: Routledge & Kegan Paul, 1985.
Thomas, Robert B. *The Old Farmer's 1991 Almanac.* Dublin, N.H.: Yankee Publishing, 1990.

Almuten

Almuten is an Arabic term for the strongest **planet** in a **natal chart** by virtue of **essential** and **accidental dignities**.

Altitude

In astrology, altitude refers to the **angular distance** (i.e., measured in degrees of an arc) that a point, **planet**, or other heavenly body is situated above or below the **horizon**. Above the horizon, altitude is measured up to a maximum angular distance of 90° (directly overhead); below the horizon, down to a maximum of -90° (directly underneath).

Ambrosia

Ambrosia, **asteroid** 193 (the 193d asteroid to be discovered), is approximately 42 kilometers in diameter and has an **orbital** period of 4.2 years. It was named after food of the ancient gods that was said to have bestowed immortality. When prominent in a **natal chart**, Ambrosia may indicate long life.

Sources:

Kowal, Charles T. *Asteroids: Their Nature and Utilization.* Chichester, West Sussex, U.K.: Ellis Horwood Limited, 1988.
Room, Adrian. *Dictionary of Astronomical Names.* London: Routledge, 1988.

America, Astrology in

See: History of Astrology in America

Amicitia

Amicitia, **asteroid** 367 (the 367th asteroid to be discovered), is approximately 20 kilometers in diameter and has an **orbital** period of 3.3 years. Its name is a personified form of the Latin word for friendship. When prominent in a **natal chart**, Amicitia indicates a friendly personality. The sign and **house** position indicate both how one interacts with friends and what one's friends are like.

Sources:

Kowal, Charles T. *Asteroids: Their Nature and Utilization.* Chichester, West Sussex, U.K.: Ellis Horwood Limited, 1988.
Room, Adrian. *Dictionary of Astronomical Names.* London: Routledge, 1988.

Amor

Amor, **asteroid** 1221 (meaning that it was the 1,221st asteroid to be discovered—in 1932) was named after the Roman god of love (corresponding to the Greek **Eros**). It has an **orbital** period of 2 2/3 years and is only 1 kilometer in diameter. Amor is one of the more recent asteroids to be investigated by astrologers. Preliminary material on Amor can be found in Demetra George and Douglas Bloch's *Astrology for Yourself,* and an **ephemeris** (table of celestial locations) for Amor can be found in the back of the second edition of George and Bloch's *Asteroid Goddesses.* Unlike the **planets**, which are associated with a wide range of phenomena, the smaller asteroids are said to represent a single principle. George and Bloch give Amor's principle as platonic "love and compassion." J. Lee Lehman associates Amor with intimacy and with nonsexual love, as well as with the loneliness and anger of being rejected.

Sources:

George, Demetra, with Douglas Bloch. *Astrology for Yourself: A Workbook for Personal Transformation.* Berkeley, Calif.: Wingbow Press, 1987.

———. *Asteroid Goddesses: The Mythology, Psychology and Astrology of the Reemerging Feminine.* 2d ed., rev. and enl. San Diego, Calif.: Astro Computing Services, 1990.

Lehman, J. Lee. *The Ultimate Asteroid Book.* West Chester, Pa.: Whitford Press, 1988.

Anahita

Anahita, **asteroid** 270 (the 270th asteroid to be discovered), is approximately 52 kilometers in diameter and has an **orbital** period of 3.3 years. It was named after a goddess of fertility in Persian mythology. When prominent in a **natal chart**, Anahita can show an exceptionally productive or "fertile" individual. By sign and **house** location, it may show an area of great potential that need only be cultivated a little to produce results.

Sources:

Kowal, Charles T. *Asteroids: Their Nature and Utilization.* Chichester, West Sussex, U.K.: Ellis Horwood Limited, 1988.

Room, Adrian. *Dictionary of Astronomical Names.* London: Routledge, 1988.

Androgynous Planet

Traditionally, most **planets** and signs were designated as either **masculine** or **feminine**. **Mercury** was the only planet in premodern astrology that was said to be neutral or androgynous. In contemporary astrology, **Uranus** has also come to be regarded as an androgynous planet.

Angle (Angular)

The term angle can be used in two different ways in astrology. In its primary, traditional meaning, angle refers to one of the four "corners" (figuratively speaking) of a chart—namely, the cusps of the first, fourth, seventh, and tenth **houses**. Planets making a **conjunction** with the angles—which are sometimes called angular planets, particularly when they are in an **angular house**—are said to exercise an especially strong influence over the entire **horoscope**. In practice, astrologers pay the most attention to angular planets in the first and tenth houses. Angle is also used sometimes as an alternative term for **aspect**, as when one talks about the angular relationship between two **planets**.

Angular Distance

The distance between points in an astrological chart is always expressed in terms of angular distance. Because the locations of the significant elements of a **horoscope** are expressed in terms of degrees (°) and minutes (') and, occasionally, seconds (") of the **zodiac**, the distance between any two points is similarly expressed as so many degrees and minutes of the arc between them. To take a concrete example, the angular distance between a **planet** located at 3°15' **Aries** and another **planet** situated at 24°27' Aries would be 21°12'.

Angular Houses

The **houses** of an astrological chart are classified into three groups of four: angular houses (the first, fourth, seventh, tenth), **succedent houses** (the second, fifth, eighth, and eleventh), and **cadent houses** (the third, sixth, ninth, and twelfth). In traditional astrology, angular houses were regarded as the most powerful houses in which **planets** could be positioned. Modern astrologers, however, tend to believe that planets placed in angular houses have the most

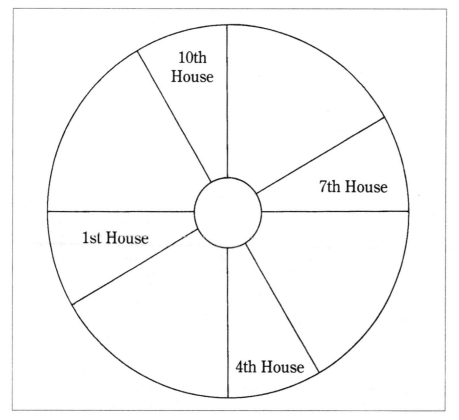

◄
Angular houses.

influence on the outer, surface aspects of a person's life, while planets placed in the cadent houses have the most impact on one's inner life. Planets located in succedent houses mediate one's inner and outer lives.

Angular Velocity

The core meaning of angular velocity is the **angular distance**, expressed in degrees (°) and minutes (′) of an arc, that a **planet** travels in the course of a day. By extension, angular velocity can also be the angular distance a heavenly body moves during any given unit of time.

Anomalistic Period (Anomaly; Anomalistic Year)

For a **planet**, an anomalistic period is the time between two successive **perihelions** (the point in a planet's **orbit** where it is closest to the **Sun**). For the **Moon**, an anomalistic period is the time between two successive **perigees** (the point where it is closest to Earth). The expression anomalistic period is derived from *anomaly,* which in astronomy refers to the **angular distance** of a planet from its perihelion or its **aphelion**. By extension, an anomalistic year is the period between Earth's perihelions, which is 365.23964 days.

Antipathy

Congruent with its use in everyday English, antipathy refers to an inharmonious relationship between certain **planets**, particularly when they make **hard aspects** to each another. The term is also used to refer to the repulsion between people whose charts interact inharmoniously with each other.

Antiscion

Antiscion is a somewhat confusing term that has, unfortunately, come to be used for more than one notion. Picture the wheel of the **zodiac** and imagine a straight line from 0° **Cancer** to 0° **Capricorn** so as to divide the circle into two equal halves. If a planet is located at an **angular distance** of 45° away from this dividing line (e.g., at 15° **Taurus**), its antiscion would be 45° in the opposite direction from the line (e.g., at 15° **Leo**). If another planet happens to be located at or very near the antiscion of the first planet, the two planets are said to have a relationship with each other comparable to a conjunction **aspect**. This is the traditional meaning of the term.

Some astrologers have extended the term to apply to points at equal angular distances from the **ascendant–descendant** axis (i.e., at equal distances above and below the **horizon**) in an individual **horoscope**.

Sources:

Brau, Jean-Louis, Helen Weaver, and Allan Edmands. *Larousse Encyclopedia of Astrology.* New York: New American Library, 1980.
Gettings, Fred. *Dictionary of Astrology.* London: Routledge & Kegan Paul, 1985.

Anubis

Anubis, **asteroid** 1,912 (the 1,912th asteroid to be discovered), is approximately 11 kilometers in diameter and has an **orbital** period of 4.9 years. Anubis was named after the Egyptian god of the dead. According to Lehman (p. 144), individuals in whose **natal chart** this asteroid is prominent "may represent someone for whom death is more than a passing issue."

Sources:

Kowal, Charles T. *Asteroids: Their Nature and Utilization.* Chichester, West Sussex, U.K.: Ellis Horwood Limited, 1988.
Lehman, J. Lee. *The Ultimate Asteroid Book.* West Chester, Penn.: Whitford Press, 1988.

Aphelion

Although they approximate circles, every **orbit** is elliptical. The point in a **satellite's** orbit where it is farthest from the **Sun** is called its aphelion (from Greek *apo,* away and *helio's,* sun).

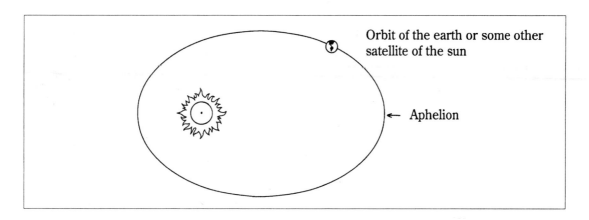

Aphelion (not drawn to scale).

Aphrodite

Aphrodite, **asteroid** 1,388 (the 1,388th asteroid to be discovered), is approximately 22 kilometers in diameter and has an **orbital** period of 5.2 years. Aphrodite was named after the Greek goddess of sex, love, and beauty, the equivalent of the Roman **Venus**. Lehman associates Aphrodite with Venus and **Astarte** (also divinities of sex and fertility), asserting that this asteroid is more "refined" than the other two.

Sources:

Kowal, Charles T. *Asteroids: Their Nature and Utilization*. Chichester, West Sussex, U.K.: Ellis Horwood Limited, 1988.

Lehman, J. Lee. *The Ultimate Asteroid Book*. West Chester, Penn.: Whitford Press, 1988.

Apogee

Every **orbit** is elliptical. When a **satellite** is at its greatest distance from the **Earth**, it is at its apogee (from Greek *apo,* away, and *geios,* earth).

Apollo

Apollo, **asteroid** 1,862 (the 1,862d asteroid to be discovered) is approximately 1.4 kilometers in diameter and has an **orbital** period of 1.8 years. Apollo was named after the Greek sun-god, patron of the fine arts, medicine, music, poetry, and eloquence. According to Lang-Wescott, Apollo indicates where we have recurrent learning experiences—where we are slow to learn to change our patterns. This asteroid's key phrase is *against the odds*. According to Lehman,

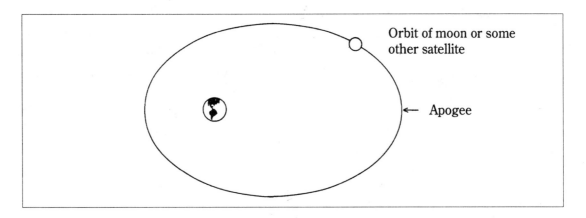

Orbit of moon or some other satellite

← Apogee

Apogee (not drawn to scale).

Apollo can manifest in one of three ways—as a personification of the **Sun**, as a personification of the traits Greek society used to portray the ideal male, and as the giver–healer of disease.

Sources:

Lang-Wescott, Martha. *Asteroids-Mechanics: Ephemerides II.* Conway, Mass.: Treehouse Mountain, 1990.
———. *Mechanics of the Future: Asteroids.* Rev. ed. Conway, Mass.: Treehouse Mountain, 1991.
Lehman, J. Lee. *The Ultimate Asteroid Book.* West Chester, Penn.: Whitford Press, 1988.

Apollon

Apollon is one of the eight **hypothetical planets** (sometimes referred to as the trans-Neptunian points or planets, TNPs) utilized in **Uranian astrology**. It indicates expansiveness and multiplicity. It can symbolize everything from commerce and science to peace and success. In combination with other celestial bodies, Apollon means lots of (or too many) irons in the fire. It may also indicate distant career opportunities and potentials, such as in another country.

Sources:

Lang-Wescott, Martha. *Mechanics of the Future: Asteroids.* Rev. ed. Conway, Mass.: Treehouse Mountain, 1991.
Simms, Maria Kay. *Dial Detective: Investigation with the 90 Degree Dial.* San Diego, Calif.: Astro Computing Services, 1989.

Aporhoea

The **Moon** is said to be in aporhoea as it **separates** from an **aspect** with one **planet** and begins to **apply** an aspect with another planet.

Apparent Motion

It has become astrological tradition to speak about the **zodiac** and the heavenly bodies as if they were revolving around the Earth while Earth remains stationary. So that other people do not regard **astrology** as locked in a pre-Copernican world view, astrologers sometimes specify that they are talking about the *apparent* motion of the **stars** and **planets**. In this custom, astrologers are following the same tradition as everyone else who refers to the daily appearance and disappearance of the **Sun**, for example, as the "rising" and "setting" of the Sun, even though most people in industrialized societies know that it is the axial rotation of the Earth that causes this apparent motion.

Applying Aspect (Approaching Aspect)

When a **transiting planet** begins to form an **aspect** vis-à-vis another planet or a **house cusp**, it is said to be applying. After the aspect has passed the point of being exact and the faster-moving planet is pulling away, the aspect is said to be **separating**. This may sound confusing, but is really quite simple. To illustrate, let us say that **Pluto** is located at 25° in the sign **Capricorn**. As transiting **Mars** gets within about 4° of Pluto (e.g., reaches 21°, 22°, 23°, or 24° Capricorn), we say that Mars is applying to (or approaching) a **conjunction** with Pluto. The conjunction becomes exact when Mars reaches 25° and is separating as soon as Mars **transits** past 25° Capricorn.

A doubly applying (or doubly approaching) aspect occurs when both planets are moving toward an aspect. In other words, if in the preceding example Pluto had been moving **retrograde** (backward through the **zodiac**) as Mars moved **direct** (forward through the **zodiac**), the aspect would have been doubly applying. For the purpose of interpretation, applying aspects are regarded as being stronger than separating aspects.

Sources:

Gettings, Fred. *Dictionary of Astrology.* London: Routledge & Kegan Paul, 1985.
Lee, Dal. *Dictionary of Astrology.* New York: Paperback Library, 1969.

Appulse

Appulse refers to a partial **occultation,** a **conjunction,** a **planet's** crossing of the **meridian,** or the entry of the **Moon** into the Earth's shadow.

Aquarius

Aquarius (from the Latin *Aquarii,* water carrier) the eleventh sign of the **zodiac,** is a **fixed air** sign. It is a positive, **masculine** sign, **ruled** by the **planet Uranus** (before the outer planets were discovered, it was said to be ruled by **Saturn**). Its symbol is the Water Bearer, and its **glyph** is a pair of wavy lines representing water (resulting in a frequent confusion about Aquarius's element, which is air rather than **water**). Aquarius is associated with the shins, ankles, and the circulatory system, and individuals with an Aquarius **sun sign** are susceptible to sprained ankles, hardening of the arteries, and varicose veins. The key phrase for Aquarius is *I know.*

Like certain other Zodiacal signs, Aquarius has been associated with more than one mythic figure. It is most often identified with Ganymede ("cup bearer of the gods"), a beautiful young man who, after being abducted by an eagle sent by Zeus, served as his cupbearer. Ganymede was also Zeus's lover, and was said to have been transformed into the **constellation** Aquarius.

Another mythical figure sometimes associated with Aquarius is Cecrops. Cecrops, half human and half serpent, was a culture hero who, as king of Attica, put an end to human sacrifice (by offering cakes instead of flesh to the gods) and founded a court. He also taught his people writing, the proper manner of burying the dead, and census taking. He is particularly remembered for deciding a contest between Athena and Poseidon in favor of Athena. In anger, Poseidon responded by flooding Attica.

Despite the myth of Ganymede, there is no special connection between Aquarius and homosexuality (**Neptune**, ruler of **Pisces**, was the ancient patron of homosexuals). However, Aquarians tend to be eccentric individuals who enjoy working with other people. In line with the story of Cecrops, **natives** of this sign tend to be humanistic social reformers, with a special aptitude for intellectual pursuits like writing. Also in line with the Cecrops myth, census taking reflects the mathematical and scientific inclinations of Aquarius. While Aquarians are known for being open-minded, they are also unusually argumentative. They tend to avoid emotions by intellectualizing them—symbolically choosing Athena (goddess of intellect) over Poseidon (ruler of water, the symbol of emotion) until they are overwhelmed (flooded).

There is a wealth of information available on the characteristics of the zodiacal signs—so much that one book would not be able to contain it all. One traditional way in which astrologers condense information is by summarizing sign and planet traits in lists of words and short phrases called key words or key phrases. The following Aquarius key words are drawn from Manly P. Hall's *Astrological Keywords:*

> *Emotional key words:* "The emotional nature is very active but in negative types not very profound; vivacious, excitable, kindly in disposition, well-liked, gentle, altruistic, domestic but changeable, unconventional, temperamental, worrying" (p. 18).

> *Mental key words:* "Inventive, intellectual, fond of literature and science, diplomatic, tolerant, reasonable, independent, discreet, optimistic, humanitarian, fixed in opinion" (pp. 21–22).

Most popular works on astrology contain data on the signs, and these can be consulted for more detailed information.

Sources:

Evans, Colin. *The New Waite's Compendium of Natal Astrology.* Revised by Brain E. F. Gardener. York Beach, Maine: Samuel Weiser, 1971. (Originally published, 1917.)

Green, Landis Knight. *The Astrologer's Manual: Modern Insights into an Ancient Art.* Sebastopol, Calif.: CRCS Publications, 1975.

Hall, Manly P. *Astrological Keywords.* 1958 Reprint. Savage, Md.: Maryland: Littlefield Adams (1975), 18, 21–22.

Aquinas, Saint Thomas

Saint Thomas Aquinas was a famous thirteenth-century Italian scholar–philosopher and the official theologian of the Catholic church. Although not an astrologer, he made some very influential assertions about the science of the **stars**. While he acknowledged planetary influence, Thomas Aquinas was also concerned with reconciling the apparent determinism of astrology with free will.

For example, he asserted that one could utilize powers of rationality to overcome such forces of determinism. The basis for this assertion was the distinction Christian philosophy drew between the immortal soul (governed by reason) and the physical body (governed by sensual desire). As an artifact of this physical world, astrological forces could, according to Thomas Aquinas, affect the physical body. The soul, however, was beyond such forces. Individuals could thus exercise their reason and overcome planetary influences.

People in groups, however, were ruled more by their passions than by reason. Thus, the actions of nations, cities, and other organizations—the sphere of **mundane astrology**—were more "fated" than the actions of individuals. Because of the clear distinction that he drew between groups and individuals, it has been said that Thomas Aquinas was the first person to distinguish **natal astrology** from mundane astrology.

Sources:

Baigent, Michael, Nicholas Campion, and Charles Harvey. *Mundane Astrology*. 2d ed. London: Aquarian Press, 1992.

Brau, Jean-Louis, Helen Weaver, and Allan Edmands. *Larousse Encyclopedia of Astrology*. New York: North American Library, 1980.

Ara

Ara, **asteroid** 849 (the 849th asteroid to be discovered), is approximately 152 kilometers in diameter and has an **orbital** period of 5.6 years. Ara was named after the American Relief Administration (ARA) and represents the giving of aid. In a **natal chart**, its sign and **house** position indicates where and how one is most likely to give aid or to be aided by others. When **afflicted** by inharmonious **aspects**, Ara may indicate lack of aid or giving aid for the purpose of self-aggrandizement or as a manipulation.

Sources:

Kowal, Charles T. *Asteroids: Their Nature and Utilization*. Chichester, West Sussex, U.K.: Ellis Horwood Limited, 1988.

Room, Adrian. *Dictionary of Astronomical Names*. London: Routledge, 1988.

Arabic Astrology

See: History of Western Astrology

Arabic Parts

The Arabic Parts are arithmetically derived points on the **ecliptic** (the path that the **Sun** appears, from our terrestrial perspective, to travel during the course of a year) that represent the synthesis of two or more astrological components (e.g., **planets**, **house cusps**, or even other Arabic Parts). The longitudinal distance between them is measured and then projected from a meaningful point in the astrological chart (usually the **ascendant**). The degree (°), minute ('), and second (") of **zodiacal longitude** that this distance reaches is called the "*part.*" Modern astrological texts (post 1800) usually do not distinguish between **diurnal** and **nocturnal** charts (astrological charts—be they **natal**, **horary**, **electional**, or other—are erected for times when the Sun is above the **horizon** or diurnal, or below the horizon or nocturnal), yet the original practice was to do so in most, if not all, cases. Thus, in diurnal charts the formula is often different from that in nocturnal charts.

For example, the most commonly used Arabic Part, the Pars Fortunae (**Part of Fortune**), is found in diurnal figures (*figure* is a traditional term for an astrological chart) by taking the distance from the Sun to the Moon (in the order of the signs) and projecting it from the ascendant (also in the order of the signs). Let it be assumed that the ascendant of a **native** born in the daytime with 12 **Pisces** 30 rising has the Sun at 4 **Aquarius** 46 in the eleventh house and the **Moon** at 0 **Taurus** 15. The distance between the *Lights* (a traditional term for the Sun and the Moon) is 85° 29'. When this distance is added to the ascendant, the part is found to be at 67° 53' or 7 **Gemini** 59.

Should the figure be nocturnal, however, the Part of Fortune is found from the Moon. Thus, the distance from the Moon to the Sun (in the order of the signs) is found to be 274° 31'. This distance, projected from the ascendant (12 Pisces 30) locates the Part at 257° 01' or 17 **Sagittarius** 01.

In traditional astrology (that practiced in Europe until the mid 17-seventeenth century), the Arabic Parts were used for several purposes: First, they were used in horary figures to assist in judgment when the planetary testimony was obscure. One circumstance in which this seems to have been done was when, in a horary figure, one planet is the **significator** of a matter and another planet **applies** to some aspect of this **significator**. In such a case the astrologer may not know if the second planet will hinder or assist the business. The astrologer might take the distance from the **aspect** in question to the significator and—making an Arabic Part of this distance—project it from the ascendant or other relevant house cusp (say, the third, if the business is about travel, siblings, etc.). The astrologer would then judge whether the application was beneficial or not by determining if the ruler of the part was a **benefic**. Likewise, a judgment as to good or evil could be made in this way, again on the basis of the benefic or **malefic** nature of the Part's ruler. The strength of the ruler of the Part and its aspect (or lack of same) to the significator could also yield helpful information. This is what Guido Bonatti obscurely alludes to when he cites Albumasar (Persian astrologer, A.D. 787–886) in his discussion of the Parts in *Liber Astronomiae* (column 616; *Guidonis Bonatti,* 1550). Lynn Thorndike, in *The History of Magic and Experimental Science* (p. 826), calls Bonatti "the most influential astrologer of the thirteenth century." Bonatti's work (*Liber Astronomiae*) was a major source for traditional medieval European astrological practice.

In his "146 Considerations" (Tractatus V of *Anima Astrologiae*), Bonatti discusses another way the concept of the parts could be used to clarify murky testimony in horary figures when the planetary indications are inscrutable. He suggests making parts of those house rulers that related to the matter considered. This is what he advocates in Considerations 144 and 146.

Jean Ganivet, in *Amicus Medicorum* (1508), provides us with an example of the use of the Parts in iatromedical diagnosis. He casts a horary figure for the dean of Vienne, seeking to determine whether the dean would survive his current illness or not. He concludes, after considering the Lights, the Part of the Killing Planet, the Part of Death, the Part of Life and the Part of Fortune, all of which were adversely placed, that the dean will fall into delirium in 24 hours and die within two days. He reports that such was the case.

In natal figures, the Parts were usually used to get a deeper understanding of the **native**'s life. For instance, the Part of Fortune was called the lunar ascendant and provided the medieval astrologer with information relating to the native's inner motivation (as opposed to outer drives imposed upon one by physical and worldly demands). The Part of the Sun (Pars Solis, Pars Futurorum, Pars Spiritus, Pars Daemonis) signifies, according to Bonatti, the soul and the body and their quality, as well as faith, prophecy, religion and the culture of God, secrets, cogitations, intentions, hidden things, etc. It is found in a way different from that in which the Part of Fortune is found: In diurnal figures, the distance from the Moon to the Sun is projected from the ascendant; in nocturnal figures, the distance from the Sun to the Moon is projected from the ascendant. Bonatti's work catalogs the Parts according to the themes of the houses. His Parts of the seventh house contains numerous Parts intended to reveal the marital fidelity of man and wife, thus providing the astrologer with material useful in **synastry**, although it is here that his medieval monkish misogyny shines forth most glaringly.

The Parts also had application in economic forecasting. Bonatti gives us an involved (and largely accurate) technique for commodities forecasting! In addition, the Parts were used in mundane figures (**ingresses**; also known as Revolutions of Years of the World).

The Parts were used extensively by the Arabic astrologers, who greatly increased their number. Bonatti, who relies on Arabic sources, lists 128 Parts. **Al-Biruni**, who is one of Bonatti's sources, lists 143. Al-Biruni advocated a rational astrology based on actual astronomical verities and expressed doubt bordering on scorn with regard to horary astrology, which he likened to sorcery. In discussing the Parts (which he calls Lots) he complained, "It is impossible to enumerate the lots which have been invented for the solution of horary questions and for answering enquiries as to prosperous outcome or auspicious time for action; they increase in number daily. . ." (p. 28).

This proliferation led to the superficial and promiscuous abuse of the Parts by shallow practitioners who did not appreciate that the Parts were never intended to replace the testimony of the primary figure. Accurate **delineation** of the Parts depends on accurate delineation of the figure. (For a fuller treatment of how the Parts are to be delineated, see Robert Zoller's *Lost Key to Prediction.*)

The history of the Parts predates their Arabic usage, stretching back to the Hellenistic Period, perhaps as early as 300 B.C., and, conceivably, even to Greco-Babylonian times. Thus, the name "Arabic" Parts is a misnomer. The Parts are found in Dorotheus's *Pentateuch* (first century A.D.) and in the *Liber Hermetis,* which Gundel and Festugiere regard as a pre-Islamic Hellenistic Hermetic text exemplifying Egyptian temple astrology of an era possibly as early as the third century B.C. Thus, the "Arabic" Parts might better be called Hermetic or Egyptian Parts.

That the Parts originated in pagan times is also implied by Bonatti's, Albumasar's, and Al-Biruni's rather vague handling of the Part of the Sun and the Part Hyleg. In the former case, Bonatti, drawing on Albumasar and Al-Biruni, seems intentionally vague in merely mentioning that the Part of the Sun was relevant to "faith, prophesy and the culture of God." He does not elaborate on this in any way. Al-Biruni, who gives symbols for many of the Parts, indicates the Part of the Sun (which he calls the Part of the Daemon) as a circle with two horns—as a crescent emerging from behind a disk. The glyph resembles the head of a medieval Roman horned demon: a figure that was not originally regarded as evil. In light of the well-attested fact that much of the astrological lore of Albumasar, Al-Biruni, Messahalla, and others came from the polytheistic Hermetic Sabian community at what is today Harran, in southeast Turkey, there has been a long-standing assumption on the part of some esotericists that the medieval astrological tradition was a vehicle for preserving the Hellenistic pagan Hermetic gnosis. This assumption appears correct. The reticence of both the Moslem and Christian writers (such as Albumasar, Al-Biruni, and Bonatti) was probably due to their wish to avoid censure by their respective religious authorities. The daemon referred to in the name Part of the Daemon may well be the Neoplatonic–Hermetic Agathodaemon, which was the chief deity of the pagan Sabians.

Another Part which receives vague treatment by Bonatti is the Part Hyleg. Bonatti says that it is the root of the other Parts and can exist without them, but they cannot exist without it and that "the ancients could have said more about it had they wanted but refrained from doing so because it was involved with other things" (Zoller, p. 94). This statement is the very epitome of obscurity. The key to the mystery of this Part is to determine how it is found and how it got its name. It is taken (by day or night) from the position of the conjunction or prevention (i.e., the new or full moon) prior to birth to the position of the Moon at the time of birth and then projected from the ascendant. It is also called the Radix Vitae (Root of Life) and comprehends the whole life of the native, which links it to the Gnostic and Hermetic mysteries of reincarnation discussed in the Corpus Hermeticum (attributed to Hermes Trismegistus). Although the Corpus Hermeticum we have today dates from the early centuries A.D., the cult whose doctrines it embodies began to coalesce in Egypt with Alexander's conquest (331 B.C.) around the notion that the Greek god Hermes and the Egyptian Thoth were one in the same, an idea that had been commonly accepted since Plato's times. The Hermetic doctrine of reincarnation, which bears resemblance to the Hindu and Buddhist concepts, is found scattered throughout the libelli comprising the Corpus, but the following are especially relevant: Libellus I, sections 13–18; Libellus III, section 4; Libellus VIII; and Libellus X, sections 16–22. In Libellus XI, sections 7–8a, the Moon is referred to as "the instrument by which birth and growth are wrought" and we are told that the Moon "divides the immortals from the mortals."

This new understanding of the antiquity of the Parts may not be the final word. If the Parts, as it now seems certain, were used as early as 300 B.C., we may be dealing with a tradition that is far older. The ancient usage of the Parts has had an effect on modern astrological practice. Besides being resurrected in the twentieth century in the context of traditional astrology, the concepts underlying the Parts have been influential in modern astrological innovations. For example, the Arabic Parts prefigure by at least 2,000 years the planetary pictures of the Hamburg School of Uranian Astrology and similar practices of the chronobiologists.

—Robert Zoller

Sources:

Al-Biruni, Abu'l-Rayhan Muhammad ibn Ahmad. *The Book of Instruction in the Elements of the Art of Astrology.* Translated by R. Ramsay Wright. London: Luzac & Co., 1934.

Bonatti, Guidonis. *The Astrologer's Guide: Anima Astrologiae.* Translated by Henry Coley (1676) and edited by William Lilly. London: Regulus, 1986. (Facsimile of 1886 edition.)

Festugiere, Le R. P., *La revelation d'Hermes Trismegiste,* Paris: Librairie Lecoffre, 1950.

Ganivet, Jean. *Amicus Medicorum.* Lyons, France: 1508.

Guidonis Bonati Forliviensis Mathematici de Astronomiae Tractatus Basel, Switzerland, 1550.

Gundel, von Wilhelm. *Dekane und Dekansternbilder.* Darmstadt, Germany: Wissenschaftliche Buchgesellschaft, 1969.

Hermetica. 4 vols. Translated and edited by Walter Scott. London: Dawsons of Pall Mall, 1968.

Thorndike, Lynn. *The History of Magic and Experimental Science.* 8 vols. New York: Columbia University Press, 1923–1964.

Zoller, Robert. *Lost Key to Prediction.* New York: Inner Traditions, 1980.

Arachne

Arachne, *asteroid* 407 (the 407th asteroid to be discovered), is approximately 104 kilometers in diameter and has an **orbital** period of 4 1/4 years. Arachne was named after a mythological woman adept at weaving who was changed into a spider. This asteroid's key words are *entangled* and *network*. According to Lang-Wescott (p. 78), Arachne indicates "reactions to people and situations that are very involved." It also represents webs (both actual and psychological), intrigue, entanglement, and perceptions of intricacy.

Sources:

Lang-Wescott, Martha. *Asteroids-Mechanics: Ephemerides II.* Conway, Mass.: Treehouse Mountain, 1990.
———. *Mechanics of the Future: Asteroids.* Rev. ed. Conway, Mass.: Treehouse Mountain, 1991.

Archer

The Archer is a popular alternative name for the sign **Sagittarius**.

Aries

Aries (from the Latin for ram), the first sign of the **zodiac**, is a **cardinal fire** sign. It is a positive, **masculine sign ruled** by the **planet Mars**. Its symbol is the Ram, and its **glyph** is said to represent a ram's horns. It takes its name from the Greek god of war, making it one of the few signs with a well-developed mythology. Aries is associated with the head, and people with an Aries **sun sign** are prone to headaches and injuries to the head and face. The association of the head with Aries is the source of the word headstrong, which characterizes people with a strong Aries nature. As the first sign, the key phrase for Aries is *I am,* representing the birth of awareness.

Although Zeus, king of the Greek gods, fathered many children, Aries was the only son by his wife, Hera. Aries ruled war and was said to delight in conflict. He was also impulsive, often defying the Fates. According to most accounts, Aries never married but had many love affairs, best known of which was his liaison with the goddess of love, by whom he fathered **Eros** (from whence erotic). His nature was simultaneously brave and insolent, and in ancient works of art he was portrayed as young and handsome.

Like its namesake, the sign Aries is youthful and impulsive. Arian nature can manifest positively as bravery in the act of standing up for one's rights. Negatively, the same nature can manifest as crudeness, pushiness, over aggressiveness, and even violence. Arians tend to be egotistical, though their egotism is the un-self-conscious egotism of a child (in contrast to the fully self-conscious egotism of those under a sign like **Leo**). They are quick to anger, but just as quick to forgive. As **natives** of the first sign of the zodiac, they are often pioneers, but they are infamous for the difficulties they have finishing what they begin—they enjoy the excitement of being the first into new territory but prefer to let others map it out. Like all fire sign natives, they are fond of physical and social activity.

There is a wealth of information available on the characteristics of the zodiacal signs—so much that one book would not be able to contain it all. One traditional way in which astrologers condense information is by summarizing sign and planet traits in lists of words and short phrases called key words or key phrases. The following Aries key words are drawn from Manly P. Hall's *Astrological Keywords:*

Emotional key words: "Courageous, enthusiastic, imaginative, energetic, excitable, proud, impulsive, audacious, not domestic, hasty, brusque, sharp, passionate, quick-tempered, intemperate" (p. 17).

Mental key words: "Executive, enterprising, pioneering, confident, ingenious, scientific, explorative, independent, expedient, precise, progressive or intolerant in religion [one extreme or the other], aggressive, competitive" (p. 20).

Most popular works on astrology contain data on the signs, and these can be consulted for more detailed information.

Sources:

Evans, Colin. *The New Waite's Compendium of Natal Astrology.* Revised by Brian E. F. Gardener. York Beach, Maine: Samuel Weiser, 1971. (Originally published 1917.)

Green, Landis Knight. *The Astrologer's Manual: Modern Insights into an Ancient Art.* Sebastopol, Calif.: CRCS Publications, 1975.

Hall, Manly P. *Astrological Keywords.* 1958. Reprint. Savage, Md.: Littlefield Adams (1975), 17, 20.

Armillary Sphere

An armillary (from Latin *armilla,* bracelet) sphere is a skeletal sphere consisting of rings that represent the more important celestial circles utilized by astrologers—the **ecliptic**, the **meridian**, the **horizon**, the **celestial equator**, etc.

Armisticia

Armisticia, **asteroid** 1,464 (the 1,464th asteroid to be discovered), is approximately 17 kilometers in diameter and has an **orbital** period of 5.2 years.

Armisticia is a concept asteroid, named after **armistice**. Lehman associates this asteroid with peace treaties.

Sources:

Kowal, Charles T. *Asteroids: Their Nature and Utilization.* Chichester, West Sussex, U.K.: Ellis Horwood Limited, 1988.

Lehman, J. Lee. *The Ultimate Asteroid Book.* West Chester, Penn.: Whitford Press, 1988.

Arroyo, Stephen

Stephen Arroyo, a contemporary astrologer, was born October 6, 1946, in Kansas City, Missouri. He was one of seven children of Dolores and Joseph Arroyo, an entrepreneur in Chicago, Illinois, and founder of Karr-Products, Inc. Stephen Arroyo studied at Drake University, Des Moines, Iowa (1964–1965), the University of California, Davis (B.A., 1968), and California State University,

◄

An armillary sphere used by the great astronomer Tycho Brahe. · Bettmann Archive

Sacramento (M.A. psychology, 1972) and holds an M.F.C.C. (marriage, family and child counselor) license in California. He has received numerous consultations and correspondence from **Dane Rudhyar**. He has also attended lectures and classes by Rudhyar as well as those of many other teachers, including Frances Sakoian and **Isabel Hickey**. He has maintained a psychological/astrological counseling practice since 1970.

Arroyo published articles in numerous national astrological magazines in the early seventies and has written a half-dozen astrology books. Awards include the Astrology Prize by the British Astrological Association, the International Sun Award by the Fraternity of Canadian Astrologers, and the Regulus Award for Spiritual and Humanistic Astrology by the United Astrology Conference. He married in 1971 and has two children.

Selected Publications:

Astrology, Psychology and the Four Elements. Reno, Nev.: CRCS, 1975.
Astrology, Karma and Transformation. Reno, Nev.: CRCS, 1978.
Relationships and Life Cycles. Sebastopol, Calif.: CRCS, 1980.
New Insights in Modern Astrology. By Arroyo and Liz Greene. Sebastopol, Calif.: CRCS, 1984.
The Practice and Profession of Astrology. Sebastopol, Calif.: CRCS, 1985.
Stephen Arroyo's Chart Interpretation Handbook. Sebastopol, Calif.: CRCS, 1989.

Artemis

Artemis, **asteroid** 105 (the 105th asteroid to be discovered), is approximately 126 kilometers in diameter and has an **orbital** period of 3.6 years. Artemis was named after the Greek goddess of the hunt. Lehman associates this asteroid with the psychological urges evoked by "the hunt"—hunting, killing, and eating (absorbing).

Sources:

Kowal, Charles T. *Asteroids: Their Nature and Utilization.* Chichester, West Sussex, U.K.: Ellis Horwood Limited, 1988.
Lehman, J. Lee. *The Ultimate Asteroid Book.* West Chester, Penn.: Whitford Press, 1988.
Room, Adrian. *Dictionary of Astronomical Names.* London: Routledge, 1988.

Arthur

Arthur, **asteroid** 2,597 (the 2,597th asteroid to be discovered), is approximately 20 kilometers in diameter and has an **orbital** period of 5.2 years. Arthur was named after the semimythic king of England. According to Lehman (p. 117), the person in whose **natal chart** this asteroid is prominent is a "hero who presides. The heroic nature of this asteroid comes from properly executing the duty of assigning someone else the job of the quest."

Sources:

Kowal, Charles T. *Asteroids: Their Nature and Utilization.* Chichester, West Sussex, U.K.: Ellis Horwood Limited, 1988.

Lehman, J. Lee. *The Ultimate Asteroid Book.* West Chester, Penn.: Whitford Press, 1988.

Ascendant (Rising Sign)

The ascendant, also called the rising sign, is the sign of the **zodiac** (or, more technically, the specific **degree** of the zodiac) that was on the eastern **horizon** at the moment for which a **horoscope** was **cast** (calculated and drawn). On a zodiacal wheel, the ascendant is the sign at the nine o'clock position. In a **natal chart**, the ascendant indicates a significant influence on the personality; only the **Sun** and **Moon** exert stronger influences. These three signs—the ascendant, the **sun sign**, and the moon sign—are considered together when someone with a knowledge of astrology beyond sun signs briefly describes her or his astrological makeup (e.g., "I'm a **Libra** with Moon in **Cancer** and **Leo** rising"). The astrologically informed listener then knows that the speaker, while primarily a Libra, is also sensitive and moody like a Cancer and will also come across as a Leo in certain settings.

When either the Moon or the ascendant is in the same sign as the Sun, the person is said to be a **double sign**. If in the foregoing example, for instance, the **native** had been born when the Moon was in Libra instead of Cancer, the person would be referred to as a double Libra. Furthermore, continuing the same example, if the Moon was in Libra and Libra was also on the eastern horizon at the birth moment, the native would be termed a triple Libra. People who are a double or triple sign usually embody purer characteristics of their sign than other individuals. No **planet** is included in these specialized rubrics. In other words, if, continuing with the same example, **Mercury** or **Venus** (or any other planet for that matter) was in Libra at the moment of birth, but neither the Moon nor the ascendant was in Libra, the native would not qualify as a double or triple Libra.

Although the ascendant is important, it is generally regarded as exerting a more superficial influence than either the Sun or the Moon; it is usually regarded as influencing the native's appearance and certain outward traits more than the depth of her or his personality. Some astrologers, however, view the ascendant as indicating traits at least as deep as the sun sign, if not deeper. One way of resolving this disagreement is to take a clue from **esoteric astrology** (spiritual astrology or the astrology of the soul).

In some systems of **esoteric astrology**, the ascendant is said to embody positive traits that the native is supposed to be "growing toward." If one was born with **Virgo** on the ascendant, for example, then the native would need to learn to become more organized or more attentive to details. If this individual is indeed learning Virgo lessons, then the person's Virgo traits will have acquired "depth"; if, on the other hand, the person is not involved in the process of personal or spiritual growth, then these same traits may exert only a superficial influence on the personality. Acquaintance with one or the other of these two types of individuals (growing or nongrowing) may explain the diverging views of astrologers on the signficance of the ascendant.

Whatever one's view of the greater or lesser "depth" of the ascendant, there is general agreement that the ascendant is a peculiarly sensitive point in the horoscope. In most systems of **house** division, the first house begins at the ascendant, and any planet in close proximity to this point—especially if it is located in the first (rather than in the twelfth) house—exerts a strong influence over the whole personality. Thus, for example, a person whose Moon is in close **conjunction** with the ascendant will be moody and sensitive, even if no other factor in the chart indicates this trait.

The planet that **rules** the ascendant is also regarded as particularly strong. Some astrologers view this planet as the "ruler" of the entire chart. In a natal chart with **Taurus** rising, for instance, Venus (the ruler of Taurus) would be the chart ruler. The ruler of the ascendant is more important in **horary astrology** than in natal astrology.

Because of the rotation of Earth, all 12 signs of the zodiac pass over the horizon during the course of any given 24-hour period. This means that the ascendant changes on the average of once every 2 hours. Hence, if someone's birth time is off by 2 hours or more, the person will be assigned an incorrect ascendant—one of the many reasons why an accurate birth time is important.

Using the ascendant as an indicator, astrologers can obtain a general idea of why a client is seeking a reading. If someone calls and makes an appointment when Libra is rising, for instance, the querent is interested in finding out about her or his marriage or some similar close personal relationship. If, on the other hand, **Capricorn** is rising, the querent is more interested in business and finance.

Sources:

Brau, Jean-Louis, Helen Weaver, and Allan Edmands. *Larousse Encyclopedia of Astrology.* New York: New American Library, 1980.

McEvers, Joan. *Spiritual, Metaphysical & New Trends in Modern Astrology.* Saint Paul, Minn.: Llewellyn Publications.

The ascendant axis is the **horizon** axis. In an astrological chart, this corresponds to the line drawn from the **ascendant** to the **descendant**.

Ascension, Long and Short

If one stands in front of a building, it may appear to be twenty feet wide. If one then walks 10 yards or so to the left or to the right and examines it from a different perspective, the building will appear to be narrower than before. Because the belt of the **zodiac** is slanted at 23 1/2° to Earth's equator, we see some astrological signs from a slanted perspective. This causes, particularly at middle-**latitudes**, a noticeable variation in the length of time it takes for different signs to rise (to ascend) over the **horizon**. Those requiring more time are referred to as signs of long ascension; those requiring less, signs of short ascension. In the Northern Hemisphere, the signs of long ascension are **Cancer, Leo, Virgo, Libra, Scorpio,** and **Sagittarius,** with the "longest" signs being Virgo and Libra. The signs of short ascension are **Capricorn, Aquarius, Pisces, Aries, Taurus,** and **Gemini,** with the "shortest" signs being Pisces and Aries. This situation is reversed in the Southern Hemisphere.

Sources:

Brau, Jean-Louis, Helen Weaver, and Allan Edmands. *Larousse Encyclopedia of Astrology.* New York: New American Library, 1980.
Lee, Dal. *Dictionary of Astrology.* New York: Paperback Library, 1969.

Ashley, Wendy Z.

Wendy Ashley, born December 14, 1942, in New York City, is a practicing mythic astrologer with an international clientele. She is a groundbreaking teacher synthesizing myth and astrology for contemporary students and practitioners. She restores symbolic elements lost from astrology when myth was deleted in the interests of modern religion and science.

In 1974, Ashley began a 10-year study of symbol and dream interpretation with archetypal psychologist Charles Ponce. It was Ponce's perspective and tutelage that inspired and supported her own research into archaeoastronomy and astromythology. Ashley returned to college when her children were in high school and earned a B.A. degree in anthropology with concentrations in astronomy and cross-cultural studies of women from the University of Maine.

Her program of study was designed to further her research into how myth, astronomy, and astrology were once fused. Since then she has returned as guest lecturer to that university's honors programs, as well to Clark University, Antioch, and elsewhere. Ashley has hosted a daily television program, been a frequent talk show guest, and taught astrology in high school and in a university planetarium. She was instrumental in forming statewide astrology groups in 1968 and again in 1974.

Ashley believes her interest in mythology and comparative religions came from her early exposure to diversity—with a Jewish father and a Buddhist–Spiritualist mother. Her grade school education was Catholic, followed by high school years with grandparents in an evangelical Baptist community. Her grandfather, an Episcopalian, was a student of the Abenaki language, so Ashley acted as hostess for him when native American visitors came to stay and confer. Today her family has Asian and Afro-American as well as white members.

Since 1985, as a mythic astrologer she has lectured to Jungian groups and has taught for astrological organizations and conferences. She has lectured on sky myth and local gods and goddesses at Celtic sites in England, as well as in Greece, and convenes the School of Mythic Astrology every summer on the coast of Maine.

Ashley has been working on recording her work in multiple books. Current manuscripts include one on Mars, another is a basic primer on mythic astrology, and another is on goddess mythology of the 12 signs.

Aspect

Aspect (from Latin *aspectus,* to view or to look at) refers to the angular relationship between various points in a **horoscope** (an astrological chart), especially to a series of named angles, such as **trines** (120°) and **squares** (90°). The twelve signs of the **zodiac**, in addition to being bands of astrological influence, also provide astrologers with a system for locating **planets** and other points in space. A circle contains 360°, so when it is divided into 12 equal regions for the 12 signs, each sign encompasses an arc of 30°. Hence, a planet located near the beginning of **Aries**, for instance, might be at 1° Aries; in the middle of Aries, at 15° Aries; and near the end of the sign, 29° Aries. Earth, which is understood to be at the center of the horoscope (unless one is using a **heliocentric** or **Sun**-centered system), constitutes the vertex for any angle between planets or between other points in the chart. Thus, for example, if **Mercury** is located at 1° Aries, it would make a **semisextile** (30°) aspect with another planet—let us say **Venus**—that is located at 1° in the very next sign, which is **Taurus**. If we move Venus forward another 30° until it is at 1° **Gemini**, Mercury and Venus would form a **sextile** (60°) aspect. Another 30° to 1° **Cancer** forms a square (90°), and so forth.

The interpretation of a horoscope is built around three primary factors—signs, **houses**, and aspects—which makes aspect interpretation one of the most fundamental components of astrology. In a **natal chart** the planets represent, among other things, the various facets of one's psyche, and aspects between them indicate how these facets conflict or work together. **Mars**, for example, represents the forceful, outgoing, aggressive side of the self, whereas **Saturn** represents the security-seeking, self-disciplined side. While everyone experiences some tension between these two principles, an individual with a Mars–Saturn square (a conflict aspect) in her or his chart experiences this conflict in an exaggerated manner, often overrepressing outgoing, aggressive urges and at other times exploding with impulsive actions or words. A trine, on the other hand, represents the easy flow of energy between two points; so an individual with a Mars-Saturn trine would find that these two facets of the personality work together easily, bringing patience and discipline (Saturn) to the side of ambitious aggression (Mars), and vice versa.

The major aspects are the **conjunction** (0°), sextile (60°), square (90°), trine (120°), and **opposition** (180°). Squares and oppositions are regarded as **hard aspects**, meaning that they usually present challenges the **native** must

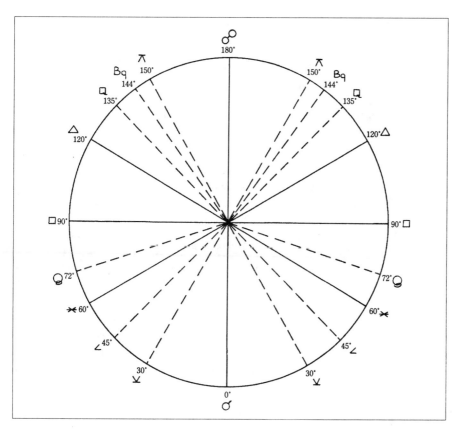

Aspects.

face and overcome. Sextiles and trines, on the other hand, are regarded as **soft aspects**, meaning that the energies represented by the planets and other points in the aspect combine in an easy, harmonious manner. The conjunction indicates a powerful blending of energies that can be easy or challenging, depending on the planets involved and the aspects that other planets make to the pair in conjunction. The traditional names for hard and soft aspects (names one still finds in older astrology books) are **malefic** and **benefic**. Beyond the obvious, undesirable connotations of malefic, these terms were dropped because malefic aspects are not always "bad," nor are benefic aspects always "good." For instance, an individual with numerous soft aspects and no hard aspects can be a lazy person who is never challenged to change and grow. On the other hand, an individual who has risen to the challenge of numerous hard aspects and overcome her or his limitations can be a dynamic, powerful person.

The "traditional" minor aspects are the semisextile (30°; sometimes called a dodecile), the **decile** (36°), the **semisquare** (45°; sometimes called an octile), the **quintile** (72°), **sesquisquare** (135°; sometimes called a sesquiquadrate or sesquare), the **quincunx** (150°; sometimes called an injunct), and the **biquintile** (144°). Other minor aspects are the **vigintile** (18°; also called a semidecile), the **semioctile** (22 1/2°; sometimes called the semi-semi-square), the **quindecile** (24°), the **novile** (40°), the **septile** (51 3/7°), and the **trecile** (108°). The ancients, who referred to the aspects as familiarities or configurations, used only the major aspects. The major hard aspects come from dividing the horoscope circle into halves and quarters, soft aspects from dividing it into thirds and sixths. Some of the minor aspects derive from further dividing the circle into eighths and sixteenths (semisquare, sesquisquare, and semioctile) and twelfths (semisextile and quincunx). Yet other minor aspects derive from 5-way and 10-way divisions (quintile, biquintile, decile, and vigintile), a 7-way division (septile), a 9-way division (novile), and a 15-way division (quindecile). For general interpretation purposes, the minor aspects are rarely used unless they are *very* precise.

Few aspects are ever exact (exact aspects are referred to as **partile** aspects). For this reason, astrologers speak of the orb—or the **orb of influence**—within which specific aspects are effective. For a sextile, for example, many astrologers use a 6° orb in a natal chart, which means that if any 2 planets are making an angle anywhere in the 54°–66° range, they are regarded as making a sextile aspect with each other. The closer an aspect is to being exact, the stronger it is. For the major aspects, astrologers often allow an orb of 8° or more; for minor aspects, 1° to 3°.

Why should some aspects produce harmony and others conflict? Although astrologers have speculated on this point (often making **numerological** speculations), the question has never been satisfactorily answered. In terms of the astrological tradition, it is easy to see that the trine, the primary soft aspect, usually brings a sign of one **element** into relationship with another sign of the same element (i.e., 15° Gemini is 120° away from 15° **Libra**, which is 120° away from 15° **Aquarius**, which, in turn, is 120° away from 15° Gemini, making a

grand trine composed entirely of **air signs**), and signs of the same element tend to blend together harmoniously. By way of contrast, the square, which is the primary hard aspect, brings signs of very different, potentially conflicting elements into relationship (e.g., a planet in a **water sign** squaring a planet in a **fire sign**).

But such an analysis breaks down as soon as we compare oppositions and sextiles, which involve precisely the same kinds of elemental combinations (e.g., the natural opposition to a planet in a water sign is a planet in an **earth sign**, and the natural sextiles to water signs also involve earth signs). Thus, at this stage in our understanding we can only observe that such and such an aspect produces such and such an effect, without fully knowing why. This should not be too bothersome as the situation is not much different from the natural sciences, in which one can describe the effects of, say, gravity without being able to explain why gravity works.

Sources:

Brau, Jean-Louis, Helen Weaver, and Allan Edmands. *Larousse Encyclopedia of Astrology.* New York: New American Library, 1980.

Donath, Emma Belle. *Minor Aspects Between Natal Planets.* Tempe, Ariz.: American Federation of Astrologers, 1981.

Hand, Robert. *Horoscope Symbols.* Rockport, Mass.: Para Research, 1981.

Whitman, Edward W. *Aspects and Their Meanings: Astro-kinetics, Vol. III.* London: L. N. Fowler, 1970.

Aspectarian

An aspectarian is a chronological list of all the **aspects** that the **planets** make with one another during a particular period of time, usually a month. In addition to the planets and their aspects, the time that an aspect becomes exact is given. (*See* illustration, p. 44.)

Assyrian Astrology

See: History of Mesopotamian Astrology

Astarte

Astarte, **asteroid** 672 (the 672d asteroid to be discovered), is approximately 19 kilometers in diameter and has an **orbital** period of 4.1 years. Astarte was named after the Middle Eastern goddess, roughly equivalent to **Venus**, also known as Ishtar. Lehman associates Astarte with Venus and **Aphrodite** (divinities of sex and fertility), asserting that this asteroid is more "primal" than the other two.

Aspectarian		
January 1992		
1	☉ P ☽	2:28	A.M.
	☽ P ♅	2:50	A.M.
	☽ ☌ ♀	9:17	A.M.
	☽ P ♂	11:49	A.M.
	☽ ⚹ ♄	7:12	P.M.
2	☿ P ♆	1:18	A.M.
	☽ □ ♃	12:22	P.M.
3	☽ ☌ ☿	0:08	A.M.
	☽ ☌ ♂	10:16	A.M.
4	☽ P ♂	3:57	A.M.
	☽ P ♅	3:00	P.M.
	☉ P ☽	7:00	P.M.
	☽ P ☿	10:55	P.M.
	☉ ☌ ☽	11:11	P.M.
	☽ ☌ ♅	11:18	P.M.
5	☽ △ ♃	0:40	A.M.
	☉ ☌ ♅	0:45	A.M.
	☽ ☌ ♆	4:18	A.M.
	♀ P ♄	5:19	A.M.
	☽ P ♆	5:31	A.M.
	☉ △ ♃	4:09	P.M.
	☽ ⚹ ♇	4:12	P.M.
	♀ ⚹ ♄	10:45	P.M.
6	☽ P ♀	0:14	A.M.
	☉ P ☿	1:24	A.M.
	☽ P ♄	1:48	A.M.
	☽ ☌ ♄	9:16	P.M.
	☽ ⚹ ♀	11:37	P.M.
7	☉ ☌ ♆	12:41	P.M.

Aspectarian (uses first week of January 1992 only).

Kowal, Charles T. *Asteroids: Their Nature and Utilization*. Chichester, West Sussex, U.K.: Ellis Horwood Limited, 1988.

Lehman, J. Lee. *The Ultimate Asteroid Book*. West Chester, Penn.: Whitford Press, 1988.

Room, Adrian. *Dictionary of Astronomical Terms*. London: Routledge, 1988.

Asteroids

An asteroid (meaning starlike or small star) is one of thousands of small planets, 95% of whose **orbits** lie between the orbits of **Mars** and **Jupiter**. Some have irregular orbits that carry them inside the orbit of Mars (the Apollo and Amor groups); some, even inside the orbit of **Mercury (Icarus)**, Earth and **Venus (Bacchus** and **Apollo)**. Others travel in the same orbital path as Jupiter (the Trojan asteroids). Initially, these planetoids were given mythological names, but as telescopes increased in strength and more and more asteroids were discovered, astronomers began naming them after places (e.g., Pretoria, Toronto, and Arizona) and people (e.g., Jonathan Murray, Rockwell Kent, and Christy Carol). Some of the smaller and more recently located asteroids have been given entertaining-sounding names, such as Bilkis (the Koranic name for the Queen of Sheba), Dudu (the dancing girl in Nietzsche's *Thus Spake Zarathustra)*, and Mr. Spock (named after the discoverer's cat).

While most asteroids are no more than a few miles across, many are much larger. **Ceres**, the largest asteroid, is 620 miles in diameter. The main group of asteroids are located where Bode's law would lead one to anticipate a **planet**, and one theory speculates that the asteroid belt is the debris of a former planet that has disintegrated into many pieces. Another theory speculates that at some distant time in the past when the **solar system** was being formed, the material circulating between Mars and Jupiter failed to coalesce into a cohesive planet, perhaps because of the disruptive influence of Jupiter's tremendous gravity.

Except for a very few whose orbital paths carry them near Earth, asteroids are invisible to the naked eye. The asteroid belt was not discovered until the nineteenth century, so they were not taken into account in traditional astrology. Even after sufficient information was available to construct **ephemerides** (tables of positions) of the major asteroids, astrologers chose to ignore them. **Alan Leo** tried to interest his fellow astrologers in asteroids but was unsuccessful. Perhaps the ongoing disputes over the astrological influences of the newly discovered planets discouraged astrologers from studying the significance of these relatively tiny bodies. Their sheer numbers would also discourage such exploration. Whatever the explanation, the astrological study of asteroids did not begin until the last quarter of the twentieth century.

The real founder of asteroid studies was Eleanor Bach, who in the early 1970s published an **ephemeris** and a set of interpretations for the first four asteroids to be discovered—Ceres, **Pallas, Juno,** and **Vesta**. This was followed in 1977 by a similar work on the Big Four by **Zipporah Dobyns**. Emma Belle

Donath also published a set of books dealing with the four major asteroids. In 1986, **Demetra George** and Douglas Bloch's *Asteroid Goddesses* was published. Building on the work of its predecessors, this book quickly became the definitive study of Ceres, Pallas, Juno, and Vesta. It contained everything needed to locate and interpret the four major asteroids in a **natal chart**. George, the primary author, also integrated the feminist theory of the primordial goddess religion (the notion that all of our more distant ancestors were goddess worshipers) into her discussion, giving *Asteroid Goddesses* tremendous appeal in a subculture where the idea of a primordial goddess religion was widely accepted. The book enjoyed such success that a new, expanded edition was published four years later. The general availability of *Asteroid Goddesses,* the basic appeal of the goddess notion, and the integration of asteroid positions into most computer chart-casting programs all combined to make Ceres, Pallas, Juno, and Vesta easy to use. Thus, the acceptance and continually expanding use of the four major asteroids by the larger astrological community is ensured.

The focus on Ceres, Pallas, Juno, and Vesta by asteroid advocates has generally eased the anxiety of astrologers who resisted the introduction of hundreds of new points demanding interpretation in a **horoscope**. Yet, the

▶
Most of the asteroid belt lies between the orbits of Mars and Jupiter. (Not drawn to scale)

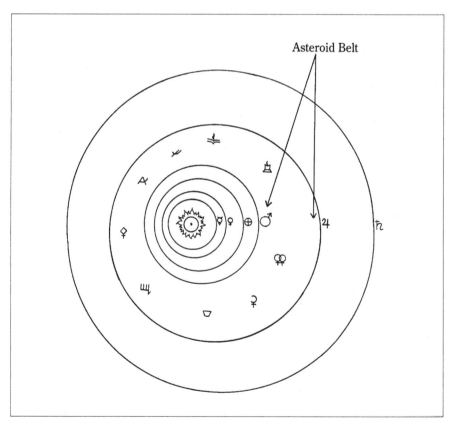

Asteroid Belt

widespread acceptance of the Big Four only made the question of the significance of the other asteroids more insistent. Those who have studied the astrological influence of asteroids have reached a consensus, which is, to quote from J. Lee Lehman's *The Ultimate Asteroid Book:* "1. The asteroids have astrological effects which may be studied. 2. The name of an asteroid has astrological significance" (p. 10).

The most common way of studying the influence of a new astrological factor is to study people in whose charts the factor is prominent, such as when an asteroid is in very close **conjunction** with a key **planet** or with the **ascendant**. The essential clue is the name of the asteroid, which gives preliminary insight into the asteroid's astrological "temperament," because the names astronomers give to newly discovered celestial bodies are not coincidental—by virtue of some nonapparent **synchronistic** influence, non-astrologically inclined astronomers give them astrologically significant names. Thus, for example, with regard to the asteroid **Eros**, an astrologer would anticipate that it was somehow related to passion, yet its name was assigned by an astronomer for whom asteroids were little more than big space rocks.

In *The Ultimate Asteroid Book* (1988), Lehman attempted to overcome some astrologers' resistance to asteroid use by asserting that asteroids have few concepts allocated to them and that their being small and numerous may allow for many very exact meanings. For example, *Eros* specifically means "passionate attachment," rather than having a broad range of meanings. (One can only wonder about the concepts associated with asteroids like Dudu.) Lehman contrasts this specificity with the multivalent significance of a planet like **Venus**, which can refer to "love, harmony, magnetic attraction, the veins, diabetes, erotica, potatoes, or a host of other things" (p. 12).

Beginning with a preliminary clue, such as (in the case of Eros) the idea that this small celestial body is somehow related to passion, the astrologer would place Eros in the charts of acquaintances as well as in those of famous people whose lives are open to public scrutiny. One would anticipate that **natives** with Eros in conjunction (or in some other close aspect) with the Sun, the ascendant, Venus, or Mars might exhibit more "erotic" inclinations than people with a less prominent Eros. One could not, however, know the specific nature of these inclinations—and how they differed from the passions of Venus, Mars, and **Pluto**—until after studying many people with Eros prominent in their chart. This approach to the study of new astrological factors is the same methodology utilized by astrologers to uncover the nature of the "new" planets **Uranus**, **Neptune**, and Pluto.

There were several reasons for the initial focus on the Big Four. Ceres, Pallas, Juno, and Vesta were the first asteroids to be discovered—in 1801, 1802, 1804, and 1807, respectively—and there was a 38-year gap before other asteroids were located. They thus belong together in a fairly natural grouping. Beyond the Big Four, however, asteroid research has not proceeded in a systematic manner. Rather than studying either the next asteroids to be discovered, or the next-largest asteroids, researchers have jumped to the study of asteroids with intriguing names like Eros and **Amor**, or asteroids with eccentric orbits, such as Adonis and Icarus. These are all relatively tiny bodies: Eros is 18 miles across at its widest, Amor is approximately 2 miles in diameter, and Adonis and Icarus are both about 1 mile wide. By comparison, Hygiea (personification of health or hygiene), Psyche (personification of the soul), Kalliope (muse of epic poetry), and Laetitia (Latin for gladness) are all larger than Juno (150 miles in diameter), but almost no information is available on any of these bodies except Psyche. (Short summary meanings of these asteroids are given in Martha Lang-Wescott's *Mechanics of the Future: Asteroids.*)

By sequence of discovery, the next four asteroids after the Big Four are Astraea (goddess of justice), Hebe (goddess of youth, who took ambrosia to the gods), Iris (goddess of the rainbow, who was a messenger between the gods and humanity), and Flora (goddess of flowering plants). Again, little information on any of these four asteroids is available except for short summaries in Lang-Wescott's survey. The clues that one would use to research any one of these "concept" or "goddess" asteroids—health, justice, poetry, gladness, and so forth—are all appealing, so the lack of attention they have attracted is surprising. Clearly, the next step in establishing the study of asteroids as a widely accepted branch of astrology will be the systematic exploration of the larger or the earlier asteroids, rather than the current piecemeal study of asteroids with idiosyncratic appeal.

Another issue that will have to be resolved before "nonasteroid" astrologers begin to take asteroids seriously is the question of sign **rulership**. It was traditionally held that the **Sun** and the **Moon** (the two **luminaries**) ruled one sign apiece, **Leo** and **Cancer**, respectively. The known planets each ruled two signs: **Mercury** ruled **Virgo** and **Gemini**, Venus ruled **Taurus** and **Libra**, Mars ruled **Aries** and **Scorpio**, **Jupiter** ruled **Sagittarius** and **Pisces**, and **Saturn** ruled **Capricorn** and **Aquarius**. When the "new" planets were discovered, astrologers determined that Uranus ruled Aquarius, Neptune ruled Pisces, and Pluto ruled Scorpio, leaving Saturn, Jupiter, and Mars as the rulers, respectively, of Capricorn, Sagittarius, and Aries. In this modified system, only Mercury and Venus still rule two signs each. The attractiveness of a balanced system in which twelve heavenly bodies rule twelve signs has often led twentieth-century astrologers to speculate that two new planets would eventually be discovered and come to be accepted as the rulers of Virgo and Libra.

Some modern-day astrologers speculate that the larger **asteroids** rule these signs. Bach, the founder of astrological asteroid studies, assigns Ceres and Vesta the rulership of Virgo, and Juno and Pallas the rulership of Libra. Dobyns, another pioneer in the field of asteroid research, appears to accept the Big Four as corulers (with Mercury and Venus) of these two signs. However, spreading out sign rulerships to more than one planet does not strike a favorable chord among nonasteroid astrologers. Not only does multiple rulership lack elegance, but it also makes certain astrological procedures, such as identifying the **significator** in **horary astrology**, somewhat schizophrenic. Beyond the question of elegance, some of the sign associations are strained. Ceres, which embodies the quality of nurture, for example, is clearly more related to Cancer than to Virgo. Another question one might ask with respect to asteroid rulerships is: Why stop with the Big Four? The asteroid Hygiea, the personification of health and hygiene, is clearly related to Virgo; the asteroid Astraea, the goddess of justice, has definite affinities to Libra; and so forth. The point is, while various asteroids may well be associated with the twelve signs of the **zodiac**, assigning rulerships to asteroids raises more problems than it resolves.

See pages xxv–xxvii, in the Introduction, for tables of astrological glyphs and illustrations.

Sources:

Brau, Jean-Louis, Helen Weaver, and Allan Edmands. *Larousse Encyclopedia of Astrology.* New York: New American Library, 1980.

Dobyns, Zipporah. *Expanding Astrology's Universe.* San Diego, Calif.: ACS Publications, 1983.

Donath, Emma. *Asteroids in the Birth Chart.* 1979. Reprint. Tempe, Ariz: AFA, 1991.

———. *Asteroids in Midpoints.* 1982. Reprint. Tempe, Ariz.: AFA, 1988.

George, Demetra, with Douglas Bloch. *Asteroid Goddesses: The Mythology, Psychology and Astrology of the Reemerging Feminine.* 2d ed., San Diego, Calif.: ACS Publications, 1990.

Lang-Wescott, Martha. *Mechanics of the Future: Asteroids.* Rev. ed. Conway, Mass.: Treehouse Mountain, 1991.

Lehman, J. Lee. *The Ultimate Asteroid Book.* West Chester, Pa.: Whitford Press, 1988.

Press, Nona. *New Insights into Astrology.* San Diego, Calif.: ACS Publications, 1993.

Astraea

Astraea, **asteroid** 5 (the 5th asteroid to be discovered—in 1845, by the German amateur astronomer Karl Ludwig Hencke), is approximately 120 kilometers in diameter and has an **orbital** period of 4.1 years. Astraea was named after the Roman goddess of justice (the familiar blindfolded goddess who holds the scales of justice in one hand and a sword in the other). According to Lang-Wescott, Astraea indicates where we have difficulty letting go of people, relationships, and situations, as well as a sense of "loose ends" afterward. This asteroid's key words are *open-ended* and *witness*. According to McKenna, Astraea represents the most important individual needs, for which one must take exceptional personal responsibility. At the same time, it is easy for the needs indicated by this asteroid to be set aside because of other needs and external influences.

Sources:

McKenna, Barry. *The Astraea Minor Planet Ephemeris.* Newtonville, Mass.: Astraea Publications, 1991.

Lang-Wescott, Martha. *Asteroids-Mechanics: Ephemerides II.* Conway, Mass.: Treehouse Mountain, 1990.

———. *Mechanics of the Future: Asteroids.* Rev. ed. Conway, Mass.: Treehouse Mountain, 1991.

Astrodiagnosis

Astrodiagnosis is the subdivision of **medical astrology** dealing with the diagnosis of disease.

Astrolabe

An astrolabe is a mechanical device that, prior to the development of the sextant, was widely used by mariners. Said to have been developed by Hipparchus, greatest of the ancient Greek astronomers (although some scholars give **Ptolemy** the honor), the astrolabe was used by astrologers to determine the positions of the **planets** when they erected **horoscopes** (prior to the development of **ephemerides**, it was necessary to actually look at the heavens when casting a horoscope). The term itself means taking the star in Greek, so it could be used to refer to any instrument for observing the stellar dome. Thus, in the early medieval period *astrolabe* was often applied to the **armillary sphere**, a different instrument. The device we now call an astrolabe is more properly termed a planispheric astrolabe. Originally Greek, this instrument was lost to western Europe until its reintroduction by Arabic sources.

Sources:

deVore, Nicholas. *Encyclopedia of Astrology.* New York: Philosophical Library, 1947.
Tester, Jim. *A History of Western Astrology.* New York: Ballantine, 1987.

Astrologer

An astrologer is one who practices astrology. The term is usually reserved for individuals who read charts for clients, although astrological researchers can appropriately claim the title. Because astrology is not accepted as a legitimate profession by the larger society, there presently exists no officially recognized agencies for training, testing, and certifying astrologers. While various tests of astrological competence and informal certifications recognizing such skills have been established, the nonofficial status of these examinations makes them largely ineffective for regulating the field.

Astrological Data

Astrological data are the basis for casting horoscopes and include name, date, place of birth, and time of birth. Astrologers base their studies on this data as they examine the patterns and positions of the **planets** and the signs as they rise, culminate and set. Whether they are doing a research study or a personal **horoscope**, the accuracy of their observations depends on the accuracy of their

The Painswick Astrolabe, resembling the drawings found in Chaucer's work on astrolabes.
· Bettmann Archive

data. Whether they are presenting a paper or delineating a chart, they cannot validate their work unless they can validate their data.

Speculative charts come from cases where the birth time is unknown and as such are pure guesswork, usually backed up with events to illustrate the supposed accuracy; **rectification** of a chart begins with an approximate birth time and corrects the chart to a specific minute. Historically, astrological data have not been presented with any source of origin. Magazines and journals blithely present charts and articles, and readers are apparently supposed to accept on faith that the data are accurate. Astrologers give lectures or present papers with no source given for the data. When one begins to examine the charts of historical figures and public figures, it may come as a shock to find that there are several times of birth given. There are over a dozen times of birth given for Ronald Reagan, and as many for Joseph Stalin, Clark Gable, and Evita Peron.

There is nothing wrong with speculative data—if they are presented as such. However, presenting data as factual when they are not is a falsehood; deliberate inaccuracy is ethically unforgivable; and presenting data without a source is amateurish, unprofessional, and misleading. Many astrological data

▶
A 17th-century English illustration of an astrologer with a client.
· **Bettmann Archive**

are time-specific, so any chart that does not state the source is open to question, and any conclusions drawn from such a chart are not acceptable as valid conclusions. When data were scarce, astrologers took what they could get. That time is past if they ever hope to gain a reputation for conducting legitimate studies. Astrological journals, schools, and teachers have a responsibility to the next generation of astrologers to set a standard in recording information. Astrology is making great strides in the latter twentieth century; never before has there been access to so much data or to computer-generated charts, and it is imperative that studies be built on a firm basis and employ empirical data.

The Rodden classification of astrological data is a simple, effective system. Many astrologers in the United States and Europe use it or a similar coding system. The first four letters of the English alphabet are used:

AA   Accurate; recorded by the family or the state

A   Accurate probably; data from the person or family

B   Biography or autobiography

C   Caution; no source of origin

DD   Dirty data; two or more quotes with none verified

◄
Illustration from a 17th-century work showing astronomers exchanging observational data.
· **Bettmann Archive**

Data are the foundation of empirical study. Astrologers should insist on quality reference works and accurate data that include the date, place, time, time zone, longitude and latitude, source, and a designation of accuracy.

—Lois M. Rodden

Astrology

Astrology is the science or study of the stars and originally encompassed both **astronomy** and what we today call astrology. The word is a combination of *astron,* Greek for star, and *logos,* a complex word originally meaning speech (in the sense of discourse). Astrology is discussed extensively in the introductory essay to this encyclopedia.

Astromancy

Astromancy refers to a kind of astrological fortune-telling that views the **stars** as predicting an irrevocable destiny for the person having her or his fortune told. Modern astrologers tend to distance themselves from this tradition of predicting specific events. Instead of predicting events, most contemporary astrologers describe upcoming planetary conditions, with the understanding that clients have the free will to respond to planetary influences in different ways. Like meteorologists, astrologers can only predict trends and probabilities—not details.

Astronomy

Astronomy is the branch of natural science that studies the celestial bodies. The word is a combination of *astron,* Greek for star, and *nomos,* Greek for law. Astrology was formerly part of astronomy, astrological determinations being viewed as a "practical application" of astronomical knowledge. Prior to the modern period, all of the great astronomers were also astrologers, including such luminaries as **Tycho Brahe** and **Johannes Kepler.**

Several hundred years ago, however, the two fields began to diverge, and today there are two distinct communities: astrologers, who are largely ignorant of astronomy, and astronomers, who know almost nothing about astrology. For the most part, contemporary astronomers despise astrology as a medieval superstition. This is not, however, because astrology fails to pass empirical tests of validity, but because astronomers reject astrology out of hand. When skeptics have actually subjected astrology to empirical tests, they have found—sometimes to their dismay—correlations between celestial and terrestrial phenomena (*see* **sTARBABY**).

For their part, astrologers are more often than not woefully ignorant of astronomy. This ignorance is sometimes compounded by an attitude that condemns all science as narrow-minded and spiritually dead. There are, however, a handful of contemporary astrologers who have explored current astronomy for potential astrological insights, including Michael and Margaret Erlewine, whose *Astrophysical Directions* offers a starting point for astrologers interested in pursuing this line of research, and Philip Sedgwick, whose *Astrology of Deep Space* is a creative follow-up on the Erlewines' work.

Sources:

Brau, Jean-Louis, Helen Weaver, and Allan Edmands. *Larousse Encyclopedia of Astrology.* New York: New American Library, 1980.

Erlewine, Michael, and Margaret Erlewine. *Astrophysical Directions.* Ann Arbor, Mich.: Heart Center School of Astrology, 1977.

Sedgwick, Philip. *The Astrology of Deep Space.* Birmingham, Mich.: Seek-It Publications, 1984.

◄
An 18th-century illustration of astronomers at the Royal Observatory in Greenwich, England.
· Bettmann Archive

Astrotherapy (Clinical Astrology)

Astrotherapy, or clinical astrology, is the application of astrology to psychotherapy. More specifically, it is the attempt to integrate astrological principles with psychological concepts and practices, especially as these relate to working with clients on an ongoing basis. Astrotherapy includes any form of treatment utilizing astrological precepts to treat emotional and behavioral problems, remove or modify existing symptoms, and promote positive personality growth and fulfillment. Just as there are many forms of psychotherapy, astrotherapy takes many forms as well. Efforts have been made to integrate astrology with humanistic, Jungian, psychoanalytic, Gestalt, psychosynthesis, object relations, and transpersonal therapies. There is, in short, no single form of astrotherapy. It is rather a general tool for fostering empathic understanding of the client's internal world.

Like an "X ray" of consciousness, a birth chart reveals the mental and emotional processes that constitute psychic structure. It assists the therapist in understanding the intrapsychic dynamics that underlie the presenting problem and so enables the therapist to better support the client's efforts at changing emotional, cognitive, and behavioral patterns. Because the language of astrology is symbolic, and thus without restricted meanings for its component variables, it can be translated into almost any psychological model or type of therapy.

Astrology as a Personality Theory

Every approach to psychotherapy is founded on certain presuppositions about the human psyche it hopes to treat. These presuppositions, in sum, constitute the personality theory that supports the therapy. According to Hall and Lindzey (1978), any adequate theory of personality must accomplish the following minimal objectives: It must (1) be comprehensive, or integrative, in that it deals with the total, functioning person; (2) account for what motivates the human being; (3) contain a set of empirical definitions concerning the various parts of the personality, thus permitting observation; (4) consist of a cluster of assumptions about behavior that are systematically related in accordance with certain rules; and (5) be useful in that it is capable of generating predictions about personality characteristics that are testable and verifiable, thus expanding knowledge.

Although astrology has dubious legitimacy in the current marketplace of ideas, it meets all the foregoing qualifications for a comprehensive theory of personality. First, astrology is a comprehensive system in that it is concerned with all the parts and processes that make up the totality of the human psyche. Second, the signs of the **zodiac** provide clear referents for the impulses, motives, and instinctual drives that govern and regulate human conduct. Third, the various signs, **planets**, and **houses** that constitute the parts of personality are empirically defined. Fourth, the rules of chart interpretation—**delineation,** synthesis, and aspect analysis—represent specific assumptions about behavior that are systematically related. And fifth, astrology is useful in that it not only explains the facts of behavior but also is capable of generating predictions or propositions that are verifiable, thus promoting research.

We can say, then, that astrology consists of a set of assumptions and definitions concerning human behavior together with rules for relating these assumptions and definitions to observable events. A simple example should suffice to illustrate this. If a person has **Saturn** on the **ascendant**, our theory would predict that the function symbolized by this planet would be a salient feature of the personality. This prediction is based on the related assumptions that (1) the ascendant is a conspicuous element of personality and (2) planets **conjunct** the ascendant will be prominent in the person's appearance and behavior. Since Saturn has an empirical definition (Saturn represents the process of *organizing* and is associated with orderly, serious behavior geared toward satisfying the need for structure and control), these assumptions can be tested by comparing them with the person's actual observed behavior? If the subject does in fact appear to be orderly, serious, structured, and the like, then the prediction is confirmed.

Astrology differs from other personality theories in that it is the only system in which there are external referents—signs and planets—for pieces of psychic structure. These external referents are visible, predictable, and capable of complexity beyond any theory of human behavior devised by psychology. Although astrology is simple in its derivation of archetypes (signs), it is complex in its ability to derive individual process from these archetypes (planets in sign, house, and aspect); each piece of psychic structure has concrete meaning yet is infinitely variable in combination. Because astrology has many shades of meaning, it is easily compatible with most psychological models, almost all of which can be subsumed into astrological language. For example, Freud's tripartite division of the mind into id, ego, and superego is roughly paralleled in astrology by the relations between **Mars** (id), the **Sun** (ego), and Saturn (superego). The many elements of astrology make it a vastly more subtle and potentially sophisticated model for depicting the structure and dynamics of the psyche.

Another difference between astrology and conventional personality theories is that astrology has no founder. It was not invented, created, or developed by any single individual or group of individuals, unlike other personality theories. Invariably a personality theory bears the stamp of its creator; that is, the theory is a self-portrait of its founder. This can be seen clearly, for example, in Freud's **horoscope,** which perfectly symbolizes the Oedipus complex that Freud universalized for every human being. This same principle holds true for the other personality theories. Each theory, with the exception of astrology, began as a projection of one person's individual viewpoint and subsequently attracted adherents to that viewpoint. In each instance, the peculiarities of the theory can be traced back to the prejudices, tendencies, issues, and cognitive styles that are clearly reflected in the horoscope of the founder. Astrology, however, has a more objective framework since it did not originate with any one individual (or even one culture), is based on empirical observation, and has stood the test of time. In this sense, it can be thought of as a metatheory that subsumes other models.

Astrology as a Diagnostic Tool

The real value of astrology, however, goes beyond its potential as a personality theory. Because every astrological chart is unique, astrology functions as a diagnostic device of unparalleled richness. Many therapists are beginning to use astrology as an assessment tool because of the advantages it presents over traditional psychological tests. Since it is based on an external frame of reference, the chart offers a character portrait entirely independent of the test responses that occur on traditional psychological questionnaires, thus eliminating any possibility of response bias by subjects who might unconsciously wish to manipulate their scores. Whereas most diagnostic tests provide a flat, static profile based on a quantitative assessment of various personality attributes, astrology presents a qualitative assessment of psychic structure based on psychological processes in interaction, e.g., conscious and unconscious dynamics, areas of repression and conflict, pathways of sublimation, projection, and the like. Thus, the horoscope more closely approximates the psychic geography that therapist and client are exploring.

Because it is based on external referents that are observable and predictable, the horoscope provides an objective reference point to balance the subjectivity of the therapeutic process. Whereas traditional tests are restricted to linear measurements that fragment the personality into a multitude of traits, motives, needs, factors, and scales, the horoscope depicts personality as the overall pattern of behaviors resulting from the unique organization of its underlying variables. Here again it is superior to devices limited to measuring parts of the personality, because such assessments cannot offer an integrated picture of the whole person.

The dysfunctional extremes of zodiacal signs can be precisely correlated to some of the major diagnostic categories of traditional psychology (Perry, 1989a, 1989b). Generally, however, astrology does not reduce people down to preformed categories with pathological diagnoses. Rather, a chart enlarges a person's sense of identity and creates a sense of possibility. Astrology suggests that the individual is not merely a consequence of multiple impinging factors like genetics or environmental conditions but a mirror of the living universe. The Hermetic doctrine of the macrocosm and the microcosm provides the philosophical foundation of astrology and is a counterpart to the modern philosophy of holism. In this view, the psyche is not merely a whole unto itself but is also a part of the greater whole that reflects it.

Not only does astrology present a comprehensive portrait of the psyche in all its rich complexity, it is also capable of looking backward into the past or projecting forward into the future. Astrology is a diagnostic time machine that allows the therapist to gain access to psychological events that span the period from birth to death. For example, by examining the transits and progressions for any year of a person's life, the astrologer is able to (1) discern clues to traumatic events that might have occurred in early childhood and (2) project into the future and target periods when the individual is liable to face new crises. Such projections do not just predict a generic crisis, but a crisis of a specific type and duration. An astrological chart assists the therapist in both diagnosis and prognosis, for where it symbolizes inborn conflicts, complexes, and areas of repression, it also points to latent potentials and areas (and times) of probable growth. In effect, the chart can be seen as a symbolic map of the process of self-actualization.

An astrological chart has another further advantage over traditional diagnostic schemes. Although every assessment device is capable of describing the personality of its subject, traditional tests do nothing to illuminate the specific types of objects that the individual is likely to encounter. In astrology, however, each symbol of the chart is a corollary to both an intrapsychic process and an environmental condition. This means that a chart presents a portrait not simply of the individual but also of the individual in dynamic relation to an environment. Because subject and object define each other, the environment is seen as a reflection of the psyche to which it adheres. The advantage of such a concept is that it shows how interpersonal problems are precisely mirrored in intrapsychic structures. Astrological indications of interpersonal problems are not of a general type, but of highly specialized relations such as potential marriage partners, children, authority figures, financial institutions, religious organizations, friends, employers and employees, and just about any other type of relation.

Traditional, Event-Oriented Astrology

It is difficult to appreciate just how far astrology has come over the last 30 years. It was not until the advent of humanistic psychology in the 1960s that astrologers began to think seriously about the astrological chart in terms of psychological growth and transformation. For those who began studying astrology only recently, it might seem that it was always that way; but it was not. Although **Jung** (1931) once said, "Astrology represents the summation of the psychological knowledge of antiquity" (p. 142), there was very little in astrology prior to the 1960s that bore much relationship to what is generally considered "psychological" today.

Ancient peoples initially perceived the planets as gods that ruled over the various processes of nature, much as a king ruled over his subjects. The conceived relationship between celestial and terrestrial events was linear, dualistic, and hierarchical: a superior power and dominion over an inferior one. While later and deeper forms of astrological philosophy recognized that the macrocosm and microcosm were actually interpenetrating and thus their relationship was not linear or dualistic, this view declined with the collapse of the Hellenistic culture in the third century. A simpler model prevailed during the medieval period and persisted in one form or another right up to the second half of this century. Human beings were perceived as fated recipients of cosmic forces that could be propitiated but not denied.

Such a gloomy determinism was reinforced by a value-laden terminology that too often described the astrological chart in ominous terms, e.g., **malefic**, evil aspect, **debilitation, affliction, detriment, fall**, destroyer of life, hell of the zodiac, and so on. Of course, there were "good" parts to astrology as well, such as benefics and exaltations, but these only served to underscore the determinism of the system. Planets were variously conceived as transmitters of mysterious rays or electromagnetic forces that affected the individual at birth. Understandably, this induced individuals to focus their attention outward to see what malice or affection the gods might have in store for them. The rigid determinism of traditional astrology did not allow for the possibility of change or growth in consciousness. Instead, people more likely consulted the stars as a means of avoiding a calamitous fate or of exploiting opportunities for manipulating circumstances to personal advantage.

The implication of traditional, event-oriented astrology was that the individual was a potential victim of an indifferent universe over which she or he had little or no control. Accordingly, astrologers were only too eager to give people what they wanted—predictions, advice, warnings, and simplistic solutions to what we now recognize to be complex psychological problems. At best, traditional astrologers were well-meaning individuals interested in predicting events and describing character, and they did no harm. At worst, they were fear-peddling parasites who exploited the insecurities and anxieties of the people who purchased their services, and they did great harm.

The vast majority of mundane predictions about illnesses, accidents, divorces, shipwrecks, earthquakes, scandals, inheritances, marriages, job promotions, and the like were utterly useless except to create an addiction to the astrologer, whose pronouncements appeared to offer some promise of control over the events in question. But no astrologer could predict with certainty exactly what the events would be, under precisely what circumstances they would take place, or how they would affect the person. Especially lacking in such predictions was the meaning and purpose that the event might have beyond its immediate effects. What relationship did it have to the consciousness of the experiencer? What opportunities did it offer for self-insight and growth in awareness?

Likewise, the traditional astrologer's description of character was generally limited to superficial trait descriptions heavily laden with moral judgments and glib advice. At best, the astrologer confirmed what the individual already intuitively knew. At worst, the astrologer confused or upset the individual with interpretations that were shallow, insensitive, judgmental, too negative, or just plain wrong. There was little if any attempt to address the deeper dimensions of the chart that hinted at unconscious beliefs and fundamental drives that underlay surface behavior. Character was seen as either static and unalterable or easily modified by following the cosmically informed counsel of one's astrologer. Such assumptions seem naive from the perspective of modern psychology. We now recognize that while changing one's inborn character can be extraordinarily difficult, it can be achieved through courage, persistence, and hard work.

The Birth of Psychological Astrology

It was the Swiss psychoanalyst Carl Jung who first recognized the vast potential of astrology as a tool for exploring the depths of the human psyche. In various writings throughout has life, Jung made reference to his profound respect for astrology. He asserted that astrology had a great deal to contribute to psychology and admitted to having employed it with some frequency in his analytic work with clients. In cases of difficult psychological diagnosis, Jung would draw up a horoscope in order to have a further point of view from an entirely different angle. "I must say," said Jung, "that I very often found that the astrological data elucidated certain points which I otherwise would have been unable to understand" (1948).

Jung regarded the signs and planets of astrology as symbols of archetypal processes that originated in the **collective unconscious**. The archetypes of the collective unconscious were the universal organizing principles underlying and motivating all psychological life, both individual and collective. In Jung's view, mythology placed emphasis on the cultural manifestations of archetypes at various times and places in history, whereas astrology used archetypes as a language for understanding the basic psychological drives of human beings. "Astrology, like the collective unconscious with which psychology is concerned, consists of symbolic **configurations**: the planets are the gods, symbols of the power of the unconscious" (Jung, 1976). The gods of mythology represented the living forces of the universe that patterned all things. Like **Plato**'s Forms, an archetype was both subjective and objective; it was evident both in the innate ideas of human consciousness as well as in the fundamental processes of nature; it informed not only human experience but also planetary motions.

It was precisely this dual nature of the archetype that enabled the chart to bridge the inner character and the outer events that reflected that character. "There are many instances of striking analogies between astrological **constellations** and psychological events or between the horoscope and the characterological disposition," wrote Jung (1976). Archetypes, he concluded, were "psychoid"; i.e., they shape matter as well as mind. An astrological configuration defined both the innate disposition of the individual and the particular kinds of outer conditions that the individual was likely to experience. In a 1954 interview, Jung stated, "One can expect with considerable assurance, that a given well-defined psychological situation will be accompanied by an analogous astrological configuration."

Jung recognized that the unique and unparalleled ability of astrology to disclose correlations between planetary motions and human experience also made it an accurate way of timing life crises: "I have observed many cases where a well-defined psychological phase or an analogous event has been accompanied by a **transit**—particularly the afflictions of Saturn and **Uranus**" (1954).

Jung's observance of correlations between psychological phenomena and astrological data contributed to the formulation of his theory of **synchronicity**. He defined synchronicity as "the simultaneous occurrence of a certain psychic state with one or more external events which appear as meaningful parallels to the momentary subjective state" (1955, p. 36). Accordingly, Jung did not hesitate to take the synchronistic phenomena that underlay astrology seriously. Astrology, he thought, worked precisely because of synchronicity; i.e., the psychic structure of the person about to be born was "meaningfully paralleled" in the positions of the planets at that time.

When looking for a way to test the hypothesis of synchronicity, Jung set up an astrological experiment that correlated planetary configurations, or cross aspects, between the charts of marital partners. He hypothesized that certain cross aspects would appear with greater frequency between the charts of marital partners than between charts of people who had no relationship. "The meaningful coincidence we are looking for is immediately apparent in astrology," said Jung, "since the astrological data. . . correspond to individual traits of character; and from the remotest times the various planets, houses, zodiacal signs, and aspects have all had meanings that serve as a basis for a character study" (1955, pp. 43–44).

Although Jung never developed any systematic theory of astrology, it appears that his own theory of analytical psychology was heavily influenced by it. There are so many parallels that one is almost forced to conclude that at least some of his major concepts were borrowed directly from astrology. In addition to his explicit endorsement of planets as archetypes, and his theory of synchronicity as a means for explaining astrological coincidences, Jung's notion of two attitude types—extrovert and introvert—is readily recognizable by astrologers as the bipolar division of the zodiac into positive/**masculine** (extrovert) and negative/**feminine** (introvert) **signs**. Likewise, his four function types—intuition, sensation, thinking, and feeling—are roughly paralleled in astrology by the four **elements**—fire, earth, air, and water. In addition to these more obvious analogues, there are additional correlations that have been explored by astrologers. These include ego/Sun, persona/ascendant, shadow/**Pluto**, anima/**Venus**, animus/Mars, and collective unconscious/**Neptune**. Difficult astrological configurations, especially those involving **hard aspects** from the outer planets to **Mercury**, Venus, Mars, the **Moon**, or the Sun, have been observed by astrologers to represent trouble spots in the personality similar to what Jung described as psychic complexes, i.e., unconscious, emotionally charged memories, images, and thoughts clustered around a central core.

In the 1930s, **Dane Rudhyar** began to reformulate modern astrology in terms of Jung's analytical psychology. He especially focused on Jung's idea that the psyche was a dynamic compound of opposing forces in equilibrium, and that the psyche was intrinsically motivated to evolve in the direction of psychic wholeness, a process Jung called individuation. Jung believed that the process of personality transformation was innate, or teleologically motivated. Personality was not merely the product of external forces, but strove purposefully toward a final goal of self-realization. As the individual learned from self-created experience, the archetypal structuring of the psyche became increasingly differentiated, integrated, and whole. Rudhyar (1936) recognized that these ideas were readily adaptable to astrology: The horoscope, too, was a dynamic compound of opposing forces (signs) in equilibrium, and the various parts of astrology with their myriad aspects and interrelations were symbolic of archetypal forces struggling to transform themselves into in integrated whole. Rudhyar realized that the process of individuation was implicit in every horoscope.

By the 1960s, Rudhyar's project of reformulating astrology received new impetus from the humanistic movement in psychology. Humanistic psychology, as embodied in the writings of Abraham Maslow, Carl Rogers, Rollo May, and others, had arisen in response to the bleak pessimism inherent in the Freudian psychoanalytic view and the robot conception of human potential implied in behaviorism. Both psychoanalysis and behaviorism were deterministic in that they conceived of personality as the effect of causes external to the person—i.e., genetics, parental influence, environmental conditions, and so on. Humanistic psychologists countered this trend by developing models that could account for the apparent purposiveness and growth-seeking behavior of human beings.

Rather than portray the individual as caught in an interminable struggle between instinctual drives and the inhibiting influence of society (psychoanalysis), or fragment the person into a multitude of conditioned behaviors (behaviorism), humanists perceived the individual as a unified organism made up of autonomous drives and functions that could be differentiated from one another and integrated into a functional whole greater than the sum of its parts. Humanistic psychologists challenged Freudian theory by postulating that instinctual drives were not dangerous forces erupting out of a primitive id, but healthy impulses that should be valued and trusted. The individual was perceived as a creative, self-actualizing, and self-determining organism capable of making responsible decisions and growing progressively toward an ideal state. Unlike behaviorists, who ignored the internal world of consciousness, humanists emphasized the primacy of the subjective element. Whereas behaviorists contended that behavior was solely conditioned by external causes, humanists focused on the relevance of intentionality as an internal cause of behavior. While behaviorists were concerned with how behavior could be manipulated and controlled, humanists emphasized the capacity for personal freedom and choice. In sum, it was not the outer environment that was of central importance to the humanistic psychologist, but the person's inner world of perceptions, values, thoughts, beliefs, attitudes, expectations, needs, feelings, and sensations.

Rudhyar was the first to recognize how astrology and humanistic psychology complemented each other. The horoscope, in effect, could be utilized as a tool for mapping the complex inner world that humanists were starting to explore. Just as humanistic psychology was a response to the determinism inherent in psychoanalysis and behaviorism, humanistic astrology was a response to the determinism inherent in traditional, event-oriented astrology. Borrowing from Carl Rogers's (1951) *Client-Centered Therapy,* Rudhyar developed *Person-Centered Astrology* (1972). Rudhyar was less concerned with whether astrology works than with how it can be used to assist the process of self-actualization. The real question was, given that astrology works, what is its proper use?

In 1969, Rudhyar founded the International Committee for Humanistic Astrology and declared that astrology was, or should be, primarily a technique for understanding human nature. He decried the implicit determinism of predictive astrology and focused instead on astrology's potential as a symbolic language. Instead of seeing planets as transmitters of physical influence, Rudhyar saw them as symbolic of human functions. As a psychological language and diagnostic tool, astrology could serve as a guide to the integration and transformation of personality. Rudhyar's approach was "person-centered" in the sense that every birth chart (horoscope) was unique; a horoscope represented the individual's total potential, in which no planet was "good" or "bad," but rather each element was part of an organic whole. Events were not interpreted as isolated occurrences with fortunate or unfortunate effects, but as purposeful, phase-specific manifestations of developmental cycles. An event derived its meaning from the stage it represented in a given planetary cycle and contributed to an ongoing process of growth that led inexorably toward self-realization.

In the 1970s, the humanistic banner was taken up by such astrologers as **Zipporah Dobyns,** Richard Idemon, **Stephen Arroyo, Robert Hand,** and others. **Humanistic astrologers** asserted that there is no absolute separation between human and divine; rather, people and planets are woven into the same seamless web of being. Every individual is a focus and channel for the numinous energies that permeate the entire cosmos. Consciousness, not matter, is the primary reality of the Universe. As the human psyche is both reflective of and embedded within the Universal Psyche, it partakes of the creative power of this parent consciousness. The psyche is bound and animated by the laws and formative principles of the One Being of which all lesser beings are parts. While the universal laws of Absolute Being cannot be violated, the individual is free and self-determining within the boundaries of these laws.

Rudhyar held that each person was born in response to a need of the universe at a particular time and place. The birth chart, in effect, represents the solution to this need; i.e., it reveals the purpose of the life and the key to one's destiny. Put another way, the horoscope is like a "seed plan" that shows a person's unique path of development. Just as a seed packet depicts a picture of the plant that enclosed seeds may eventually become, so the horoscope symbolizes the kind of adult that the individual may become. In this view, nothing occurs in a human life except for a purpose, and this purpose is the purpose of the whole acting through the individual. This whole is often referred to as the core self, the indwelling divinity that is rooted in a living, purposive universe. The question then becomes not What is going to happen, but What is its meaning? Astrology, said Rudhyar, can be utilized as a kind of "karma yoga" in which everything that happens is related to who the person is and may become. Thus, the humanistic astrologer should not be concerned with events per se, but only with the response or meaning that the client gives to them. "It is not the predictable events which are important, but the attitude of the individual person towards his own growth and self-fulfillment" (1972, p. 54).

The advantage of the birth chart is that it depicts the individual as a whole and thus provides a means for understanding how internal conflicts result in personality fragmentation and the exteriorization of conflict. Individuals split off and deny certain parts of themselves when the needs that underlie the expression of these parts meet with pain and frustration. Various functions get repressed and projected, and thus the individual is reduced to only part of what she or he potentially is. Unintegrated functions are typically experienced in the outer world in the guise of people and situations the individual attracts. What the individual experiences as a problematic situation or relationship can be seen in the chart as an aspect of the person's own psyche. In this way, the horoscope indicates what functions have been denied and projected and through what circumstances (houses) they will likely be encountered.

While the birth chart provides insight into a person's internal conflicts, **transits** and **progressions** tell when these conflicts will be targeted for healing. These planetary movements indicate the nature, meaning, and duration of various developmental periods, each of which presents its own challenges and opportunities. Although transits may correlate with outer events that seem to impinge upon the individual, astrology suggests that these events are the synchronous external manifestation of inner changes. The outer events serve as the trigger or stimulus to promote inner psychological growth. Seen in this way, transits reveal those parts of a person's nature which are ready to be consciously integrated, explored, or transformed. Reengaging a split-off part usually results in crisis since it means that the old order has to die in order for a new, more inclusive order to emerge. The humanistic astrologer, says Rudhyar,

> welcomes crises as signs of growth. He attempts to help the client or patient to reorient himself toward the causes of the crisis, to reassess his goals as well as his motives, to accept what is, but in a new and holistic manner. . . which eventually should lead to harmony, inner peace, wisdom and compassion (1975, pp. 56–57).

The value of astrology, then, is not in its power to predict what the gods have in store for humans, but in its ability to reveal the godlike powers that reside in the depths of every human being. Accordingly, the focus in humanistic astrology is inward, not outward, and interpretations are made in terms of personal growth and fulfillment. Simply put, the goal is to help the client realize the potentials that are symbolized by the horoscope. For example, Saturn opposed Venus in the natal chart indicates not simply "misfortune in love" but also the potential to love deeply, enduringly, and responsibly, along with the patience and determination to overcome obstacles. Although realization of this potential may require a certain amount of hardship and suffering, to predict only hardship and suffering with no understanding of the potential gains involved is shortsighted at best and damaging at worst. Dobyns put it this way:

> Telling people they are fated to experience specific negative events can be highly destructive. The view taken here is that character is destiny, and that by changing our character (our habitual attitudes, beliefs, and actions) we can change our destiny. With self-knowledge, we can integrate conflicts, overcome weaknesses, further develop talents, and move toward balance. As humanistic psychology puts it, we can achieve self-actualization and self-transcendence (1973, p. 2).

In many ways, humanistic astrology represents a genuine advancement in the theory of humanistic psychology. Both Jungian and humanistic psychologies have been criticized for their lack of precision in describing the inner nature of the human being. References to archetypes, faculties, functions, impulses, and the like tend to be vague and speculative, with no concrete referents for outlining in a systematic manner the structure of the psyche. Humanistic psychology is more a set of attitudes toward the person than a precise and useful theory of personality and human growth. Astrology, on the other hand, provides objective, predictable correlates for the structure and dynamics of the psyche while also indicating the directions that growth might occur. The person with Saturn opposed Venus, for example, may shift over time from a negative, fearful attitude toward relations (e.g., "I will resist being controlled by my domineering partner") to one of responsible and loyal commitment. Such a shift would reflect a more mature, realistic attitude toward relationships, (e.g., "a good marriage requires patience, humility, and hard work") while still being consistent with the astrological meaning of Saturn opposed Venus.

Fate and Causality

As a theory of causality, humanistic astrology is radically opposed to the mechanistic determinism implicit in most psychological models. It does not assume that psychological problems are invariably the by-products of an unhealthy culture, traumatic experiences, or faulty child rearing. Because the precise nature of the person as well as the person's environment is implicit in the symbolism of the chart from the first breath, astrology suggests that character and destiny are fated. But as Greene (1984) points out, what we call fate is indissolubly bound up with justice and law rather than a random predetermining force that dictates a person's every action and experience. Fate was personified as the goddess Moira by the Greeks and evolved from a vision of an orderly, interconnected cosmos. As the guardian of justice, Moira was simply natural law raised beyond the status of a deity. She embodied the principle that because humans are part of nature they cannot violate nature's laws without suffering the consequences; i.e., they cannot repudiate an archetype or express an archetype to excess without exacting a penalty designed to correct the transgression. In this regard, fate is a cause-and-effect principle analogous to the eastern doctrine of karma. Fate is not simply a mysterious power dispensing blessing or punishment, but a corrective process in the service of a transcendent purpose—that the individual evolve toward a fuller realization of the divine order that humans naturally embody.

By combining the doctrine of karma with the theory of astrology, one can account for the fated quality of a person's life and character; the chart may be seen as a seed plan or blue print of destiny, but in the end it reflects a self-created fate. This perspective suggests that the infinite wisdom of the cosmos decrees that a person is born when the planets are arranged in a structure that reflects the fate which that individual has earned on the basis of past actions in past lives. Subsequent experiences with one's culture and caretakers derive from a preexistent psychic structure. The environment, then, beginning with the body, is not so much a primary as a secondary cause of behavior; it is a mirror reflecting the soul's already existing internal structure. Thus, for a pathological condition, the environment confirms—but does not originate—the child's primary anxieties and inner conflicts. Of course, one cannot dispute environmental deficits and their effects. What needs to be emphasized, however, is the individual's accountability. In this view, the experienced environment constitutes karmic feedback to activate, correct, and refine a person's innate character, however long and painful this process may be. Recent developments in past-lives therapy suggest that a given life may be but a single chapter in a long and ongoing evolutionary process (Moody, 1990; Weiss, 1992; Woolger, 1988).

Basic Needs and Psychopathology

The application of astrology to clinical practice can take many and varied forms. Whatever method is employed, however, an immediate advantage of astrology is that it provides a clear framework for understanding a client's needs. Each sign of the zodiac represents a fundamental human need or motivational drive (Perry, 1989a, 1989b). Although all 12 signs are operative in consciousness, constituting the archetypal structure of the psyche, the signs the planets occupy show those needs that are going to be highlighted in the personality. The practitioner needs to assess how the planets are organized in the chart, i.e., what kinds of relations they form to one another. The overall network of planetary aspects symbolizes cognitive structure—that relatively enduring organization of ideas, attitudes, and expectancies by which individuals interpret their world and direct their behavior.

If, for example, a person's Sun squares Neptune, the underlying needs which these planets rule are in conflict (square aspect). The need for validation (Leo) and the capacity for creative self-expression (the Sun) are in conflict with the need to surrender ego in selfless service to the whole (Pisces/Neptune).

This conflict will emerge into consciousness as a particular way of thinking (the person may not *believe* that she or he deserves recognition), perceiving (others are *perceived* as more important, or disinterested, or invalidating), and behaving (the person's will is weakened, intentions are unclear, and there is likely to be a tendency toward self-sacrifice, self-sabotage, or self-delusion).

The result of such a mind-set may likewise be deception in dealings with others. Duplicity or fraudulent behavior is a central feature of "the false self" that is characteristic of narcissistic personality disorder; the individual may over-compensate for his perceived deficiencies by developing a behavioral style that seems to say, "I'm special, wonderful, perfect, and superior, while you (all other people) are nothing." The signs that the planets occupy show the particular way this process is likely to unfold.

The point is, beliefs are cognitive structures that emerge from the relative integration of underlying needs, whereas behavior is the observable expression of these internal structures. By examining the client's birth chart, the astrotherapist is able to gain insight into the core ideas that underlie the presenting problem. Psychopathology can be seen as a product of grim, unconscious, pathogenic beliefs that result from a lack of integration of basic needs. These negative or false beliefs predispose the individual to hurt herself or himself or others by attempting to satisfy specific needs. Invariably, false beliefs are rooted in painful childhood relationships that offer the first, and thus prototypical, relational experiences, which will later be re-created in adult life. These early formative experiences are the externalization of intrapsychic patterns symbolized by the birth chart. In other words, the pathogenic beliefs that develop in response to painful childhood experiences are symbolized by certain planetary configurations.

Psychological astrology has, like the Roman god Janus, two faces. One looks inward into the underlying motives, complexes, and family inheritance that lie behind the manifest problems and difficulties the individual faces; the other looks outward toward the myriad events, circumstances, and relation-ships that mirror this inner world. The symbols of the chart form a metaphorical bridge between subjective and objective reality, showing how they are but two faces of the same reality.

A personality theory particularly compatible with psychological astrology is object relations theory. According to this model, the human personality evolves through the internalization of primary objects, e.g., parents and siblings. Early childhood relationships with these primary objects become the main determinants of personality formation through a process that commits these relationships to memory as internal objects. (An internal object is a piece of psychic structure that formed from the person's experience with an important caretaking person in early life.) As a mental representation of this earlier relationship, an internal object is associated with the relative satisfaction of a specific need *by* the object (e.g., the need for protection, approval, autonomy, security, and the like). These experiences of need satisfaction are incorporated into the self as a trace of the earlier relationship. Internal objects thus exist in relation to parts of the self. Intrapsychic relations between self-parts (primary needs and capacities) and object-parts (the internalization of the object's response to specific needs) are bound together by affects that derive from the original object relationship.

Consider again the individual with Sun square Neptune. His need for validation might have been frustrated by a father (Sun) who appropriated him for the father's own needs. For example, the father might have only responded to the child when the child thought, felt, or acted in a manner that validated the father (for example, the child expressed an interest in football because the father had been a football player). Who the child was as a distinct individual was more or less ignored. To gain the father's approval required the child to sacrifice (Neptune) his real identity, deny feelings and interests that were different from the father's, and so deceive the father into thinking that father and son were one. Not surprisingly, this child grew up confused about who he really is. He is likely to feel unimportant, sacrifice himself for others, lack confidence, overcompensate—in short, express the various behavioral attributes characteristic of Sun square Neptune. This aspect, then, symbolizes a psychic structure that represents both a quality of the self and a quality of the father (object). More to the point, it symbolizes a relationship that is both intrapsychic and interpersonal.

Kohut (1977) refers to the psychic structures that result from early developmental experiences as self-objects. A self-object represents an affect-laden image of the self in relation to an object. In other words, the core structures of the self are composed of internalized relations with significant others (objects) around particular needs. Self-objects are made up of two parts: (1) the basic drive and (2) a belief about the object toward which the drive is directed. Thus, an internal object is more than a memory; it is part of the self's being; it contributes to beliefs, attitudes, and expectations about ourselves and about the world in general.

For another example, consider an infant's need for security. If the infant's mother is consistently unavailable, erratic in her responses, or rejecting, the pain of this unmet need will become associated with a depriving object. Later, whenever the child or adult experiences a need for attachment, her capacity to satisfy this need will be compromised by unconscious aversion; i.e., the need may be denied, projected, or expressed in a dysfunctional way. The child has an unconscious belief that others will respond to her need for attachment in the same way that her mother did. Once such beliefs are in place, they regulate behavior in a manner that functions like a self-fulfilling prophecy. The individual who expects that others are likely to reject her need for attachment will unconsciously choose someone who cannot tolerate this need. The relationship with the original object is then reexperienced in the relationship with the current object.

Like object relations theory, astrology provides a system of constructs that have dual meanings. On the one hand, a planet represents a capacity for the satisfaction of a specific need (e.g., Venus represents the capacity to satisfy the need for security and attachment). On the other hand, a planet represents an object; e.g., Venus symbolizes the beloved, material goods, and beautiful things. A planet, therefore, is a Janus-faced entity that correlates to the concept of self-object; it is a piece of psychic structure that represents both a need or drive and an object that is associated with the satisfaction of that need/drive.

The tendency to re-create past object relations in current relationships preserves and confirms the personality as a closed system of parts in fixed relation to one another. While this need to confirm and preserve psychic structure is very real, there is a countertendency to change dysfunctional patterns established in earlier relationships by disconfirming the negative beliefs that perpetuate the old order (Weiss & Sampson, 1986). In other words, the psyche has an intrinsic need to evolve and grow.

In object relations theory, the process by which this occurs is called projective identification, which refers to the psychological mechanism of exporting dangerous and painful aspects of the self into the external object for safekeeping (Ogden, 1982). The object is perceived as embodying the negative qualities that the subject cannot assimilate; i.e., one identifies in the other what oneself has projected. The recipient is not only perceived as embodying these split-off qualities, but actually begins to feel and behave in a manner that is congruent with the projection—the recipient is pressured to identify with a specific, disowned aspect of the projector. If, however, the recipient is able to contain the projection and talk about it in a way that disconfirms the pathogenic belief behind the project, healing can be experienced in the relationship. In this way, the psyche may be a self-correcting process structure that evolves by experiencing the consequences of its own internal states.

Ideally, this is what happens in object relations therapy. Transference is the expression of projective identification in the therapeutic relationship. The client transfers his internal object relations onto and into the therapist. Countertransference is the feelings, fantasies, and attitudes stirred up in the therapist in response to the transference. The subjective experience of the therapist thus forms a model of what happens inside the people with whom the patient is in relationship. By thoughtfully examining the ideas, associations, and fantasies that occur in response to the patient's behavior, the therapist is provided with a set of clues as to the patient's problems in relationships. The countertransference informs the ensuing interpretation of the transference, which, it is hoped will have a healing impact (Scharff, 1992).

Because of the nature of transference phenomena, it is almost impossible for the therapist to observe the patient dispassionately. Rather, the therapist becomes drawn into and submerged in the client's inner world; one could even say the therapist becomes part of the client's unconscious world. Without the benefit of the horoscope as a reliable guide for exploring these otherwise uncharted waters of the unconscious, the therapist is like a deep-sea diver in the night with nothing to illuminate the black waters into which he is descending. Suppose these murky depths are populated with all manner of creatures (objects) that periodically brush up against, or even attack, the therapist-explorer. With only his senses and imagination to guide his way, he has no way of knowing with any certainty what strange creatures he is encountering.

With the horoscope, however, the therapist is provided a penetrating light that can illumine the deepest and darkest recesses of the client's psyche. Here the terms *object* and *object relations* take on new significance. Astrology furnishes no imaginary objects with speculative features, but planetary symbols that provide concrete, objective referents to the client's object relations. These referents have precise definitions and rules of interaction that help to clarify and articulate the client's inner world. Thus, the therapist has an objective reference point to balance the subjectivity of the therapeutic process.

An astrotherapist will almost never explicitly introduce information about the chart into the session. To do so would contaminate the transference, and it is the transference that drives the therapy. To talk about the chart would put the therapist in the specific role of "astroguru," with seemingly magical powers to interpret the stars, see into the client's future, and speak with the authority of the cosmos. This would constitute a massive violation of the principle of neutrality, which enables the transference to develop. Also, a chart interpretation tends to pull the client out of the process of exploring her subjective world of feelings and perceptions, especially as these relate to the therapist. Psychopathology is rooted in emotionally significant childhood experiences of *relationship*. Accordingly, it is through relationship that healing can best occur. No amount of teaching or advising, however powerful and revealing the information might be, can substitute for a long-term relationship (6 months or more) with a therapist who can truly see, understand, and accept the client in all her outrageous humanity.

The specific advantage of the chart is that it deepens the therapist's capacity; while the therapist will use his countertransference response to inform the ensuing interpretation of the transference, it is the chart that helps to inform the countertransference itself. That is, the therapist can read in the chart a virtual description of what he is actually experiencing in relation to the client. If, for example, the therapist is feeling hopeless, helpless, and overwhelmed by the sheer depth and intensity of the client's despair, he may note that her Pisces moon is the focal point of a powerful **yod** involving Neptune and Pluto. Such a moon/object suggests that the client might have had a mother who was hopeless, helpless, and ineffectual in dealing with her daughter's pain—the same feelings the therapist is experiencing. The client, in effect, is projecting into the therapist an image of a weak and ineffectual mother too easily overwhelmed by her daughter's negative feelings. If the therapist can contain the projection, however, and not give in to the temptation to deny the client's pain, but instead be an effective container offering empathy, compassion, and understanding, then this new experience will modify the client's internal object relations. In astrological terms, it will help the client to integrate her Pisces moon in such a way that she has deeper compassion for herself, is more understanding and accepting of her emotional needs, and is not so easily overwhelmed by her negative feelings.

The therapist can also use his understanding of the chart to formulate an interpretation of the transference. He may, for example, inquire what it is like for the client to share her pain with him. When she confesses that she feels guilt and worries that her feelings are "too much" for the therapist, he can suggest that she is experiencing him as if he were her mother, i.e., that she thinks he will feel burdened and overwhelmed by her needs just as she perceived her mother to be burdened and overwhelmed. This will help the client to modify her pathogenic belief that other people, like her mother, are unable to tolerate her feelings. So, instead of the client's denying her Piscean feelings, or collapsing into them in a way that makes her appear inconsolable, she becomes able to express them in a manner that allows others to offer her the empathy she requires.

—Glenn Perry

Sources:

Dobyns, Z. *The Astrologer's Casebook*. Los Angeles: TIA Publications, 1973.

Hall, C., and Lindzey, G. *Theories of Personality*. New York: John Wiley & Sons, 1978.

Greene, Liz. *The Astrology of Fate*. York Beach, Maine: Samuel Weiser, 1984.

Jung, C. "Commentary." In *The Secret of the Golden Flower,* translated and edited by R. Wilhelm. New York: Harcourt, Brace, & World, 1931.

———. "Interview with André Barbault." *Astrologie Moderne* (May 26, 1954).

———. *Jung: Letters (Volume II)*. Edited by G. Adler and A. Jaffe; translated by R. F. C. Hull. London: Routledge and Kegan Paul, 1976.

———. "Letter to Professor B. V. Raman." *American Astrology* (June 1948).

———. "Synchronicity: An Acausal Connecting Principle." In *The Interpretation of Nature and Psyche,* C. Jung and W. Pauli, 1–146. New York: Pantheon, 1955.

Kohut, H. *The Restoration of the Self.* New York: International Universities Press, 1977.

Moody, R. *Coming Back: A Psychiatrist Explores Past-Life Journeys*. New York: Bantam, 1990.

Ogden, T. *Projective Identification & Psychotherapeutic Technique*. New York: Jason Aronson, 1982.

Perry, G. "Psychopathology of the Zodiac (Part I)." *The Astrotherapy Newsletter* 2, no. 3 (1989a): 1–6.

———. "Psychopathology of the Zodiac (Part II)." *The Astrotherapy Newsletter* 2, no. 4 (1989a): 1–6.

Rogers, Carl D. *Client Centered Therapy*. Boston: Houghton Mifflin, 1951.

Rudhyar, D. *The Astrology of Personality*. Garden City, N.Y.: Doubleday & Company, 1936.

———. *From Humanistic to Transpersonal Astrology*. Palo Alto, Calif.: The Seed Center, 1975.

———. *Person-Centered Astrology*. Lakemont, Ga.: CSA Press, 1972.

Scharff. J. S. *Projective Identification and the Use of the Therapist's Self.* Northvale, N.J.: Jason Aronson, 1992.

Weiss, B. *Many Lives, Many Masters*. New York: Simon & Schuster, 1992.

Weiss, J., and H. Sampson. *The Psychoanalytic Process*. New York: Guilford Press, 1986.

Woolger, R. *Other Lives, Other Selves*. New York: Bantam, 1988.

Ate

Ate, **asteroid** 111 (the 111th asteroid to be discovered), is approximately 156 kilometers in diameter and has an **orbital** period of 4.2 years. It was named after the goddess of blind folly and mischief. According to Greek tragedians, Ate was behind the avenging curse which was the ultimate cause of the Trojan War. The natal position of Ate by sign and **house** may indicate where one is most prone to folly. When **afflicted**, Ate may show where one is likely to respond to real or imagined insults in an exaggerated fashion.

Sources:

Kowal, Charles T. *Asteroids: Their Nature and Utilization*. Chichester, West Sussex, U.K.: Ellis Horwood Limited, 1988.
Room, Adrian. *Dictionary of Astronomical Names*. London: Routledge, 1988.

Athazer

The **Moon** is said to be athazer either when it is in an exact **conjunction** with the **Sun** or when it makes an exact **aspect** with the Sun.

Athene

Athene, **asteroid** 881 (the 881st asteroid to be discovered), is approximately 12 kilometers in diameter and has an **orbital** period of 4.2 years. Athene was named after the Greek warrior goddess Athena. Lehman associates this asteroid, as well as the asteroids **Pallas** and **Minerva,** with "interest or ability in areas which combine the functioning of the mind and the body" (p. 24). Athene, in contrast with Pallas and Minerva, indicates more interest in being competent than in being right (Pallas) or accomplished (Minerva).

Sources:

Kowal, Charles T. *Asteroids: Their Nature and Utilization*. Chichester, West Sussex, U.K.: Ellis Horwood Limited, 1988.
Lehman, J. Lee. *The Ultimate Asteroid Book*. West Chester, Penn.: Whitford Press, 1988.
Room, Adrian. *Dictionary of Astronomical Names*. London: Routledge, 1988.

Atlantis

Atlantis, **asteroid** 1,198 (the 1,198th asteroid to be discovered), is approximately 2.8 kilometers in diameter and has an **orbital** period of 3.4 years. Atlantis was named after a mythological continent, said by Plato to have existed in the Atlantic Ocean, that was destroyed by cataclysmic earthquakes. According to Lang-Wescott, the location of Atlantis indicates where we experience a sense of imminent doom, as well as a willingness to "pay for" real or imagined errors or unworthiness from the past. This asteroid's key words are *expiation* and *ethics*.

Sources:

Lang-Wescott, Martha. *Asteroids-Mechanics: Ephemerides II.* Conway, Mass.: Treehouse Mountain, 1990.
———. *Mechanics of the Future: Asteroids.* Rev. ed. Conway, Mass.: Treehouse Mountain, 1991.

Attila

Attila, **asteroid** 1,489 (the 1,489th asteroid to be discovered), is approximately 15 kilometers in diameter and has an **orbital** period of 5.7 years. Attila was named after the West's most famous barbarian, Attila the Hun. Lehman (p. 43) associates this asteroid with power and dominance issues. Attila, she says, "signifies the fighter. The Attila type does not retire gracefully."

Sources:

Kowal, Charles T. *Asteroids: Their Nature and Utilization.* Chichester, West Sussex, U.K.: Ellis Horwood Limited, 1988.
Lehman, J. Lee. *The Ultimate Asteroid Book.* West Chester, Penn.: Whitford Press, 1988.

Autumnal Equinox (Fall Equinox)

Equinox, Latin for "equal night," refers to one of the two days of the year on which daytime and nighttime are equal in duration. The autumnal equinox takes place on or around September 23, and marks the beginning of both the sign **Libra** and the fall season.

Axial Rotation

Axial rotation is the turning of Earth on its axis and, by extension, the spinning of any heavenly body on its axis. It is Earth's daily rotation that is responsible for the **apparent motion** of the **Sun**, **Moon**, **planets**, and **stars** across the sky.

Azimuth

One can locate a specific celestial object in several ways, most of which involve specifying two coordinates. The azimuth is one of the coordinates of such a system. Although the notion of azimuth is basically simple, it is not simple to explain. Imagine that a group of people are looking at a **star**. From where they are standing, they can measure the angle between the horizon and the star. This gives them one coordinate in terms of **angular distance** (called the **altitude**, for obvious reasons). Then imagine a geometric plane that, like some kind of gigantic wall, cuts through Earth, intersecting the north and south poles, the place where they are standing, and the point directly over their heads (the zenith). They then measure another angle with their surveying instrument, this time between the imaginary wall and the star. This angular distance gives them the azimuth.

Sources:

Filbey, John, and Peter Filbey. *The Astrologer's Companion.* Wellingborough, Northamptonshire, U.K.: Aquarian Press, 1986.

Gettings, Fred. *Dictionary of Astrology.* London: Routledge & Kegan Paul, 1985.

Aztec Astrology

See: Mesoamerican Astrology

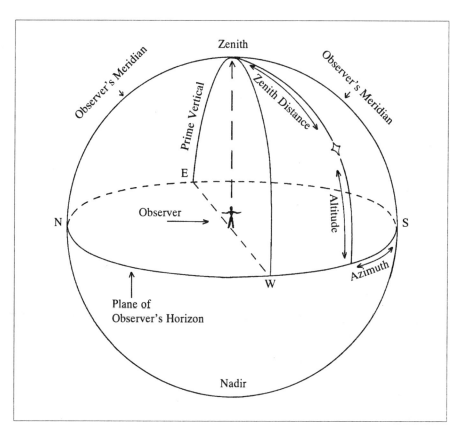

◀
Azimuth.

B

Babylonian Astrology

See: Mesopotamian Astrology

Bacchus

Bacchus is **asteroid** 2,063 (the 2,063d asteroid to be discovered). It is approximately 1.2 kilometers in diameter and has an **orbital** period of 1.1 years. Bacchus was named after the god of wine, the Roman equivalent of the Greek Dionysus. According to Lang-Wescott, Bacchus is related to addictive syndrome, particularly to the denial, substitution, and management of uncomfortable emotions. This asteroid's key word is *denial.* According to Lehman (p. 65), "Bacchus represents the way that a person seeks ecstasy through direct experience or passion."

Bacchus is also one of the names given to the hypothetical planet that some astrologers assert is orbiting beyond Pluto.

Sources:

Lang-Wescott, Martha. *Asteroids-Mechanics: Ephemerides II.* Rev. ed. Conway, Mass.: Treehouse Mountain, 1990.
Lehman, J. Lee. *The Ultimate Asteroid Book.* West Chester, Penn.: Whitford, 1988.

Bacon, Francis

Francis Bacon (1561–1626) was an English philosopher often regarded as the father (or one of the fathers) of modern science. He was famous for his advocacy of the empirical method. Perhaps because he perceived it as resting on an empirical base, he was an ardent champion of astrology.

Bailey, Alice A.

Alice A. Bailey, a well-known Theosophist who left the Theosophical Society to form the Arcane School in 1919, was born in Manchester, England, on June 16, 1880. Born Alice La Trobe-Bateman, she married the theosophist Foster Bailing in 1920. In the field of astrology, she is best known for a treatise on **esoteric astrology** that was dictated to her by Master D.K. (also known as The Tibetan). She also transcribed a volume on the astrology of countries, *The Destiny of Nations.* She asserted that she knew nothing about astrology herself. Her dense tome on esoteric astrology has been the single most influential book in this area of astrology for many decades. Bailey died in 1949.

Selected Publications:

The Destiny of the Nations. New York: Lucis Publishing Co., 1949.
Esoteric Astrology. New York: Lucis Publishing Co., 1950.
The Unfinished Autobiography of Alice A. Bailey. New York: Lucis Publishing Co., 1951.

Sources:

Holden, James H., and Robert A. Hughes. *Astrological Pioneers of America.* Tempe, Ariz.: American Federation of Astrologers, 1988.

Bailey, E. H.

E. H. Bailey, born November 29, 1876, in Kent, England, was an astrologer and an author. It is said that he became interested in astrology after reading Zadkiel's almanac (a popular astrology almanac of the times) as a boy. About 1900, he worked briefly for the well-known astrologer **Alan Leo.** He initiated the astrological periodical *Destiny* in 1904, but it was unsuccessful. He later took a job editing *The British Journal of Astrology* and became a fellow of the Astrological Society of America.

Bailey is best remembered for his work on the "prenatal epoch" (determining an individual's time of conception), a topic he became interested in after reading some pieces by **W. Gorn Old** (Sepharial) in *Astrologer's Magazine.* He communicated with Sepharial as he developed his own theory. The basic technique for determining the conception date from the birth date goes back to antiquity and can also be utilized to rectify a birth time. Bailey and Sepharial developed the method further, but their work evoked strong opposition from certain other astrologers. Bailey studied the prenatal epoch in hundreds of cases, many of them collected from the public records and others obtained with the help of obstetricians. Considering the period in which it was written, *The Prenatal Epoch* was a well-researched and well-developed book. Astrological interest in this topic has waned considerably since Bailey's time, however. He died on June 4, 1959.

Selected Publications:

The Prenatal Epoch. N.p., 1916

Sources:

Holden, James H., and Robert A. Hughes. *Astrological Pioneers of America.* Tempe, Ariz.: American Federation of Astrologers, 1988.

Barbault, André

André Barbault, born October 1, 1921, in Champigneulles, France, was a prominent astrologer and writer. He was active in the Centre International d'Astrologie from its beginning in 1946, serving as vice-president from 1953 to 1967. In 1967, he started marketing computer **horoscopes** under the name Astroflash. Barbault's particular interest is in **mundane astrology,** a subject about which he has published several volumes. In the area of **natal astrology**, he has developed a synthesis of astrology and psychoanalysis.

Selected Publications:

De la psychanalyse de l'astrologie. Paris: Editions du Seuil, 1961.
Traité pratique d'astrologie. N.p., 1961.

Sources:

Holden, James H., and Robert A. Hughes. *Astrological Pioneers of America.* Tempe, Ariz.: American Federation of Astrologers, 1988.

Barren Signs

The barren signs are the signs of the **zodiac** traditionally said to deny children (i.e., to indicate sterility) when placed on the **cusp** of the fifth house, the house of children. These signs are **Gemini**, **Leo**, and **Virgo**. A number of other signs are regarded as being somewhat barren. The traditional barren **planets** are **Mars** and **Saturn** (some astrologers now add **Uranus**). The fertile signs and planets are referred to as **fruitful**. The classification of the zodiac into degrees of barrenness and fruitfulness has been largely abandoned because contemporary astrological research has failed to verify this traditional interpretation. Some modern astrologers, however, hold the modified view that barren signs limit the

---

number of children, rather than actually deny them. The traditional barren signs are still regarded as unfruitful in **agricultural astrology**, however.

Sources:

Gettings, Fred. *Dictionary of Astrology*. London: Routledge & Kegan Paul, 1985.
Lee, Dal. *Dictionary of Astrology*. New York: Paperback Library, 1969.

Beer

Beer, **asteroid** 1,896 (the 1,896th asteroid to be discovered), is approximately 6.6 kilometers in diameter and has an **orbital** period of 3.8 years. Beer was named after a prominent astrologer. Lehman, perhaps unaware of the astronomer Beer, gives this asteroid a "literal" interpretation, associating it with addiction, particularly addiction to alcoholic substances.

Sources:

Kowal, Charles T. *Asteroids: Their Nature and Utilization*. Chichester, West Sussex, U.K.: Ellis Horwood Limited, 1988.
Lehman, J. Lee. *The Ultimate Asteroid Book*. West Chester, Penn.: Whitford Press, 1988.

Beholding

Beholding signs are pairs of signs of the **zodiac** that have the same **delineation**—i.e., the signs that are equidistant from the tropical signs (**Cancer** and **Capricorn**). These pairs of signs are **Aries** and **Libra**; **Taurus** and **Virgo**; **Gemini** and **Leo**; **Aquarius** and **Sagittarius**; and **Pisces** and **Scorpio**.

Bellona

Bellona, **asteroid** 28 (the 28th asteroid to be discovered), is approximately 124 kilometers in diameter and has an **orbital** period of 4.6 years. It was named after the Roman goddess of war, who some myths say was the wife of **Mars**; other accounts maintain that she was his sister. The goddess did not have a developed mythology of her own. The asteroid Bellona may be **delineated** in somewhat the same way as Mars. Its prominence in a **natal chart** indicates an energetic, assertive person. When inharmoniously **aspected**, Bellona may show a bellicose personality.

Kowal, Charles T. *Asteroids: Their Nature and Utilization.* Chichester, West Sussex, U.K.: Ellis Horwood Limited, 1988.

Room, Adrian. *Dictionary of Astronomical Names.* London: Routledge, 1988.

Benefic (Benefic Aspects; Benefic Planets)

Benefic is a traditional term still found in older astrological works. It refers to **aspects** and **planets** regarded as having a fortunate, harmonious influence. Benefic aspects are angles like **trines** and **sextiles** (often called **soft aspects** by current astrologers) and planets like **Venus** (the Lesser Benefic) and **Jupiter** (the Greater Benefic). The antonym of benefic is **malefic**.

Benjamine, Elbert (C. C. Zain)

Elbert Benjamine, one of America's most prominent astrologers and founder of the **Church of Light**, was born in Iowa on December 12, 1882. He studied the occult at an early age and discovered the Brotherhood of Light and its more public teaching agency, the Hermetic Brotherhood of Luxor, when he was 18. He studied astrology under Minnie Higgins, a leader of the Hermetic Brotherhood. At Lake Charles, Louisiana, on December 8, 1907, he felt that he communicated with the invisible spiritual hierarchy, a communication in which he was informed that he was destined for importance.

Higgins died in 1907, and Benjamine went to the order's Denver headquarters to take her position as one of the organization's three leaders. The other two leaders requested that he compose and write a series of lessons to assist with public outreach. He resisted undertaking this task until 1908, when he began his research for the lessons. He began writing in 1914, but soon afterward the Hermetic Brotherhood was closed down.

Benjamine moved to Los Angeles in the spring of 1915 and began holding small, private classes based on early drafts of the course he was writing. He used the pen name C. C. Zain. He opened his classes to the public on Armistice Day in 1918. One of his new students, Elizabeth Dorris, became his wife in 1919. In 1932, Benjamine incorporated the Church of Light. This successor organization to the Brotherhood of Light emphasizes evolution within a tradition supposedly dating from the Brotherhood of Light in ancient Egypt.

In 1934, Benjamine completed all 21 of the proposed public outreach courses. He published his personal statements on astrology under his own name in such books as *Astrological Lore of All Ages* (1945) and led the Church of Light until his death in 1951.

Selected Publications:

Brotherhood of Light Lessons. 21 vols. Los Angeles: Church of Light, 1922–1932.
Astrological Love of All Ages. Chicago: Aries Press, 1945.

Sources:

"The Founders of the Church of Light." *The Church of Light Quarterly* 45, no. 1 (February 1970): 1–2.
Melton, J. Gordon. *Religious Leaders of America.* Detroit, Mich.: Gale Research, 1991.

Bennett, Sidney Kimball (Wynn)

Sidney Kimball Bennett, born February 10, 1892, in Chicago, was a prominent astrologer of the early twentieth century. Under the pseudonym Wynn, he published *Wynn's Astrology Magazine* in the thirties and forties. He began studying astrology as a young man (about 1915) and was practicing professionally by the twenties.

In *The Key Cycle,* Bennett relates that a number of his clients had complained that his prognostications, based on the techniques of **progressions and directions** had failed. He regarded these failures as being traceable to mistaken birth times. These faulty predictions struck home, however, in May 1926 when he failed to foresee an accident in which he was almost killed by a hit-and-run driver. At the time, Bennett was traveling in California on a business trip during which he was attempting to take advantage of a "marvelous combination of progressions." However, from a business standpoint the trip was a total failure. Reflecting upon these events and calling to mind his clients' complaints, he was persuaded to give up progressions and directions.

He then began to experiment with other predictive methods, such as **solar return.** Bennett devised a technique for utilizing this method for intermediate dates, and this was the origin of the predictive system he called The Key Cycle.

In the early thirties, Bennett wrote an astrology column for the New York *Daily News.* In 1932, he foretold a week of financial turmoil for early March 1933. One of Roosevelt's first official acts as president after he was inaugurated on March 4, 1933, was to proclaim a "bank holiday," closing all the banks in the United States. Many banks did not reopen, and depositors suffered a complete loss. This act shook the nation and threw the financial markets into chaos. Bennett became famous for his prediction. In later life, he lived in Australia, where he is thought to have died in the late fifties.

Selected Publications:

Your Life till 1954. . . Your next 20 years. . . with 20-year World Prediction, interpreted by Wynn. New York: Wynn Publishing Co., 1933.

Astrology: Your Path to Success. Philadelphia: David McKay Co., 1938.
Astrology, Science of Prediction. Los Angeles: Wynn Publishing Co., 1945.
The Key Cycle. 1931. Reprint. Tempe, Ariz.: American Federation of Astrologers, 1970.

Sources:

Holden, James H., and Robert A. Hughes. *Astrological Pioneers of America*. Tempe, Ariz.: American Federation of Astrologers, 1988.
Wynn's Astrology Magazine. New York: Wynn Publishing Co., 1931–194[?].

Berosus

Berosus was a famous Mesopotamian priest and astrologer born about 330 B.C. He left his native land, settled on the Greek island of Kos, and taught astrology. Berosus is attributed with introducing astrology to the Greeks, in whose hands it was transformed from a priestly art into an empirical science.

Besieged

Besieged is a traditional term used to describe the situation of a **planet** (particularly a **significator**) placed between two other planets and falling within both of their **orbs of influence.** The conflicting connotations of the word besieged derive from the tendency of an older generation of astrologers to call attention to **conjunctions** in which a **benefic** planet (e.g., **Venus**) was placed between two **malefics** (e.g., **Mars** and **Saturn**). A planet can be favorably besieged, however, as when placed between two benefic planets.

Bestial Signs

The bestial signs are the signs of the **zodiac** represented by animals. Those classified as bestial vary, but always include **Aries** the Ram, **Taurus** the Bull, **Leo** the Lion, and **Capricorn** the Goat. The three **water signs** are also symbolized by animals, but water sign animals are not four-footed "beasts." Hence, the water **triplicity**—**Cancer** the Crab, **Scorpio** the Scorpion (sometimes the Eagle), and **Pisces** the Fish—is sometimes included, sometimes not, in the bestial list. **Sagittarius** the Archer is often represented as a centaur—half human and half horse. When represented as an archer, Sagittarius is classified as nonbestial; when represented as a centaur, bestial.

The signs that are not bestial are **human signs: Gemini** the Twins, **Virgo** the Virgin, **Aquarius** the Water Bearer, and, when considered as the Archer, Sagittarius. Only **Libra** is represented by a nonliving artifact, the Scales (although the old symbol for Libra was a woman holding a scale, which would make it a human sign). This grouping of signs into bestial and nonbestial contrasts with the signs found in East Asian astrological systems (e.g., **Chinese astrology**), all of which are bestial.

Unlike most other schemes of classification, such as the **elements** (earth, air, fire, and water) and the **qualities** (**cardinal, mutable,** and **fixed**), the bestial/nonbestial contrast does not carry practical consequences for interpretation (e.g., persons born under animal signs are not more "beastly" than others). For this reason, as well as because of the negative connotation of the term beast, the expression bestial sign has dropped out of general usage in modern astrology.

Sources:

Bach, Eleanor. *Astrology from A to Z: An Illustrated Source Book.* New York: Philosophical Library, 1990.
Lee, Dal. *Dictionary of Astrology.* New York: Paperback Library, 1969.

Bettina

Bettina, **asteroid** 250 (the 250th asteroid to be discovered), is approximately 128 kilometers in diameter and has an **orbital** period of 5.6 years. It was named after the baroness Rothschild, who had subsidized its discoverers. In a **natal chart**, Bettina may show where one gives or is otherwise generous with an expectation of reward.

Sources:

Kowal, Charles T. *Asteroids: Their Nature and Utilization.* Chichester, West Sussex, U.K.: Ellis Horwood Limited, 1988.
Room, Adrian. *Dictionary of Astronomical Names.* London: Routledge, 1988.

The Bible and Astrology

The Hebrew and Christian Bible is a complex set of documents. To advocates of astrology, it is not difficult to find passages presenting the science of the stars in a positive light. If, on the other hand, one wishes to attack astrology, it is also possible to find passages condemning stargazing. Certain Scriptures appear—at least in the King James Version (KJV)—to condemn astrologers as those who keep, watch, or observe the times; e.g., "Ye shall not eat anything with the blood, neither shall ye use enchantment, nor observe times" (Lev. 19:26). This allusion to astrology, however, was an interpolation by KJV translators. In modern translations, it is clear that the original biblical condemnation was against divination in general, rather than astrology in particular: "You shall not eat meat with the blood in it. You shall not practise divination or soothsaying" (New

English Bible); and "You shall not eat any flesh with the blood in it. You shall not practice augury or witchcraft" (Revised Standard Version).

Advocates of astrology, however, can point to such passages as "God created lights in the heavens, and He made them for signs and for seasons" (Gen. 1:14), which is capable of being interpreted as a reference to astrology. More generally, because the God of Western religions is a sky-god, many different scriptural passages portray God as utilizing heavenly signs to instruct the faithful. These signs are often ambiguous enough to be given an astrological interpretation. With a little reworking, it is not difficult to read many otherwise innocent passages in an astrological manner, for example, the Lord's Prayer:

Our Father who lives in the heavens,

Let your name be honored,

Let your Kingdom come,

Let your will be done down here on the earth,

As perfectly as it is in the sky.

—Don Jacobs, *Astrology's Pew in the Church*

From these examples, it is not difficult to see that both supporters and detractors must "massage" various biblical passages to get an unambiguous message on the status of astrology. One of the few biblical accounts in which we can clearly perceive the practice of astrology is the story of The Three Wise Men. The Magi were clearly astrologers, and The **Star of Bethlehem**, as scholars have long pointed out, was actually a major planetary **conjunction**. The Magi believed, as do many of our contemporaries, that our **planet** was on the verge of entering a "new age," and this particular conjunction was taken to indicate the birth of a new world teacher.

Sources:

Jacobs, Don. *Astrology's Pew in the Church*. San Francisco: The Joshua Foundation, 1979.
Simms, Maria Kay. *Twelve Wings of the Eagle: Evolution through the Ages of the Zodiac.* San Diego, Calif.:, 1988.

Bicorporeal

Bicorporeal signs are signs of the **zodiac** said to be "double bodied": **Gemini, Sagittarius,** and **Pisces.** As originally used by **Ptolemy,** bicorporeal referred to all of the **mutable** signs, which are the three signs mentioned above plus **Virgo.**

Biquintile

A biquintile is a minor **aspect** of 144°, created by subdividing a circle (360°) into five parts. As the name indicates, a biquintile is equivalent to two **quintiles** (72° aspects). The great astronomer **Johannes Kepler** devised quintiles and biquintiles for his astrological work. Underresearched, its influence is sometimes said to be similar to that of a quintile. It is given an **orb of influence** of 1° to 2°.

Birth Control, Astrological

While the expression astrological birth control could have several referents, it is usually taken to refer to the system discovered and elaborated by the Czech psychiatrist Eugen Jonas. Jonas's initial discoveries were summed up by his three fundamental rules—conception, determination of sex, and life capability of the fetus—which he first formulated on August 15, 1956 (Ostrander & Schroeder 1970, 49).

> 1. The time of fertility [a second period of fertility, independent of the ovulation cycle] occurs during the same phase of the **moon** as that in which the woman was born.
>
> 2. The sex of the future child will be determined by the position of the moon during the time of the woman's fertility—whether the moon is found in the positive or in the negative field (i.e., in a **positive, masculine sign** or in a **negative, feminine sign**) of the **ecliptic** (or **zodiac**).
>
> 3. Unfavorable distribution of gravitational forces of the nearer celestial bodies at the time of conception produces complications during pregnancy, particularly for the fetus.

These discoveries became the basis for an astrological birth control clinic that, after overcoming much resistance, Jonas was able to establish in Czechoslovakia.

The first rule became the basis for a system of birth control that is basically an elaboration and development of the old rhythm method. Rather than abstaining only during the period of a woman's ovulation, a couple also abstains on (and for several days prior to) the day that the **Sun** and Moon repeat the exact angle they made with each other at the moment of the woman's birth. For instance, a woman born at the exact moment of the full moon (when, with Earth as the vertex, the Sun and Moon make a 180° angle to each other) would abstain during, and for several days prior to, the full moon. When combined with abstention during ovulation, this modified rhythm method is, according to Czech researchers, 98% effective as a birth control method.

Jonas became interested in astrology as a student but kept this interest separate from his profession during the early part of his career. In the mid-1950s, however, neighboring Hungary legalized abortion. This motivated Jonas, a practicing Catholic, to search for alternatives, even in such unlikely subject areas as astrology. From the ancient system of **Mesopotamian astrology,** he found a fragment asserting that "woman is fertile during a certain phase of the moon" (Ostrander & Schroeder 1979, 61). No other clues illuminating this statement survived. Using this assertion as a starting place, however, Jonas painstakingly researched birth records until he broke the code of ancient astrological science: A woman is fertile during the phase of the Moon that replicates the phase the Moon was in at the moment of her birth.

Jonas's second rule is based on the Pythagorean notion that odd numbers are male and even numbers female. Hence, since ancient times, the first, third, fifth, seventh, ninth, and eleventh signs of the zodiac (**Aries, Gemini, Leo, Libra, Sagittarius,** and **Aquarius**) were regarded as masculine, while the second, fourth, sixth, eighth, tenth, and twelfth signs (**Taurus, Cancer, Virgo, Scorpio, Capricorn,** and **Pisces**) were regarded as feminine. The Moon, as the traditional **ruler** of conception and motherhood, might well have been anticipated as the key to influencing the sex of a child. Using the sign of the Moon at the time of conception, Jonas found that he could predict the sex of a child with 85% accuracy. This effect of the Moon sign was apparently known to Hellenistic astrologers—another item of ancient wisdom discarded in the crusade to rid the world of "superstition."

The third rule flows out of Jonas's search for possible astrological factors in miscarriages and birth defects. Jonas found a significant correlation between such complications and the presence of **opposition** (180°) angles—particularly when the Sun was involved—during conception. While this particular finding has no known correlate with traditional astrology, the negative effect of an opposition **aspect** in a **natal chart** (in contrast to a conception chart) has been well known since antiquity. That the Sun, as the traditional ruler of vitality and life force, is involved in such complications is not surprising.

As Jonas's work became established and grew, his center counseled couples in all three of the areas covered by his three rules: birth control, selecting the sex of children, and avoiding birth complications. This work flourished during Czechoslovakia's "springtime of freedom," the country's short-lived experiment with an open society prior to the Soviet invasion in the late summer of 1968. Jonas's center remained in operation another year and half following the invasion before being closed by the government. The doctor was demoted and his work stopped. It is hoped that the changes which have occurred in Czech society since the collapse of the iron curtain signal a new beginning for Jonas and his colleagues, and that the results of their careful research will soon be made available.

Although most of the relevant research of Jonas and colleagues is contained in untranslated books, pamphlets, and articles, since 1972 the English-speaking world has had the basic information on astrological birth control available to it through the book *Astrological Birth Control.* The authors, Sheila Ostrander and Lynn Schroeder, had discovered Jonas's work while researching their popular *Psychic Discoveries Behind the Iron Curtain.* They collected materials on astrological birth control and, having copies of most of the relevant information at the time of the Soviet invasion, Ostrander and Schroeder decided to have the materials in their possession translated. From these and other sources they wrote *Astrological Birth Control*. (The book is also useful for its overview of scientific research on astrological effects up to 1972.) Enough technical material is included that any competent astrologer can cast an astrological birth control chart, although the authors were careful to include the caveat that they were not recommending the system. The reports from non–iron curtain researchers who have investigated Jonas's system since the publication of Ostrander and Schroeder's book are mixed; some claim to have replicated his results, while others report disconfirmation.

Sources:

Naish, Francesca. *The Lunar Cycle: A Guide to Natural and Astrological Fertility Control*. Bridport, Dorset, U.K.: Prism Press, 1989.

Ostrander, Sheila, and Lynn Schroeder. *Astrological Birth Control*. Englewood Cliffs, N.J.: Prentice-Hall, 1972. (Reissued in paperback as *Natural Birth Control*.)

———. *Psychic Discoveries Behind the Iron Curtain*. Englewood Cliffs, N.J.: Prentice-Hall, 1970.

Birth Moment

Although determining the exact birth moment—first appearance of the baby's head, delivery, severing of the umbilical cord, first breath, first cry, etc—has sometimes been the subject of debate, the consensus among most astrologers is that the **natal chart** should be cast for the individual's first breath. Clients sometimes tell astrologers that their **nativity** should have been earlier or later than was recorded on their birth certificate (e.g., that the chart cast for their moment of birth is somehow wrong, because they were born premature). Such people misconceive the nature of astrological influence: The individual's first independent breath is like the clicking of a camera shutter, exposing the "film" of their soul to the imprint of celestial influences.

Sources:

Bach, Eleanor. *Astrology from A to Z: An Illustrated Source Book*. New York: Philosophical Library, 1990.

Leo, Alan. *Dictionary of Astrology*. Reprint. New York: Astrologer's Library, 1983.

Birthplace System

An alternative name for the **Koch house** system. By extension, Koch houses are sometimes called birthplace houses.

Bitter signs is an archaic term applied to the **fire signs**, which were said to be fiery, hot, and bitter. The antonym is **sweet signs.**

Blue Moon

The **Moon** can sometimes appear bluish because of atmospheric conditions, but the expression once in a blue Moon refers to a month during which two full moons occur—one at the beginning and the other near the end of the month. This happens only once every few years.

Blumenthal, Marian

Marian Blumenthal, an ordained minister and astrologer, uses hyperdimensional awareness modalities in her practice of spiritual psychology. The cross-cultural techniques she has perfected come from early experiences with native Americans and gypsy bands who camped on her parents' Wyoming land. She was born July 25, 1933, into an astrology family with more than 200 years of practice on the maternal line. She credits "The Grandmothers" of Wyoming and the Dakotas for focusing her life's work. Blumenthal is a graduate of the Famous Writers School (1964) of Newport, Connecticut; Eastern Nebraska Christian College (A.A., 1970); St. John's University, located near Shreveport, Louisiana (B.A., psychology, 1972; M.A., sociology, 1976); and the Metaphysical Institute of Los Angeles, California (1978). She is founder of Sea Bri, a nonprofit educational foundation, and has conducted classes through the Las Vegas, Nevada, adult evening school program. She has hosted her own television show in Palm Springs, California, and writes a metaphysical by-line column for the *Seafarer* periodical.

Boomerang

A boomerang is a **configuration** resembling a **yod** but involving a fourth **planet** directly opposed to the "action planet" at the tip of the yod. In a yod, two planets form a **sextile** (60°) **aspect** and both in turn form a **quincunx** (150°) aspect with a third planet. If lines were drawn to the center of the **horoscope** from all three planets, the resulting pattern would look like a capital *Y.* The planet at the bottom tip of the *Y* is said to be the action planet because its **house** placement is where the action takes place when the configuration is activated by a **transit** or a **progression**. The interpretation often given to a yod in a **natal chart** is that it indicates a life that proceeds along in a certain pattern for a period of time until the established pattern is abruptly interrupted and the **native** is forced to proceed in a new direction, though the new direction is one for which the person had actually been preparing for some time. A completely unanticipated promotion in one's chosen profession, for example, might be brought about by an activated yod configuration.

When a fourth planet is involved in a yod so that it forms an **opposition** (180°) aspect to the action planet and **semisextile** (30°) aspects to the remaining two planets, the resulting formation is called a boomerang, a designation coined by Joan McEvers. In a boomerang, the situation anticipated at the point of the action planet "boomerangs" when the configuration is activated. One example McEvers uses in her explanation of the boomerang is Ralph Waldo Emerson, who had such a configuration in his natal chart and who, when fortune placed the 26-year-old minister in the pulpit of Boston's Old North Church, found himself in a situation with which his nonconformist temperament had difficulty coping. He was eventually forced to leave the ministry. Thus, Emerson's opportunity "boomeranged."

Sources:

Escobar, Thyrza. *Side Lights of Astrology.* 3d ed. Hollywood, Calif.: Golden Seal Research, 1971.

▶
Boomerang.

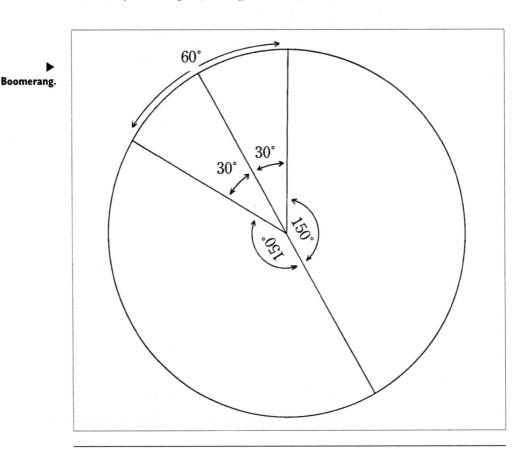

McEvers, Joan. "The Boomerang: A New Configuration." In *Astrology: Old Theme, New Thoughts* (p. 95–106). Edited by Marion D. March and Joan McEvers. San Diego, Calif.: Astro Computing Services, 1984.

Boreal Signs

Boreal signs is an archaic term referring to the northern signs, **Aries** through Virgo. The term is derived from Boreas, the Greek personification of the north wind.

Bowl Pattern

A bowl, or hemispheric, pattern is a **horoscope** in which all of the **planets** are in half of the chart. Ideally, they are spread out so as to create the visual impression of a bowl.

Bradley, Donald A. (Garth Allen)

Donald A. Bradley, born in Nebraska on May 16, 1925, was a leader of the "siderealist" movement and research director of the Llewellyn Foundation for Astrological Research. He carried out several statistical studies, including an astrological analysis of 2,492 clergymen and an extensive study of rainfall. His results, while initially greeted with enthusiasm, were later shown to be largely insignificant, either because of faulty design or neglected statistical considerations.

Bradley was an enthusiastic adherent of the **sidereal zodiac** as advocated by **Cyril Fagan** and wrote many books and articles on siderealism. He published his early work under his own name but later used the pseudonym "Garth Allen." A regular contributor to *American Astrology Magazine,* he was senior editor when he died of cancer on April 25, 1974, in Tucson, Arizona.

Selected Publications:

Profession and Birthdate. Los Angeles: Llewellyn Publications, 1950.
Stock Market Prediction. Los Angeles: Llewellyn Foundation for Astrological Research, 1950.
Picking Winners. Saint Paul, Minn.: Llewellyn Publications, 1954.
Solar and Lunar Returns. 2d ed. Saint Paul, Minn.: Llewellyn Publications, 1968.

Sources:

Holden, James H., and Robert A. Hughes. *Astrological Pioneers of America.* Tempe, Ariz.: American Federation of Astrologers, 1988.

Brahe, Tycho

Tycho Brahe, an eminent Danish astronomer and **astrologer**, was born April 13, 1546, in Kundstorp, Denmark. He taught **astronomy** at the University of Copenhagen and established an observatory on the island of Hven under the patronage of King Frederick II. He moved to Prague after the king's death, where he took **Johannes Kepler** as his assistant.

Dissatisfied with inexactness of most existing observations of the celestial bodies, Brahe designed instruments that enabled him to make the most precise observations of the heavens to be recorded prior to the invention of the telescope and discovered the phenomenon of exploding novas. (The accuracy of Brahe's observations enabled Kepler to discover some of the laws governing planetary motions.) Brahe was also a **mundane astrologer**. He contributed to **aspect** theory and did work on the connection between the natural cataclysms and **conjunctions**. Brahe died October 21, 1601, in Prague.

Sources:

Brau, Jean-Louis, Helen Weaver, and Allan Edmands. *Larousse Encyclopedia of Astrology.* New York: New American Library, 1980.

Kitson, Annabella, ed. *History and Astrology: Clio and Urania Confer.* London: Mandala, 1989.

Broken Signs (Mutilated Signs; Imperfect Signs)

Broken signs (also called mutilated signs or, in more recent works, imperfect signs) is an archaic term referring to certain signs that, when on the **ascendant** and **afflicted**, are said to result in a twisted body or limbs. The broken signs are variously listed, usually including **Leo** and **Pisces**, sometimes **Scorpio** or Virgo, and occasionally **Capricorn** and **Cancer**. This classification has been abandoned by modern astrologers. Almost any severely **afflicted planet** in any sign when placed in the first house (the **house** of the physical body) could result in physical difficulties. The antonym term is **whole sign** (perfect sign).

Broughton, Luke Dennis

Luke Dennis Broughton, a leader in the astrology revival of the late nineteenth century, was born on April 20, 1828, in Leeds, England. At a time when astrology was unpopular, his family continued to practice it. This custom originated with his grandfather, a doctor who used **Nicolas Culpepper's** herbal compendium (*Culpepper's English Physician and Herbal Remedies,* originally published in 1652), which correlated astrological signs with medicinal herbs. Luke Broughton's father, also a physician, followed in his father's footsteps, and Luke, in turn, followed his father. Mark Broughton, Luke's older brother, headed an astrological society in Leeds and published an **almanac** as well as an **ephemeris** (a table indicating planetary positions). After arriving in America, Mark Broughton initiated an astrological periodical, *Broughton's Monthly Horoscope.*

Luke Broughton married at age 24, and he moved to the United States 2 years later. He intended to follow his family's medical occupation. Settling in Philadelphia, he worked as a weaver and later as a laboratory technician while a student at Eclectic Medical College. (Eclecticism was a school of medicine based on such natural remedies as Culpepper's herbs.) After his brother's magazine ceased publication in 1860, Luke initiated *Broughton's Planet Reader and Astrological Journal,* which was published until 1869.

Antiastrology laws were passed in Philadelphia not long after Luke Broughton began his journal. It is not known whether these laws were prompted, in whole or in part, by Broughton's public astrology activity. In 1863, he moved his medical office to New York City, where he continued to practice astrology. After the Civil War, Broughton began renting a lecture hall and speaking regularly on astrology. Experiencing marked success in his lectures, he opened an office devoted completely to astrology and began dividing his time between medicine and the science of the stars. Broughton also trained astrologers, and most of the important astrologers of the early twentieth century were his students. He also distributed British astrological literature, including the technical works necessary for erecting **astrological charts**. He wrote *Remarks on Astrology and Astromedical Botany* (1880) as well as several texts, including *Planetary Influence* (1893) and *The Elements of Astrology* (1898).

As evidenced by the antiastrology laws adopted in Philadelphia, the astrological revival brought controversy in its wake, and Broughton situated himself in the middle. While he denounced astrologers he thought were incompetent or in error, he was also an outspoken defender of astrology. He served as an expert witness in cases where astrologers were arrested for telling fortunes. Broughton taught thousands of astrologers and was a pivotal individual in making astrology a widely practiced art in the United States. He died in 1898, and his daughter carried on his New York practice. Several of his sons also became astrologers.

Selected Publications:

Remarks on Astrology and Astromedical Botany. New York: Privately printed, 1880.
Planetary Influence. New York: Privately printed, 1893.
The Elements of Astrology. New York: Privately printed, 1898.

Sources:

Culpepper's English Physician and Herbal Remedies. North Hollywood, Calif.: Wilshire Book Co., 1971.
Holden, James H., and Robert A. Hughes. *Astrological Pioneers of America.* Tempe, Ariz.: American Federation of Astrologers, 1988.
Melton, J. Gordon. *New Age Encyclopedia.* Detroit: Gale Research, 1990.

Brutish Signs

Brutish signs is an archaic term referring to **Leo** and the last third (the Leo **decan**) of **Sagittarius**, which, when occupied by **planets** under unfavorable **aspects** or in some other manner **afflicted**, was said to produce **natives** with coarse, "brutish" natures. This term, as well as the connotations of afflicted planets in these two arcs, has been abandoned by modern astrologers.

Bucket Pattern

A bucket pattern is a specific planetary arrangement in which all of the **planets** but one are on one side of an astrological chart. In the case of a **natal chart**, the isolated planet, called the handle or **singleton**, represents a point of focus for the **native's** life. Because of the focus of energies on the singleton, a bucket chart is sometimes also called a funnel chart.

Bull

The Bull is a popular name for the sign **Taurus**.

Bundle Pattern

A bundle, or cluster pattern is a **horoscope** arrangement in which all of the **planets** are contained in one 120° arc.

Business Astrology

Astrology is basically a study of cycles. All dynamic phenomena—whether the lives of individual human beings or the ebb and flow of economic activity—are subject to cycles. Many different cycles are interwoven with one another through time, which is why we can sometimes make predictions about business and economic trends. But there is one cycle that is very clear and is fairly predictive in terms of business trends or business and career decisions for an individual—the nodal cycle, which is always accompanied by the **eclipses**.

The **lunar nodes** (the two imaginary points, 180° apart from other, where the **orbit** of the **Moon** around Earth appears to cross the path of the Earth's orbit around the **Sun**) travel backward through the **zodiac** on a cycle of 18–19 year. They spend approximately 1 1/2 years in two opposite signs of the zodiac and then move back to the next sign for the next 1 1/2 years. In total, the full cycle takes about 18–19 years to complete, which is one reason many of the more common cycles of interest rates, real estate values, and trend cycles are thought to have this same approximate length.

The ancient Chinese believed that when the Sun disappeared during a solar eclipse it was being eaten by a dragon. We know that this is not true, but the image bears watching because of its symbolism. Why is the dragon eating the Sun? There are many different explanations, including one maintaining that the dragon needs the Sun for food, for sustenance, and to shed its skin and grow.

In many ways, the **house** in which the transiting north node (the point where the Moon crosses the **ecliptic** from south to north, called the Dragon's Head in traditional astrology) is moving for approximately 1 1/2 years is where an individual is "eating the Sun" and "growing"—where the opportunity lies. Where the corresponding south node (the point where the Moon crosses the ecliptic from north to south, called the Dragon's Tail in traditional astrology) is moving is where a person is being asked to let go of old, outgrown behavior patterns (even though they may be quite comfortable). But, as in the childhood game Crack the Whip, if the person keeps hanging on for dear life, she or he will be thrown violently.

The eclipses accompany this traveling axis and about every 6 months at about 2 weeks apart there is a solar eclipse (a new moon) and a lunar eclipse (a full moon); if they exactly **conjunct** or **square** a natal **planet,** they trigger massive change within 3, 6, 9, or 12 months. But consider the bigger picture of the transiting nodal axis and how it affects business trends. Since the lunar nodal axis is the intersection of the ecliptic and the Moon's orbit, the lunar nodes have much to do with public pulse; and because the Moon in business astrology can sometimes indicate the public's response, then it can be argued that the nodal axis indicates trends.

When the north node entered **Aquarius** in late May 1989, an Aquarian dilemma arose that affected world politics and history. Aquarius is the sign of human rights and collective thinking. The United States was founded on the principle of human rights, which is supposedly what democracy is about. That spring of 1989 witnessed the student uprising in Beijing, China, that ended tragically with the slaughter of young students and ushered in a period of world consciousness about human rights. Throw in a couple of other cycles like the **synodic periods** of **Saturn** conjunct **Neptune** (indicating the beginning of new eras), the recently completed Saturn–**Uranus** conjunction (Uranus rules human rights), and the world was ready for change.

When the north node enters **Capricorn**, major depression and recessionary cycles are likely. Unfailingly, when this occurs, interest rates and real estate values drop, which does not help the real estate industry, but which invites the most astute buyers to purchase investments at a great time. Remember what Bernard Baruch, the wealthy financier said when asked the secret of his success: "I buy my straw hats in the fall!" If we read the symbolism of Capricorn, which occurs in the dead of winter when the world in the Northern Hemisphere is its coldest, we see death and cold on the surface, but underneath the cold and icy snow, new life is stirring. The sign of Capricorn is most functional when it is most uncomfortable, and so this nodal cycle, though quite difficult, paves the way for another nodal cycle as the north node enters **Sagittarius**, which occurred in early August 1992.

Sagittarius rules wide open spaces, country/western, truth, religion, publishing, travel, education, and native Americans, to name just a few **rulerships**. Since the lunar eclipse at 29° Sagittarius in December 1991, the fashion industry has been displaying denim, boots, and backpack-looking purses, to name just a few fashion statements. Major public figures have purchased large bodies of land in Montana and the Dakotas. We should be seeing a reclaiming of native American rights during this period as well as landmark educational changes coming from the private sector. Since the north node has just begun its run, travel prices may skyrocket and then new alternatives may develop over the 1 1/2 year cycle.

Many times during these cycles, major shifts occur at the very beginning and then at the very end; as the north node leaves a sign and completes its last two eclipses in the same sign, the problem is resolved. (An issue—"problem"—is raised during the node's entry into the relevant sign. The last "words" are said about the problem/issue as it leaves the sign, which constitutes whatever "resolution" is going to take place—whether or not it is satisfactory.) Because of this, we may not see any major changes in education until the north node is about to leave Sagittarius in January 1994, which will also be the completion months for the Uranus–Neptune conjunction. New alternatives for education may occur whereby there will be more and more video education. This might suggest that the educational market for video has arrived. Easier methods may be introduced to help people get through the legal system and the courts, and new job openings may multiply in this sector. Because Neptune also indicates "overseas," foreign countries may need more teachers.

In 1993, the European Common Market is set to begin proceedings at exactly the time of the precise conjunction of Uranus and Neptune. Since the world is truly a very small place now, the need for teachers of high-quality education will be maximized. This may be when the United States ("born" on July 4) finds itself using its greatest ability as a **Cancer** with **Gemini** rising, as a supplier of teachers throughout the world. Opportunities for teaching foreign languages, skills, and customs are just the tip of the iceberg with the north node traveling through the sign of Sagittarius.

Since Sagittarius rules belief systems, philosophies, religions, and metaphysics, 1991–94 may be a wonderful and also a terrible time for metaphysical thought. It may be wonderful in the sense that people begin looking again at their visions and try to leave the survival mode, as the north node left Capricorn and the last solar eclipse at 2° Capricorn occured on December 24, 1992. It may be a terrible time in that this last eclipse may trigger some type of banking or business crisis, because Sagittarius is not only optimism but also inflation and overindulgence.

—Georgia Strathis

Sources:

Baigent, Michael, Nicholas Campion, and Charles Harvey. *Mundane Astrology*. London: Aquarian Press, 1984.

Campion, Nicholas. *The Practical Astrologer*. New York: Harry N. Abrams, 1987.

McEvers, Joan, ed. *Financial Astrology for the 1990s*. Saint Paul, Minn.: Llewellyn Publications, 1989.

Townley, John. *Astrological Life Cycles: A Planetary Guide to Personal and Career Opportunities*. Rochester, Vt.: Destiny Books, 1980.

Byzantium, Astrology in

See: History of Western Astrology

Cadent Houses

The **houses** of an astrological chart are classified into three groups of four: **angular houses** (the first, fourth, seventh, and tenth), **succedent houses** (the second, fifth, eighth, and eleventh), and cadent houses (the third, sixth, ninth, and twelfth). Traditionally, the cadent houses have been referred to as the

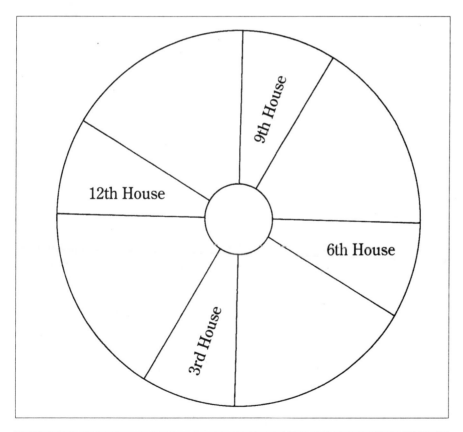

9th House

12th House

6th House

3rd House

◀
Cadent houses.

mental houses, although this ascription applies best to the third house and the ninth house (the houses of the "lower" and "higher" mind). In classical astrology, cadent houses were regarded as the least powerful houses in which **planets** could be positioned, while angular houses were the most powerful. Modern astrologers, however, tend to think that planets placed in the angular houses have the most influence on the outer, surface aspects of a person's life, and planets placed in the cadent houses have the most impact on one's inner life. Planets located in succedent houses mediate inner and outer lives.

Sources:

Brau, Jean-Louis, Helen Weaver, and Allan Edmands. *Larousse Encyclopedia of Astrology.* New York: New American Library, 1980.
Hand, Robert. *Horoscope Symbols.* Rockport, Mass.: Para Research, 1981.

Calendar

Astrology is built upon an accurate accounting of time. Fundamental to this accounting is a calendrical system that takes into consideration the irregular manner in which days, months, and years fit together. A calendar in the broadest sense consists of the set of rules that a society uses for deciding which days are ordinary days and which are holidays (a variant of "holy days"). Societies in the past evolved many different kinds of calendars, and a surprisingly large number of them are important for understanding the details of the Western civil calendar.

Origins of the Calendar

There are three natural divisions of time on Earth. The most obvious is the alternation of night and day, and all calendars are organized in terms of the 24-hour day (that being the approximate average length). Not all calendars are organized in terms of hours with a fixed length, however. Our ability to measure seconds and even minutes accurately was achieved only in modern times. A medieval sundial divided the hours of sunlight into 12 hours, but, obviously, in northern latitudes an hour during a long summer day might be twice as long as an hour during a short winter day. The Western civil calendar that is now used internationally is based on hours of a precisely defined fixed length; but there are still some local or folk calendars in which the length of an hour is much more flexible.

The next most obvious way to divide time is to use the phases of the **Moon**. Originally, a month was a "moonth": It represented the period from one full moon or new moon to the next. We cannot know how people measured time during the tens or hundreds of millennia that all human beings existed as bands of hunters and gatherers, following the herds and the ripening fruits and grains in an annual migration north and south. During the last ice age (from roughly 100,000 to 20,000 years ago), when human beings were forced to live in caves and develop new stoneware technology in order to survive, they may have begun tallying the phases of the Moon more carefully than before in attempting to calculate the length of the lunar month. In the Western civil calendar, months are arbitrary groups of days, ranging from 28 to 31 days in length, that are not correlated with the phases of the moon. All major religious calendars (Christian, Jewish, Moslem, Buddhist, and Hindu) still depend wholly or partly on having months that are exactly in phase with the Moon; so in the next section we consider in some detail just what is involved in constructing such a lunar calendar.

The third most obvious time division is marked by the seasons, by the annual migration north and south of the **Sun's** rising and setting points. Probably for a long time, years were labeled only relatively, as the regnal year of a king, by the number of years since some memorable event, and so on; and this starting point would be changed with every new generation. Only rather late in the history of civilization did years begin to be numbered from some fixed point

◀
A calendar from ancient Crete.
· **Bettmann Archive**

in the distant past, such as the first Olympiad, the founding of the city of Rome, or the birth of Jesus of Nazareth.

Constructing a Calendar

As could their predecessors, agricultural villagers today can coordinate their annual activities by word of mouth, but citizens of an empire cannot. It obviously will not work to have the arrival times of people coming to a three-day festival in the capital city spread out over a week. Hence, about 5,000 years ago the administrators in Egypt and Sumeria were faced with the problem of constructing a calendar that everyone could use to see, on each day, how many more days it would be until some scheduled event. But to construct such a calendar, these people had to deal with four basic questions:

1. How long is a day?

2. How long is a month? (Or, equivalently, how many days are there in a month?)

3. How long is a year?

4. How many months are in a year?

Being used to our modern answers to these questions, we may think them obvious; but they are not, and adequate answers to them were found only by centuries of ongoing observations, measurements, and calculations.

How Long Is a Day?

The technique of dividing day and night into 12 hours each was devised by the Babylonians, who calculated with a number system that used a base of 12 rather than 10. Hours were introduced into the Roman calendar only rather late in Roman history, when the seven-day week (also a Babylonian invention) was generally adopted. Originally the Romans had divided day and night into watches, each several hours in length.

In our modern usage, a day is defined as being 24 hours long; an hour is defined as 60 minutes times 60 seconds, or 3,600 seconds long; and a second is defined as so many vibrations of a specific line in the spectrum of a specific isotope. Naturally, this definition was worked out in a way that makes 24 hours equal to the traditional average length of a day. It was finding this average length that was the problem in the ancient world, for several reasons.

First, where do you measure from? The convention of starting each calendar day at midnight was agreed upon only in modern times. In most ancient calendars, each day began at sunset and ended at the following sunset (some ancient peoples, such as the Egyptians, counted a day as running from one dawn to the next); this is why the "eve" before many traditional holidays is still important and why the Jewish Sabbath celebration begins at sunset on Friday. But exactly when is sunset? It takes about 15 minutes for the Sun to sink completely below the horizon, which appears higher on land than it does at sea. This ambiguity is why the Talmud prescribed that all activities not allowed on the Sabbath should cease two hours before sunset. Some conventional definition—such as measuring from the moment the disc of the sun first touches the horizon—had to be introduced and adhered to.

Furthermore, since the days (in the sense of hours of light) grow longer (how much longer depends on the latitude) during half the year, shorter during the other half, an accurate measurement needs to be correct to within less than a minute to be useful for constructing a calendar. But there were no accurate techniques before modern times—even measuring a quarter hour accurately was difficult—and so the ancient calendars tended to accumulate an error of a day every few years.

How Many Days Are in a Month?

In most ancient calendars, a month was a lunar month, that is, one full cycle of the Moon's phases. We know now that the average length of a lunar month, measured from one astronomical new moon to the next, is 29.5306 days. However, an ancient month began not at the astronomical new moon, which is an invisible event, but at the first visible crescent. Many factors affect when the crescent of the new moon will be visible at a particular location. Usually the interval from each first crescent to the next will alternate between 29 and 30 days—and so the length of the months will alternate likewise—but it is easily possible for two or even three intervals of 29 days or 30 days to fall successively. Hence, it was quite late in history—long after the length of the year was well known—before the average length of the lunar cycle was known with usable accuracy.

How Many Days Are in a Year?

We know now that the average length of the year is 365.2422 days, but this precise value was taken into account only by the Gregorian reform of the calendar in 1582. The Julian calendar (devised by Julius Caesar), which the Gregorian calendar replaced, assumed the year to be 365.25 days long (as we all do for ordinary purposes), and the earlier Roman calendar that Julius replaced apparently assumed the year to be 366.25 days. The Egyptian calendar, which Julius borrowed as the basis for his, assumed the year to be exactly 365 days.

The problem in the ancient world again was finding a fixed point from which to measure the length of (or to begin) the year. The most popular choices were the winter **solstice**, when the days begin growing longer again, and the spring **equinox**, when the hours of sunlight and darkness are equal, but many others were also used. Measuring the moment of winter solstice would seem a difficult task for ancient peoples, but it now seems clear that the people who built Stonehenge about 3000 B.C. could do so quite accurately. They could also predict all **eclipses** of the Sun and the Moon. The Egyptians seem to have solved the problem by observing the **heliacal** rising of Sirius each year: The **fixed stars**, including Sirius, appear to rotate about the Earth each **sidereal day**, which is always the same length. Which stars are visible in the night sky depends on where the Earth is in its annual **orbit** around the Sun. Sirius (and any other star) will always first become visible after sunset (weather and local conditions allowing) on the same day each year relative to the solstices and equinoxes; this is its heliacal rising. In classical times the Mesopotamians claimed that they had also solved the problem in another way, as early as the Egyptians had, but it is not certain that they had done so before the seventh century B.C.

How Many Months Are in a Year?

This is the most difficult of the four questions (and the one that causes the most differences between calendars), because the length of the solar year is not a simple multiple of the length of the lunar month. Hence, if the months are wanted to stay in phase with the Moon, there are many problems.

Twelve months that alternate between 29 and 30 days produce a year of $29.5 \times 12 = 354$ days, which is 11.2422 days short of an average solar year. Every 3 years this difference will add up to 33.7266 days, allowing an extra lunar month—of, say, 30 days—to be added. This still leaves a difference of 3.7266 days, which will add up to 33+ days after 27 years, allowing an extra lunar month to be inserted, and so on. It seems clear, however, that people generally do not like to have a feature in their calendars that appears only once in 27 years; for example, what would this extra month be called? Would it contain any holidays?

Only two basic kinds of calendars have succeeded in dealing adequately with the various problems of timekeeping: (1) the lunisolar calendar of the Mesopotamians, which added lunar months during years 3, 5, and 8 of 8-year cycles, and (2) the purely solar calendar, devised by the Egyptians. Despite the retention of 30 to 31-day periods that we still term months, the Western calendar is a solar calendar.

The **zodiac** bears the imprint of all three means of measuring time (days, months, and years), but does not correspond precisely with any of them. The astrological year and the solar year, for example, are of equal lengths, but the astrological year begins at the exact moment the Sun enters the sign **Aries** (the **spring equinox**) rather than on January 1. Also, the sun resides in each sign for approximately 1 month, but neither the lunar months (which vary every year) nor the months of the Western calendar correspond with this residence (the Sun enters each sign between the eighteenth and the twenty-fourth of each month). For these reasons and others, astrologers must use their own calendars, termed **ephemerides**, to determine the precise positions of the heavenly bodies.

—Aidan A. Kelly

Sources:

Colson, F. H. *The Week*. Cambridge: Cambridge University Press, 1926.
Hawkins, Gerald S. *Stonehenge Decoded*. New York: Doubleday, 1965.
Hoyle, Sir Fred. *Stonehenge*. San Francisco: W. H. Freeman, 1976.
Nilsson, Martin P. *Primitive Time-Reckoning: A Study in the Origins and First Development of the Art of Counting Time Among the Primitive and Early Culture Peoples*. Lund, Norway: Gleerup, 1920.
O'Neil, W. M. *Time and the Calendars*. Sydney: Sydney University Press, 1975.
Parise, Frank, ed. *The Book of Calendars*. New York: Facts on File, 1982.
Wilson, P. W. *The Romance of the Calendar*. New York: Norton, 1937.
Wright, Lawrence. *Clockwork Man: The Story of Time, Its Origins, Its Uses, Its Tyranny*. New York: Horizon, 1968.

Campanus System

A Campanus system of **house** division (advanced by Giovanni Campano, a thirteenth-century mathematician–astrologer) is generated by equally dividing the **prime vertical**. By the twentieth century it had fallen into disuse, but was partially revived as a result of the advocacy of **Dane Rudhyar**.

Campion, Nicholas

Nicholas Campion was born March 4, 1953. He was educated at Queens' College, Cambridge (B.A., history, 1974; M.A., 1976). He attended London University and studied Southeast Asian politics and history at the School of Oriental and African Studies and international relations at the London School of Economics. After graduating, he taught history and English. He also worked in computing, housing administration, and theater management before becoming a full-time astrologer. He is currently a director of Cinnabar theater company and active in environmental politics.

Campion first became interested in astrology through newspaper sun sign columns and had his first personal **horoscope** cast in 1965 at age 12. He began studying astrology in 1971 and has been a full-time professional since 1984. He is a member of the Association of Professional Astrologers and a former president of the Astrological Lodge of London. Aside from his newspaper and magazine work, he specializes in political astrology and has a worldwide reputation in this field.

In 1992, the National Astrological Society of the U.S.A awarded Campion the Marc Edmund Jones Award for scholarly and innovative work, especially the research for *The Book of World Horoscopes*. He has served as vice-chairman (1983–84) and chairman (1985–86) of the U.K. Advisory Panel for Astrological Education and has been a member of the Astrological Lodge of London Committee since 1984, serving as president from 1985 to 1988 and from 1992 until the present. He has lectured on astrology to astrological, astronomical, and literary societies across the United Kingdom and in the United States, Spain, Switzerland, and Denmark.

Selected Publications:

The Book of World Horoscopes. Wellingborough, Northamptonshire, U.K.: Aquarian Press, 1988.
"Astrological Historiography in the Renaissance: The Work of Jean Bodin and Louis Le Roy." In *History and Astrology.* Edited by Annabella Kitson. London: Mandala, 1989.
"The Age of Aquarius: A Modern Myth." In *The Astrology of the Macrocosm.* Edited by Joan McEvers. Saint Paul, Minn.: Llewellyn Publications, 1990.

Cancer

Cancer (Latin for crab), the fourth sign of the **zodiac**, is a **cardinal water sign**. It is a negative (in the value-neutral sense of being negatively *charged)*, **feminine** sign **ruled** by the **Moon**. Its symbol is the crab, and its **glyph** is said to represent the two claws of a crab. It takes its name from the Latin word for crab. A moody sign, Cancer is the source of the term crabby. Cancer is associated with the breasts and the stomach, and people with a Cancer sun sign are prone to digestion and weight problems. The key phrase for Cancer is *I feel.*

Cancer, like many of the other signs of the zodiac, does not have a developed mythology. During the second labor of Hercules (it might be better termed the second feat or test), while he was struggling against the many-headed hydra, a giant crab bit him on the heel to create a diversion. Hercules, however, crushed it underfoot. This crab, Carcinus (Greek for crayfish), was an ally of Hera, queen mother of the gods, who opposed Hercules. The crab was rewarded for self-sacrificing loyalty when Hera promoted it to distinction as the **constellation** Cancer. The sign Cancer is often compared with a turtle (the symbol for Cancer in the Babylonian zodiac), and a rich source of symbolic associations for Cancer can be found in the image of the turtle, another shoreline dweller.

Cancerians are best known for their attachment to home and, like the turtle, would be happy to carry their house everywhere (if only they could!). Although homebodies, they enjoy travel if they know they have a secure home to which they can always return. Like Carcinus, they are strongly attached to their mother (or to the more nurturing parent) and tend to be nurturing parents themselves. They are highly sensitive individuals who are easily "crushed," which is why they have developed an emotional "shell" within which they can retreat. They are moodier than any of the other signs of the zodiac, and food represents emotional security to them. Like all water signs, they regard emotions as more real than any other aspect of life.

There is a wealth of information available on the characteristics of the zodiacal signs—so much that one book would not be able to contain it all. One traditional way in which astrologers condense information is by summarizing sign and planet traits in lists of words and short phrases called key words or key phrases. The following Cancer key words are drawn from Manly P. Hall's *Astrological Keywords:*

Emotional key words: "Artistic and dreamy, maternal, kindhearted, romantic, domestic, impressionable, psychic, imaginative, serene, intuitive, restless, despondent, sometimes lazy and self-indulgent" (p.17).

Mental key words: "Versatile, self-sacrificing, receptive, expresses great veneration for ancestry and precedent, thorough, persevering, cautious, reserved, brooding" (p. 20).

Most popular works on astrology contain data on the signs, and these can be consulted for more detailed information.

Sources:

Evans, Colin. *The New Waite's Compendium of Natal Astrology.* Revised by Brian E. F. Gardener. York Beach, Maine: Samuel Weiser, 1971. (Originally published 1917.)

Green, Landis Knight. *The Astrologer's Manual: Modern Insights into an Ancient Art.* Sebastopol, Calif.: CRCS Publications, 1975.

Hall, Manly P. *Astrological Keywords.* 1958. Reprint. Savage, Md.: Littlefield Adams (1975): 17, 20.

Canes, Moira

Moira Canes, an astrology counselor and gestalt therapist, was born in Johannesburg, South Africa. She completed a B.A. degree and earned a Higher Education diploma at the University of Witwatersrand. In 1977, she immigrated to Toronto, Canada. Although she had been reading books on astrology since age 16, it was not until 1979 that she began to study the subject formally, at the IAO Research Centre in Toronto. Around the same time she also began to train at the Gestalt Institute of Toronto. As a consequence of this simultaneous study, she was able to creatively incorporate these two disciplines.

Canes has taught English and theater arts to high school students and is currently on the faculty at the Gestalt Institute of Toronto. She also maintains a private practice as an astrologer and as a gestalt therapist. She is one of the pioneers of the new area of astrology that has been referred to as experiential astrology.

Capricorn

Capricorn (Latin for goat-horn), the tenth sign of the **zodiac**, is a **cardinal earth sign**. It is a negative (in the value-neutral sense of being negatively *charged),* **feminine** sign **ruled** by the **planet Saturn.** Its symbol is a goat with a fish tail, and its **glyph** is said to reflect this symbol. It takes its name from the Latin *Capricornus,* which means goat horn. Capricorn is associated with the bones and especially with the knees, and individuals with a Capricorn **sun sign** are susceptible to bone and joint problems, particularly knee problems. The key phrase for Capricorn is *I use.*

Capricorn has a confused association with two distinct mythological figures. Aegipan, son of Zeus and the nymph Aex, assisted Hermes with the recovery of Zeus's sinews from Typhon and then transformed himself into a goat-fish in order to escape. In gratitude, Zeus is said to have turned him into the constellation Capricorn. A more complex mythological association is the goat who suckled the newborn Zeus—usually said to be owned by the nymph Amalthea, though in other versions identified as her—and was later transformed into the **star** Capella. Zeus broke off the horn of the goat and gave it to Amalthea, promising her that she would be able to obtain anything she wished from the horn. This is the origin of the famous cornucopia, or horn of plenty. It was later given to the river god Achelous, who used it to replace his broken horn. Hence, Achelous became, in a sense, a blended goat and marine creature, the very image of Capricorn.

Of all the signs of the zodiac, Capricorn has the most distant relationship with its mythology. Through its association with big business, Capricorn has a certain natural connection with wealth, but it is wealth gained through work and wisdom rather than the "instant" wealth of the horn of plenty. Like their sign's sometime symbol the mountain goat, Capricorns strive to climb to the top of mountains, but in a practical, cautious, self-sufficient, step-by-step manner. Capricorns are known as planners and organizers, capable of infinite patience. They tend to be reserved, conservative, sober, and highly motivated. Typically, they view pleasure-seeking as an idle waste of time. Capricorns can be intensely loyal and will go out of their way to repay a kindness. Few astrologers have pointed out that this sign's fish tail (indicating water, the symbol of emotion) indicates that there is a highly sensitive side to Capricorns, which is hidden underneath their reserved exterior.

There is a wealth of information available on the characteristics of the zodiacal signs—so much that one book would not be able to contain it all. One traditional way in which astrologers condense information is by summarizing sign and planet traits in lists of words and short phrases called key words or key phrases. The following Capricorn key words are drawn from Manly P. Hall's *Astrological Keywords:*

> *Emotional key words:* "Inhibited, feelings are often turned upon native himself resulting in self-pity, unforgiving, cold, irritable, timid in action, the mind rules the heart too completely" (p. 18).

> *Mental key words:* "Powerful, concentrative, laborious, forceful, cautious, economical, conservative, thifty, scrupulous, trustworthy, detailed thinkers, fatalistic, stubborn, domineering, good friends and bad enemies, brooding, egotistic" (p. 21).

Most popular works on astrology contain data on the signs, and these can be consulted for more detailed information.

Sources:

Evans, Colin. *The New Waite's Compendium of Natal Astrology.* Revised by Brian E. F. Gardener. York Beach, Maine: Samuel Weiser, 1971. (Originally published 1917).

Green, Landis Knight. *The Astrologer's Manual: Modern Insights into an Ancient Art.* Sebastopol, Calif.: CRCS Publications, 1975.

Hall, Manly P. *Astrological Keywords.* 1958. Reprint. Savage, Md.: Littlefield Adams Quality Paperbacks (1975), 18, 21.

Caput Draconis

Caput Draconis (Latin for Dragon's Head), is an older term for the north **lunar node**.

Cardinal Signs

The 12 signs of the **zodiac** are subdivided according to three **qualities**: **cardinal, mutable,** and **fixed.** The 4 cardinal signs (the cardinal quadruplicity

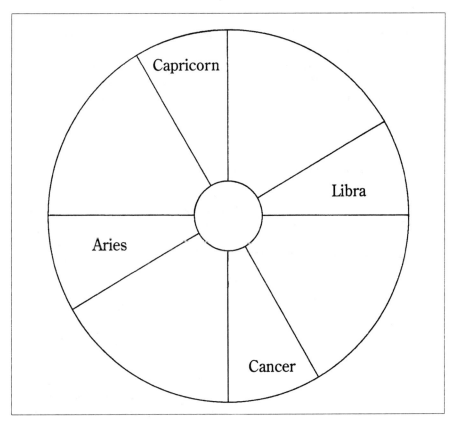

◄

Cardinal signs.

or cardinal cross) are **Aries, Cancer, Libra**, and **Capricorn**. The entrance of the **Sun** into each of these 4 signs begins a new season: Aries, spring; Cancer, summer; Libra, fall; and Capricorn, winter. The identifying trait of the cardinal signs is captured by their various alternative names: initiating, moving, or movable signs. Cardinal signs thus tend to initiate new activities and to act (to move) on the present situation. Negatively, they are said to lack staying power (a traditional characterization that applies most to Aries and not at all to Capricorn).

Carter, Charles E. O.

Charles Ernest Owen Carter, born January 31, 1887, in Parkstone, England, was a well-known and highly prolific astrologer of the early twentieth century. He graduated from the University of London and began to practice law in 1913. He was also in the army during the First World War. Carter became deeply involved with astrology in 1910 and met such eminent practitioners as **Alan Leo**. He started composing practitioners handbooks in the twenties, which were well received by the astrological community. He also wrote many articles that appeared in such periodicals as *Astrology* and *The Astrologers' Quarterly,* issued by the London Astrological Lodge.

In later life, Carter came to be considered the dean of British astrologers. He served as first principal of the London Faculty of Astrological Studies, as president of the Astrological Lodge of the Theosophical Society from 1920 to 1952, and as editor of *The Astrologers' Quarterly* from 1926 to 1959. He died on October 4, 1968, in London.

Selected Publications:

Some Principles of Horoscopic Delineation. London, 1934.
An Introduction to Political Astrology. London: L. N. Fowler, 1951.
Astrology of Accidents. 2d ed. London: Theosophical Publishing House, 1961.
Encyclopedia of Psychological Astrology. 4th ed. London: Theosophical Publishing House, 1964.
Astrological Aspects. 11th ed. London: L. N. Fowler, 1971.

Sources:

Holden, James H., and Robert A. Hughes. *Astrological Pioneers of America.* Tempe, Ariz.: American Federation of Astrologers, 1988.

Casting the Horoscope

Casting the horoscope, also referred to as chart casting, is a commonly used expression for the process of calculating and drawing up an astrological chart.

Delineating (interpreting) a chart is a distinct operation from casting a chart. A simplified method for chart casting is contained in Appendix A.

Cauda Draconis

Cauda Draconis (Latin for **Dragon's Tail**), is an older term for the south **lunar node**.

Cazimi

Cazimi (an Arabic term meaning heart of the Sun) refers to a very close **conjunction**—within 17 feet—between a **planet** and the **Sun**. In contrast to the wider **combust** conjunction, which supposedly weakened a planet, the cazimi position was traditionally said to strengthen the influence of the planet involved. Partially because contemporary astrologers do not regard the combust position as having a **debilitating** effect—hence, making the combust/ cazimi distinction one with no practical consequence—this term has dropped out of usage.

Celestial Coordinates

Celestial (sky) coordinates are most easily understood by comparing them to terrestrial (earthly) coordinates. Terrestrial coordinates allow a location to be specified in terms of degrees of **longitude** and **latitude**. Celestial coordinates similarly specify location in terms of two measurements of distance, expressed in terms of degrees of a circle. Rather than measuring degrees along the surface of **planet** Earth, however, celestial coordinates are measured against the **celestial sphere,** which is the sphere created by imagining that all of the objects in the sky are stuck against the inside of a gigantic, hollow sphere, with Earth located at the exact center.

There are several systems of celestial coordinates. The *altitude-azimuth system* begins from any given location on the Earth's surface, and uses the horizon, the **zenith**, and the north-south axis as points of reference. The *equatorial system* uses the **celestial equator** and the **vernal point** as its primary reference points. Astronomers most often use this system. The *ecliptic system* uses the **ecliptic** and the vernal point. Astrologers most often use the ecliptic system.

Celestial Equator

The celestial equator, also termed the equinoctial, is the terrestrial equator imaginarily projected outward from Earth and onto the background of the **stars** (i.e., against the backdrop of the **celestial sphere**). Because of the tilt of the Earth on its axis, the celestial equator intersects the **ecliptic** at an angle of 23 1/2°. Similarly, the celestial poles are the north and south poles projected outward against the backdrop of the celestial sphere.

Celestial Sphere

The celestial sphere can be understood by imagining that all of the objects in the sky are stuck against the inside of a gigantic hollow sphere, with Earth located at the exact center. The basic notion of the celestial sphere is assumed in various systems for locating celestial bodies in terms of celestial coordinates. Very much like terrestrial coordinates, which involve specifying a location in terms of **longitude** and **latitude**, celestial coordinates require two measurements of distance, expressed in terms of degrees of a circle. The *altitude-azimuth system* begins by situating itself at a specific location on the Earth's surface, and uses the **horizon**, the **zenith**, and the north-south axis as points of reference. The *equatorial system* uses the **celestial equator** (Earth's equator extended out into space and projected against the backdrop of the celestial sphere) and the **vernal**

► Celestial equator.

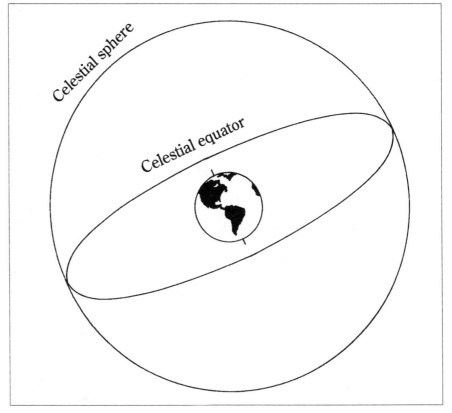

point (where the **Sun** is located at the point of the spring **equinox**) as its points of reference. Astronomers most often use the equatorial system. The *ecliptic system* uses the **ecliptic** (the **orbit** of Earth around the Sun, projected outward against the celestial sphere) and the vernal point. Astrologers use the ecliptic system.

Sources:

Brau, Jean-Louis, Helen Weaver, and Allan Edmands. *Larousse Encyclopedia of Astrology.* New York: New American Library, 1980.

Filbey, John, and Peter Filbey. *The Astrologer's Companion.* Wellingborough, Northamptonshire, U.K.: Aquarian Press, 1986.

Centiloquium

The Centiloquium refers to a set of 100 astrology aphorisms that was traditionally (but mistakenly) attributed to **Ptolemy**.

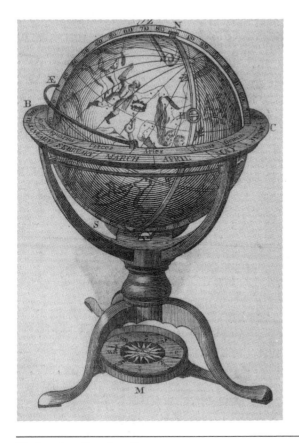

◀
An 18th-century engraving showing a celestial globe (a representation of the celestial sphere.)
· **Bettmann Archive**

Ceres

Ceres is the largest **asteroid** and one of the first four (along with the asteroids **Juno, Vesta**, and **Pallas**) to be investigated by astrologers. It was named after the Roman goddess of fertility (the equivalent of the Greek Demeter). The first asteroid to be discovered, Ceres was detected in 1801 by the Italian astronomer Giuseppi Piazzi. It has a diameter of 940 kilometers, and **orbits** the **Sun** in a bit more than 4 1/2 terrestrial years. Because Ceres was one of the earlier asteroids to be researched, a fair amount of material on it is available. Ceres represents the attribute of nurturance, either where and how we are nurtured in life, or where and how we nurture others.

Sources:

Donath, Emma Belle. *Asteroids in the Birth Chart.* Tempe, Ariz.: American Federation of Astrologers, 1979.

George, Demetra with Douglas Bloch. *Asteroid Goddesses: The Mythology, Psychology and Astrology of the Reemerging Feminine.* 2d ed. Rev. and enl. San Diego, Calif.: ACS Publications, 1990.

———. *Astrology for Yourself: A Workbook for Personal Transformation.* Berkeley, Calif.: Wingbow Press, 1987.

Chaldean Astrology

See: Mesopotamian Astrology

Chaney, W. H.

William Henry Chaney was born January 13, 1821, in Chesterville, Maine. He was called Professor Chaney (in the preceding century, professor was often applied to any prominent teacher), and taught astrology for nearly 40 years. He worked for local farmers until aged 16, worked on a fishing schooner for several years, and also spent some time in the navy. He eventually settled in Wheeling, West Virginia, where he studied and practiced law and also edited a newspaper.

In 1866, he was in New York City, where he met **Luke Broughton**, through whom he became acquainted with astrology. He was to become Broughton's most famous pupil. Chaney thereafter devoted himself to the study, practice, and teaching of astrology.

In 1867, the *New York Herald* led a crusade against the science of the stars, resulting in Chaney's imprisonment for half a year. He resumed his practice and lecturing after his release and moved to California in 1869. He moved from one place to another in California, Oregon, and Washington. His fourth marriage, to Flora Wellman, took place in 1876, and this union produced the well-known novelist Jack London (who took the name of his stepfather, John London). In 1889 Chaney moved again, this time to St. Louis, where he wrote and published his major work, *Chaney's Primer of Astrology and American Urania*. Finally, in 1892, he moved to Chicago, where he married for the last time and remained until his death. His sixth wife's name was Daisy, and they published a magazine called *The Daisy Chain*. Chaney died January 6, 1903.

Selected Publications:

Chaney's Annual: with the magic Circle Astrology Almanac. Saint Louis, Mo.: Magic Circle Publishing Co., 1890.
Chaney's Primer of Astrology and American Urania. Saint Louis, Mo.: Magic Circle Publishing Co., 1890.
The Astrology's Vade Mecum. Baltimore, Md.: Eureka Publishing Co., [1902].

Sources:

Holden, James H., and Robert A. Hughes. *Astrological Pioneers of America*. Tempe, Ariz.: American Federation of Astrologers, 1988.

Charis

Charis, **asteroid** 627 (the 627th asteroid to be discovered), is approximately 36 kilometers in diameter, and has an **orbital** period of 4.9 years. It was named after a Greek goddess who was surrounded by delight, graces, and pleasures. In a **natal chart**, Charis's sign and **house** position indicates where and how one experiences delight. When **afflicted** by inharmonious **aspects**, Charis may show the opposite of delight or the derivation of pleasure from unhealthy activities.

Sources:

Kowal, Charles T. *Asteroids: Their Nature and Utilization*. Chichester, West Sussex, U.K.: Ellis Horwood Limited, 1988.
Room, Adrian. *Dictionary of Astronomical Names*. London: Routledge, 1988.

Chart, Astrological

See: **Natal Chart.**

Chinese Astrology

The Chinese were one of the few cultures to develop a complex system of astrology entirely independent of Mesopotamian influences. (**Mesopotamian astrology** is the starting point for both Western astrology and **Hindu astrology**.) In much the same way that popular astrology in the West is confined to a knowledge of the 12 **sun signs**, most people's awareness of Chinese astrology is confined to the 12 animal "year signs." Many of the intricacies of the tradition dropped out of currency, even among Chinese astrologers, after the Golden Age of Chinese Astrology during the Chou and Han dynasties, but some contemporary astrologers have attempted to resuscitate classical Chinese astrology. The present discussion depends heavily on the discussion in Derek Walters's *Chinese Astrology* and *The Chinese Astrology Workbook.*

As might be anticipated, the Chinese system differs significantly from Mesopotamian-derived systems. In the first place, the Chinese group the **stars** into quite different **constellations**. Second, the Chinese locate heavenly bodies with respect to the celestial north pole and the **celestial equator** (called the Red Path by the Chinese) rather than with respect to the **ecliptic** (termed the Yellow Path). In the third place, while Western systems emphasize the placement of the **planets** along the ecliptic, the Chinese traditionally gave primary importance to the **Moon's** placement in the daily **lunar mansions** (a kind of 28-sign lunar **zodiac**). Fourth, the Chinese assigned meanings to the general appearance of a planet as modified by Earth's atmosphere, meaning that, unlike Western astrologers, who examine the stars only indirectly through tables, traditional Chinese astrologers maintained a continual watch of the heavens.

At points where cultural traditions differed, these differences naturally worked out as differences between astrological systems. For example, the four classical **elements** of the Western world—earth, air, fire, and water—are comparable to, yet contrast with, the five elements of East Asian philosophy— earth, fire, water, metal, and wood. The Chinese associated these five elements with the five visible planets—**Saturn** (earth), **Mars** (fire), **Mercury** (water), **Venus** (metal), and **Jupiter** (wood). The meanings the Chinese assigned to the first three planets are roughly comparable to their meanings in Western systems. Jupiter the wood planet, however, is associated with birth and springtime, associations that distinguish the meaning of the Chinese Jupiter from the Western Jupiter. And Venus, as a metal planet, is associated with martial, masculine characteristics, traits alien to the Western Venus.

While all traditional civilizations evince an interest in divination, the Chinese appear to have had a peculiarly strong interest in foretelling the future. For example, some of the earliest written artifacts of Chinese civilization are found on the so-called dragon bones, inscribed pieces of tortoise shell used by the ancients for divination. In the contemporary period, one of the most widespread tools of divination is the *I Ching* (*The Book of Changes*), a traditional Chinese work that has become popular in the Western world. The *I Ching,* however, is much more than just a fortune-telling device. Querents seek to know not only how the future will unfold but also how and when they ought to act. Similar concerns manifest in traditional Chinese astrology, which is more concerned with divining the future and determining the proper times to act than with understanding personality characteristics.

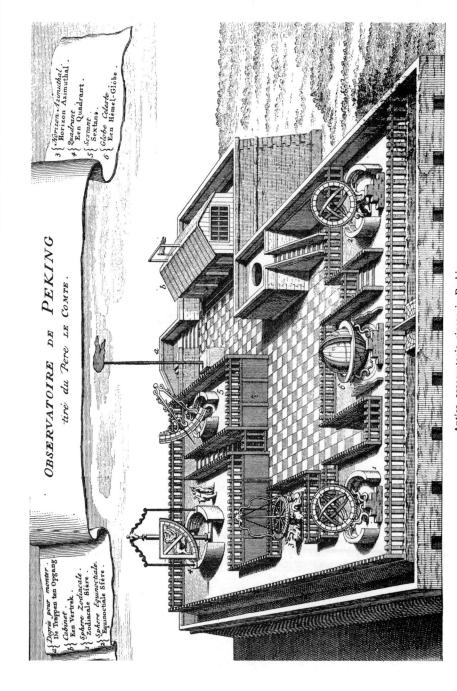

OBSERVATOIRE DE PEKING
tiré du Pere LE COMTE.

a { Degrè pour monter .
   { De Trappen ten Opgang .
b { Cabinet .
   { Een Vertrek .
4 { Sphere Zodiacale .
   { Zodiacale Sfære .
5 { Sphere Equinoctiale .
   { Equinoctiale Sfære .

3 { Horizon Azimuthal .
   { Horizon Azimurthal .
4 { Quadrant .
   { Een Quadrant .
5 { Sextant .
   { Sextant .
6 { Globe Celeste .
   { Een Hemel-Globe .

Antico osservatorio cinese in Pechino.
Da una incisione in rame dell'*Histoire des Voyages* dell'anno 1747.
a. Scala d'ascesa. – *b.* Stanza di osservazione. – 1. Sfera zodiacale. – 2. Sfera equinoziale. – 3. Cerchio orizzontale. – 4. Quadrante.
5. Sestante. – 6. Globo celeste.

The Peking Observatory. · **Bettmann Archive**

The 28 lunar mansions, for instance, are particularly important for determining which action is most appropriate for a given day. There is more than one manner in which the mansions may be utilized. In one approach, used in the calculation of Chinese **almanacs**, the mansions **rule** each day in sequence. To determine the mansion for any given day, astrologers add the code number of the day from Table 1 to the code number for the year from Table 2. If it is February 29 or after on a leap year, an additional 1 is added. And if the resulting number is greater than 28, then 28 is subtracted from it. The final number is the number of the mansion for that day. For example, suppose a couple wished to determine whether July 11, 1991, is an appropriate marriage date. From Table 1, they find that the code number for July 11 is 24. They add this to the year number for 1991, which is 5, and obtain 29. As this is greater than 28, they then subtract 28 and obtain 1. This is the number of the first lunar mansion, the Horn, which is a highly auspicious day for marriage.

The mansions are traditionally grouped into four categories, corresponding to the four phases of the Moon: The Green Dragon of Spring, The Black Tortoise of Winter, The White Tiger of Autumn, and The Red Bird of Summer. Following are brief delineations for each of the lunar mansions, condensed from the interpretations found in Walters's Chinese Astrology Workbook:

The Green Dragon of Spring

1. The Horn. Fortunate for commencing any project, beginning the construction of a building, buying land that is going to be used for a long time, or even embarking on a long-term partnership. It is believed that a man who chooses this day to marry will receive promotion, acclaim, and great honors. It is ideal for those entering into a political career. On the other hand, it is not a good day for finishing projects, and winding up affairs ought to be left to a more appropriate day. Indeed, it would be extremely unlucky to arrange funeral or memorial services on this day (p. 65).

2. The Neck. Not a good day to begin work on any large undertaking, or for construction. A man who accepts a promotion on such a day will lose office eventually. All family gatherings should be avoided; neither weddings nor funerals should be contracted on this day (pp. 65–66).

3. The Base. Unlucky for getting engaged. The children born of a marriage contracted on this day would be poor and unable to express themselves. There are further warnings against traveling by boat on this day, since it is likely to be wrecked (p. 66).

4. The Room. Those who erect buildings on a Room day will eventually extend their buildings, increase their holdings and adjoining land, and reap the advantages of a prosperous business. Although the usual case is that those days which are fortunate for joyous events are unsuitable for sorrowful ones, the Room is so fortunate a constellation that it is even propitious for funerals and burials to be held on this day, since one's ancestors would be delighted to help in securing promotion, riches, and recognition by those in authority (pp. 66–67).

Table 1. Code Numbers for the Days of the Year

Reprinted with permission from *The Chinese Astrology Workbook* by Derek Walters.

Aquarian Press, an imprint of HarperCollins Publishers Ltd., 1988.

	day no.	code		day no.	code		day no.	code
Jan.	1	1	Feb.	1	4	Mar.	1	4
	2	2		2	5		2	5
	3	3		3	6		3	6
	4	4		4	7		4	7
	5	5		5	8		5	8
	6	6		6	9		6	9
	7	7		7	10		7	10
	8	8		8	11		8	11
	9	9		9	12		9	12
	10	10		10	13		10	13
	11	11		11	14		11	14
	12	12		12	15		12	15
	13	13		13	16		13	16
	14	14		14	17		14	17
	15	15		15	18		15	18
	16	16		16	19		16	19
	17	17		17	20		17	20
	18	18		18	21		18	21
	19	19		19	22		19	22
	20	20		20	23		20	23
	21	21		21	24		21	24
	22	22		22	25		22	25
	23	23		23	26		23	26
	24	24		24	27		24	27
	25	15		25	28		25	28
	26	26		26	1		26	1
	27	27		27	2		27	2
	28	28		28	3		28	3
	29	1		(29)			29	4
	30	2					30	5
	31	3					31	6

Table I. Code Numbers for the Days of the Year

(continued)

	day no.	code		day no.	code		day no.	code
Apr.	1	7	May	1	9	June	1	12
	2	8		2	10		2	13
	3	9		3	11		3	14
	4	10		4	12		4	15
	5	11		5	13		5	16
	6	12		6	14		6	17
	7	13		7	15		7	18
	8	14		8	16		8	19
	9	15		9	17		9	20
	10	16		10	18		10	21
	11	17		11	19		11	22
	12	18		12	20		12	23
	13	19		13	21		13	24
	14	20		14	22		14	25
	15	21		15	23		15	26
	16	22		16	24		16	27
	17	23		17	25		17	28
	18	24		18	26		18	1
	19	25		19	27		19	2
	20	26		20	28		20	3
	21	27		21	1		21	4
	22	28		22	2		22	5
	23	1		23	3		23	6
	24	2		24	4		24	7
	25	3		25	5		25	8
	26	4		26	6		26	9
	27	5		27	7		27	10
	28	6		28	8		28	11
	29	7		29	9		29	12
	30	8		30	10		30	13
				31	11			

Table 1. Code Numbers for the Days of the Year

(continued)

	day no.	code		day no.	code		day no.	code
July	1	14	August	1	17	Sept.	1	20
	2	15		2	18		2	21
	3	16		3	19		3	22
	4	17		4	20		4	23
	5	18		5	21		5	24
	6	19		6	22		6	25
	7	20		7	23		7	26
	8	21		8	24		8	27
	9	22		9	25		9	28
	10	23		10	26		10	1
	11	24		11	27		11	2
	12	25		12	28		12	3
	13	26		13	1		13	4
	14	27		14	2		14	5
	15	28		15	3		15	6
	16	1		16	4		16	7
	17	2		17	5		17	8
	18	3		18	6		18	9
	19	4		19	7		19	10
	20	5		20	8		20	11
	21	6		21	9		21	12
	22	7		22	10		22	13
	23	8		23	11		23	14
	24	9		24	12		24	15
	25	10		25	13		25	16
	26	11		26	14		26	17
	27	12		27	15		27	18
	28	13		28	16		28	19
	29	14		29	17		29	20
	30	15		30	18		30	21
	31	16		31	19			

Table I. Code Numbers for the Days of the Year

(continued)

	day no.	code		day no.	code		day no.	code
Oct.	1	22	Nov.	1	25	Dec.	1	27
	2	23		2	26		2	28
	3	24		3	27		3	1
	4	25		4	28		4	2
	5	26		5	1		5	3
	6	27		6	2		6	4
	7	28		7	3		7	5
	8	1		8	4		8	6
	9	2		9	5		9	7
	10	3		10	6		10	8
	11	4		11	7		11	9
	12	5		12	8		12	10
	13	6		13	9		13	11
	14	7		14	10		14	12
	15	8		15	11		15	13
	16	9		16	12		16	14
	17	10		17	13		17	15
	18	11		18	14		18	16
	19	12		19	15		19	17
	20	13		20	16		20	18
	21	14		21	17		21	19
	22	15		22	18		22	20
	23	16		23	19		23	21
	24	17		24	20		24	22
	25	18		25	21		25	23
	26	19		26	22		26	24
	27	20		27	23		27	25
	28	21		28	24		28	26
	29	22		29	25		29	27
	30	23		30	26		30	28
	31	24					31	1

5. The Heart. Unfortunate for construction—misfortune will result—or for those involved in criminal charges—the verdict is likely to be guilty and the sentence imprisonment. Marriage should not be contracted on this day lest the children be afflicted (p. 67).

6 The Tail. Fortunate for building and for finding hidden treasure. Those whose marriages have been negotiated on a Tail day will have numerous descendants and be promoted to high office later in life (p. 67).

7. The Basket. Ideal for starting new ventures, which will enjoy a year of good fortune. Business will thrive and profits will be handsome. It is a good day to acquire new property or to open a new "door" (in present-day terms, this indicates a fortunate day to add extensions to property, to move into new premises, or perhaps to enroll in a new organization if it would involve moving into new buildings), as those who do so can be sure of rewards for themselves and their families (pp. 67–68).

The Black Tortoise of Winter

8. The Ladle. Fortunate for digging and any kind of physical labor. It is an exceedingly fortunate sign, revealing promotion and increase in wealth (p. 68).

9. The Ox-Boy. Unlucky, particularly for marriage. Generally unsuitable for contracting any kind of business, as the parties to the contract are deemed likely to lose interest in the project (pp. 68–69).

10. The Maiden. Unsuitable for funerals, which if carried out on a Maiden day, will result in epidemics and illness, particularly of the bowels, befalling the family (p. 69).

11. The Void. Days ruled by the Void portend domestic quarrels. It is not a suitable day for digging or construction, while those unwise enough to marry on a Void day can expect to have delinquent children (pp. 69–70).

12. The Rooftop. Fraught with danger for those on the move. Traveling should be avoided; those going by land are in danger of being attacked, while ships may run aground or capsize. A much wiser course would be to confine activities to those which can be carried out in one place, such as repairs or refurbishment of houses, especially, of course, of the roof (p. 70).

13. The House. Fortunate construction and building. It is favorable for all projects initiated on this day. Those in authority will recognize good work and give rewards from which the whole family will be able to benefit (p. 70).

14. The Wall. Fortunate for expansion, construction, building and digging. It is a favorable time to embark on new ventures or enter through new doors. Those who marry on a Wall day will have extremely talented children (p. 70).

15. Astride. Unfavorable for construction work or digging. Riches will not be attracted to any buildings erected on an Astride day, while those who dig trenches on this day will encounter misfortune (p. 71).

16. The Mound. Favorable for family gatherings, social events, parties, festivities, and assemblies of all descriptions. It is a fortunate day for all kinds of building and construction, digging trenches, and opening water courses. In particular, it is the ideal day for erecting a triumphal arch, which by extension means unveiling monuments or erecting dedicatory plaques (p. 71).

17. The Stomach. Good for putting away savings. The stomach is a fortunate day for any matters involving the earth element, such as digging, building walls, and even burying the dead. Those who are wise enough to choose this day to marry will have children destined to meet the head of state (p. 71).

18. The Pleiades. Unlucky. The Pleiades is not a favorable time to begin construction, dig or undertake any kind of family activity. Those unfortunate enought to marry on a Pleiades day will soon separate (p. 72).

19. The Net. Generally fortunate, whether for construction work, or burial. Those who marry on a Net day will have long-lived children (p. 72).

20. The Beak. Not generally a fortunate sign; many of the portents are concerned with punishment and retribution for wrongdoing. On days ruled by the Beak, it is important to be extremely careful in one's conduct (pp. 72–73).

21. Orion. Days ruled by Orion are fortunate in some respects, unfortunate in others. Merit will be achieved through building or beginning new projects. New ventures prosper. Any labor or industry undertaken on an Orion day will be rewarded, whether it is already under way or just commenced. Conversely, Orion has an adverse influence on attempts to bring any affairs to a close; matters will not end as hoped but will continue to make demands on time and finance. Marriages and betrothals ought not be contracted on this day, lest they end in separation. Nor is it a good day for interments, as this may forebode the death of a distant relative (p. 73).

The Red Bird of Summer

22. The Well. Favorable for most courses of action, although for those taking examinations that come under the aegis of the element water, the signs are particularly encouraging. Wood (representing plants) and water suggest that the Well is a beneficial sign for herbivorous animals—cattle, sheep, horses, deer, rabbits—and animal husbandry generally. It also augurs good propspects for widows who own land; the land will increase in value, bringing them the security of an income and the chance of a second husband. A Well day is regarded as an unfortunate time to lay work aside; that which has been commenced ought to be completed or continued during the influence of the Well, which favors industriousness rather than leisure. Burials and funerals are not advised on a Well day (pp. 73–74).

23. Ghosts. Days ruled by Ghosts are unfavorable; any new projects will end in disaster. It is inadvisable to go through doors through which one has not passed before. Women who marry on a Ghosts day will be widows longer than wives. But prayers for the dead, memorial services, and visits to cemeteries to visit the tombs of ancestors will bring great merit and respect and honors to one's own descendants (p. 74).

24. The Willow. No transactions are appropriate for a Willow day, and contrary to what might be expected, they are even regarded as unsuitable for funerals. Carelessness will be followed by discord, misdeeds by illness, and harmful actions by ruin (p. 74).

25. The Bird. Ideally suited to building; those who carry out construction work on a Bird day will gain promotion. But it is not an auspicious day for weddings or funerals; the woman who marries this day will fall prey to a ravisher, and those who bury their dead will see separation (pp. 74–75).

26. The Bow. Generally favorable. The Bow shows thriving business, official success, acquisition of new property, and happy personal relationships (p. 75).

27. The Wings. Those who marry on a Wings day will suffer from chronic illness; men who leave home on business will return to find their wives in the arms of lovers. Nor is it an auspicious day to offer sacrifices to one's ancestors, as it foreshadows separation from one's own children, who will leave the country in later life (p. 75).

28. The Carriage. Auspicious for all kinds of mercantile business, and great profit will result. The Carriage is an ideal day for the landscape gardener, and if "dragon terrace" is constructed, it will bring the artisan and the owner great honor. It is a favorable time to arrange obsequies and funeral rites for ancestors and also to contract marriages; those who do either will find their own children developing rare talents, so bringing great honor to their parents (pp. 75–76).

These lunar mansions constitute the oldest Chinese "zodiac." The 12 animal signs were incorporated into the system much later. Some speculate that these later signs originated outside of China proper, perhaps in northern central Asia. These 12 signs derive not from the 12 months of the year, but from the 12 years of the Jupiter cycle (Jupiter takes approximately a dozen years to complete one orbit of the Sun). Attempts to correlate the 12 signs of the Chinese zodiac with the 12 signs of the Western zodiac are problematic, to say the least. The 12 animal signs are the Rat, Ox, Tiger, Rabbit (or Cat), Dragon, Snake (Serpent), Horse, Sheep (Goat), Monkey, Cock, Dog, and Pig (Boar). It is relatively easy to obtain books on East Asian astrology that delineate the characteristics of each animal sign in detail. Walters provides a short summary of the personality traits associated with each sign in *The Chinese Astrology Workbook:*

Rat. The Rat is a nocturnal animal; hence, one with a Rat personality works best at night in the quiet hours. The Rat is studious, persevering, and quick witted. The Rat is often extremely likable, characterized by charm and sociability. The Western use of the word rat in the derogatory sense does not apply. Years: 1900, 1912, 1924, 1936, 1948, 1960, 1972, 1984, 1996 (p. 116).

Ox. The Ox represents solid dependability, method, and routine. Through sheer perseverance, the Ox can succeed where all others fail. Very down-to-earth, cautious, and unlikely to take to new ideas. Years: 1901, 1913, 1925, 1937, 1949, 1961, 1973, 1985, 1997 (p. 116).

Tiger. Rash and brash; fiercely competitive, but magnetic. An iron fist in a velvet glove. Proud and defensive with unpredictable moods. Often enters uniformed services. Years: 1902, 1914, 1926, 1938, 1950, 1962, 1974, 1986, 1998 (p. 116).

Rabbit. Benevolent and caring. Often involved in healing, cosmetics, or pharmaceuticals. Avoids confrontation where possible but shows bravery against high odds. Years: 1903, 1915, 1927, 1939, 1951, 1963, 1975, 1987, 1999 (p. 116).

Dragon. Exotic, willful, elegant, with a leaning toward the occult. Tends to make sudden decisions—impulsive—and often short-tempered. Tends to take risks and often enters the world of entertainment. Years: 1904, 1916, 1928, 1940, 1952, 1964, 1976, 1988, 2000 (p. 116).

Snake. Quietly methodical, with a reputation for wisdom. Elegant and epicurean—a connoisseur. Despite this, has a certain naïveté, and can be easily scandalized. May turn to fictional writing as a pastime or career. Years: 1905, 1917, 1929, 1941, 1953, 1965, 1977, 1989, 2001 (p. 117).

Horse. The Horse is the symbol of yang, or masculine ambitions and possessions. Sociable among their own kind. Horse personalities often have difficulties in relating to and understanding the opposite sex. Team sports are preferred to individual attainment. Years: 1906, 1918, 1930, 1942, 1954, 1966, 1978, 1990, 2002 (p. 117).

Sheep. The Sheep is the complementary sign to the Horse and represents the essence of the yin, the feminine passive principle. It is a peaceful, retiring, and contemplative sign and reveals interest in music, poetry, and painting. A monastic or contemplative life is often associated with the Sheep. Years: 1907, 1919, 1931, 1943, 1955, 1967, 1979, 1991, 2003 (p. 117).

Monkey. Whereas the Horse represents masculine leisure activities, the Monkey represents masculine technological prowess. It shows skills, dexterity and an interest in machines. The character associated with the Monkey shows humor and mischief. Years: 1908, 1920, 1932, 1944, 1956, 1968, 1980, 1992, 2004 (p. 118).

Cock. The Cock sign reveals aggressive competitiveness. Despite the Cock's being a male bird, it represents feminine interests, in particular fashion and the garment industry. It is therefore also associated with weaving and embroidery and to a lesser extent with popular art. Years: 1909, 1921, 1933, 1945, 1957, 1969, 1981, 1993, 2005 (p. 118).

Dog. The sign of the Dog shows defense, protection, and devotion to family. The Dog makes a firm friend and will stand by loyally when all others have abandoned an apparently hopeless cause. The Dog is usually skilled at matters connected with the fabric or furnishings of a house. Years: 1910, 1922, 1934, 1946, 1958, 1970, 1982, 1994, 2006 (p. 118).

Pig. The Pig shows concern for welfare, children, and comfort. Pig personalities are drawn toward careers involving young children, such as teaching, nursing, and midwifery. Pig personalities are homemakers rather than homebuilders. Years: 1911, 1923, 1935, 1947, 1959, 1971, 1983, 1995, 2007 (p. 119).

In contrast to the Western year, the Chinese year begins on variable dates (on the second new moon after the winter **solstice**) in late January or early February. Hence, someone born on January 10, 1911, for instance, would be a Dog rather than a Pig.

Table 2. Year Numbers to Find Lunar Mansion

Reprinted with permission from *The Chinese Astology Workbook* by Derek Walters.

Aquarian Press, an imprint of HarperCollins Publishers Ltd., 1988.

Year	No.	Year	No.	Year	No.	Year	No.
1977	16	1985	26	1993	8	2001	18
1978	17	1986	27	1994	9	2002	19
1979	18	1987	0	1995	10	2003	20
1980	19	1988	1	1996	11	2004	21
1981	21	1989	3	1997	13	2005	22
1982	22	1990	4	1998	14	2006	23
1983	23	1991	5	1999	15	2007	24
1984	24	1992	6	2000	16	2008	25

Much is often made of the compatibility between the signs of the Chinese zodiac. Harmonious unions, particularly marriages, are regarded as best between Rats, Dragons, and Monkeys; between Oxen, Snakes, and Cocks; between Tigers, Horses, and Dogs; and between Rabbits, Sheep, and Pigs. The most inharmonious relationships are between Rats, Rabbits, Horses, and Cocks; between Oxen, Dragons, Sheep, and Dogs; and between Tigers, Snakes, Monkeys, and Pigs.

From the pattern shown in Table 2—beginning with zero for the year 1987 and numbering each successive year in numerical order from 1 to 27, but skipping a number after each leap year—it should be relatively easy to project this table into the past or future to obtain numbers for years prior to 1977 and after 2008.

Adapted from Walters, Derek, *The Chinese Astrology Workbook,* 1988. Wellingborough, Northamptonshire, U.K.: Aquarian Press.

Sources:

Brau, Jean-Louis, Helen Weaver, and Allan Edmans. *Larousse Encyclopedia of Astrology.* New York: New American Library, 1980.

Logan, Daniel. *Your Eastern Star: Oriental Astrology, Reincarnation and the Future.* New York: William Morrow & Company, 1972.

Walters, Derek. *Chinese Astrology: Interpreting the Revelations of the Celestial Messengers.* Wellingborough, Northamptonshire, U.K.: Aquarian Press, 1987.

———. *The Chinese Astrology Workbook: How to Calculate and Interpret Chinese Horoscopes.* Wellingborough, Northamptonshire, U.K.: Aquarian Press, 1988.

Chiron

Chiron is a **comet** about 150 miles in diameter traveling in an erratic **orbit** between **Saturn** and **Uranus**. It was discovered by astronomer Charles Kowal on November 1, 1977, at approximately 10 A.M. in Pasadena, California. Chiron was thought to be a small **planet,** or planetoid, until 1990, when astronomers discovered an atmosphere of gas and dust, which meant it had to be a comet— by far the largest one in the **solar system.**

Ephemerides were available within a year of Chiron's discovery, computed (in right ascension/declination) by Brian Marsden, director of the Smithsonian Institution Astrophysical Observatory Minor Planet Center, and (in longitude and latitude) by Joelle K. D. Mahoney, director of the Astrological Research Centre, and Maria E. Bianco. A Chiron committee for further research was formed, and the world's first astrological ephemeris of Chiron was published at a meeting of the Astrologer's Guild of America in June 1978. Later that year, Zane B. Stein founded the Association for Studying Chiron and its newsletter, *The Key.* The first publications about Chiron came in 1983: Stein's historic pamphlet, *Interpreting Chiron,* Erminie Lantero's book *The Continuing Discovery of Chiron,* and Richard Nolle's book *Chiron: The New Planet in Your Horoscope.*

As is customary, astrologers looked to the mythical character after which the new planet was named for insight into its astrological meaning. Because our easily accessed sources of Greek mythology focus on the stories of powerful gods and remarkable heros, by comparison Chiron seems merely a frequently mentioned supporting character. However, astrologer Dale O'Brien has assembled perhaps the most complete version of the myth, encompassing many different facets of Chiron's story. In O'Brien's *The Myth of Chiron,* Chiron is far more than just a "wounded healer," which is the most frequent description of him.

Apparently, the Chiron myth was derived from the shamanistic culture in the vicinity of northern Greece. Chiron, the first centaur, was the mentor and trainer of a long line of heroes and other notables. The first and greatest astrologer, he was trained by both Apollo and Artemis in many different areas of expertise, including physical, cultural, and metaphysical arts. Many components of the Chiron myth parallel the later story of the life of Christ.

In the strictest sense and to the best of our knowledge, there has been no statistically legitimate research on Chiron's astrological placements equal in caliber to the Gauquelin research on planetary placement and successful careers. However, in terms of anecdotal research, Zane Stein's *Chiron, essence et interpretation* (1989) specifically references approximately 1,000 famous individuals' natal Chiron placements. Further, since 1988, Dale O'Brien has been compiling anecdotal research on over 2,000 charts, including hundreds of full- and part-time astrologers, living and dead, along with the charts of scores of serious astrology students and astrological clients. Notably, the **Gauquelin** angular sectors correspond significantly to the placement of Chiron in astrologers' charts. Most significantly represented sectors are near the midheaven (and tenth house) and especially near the **ascendant** (and first house), and near particularly tight **conjunctions** of Chiron to the ascendant. Whether angular or not, Chiron in these charts tends to be significantly **aspected**.

Although Chiron became of interest to the astrological community in the early 1980s, perhaps only 10% of astrologers use Chiron regularly in chart readings. Interest in Chiron continues to grow, however, and it appears that up to 20% of astrologers accept and use Chiron at some level in their work. The two most recently published books on Chiron are *Chiron: Rainbow Bridge Between the Inner and Outer Planets* (1987) by Barbara Hand Clow and *Chiron and the Healing Journey* (1989) by Melanie Reinhardt. No formal organizations for the study of Chiron are known to exist today. The newsletter *Chironicles* began publication in April, 1992.

There have been two primary theories about Chiron's **rulership**. Because mythological Chiron was a centaur and a great teacher, some astrologers (e.g., Reinhardt) believe Chiron rules **Sagittarius**. Others (particularly Clow) make a case for **Virgo** rulership, based on Chiron's work as a holistic healer and herbalist, as well as his unselfish service to the many would-be heroes he mentored, such as Jason, Hercules, and Asclepias. The surge in holistic healing and the reawakening of esoteric knowledge around the time of the astronomical discovery of Chiron further supports this theory. Yet others theorize some connection between Chiron and **Libra**, the sign it occupies at **perihelion**. A less frequently held but significant early theory focused on Chiron's legendary skills as a surgeon—a case for **Scorpio**.

An updated view: The discovery that Chiron is a comet makes rulership moot, since comets do not rule **zodiac** signs. This does not appear to decrease Chiron's well-observed astrological influence (Morrison's introduction in Stein, 1988). Rulership aside, students of what author Erminie Lantero aptly calls "the continuing discovery" have come to connect Chiron with holism and some of the following concepts: a key, a doorway, a change in consciousness, a different perspective, a bridge between established ways and evolutionary change, alternatives, holistic healing, and ecology. Chiron seems to represent a reawakening of shamanism, where the spirit's journey to the underworld is the path to healing—i.e., reexperiencing the wounding or cause of spiritual, emotional, or physical disease and retrieving the scattered parts of the soul.

Because Chiron the Centaur was the first astrologer, discovery of Chiron the planet may suggest a new path for astrological counseling, mentoring clients to express their unique talents and the highest potentials in their chart (O'Brien). For this reason, astrological Chiron may be most affiliated with chart **synthesis** (Mason). Chiron presents a virtual wild card that several astrologers have independently described as the critical missing factor in chart interpretation. In a new theory, Chiron may be connected to a process of "inner marriage": the union of male/female and light/dark aspects in individuals that is the prelude to success in outer marriage or partnership (Mason).

This concept is based on preliminary responses to rulership, those most likely to come from the **collective unconscious**. Most astrologers link Chiron with signs in the Virgo-to-Sagittarius sector of the zodiac, an area which represents a process of self-possession or inner marriage (Virgo) through sharing self (Libra and Scorpio) and reaping the rewards of both inner and outer marriage in the sign of higher philosophy (Sagittarius), ruled by the planet of prosperity (**Jupiter**). Those who achieve successful relationships become models in an age where successful relating is of utmost importance—the prelude to balancing the masculine and feminine principles on a global level, assimilating polarities for the sake of wholeness and survival.

Comets throughout history have been viewed as omens. Some believe Chiron's discovery may point to the balance needed to move humanity into an alternative life-style of holism that will support Earth and all life upon it in abundance.

—*Joyce Mason and Dale O'Brien*

Sources:

Chronicles: A newsletter dedicated to the myth and astrology of Chiron, and the practice of astrology from a Chironic perspective. Published three times per year. (Available from *Chronicles*, P.O. Box 41127, Sacramento, Calif. 95841.)

Clow, Barbara Hand. *Chiron: Rainbow Bridge Between the Inner and Outer Planets.* Saint Paul, Minn.: Llewellyn Publications, 1987.

Lantero, Erminie. *The Continuing Discovery of Chiron.* York Beach, Maine: Samuel Weiser, 1983.

Mason, Joyce. "The Radical Virgo." *The Mountain Astrologer,* Apr./May 1992.

"The mother of all short comets." *Discover,* Feb. 1991, p. 8.

Nolle, Richard. *Chiron: The New Planet in Your Horoscope.* Tempe, Ariz.: AFA, 1983.

O'Brien, Dale. *The Myth of Chiron,* 1991. Audiotape. (Available from Dale O'Brien, 5154 St. Barnabas Rd., Temple Hills, Md. 20748.)

Reinhardt, Melanie. *Chiron and the Healing Journey: An Astrological and Psychological Perspective.* London: Arcana, 1989.

Stein, Zane B. *Essence and Application: A View from Chiron. 3d ed.* New York: Al H. Morrison's CAO
Times, 1988. (Translated as *Chiron, essence et interpretation* in 1989.)
———. *Interpreting Chiron.* [Pamphlet.] New York, The Author, 1983.

Choisnard, Paul

Paul Choisnard, born February 13, 1867, in Tours, France, was an eminent
astrologer. A graduate of L'Ecole Polytechnique in Paris, his first career was as a
major in the field artillery. He became interested in astrology, especially
"scientific astrology," and took it up as a significant side interest. He was
particularly interested in astrological research involving statistical methods. To
avoid conflict within his first profession, he used the pseudonym Paul Flambart
until after he retired. He was a prolific writer, though little known in the United
States.

Choisnard was important for his role in helping revive astrology in France
and for his pioneering role in applying statistical methods to astrology. He was
succeeded in the latter role by the Swiss astrologer Karl Ernst Krafft, who was in
turn followed by **Michel Gauquelin**. Choisnard died February 9, 1930, at St.
Geni-de-Saintange.

Selected Publications:

Influence astrale. Paris, 1901.
Etude nouvelle sur l'hérédité. Paris, 1903.
Langage astral. Paris, 1903.

Sources:

Holden, James H., and Robert A. Hughes. *Astrological Pioneers of America.* Tempe, Ariz.: American
Federation of Astrologers, 1988.

Choleric

Choleric is the traditional name for the personality temperament indicated by an
excess of the **element** fire.

Christianity and Astrology

Historically, astrology was integrated into the Church along with other aspects
of Hellenistic civilization. From time to time, various Christian thinkers worried
about the tension between free will and the apparent determinism of astrology,
but by and large the science of the stars occupied an honorable position in the
Western tradition. Although some of the biblical prophets disparaged stargaz-

ing, The Three Wise Men were clearly astrologers, and in certain other scriptural passages it was evident that God regularly used heavenly signs to instruct the faithful.

Despite certain tensions between them, astrology and Christianity were not separated until the fundamentalist movement of the early twentieth century. For various reasons, but particularly because of astrology's association with metaphysical religion (e.g., the New Age movement), fundamentalists—and, later, most other varieties of conservative Christians—rejected astrology as a delusion at best and as a tool of Satan at worst. (*See also:* **The Bible and Astrology; History of Astrology.**)

Sources:

Jacobs, Don. *Astrology's Pew in the Church.* San Francisco: The Joshua Foundation, 1979.
Simms, Maria Kay. *Twelve Wings of the Eagle. Our Spiritual Evolution through the Ages of the Zodiac.* San Diego, Calif.: Astro Computing Services, 1988.

Chronocrators

The chronocrators, the "markers or rulers" of time, are the periodic **conjunctions** of **Jupiter** and **Saturn** that occur every 20 years. Because Jupiter and Saturn were the slowest-moving **planets** in the then-known **solar system,** their conjunction was perceived by the ancients as particularly significant. These celestial meetings indicated important events, as well as the beginning and ending of important periods of time. It has been speculated that the **Star of Bethlehem**, for example, was actually a Jupiter–Saturn conjunction. There exists considerable traditional astrological literature on chronocrators. This literature develops, among other things, longer cycles out of the patterns of successive chronocrators (e.g., the 2-century cycle during which chronocrators occur in the same **element**) and speculates about the significance of these longer time periods. Few modern astrologers have more than passing familiarity with this phase of astrology.

Chronos

Chronos is an older name for **Saturn**. Mythologically, Chronos was regarded as the Greek god equivalent to the Roman Saturn.

Church of Light

Elbert Benjamine (C. C. Zain) incorporated the Church of Light in Los Angeles in 1932, although its roots lie in Emma Harding Britten's 1876 book *Art Magic.* The Church of Light views itself as an outgrowth of the Brotherhood of

Light, which it says separated from Egyptian theocracy in 2400 B.C. and subsequently became a secret order.

The Church of Light teaches that there is only one religion, the laws of nature. Astrology is emphasized as a vehicle for interpreting the laws of nature, although all occult sciences are recognized. The core teaching of the church is contained in 21 courses. After completion, members are given a Hermetic certificate. Service to others is stressed.

The Church of Light is important to the history of astrology in the United States. The church was one of the few organizations offering high-quality correspondence courses in astrology in the early twentieth century, and many older contemporary astrologers studied with the Church.

Sources:

Burgoyne, Thomas H. *The Light of Egypt.* 2 vols. Albuquerque, N. Mex.: Sun Publishing Company, 1980.
Church of Light, *Astrological Research & Reference Encyclopedia.* 2 vols. Los Angeles, 1972.
Wagner, H. O., comp. *A Treasure Chest of Wisdom.* Denver, Colo.: H. O. Wagner, 1967.

Circe

Circe, **asteroid** 34 (the 34th asteroid to be discovered), is approximately 112 kilometers in diameter and has an **orbital** period of 4.4 years. Circe was named after the Greek enchantress who detained Odysseus on her island. She was a sorceress known for her knowledge of magic and poisonous herbs. According to Lang-Wescott, Circe represents where we facilitate and assist others, as well as where we seek help. This asteroid's key word is *rescue.* According to Lehman, Circe has a magical and temptress side and indicates where we have the power to influence others, for good or for bad.

Sources:

Lang-Wescott, Martha. *Asteroids-Mechanics: Ephemerides II.* Conway, Mass.; Treehouse Mountain, 1990.
———. *Mechanics of the Future: Asteroids.* Rev. ed. Conway, Mass.: Treehouse Mountain, 1991.
Lehman, J. Lee. *The Ultimate Asteroid Book.* West Chester, Penn.: Whitford, 1988.

Clark, Vernon E.

Vernon E. Clark was born August 29, 1911, in Baltimore, Maryland. He studied art at the Maryland Institute of Art and at Columbia University Teachers College and graduated from Columbia University. He practiced as a clinical psychologist in the U.S. Army, at Downey Veterans Hospital, and, after 1950, from his home.

In 1927, Clark became interested in astrology, joining the American Federation of Astrology in 1959. He served as a trustee of the American Federation of Astrologers Building Fund and, in 1958, was the first American to win the Gold Medal of the Faculty of Astrological Studies in London. Clark is remembered for the blind trial experiments of natal chart interpretation that he conducted from 1959 to 1961, which generally supported the thesis that natal **horoscopes** are potentially indicative of the life circumstances of the **natives**. He died on November 6, 1967, in Evanston, Illinois.

Sources:

Dean, Geoffrey. *Recent Advances in Natal Astrology.* Subiaco, Australia: Analogic, 1977.

Holden, James H., and Robert A. Hughes. *Astrological Pioneers of America.* Tempe, Ariz.: American Federation of Astrologers, 1988.

Clementina

Clementina, **asteroid** 252 (the 252nd asteroid to be discovered), is approximately 45 kilometers in diameter and has an **orbital** period of 5.6 years. Its name, the personification of mercy (clemency), is derived from the Latin *clementia*. When prominent in a **natal chart**, this asteroid shows a forgiving person. Its location by sign and **house** indicates where one forgives or experiences forgiveness.

Sources:

Kowal, Charles T. *Asteroids: Their Nature and Utilization.* Chichester, West Sussex, U.K.: Ellis Horwood Limited, 1988.

Room, Adrian. *Dictionary of Astronomical Names.* London: Routledge, 1988.

Climacteric Conjunction

A climacteric conjunction is a **conjunction** of **Jupiter** and **Saturn**. As the slowest-moving **planets** known to the ancients, the periodic (every 20 years) conjunction of these two celestial bodies was regarded as especially significant.

Clio

Clio, **asteroid** 84 (the 84th asteroid to be discovered), is approximately 88 kilometers in diameter and has an **orbital** period of 3.6 years. It was named after the muse of history. Clio's location by sign and **house** shows where one tends to keep alive memories—or even a written record—of the past. When prominent in a mental house (third or ninth) or in a close **aspect** with **Mercury** (planet of the mind), Clio may show a **native** who is always bringing the past to bear on the present. When prominent and **afflicted**, Clio may show someone who tends to live in the past or who is somehow stuck in the past.

Sources:

Kowal, Charles T. *Asteroids: Their Nature and Utilization*. Chichester, West Sussex, U.K.: Ellis Horwood Limited, 1988.
Room, Adrian. *Dictionary of Astronomical Names*. London: Routledge, 1988.

Cochrane, David

David Cochrane was born May 1, 1949, in East Meadow, New York. He received his B.A. degree in psychology in 1972. After graduating from college, he turned down a scholarship for graduate school in order to devote full attention to astrology. He was a full-time astrologer until the early 1980s. Cochrane developed a system of astrological analysis based primarily on **harmonics** and **midpoint** structures, and his ideas were published in several articles.

In the early 1980s, he switched to full-time computer programming, and the first version of KEPLER, an astrology software program, was made available in 1986. At present, his greatest interest is developing the tools necessary for astrology to become more precise, accurate, practical, and useful so that eventually it will be acceptable to the academic community and used more widely by various professionals. In 1990, he was selected for membership in *Who's Who in the Computer Industry*. He is married and has one child.

Cold

The signs are numbered from 1 to 12 according to their order in the **zodiac** (e.g., **Aries** = 1, **Taurus** = 2, etc.). Cold and hot was one of the sets of categories used in premodern physics, and the ancients classified all even-numbered signs (all water and **earth signs**) as cold. Traditionally, the **Moon** and **Saturn**, and sometimes other **planets**, were also considered to be cold. The terms hot and cold are infrequently used in modern astrology.

Collective Unconscious (Archetypes)

The collective unconscious, a term coined by the psychologist **Carl Jung**, refers to the storehouse of myths and symbols to which all human beings have access. Much of traditional Jungian analysis focuses on the interpretation of dreams. Jung found that the dreams of his clients frequently contained images with which they were completely unfamiliar but which seemed to reflect symbols that could be found somewhere in the mythological systems of world culture; the notion of the collective unconscious was used to explain this phenomenon.

Jung further found that he could often interpret his patients' dreams if he studied and reflected upon the particular myth or symbol to which the dream image seemed to allude. In certain cases, deeper and more complete significance for the dream image could be uncovered by locating similar images in more than one cultural system. Researching such images in the quest for deeper meanings is referred to as amplification.

Jung's unique contribution to modern psychology begins with the observation that the basic structure of many symbols and myths is nearly universal, even between cultures with no historical influence on one another. Most traditional societies, for example, tell hero myths, use circles to represent wholeness, the sky to symbolize transcendence, etc. Jung theorized that this universality resulted from unconscious patterns (genetic or quasi-genetic predispositions to utilize certain symbolic and mythic structures) that we inherited from our distant ancestors. The reservoir of these patterns constitutes a collective unconscious, distinct from the individual, personal unconscious that is the focus of Freudian psychoanalysis.

Jung referred to the unconscious, predisposing patterns for particular myths and symbols as archetypes; hence, one can talk about the mandala (i.e., the circle) archetype, the hero archetype (the latter made famous by the Jungian thinker Joseph Campbell), and so forth. Astrologers adopted this kind of language for discussions about the elements of their craft, e.g., the "**Mars** archetype," the "**Venus** archetype," etc.

Sources:

Burt, Kathleen. *Archetypes of the Zodiac.* Saint Paul, Minn.: Llewellyn Publications, 1990.
Valentine, Christine. *Images of the Psyche: Exploring the Planets Through Psychology and Myth.* Shaftesbury, Dorset, U.K.: Element Books, 1991.

Colors and the Zodiac

Human beings have often perceived colors as constituting a kind of symbolic alphabet, so it is natural that colors would come to be associated with the signs of the **zodiac** as well as with the **planets.** There is, however, more than one system of correlations between the colors and the signs. The following color–sign associations should thus be regarded as illustrative rather than definitive:

> *Aries:* Red and other "flaming" colors
>
> *Taurus:* Pink, pale blue, and other pastels
>
> *Gemini:* Yellow and violet
>
> *Cancer:* Green, smoky-gray, silver, and silvery blue colors
>
> *Leo:* Orange and gold
>
> *Virgo:* Green and dark brown
>
> *Libra:* Pink, pale green, and various shades of blue

Scorpio: Deep red, maroon, dark brown, black

Sagittarius: Dark blues and purples

Capricorn: Brown, gray, black, dark green, and earth tones

Aquarius: Turquoise, aquamarine, white, electric blue

Pisces: Sea green, lavender, lilac

Natives born under the influence of one of these signs (particularly, but not exclusively, as this influence manifests in their **sun sign**) usually feel a special affinity with their sign's colors. This affinity can manifest as a tendency to wear clothes of—or to decorate homes with—the associated zodiacal colors.

Combust

A **planet** is said to be combust when it is within 8° 30′ (many would say less) of the **Sun**. In traditional astrology, this was regarded as having a weakening (**debilitating**) effect on the planet involved. Contemporary astrologers have not found that this close **conjunction** with the Sun weakens planets, and, to the contrary, some researchers have asserted that such a position tends to strengthen the influence of the planets involved. The notion of combust might have been based on the observation that during **partile** conjunctions in which the Sun actually came between a particular planet and Earth (i.e., during **occultations**), the matters and processes ruled by the planet involved in the conjunction were weakened. Certain twentieth-century experiments, such as those supporting the **Kolisko effect** (in which the **metal** associated with a given planet was less reactive during the planet's occultation), would support such an interpretation.

Mercury, as the planet closest to the Sun, is most often involved in close conjunctions with the greater **luminary**. Observing people with combust Mercury, many modern astrologers have noted greater mental energy as well as greater powers of concentration in these **natives**. However, it has also been observed that this position, unless counteracted by other factors in the **natal chart**, causes people with combust Mercurys to be less able to see points of view other than their own.

Sources:

Bach, Eleanor. *Astrology from A to Z: An Illustrated Source Book.* New York: Philosophical Library, 1990.

deVore, Nicholas. *Encyclopedia of Astrology.* New York: Philosophical Library, 1947.

Comets

A comet (from Greek *kometes,* long-haired) is a celestial body composed of ice, rock, and frozen gases that has been quaintly described as a dirty snowball. Almost all comets observed from **Earth** are part of our **solar system**, following long eliptical **orbits** that bring them from outside the orbit of **Pluto**, close to the **Sun**, and then back beyond Pluto. Many become involved with gravitational forces in the planetary system, so that they subsequently follow paths that keep them considerably inside Pluto's orbit—some even become trapped inside **Jupiter's** orbit. The so-called tail of a comet is produced when the comet passes close enough to the Sun for sunlight to heat it up, causing gas and dust particles to escape from the nucleus and form a glowing tail.

As extraordinary heavenly phenomena that did not appear to follow the same regular patterns as the **stars** or the **planets**, comets were traditionally regarded as signs of unusually important events. In Western countries in particular, they were regarded as omens of disaster—plagues, famines, war, and so forth. In China they were also traditionally regarded as omens, but they could be omens of either good or evil. To modern people who rarely look at the night sky—much less ever having seen a comet—this explanation appears unreasonable. To understand ancients' response to comets, one must empathize with them and understand that they saw celestial events as messages from the gods. Furthermore, our generation has not had the opportunity to view any truly spectacular comets—fiery visitors that in times past lit up the night sky

▶
In many cultures, comets have been regarded as portents of momentous events. This 16th-century woodcut is from an astrological tract by Paracelsus. · Bettmann Archive

with a spectacle of brilliance exceeding the glow of a full Moon. With these considerations in mind, it is easier to understand the response of the French surgeon Ambroise Paré to a comet that appeared over Europe in 1528: "It appeared to be of great length and the color of blood. At its summit was visible the figure of a bent arm, holding in its hand a great sword as if ready to strike. On either side of the tail were seen a great number of axes, knives, and bloodstained swords, among which were hideous human faces with beards and bristling hair. The comet was horrible and produced such great terror among the common people that many died of fear and many others fell sick" (Ritchie, p. 1).

Many meteors are constituted by the residue of comets. This residual matter is drawn into Earth's gravitational field, burns up as it passes through the atmosphere, and occasionally creates a visible flash that we call a falling star or a shooting star. Less frequently, enough mass is left after the journey through the atmosphere for a meteor to actually strike the surface of Earth. In this situation, the meteor becomes a **meteorite**.

Despite the importance that earlier generations of astrologers attributed to comets, modern astrologers have tended to ignore them. There exist, however, **ephemerides** of such well-known comets as Halley's, so it is possible to place at least these in **horoscopes** and study their influence. It is also relevant to note that **Chiron**—a large planetoid orbiting between **Saturn** and **Uranus** that has been given an extraordinary amount of attention by contemporary astrologers—is a comet. It is thus entirely possible that comet studies will find a place in modern astrology in the not-too-distant future.

Sources:

Brandt, John C. *Comets: Readings from Scientific American*. San Francisco: W. H. Freeman and Co., 1981.
Krupp, E. C. *Beyond the Blue Horizon: Myths and Legends of the Sun, Moon, Stars, and Planets*. New York: HarperCollins, 1991.
Ritchie, David. *Comets: The Swords of Heaven*. New York: Plume, 1985.

Commanding (Obeying)

In traditional astrology, the commanding signs were **Taurus** through **Virgo**. The complementary signs, termed obeying, were **Scorpio** through **Pisces**. The schema commanding/obeying was a way of designating equal distances from the **Aries–Libra** axis, rather than an assertion about the characteristics of the relevant signs.

Common

Mercury is a neutral **planet** in the sense that it is neither **feminine** nor **masculine**, neither **malefic** nor **benefic**, etc. As a planet that tends to take on the traits of its sign and **house** placement more readily than other planets, the astrological tradition has characterized Mercury as a common (meaning, in this case, neutral) planet. Common signs is another designation for **mutable signs** (**Gemini, Virgo, Sagittarius**, and **Pisces**); the mutable signs represent a kind of halfway point between the two extremes of **cardinal** and **fixed signs** and are thus common (again in the sense of neutral).

Common Planet

The **planet Mercury** is sometimes referred to as a common planet, perhaps because of its **androgynous** character.

Composite Chart

A composite chart is a form of **synastry** in which the **horoscopes** of two individuals (or of some other entity, such as a corporation) being compared are overlaid, the **midpoints** between the **planets** and the **house cusps** calculated, and a third chart generated consisting entirely of these midpoints. For example, if one individual's **Sun** was located at 15° **Scorpio** and the other person's Sun at 15° **Virgo,** the Sun in the composite chart would be placed at 15° **Libra.** The same operation is carried out for all of the planets and houses.

A composite chart, like other methods of chart comparison, is supposed to reveal how two different people or entities interact. Many astrologers, however, have criticized the composite method, finding it less than satisfactory for uncovering interpersonal dynamics. An alternative interpretation is that, rather than providing insight into the interpersonal dimension, the composite chart shows how the pair of people in the relationship *operate together in the world.* According to this line of interpretation, a composite chart would provide insight into the "personality" of a marriage or the "personality" of a business partnership.

Computers and Astrology

The astrologer's craft consists of two very different skills: (1) **casting charts,** (erecting) the mathematical construction of an astrological chart; and (2) **delineation**, interpreting the meaning of a chart.

Although delineation is the core technique of modern astrology, an accurate interpretation obviously depends upon having initially erected the **horoscope** correctly. However, because the math involved with constructing an astrological chart is quite tedious and fairly lengthy, it is easy for errors to creep in—errors that can skew the meaning of the entire chart. As devices that do not become bored with with tedious calculations, computers are clearly the answer to this problem, and some astrologers began utilizing computers as early as the late 1960s. The full potential of astrological computer methods did not begin to manifest itself, however, until after the advent of the personal computer revolution in the late 1970s. This revolution has transformed the practice of astrology so that, at the present time, the vast majority of astrologers cast charts with computers.

Computers not only avoid computational errors (as long as the data are correctly entered) but also save the astrologer many hours of time. In this regard, Hank Friedman, the author of *Astrology on Your Personal Computer,* begins his book with an instructive example:

> I had just finished dinner when I suddenly remembered that a couple would be arriving in an hour for an astrological consultation. I needed to prepare two charts, a comparison between them, and a set of progressions for each person. In the old days, before I'd purchased my computer system and astrological software, my goose would have been cooked. It took me at least four hours to prepare all of that material using my reference books and a calculator. Instead of frantically rushing to get everything done, I calmed myself down, turned on my computer, and got to work. . . . (p. 1).

> It took me about ten minutes to complete all of the steps, and the computer about 15 minutes to calculate and print out a complete set of wheels and aspects for both people, both of their progressed charts including timed progressed hits, and a combined bi-wheel with interaspects. I even had enough time left over to review the charts before they arrived (p. 4).

Friedman was using an early 1980s system. More recent state-of-the-art systems could have performed the same operations in less than 5 minutes.

The time-saving aspect of computerized charts also encourages astrologers to explore approaches they might have otherwise avoided. Thus, for example, the many **Arabic Parts** beyond the **Part of Fortune**—points in the chart that are exceedingly time-consuming to calculate manually—can be all located with the press of a button. This time-saving feature of computer astrology also makes **astrological research** far easier that it has been in the past.

A more problematic aspect of this innovation in astrological practice has been the application of computer methods to the actual delineation of horoscopes. The building blocks of chart interpretation are the meanings of each particular sign position, **house** position, and **aspect.** Computer programs are perfectly capable of storing such information and generating a list of interpretations for any given person. No professional astrologer, however, would simply list interpretations of each component of a horoscope. In fact, the very mark of an experienced astrologer is the ability to meaningfully **synthesize** such information into a coherent whole. This is especially important when two or more elements of a horoscope give contrary indications.

For example, a **Capricorn** moon in a **natal chart** usually indicates a **native** who is not emotionally sensitive to others. If, however, this same individual's natal moon is also in the first house, **conjunct** both the **ascendant** and **Neptune,** she or he will be extremely sensitive—probably oversensitive—

to other people. Experienced astrologers would immediately recognize this and avoid the mistake of telling this particular client that she or he was emotionally insensitive.

Interpretive computer programs, no matter how sophisticated, cannot ever do much more than list the meanings of each element of a horoscope. No existing program would avoid, for instance, the error of informing Capricorn moon natives about their insensitivity. Thus, while computer readings may have a certain place as a preliminary step in astrological science, they will have to become far more sophisticated before they begin to approximate the skill of an experienced astrologer.

Sources:

Brau, Jean-Louis, Helen Weaver, and Allan Edmans. *Larousse Encyclopedia of Astrology.* New York: New American Library, 1980.

Foreman, Patricia L. *Computers and Astrology: A Universal User's Guide and Reference.* Burlington, Vt.: Good Earth Publications, 1992.

Friedman, Hank. *Astrology on Your Personal Computer.* Berkeley, Calif.: SYBEX, 1984.

Concept Asteroids

Asteroids are thousands of small planetoids, 95 percent of whose **orbits** lie between those of **Mars** and **Jupiter.** Initially these asteroids were given mythological names, but as more asteroids were discovered, astronomers began naming them after places, people, and, eventually, concepts. Astrologers who have studied the influence of asteroids have reached the conclusion that the name of an asteroid gives one preliminary insight into the asteroid's astrological effects.

The early asteroids studied by astrologers were named after mythological figures, and an exploration of the relevant myths provided a preliminary clue to the nature of these tiny planetoids' influence. When researchers began shifting away from explicitly mythological asteroids and began examining asteroids named after concepts, they continued to follow their previous line of exploration by finding initial clues to the astrological influences of such asteroids in the concepts after which they were named. **Pax,** for example, is the Latin word for "peace," which is a clue to the presumably "peaceful" or "pacifying" influence of the asteroid Pax.

Conception (Conception Charts)

Although **genethliacal astrology (natal astrology)** has settled on the birth time as the moment for **casting the horoscope,** astrologers have long felt that it would also be desirable to cast charts for the moment of conception. **Ptolemy,** for example, asserted that gender as well as certain other prenatal events could be deduced from the **planets** at the time of conception. However, the obvious difficulties that would be involved in determining precise conception moments have effectively frustrated astrological research in this area. For the most part, the observation that Nicholas deVore made earlier in this century still applies: "The entire subject of prenatal cosmic stimulation is a welter of confused theorizing, which yet lacks confirmation in practice sufficient to bring about any unanimity of opinion" (pp. 61–62).

Some contemporary thinkers, nevertheless, have been intrepid enough to explore this largely uncharted domain. Of greatest significance has been the work of Eugen Jonas, a Czech psychiatrist who developed a system of astrological **birth control** based on the discovery that women have a cycle of fertility beyond the normal ovulation cycle—one based on the phase of the **Moon.** Jonas found, among many other interesting things, that the sign the Moon (which **rules** the principal of conception and motherhood) was in during conception determined the offspring's sex—male in the case of **masculine** signs and female in the case of **feminine** signs.

In an effort to construct usable conception charts, some twentieth-century astrologers have picked up on the *trutine of Hermes,* an ancient principle for casting conception charts ascribed to the legendary Hermes Trismegistus that asserts that "the place of the Moon at conception was the **Ascendant** of the birth figure [i.e., **conjunct** the ascendant of the **natal chart**] or its opposite point [conjunct the **descendant**]." If Hermes was correct, then the trutine could be used to determine the precise time of conception in cases where the date and time of conception were known approximately. Prenatal charts relying on the trutine were seriously proposed early in this century by Walter Gorn Old (who wrote under the pen name Sepharial) in *The Solar Epoch* and by E. H. Bailey in *The Prenatal Epoch.*

Sources:

Bailey, E. H. *The Prenatal Epoch.* N.p., 1916

Brau, Jean-Louis, Helen Weaver, and Allan Edmands. *Larousse Encyclopedia of Astrology.* New York: New American Library, 1980.

deVore, Nicholas. *Encyclopedia of Astrology.* New York: Philosophical Library, 1947.

Gettings, Fred. *Dictionary of Astrology.* London: Routledge & Kegan Paul, 1985.

Ostrander, Sheila, and Lynn Schroeder. *Astrological Birth Control.* Englewood Cliffs, NJ: Prentice-Hall, 1972.

Sepharial [Walter Gorn Old]. *The Solar Epoch.* Santa Fe, N. Mex.: Sun Publishing Co., 1991.

Conceptive Signs

The conceptive signs are the four **fixed signs.**

Concordia

Concordia, **asteroid** 58 (the 58th asteroid to be discovered), is approximately 104 kilometers in diameter and has an **orbital** period of 4.4 years. It was named after a Latin word for peace. Concordia shows peacefulness—or the seeking of peace—by its **house** and sign position (e.g., peace with relatives in the third house, peace with employees in the sixth, and so forth).

Sources:

Kowal, Charles T. *Asteroids: Their Nature and Utilization.* Chichester, West Sussex, U.K.: Ellis Horwood Limited, 1988.

Room, Adrian. *Dictionary of Astronomical Names.* London: Routledge, 1988.

Configuration

Traditionally, the term configuration was used to refer to any **aspect**. In contemporary astrology the term is reserved for sets of interrelated aspects involving three or more **planets**, such as **T-squares**, **grand trines**, and so forth. By extension, the configuration is sometimes used to refer to the pattern presented by the entire **horoscope**.

Conjunction

A conjunction is, as the name implies, an **aspect** in which two points—such as two **planets**—are close enough that their energies join. A conjunction is a major **aspect,** regarded as harmonious or inharmonious depending on the planets involved; a conjunction involving planets like **Jupiter** and **Venus**, for instance, would exert a generally fortunate influence, while a conjunction involving **Saturn** or **Pluto** would be challenging, to say the least. It is sometimes called the aspect of prominence because it brings the planets involved into prominence in a chart.

Constantia

Constantia, **asteroid** 315 (the 315th asteroid to be discovered), is approximately 8 kilometers in diameter and has an **orbital** period of 3.4 years. Its name is a personified form of constancy. In a **natal chart**, its location by sign and **house** indicates where one experiences or seeks constancy. When **afflicted** by inharmonious **aspects**, Constantia may show inconstancy or a false sense of stability. If prominent in a chart (e.g., **conjunct** the **Sun** or the **ascendant**), it may show an exceptionally fair person or someone for whom constancy and the seeking of stability and security are dominant life themes.

Kowal, Charles T. *Asteroids: Their Nature and Utilization.* Chichester, West Sussex, U.K: Ellis Horwood Limited, 1988.

Room, Adrian. *Dictionary of Astronomical Names.* London: Routledge, 1988.

Constellation

A constellation (from Latin *con,* with, and *stella,* star) is a collection of **stars** that the ancients grouped together, identified with a figure from mythology, and named after that figure. In astrology, the names of the various signs of the **zodiac** are taken from 12 **constellations** intersected by the **ecliptic**. The untutored eye has a difficult time discerning the relationship between these star groups and the figures they are said to represent: Unlike the ancients, who gazed upon a sky filled with legends, heroes, and heroines, we moderns look up to see only a confused mass of tiny lights.

Contraparallel

The **orbits** of most of the **planets** in the **solar system** lie in approximately the same geometric plane, which is why we are able to draw an astrological chart using only a two-dimensional representation rather than one with three dimensions. There is, nevertheless, a variation in the tilt or angle of these orbits, and at any given time most planets are positioned north and south of the **celestial equator** (the plane described by projecting the Earth's equator against the background of the **stars**). This variation is measured in degrees of **declination**. Two planets are **contraparallel** when they lie on opposite sides of the celestial equator and have the same degree of declination (e.g., one planet at 10° declination and the other at -10°). Planets with opposite declinations are said to have a relationship similar to an **opposition**. Relatively few astrologers take contraparallels into account when interpreting a **horoscope**.

Sources:

deVore, Nicholas. *Encyclopedia of Astrology.* New York: Philosophical Library, 1947.

Hand, Robert. *Horoscope Symbols.* Rockport, Mass.: Para Research, 1981.

Contrascion

Picture the wheel of the **zodiac** and draw a straight line from 0° **Aries** to 0° **Libra** so as to divide the circle into equal halves. If a **planet** is located at an **angular distance** of 45° away from this dividing line (e.g., at 15° **Taurus**), its contrascion would be 45° in the opposite direction from the line (e.g., at 15° **Aquarius**). If another planet happens to be located at or very near the contrascion of the first planet, the two planets are said to have a relationship with each other comparable to an **opposition** aspect.

Converse Directions

Converse directions refers to progressing **planets** backward rather than forward in an **ephemeris** during **prognostication**.

Copernicus, Nicolaus

Nicolaus Copernicus, famous for the theory that Earth revolves around the **Sun** rather than the reverse, was born on February 19, 1473, in Torun, Poland. This theory had been put forward by the ancient Greeks, most notably by Aristarchus of Samos, but did not make much headway until Copernicus's *De revolutionibus orbium coelestium,* which was not published until 1543, although it had been written more than a dozen years prior.

Many commentators have asserted that the triumph of the Copernican over the Ptolemaic view led more or less directly to the discrediting of astrology. This assertion is naive, however, as astrology does not depend upon a geocentric cosmology. Astrology studies the position of the **planets** relative to Earth, a positioning that worked equally well in a geocentric or heliocentric frame of reference. Copernicus himself cast birth charts, and he gave one manuscript to Joachim Rheticus, an astrologer, to publish. Copernicus died on May 24, 1543, in Frombork, Poland.

Sources:

Brau, Jean-Louis, Helen Weaver and Allan Edmands. *Larousse Encyclopedia of Astrology.* New York: New American Library, 1980.
Kitson, Annabella, ed. *History and Astrology: Clio and Urania Confer.* London: Mandala, 1989.

Correction

In astrology, correction refers to the translation of one's birth time into **sidereal time**.

Correspondences, Law of

The law of correspondences refers, primarily, to the notion—widely accepted in occult circles—that everything in this world is the manifestation of some spiritual principle. The expression "as above, so below" partially articulates this idea. Because the premodern world believed that celestial bodies were spiritual (or at least semispiritual), the law of correspondences was invoked to explain astrological influences. The ancient notion of correspondences is sometimes equated with the modern idea (derived from **Jungian** psychology) of **synchronicity.** Synchronicity, however, applies to any meaningful coincidence—not simply to parallels between events "above" and events "below." Synchronicity also does not carry the same metaphysical connotations usually associated with the law of correspondences.

Co-significator

Co-significator, a term used particularly in **horary astrology,** refers to a **planet** or sign that in some way relates to the matter under consideration by virtue of certain traditional astrological associations.

Cosmobiology

Cosmobiology is a contemporary form of scientific astrology that is especially popular in Europe. Cosmobiology utilizes modern-day methods of scientific research, such as statistics, analysis, and computer programming to study the influence of the cosmos on individuals. The word cosmobiology was coined by Austrian physician Dr. Feerhow and was later used by Swiss statistician **Karl Ernst Krafft** to designate the branch of astrology based on scientific foundations and keyed to the natural sciences. Cosmobiology has, through the work of **Reinhold Ebertin**, become increasingly well-known within the last 50 or so years.

Despite the great diagnostic value of cosmobiology in the fields of character study (characterology) and psychology, one should not forget that the individual's natal constellation can only be seen and properly interpreted in connection with his or her life history (including medical history, upbringing, time and circumstances in which he lives, religion, manners, morals, environment, etc.).

The Cosmogram

Cosmogram is the cosmobiological term for **horoscope**. The foundation for casting the cosmogram is the **zodiac**, through which the **Sun** moves in one year. Each of the 12 **signs** of the zodiac encompasses 30 smaller divisions, called **degrees** (°), so that the whole circle contains 360°.

To locate the positions of the stellar bodies in the zodiac more exactly, 1° is divided into 60′ (60 minutes) and every minute is divided into 60″ (60 seconds). The position of each stellar body is expressed in degrees, minutes, and, sometimes, seconds. To distinguish subdivisions of degrees from subdivisions of hours, one uses the symbols *h* (for hour), *m* (minute), and *s* (second) when discussing time, and the symbols ' for minute and " for seconds when discussing degrees.

The 90 Degree Dial

Traditionally, the horoscope is divided into one of several **house** systems, which allow astrologers further interpretations. Cosmobiology does not utilize a house system. Instead, the focus is on planetary influences.

The cosmogram, composed of two circles, is the basic form used for interpretation in Cosmobiology. One circle is the standard 360° circle for the regular planetary distribution; the other is a 90° circle—or 90° dial.

The 360° circle is a recognized measuring device. To simplify the process of investigation, the 360° circle is reduced to a fourth; i.e., the regular 360° circle is quartered into four equal parts to provide a structure for the angular distribution of the stellar bodies. The resulting 90° "circle" groups are called **cardinal, fixed,** and mutable quadruplicites (**mutable signs**), with each quadruplicity occupying 30° of the 90° circle.

Prior to constructing a cosmogram, one must have a chart locating the stellar bodies on a 360° circle. This can be derived from standard chart erection methods, so it is suggested that the astrologer begin by constructing the type of horoscope she or he is accustomed to, then transcribe the planets to the cosmogram in their locations.

Cosmobiology utilizes much smaller **orbs** of influence in ascertaining **aspects** than those used in standard methods of astrology. An orb of only 1-and-1/2° on each side is allowed, except in the case of aspects personal points (**Sun, Moon,** MC and **Ascendant**), in which an orb of 50° may be used.

As in a traditional horoscope, the **planets** are placed in the inner circle of the cosmogram. However, the **ascendant** (ASC) and **midheaven** (medium-coeli, MC) positions are treated the same as **planets**, and are located according to sign position.

Like traditional astrology, Cosmobiology utilizes the Moon's Node (**Dragon's Head**), but in the 90° circle there is no distinction between the north and south nodes, as they are posited in the same place. (In the 90° circle, oppositions are in **conjunction**.) Cosmobiology pays almost no attention to **sextiles** and **trines** since they generally signify a harmonious state of affairs but seldom denote concrete events. The cosmogram shows only **conjunctions** (0°) **semi-squares** (45°), **squares** (90), **sesqui-squares** (135°) and **oppositions** (180°). These **hard** aspects indicate actual events.

The 90° (outer) circle begins with 0° (located at the top of the chart) and ends at the same spot with 90°. Each 30° sector of the 90° circle is occupied by one of the three quadruplicities, and will contain only those stellar bodies that correspond to the zodiacal signs of that quadruplicity. All stellar bodies are entered in a counter-clockwise manner, beginning from point zero (0°).

A boundary line between each 30° segment of the 90° circle aids accuracy as one inserts each stellar body on the cosmogram. If the position of the **sun**, for instance, is 15° of Libra, one would locate the 15° mark in the Cardinal sector of the cosmogram (0-30°) and draw the appropriate symbol. If the **moon** were posited in 27° of Scorpio, one would locate the 27° mark of the Fixed sector of the cosmogram (30-60°) or, when considering the whole circle, locate 57° and draw in the appropriate symbol. If Venus is at 12° Virgo it will be entered at 12° of the Mutable sector of the cosmogram (60-90°) or, when considering the whole circle, at 72°.

All symbols should be entered as if on a vertical line to the center of the circle, so that when the sheet is turned the symbols will always be in an upright position (Figure 1.) Precision is the key to accurate interpretations.

The "individual" points in a birth chart are:

M = MC = the medium coeli

A = ASC = the ascendant

These are known as the individual points because they move about 1° in 4 minutes. With the aid of the dial, these points can be rectified (*see* **rectification**)

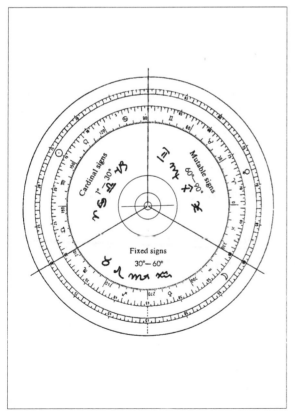

◄

Figure I.

and the precise time of birth confirmed. In the past, the ascendant was considered the most important individual factor; but recently, the MC has been given greater importance. The ascending degree is the degree of the **ecliptic** rising on the eastern horizon at the time of birth—the apparent meeting point of ecliptic and horizon. Since we live and move on the horizontal plane, the individual's ascendant may be interpreted as her/his point of contact with other people and the mutual relationship between the individual and her/his environment. However, it would be a mistake to identify character with the ascendant since the ascendant correlates more with **Jung**'s use of the term "persona" in the sense of a "mask," which a person wears and through which a person plays a "part" in the world. The MC, on the other hand, seems to relate to the actual "inner life"—to one's "ego"—including one's inner ambitions and will to make decisions.

Midpoints

In cosmobiology, not only are the so-called hard aspects given more attention than in traditional astrology, but a unique angular/distance relationship between two stellar bodies is utilized—the midpoint.

Alfred Witte, the founder of the Hamburg School of Astrology, is credited with the introduction of the midpoint system to modern astrology (traditional astrology does not use midpoints). Later, midpoints became the object of intense research by Reinhold Ebertin, and were later incorporated by him into a system that now dominates astrology.

Although midpoints are the primary tools of cosmobiological interpretations, they are not the exclusive property of cosmobiology: Uranian astrologers also use midpoints in conjunction with the eight trans-Neptunian planets, **Cupido, Hades, Zeus, Kronos, Appolon, Admetos, Vulcanus** and **Poseidon**.

The midpoint theory, as the name implies, involves the zodiacal-calculated half-way point between two stellar bodies. Midpoints (also called half-sums) are calculated using the standard mathematical midpoint formula.

Moon	= 5°51′ Cancer	= 95°51′
Node	= 1°51′ Scorpio	= 211°51′

Sum: Moon + Node	= 307°42′
Midpoint Moon/Node	= 153°51′
or	= 3°51′ Virgo/Pisces

In exact investigations one writes the degree-numbers below the names of the stellar bodies, in this way:

Uranus	= Moon/Node
3°46′	3°51′

The midpoint is exact within 5′ (minutes of arc).

In Figure 2 Moon, Uranus, and the node form a grand trine; they are a distance of approximately 120° from one another. According to traditional astrology, one would interpret this stellar grouping as a grand trine only, but according to cosmobiology, there is a direct midpoint as well, since Uranus is in the center, between Moon and Node. The midpoint is expressed as:

Uranus   = Moon/Node

The Solar Arc Direction

Precise work requires not only coordinating number of degrees with years of life but also the calculation of the individual solar arc. The solar arc for a particular year of life denotes the distance between the solar position on the day of birth and the number of days that corresponds to the year of life in question.

◀
Figure 2.

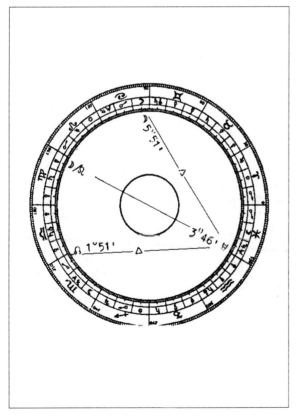

This is also expressible in a formula:

　　birthday
+　days as years of life
_____

=　index day
　　solar position on index day
−　solar position on birthday
_____

=　solar arc

Example: Male born June 20.1971

+　21 days
_____

=　June 41

In June there are

−　30 days
_____

=　July 11.1971 = index day.

The Sun is at 28°55′ Gemini on June 20.1971

The Sun is at -19°01′ Cancer on July 11.1971
_____

　18°54′ = solar arc for 26 days

We now have to calculate the progressed positions to the planets by adding the solar arc of 18°54′ to each planet. In order to differentiate the positions of the natal chart and the progressed positions, the natal chart is on the inside of the 90° wheel and planets are marked in black. The progressed positions are on the outside of the 90° wheel and marked in red (or any other color), thus making the relationships between the progressed cosmogram and the natal figure recognizable. Those configurations that immediately hit the eye are usually the most significant ones. (*See* Figure 3, p. 153.)

It is very important to consider the points lying 180° opposite as well, because these constitute the semi-squares and sesqui-quadrates. These aspects are sometimes ignored because they are difficult to determine. However, statistics show that these aspects are at least equal in importance to other aspects. In the cosmogram they are easy to spot.

Transits

The word **transit** means going over, and in cosmobiology, it refers to one planet's passage over another. Stellar bodies in the cosmogram are primarily considered as the **radix** (or **natal**) and each of the radical stars is marked by *r*. The planets in motion are designated as progressing, abbreviated *pr*.

A differentiation must be made between strong and weak transits—between those that can bring about a change in life, and those that merely have an influence in shaping ordinary, everyday events. The slower a planet moves, the stronger its influence. Whoever has stood under the influence of the transits of Pluto, Neptune or Uranus, all of which are slow-moving planets, is thought to be profoundly affected by them.

The 45° Graphic Ephemerides

Cosmobiologists work with the 45° geocentric and heliocentric ephemerides (**ephemeris**) and the 45° midpoint ephemerides. Reinhold Ebertin introduced the 45° ephemerides, which enables one to obtain—within a few minutes of time—an overview of the year to come by writing the positions from the natal chart in the margin and then drawing straight lines through the graphic ephemeris.

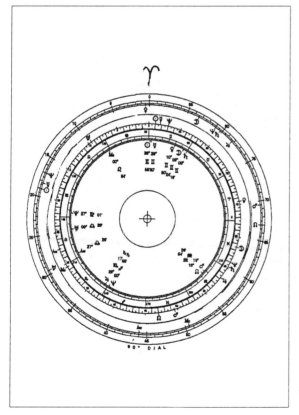

◄

Figure 3.

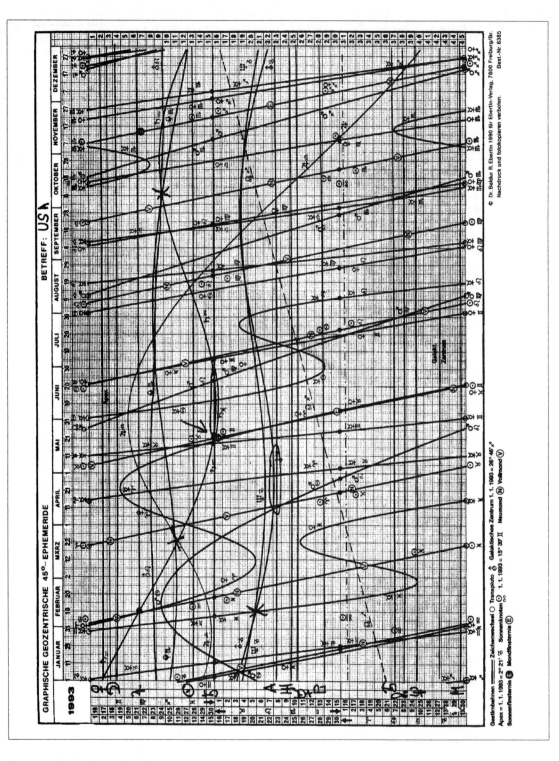

Figure 4: the graphic ephemeris.

In the graphic ephemeris (*see* Figure 4, p. 154), the month of the year can be found at the top, and just below are the periods of 10 years. On the sides are the divisions into degrees, with the right side ranging from 1° to 45°, and on the left side the markings for each sign.

By drawing horizontal lines across the page, points of intersection of the various stellar orbits will become evident. Note that the orbits of the slow-moving planets take on a fairly flat form, whereas the fast-moving planets move in an almost vertical plane. In solar motion the small circles are marked by *N* for new moon and *V* for full moon (from the German *voll-full*). An *E* in the circle indicates an eclipse.

—Irmgard Rauchhaus

Sources:

Ebertin, Elsbeth, and Georg Hoffman. *Fixed Stars and Their Interpretation.* Tempe, Ariz.: American Federation of Astrologers, 1971.

Ebertin, Reinhold. *Applied Cosmobiology.* Tempe, Ariz.: American Federation of Astrologers, 1972.

———. *Directions, Co-Determinants of Fate.* Tempe, Ariz.: American Federation of Astrologers, 1976.

———. *Transits.* Tempe, Ariz.: American Federation of Astrologers, 1976.

Harding, Michael, and Charles Harvey. *Working with Astrology.* New York: Arkana Publications, 1990.

Kimmell, Eleonora. *Patterns of Destiny.* Tempe, Ariz.: American Federation of Astrologers, 1985.

Savalan, Karen Ober. *Midpoint Interpretation Simplified.* Tempe, Ariz.: American Federation of Astrologers, 1983.

Simms, Maria Kay. *Dial Detective.* San Diego: AstroComputing Services, 1989.

Cox, Susie

Susie Cox, born June 17, 1949, in Tucson, Arizona, is an astrology entrepreneur who promotes global communication among astrologers. She publishes the *International Directory of Astrologers,* a worldwide listing of individual astrologers and astrology organizations and businesses from 56 countries. She is an independent producer of astrology videos and produces theatrical entertainment for international conferences. She has been the staff astrologer at Canyon Ranch Health Resort in Tucson since 1981 and is listed in *Marquis' Who's Who in America.*

Cox began the study of astrology at age 7 and has been a professional astrologer since 1971. She studied astronomy at the University of Arizona and teaches experiential workshops in celestial mechanics and astrodrama in the United States, England, and France.

Cox has owned a metaphysical bookstore, published two astrology periodicals, and has interpreted over 20,000 astrology charts. She lives in Tucson.

Selected Publications:

The International Directory of Astrologers. Tucson, Ariz.: Susie Cox, Publisher, 1992.

Crab

The Crab is a popular name for the sign **Cancer**. Its association with moody Cancer is the ultimate source of the term crabby.

Crescentia

Crescentia, **asteroid** 660 (the 660th asteroid to be discovered), is approximately 42 kilometers in diameter and has an **orbital** period of 4 years. Its name is the personification of a Latin word for increase. In a **natal chart**, its location by sign and **house** indicates where and how one is most likely to experience expansion. When **afflicted** by inharmonious **aspects**, Crescentia may show decrease, or less than desirable increase. If prominent in a chart (e.g., **conjunct** the **Sun** or the **Ascendant**), it may show an exceptionally expansive person.

Sources:

Kowal, Charles T. *Asteroids: Their Nature and Utilization.* Chichester, West Sussex, U.K.: Ellis Horwood Limited, 1988.
Room, Adrian. *Dictionary of Astronomical Names.* London: Routledge, 1988.

Crowley, Aleister

Aleister Crowley, a famous English occultist and writer, was born on October 12, 1875, in Leamington, Warwick, England. He was a wealthy eccentric who inherited a fortune and was educated at Cambridge. He joined The Hermetic Order of the Golden Dawn, founded the Magickal group, and wrote numerous books. He was married many times, outraged polite British society, and died of a drug overdose.

He lived in the United States during World War I and had a brief association with **Evangeline Adams** during which he proposed a joint book on astrology, a project never manifested. Crowley did write an astrology book prior to leaving America in 1919, but this manuscript was not published until 1974. Despite the character of the author, Crowley's *Complete Astrological Writings* book is suggestive and merits reading.

He also wrote a short piece, "How Horoscopes are Faked," under the pseudonym Cor Scorpionis (Latin for Scorpion's Heart) that appeared in a small-circulation New York periodical in 1917. This article was a thinly disguised attack on Adams, whom Crowley accused of practicing astrology for profit

(Crowley was wealthy and did not need to work for a living) and other sins. The piece was clearly sour grapes, written after the book project was rejected. Crowley died on December 1, 1947.

Selected Publications:

Aleister Crowley/The Complete Astrological Writings. Edited by John Symonds and Kenneth Grant. London: Gerald Duckworth & Co., 1974. Dallas: Duckworth, 1979.

Sources:

Holden, James H., and Robert A. Hughes. *Astrological Pioneers of America.* Tempe, Ariz.: American Federation of Astrologers, 1988.

Culmination

Culmination usually refers to the arrival of a celestial body at the **midheaven**, the highest point in a chart. It may also refer to the arrival of a celestial body at a point where an **aspect** becomes exact.

Culpepper, Nicolas

Nicolas Culpepper, astrologer and herbalist, was born in Ockley, England, on October 18, 1616, to a wealthy family that owned property throughout Kent and Surrey. His father died before he was born, and he was brought up by his mother in Isfield, where her father was a Church of England minister with Puritan leanings. As a child, he learned Latin and Greek from his grandfather. He was sent to Cambridge, where he majored in classical studies.

Culpepper became engaged and persuaded his fiancée to run away with him and get married. However, while on her way to the rendezvous, she was struck and killed by lightning. Culpepper had a nervous breakdown; after he recovered, he refused to return to his schooling or to enter the ministry. This refusal caused him to lose his inheritance from his mother's family, and he had exhausted the inheritance from his father. He was thus apprenticed to an apothecary.

His apprenticeship was at St. Helens, Higgate, and he inherited and continued the practice of his employer. Culpepper also developed skill in astrology, a field that had intrigued him from a young age. At some point he began correlating astrology and the medicines he was studying as an apothecary. This association may have been suggested by certain contemporary German books that linked the two.

Culpepper married Alice Fields in 1640 and through her wealth was able to set up practice in the East End of London, on Red Lion Street, Spitalfields. He joined the forces opposed to King Charles I in 1642 and fought in the Battle of Edgehill. He was wounded during the battle, and this wound may have triggered the tuberculosis that bothered him for the balance of his life. He evoked the hostility of the medical profession when he published an English translation of the *Pharmacopea* in 1649. Detailed information about herbs and other medical substances had been a professional secret before Culpepper's translation, and other doctors were angry. His incorporation of astrology in this publication was held up for ridicule. He continued in medical practice for the five final years of his life. His wife's money allowed him to devote his time to caring for the poor. He died at the youthful age of 38 on January 10, 1654.

Culpepper's translation of the *Pharmacopea* became known as *Culpepper's Herbal,* and gave him a certain amount of fame. It became a standard reference book and was reprinted often. When herbal medicine was making a comeback in the present century, *Culpepper's Herbal* again became important for its summary of the herbal lore of earlier times. It became a resource for healers and others who wanted alternatives to the harsh chemicals of mainstream medicine.

Selected Publications:

Culpepper, Nicolas. *Culpepper's English Physician and Herbal Remedies.* North Hollywood, Calif.: Wilshire Book Company, 1971. (Originally published 1649.)

Sources:

Inglis, Brian, and Ruth Inglis. *The Alternative Health Guide.* New York: Alfred A. Knopf, 1983.
Melton, J. Gordon. *New Age Encyclopedia.* Detroit: Gale Research, 1990.

Cunningham, Donna

Donna Cunningham is a contemporary astrologer best known for her contributions in the areas of astrology and counseling/healing. She was born in Onawa, Iowa, and holds degrees in psychology from Grinnell College (B.S., 1964, *Phi Beta Kappa*) and in social work from Columbia University (M.S.W., 1967). Cunningham is a licensed social worker in New York and California with over 25 years of counseling experience in alcoholism, women's health, hospitals, psychiatric clinics, and private practice. She has also been a consulting astrologer since 1970, is certified as a professional astrologer by the American Federation of Astrologers and Professional Astrologers Incorporated, and is a member of the National Council for Geocosmic Research and the American Federation of Astrologers Network. She teaches astrology, giving seminars and lectures nationally and internationally, and is the author of 9 books, including *An Astrological Guide to Self-Awareness* (1979), *Healing Pluto Problems* (1986), and *Moon Signs* (1988), as well as hundreds of magazine articles. In 1986, Professional Astrologers Incorporated gave her its annual award for her contributions to the field. Her current emphasis is on professional training for advanced students and astrologers on applying counseling principles to astrological practices—training that includes seminars, a tape series, and, ultimately, a book.

Cunningham uses healing tools like **flower remedies** in her work with clients and has been a flower remedy practitioner since 1981. She edited *Shooting Star,* an independent quarterly integrating astrology and flower remedies, from 1989 to 1991. She also does flower remedy consultations through *Flowers by Mail.*

Selected Publications:

An Astrological Guide to Self-Awareness. Sebastapol, Calif.: CRSC Publications, 1979.
Healing Pluto Problems. York Beach, Maine: Samuel Weiser, 1982.
Astrology and Vibrational Healing. San Rafael, Calif.: Cassandra Books, 1988.
Moon Signs: The Key to Your Inner Life. Westminster, Md.: Ballantine, 1988.

Cupido

Cupido is one of the eight **hypothetical planets** (sometimes referred to as the trans-Neptunian points or planets, TNPs) utilized in Uranian astrology. Cupido is related to small groups, such as the family. It is also, by extension, connected with attitudes toward home and property. Finally, this hypothetical planet is associated with art, the appreciation of beauty, artists, and craftspeople.

Sources:

Lang-Wescott, Martha. *Mechanics of the Future: Asteroids.* Rev. ed. Conway, Mass.: Treehouse Mountain, 1991.
Simms, Maria Kay. *Dial Detective: Investigation with the 90 Degree Dial.* San Diego, Calif.: Astro Computing Services, 1989.

Cusp

In astrology, the term cusp refers to two different but related divisions. First, a cusp is the dividing line separating a sign from its preceding sign. For example, someone born just prior to the **Sun's** movement out of **Cancer** and into **Leo** is said to be "on the cusp of Leo" or "on the Cancer-Leo cusp." An individual born on a cusp is said to manifest traits of both signs.

Second, the cusp is the dividing line separating a **house** from the preceding house. Thus, for example, if an individual's seventh house begins at 10° **Aries** and ends at 13° **Taurus**, the person's seventh house cusp is at 10° Aries. **Planets** located at the end of one house so that they are very close (usually within 5°) to the next house are said to influence the affairs of both houses. Thus, to continue using the previous example, a natal **Venus** located at 8° Aries in the sixth house would exert—over and above its influence in the sixth house—an influence in the seventh house because it is only 2° away from the seventh-house cusp.

Sources:

Brau, Jean-Louis, Helen Weaver, and Allan Edmands. *Larousse Encyclopedia of Astrology.* New York: New American Library, 1980.
Leo, Alan. *Dictionary of Astrology.* Reprint. New York: Astrologer's Library, 1983.

Custer, Edith

Edith Custer, born January 5, 1923, in Whitestone, New York, is a well-known contemporary astrologer. She started studying around 1968 and is fortunate to be able to count some of the best teachers in astrology as her instructors.

Since 1974, with the exception of three years, she has been the editor and publisher of *The Mercury Hour,* an international astrology magazine. She began lecturing and teaching in 1974 and has lectured in almost every state in the union as well as Australia and New Zealand. She has also been chairperson for the advisory board of the National Council for Geocosmic Research (NCGR) since the late 1970s and is now a member of the board of directors.

In 1984, Custer received the Marc Edmund Jones Award; in 1989, received one of the first Regulus Awards, presented by the UAC; and has received several other awards.

D

Daily Motion

Daily motion is the **angular distance**, expressed in degrees (°) and minutes (′) of an arc, that a **planet** travels in the course of a day.

Day Horoscope

A day horoscope is a **horoscope** in which the **Sun** is above the **horizon**.

Days of the Week

In ancient times, astrology was a universal language or symbolic code that was applied to the interpretation of every imaginable phenomenon. As far back as Roman times, the days of the week were correlated with the traditional **planets** (the **Sun**, the **Moon**, and the five planets visible to the naked eye): Monday was thought to be **ruled** by the Moon ("moonday"), Tuesday by **Mars**, Wednesday by **Mercury**, Thursday by **Jupiter**, Friday by **Venus**, Saturday by **Saturn** ("saturnday"), and Sunday by the Sun ("sunday"). These days were regarded as lucky for people ruled by the corresponding planets (e.g., Monday was regarded as lucky for **Cancer**, the sign ruled by the Moon), and an activity ruled by a particular planet was said to be enhanced when carried out on a day ruled by the same planet (e.g., Mercury-ruled Wednesday was good for writing and sending letters—activities ruled by the planet Mercury). Weeks, unlike months and years, appear to be unnatural periods not correlated with any natural phenomenon; but, in fact, weeks are based on subdivisions of the lunar cycle in quarters: new moon, first quarter, full moon, and last quarter. While modern **astrologers** are aware of these **rulerships**, they are rarely utilized for practical astrological purposes.

Sources:

Hall, Manly P. *Astrological Keywords.* 1958. Reprint. Savage, Md.: Littlefield Adams, 1975.
Rasmussen, Steven C. "Secrets of the Seven-Day Week." *The Mountain Astrologer* 292 (February/
    March 1992): 3–6.

Death Chart

A death chart is, as the name indicates, a **horoscope** calculated for the time of death.

Debility

A debility is a weakening of a **planet** through its placement in certain signs and **houses**. Planets in the sign of their **detriment** or **fall**, or in the house opposed to the **natural house** ruled by the planet, are said to be debilitated. The basic idea informing the notion of debility is that there are certain signs or houses whose energies are incompatible with the characteristics of certain planets, and that this inharmonious blending of energies serves to lessen the strength of a planet's influence. For various reasons, but principally because the influence of planets so placed does not actually seem to be weakened, contemporary astrologers have largely abandoned the use of this term.

Decan (Decante)

Each sign of the **zodiac** occupies an arc of 30° (the 360° of a circle divided by 12 signs equals 30° per sign). Every sign is subdivided into 3 decans or decantes of 10°, each of which is associated with 3 signs of the same **element**. Thus, for example, **Scorpio**, a **water sign**, is subdivided into a Scorpio decan (from 0° Scorpio to 10° Scorpio), a **Pisces** decan (from 10° Scorpio to 20° Scorpio), and a **Cancer** decan (from 20° Scorpio to 30° Scorpio). The uniform pattern of the decans is for the first 10° of every sign to be associated with the same sign. In other words, the first decan of **Aries** is the Aries decan, the first decan of **Taurus** is the Taurus decan, and so forth.

The second decan is associated with the next sign of the same element in the natural order of the zodiac. Thus, for instance, the second decan of Aries is the **Leo** decan (the next **fire sign**), the second decan of Taurus is the **Virgo** decan (the next **earth sign**), etc.

The third decan is associated with the remaining sign of the same element. To continue with the same examples, the third decan of Aries is the **Sagittarius** decan, and the third decan of Taurus is the **Capricorn** decan.

For signs placed later in the zodiac, one continues around the zodiac, past the Pisces-Aries **cusp** (the boundary between the last and first signs), to pick up the next signs of the same element past this cusp. For example, for the sign **Aquarius**, which is the last **air sign** in the zodiac, the first decan is the Aquarius decan, the second decan is the **Gemini** decan (Gemini is the next air sign after one crosses the Pisces-Aries divide), and the third decan is **Libra** (the next air sign in succession). These relationships are clearer in outline form:

Aries–Aries decan, 0°–10°; Leo decan, 10°–20°; Sagittarius decan, 20°–30°; Taurus–Taurus decan, 0°–10°; Virgo decan, 10°–20°; Capricorn decan, 20°–30°; Gemini–Gemini decan, 0°–10°; Libra decan, 10°–20°; Aquarius decan, 20°–30°; Cancer–Cancer decan, 0° –10°; Scorpio decan, 10°–20°; Pisces decan, 20°–30°; Leo–Leo decan, 0°–10°; Sagittarius decan, 10°–20°; Aries decan, 20°–30°; Virgo–Virgo decan, 0°–10°; Capricorn decan, 10°–20°; Taurus decan, 20°–30°; Libra–Libra decan, 0°–10°; Aquarius decan, 10°–20°; Gemini decan, 20°–30°; Scorpio–Scorpio decan, 0°–10°; Pisces decan, 10°–20; Cancer decan, 20°–30°; Sagittarius–Sagittarius decan, 0°–10°; Aries decan, 10°–20°; Leo decan, 20°–30; Capricorn–Capricorn decan, 0°–10°; Taurus decan, 10°–20°; Virgo decan, 20°–30°; Aquarius–Aquarius decan, 0°–10°; Gemini decan, 10°–20°; Libra decan, 20°–30°; Pisces–Pisces decan, 0°–10°; Cancer decan, 10°–20°; Scorpio decan, 20°–30°

The decans indicate a subsidiary influence. For example, someone born when the **Sun** was in the middle of Scorpio will be slightly influenced by the sign Pisces (because the Sun was in the Pisces decan of Scorpio); although the person will still be Scorpio, the normal intensity of this sign will be somewhat moderated by Pisces. This modification is relatively minor and is usually ignored, unless one is examining the subtleties of a particular chart. When decans are used at all, the focus is almost always the **sun sign**; (for example, the decans of the **planets** and the other points in a **natal chart**, with the possible exception of the **Moon** and the **ascendant** (rising sign), are usually ignored).

Sources:

Bach, Eleanor. *Astrology from A to Z: An Illustrated Source Book.* New York: Philosophical Library, 1990.
Lee, Dal. *Dictionary of Astrology.* New York: Paperback Library, 1969.

Decile

A decile is a minor **aspect** of 36°, created by subdividing a circle (360°) into 10 parts. It is half of a **quintile** (72°) and is thus related to the family of aspects derived from dividing a circle into fifths. Like quintiles, deciles refer to the aptitudes or talents related to the **planets** involved in the aspect, though the influence of a decile is less marked. It is given an **orb of influence** of 1°–2°.

Declination

The **solar system** lies more or less in one geometric plane, which is why astrological charts can be drawn in two dimensions. If the **celestial equator** (which is the terrestrial equator extended out into space, and projected against the background of the **stars**) is used as a point of reference, it is found that, at any given time, most celestial bodies do not lie exactly in the same plane, but, rather, are located somewhat north or south of the celestial equator. The **angular distance** (distance expressed in degrees [°] and minutes [']) of these bodies north or south of the celestial equator is their declination. Because some astrologers regard **planets** at the same declination as being in **aspect** with one another, planets' declinations are often recorded in **ephemerides**.

Decreasing or Increasing in Light

From the new to the full moon, the **Moon** is said to be increasing in light, for obvious reasons. Similarly, the Moon is said to be decreasing in light from full to new moon.

Decumbiture Chart

A decumbiture chart is a **horoscope** calculated for the moment one goes to bed at the start of an illness. It is sometimes used in **medical astrology** for prognosis.

Degree

A unit of angular measurement, a degree is 1/360th the circumference of a circle. The number 360 probably comes from older notions about the year's being 360 days in length.

A degree (°) is divided into minutes: one minute (') is 1/60th of a degree. And a minute is divided into seconds: one second (") is 1/60th of a minute.

Degree Rising

The degree rising is the degree of the sign of the **zodiac** on the **ascendant**.

Degrees, Meanings of

In astrologers' quest for subsidiary bands of influence, the 12 signs of the **zodiac** have been subdivided in various ways. **Decans** (10° arcs) and **dwads** (2 1/2° arcs) are two such subdivisions. It was almost inevitable that astrologers would eventually speculate about the astrological meanings of the individual degrees of the zodiac. Unfortunately, there has been less general agreement on the meanings of the degrees than on the meaning of other subdivisions. One contemporary author, for example, counts no less than 17 distinct systems for assigning significance to the degrees. This lack of unanimity is less important, however, than astrologers' disagreement over other issues, because, for purposes of individual chart interpretation, degree meanings provide a level of detail that astrologers rarely have time to develop and, hence, most do not use them. Probably the most widely used system among those who do consider degree meanings is the Sabian Symbols popularized by **Marc Edmund Jones** and **Dane Rudhyar.**

Sources:

Jones, M. E. *The Sabian Symbols.* New York: Sabian Publishing Society, 1953.
Rudhyar, Dane. *The Astrology of Personality.* New York: Lucis Trust, 1936.

Delineation

Delineation is an alternative term for astrological interpretation. Traditionally, delineation meant the interpretation of specific components of an astrological chart, and the term **synthesis** was reserved for the interpretation of the chart as a whole. In current usage, however, delineation can mean any level of interpretaiton.

Dembowska

Dembowska, **asteroid** 349 (the 349th asteroid to be discovered), is approximately 164 kilometers in diameter and has an **orbital** period of 5 years. It was named after the Italian astronomer Baron Ercole Dembowska. The unusual name of this planetoid—which seems to suggest an unusual mythological figure, but which does not appear in any mythological dictionaries—led to its inclusion in *The Asteroid Ephemeris: Dudu, Dembowska, Pittsburgh, Frigga,* Batya Stark and Mark Pottenger's tour de force of astrological humor.

Sources:

Kowal, Charles T. *Asteroids: Their Nature and Utilization.* Chichester, West Sussex, U.K.: Ellis Horwood Limited, 1988.
Room, Adrian. *Dictionary of Astronomical Names.* London: Routledge, 1988.
Stark, Batya, and Mark Pottenger. *The Asteroid Ephemeris: Dudu, Dembowska, Pittsburgh, Frigga.* San Diego, Calif.: Astro Computing Services, 1982.

Demeter

Demeter, **asteroid** 1,108 (the 1,108th asteroid to be discovered), is approximately 21 kilometers in diameter and has an **orbital** period of 3.8 years. Demeter, whom the Romans equated with Ceres was one of the 12 great Olympian deities of the Greek pantheon. She was the goddess of agriculture and the guardian of the institution of marriage. According to Lang-Wescott, Demeter represents nurturance. This nurturance can manifest as nurturance of others or of self. This asteroid's key words are *mother* and *child*. Lehman believes Demeter has an influence similar to that of the asteroid Ceres but is less practical and more spiritual than her Roman parallel. Demeter, in other words, represents more of a spiritual nurturance than Ceres. Also, to take an example proffered by Lehman, Ceres represents vocational work, whereas Demeter represents more avocational work.

Sources:

Lang-Wescott, Martha. *Asteroids-Mechanics: Ephemerides II*. Conway, Mass.: Treehouse Mountain, 1990.
———. *Mechanics of the Future: Asteroids*. Rev. ed. Conway, Mass.: Treehouse Mountain, 1991.
Lehman, J. Lee. *The Ultimate Asteroid Book*. West Chester, Penn.: Whitford Press, 1988.

Depression

In traditional astrology, depression is an alternate term for **fall**.

Descendant

The descendant is the **cusp** (beginning) of the seventh house. In a **natal chart**, it corresponds to the western horizon at the moment of birth and is thus the point where, over the course of a 24-hour period, **planets** "descend" out of the sky. As one of the four **angles**—the others being the **ascendant** (first-house cusp), the midheaven/**medium coeli** (tenth-house cusp), and the **nadir/ imum coeli**-(fourth-house cusp)—the descendant is one of the more powerful locations for a planet. Thus, a planet in a close **conjunction** with the descendant is traditionally regarded as having a strong influence over the entire chart, although such influences are more marked in the case of planets conjunct with the ascendant and the midheaven.

Sources:

Bach, Eleanor. *Astrology from A to Z: An Illustrated Source Book*. New York: Philosophical Library, 1990.
Fleming-Mitchell, Leslie. *Running Press Glossary of Astrology Terms*. Philadelphia: Running Press, 1977.

Detriment

The term detriment is part of a traditional way of classifying certain sign placements of **planets**. A planet is said to be in its **dignity** when it is in the sign it **rules** (e.g., **Mars** in **Aries,** the **Sun** in **Leo,** etc.). There are also certain placements said to be especially favorable for a planet that are traditionally termed **exaltations** (to continue with the foregoing example, Mars in **Capricorn,** the Sun in Aries). When a planet is placed in the sign opposite its exaltation, it is said to be in its **fall** (Mars in **Cancer,** the Sun in **Libra**). A planet is said to be in its detriment when placed in the sign opposite the sign that it rules (Mars in **Libra,** the Sun in **Aquarius**). For example, because **Venus** rules **Taurus,** this planet is in detriment when placed in the sign **Scorpio.** As the name implies, being in detriment is regarded as an unfortunate placement. A planet in its detriment is traditionally regarded as being out of harmony with the sign and consequently weakened (in a position of **debility**).

For the most part, contemporary astrological research has tended to disconfirm that a planet in its traditional detriment is weakened. However, it is sometimes the case that planets in detriment have unfortunate effects. In the example cited, Venus, as the planet of love, harmony, and relationships is not well placed (especially in a **natal chart**) in Scorpio, a sign noted for jealously, possessiveness, and sexual obsession. There are, nevertheless, certain obvious problems with this traditional understanding. The Sun, for example, rules Leo, the sign opposite Aquarius. This means that the 1-out-of-12 people in the world born with an Aquarius **sun sign** have their sun in the sign of its detriment. This particular placement is not normally regarded as being unfortunate, however, making **detriment** appear inapplicable in this case. More generally, all of the traditional detriments should be regarded with caution, used when relevant to a particular individual's chart and rejected when not.

Sources:

Brau, Jean-Louis, Helen Weaver, and Allan Edmands. *Larousse Encyclopedia of Astrology.* New York: New American Library, 1980.
deVore, Nicholas. *Encyclopedia of Astrology.* New York: Philosophical Library, 1947.

Dexter

Dexter (from a Latin term meaning right), refers to one of the many ways of classifying astrological **aspects**. The antonym is **sinister** (meaning "left," not "evil"). A dexter aspect occurs when a faster-moving **planet** makes an aspect with a slower-moving planet that is located clockwise from it (to the "right") in the **zodiac**. While astrologers from **Ptolemy** onward have regarded dexter and sinister aspects as having somewhat different influences, the differences are comparatively minor. In most general chart readings this distinction is ignored.

Diana

Diana, **asteroid** 78 (the 78th asteroid to be discovered), was named after the Roman goddess of the hunt and the **Moon**. Its orbital period is a little over 9 years, and it is 144 kilometers in diameter. Diana is one of the more recent asteroids to be investigated by astrologers. Preliminary material on Diana can be found in Demetra George and Douglas Bloch's *Astrology for Yourself,* and an **ephemeris** (table of celestial locations) for Diana can be found in the back of the second edition of George and Bloch's *Asteroid Goddesses.* Unlike the **planets**, which are associated with a wide range of phenomena, the smaller asteroids are said to represent a single principle. George and Bloch give Diana's principle as "survival and self-protection." J. Lee Lehman finds that Diana's position in a chart "shows the place and area of life in which a person expects absolute respect and obedience, as if s/he were divine" (p. 75). She also observes that individuals with a prominent Diana are intolerant of those they regard as "lesser types."

Sources:

Dobyns, Zipporah. *Expanding Astrology's Universe.* San Diego, Calif.: Astro Computing Services, 1983.

George, Demetra, with Douglas Bloch. *Astrology for Yourself: A Workbook for Personal Transformation* . Berkeley, Calif.: Wingbow Press, 1987.

———. *Asteroid Goddesses: The Mythology, Psychology and Astrology of the Reemerging Feminine.* 2d ed. San Diego, Calif.: Astro Computing Services, 1990.

Lehman, J. Lee. *The Ultimate Asteroid Book.* West Chester, Pa.: Whitford Press, 1988.

Dignity

The term dignity is part of a traditional schema for classifying certain sign placements of **planets**. A planet is said to be in its dignity (or in its **domicile**) when in the sign it **rules**. For example, because **Mercury** rules **Gemini**, it is in dignity when in the sign Gemini. As the name of the term implies, this is regarded as a fortunate placement; a planet in its dignity is traditionally regarded as being in harmony with the sign and consequently strengthened. For example, a person born during a period when Mercury was in Gemini has—unless other factors in the **natal chart** mitigate against it—a good mind and good basic communication skills.

The attitude of modern astrologers toward the traditional dignities is mixed, partly because planets placed in their dignities are not always the unmitigated blessings one might anticipate. The **Moon** in the sign of its dignity, **Cancer**, for example, is a highly sensitive placement that, unless counterbalanced by other factors, tends to make a person too sensitive and moody. More generally, all of the traditional dignities should be utilized with caution, accepted when relevant to a particular individual's chart and rejected when not.

Brau, Jean-Louis, Helen Weaver, and Allan Edmands. *Larousse Encyclopedia of Astrology.* New York: New American Library, 1980.

deVore, Nicholas. *Encyclopedia of Astrology.* New York: Philosophical Library, 1947.

Direct

When a **planet** is moving from west to east in the natural order of the **zodiac,** it is said to be moving direct. Direct is the antonym to **retrograde,** which is the **apparent movement** of a planet backward through the zodiac.

Directions

Directions is an alternative designation for **progressions.**

Dispositor

A **planet** is the dispositor of other planets when they are located in the sign the first planet **rules**. For instance, if both **Mercury** and **Mars** are in the sign **Taurus,** then **Venus,** the ruler of Taurus, is the dispositor of Mercury and Mars. One would say that Mercury and Mars are "disposed by" or "disposed of by" Venus. A planet in its own sign, such as Venus in Taurus, is said to dispose itself (or, sometimes, to dispose of itself). In some charts, one can trace a chain of dispositors (e.g., Venus is the dispositor of Mercury and Mars, while Jupiter is the dispositor of Venus, and so on) until stopping at a single planet that is the final or ultimate dispositor of every other planet in the chart; such a planet is regarded as having an especially strong influence over the entire **horoscope.**

Sources:

Bach, Eleanor. *Astrology from A to Z: An Illustrated Source Book.* New York: Philosophical Library, 1990.

Brau, Jean-Louis, Helen Weaver, and Allan Edmands. *Larousse Encyclopedia of Astrology.* New York: New American Library, 1980.

Dissociate Aspects

Dissociate aspect was at one time an alternate term for **quincunx.** In contemporary astrology, this expression usually refers to an **aspect** in which the component **planets** are not in the anticipated signs. For example, it is normally the case that the planets making a **trine** aspect (120°) are in the same **element.** Thus, a planet in **Scorpio** will usually makes trines only with planets in the other **water signs, Cancer** and **Pisces**; a planet in **Taurus** makes trines with planets in other **earth signs**; etc. However, because an aspect does not have to be exact to be regarded as effective, sometimes—to continue using the trine example—two planets in a trine can be in signs of different elements. In this case, the trine would be termed dissociate.

Dissociate Signs

Dissociate signs are signs of the **zodiac** that are either in adjacent signs or are five signs away from each other.

Diurnal

Diurnal means "of or belonging to the day." In classical astrology, particular **planets** were classified as diurnal and others as **nocturnal**, no matter where they were in a **horoscope**. In contemporary astrology, planets are diurnal if they are located above the horizon (in **houses** 7 through 12). Often astrologers will say that planets above the horizon line show their influence more in the public

▶
Diurnal.

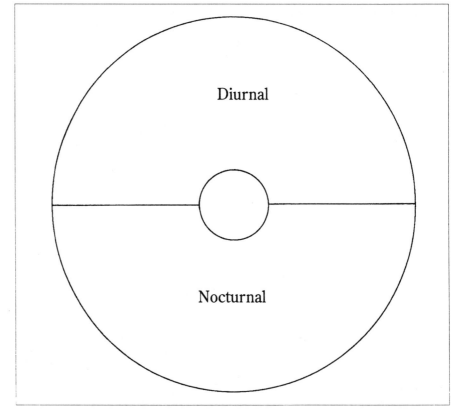

sphere, whereas planets below the horizon are more private, but this distinction clearly breaks down when considering planets in such locations as the twelfth house (a largely private house situated above the horizon). The term diurnal arc refers to the distance, expressed in degrees (°) and minutes (′) of a circle, that a planet traverses between its rising in the east and its setting in the west. Classical astrology also classified signs as diurnal (the **masculine signs**) and nocturnal (the **feminine signs**). Contemporary astrologers no longer use the expression diurnal sign.

Sources:

Bach, Eleanor. *Astrology from A to Z: An Illustrated Source Book*. New York: Philosophical Library, 1990.
Brau, Jean-Louis, Helen Weaver, and Allan Edmands. *Larousse Encyclopedia of Astrology*. New York: New American Library, 1980.

Doane, Doris Chase

Doris Chase Doane, born April 4, 1913, in Mansfield, Massachusetts, was the eldest of five children of Willis E. Chase and Rose Beaulac Chase. She graduated from Mansfield High School (1931), Wilfred Academy (1936), and UCLA (1944), where she earned a degree in psychology. She became interested in astrology in 1936, and began teaching it in 1938. In 1944, she received the Hermetician Certificate from the **Church of Light** after passing the 21 Brotherhood of Light courses and began teaching classes at the Los Angeles Church of Light. In 1946, she married a minister of that organization, Edward Doane, becoming an ordained minister herself in 1946. Doane was associated with the Church of Light from the 1940s to 1972, when she moved from Los Angeles.

She began writing in 1945 and has since published over 1,500 articles and books, several of which have become standard reference works, including the *Index to the Brotherhood of Light Lessons* and *Horoscopes of the U.S. Presidents*. President of the American Federation of Astrologers since 1979, Doane is cofounder of Professional Astrologers, Inc., a charter member of the Athena Astrological Society, and a member of the Astrologers Guild of America and several other astrological organizations. She has traveled widely lecturing and conducting workshops and has received many awards from American as well as foreign astrological groups. She is a strong advocate of professionalism and certification in astrological practice.

Selected Publications:

Astrology—30-Years Research. Los Angeles: The Church of Light, 1956.
Astrological Rulerships. Redondo Beach, Calif.: Foundation of Scientific Spiritual Understanding, 1970.
Horoscopes of the Presidents. 2d ed. Hollywood Calif.: Professional Astrologers Inc., 1971.

How to Prepare and Pass an Astrologer's Certificate Exam. San Francisco: Quarto Productions, 1973.
Progressions in Action. Tempe, Ariz.: American Federation of Astrologers, 1977.
Astrology as a Business. Tempe, Ariz.: American Federation of Astrologers, 1986.

Sources:

Holden, James H., and Robert A. Hughes. *Astrological Pioneers of America.* Tempe, Ariz.: American Federation of Astrologers, 1988.

Dobyns, Zipporah

Zipporah Dobyns is a prominent contemporary astrologer best known for her formulation of the astrological "alphabet" and for her pioneering work in **asteroid** studies. Born in Chicago, Illinois, on August 26, 1921, she graduated from the University of Chicago (B.A., anthropology, 1944, *Phi Beta Kappa*) and pursued graduate work in anthropology at the University of Chicago and the University of Arizona. She married Henry F. Dobyns in 1948 and had four children, all of whom eventually chose to take her maiden name: Rique Pottenger, William Pottenger, **Maritha Pottenger**, and Mark Pottenger. She was separated from her husband in 1956.

Dobyns began to study astrology in 1956, initially being taught by a student of the Church of Light. She was one of the first people to take the American Federation of Astrologers exams in 1960, the first time the organization gave such tests. She went to school at the University of Arizona at Tucson, where she completed masters and doctoral programs in clinical psychology (M.A., 1966; Ph.D., 1969). While in Tucson, she also hosted a daily radio program as well as a weekly newspaper column. She was ordained in the Los Angeles Community Church of Religious Science in 1968 and moved to Los Angeles in 1969 to work with the church.

Dobyns has lectured in 38 states and 13 countries. She has received numerous recognitions of her contributions to astrology, including the Regulus Award for contributions to astrological education (1992) and certificates for contributions to the field from Professional Astrologers Incorporated of California. She is a board member of the International Society for Astrological Research and an advisory board member for the National Council for Geocosmic Research and the Association for Astrological Networking. She is the primary contributor to two periodicals, *The Mutable Dilemma* and *Asteroid-World,* and the author of *Evolution Through the Zodiac* (1964), *Finding the Person in the Horoscope* (1973), *The Zodiac as a Key to History* (1977), *Expanding Astrology's Universe* (1983), and, (written with Nancy Roof) *The Astrologer's Casebook* (1973).

Selected Publications:

Evolution Through the Zodiac. 1964. Reprint. Louisiana: TIA Publications, 1972.
The Astrologer's Casebook. By Dobyns and Nancy Roof. Louisiana: TIA Publications, 1973.
Finding the Person in the Horoscope. 2d. ed. Louisiana: TIA Publications, 1976.
The Zodiac as a Key to History. 2d. ed. Louisiana: TIA Publications, 1977.
Expanding Astrology's Universe. 2d ed. San Diego, Calif.: Astro Computing Services, 1988.

Dog Days

Dog days is a 40-day period, usually given as July 4 to August 11, that is regarded as being the hottest time of the year. This period was originally calculated from the **heliacal** rising of Sirius, the Dog Star, after which dog days received its name.

Dolphin

The Dolphin is a traditional alternate name for the sign **Pisces**.

Domal Dignity

A **planet** is in its domal dignity when it is placed in the sign it **rules**. Traditional astrology referred to such a planet as domiciliated.

Domicile

In traditional astrology, a **planet** placed in the sign that it **rules** was said to be in domicile, a word derived from the Latin for home. Thus, a planet in domicile (e.g., **Mercury** in **Gemini**, **Mars** in **Aries**, etc.) is "at home," a location that allows the planet to express its nature freely. A planet in domicile is in the sign of its **dignity**, and an alternative term for domicile is domal dignity. The term domicile is infrequently used in modern astrology; when it is, it is often used in a more general sense to denote location, as when someone says that such and such a planet is "domiciled" in such and such a **house**.

Doryphory

A doryphory, or "spearbearer," is a **planet** that rises shortly before the **Sun** rises—or shortly *after* the **Moon** rises—in the same or in a contiguous sign.

Double Signs

The double signs, also called the double-bodied signs or the bicorporeal signs, are **Gemini**, **Pisces**, and **Sagittarius**. This expression comes from the symbols for these signs, which are twins for Gemini, two fish for Pisces, and a part human, part horse (centaur) for Sagittarius. **Virgo** is sometimes also included in this category, which would make all of the **mutable signs** double signs. Double signs, particularly Gemini and Pisces, are sometimes used to indicate "twos" in a chart interpretation. Thus, for example, someone with a double sign on the **cusp** (beginning) of her or his seventh **house** (the house of partnerships) might be told that she or he will have two marriages, or someone with a double sign on the cusp of the fifth house (which refers to children, among other things) might be told that she or he will have two children, with the possibility of twins.

Sources:

Brau, Jean-Louis, Helen Weaver, and Allan Edmands. *Larousse Encyclopedia of Astrology*. New York: New American Library, 1980.
Gettings, Fred. *Dictionary of Astrology*. London: Routledge & Kegan Paul, 1985.

Dragon's Head

An alternate term for the north **lunar node**. As a point where **eclipses** occur, the lunar nodes were linked to ancient mythological notions about a celestial dragon that swallowed and regurgitated the **Sun**—hence the name.

Dragon's Tail

Dragon's Tail is an alternate term for the south **lunar node**.

Druids and Astrology

See: History of Western Astrology

Dudu

Dudu, **asteroid** 564 (the 564th asteroid to be discovered), is approximately 50 kilometers in diameter and has an **orbital** period of 4.6 years. It was named after a character in Nietzsche's *Thus Spake Zarathustra*. The unusual name of this planetoid (the connotations of which are obvious enough) led to its inclusion in *The Asteroid Ephemeris: Dudu, Dembowska, Pittsburgh, Frigga,* Batya Stark and Mark Pottenger's tour de force of astrological humor.

Sources:

Kowal, Charles T. *Asteroids: Their Nature and Utilization.* Chichester, West Sussex, U.K.: Ellis Horwood Limited, 1988.

Room, Adrian. *Dictionary of Astronomical Names.* London: Routledge, 1988.

Stark, Batya, and Mark Pottenger. *The Asteroid Ephemeris: Dudu, Dembowska, Pittsburgh, Frigga.* San Diego, Calif.: Astro Computing Services, 1982.

Dwad

Dwad, or *dwadashamsa,* derived from the Sanskrit for 12-division, refers to the 12 subdivisions of 2 1/2° that comprise a sign. It is one of the few concepts from **Hindu astrology** that have been regularly utilized by Western astrologers. Each of the 12 dwads is associated with one of the 12 signs, with the first dwad being associated with the larger sign being subdivided into twelfths. The second dwad is then associated with the next sign in the order of the **zodiac,** and so forth through all 12 signs. Thus, for example, the first dwad of **Scorpio** is the Scorpio dwad; the second dwad of Scorpio is the **Sagittarius** dwad; the third, **Capricorn;** the fourth, **Aquarius;** etc.

The dwads indicate a subsidiary influence. Thus, for example, someone born when the **Sun** was at 6° Scorpio will be slightly influenced by the sign Capricorn; although she or he will still be Scorpio, the normal influence of this sign will be somewhat modified by Capricorn. This modification is relatively minor and is usually ignored by Western astrologers unless they are examining the subtleties of a particular chart. When dwads are used at all, the focus is almost always the **sun sign** (the dwads of the other **planets** are usually ignored).

Sources:

Gettings, Fred. *Dictionary of Astrology.* London: Routledge & Kegan Paul, 1985.

Lee, Dal. *Dictionary of Astrology.* New York: Paperback Library, 1969.

E

Eagle

The **constellation** Aquila is an eagle, but in astrology it is sometimes taken as an alternate term for the sign **Scorpio**. The notion here is that Scorpio rules the principle of metamorphosis and regeneration. The lowly, stinging scorpion is an adequate symbol for the unregenerate Scorpio but does not appropriately describe transformed members of this sign. The image of the noble eagle, however, captures the highest potential of Scorpio.

Eaks, Duane L.

Duane L. Eaks was born on March 6, 1940, in Montrose, Colorado. He was educated at Northern Colorado University (B.A, chemistry, 1963), San Diego State University (M.A., guidance and counseling, 1967), and the University of California at Berkeley (Ed.D., counseling psychology, 1972). Eaks commenced astrology study in Australia in 1977 at the Melbourne Academy of Cosmobiology, studying under Pamela Rowe, Gillian Murray (Helfgott), and Doris Greaves, founder of the Federation of Australian Astrologers (FAA). He completed certificate exams in 1978 and has since done extensive study of traditional and humanistic astrology via workshops, lectures, and personal study.

Eaks has been a member of the National Executive Committee of the FAA since 1982 and was national secretary from 1982 to 1988. He has also been treasurer of the Victoria FAA branch and newsletter editor and past president of the Regulus Ebertin Study Group, Melbourne. He was appointed professional member of the FAA in 1985 and elected fellow member in 1988.

Eaks has lectured extensively in Australia on astrological counseling and astrological psychology incorporating Jung's theories. Other areas of special interest are astrodrama and investigation of gay life-styles via astrology and psychology. Eaks has been a senior lecturer and counseling psychologist for the past 20 years at the Royal Melbourne Institute of Technology in Victoria. He also serves as a psychological consultant to various community agencies including the Victoria AIDS Council.

Selected Publications:

"Symbolic Analogies of the Elements." *Regulus-Ebertin Newsletter* 1, no. 1 (September 1981): 6–7.
"Astro-Biographical Sketch of John Hinckley." *Regulus-Ebertin Newsletter* 2, no. 1 (August 1982).
Student Project Guide on Astrology, edited by Eaks. Heidelberg, Victoria, Australia: Federation of Australian Astrologers, 1991.
"Projection—The Unconscious Mirror." *The FAA Journal* 21, no. 4 (December 1991): 23–33.

Earth Signs

The 12 signs of the **zodiac** are subdivided according to the four classical **elements** (earth, air, fire, and water). The earth signs (the earth triplicity or earth trigon) are **Taurus, Virgo,** and **Capricorn.** Astrologically, earth refers to practicality. Earth sign practicality manifests as an aptitude for the financial and material dimension of life.

The practicality of the earth element shows itself somewhat differently in each of the signs of the earth **triplicity.** Taurus's earthy nature emerges as interest and skill in the accumulation of material resources. Virgo's comes through as attention to details, attention to physical health, and the ability to

▶
Earth signs.

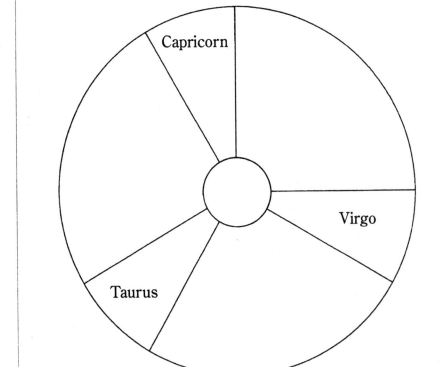

construct material objects. Capricorn's earthy nature typically manifests as the talent to manage business.

Negative earth people can be so practical that they miss the other dimensions of life. Unless counterbalanced by other factors, excessive earth in a chart indicates an individual who is materialistic, insensitive, and unimaginative. Conversely, lack of earth can indicate a person who is impractical and unreliable.

Sources:

Hand, Robert. *Horoscope Symbols.* Rockport, Mass.: Para Research, 1981.
Sakoian, Frances, and Louis S. Acker. *The Astrologer's Handbook.* New York: Harper & Row, 1989.

Earthquakes

Astrologers have been concerned with correlations between celestial events and terrestrial traumas from the very beginning of astrology. The Mesopotamians, as well as other ancient peoples, viewed earthquakes, plagues, droughts, and the like as being tied to such unusual heavenly occurences as **eclipses** and **comets**. For their part, contemporary astrologers have viewed everything from the **heliocentric nodes of the planets** to the interaction of **Uranus** with specific planetary **configurations** as influencing earthquakes. The problem with all current methods is that, *after* an upheaval has occurred, it is easy enough to look back at a chart for the given day and point out the various factors that appear to be correlated with the event. Prediction, however, is another matter. Although many have claimed to have found the key to earthquake prediction, no factor yet discovered dependably predicts such upheavals.

The closest thing to a reliable "earthquake factor" is a **syzygy** (an alignment of three celestial bodies in a straight line) involving Earth, the **Sun**, and the **Moon**. Syzygys occur every new and full moon; exact syzygys occur during eclipses (a partial verification of ancient astrology). Researchers who have observed this correlation speculate that it is the larger gravitational force—generated by the combined gravity of the Sun and the Moon pulling together (or apart) along the same axis—that disturbs the crust of the Earth and sets the stage for an earthquake (which may occur immediately or within a week of the syzygy).

In addition to the exactness of the alignment, people involved in earthquake prediction–such as Jim Berkland, author and publisher of *Syzygy: An Earthquake Newsletter*—also pay attention to the distance of the Moon from Earth (and, to a lesser extent, the distance of the Sun from Earth). The Moon's **orbit** is eliptical rather than circular. The point farthest away from Earth is the Moon's **apogee**; the closest point is the Moon's **perigee**. The distance between Earth and the Moon varies 14% every 15 days. Clearly, the gravitational force exerted by the Moon on Earth is greatest during a perigee, making the potential for earthquakes greater when syzygys occur during perigees (e.g., the Santa Cruz, California, earthquake of October 1989 took place a few days after a perigean full moon). The combination of an eclipse with a lunar perigee is almost certain to lead to a terrestrial upheaval somewhere on our **planet**. A good reference source for determining both perigees and eclipses is Neil F. Michelsen's *Tables of Planetary Phenomena.*

Another, nonastrological factor that acts as a predictor is the odd behavior of animals prior to an earthquake. Berkland observes that the number of missing animals reported in newspapers, for instance, shoots up just before an earthquake, as if they were somehow responding to a change in Earth's magnetic field. In the March 1992 issue of his newsletter (p. 7), Berkland refers to a passage in Helmut Tributsch's *When the Snakes Awake,* "based on a popular brochure printed in China in 1973," that describes the behavior of animals before an earthquake: "Cattle, sheep, mules and horses do not enter corrals. Pigs do not eat, and dogs bark madly. Ducks do not enter water and stay on shore. Chickens fly up into trees and scream loudly. Rats move their homes and flee. Hibernating snakes leave their burrows early and may freeze. Big cats pick up little ones and run. Frightened pigeons continuously fly and do not return to nests. Rabbits raise their ears, jump aimlessly and bump things. Fish are frightened and jump above water surface. Bees move their hives, making noise."

Therefore, beware of perigean syzygys. And if Fido starts acting strangely around the time of an eclipse, watch out!

Sources:

Berkland, James O. *Syzygy: An Earthquake Newsletter.* (Available from James D. Berkland, 14927 East Hills Drive, San Jose, Calif. 95127.)

Michelsen, Neil F. *Tables of Planetary Phenomena.* San Diego, Calif.: Astro Computing Services Publications, 1990.

Nolle, Richard. "The Supermoon Alignment." In *The Astrology of the Macrocosm.* Edited by Joan McEvers. Saint Paul, Minn.: Llewellyn Publications, 1990.

Rosenberg, Diana K. "Stalking the Wild Earthquake." In *The Astrology of the Macrocosm.* Edited by Joan McEvers. Saint Paul, Minn.: Llewellyn Publications, 1990.

East Point

The east point is sometimes used to refer to the **ascendant**—the point where the eastern **horizon** intersects the **ecliptic** for any given astrological chart.

Ebertin, Reinhold

Reinhold Ebertin, born February 16, 1901, in Görlitz, Saxony, was an eminent German astrologer who developed **cosmobiology**, which has proven popular with many astrologers, especially in Europe. He became interested in astrology in 1916 and by 1923 had taken up a career as a professional astrologer. He was initially a student of Alfred Witte's **Uranian Astrology** but came to reject the elements of **hypothetical planets** and **house** interpretations. Ebertin also simplified Witte's **midpoint** combinations. The resulting system was a stream-lined version of Witte's.

Ebertin initiated the periodical *Mensch in All* in 1928. It was suppressed by the Nazis but resumed after the war with the new title *Kosmobiologie*. Ebertin wrote more than 60 books, many of which have not been translated into other languages. Several of his books have been translated into English. Ebertin died March 14, 1988.

Selected Publications:

Fixed Stars and Their Interpretation. By Ebertin and Georg Hoffman. Aalen, Germany: Ebertin Verlag, 1971.
Applied Cosmobiology. Aalen, Germany: Ebertin Verlag, 1972.
Combination of Stellar Influences. Aalen, Germany: Ebertin Verlag, 1972.

Sources:

Holden, James H., and Robert A. Hughes. *Astrological Pioneers of America.* Tempe, Ariz.: American Federation of Astrologers, 1988.

Eccentric

In astronomy, eccentricity refers to an elliptical **orbit,** specifically to the extent to which the ellipse described by a celestial body's orbit departs from a perfect circle, expressed by the ratio of the major to the minor axis.

Eclipse

An eclipse is (1) the full or partial obscuring of the **Sun** by the **Moon** (a solar eclipse), or (2) the full or partial obscuring of the Moon by the Sun (a lunar

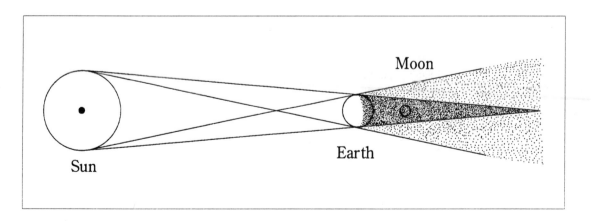

Lunar eclipse.

eclipse). When **planets** and **stars** are obscured by another celestial body (particularly by the Moon), it is called an **occultation**. The **orbits** of the Sun and Moon intersect so are not parallel; if they were parallel, we would experience a solar eclipse every new moon and a lunar eclipse every full moon. Eclipses can only occur when the Sun and Moon intersect the **lunar nodes**.

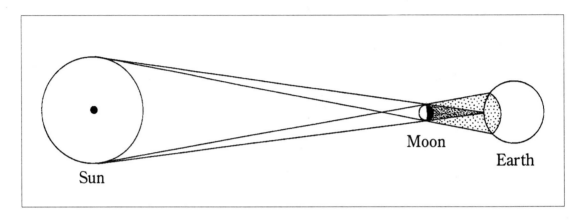

Solar eclipse.

Traditionally, the influence of eclipses, whether full or partial, has been regarded as negative, portending famine, war, and the like. Also, with respect to individual **natal charts**, the traditional interpretation is that an eclipse exerts a **malefic** influence, particularly if it falls on or near (within 5° of) a natal planet or an **angle**. Contemporary astrologers tend to see eclipses as indicating emphasis or a crisis in the affairs related to the **house** in which the eclipse occurs. For instance, should an eclipse occur in a person's second house, she or he may be

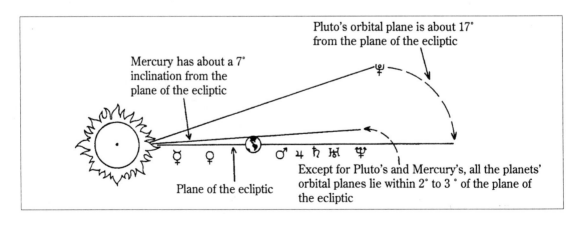

Solar system (not drawn to scale).

compelled to attend to financial matters. Should the eclipse occur near (within 5° of) a natal planet or be directly opposed to (180° away from, give or take 5°) a natal planet, the crisis will be a major one and will be colored by the nature of the planet or planets involved.

Sources:

Brau, Jean-Louis, Helen Weaver, and Allan Edmands. *Larousse Encyclopedia of Astrology*. New York: New American Library, 1980.

Jansky, Robert Carl. *Interpreting the Eclipses*. San Diego, Calif.: Astro Computing, 1979.

Michelsen, Neil F. *Tables of Planetary Phenomena*. San Diego, Calif.: Astro Computing, 1979.

Ecliptic (*Via Solis,* the Sun's Path)

The ecliptic is the **orbit** of Earth as viewed from the **Sun**. For most astrological purposes, however, the ecliptic is taken to be the orbit that the Sun appears to describe around the Earth (the *via solis,* or the Sun's path). The *via solis* acquired the name ecliptic because it is along its path, at the points where it intersects the **celestial equator** (the equator of the Earth projected outward

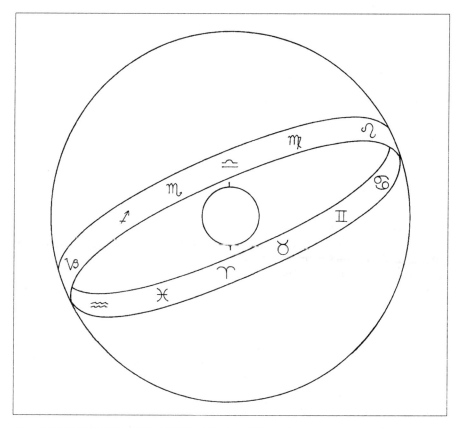

◄
Ecliptic.

onto the background of the **celestial sphere**) that eclipses occur. Owing to the tilt of the Earth on its axis, the ecliptic intersects the celestial equator at an angle of 23 1/2°. The 12 signs of the **zodiac**, through which the Sun appears to pass over the course of a year, lie around the outside of the ecliptic.

Egyptian Astrology

The ancient Greeks viewed Egypt as an exotic, mysterious land, somewhat as contemporary Westerners regard India. Thus, anything Egyptian carried with it an aura of prestige that artifacts or ideas from other areas of the world did not enjoy. For this reason, Greeks such as Herodotus tended to associate astrology with Egypt, although Egyptian astrology had been adopted wholesale directly from **Mesopotamian astrology**, and the Egyptians had added little to the science of the stars. It was only later, after Hellenistic culture had been imposed upon the land of the Nile, that Egyptians contributed to astrology.

Sources:

Baigent, Michael, Nicholas Campion, and Charles Harvey. *Mundane Astrology.* 2d ed. London: Aquarian Press, 1992.
Brau, Jean-Louis, Helen Weaver, and Allan Edmands. *Larousse Encyclopedia of Astrology.* New York: New American Library, 1980.

Electional Astrology

Electional astrology is the branch of astrology dealing with selecting (electing) the best time to initiate any given activity or project. Electional astrology is traditionally regarded as a subdivision of **horary astrology** because it involves a reverse application of horary principles. In other words, instead of examining an event that began at a particular time and forecasting the outcome, one determines the outcome one wishes to achieve and works backward to find an appropriate moment to begin.

Electional methods have been applied in selecting the time for marriage, planting (**agricultural astrology**), beginning journeys, opening businesses, buying land, contructing buildings, initiating lawsuits, and so forth. Prior to the advent of modern, psychologically oriented astrology, choosing the proper time to begin an activity was one of the chief reasons for consulting astrologers. There exists a vast traditional literature on the subject that stretches back to before the time of **Ptolemy**.

Some sense of the complexity of electional astrology can be gained from reading the entry on horary astrology. The astrologer must not only construct an *inceptional figure* (electional chart) that will accomplish the intended purpose but also select a moment that will bring concurrent influences in the client's **natal chart** into alignment with the desired end. In other words, contrary influences in the client's chart will counteract favorable influences in the election chart.

There is, however, a shorthand approach, using the position of the **Moon**, for selecting the proper moment to initiate actions. As the nearest and fastest-moving celestial body to Earth, the Moon has the most influence over the continuously changing astrological "atmosphere" of our home **planet**. For day-to-day choices, it is thus the most significant planet to examine. The first rule of thumb in electing actions by the position of the Moon is to pay attention to the Moon's waxing and waning cycle: Activities one hopes will quickly expand, such as a new business venture, should be initiated during a waxing moon (increasing in size from new to full). On the other hand, activities one hopes to stop or slow, such as the growth of hair after a haircut, should be undertaken during a waning moon (decreasing in size from full to new).

A second consideration when using the position of the moon in electional astrology is the variable speed of the Moon. The Moon travels in an eliptical **orbit** around Earth. During its **perigee** (the point at which it passes closest to Earth), it is traveling faster than during its **apogee** (the point farthest away from Earth). As with the waxing and waning cycle, activities one wants to come quickly to fruition should be undertaken close to the Moon's perigee, and activities one wants to stop or slow down should be undertaken close to its apogee. The Moon's perigee and apogee points can be found in such sources as Michelsen's *Tables of Planetary Phenomena.*

A third consideration is to avoid certain actions when the Moon is void of course (often abbreviated VOC). A planet is void of course after it makes its last major **aspect** with another planet before **transiting** out of a given sign. It remains void of course until it enters a new sign (referred to as **ingress**). The influence of void-of-course moons is on par with **retrograde** motion—these are poor periods during which to sign contracts, initiate new projects, or acquire new possessions. They are good times, however, to reflect and "recharge." Many of the major **ephemerides** (tables of planetary positions) note when the Moon goes void of course as well as when the Moon enters a new sign. Michelsen's popular *American Ephemeris,* for instance, contains last-aspect and -ingress information for the Moon at the bottom of each page. Astrologers who have studied void-of-course moons assert that the last aspect must be a major one—**conjunction, sextile, square, trine,** or **opposition**—with the **Sun** or one of the planets (**asteroids** and other celestial bodies are not considered significant for the purpose of determining VOC moons).

A fourth consideration in using the Moon's position is the nature of the Moon's last aspect before going void of course; this concluding aspect shows the outcome of any action undertaken while the Moon was in that sign. A **hard aspect**, such as a square or an opposition, tends to indicate an unfavorable outcome, whereas a sextile or a trine indicates a favorable one. A conjunction is usually regarded as favorable, although conjunction with a difficult planet such as **Saturn** might cause delays.

As an example of how VOC/last aspect works, consider Bill Clinton's inauguration on January 21, 1993. *The American Ephemeris,* at the bottom of the page for January and February, indicates that the Moon entered **Capricorn** at 2:46 A.M. **Greenwich Time** on January 20, 1993 (which corresponds with 9:46 P.M. EST on January 19). The Moon was thus in Capricorn during the inauguration. The Moon's last aspect before leaving this sign was a sextile with **Pluto** at 3:29 A.M. Greenwich time on January 22 (10:29 P.M. EST on January 21). This last aspect indicates a positive outcome to the Clinton presidency, which, if campaign promises are fulfilled, will *transform* (the effect of Pluto) the economy (associated with the sign Capricorn). Progress toward this goal is likely to be slow, however, because the Moon was waning on January 20 and because it was closer to its apogee (which occurred on January 26) than to its perigee (January 10).

A fifth consideration when using the lunar position to determine timing is the next aspect the Moon makes after an action is taken (called the **applying aspect**). Thus, if one goes to a job interview when the Moon is applying a square to **Neptune**, confused communication or even a sense of deception is likely to interfere with the interview. This need not spell doom for one's job propects, however. If the last aspect before the Moon goes void of course in the sign of the **zodiac** it was in during the interview gives a more positive indication, such as a trine to **Jupiter**, the outcome of the interview is likely to be positive. In the case of the Clinton inauguration, the Moon was beginning to move into an opposition with **Mars**, which indicates a presidency that has to deal with opposition. Mars, the ruler of war, shows that this conflict will be quite sharp. It could even indicate that the Clinton administration will have to divert its attention from the president's domestic agenda and give significant attention to overseas conflicts (Mars was in the water sign **Cancer**).

A sixth and final consideration is the sign the Moon is in at the time a project is undertaken. For example, if one wished to undertake a project that involves attention to detail, it might be best to do so when the Moon is in **Virgo** (a sign associated with detailed organization); to establish a partnership, it might be best to wait until the Moon is in **Libra** (a sign associated with marriage and business partnerships); and so forth. In the case of the Clinton presidency, the new president was inaugurated when the Moon was in Capricorn, a sign associated with economic matters.

Small astrological **almanacs** that keep track of all the data associated with the Moon's changing signs and aspects for each year can sometimes be found at larger bookstores, though one must usually go to a specialty bookseller. In addition, the *Simplified Scientific Ephemerides* published annually by the Rosicrucian Fellowship, is widely available. These tables of ephermerides have the advantage over the Michelsen ephemerides of supplying an **aspectarian** (a table that notes the day and time that aspects between planets become exact), although they have the disadvantage of not explicitly noting the last aspect the Moon makes before it goes void of course.

On a day-to-day basis, it is frequently difficult to schedule the most ideal time for any given action. Often the best one can do is to avoid the least favorable moments. Neverthless, watching the Moon with a small pocket almanac provides anyone with a minimum of astrological expertise with a quick, rough method for electing the best times to schedule everyday tasks. It would, of course, be wise to become more proficient—or to consult a professional astrologer—before selecting times for events of greater significance.

Sources:

deVore, Nicholas. *Encyclopedia of Astrology.* New York: Philosophical Library, 1947.
Michelsen, Neil F. *The American Ephemeris for the 20th Century.* San Diego, Calif.: ACS Publications, 1988.
———. *Tables of Planetary Phenomena.* San Diego, Calif.: Astro Computing Services Publications, 1990.
Morrison, Al H. "Notes on the 'Void-of-Course' Moon." *The Mountain Astrologer* 889: (August/September 1989). 11, 29.
Rosicrucian Fellowship. *Simplified Scientific Ephemeris 1993.* Oceanside, Calif.: 1992.

Elements

The primary categories by which the signs are classified are the four elements (earth, air, fire, and water) and the three **qualities** (cardinal, mutable, and fixed). Each of the 12 signs of the **zodiac** is a unique combination of an element and a quality (e.g., **Aries** is a **cardinal fire sign**, **Taurus** a **fixed earth sign**, **Gemini** a **mutable air sign**, and so forth). The elemental nature of a sign is said to refer to its basic temperament, while its quality refers to its mode of expression.

People whose only contact with the word element was in a science class immediately think of the materials diagrammed by the periodic table—oxygen, iron, hydrogen, silicon, and the like—when they hear the term. It thus strikes them as strange to consider earth, air, fire, and water by this designation. The astrological elements derive from the elements of ancient Greek philosophy. Classical philosophy and modern science share an interest in discovering the basic—the "elementary"—building blocks of the world. Prior to the advent of contemporary atomic theory, intelligent people examining the world in which they lived observed that all tangible things could be classified as solids (earth), liquids (water), or gases (air). Sources of heat and light, such as fire and the **Sun**, seemed to constitute a fourth factor (fire), which we might think of as "energy." When reworded as solid, liquid, gas, and energy, this ancient scheme of classification is not really so strange.

When the ancients analyzed the human being in terms of these four factors, it appeared to them that the physical body was earthy, feeling and emotions watery, and thoughts airy. The fire element provided the spark of life that animated the human frame with activity. From this way of looking at human nature, it was but a short step to regarding sensitive, emotional people as having more of the water "element" in their constitution than their fellows, mental people as having more air, practical people as having more earth, and energetic, active people as having more fire. When astrology was being systematized in ancient Greece, this "psychological" system was applied to the 12 signs, resulting in a classification according to the 4 classical elements: the fire **triplicity**, Aries, **Leo**, and **Sagittarius** (energy signs); the earth triplicity, **Taurus**, **Virgo**, and **Capricorn** (practical signs); the air triplicity, Gemini, **Libra**, and **Aquarius** (mental signs); and the water triplicity, **Cancer**, **Scorpio**, and **Pisces** (emotional signs).

Sources:

Brau, Jean-Louis, Helen Weaver, and Allan Edmands. *Larousse Encyclopedia of Astrology.* New York: New American Library, 1980.
Hand, Robert. *Horoscope Symbols.* Rockport, Mass.: Para Research, 1981.
Tester, Jim. *A History of Western Astrology.* New York: Ballantine, 1987.

Eleutheria

Eleutheria, **asteroid** 567 (the 567th asteroid to be discovered), is approximately 84 kilometers in diameter and has an **orbital** period of 5.5 years. It was named after the Greek goddess of liberty. There was also a festival instituted after the victory of the Greeks over the Persians that was called Eleutheria. The sign and **house** position of this planetoid in a **natal chart** indicates where and how one seeks greater freedom, as well as how one struggles for liberty. If prominent in a natal chart (e.g., **conjunct** the **Sun** or the **ascendant**), it may show a person for whom liberty and victory over obstacles are life themes.

Sources:

Kowal, Charles T. *Asteroids: Their Nature and Utilization.* Chichester, West Sussex, U.K.: Ellis Horwood Limited, 1988.
Room, Adrian. *Dictionary of Astronomical Names.* London: Routledge, 1988.

Elevation

Elevation is the **angular distance** of a celestial body above the **horizon**. An elevated **planet** in a **natal chart**, especially if it is near the **midheaven** and in the tenth house, is said to exert a particularly strong influence on the entire chart. In traditional astrology, elevated **malefic** planets, especially when elevated above the **Sun** and **Moon**, were said to exert an unfavorable influence over the entire chart. Modern astrologers have largely rejected this interpretation. For instance, a well-**aspected Saturn** (traditionally considered the Greater Malefic) placed in the tenth house is in the **house** of its **accidental dignity**, and although this placement may indicate delay, it also indicates ultimate success (should other factors support this interpretation) in one's profession.

Elongation

Elongation, in astrological parlance, is the maximum **angular distance** that **Mercury** and **Venus** travel from the **Sun**. Because the **orbits** of Mercury and Venus lie between Earth and the Sun, these two **planets** appear to always travel with the Sun, so that, from the position of Earth, Mercury is always within 28° of the Sun, and Venus always within 46°. Elongation also refers to the maximum apparent distance that a **satellite** travels from the body around which it moves (e.g., the maximum distance the Moon travels from Earth).

Elpis

Elpis, **asteroid** 59 (the 59th asteroid to be discovered), is approximately 164 kilometers in diameter and has an **orbital** period of 4.5 years. It was named after the Greek word for hope. The **house** and sign positions of Elpis in a **natal chart** indicates sources of hope as well as the area of life where the **native** invests her or his hopes. When prominent in a chart, Elpis may show a generally hopeful person. When **afflicted**, it may show disappointment or lack of hope.

Sources:

Kowal, Charles T. *Asteroids: Their Nature and Utilization.* Chichester, West Sussex, U.K.: Ellis Horwood Limited, 1988.
Room, Adrian. *Dictionary of Astronomical Names.* London: Routledge, 1988.

Enlightenment, Astrology during the

See: History of Western Astrology

Ephemeral Map

The ephemeral map is the astrological chart cast in **horary astrology** for the event in question.

Ephemeral Motion

Ephemeral motion refers to the motion of the **planets** and other celestial bodies along their **orbits**, as distinct from **progressed** motion.

Ephemeris

An ephemeris (*pl.,* ephemerides) is an astronomical/astrological **almanac** listing the daily positions of the **Sun**, the **Moon**, and the **planets**, as well as other information (including, in astrological ephemerides, certain information necessary for calculating an astrological chart). The word is derived from the

---

Greek *ephemeros,* meaning existing no longer than a day, from which we also get the word ephemeral. The use of such tables is very old, and ephemerides are used by navigators, astronomers, and astrologers. During the nineteenth century and the early twentieth century, most of the readily available ephemerides listed planetary positions for noon at Greenwich, England (0° longitude). By the late twentieth century, however, ephemerides had proliferated to the point that tables of planetary positions for midnight **Greenwich mean time** and noon and midnight Eastern Standard Time (North America), **sidereal** ephemerides, and **heliocentric** (Sun-centered) emphemerides were all readily available. The personal computer revolution has partially eliminated the need for such tables, as ephemerides have been incorporated into chart-casting programs. An interesting approach to portraying the ever-changing planetary positions that gives a quick visual sense of what all the planets are doing is the so-called graphic ephemeris (see Roxana Muise's *A-Year-At-A-Glance*).

Sources:

Bach, Eleanor. *Astrology from A to Z: An Illustrated Source Book.* New York: Philosophical Library, 1990.

Muise, Roxana. *A-Year-At-A-Glance: The 45 Degree Graphic Ephemeris for 101 Years, 1900–2001.* Bellevue, Wash.: South Western Astrology Conference, 1986.

Sepharial [W. Govn Old]. *New Dictionary of Astrology.* New York: Arco, 1964.

Epicycle

When Earth was viewed as the **stationary** center of the universe, the **retrograde** motion of the **planets** was explained in terms of epicycles—smaller **orbits** that circled in the reverse direction from the planets' usual motion.

Equal House System

When the casual observer looks at an astrological chart for the first time, it is easy to make the incorrect assumption that the 12 "pie pieces" are the 12 signs of the **zodiac**. These lines indicate the **house** divisions (sign divisions are usually not represented), which can begin or end at different places in different signs. Astrologers disagree about how to draw the houses, although most agree that the first house should begin on the eastern horizon and the seventh house (180° away) should begin on the western horizon. All of the other divisions are disputed, although the great majority of systems begin the tenth house at the **degree** of the zodiac that is highest in the heavens and the fourth house at exactly 180° away from the **cusp** of the tenth house. The equal house system is one of the very few systems of house division that utilize a different axis for the tenth and fourth houses.

In equal house system, as the name implies, all the houses are equal in width. Thus, someone born when the eastern **horizon** intersected **Virgo** at 26° would have a first house that began at 26° Virgo, a second house that began at

26° **Libra**, a third house that began at 26° **Scorpio**, and so forth. It is an ancient system of house division that is still used in **Hindu astrology**. For the most part, it had passed out of circulation among Western astrologers until fairly recently. Several of popular books, particularly Derek and Julia Parker's *The Compleat Astrologer* (first published in the United States in 1971), have propagated the equal house system because it is the easiest system to use. The increasing popularity of Hindu astrology in the West has also helped the equal house system make a comeback. Most contemporary astrologers who do not use the system are severely critical of it.

Sources:

Gettings, Fred. *Dictionary of Astrology.* London: Routledge & Kegan Paul, 1985.

Parker, Derek, and Julia Parker. *The Compleat Astrologer.* 1971. Reprint. New York: Bantam, 1975.

Equator

The equator is the imaginary line drawn around Earth (and, by extension, other celestial bodies) separating it into northern and southern **hemispheres**. The **celestial equator** refers to the circle that results when one imaginarily projects the terrestrial equator against the background of the **fixed stars**.

Equinoctial Signs

The equinoctial signs are **Aries**, which begins on the **vernal** (spring) **equinox**, and **Libra**, which marks the **autumnal equinox**.

Equinox

The equinoxes (from the Latin for equal night) are the two points in the year when the length of the day is equal to that of the night. These are the vernal (spring) equinox, which occurs on the first day of spring (on or around March 21), and the autumnal equinox, which takes place on the first day of fall (on or around September 23). In astronomical terms, the equinoxes occur when Earth reaches a place in its **orbit** where, from our point of view, the **Sun** appears to be situated at the exact intersection of the **celestial equator** and the **ecliptic**. The vernal equinox is especially important for Western astrologers, who regard the Sun's position against the backdrop of the **stars** at the spring equinox (the **vernal point**) as the place where the **zodiac** begins.

Sources:

Filbey, John, and Peter Filbey. *The Astrologer's Companion.* Wellingborough, Northamptonshire: Aquarian Press, 1986.

Tester, Jim. *A History of Western Astrology.* New York: Ballantine, 1987.

Erato

Erato, **asteroid** 62 (the 62d asteroid to be discovered), is approximately 64 kilometers in diameter and has an **orbital** period of 5.5 years. Erato was named after the Greek muse of love poetry. Lehman associates this asteroid with the *inspiration* of love, as distinct from its consummation.

Sources:

Kowal, Charles T. *Asteroids: Their Nature and Utilization.* Chichester, West Sussex, U.K.: Ellis Horwood Limited, 1988.
Lehman, J. Lee. *The Ultimate Asteroid Book.* West Chester, Penn.: Whitford Press, 1988.
Room, Adrian. *Dictionary of Astronomical Names.* London: Routledge, 1988.

Eros

Eros, **asteroid** 433 (the 433d asteroid to be discovered—in 1898) was named after the god of love in Greek mythology, the son of Ares (**Mars**) and Aphrodite (**Venus**). It was the first known asteroid to pass inside the **orbit** of Mars. It has an orbital period of 1 3/4 years and is 22 kilometers in diameter. Eros is one of the more recent asteroids to be investigated by astrologers. Preliminary material on Eros can be found in **Demetra George** and Douglas Bloch's *Astrology for Yourself,* and an **ephemeris** (table of celestial locations) for Eros can be found in the back of the second edition of George and Bloch's *Asteroid Goddesses.* Unlike the **planets**, which are associated with a wide range of phenomena, the smaller asteroids are said to represent a single principle. George and Bloch (1987) give Eros's principle as "vitality and passion." Zipporah Dobyns associates Eros with romantic love. J. Lee Lehman contends that Eros is the ruler of romance and passionate attachment. Lehman contrasts **Sappho,** which she regards as raw sexual drive, with Eros, which she sees as more mental—the conceptualization of attraction.

Sources:

Dobyns, Zipporah. *Expanding Astrology's Universe.* San Diego, Calif.: Astro Computing Services, 1983.
George, Demetra, with Douglas Bloch. *Asteroid Goddesses: The Mythology, Psychology and Astrology of the Reemerging Feminine.* 2d ed. rev. and enl. San Diego, Calif.: Astro Computing Services, 1990.
———. *Astrology for Yourself: A Workbook for Personal Transformation.* Berkeley, Calif.: Wingbow Press, 1987.
Lehman, J. Lee. *The Ultimate Asteroid Book.* West Chester, Pa.: Whitford Press, 1988.

Erratics

The erratics, or erratic stars, was a term used in traditional astrology to refer to the **planets**, as distinct from the **fixed stars**.

Esoteric Astrology

Esoteric (from Greek *esoteros*, inner; derived from *eso*, within) astrology is the general term for various schools of astrology whose practitioners view themselves as studying the "ancient widsom" behind the science of the stars. The original sense of the word esoteric was that it was hidden from, or otherwise inaccessible to, the uninitiated. However, contemporary esoteric astrology is openly accessible to anyone who is able to read. The contrasting term to esoteric is exoteric (meaning external, as opposed to the "inner" significance of the esoteric approach), and, from an esoteric standpoint, all of astrology that is not esoteric is exoteric. Although modern esoteric astrology can appropriately claim an ancient lineage, the reformulation of the ancient wisdom tradition as put forward by Helena Blavatsky and the Theosophical Society in the nineteenth century has been the single most important shaper of contemporary astrology.

Esoteric astrologers are more interested in utilizing the elements of astrology for philosophical speculation than in the practical application of astrology to the concerns of everyday life. Hence, the erection and interpretation of individual **horoscopes** plays a relatively small role. Fred Gettings (p. 116) describes esoteric astrology as "founded on the premise that the cosmos is a living being, that the destiny of the solar system is intimately bound up with the destiny of humanity, and that human beings reincarnate periodically onto the earth."

Sample speculations characteristic of the esoteric approach are the notion that the individual soul incarnates in each of the 12 signs of the **zodiac** in succession (**Manly Palmer Hall**) and that each of the zodiacal signs has an "esoteric **ruler**," different from their "exoteric rulers" (**Alice A. Bailey**). Other significant features are utilization of the notions of **reincarnation and karma** to explain **hard aspects** and **soft aspects**, the correlation of the **planets** with the *chakras* (the "energy centers" of the Hindu yoga tradition), and a spiritual interpretation of the **elements**. Beyond the thinkers already mentioned, other key shapers of modern esoteric astrology are **Alan Leo**, **Max Heindal**, and Rudolf Steiner.

Sources:

Gettings, Fred. *Dictionary of Astrology.* London: Routledge & Kegan Paul, 1987.
McEvers, Joan, ed. *Spiritual, Metaphysical and New Trends in Modern Astrology.* Saint Paul, Minn.: Llewellyn, 1988.
Simms, Maria Kay. *Twelve Wings of the Eagle: Our Spiritual Evolution through the Ages of the Zodiac.* San Diego, Calif.: Astro Computing Services, 1988.

Esoteric Rulerships

In **esoteric astrology**, the 12 signs of the **zodiac** are said to have esoteric rulers—**rulerships** by **planets** other than their usual planetary rulers—that are activated only in "highly evolved" (spiritually evolved) individuals.

Essential Dignity

When a **planet** or one of the **luminaries** (the **Sun** or the **Moon**) is located in one of the signs of the **zodiac** it is said to **rule**, then it is in its essential dignity, as distinct from its **accidental dignity**. **Mars,** for example, would be said to be in its essential dignity if found in the sign **Aries.**

Esther

Esther, **asteroid** 622 (the 622d asteroid to be discovered), is approximately 28 kilometers in diameter and has an **orbital** period of 3.8 years. It was named after the biblical heroine Esther. Queen Esther, herself a Jew, intervened to prevent a genocidal campaign against the Jewish people. Like its namesake, the asteroid represents opposition to genocide and a kind of "rescuer" impulse. In a **natal chart,** its location by sign and **house** indicates where and how one is most likely to be a "rescuer." When **afflicted** by inharmonious **aspects,** Esther may show a rescuer complex—an individual who engages in rescue behavior for self-aggrandizement. If prominent in a chart (e.g., **conjunct** the **Sun** or the **ascendant**), it may show an individual who becomes involved in a rescue-related career or in a humanitarian group like Amnesty International.

Sources:

Kowal, Charles T. *Asteroids: Their Nature and Utilization.* Chichester, West Sussex, U.K.: Ellis Horwood Limited, 1988.

Room, Adrian. *Dictionary of Astronomical Names.* London: Routledge, 1988.

Ethics and Astrology

Astrological organizations often promulgate explicit codes of ethics, partly because no government agencies regulate the behavior of astrologers and partly because of the tendency of astrology's critics to portray astrologers as unethical charlatans. These codes of ethics go back at least as far as Firmicus Maternus (330 B.C.), who in *Mathesis* sets high standards for astrologers:

> Shape yourself in the image and likeness of divinity, so that you may always be a model of excellence. He who daily speaks about the gods must shape his mind to approach the likeness of divinity. Be modest, upright, sober, and content with few goods, so that the shameful love of money may not defile the glory of this divine science. Outdo the training and principles of worthy priests. For the acolyte of the Sun and Moon and the other gods, through whom all earthly things are governed, must educate his mind to be proved worthy in the sight of all mankind. See that you give your responses publicly in a clear voice, so that nothing illegal may be asked of you. Do not give a response about the condition of the Republic or the life of the Emperor–that is illegal. Have a wife, a home, friends; be constantly available to the public; keep out of quarrels; do not undertake any harmful business; do not be tempted by the offer of money; keep away from all passion of cruelty; never

take pleasure in others' quarrels or capital sentences or fatal enmities. . . . Be generous, honest and truthful. . . . Be reticent about people's vices. . . . Do not give away the secrets of this religion to wicked men, for the astrologer must be pure.

Later astrologers, like the seventeenth-century British astrologer **William Lilly,** based their ethical admonitions on Firmicus Maternus's. In Lilly's case, this is clear from certain passages in his celebrated *Christian Astrology,* one of which (Kitson, pp. 25-26) says,

as thou daily conversest with the heavens, so instruct and form thy mind according to the image of divinity; learn all the ornaments of vertue, be sufficiently instructed therein; be human, courteous, familiar to all. . . . covet not an estate, give freely to the poor. . .let no worldly wealth procure an erroneous judgment from thee, or such as may dishonour the Art, or this divine Science. . . . Be sparing in delivering Judgment against the Commonwelth thou livest in. Give not judgment of the death of the Prince. . . . Marry a wife of thy own, rejoice in the number of thy friends.

In the English-speaking world, almost all explicit ethical codes for astrologers can be traced back to Lilly. Other points usually mentioned in professional codes of ethics are confidentiality, both of personal information shared by the client and of the **natal chart** itself; disclaiming the ability to predict events in precise detail; de-emphasis on potentiality for future illnesses, accidents, or disasters; and avoiding approaches that would in any way encourage clients to become dependent upon the astrologer or to in any way abdicate responsibility for their life. Astrologers are further admonished to educate the general public on the true nature of the science of the stars; establish professional standards that exclude charlatans; propagate serious astrology through teaching, writing, and so forth; and support any serious, open-minded research on astrology.

In *The Practice of Astrology* and in other writings, **Dane Rudhyar** was especially concerned with the moral responsibility of the astrologer. He warned astrologers to avoid giving clients information they were unable to assimilate, and especially to avoid inducing a state of fear. Rudhyar wrote that an astrologer failed her or his clients when, "instead of helping the client to overcome his semi-conscious fears, he accentuates and gives a mysterious power to these fears by giving them a justification against which there can be no recourse" (p. 24). He also believed that prediction has value only as it contributes to the person's development and essential welfare. The goal of the astrologer should be to open clients to their highest potential, rather than to impress them with her or his knowledge.

Sources:

Brau, Jean-Louis, Helen Weaver, and Allan Edmands. *Larousse Encyclopedia of Astrology.* New York: New American Library, 1980.

Kitson, Annabella, ed. *History and Astrology: Clio and Urania Confer.* London: Mandala, 1989.

Lilly, William. *Christian Astrology.* Exeter, U.K.: Regulus Publishing Co., 1985. [Facsimile reprint of the 1647 edition with color portrait and supplementary comments by Patrick Curry and Geoffrey Cornelius.]

Rudhyar, Dane. *The Practice of Astrology: As a Technique in Human Understanding.* New York: Penguin, 1968.

Eunice

Eunice, **asteroid** 185 (the 185th asteroid to be discovered), is approximately 188 kilometers in diameter and has an **orbital** period of 4.5 years. Its name is Greek for good victory. The asteroid indicates good luck and a fortunate outcome to activities undertaken in matters associated with its sign and **house** position.

Sources:

Kowal, Charles T. *Asteroids: Their Nature and Utilization.* Chichester, West Sussex, U.K.: Ellis Horwood Limited, 1988.

Room, Adrian. *Dictionary of Astronomical Names.* London: Routledge, 1988.

Euphrosyne

Euphrosyne, **asteroid** 31 (the 31st asteroid to be discovered), is approximately 270 kilometers in diameter and has an **orbital** period of 5.5 years. Euphrosyne, whose appelation means cheerfulness or joy, was named after one of the three Graces. She was a daughter of Zeus and Eurynome. Like its mythological namesake, the asteroid confers the "grace" of joy to **natives** in whose chart it is prominent.

Sources:

Kowal, Charles T. *Asteroids: Their Nature and Utilization.* Chichester, West Sussex, U.K.: Ellis Horwood Limited, 1988.

Room, Adrian. *Dictionary of Astronomical Names.* London: Routledge, 1988.

Europe, History of Astrology in

See: History of Western Astrology

Euterpe

Euterpe, **asteroid** 27 (the 27th asteroid to be discovered), is approximately 88 kilometers in diameter and has an **orbital** period of 4.3 years. It was named after the Greek muse of lyric poetry and music, who some myths say invented the flute; she also is said to have had a special affection for "wild" melodies. The prominence of Euterpe in a **natal chart** indicates talent in wind instruments and a preference for "wild" music.

Sources:

Kowal, Charles T. *Asteroids: Their Nature and Utilization.* Chichester, West Sussex, U.K.: Ellis Horwood Limited, 1988.
Room, Adrian. *Dictionary of Astronomical Names.* London: Routledge, 1988.

Exaltation

The term exaltation is part of a traditional system of classifying certain sign placements of **planets**. A planet is said to be in its **dignity** when it is in the sign it **rules**. These are considered to be favorable placements. Exaltations are sign positions said to be more favorable for a planet than even the signs it rules. **Mars**, for example, rules **Aries** and is said to be well placed (in its dignity) in that sign. But Mars is even better placed in **Capricorn**, the sign of its exaltation. In this example, we can see that while Aries would allow Mars to express its outgoing, assertive nature quite well, Capricorn would be a better placement because, without blunting one's assertiveness, Capricorn could discipline Mars so that one would not be inclined to impulsiveness (a trait characteristic of Mars in Aries).

The reception of the traditional exaltations among modern astrologers is mixed. This is partially because exalted planets are not always the unmitigated blessings that one might anticipate. **Venus** in the sign of its exaltation, **Pisces**, for example, is a highly idealistic, mystical placement that, unless counterbalanced by other factors in a **natal chart**, tends to make a person too impractical about human relationships, particularly romantic involvements. More generally, all of the traditional dignities should be taken with a grain of salt, used when relevant to a particular individual's chart and rejected when not.

Sources:

Brau, Jean-Louis, Helen Weaver, and Allan Edmands. *Larousse Encyclopedia of Astrology.* New York: New American Library, 1980.
deVore, Nicholas. *Encyclopedia of Astrology.* New York: Philosophical Library, 1947.

Executive Type

Executive type refers to the determination of those **natives** born when the **Sun** was in one of the **fixed signs**—**Taurus, Leo, Scorpio,** or **Aquarius.**

Externalize

Astrological influences are often thought of as affecting the inner side of life first (e.g., emotionally or mentally) and then manifesting as an event in the outer world. The term externalize is often used to describe this outward manifestation.

F

Face

Face is a term that refers to the division of the **zodiac** into 72 equal arcs of 5° each. Some astrologers have used the appelation interchangeably with **decan**, which divides the zodiac into 36 equal arcs of 10° each. Contemporary astrologers rarely employ the term.

Fagan, Cyril

Cyril Fagan, an eminent Irish astrologer, was born on May 22, 1896, in Dublin, Ireland, and died on January 5, 1970, in Tucson, Arizona. Deafness kept him from following the family profession, medicine, and he eventually took up astrology. He later settled in Tucson, Arizona.

In the thirties Fagan founded the Irish Astrological Society, serving as president for some years. He took up the cause of the fixed or **sidereal zodiac** and became the leader of sidereal astrologers in America. *Zodiacs Old and New* (1950) articulates most of his ideas on siderealism. Fagan had a dogmatic style that convinced some and repelled others. **Ernest Grant** was the initial publisher of his *Fixed Zodiac Ephemeris for 1948.*

Despite the support of Fagan's views on siderealism, however, most astrologers continued to use the moving or **tropical zodiac**, and some who converted to siderealism later returned to the tropical fold. Fagan began a long-running feature, "Solunars," in *American Astrology Magazine* (1954–1970) in which he put forward his theories and also discussed **horoscopes** of many historical personages based on careful research into correct birth dates and birth times. Beyond siderealism, Fagan denounced the use of **house** rulers in **natal astrology**, tried to revive the ancient use of simultaneous rising stars, and advocated the Campanus house system (although he later advocated an 8-fold division of the chart).

He was a strong advocate of precise data and accurate calculation and criticized use of speculative charts and unjustified **rectification** of birth times.

These contributions were eclipsed, however, by his advocacy of siderealism. Following Fagan's and his principal supporters' death in the seventies, the sidereal zodiac faded from the scene. The fixed zodiac has only recently returned to prominence, in the works of **Hindu astrologers.**

Selected Publications:

Fixed Zodiac Ephemeris for 1948. Washington, D.C.: National Astrology Library, 1948.
Zodiacs Old and New. 2d ed. Los Angeles: Llewellyn Publications, London: Anscombe, 1951.
A Primer of the Sidereal Zodiac. By Fagan and R.C. Firebrace. London: R. C. Firebrace, 1961.

Sources:

Holden, James H., and Robert A. Hughes. *Astrological Pioneers of America.* Tempe, Ariz.: American Federation of Astrologers, 1988.

Fall

The term fall is part of a traditional way of classifying certain sign placements of **planets.** A planet is said to be in its **dignity** when it is in the sign it **rules** (e.g., **Mars** in **Aries,** the **Sun** in **Leo**). There are also certain placements said to be especially favorable for a planet that are traditionally termed **exaltations** (to continue with the same examples, Mars in **Capricorn,** the Sun in Aries). When a planet is placed in the sign opposite its dignity, it is said it is said to be in its **detriment** (Mars in **Libra,** the Sun in **Aquarius**). A planet is in its fall when it is placed in the sign opposite the sign of its **exaltation** (Mars in **Cancer,** the Sun in Libra). For example, because the **Moon** is exalted in **Taurus,** it is in its fall when placed in the sign **Scorpio**; as the name implies, this is regarded as an unfortunate placement. A planet in its fall is traditionally regarded as being out of harmony with the sign and consequently weakened (in a position of **debility**).

For the most part, contemporary astrological research has tended to disconfirm that a planet in its traditional fall is weakened. However, it is sometimes the case that planets in fall have unfortunate effects. In the example cited, the Moon, as the planet of receptivity and sensitivity, is not well placed (especially in a **natal chart**) in Scorpio, a sign noted for possessiveness, obsessiveness, and intense emotions. There are, nevertheless, certain obvious problems with this tradition. The Sun, for example, is exalted in Aries, the sign opposite **Libra.** This means that the 1-out-of-12 people in the world born with a Libra **sun sign** have their sun in its fall. This particular placement of the Sun, however, is not normally regarded as being unfortunate, making the traditional ascription appear inapplicable, at least in this case. Generally, all the traditional falls should be taken with a grain of salt, used when relevant to a particular individual's chart and rejected when not.

Sources:

Brau, Jean-Louis, Helen Weaver, and Allan Edmands. *Larousse Encyclopedia of Astrology.* New York: New American Library, 1980.
deVore, Nicholas. *Encyclopedia of Astrology.* New York: Philosophical Library, 1947.

Familiarity

Familiarity is an older term for the **aspects** between the **planets**.

Fanatica

Fanatica, **asteroid** 1,589 (the 1,589th asteroid to be discovered), is approximately 14 kilometers in diameter and has an **orbital** period of 3.8 years. Fanatica is a concept asteroid, named after fanaticism. Lehman associates this asteroid with fanatical temperaments and activities.

Sources:

Kowal, Charles T. *Asteroids: Their Nature and Utilization.* Chichester, West Sussex, U.K.: Ellis Horwood Limited, 1988.
Lehman, J. Lee. *The Ultimate Asteroid Book.* West Chester, Penn.: Whitford Press, 1988.

Fate (Destiny, Predestination)

Fate (destiny or predestination) is the belief that events—and, especially, human lives—follow an irrevocable script: What we are experiencing at this moment was inevitable and could not have possibly been different. The belief implies that the future is predetermined, in that there is no way of avoiding what will happen.

Because the word "prediction" seems to connote an irrevocable destiny, and because astrologers sometimes talk about "predicting" the future, astrology has often been accused of assuming—or even of advocating—a notion of rigid predetermination. However, the nature of astrological consulting work refutes this perception: Clients consult astrologers about the future to better direct their lives. One might, for example, consult an astrologer in order to select the best time to sign a contract. Selecting an auspicious moment clearly implies freedom of choice (i.e., freedom to select from several different possible futures). In other words, if the outcome of the contract and the time one signed it were rigidly fated, it would make no sense to make an effort to choose the best moment.

Rather than "predicting the future," what astrologers actually do is describe upcoming planetary conditions, with the understanding that clients have the free will to respond to planetary influences in different ways. A traditional astrological adage is that "The stars incline; they do not compel." Like a meteorologist forecasting the weather, an astrologer can only predict upcoming planetary conditions. Whether or not one chooses to go for a picnic on the day a meteorologist predicts rain—or on the day an astrologer advises that one stay at home—is one's free choice.

Felicia

Felicia, **asteroid** 294 (the 294th asteroid to be discovered), is approximately 35 kilometers in diameter and has an **orbital** period of 5.5 years. Its name means lucky or happy. When prominent in a **natal chart,** Felicia indicates a lucky person with a generally positive attitude. Its location by sign and **house** indicates potential sources of luck or happiness. When involved in many inharmonious **aspects,** Felicia may show an unlucky or unwisely optimistic person.

Sources:

Kowal, Charles T. *Asteroids: Their Nature and Utilization.* Chichester, West Sussex, U.K.: Ellis Horwood Limited, 1988.
Room, Adrian. *Dictionary of Astronomical Names.* London: Routledge, 1988.

Felicitas

Felicitas, **asteroid** 109 (the 109th asteroid to be discovered), is approximately 76 kilometers in diameter and has an **orbital** period of 4.4 years. It was named after the Roman goddess of happiness. When prominent in a **natal chart,** Felicitas indicates a person with a generally positive attitude. Its location by sign and **house** position indicates potential sources of happiness. When involved in many inharmonious **aspects,** Felicitas may show a person who is glad about the wrong things, or an unwisely optimistic person.

Sources:

Kowal, Charles T. *Asteroids: Their Nature and Utilization.* Chichester, West Sussex, U.K.: Ellis Horwood Limited, 1988.
Room, Adrian. *Dictionary of Astronomical Names.* London: Routledge, 1988.

Feminine Signs (Negative Signs)

The 12 signs of the **zodiac** are classified in a number of different ways, including a division into positive, **masculine signs** and negative, **feminine signs** (using negative and positive in the neutral sense of opposite polarities rather than as value judgments about "good" and "bad"). The feminine signs include all the earth signs (Taurus, Virgo, Capricorn) and all the **water signs (Cancer, Scorpio, Pisces)**. The gender of the signs was originally determined by the Pythagorean notion that odd numbers are male and even numbers female. This caused the signs that came second (Taurus), fourth (Cancer), sixth (Virgo), etc. in the zodiac to be classified as feminine. By comparison with the masculine signs, the feminine signs tend to be more receptive and introverted.

Sources:

Leo, Alan. *Dictionary of Astrology.* Reprint. New York: Astrologer's Library, 1983.
Tester, Jim. *A History of Western Astrology.* New York: Ballantine, 1987.

Feral

Feral is a term used to refer to a wild animal. Feral signs is an older designation, more or less equivalent to the term **bestial signs**. In traditional astrology, the **Moon** was also sometimes said to be feral when it was **void of course**.

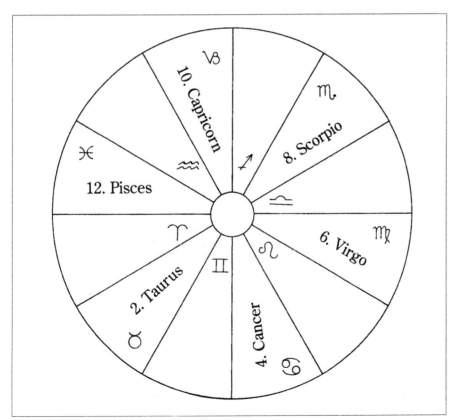

◄
Feminine signs.

Feronia

Feronia, **asteroid** 72 (the 72d asteroid to be discovered), is approximately 96 kilometers in diameter and has an **orbital** period of 3.4 years. It was named after the Roman goddess of freed slaves (it was named at the beginning of the American Civil War), who was also goddess of groves, woods, and orchards. Her shrine on Mount Soracte in Etruria was the scene of an annual fire-walking ritual. In a **natal chart**, the asteroid's location by sign and **house** may indicate where one feels free from social bonds or from the bondage of the past. A **native** with a prominent natal Feronia also feels an attraction for sylvan environments.

Sources:

Kowal, Charles T. *Asteroids: Their Nature and Utilization.* Chichester, West Sussex, U.K.: Ellis Horwood Limited, 1988.
Room, Adrian. *Dictionary of Astronomical Names.* London: Routledge, 1988.

Fides

Fides, **asteroid** 37 (the 37th asteroid to be discovered), is approximately 94 kilometers in diameter and has an **orbital** period of 4.3 years. It was named after the Roman goddess of faith, honesty, and oath. Like its mythological namesake, the asteroid confers faithfulness and honesty to **natives** in whose chart it is prominent (e.g., **conjunct** the **Sun** or the **ascendant**). Fides relates particularly to overt displays of honesty and to the outward performance of duty. Negatively, it may manifest itself as blind faith, as the tendency to use honesty as an excuse for expressing unkind remarks, or as the trait of emphasizing the duties others have toward oneself as a way of manipulating their behavior.

Sources:

Kowal, Charles T. *Asteroids: Their Nature and Utilization.* Chichester, West Sussex, U.K.: Ellis Horwood Limited, 1988.
Room, Adrian. *Dictionary of Astronomical Names.* London: Routledge, 1988.

Fiducia

Fiducia, **asteroid** 380 (the 380th asteroid to be discovered), is approximately 78 kilometers in diameter and has an **orbital** period of 4.4 years. Its name is a personified form of the Latin word for confidence or trust. In a **natal chart**, its location by sign and **house** position indicates where and in what manner one is most likely to be trustworthy, as well as where one experiences trust issues. When **afflicted** by inharmonious **aspects**, Fiducia can show untrustworthiness or a tendency to misplace trust. If prominent in a chart (e.g., **conjunct** the **Sun** or the **ascendant**), it may show an exceptionally trustworthy person or someone for whom trust is a dominant life theme.

Sources:

Kowal, Charles T. *Asteroids: Their Nature and Utilization.* Chichester, West Sussex, U.K.: Ellis Horwood Limited, 1988.
Room, Adrian. *Dictionary of Astronomical Names.* London: Routledge, 1988.

Figure

Figure is an old term for an astrological chart.

Fire Signs

The 12 signs of the **zodiac** are subdivided according to the 4 classical **elements** (earth, air, fire, and water). The 3 **fire signs** (the fire triplicity or fire trigon) are

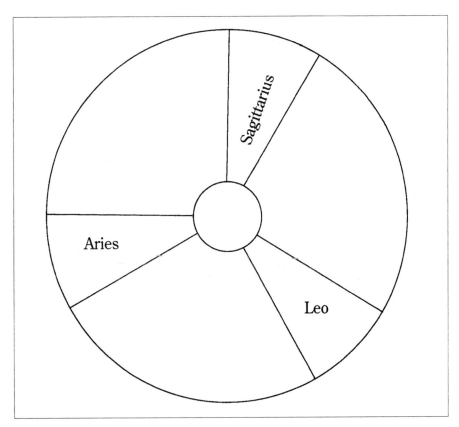

◄
Fire signs.

Aries, **Leo**, and **Sagittarius**. Astrologically, fire refers to activity. Fire sign activity can manifest as inspiration and leadership. For people with a predominance of this element, action is the most important aspect of life.

The activity of the fire element shows itself somewhat differently in each of the signs of the fire **triplicity**. Aries' fiery nature typically manifests as bravery, curiosity, and originality. Leo's comes through in the qualities of leadership and acting ability. Sagittarius's fiery nature emerges as a striving upward toward high social or religious ideals.

Negative fire people can be egotistical, pushy, and excessively concerned about the opinions others hold of them. Unless counterbalanced by other factors, excessive fire in a chart indicates an individual who is overactive, impulsive, and even violent. Conversely, lack of fire can indicate a person who is low in energy and self-esteem.

Sources:

Hand, Robert. *Horoscope Symbols.* Rockport, Mass.: Para Research, 1981.
Sakoian, Frances, and Louis S. Acker. *The Astrologer's Handbook.* New York: Harper & Row, 1989.

▶
Fixed signs.

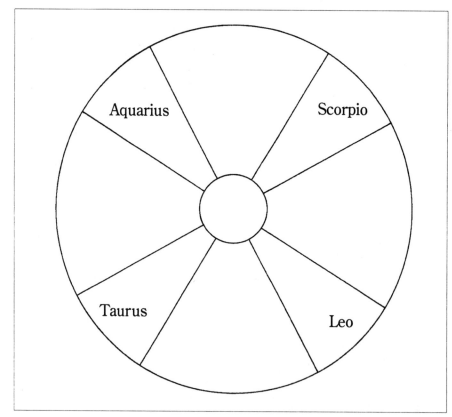

First Point

First point refers to zero **degrees Aries**, the point along the **ecliptic** where the **zodiac** begins.

First Station

When, from the perspective of Earth, it appears that a **planet** pauses and then reverses direction (i.e., appears to go backward in its **orbit**), the point at which it pauses is called the first station.

Fish

The Fish (or Fishes) is a popular name for the sign **Pisces**.

Fixed Signs

The 12 signs of the **zodiac** are subdivided according to 3 **qualities**: cardinal, mutable, and fixed. The 4 fixed signs (the *fixed quadruplicity* or *fixed cross*) are **Taurus, Leo, Scorpio,** and **Aquarius**. The **Sun** moves through these signs when the seasons are at their peak: Taurus in spring, Leo in summer, Scorpio in fall, and Aquarius in winter. The identifying trait of the fixed signs is captured by the connotation of *fixed*: In response to changing circumstances, fixed signs tend to persist in acting according to preestablished patterns. Positively, the fixed quality can manifest as strength and persistence; negatively, as inflexibility and stubbornness.

Fixed Stars

In astrology, the fixed stars refer to all the heavenly bodies we familiarly call **stars**, with the exception of our own **Sun.** The expression *fixed stars* was originally devised to distinguish the stars from the so-called wandering stars, which was the ancient designation for the **planets.** Since antiquity, the fixed stars have been regarded as having astrological influences, particularly if a star is in close **conjunction** with a key planet or some other sensitive point in an astrological chart. Traditional systems of interpretation for the fixed stars described their nature in terms of their similarities to planetary influences. Thus, for example, the star Vega is regarded as having a blend of venusian (**Venus**-like) and mercurial (**Mercury**-like) natures.

Despite the traditional importance assigned to these celestial bodies, few modern astrologers are interested in them. This lack of interest is indicated by computer chart-casting programs, which do not include the fixed stars. One reason for this is that most modern professional astrologers are forced to confine their consulting sessions to 1- or 2-hour periods. An astrologer is lucky to cover even the basics of planetary influence in that span of time. The techniques that provide more refined interpretations—whether they be ancient methods involving the fixed stars or modern methods involving the **asteroids**—are thus left out for lack of time. The fixed stars would provide aspiring astrological researchers with a potentially fruitful field for investigation, however, particularly as traditional interpretations for the principal fixed stars are already in existence and could serve as a starting point for further research.

Sources:

Brau, Jean-Louis, Helen Weaver, and Allan Edmands. *Larousse Encyclopedia of Astrology.* New York: New American Library, 1980.
Ebertin, Reinhold, and George Hoffmann. *Fixed Stars and their Interpretation.* Translated by Irmgard Banks. Tempe, Ariz.: American Federation of Astrologers, 1971.

Flower Remedies and Astrology

The flower remedies—also known as flower essences—are liquids that catalyze changes in problematic patterns or emotions, such as guilt or low self-esteem. They are not herbs or aromatherapy oils, but a greatly diluted essence of the flower of the plant, similar in nature to homeopathic remedies or cell salts. They are sold in many health food stores in concentrate form, four drops of which are mixed in an ounce of spring water. The resulting mixture is taken by mouth at the rate of four drops four times a day. The best known are the Bach remedies, developed in England in the 1930s, and the so-called California remedies, developed by the Flower Essence Society (FES) in the 1970s. By the 1990s, however, companies all over the world were making remedies from their local flowers.

The remedies are an easily learned tool to incorporate into the practice of astrology. The astrologer's reading clearly identifies character patterns in the birth chart and current issues brought up by **transits** or **progressions**. The astrologer can then give a mixture of remedies relevant to those patterns or issues to clients who want to continue to work with the insights gained in the reading. In taking the remedies, clients reportedly gain new perceptions and conscious awareness of where their difficulties stem from. As more clarity is gained, some clients have claimed that even long-standing patterns have been gradually released and replaced with a healthier outlook.

The guilt-ridden client, for instance, may be given Pine by Bach, while the client with low self-esteem may benefit from FES's Sunflower. The child who continually demands to be the center of attention may be given Bach's *Chicory.* FES's *Lotus* is useful for those who wish to pursue meditation and spiritual development. The first remedy the astrologer may wish to acquire is Bach's famous Rescue remedy, which can be given to clients who are in a crisis situation or who are emotionally upset. A few drops of the concentrate to sip in a glass of water or a cup of tea are used to quickly restore calm.

As astrologers become more skilled in using the remedies, they can more easily link them with the concerns of various **planets** or signs. Issues related to the planet **Pluto**, for example, include control (treated with Vine), resentment (assuaged with Willow), and envy or the desire for revenge (mollified with Holly)—all of these therapies for Pluto ailments are Bach remedies. FES's offerings abound with remedies for **Venus** concerns, such as Dogwood, for gentleness and grace in relationships, Bleeding Heart, for the brokenhearted, and Quince, for developing the positive power of love. For the discouragement that often accompanies a **Saturn** transit, the astrologer may suggest Bach's Elm, Gentian, or Gorse.

The astrologer may also be intrigued with certain formulas designed to address various chart factors. For instance, one of Desert Alchemy's founders, Cynthia Kemp, is herself an astrologer and has devised premixed formulas for transits from **Jupiter** and **Chiron** on out to Pluto. She also mixed combination formulas for the **house** axes, such as the axes for the first and seventh houses, the second and eighth **houses**, and the third and ninth **houses**. Pegasus Products also features remedies for issues related to the planets and several of the **fixed stars** in their Star-lite Elixir line. Earthfriends, founded by astrologer John Stowe, features planetary oils that incorporate both flower remedies and aromatherapy oils.

Addresses of some major essence companies are:

Alaskan Flower Essences
Box 1561
Fritz Creek, AK 99603-6161

Desert Alchemy
Box 44189
Tucson, AZ 85733

Earthfriends
Box 8468
Atlanta, GA 30306

Ellon-Bach U.S.A., Inc.
644 Merrick Road
Lynnbrook, NY 11563

Flower Essence Services
Box 586
Nevada City, CA 95959

Pegasus Products
Box 228
Boulder, CO 80306

—Donna Cunningham

Sources:

Barnard, Julian, and Martine Barnard. *The Healing Herbs of Edward Bach.* Hereford, U.K.: Bach Educational Programme, 1988.
Chancellor, Philip M. *Handbook of the Bach Flower Remedies.* New Canaan, Conn.: Keats Health Books, 1980.
Cunningham, Donna. *Flower Remedies Handbook.* New York: Sterling Publishing, 1992.
Gurudas. *Flower Essences and Vibrational Healing.* Rev. ed. San Rafael, Calif.: Cassandra Press, 1989.
Kamiski, Patricia, and Richard Katz. *Flower Essence Repertory.* Rev. ed. Nevada City, Calif.: Flower Essence Services, 1992.

Forming

When two **planets** are beginning to enter into an **aspect** with each other, but before the aspect has become exact, the aspect is said to be forming.

Forrest, Steven

Steven Forrest is a contemporary astrologer best known for his work on personal, individual applications of astrological symbolism. He was born in Mount Vernon, New York, on January 6, 1949, and educated at the University of North Carolina at Chapel Hill (B.A. religion, 1971). Shortly after graduation he began his astrological practice. He is the author of *The Inner Sky* (1984), *The Changing Sky* (1986), and, with his wife Jodie, *Skymates* (1988). His fourth book, *The Night Speaks,* will be an extended argument for the intellectual plausibility of astrology. Forrest's work has been translated into several languages, and he travels throughout the United States and Canada lecturing on astrological topics.

Forrest has written technical articles for most of the major astrological journals and composed the popular The Sky Within report writer for Matrix Software (the largest producers of astrological software). Currently he is composing a second report writer for Matrix. Forrest won the 1985 Professional Astrologer Incorporated Award for Outstanding Contribution to the Art and Science of Astrology. The strong point of his astrological work, both as an author and as a consultant, lies in his ability to relate broad, abstract notions to the down-to-earth realities of everyday life. He lives in the woods near Chapel Hill with his wife and cats.

Selected Publications:

The Inner Sky. 1984. Reprint. San Diego, Calif.: Astro Computing Services, 1988.
The Changing Sky. 1986. Reprint. San Diego, Calif.: Astro Computing Services, 1989
The Night Speaks. Forthcoming.
Skymates. By Steven Forrest and Jodie Forrest. 1989. Reprint. San Diego, Calif.: Astro Computing Services, 1992.

Fortified

A **planet** is said to be fortified when it is **elevated**, favorably-**aspected**, or in a sign that it **rules**.

Fortunes

Fortunes is an older term for the so-called **benefic planets**, **Jupiter** (the Greater Fortune) and **Venus** (the Lesser Fortune).

Foundation Chart

A foundation chart is a **horoscope** calculated for the moment construction on a building is begun. Although such charts can be **cast** retrospectively, in traditional astrology they were part of **electional astrology**—the branch that deals with the most appropriate times to begin things.

Four-footed Signs

The traditional four-footed signs were, as one might anticipate, **Aries, Taurus, Leo, Sagittarius** and **Capricorn**.

Fraternitas

Fraternitas, **asteroid** 309 (the 309th asteroid to be discovered), is approximately 32 kilometers in diameter and has an **orbital** period of 4.4 years. Its name is derived from the Latin word for brotherhood. When prominent in a **natal chart**, Fraternitas indicates a friendly personality, interested in universal brotherhood. The sign and **house** position indicates both how we interact with friends as well as what our friends are like.

Sources:

Kowal, Charles T. *Asteroids: Their Nature and Utilization.* Chichester, West Sussex, U.K.: Ellis Horwood Limited, 1988.

Room, Adrian. *Dictionary of Astronomical Names.* London: Routledge, 1988.

Frieda

Frieda, **asteroid** 722 (the 722d asteroid to be discovered), is approximately 15 kilometers in diameter and has an **orbital** period of 3.2 years. Its name means peace in German. In a **natal chart**, its location by sign and **house** indicates where and how one is most likely to seek or experience peace. When **afflicted** by inharmonious **aspects**, Frieda may show conflict or peace-seeking in situations where a peaceful response is inappropriate. If prominent in a natal chart (e.g., **conjunct** the **Sun** or the **ascendant**), it may show an exceptionally tranquil person.

Sources:

Kowal, Charles T. *Asteroids: Their Nature and Utilization.* Chichester, West Sussex, U.K.: Ellis Horwood Limited, 1988.
Room, Adrian. *Dictionary of Astronomical Names.* London: Routledge, 1988.

Frigga

Frigga, **asteroid** 77 (the 77th asteroid to be discovered), is approximately 66 kilometers in diameter and has an **orbital** period of 4.4 years. It was named after the Norse goddess of marriage, the wife of Odin (the Roman equivalent to Juno). The unusual name of this planetoid—which seems to suggest an obscene gesture—led to its inclusion in *The Asteroid Ephemeris: Dudu, Dembowska, Pittsburgh, Frigga,* Batya Stark and Mark Pottenger's tour de force of astrological humor.

Sources:

Kowal, Charles T. *Asteroids: Their Nature and Utilization.* Chichester, West Sussex, U.K.: Ellis Horwood Limited, 1988.
Room, Adrian. *Dictionary of Astronomical Names.* London: Routledge, 1988.
Stark, Batya, and Mark Pottenger. *The Asteroid Ephemeris: Dudu, Dembowska, Pittsburgh, Frigga.* San Diego, Calif.: Astro Computing Services, 1982.

Fruitful (Fertile Signs and Planets)

The fruitful signs are the signs of the **zodiac** traditionally said to indicate children (i.e., to indicate fertility) when placed on the **cusp** of the fifth house, the house of children. These signs are the *water triplicity* (**Cancer, Scorpio,** and **Pisces**). Several other signs are regarded as being somewhat fruitful. The fruitful **planets** are the **Sun,** the **Moon, Venus,** and **Jupiter** (with **Neptune** being added by certain modern astrologers). **Mercury** is regarded as moderately fruitful. The infertile signs and planets are designated **barren.** The classification of the zodiac into degrees of barrenness and fruitfulness has been largely abandoned because contemporary astrological research has failed to verify this traditional interpretation. However, the traditional fruitful signs are still regarded as fertile in **agricultural astrology**.

Sources:

Lee, Dal. *Dictionary of Astrology.* New York: Paperback Library, 1969.
Leo, Alan. *Dictionary of Astrology.* Reprint. New York: Astrologer's Library, 1983.

G

Gadbury, John

John Gadbury, an English astrologer, was born in Wheatley, Oxon, England, on January 1, 1627. He was the son of a farmer, William Gadbury, and was initially apprenticed to a tailor. He left him in 1644, however, when his mother's father, Sir John Curson, offered to provide the funds for an Oxford education. After graduation, he worked with a London merchant, marrying in about 1648. After he returned to Oxfordshire, he studied astrology with Nicholas Fiske and in 1652 published his first book on the science of the stars. His *Doctrine of Nativities,* a general treatise on **natal astrology**, was published in 1658.

Gadbury became an associate of the eminent astrologer **William Lilly**, although they differed in their politics. Lilly even wrote an introduction to one of Gadbury's books. However, when in 1659 the Swedish King Charles X sent Lilly a gift of a gold chain and medal, Gadbury became jealous. The gift came after a favorable forecast Lilly had given Charles in his **almanac** of 1658. Gadbury published an opposed forecast, and, as it turned out, King Charles died unexpectedly in 1660.

This naturally led to a rift between the two men, which culminated in the so-called Scorpio quarrel of 1675. Displeased with Lilly's negative characterization of **Scorpio**, Gadbury, who had a Scorpio **ascendant**, attacked Lilly in his *Obsequium Rationabile.* Gadbury was answered by some tracts and broadsides printed by Lilly's associates. The quarrel climaxed with the 1693 publication of John Partridge's *Black Life of John Gadbury.* Gadbury is remembered primarily for his *Collectio Geniturarum,* a compilation of 150 **horoscopes**. This collection was often referred to by later astrologers. Gadbury also authored almanacs and tables of planetary positions, but his success was mild compared with other London astrologers, particularly Lilly. He died in London on March 28, 1704.

Selected Publications:

Astronomical Tables. (Invented by George Hartgill.) Introduction by William Lilly. London, 1654.
Genethlialogia, or the Doctrine of Nativities. 2d ed. London, 1661.

Collectio Geniturarum. London: James Cottrel, 1662.
Obsequium Rationabile, or a Reasonable Service performed for the Coelestial sign Scorpio. . . against. . . that grand (but fortunate) Imposter, Mr. William Lilly. London, 1675.

Sources:

Holden, James H., and Robert A. Hughes. *Astrological Pioneers of America.* Tempe, Ariz.: American Federation of Astrologers, 1988.

Gaea

Gaea, **asteroid** 1,184 (the 1,184th asteroid to be discovered), is approximately 20 kilometers in diameter and has an **orbital** period of 4.4 years. Gaea was named after the Greek earth goddess. Lehman associates this asteroid with what she calls the "ground of being."

Sources:

Kowal, Charles T. *Asteroids: Their Nature and Utilization.* Chichester, West Sussex, U.K.: Ellis Horwood Limited, 1988.
Lehman, J. Lee. *The Ultimate Asteroid Book.* West Chester, Penn.: Whitford Press, 1988.

Galactic Center

We are located in a spiral-shaped galaxy approximately 100,000 light-years in diameter. Our **solar system** lies on the outskirts of the galaxy, about 30,000 light-years away from the galactic center (GC). From our location, the GC is located in the latter degrees of the sign **Sagittarius**. (Owing to the **tropical** or moving **zodiac** that most Western astrologers use, the exact position of the GC appears to be is gradually shifting.) The GC is such an intense source of infrared emissions and microwaves that astrophysicists have speculated that an explosion took place there 10 million years ago. Because our solar system is actually rotating around the GC, the GC can be thought of as a bit like the sun of our solar system. The 250 million years that it takes for our solar system to complete one rotation is called a cosmic year.

Astrologers who have studied the effects of the galactic center in **horoscopes** have found that it exerts a powerful influence within a narrow **orb** of 2°, with some effect out to 4°. Individuals with inner **planets** or one of the **angles conjunct** the GC have, in the words of Philip Sedgwick, a potential link "with whatever it is behind all this" (p. 91). When this transpersonal link is ignored, the individual can experience stress and confusion; when it is consciously appropriated, information can be grasped that the individual may seem to have no outward way of knowing. The GC is not significant in such natural events as earthquakes, but it does appear to be prominent in important events involving technology. It also seems to play a major role in human inventiveness, especially technological inventiveness.

Given the many points occupying contemporary astrological space—heliocentric planets, multiple **midpoints**, thousands of **asteroids**, and so forth—everyone surely has some such point in the latter degrees of Sagittarius. On this basis, some astrologers find it useful to examine the position of the galactic center in every chart, and, by its **house** placement, determine to which area of the **native**'s life the cosmos is "speaking." The GC was located at 26° 09′ Sagittarius in 1950, at 26° 34′ in 1980, and will be at 26° 51′ in the year 2000.

Sources:

Brau, Jean-Louis, Helen Weaver, and Allan Edmands. *Larousse Encyclopedia of Astrology.* New York: New American Library, 1980.
Sedgwick, Philip. *The Astrology of Deep Space.* Birmingham, Mich.: Seek-It Publications, 1984.

Galahad

Galahad, **asteroid** 2,082 (the 2,082d asteroid to be discovered), is approximately 14 kilometers in diameter and has an **orbital** period of 5 years. Galahad was named after the knight of the Round Table. Lehman associates this asteroid with the challenge of merging action and contemplation, with reminding us that our movement through life is a spiritual process.

Sources:

Kowal, Charles T. *Asteroids: Their Nature and Utilization.* Chichester, West Sussex, U.K.: Ellis Horwood Limited, 1988.
Lehman, J. Lee. *The Ultimate Asteroid Book.* West Chester, Penn.: Whitford Press, 1988.

Galaxy

Contrary to what one might anticipate, **stars** are not evenly distributed throughout the universe. Instead, they cluster together in galaxies (from Greek *gala,* milk), which are large groupings containing billions of stars. Our galaxy is called the Milky Way.

The astrological effects of the **fixed stars** were the only influences from outside the **solar system** considered in traditional astrology. More recently, astrological researchers have begun to explore the potential astrological significance of galactic as well as extragalactic phenomena—phenomena such as the **galactic center**, black holes, pulsars, quasars, and so forth. This area of study is still very much in its infancy, with little information immediately applicable to the interpretation of individual **natal charts**.

Sources:

Erlewine, Michael, and Margaret Erlewine. *Astrophysical Directions.* Ann Arbor, Mich.: Heart
    Center School of Astrology, 1977.
Sedgwick, Philip. *The Astrology of Deep Space.* Birmingham, Mich.: Seek-It Publications, 1984.

Galilean Moons (Moons of Jupiter)

The largest **planet** in the **solar system, Jupiter** has, as one might anticipate, a
large number of **satellites**—16 at last count (one less than **Saturn**, which holds
the current record of 17). Four of these, called the Galilean moons because they
were discovered by **Galileo**, are large bodies—Ganymede (3,270 miles in
diameter), Callisto (2,980 miles), Io (2,260 miles), and Europa (1,950 miles)—
all larger than **Pluto** (estimated diameter, 1,457 miles). These moons **orbit**
between 262,000 miles and 1,170,000 miles away from Jupiter. Their orbital
periods range from less than 2 terrestrial days (Io) to more than 16 (Callisto). All
the non-Galilean moons are less than 120 miles in diameter, clearly distinguish-
ing them from Jupiter's Big Four.

The moons of **Mars** constitute the most useful starting point for the new
field (new for astrology) of **planetary moon** studies (see **Phobos and Deimos**).
The Jovian moons are also useful for this purpose, however, particularly in the
ways they contrast with the Martian system. Next to Phobos and Deimos, the
Galilean moons have attracted the attention of human beings more than the
moons of any other celestial body (indicating that their astrological significance
should be relatively easy to retrieve from the **collective unconscious**). To
begin with, they were the first nonterrestrial moons to be discovered, and their
discovery (in 1610) was an important factor in overturning the medieval
European view of extraterrestrial space: In the seventeenth century they
produced a sensation, comparable to the discovery of mountains on the surface
of the Moon. In more recent years, as *Pioneer* and *Voyager* probes have sailed
past Jupiter and taken dramatic photographs, the Big Four Jovian moons have
become the focus of considerable astronomical and popular interest.

It would be difficult to dispute the idea that four celestial bodies larger
than Pluto that are, even at their greatest distance away from us, always more
than four times nearer than Pluto's closest approach to Earth should have some
sort of astrological influence. The operative question, however, is, Does the
study of Jovian satellites add anything to our understanding of Jupiter, or are
these influences indistinguishably blended with Jupiter's? An initial clue from
astrological studies of Phobos and Deimos is that the Jovian moons may
represent a polar opposite principle (or, perhaps, another, related principle) to
some key Jupiterian principle. Another clue, taken from **asteroid** studies, is that
the mythology associated with the name of a newly explored celestial body
provides an initial guide to its astrological significance.

Zeus (the Greek equivalent of the Roman Jupiter), as anyone familiar with
classical mythology knows, had an unpleasant propensity to rape everyone to

whom he took a fancy, and all four of the figures after whom the Galilean moons are named were victims of the god's lust. Ganymede was a young man whom Zeus kidnapped to become his lover and cupbearer, while Io, Europa, and Callisto were all young women raped by the king of the gods. Zeus, however, seems to have been plagued by guilt for his misdeeds, because he tried in various ways to make it up to his victims. In the case of Ganymede, Zeus gave the youth's royal father a pair of fine mares and a golden grapevine, and Ganymede himself was immortalized as a **constellation (Aquarius)**. Callisto was similarly transformed into a constellation (the Big Bear), Europa was given a set of unusual gifts (see **Taurus**), and Io became a queen and the ancestress of dynasties, as well as an ancestress of the hero Hercules.

Because many of the ancient gods (including the ones after whom the outer planets are named) were portrayed as rapists, focusing on the purely sexual aspect of these tales probably does illuminate the astrological/psychological principles represented by the Jovian moons. Zeus differed from many other Olympian rapists in that he showered his victims with gifts. This, of course, ties in with Jupiter's astrological characteristic as (among other things) the principle of generosity. With a little reflection, it is not difficult to see that these myths give us some less than pleasant insights into gift-giving: Rather than being "freely given," as the saying goes, gifts are often given to compensate victims for abuse—or, to translate this basic principle into something closer to home, to compensate for the more subtle abuse of neglect (as when parents who feel guilty about not devoting enough time to their children shower them with gifts).

In another myth, Zeus promised to give Sinope (after whom Jupiter's outermost satellite was named) anything in exchange for her favors, so she tricked him into granting her the gift of perpetual virginity. Here we see another shadow side of generosity—giving gifts because we want something—that represents the polar opposite principle of generosity: greed. This principle is usually associated with **Saturn**, but Saturnian greed is a thrifty greed that flows out of a sense of lack. Jovian greed, by way of contrast, flows out of a sense of abundance and expansion, an expansiveness directed solely toward continuing to grow and accumulate. (In **medical astrology**, Jupiter is often associated with cancer.)

An analysis of these myths has given us another perspective on generosity: Most people give gifts out of guilt or because they want something in return (e.g., when someone who has been generous requests a favor of us, we feel guilty if we do not comply). Thus, the placement of Jupiter by sign and—especially—by **house** tells us where we experience at least one form of guilt (other forms of guilt are associated with Saturn) or where we are prone to be generous in order to get something (greed). This analysis of the Jovian moons provides astrologers with new meanings for Jupiter, meanings that were not part of traditional astrological thinking about the planet. And, as astrologers continue to explore the astrological meanings implicit in the Jovian system, more insights are likely to emerge.

Sources:

Lewis, James R. *Martian Astrology*. Goleta, Calif.: Jupiter's Ink, 1992.
McEvers, Joan, ed. *Planets: The Astrological Tools*. Saint Paul, Minn.: Llewellyn Publications, 1989.
Room, Adrian. *Dictionary of Astronomical Names*. London: Routledge, 1988.

Ganymed

Ganymed is **asteroid** 1,036 (the 1,036th asteroid to be discovered). It is approximately 40 kilometers in diameter and has an **orbital** period of 4.3 years. It was named after the youth who was kidnapped to become the cupbearer of Zeus. According to Lehman (p. 67), "the asteroid Ganymed shows how we are able to submit ourselves to that which is beyond our personal power. In negative form, it is the way we evade even the awareness that there *is* anything beyond our own powers."

Ganymed is also one of the moons of **Jupiter**.

Sources:

Kowal, Charles T. *Asteroids: Their Nature and Utilization*. Chichester, West Sussex, U.K.: Ellis Horwood Limited, 1988.
Lehman, J. Lee. *The Ultimate Asteroid Book*. West Chester, Penn.: Whitford Press, 1988.

Gauquelin, Françoise

Françoise Schneider Gauquelin, psychologist and statistician, was born in Switzerland in 1929. She first studied psychology in Geneva, then in Paris, where she met **Michel Gauquelin,** also a psychology student, who introduced her to the scientific investigation of astrology.

Their 30-year collaboration in this field yielded important discoveries, now often summarized as "the Gauquelin **Mars effect** with Sports Champions." But actually their significant findings were not confined to **Mars** only but involve the four most visible planets: **Venus, Jupiter, Saturn,** and the **Moon.** These bodies are not correlated with athletes only, but with all kinds of famous professionals: actors, politicians, scientists, writers, painters, musicians, etc. After investigating data from some 15,000 professionals, the Gauquelins explored also some 16,000 parent-children pairs, which showed that similar planetary constellations preside at the birth of parents and their children in a statistically significant pattern. These outcomes appear to stem from to a correlation of the planets with inborn character traits of each individual.

Although such statements are based on a sound scientific methodology, they were received with much skepticism and scorn by the scientific establishment in general. In Europe and in the United States, scientific committees joined forces to prove them fallacious. But the Gauquelins' results successfully withstood even the most severe tests. According to the famous British astrologer **John Addey**, "The specific importance of the Gauquelins is not in their direct contribution to the knowledge of astrological principles as such, though this has been valuable in some instances, but in the fact that, confronted by a mountain of prejudice against astrology in an age which demands secure empirical evidence, they have by dint of immense courage, tenacity, and intelligence, provided this on a massive scale and in a form which has never been refuted, despite repeated attempts by hostile critics in the scientific world."

Michel and Françoise Gauquelin's collaboration lasted until 1980. At that point each of them continued their research work separately. Françoise has written numerous technical books and articles dealing with the Gauquelin methodology. She also wrote *Psychology of the Planets* (1982), which shows how strikingly similar are the traditional psychological traits associated with the planets and the modern outcomes of the Gauquelins' statistical studies. Her research journal *Astro-Psychological Problems* (1982–1988) convincingly shows that not only the famous professionals are born under typical planetary constellations, but unknown individuals as well. *The Horoscope Revisited* explains how to use the Gauquelin findings in current practice.

Selected Publications:

Series A: Professional Notabilities. 6 vols. Paris: Laboratoire d'Etude des Relations entre Rythmes Cosmiques et Psychophysiologiques, 1970–71.
Series B: Heredity Experiments. 6 vols. Paris: Laboratoire d'Etude des Relations entre Rythmes Cosmiques et Psychophysiologiques, 1970–71.
Series C: Psychological Monographs. 5 vols. Paris: Laboratoire d'Etude des Relations entre Rythmes Cosmiques et Psychophysiologiques, 1972–77.
Series D: Scientific Documents. 10 vols. Paris: Laboratoire d'Etude des Relations entre Rythmes Cosmiques et Psychophysiologiques, 1976–82.

Gauquelin, Michel

Michel Gauquelin, a French researcher prominent for his statistical investigation of astrology, was born on November 13, 1928, in Paris. He received his doctorate in psychology and statistics from the Sorbonne. Together with that of his wife, **Françoise Gauquelin**, his work has provided the most rigorous scientific evidence for the validity of astrology, although their work departs from traditional astrology on certain points.

Investigating earlier statistical studies of astrology, the Gauquelins found them lacking proper controls and other elements of sound research. Beginning in 1949, they collected birth data on thousands of people from records across Europe and analyzed natal planetary positions with respect to such factors as profession and personality. Their most celebrated discovery was that for specific professions—particularly for writers, sports champions, and scientists—the positions of certain **planets** were found in statistically significant patterns. The planet **Mars**, for instance, was often found to be near the horizon or near the meridian of the birth charts of sports champions (the so-called **Mars effect**). The **horoscopes** of eminent scientists exhibited a similar pattern with respect to the planet **Saturn**; the writers' with respect to the **Moon**.

The Gauquelins' studies have withstood repeated attacks, and replications of their research by others have verified the original findings. Through their laboratory they published a complete record of their research, which filled 23 volumes. They also published numerous short works, including *The Cosmic Clocks* (1967), *The Scientific Basis of Astrology* (1969), *Cosmic Influences on Human Behavior* (1973), and *Birthtimes: A Scientific Investigation of the Secrets of Society* (1983). To avoid professional prejudice against them, the Gauquelins have tended to discuss their findings in terms of "cosmic genetics," "planetary heredity," or "cosmobiology."

Because the Gauquelins' work differs in many respects from traditional astrology, astrologers tend to refer to it as "neoastrology." The significance of their work is such that no research validating astrology is more frequently cited. Michel Gauquelin died in Paris on May 20, 1991.

Selected Publications

The Cosmic Clocks: From Astrology to a Modern Science. Chicago: Henry Regnery, 1967.
Birthtimes: A Scientific Investigation of the Secrets of Astrology. New York: Hill & Wang, 1983.
Neo-Astrology: A Copernican Revolution. New York: Arkana, 1991.

Sources:

Brau, Jean-Louis, Helen Weaver, and Allan Edmands. *Larousse Encyclopedia of Astrology*. New York: New American Library, 1980.
"In Memoriam: Michel Gauquelin—November 13, 1928–May 20, 1991." *Astroflash* (Summer 1991): 9–10. (Available from Astro Computing Services, San Diego, Calif.)

Gemini

Gemini, the third sign of the **zodiac**, is a **mutable air** sign. It is a positive, **masculine sign ruled** by the **planet Mercury**. Its symbol is the Twins, its **glyph** is said to represent twins, and it takes its name from the Latin word for twins. Gemini is associated with the shoulders, arms, hands, and lungs, and individuals with a Gemini **sun sign** are prone to accidents involving the arms, and to lung problems. The key phrase for Gemini is *I think*.

While Gemini has been associated with different pairs of people, the primary association is with Castor and Pollux (the Roman version of the Greek Castor and Polydeuces). Castor and Pollux were the sons of Leda, who coupled with the god Zeus and then, in some accounts, lay with her husband, King Tyndareus; the resulting offspring were Pollux, the son of Zeus, and Castor, the son of Tyndareus. They were warriors and members of the Argonauts' crew (the band of mythological adventurers who sailed with Jason in quest of the Golden Fleece) and came to be regarded as patron deities of sailors and navigators. During a cattle-stealing adventure, Castor was slain. Pollux, the immortal brother, asked Zeus that either he might die also or his dead brother might share his immortality. In deference to his son's wish, Zeus allowed the brothers to alternate so that one spent a day in the underworld while the other was among the gods; on successive days they traded places.

The primary Gemini trait reflected in this tale is the sign's well-known dual nature. People who do not understand Geminis frequently regard them as "two-faced," but people born under this sign are, more often than not, sincerely schizophrenic— they sincerely identify with both their personalities. Positively, this dual nature manifests as an ability to see both sides of every disagreement; a typical Gemini remark is, "There's two sides to everything." Like Castor and Pollux, Geminis are highly social beings with greatly developed communication skills. Also like the twins of mythology, they are associated with travel and trade (and sometimes "cattle rustling") and enjoy travel. Like all air signs, they are at home in the mental realm; many academics and teachers are Geminis.

There is a wealth of information available on the characteristics of the zodiacal signs, so much that one book would not be able to contain it all. One traditional way in which astrologers condense information is by summarizing sign and planet traits in lists of words and short phrases called key words or key phrases. The following Gemini key words are drawn from Manly P. Hall's *Astrological Keywords:*

Emotional key words: "Lack concentration, sensitive, eloquent, humane, fond of travel, not domestic, good company, changeable, unsympathetic but genial, quick-tempered" (p. 17).

Mental key words: "Dextrous in manual expression, inventive, literary, versatile, adaptable, self-expressive, democratic, curious, analytical if highly evolved, sometimes scatterbrained, tricky" (p. 20).

Most popular works on astrology contain data on the signs, and these can be consulted for more detailed information.

Sources:

Evans, Colin. *The New Waite's Compendium of Natal Astrology.* Revised by Brian E. F. Gardener. York Beach, Maine: Samuel Weiser, 1971. (Originally published 1917.)

Green, Landis Knight. *The Astrologer's Manual: Modern Insights into an Ancient Art.* Sebastopol, Calif.: CRCS Publications, 1975.

Hall, Manly P. *Astrological Keywords.* 1958. Reprint. Savage, Md.: Littlefield Adams (1975), 17, 20.

Gemstones and Astrology

Quite a bit has been written on the correlations between gemstones, signs, and **planets**; unfortunately, much of what has been written is not in agreement. Some of this disagreement seems to stem from the gem industry's attempt to "translate" these correlations into "birthstones" for each month even though **sun signs** "straddle" two months rather than begin and end neatly with the beginning and end of each month. This confusion is compounded because European birthstone selections, especially those of the German-speaking countries, do not always coincide with North American ones.

The rationale for correlating gemstones with signs and planets is that since everything is energy—and since everything is interrelated—correspondences between gems, signs, and planets can be made by looking at properties such as hardness, color, mineral families, crystal systems, chemical elements, inclusions, and many other things (including, of course, mythology). Again confusion arises, in part from subjectivity (what is "red" to one person may be "crimson" or "purple-red" to another) and in part because no two gemstones are precisely alike. While we may be content to call a certian mineral an agate, agates come in a variety of colors and may be banded, layered, or a single color. Moreover, agates are a form of chalcedony, which in turn is part of the quartz family. Furthermore, agate nodules such as geodes may contain opal, quartz crystal, or calcite, among other things. So no gemstone partakes "purely" of one sign or planet.

Even though classifying gems by sign is much like saying all Librans are identical, it *is* a starting point. According to both gemological and mythological tradition, gems are symbolic of certain attributes. An astrologer trained in working with gems can, through the premise that everything is energy, use them to enhance, balance, or redirect certain energies within the person by using an appropriate gem to create an awareness of potentials and to stimulate direction of those potentials along appropriate lines. (Contrary to some schools of magic, astrologers do not believe that one can use a gem to create a potential that is not already inherently present and shown by the **natal chart, progressions and directions,** or **transits**). Ideally, the astrologer would suggest the class of gem, but the client would go to the store and select the gem, the theory being that color variations or inclusions might be meaningful to the client. This runs counter to **Hindu astrology**, in which the astrologer chooses the gem and even the specific weight.

Following is a list of commonly accepted correspondences between gems, signs, and planets:

Aries: Diamond, red jasper, red carnelian, bloodstone sard

Taurus: Blue sapphire, orange carnelian, rose quartz, emerald, selenite

Gemini: Agate, citrine, tiger's eye, apatite, aquamarine

Cancer: Pearl, green aventurine quartz, chrysoprase, moonstone, moss agate

Leo: Ruby, clear quartz crystal, any "golden" quartz (e.g., citrine, the gold-brown form of aventurine quartz, tiger's eye), jasper, onyx

Virgo: Sardonyx, yellow agate, yellow citrine, amazonite, peridot

Libra: Padparadschah sapphire, orange citrine, smoky quartz, elbaite, nephrite/jade

Scorpio: Opal, blood-red carnelian, sard, almandine garnet, rubellite

Sagittarius: Topaz, blue quartz, chalcedony, azurite, labradorite

Capricorn: Turquoise, onyx, quartz cat's eye, fire agate, green tourmaline

Aquarius: Amethyst, hawk's eye, turquoise, quartz crystal, uvarovite

Pisces: Bloodstone, moonstone, amethyst, amethyst quartz, jade

Sun: Chrysoberyl, diamond, quartz crystal, amber, gold

Moon: Moonstone, pearl, emerald, chalcedony, calcite

Mercury: Yellow sapphire, topaz, citrine, lodestone, cinnabar

Venus: All sapphires but yellow, hyacinth (a yellow-red zircon), rose quartz, nephrite, chrysoprase

Mars: All red garnets, ruby, jasper, hematite, iron

Jupiter: Amethyst, lapis lazuli, blue sapphire, hyacinth, iris agate

Saturn: Aquamarine, blue spinel, onyx, jet, obsidian

Uranus: Turquoise, malachite, amazonite, barite, amethyst

Neptune: Amethyst, opal, most shells, fluorite, bloodstone

Pluto: Bloodstone, dark red agates, almandine and pyrope garnets, alexandrite, flint

Overlaps in correspondence in many cases reflect both color variations and philosophical variations.

—*Donna Van Toen*

Sources:

Bauer, Jarsolav, and Vladimir Bouska. *A Guide in Color to Precious and Semi-Precious Stones.* Secaucus, N.J.: Chartwell Books, 1989.

Matteson, Barbara J. *Mystic Minerals.* Seattle, Wash.: Cosmic Resources, 1985.

Raphaell, Katrina. *Crystal Enlightenment, Volume 1.* New York: Aurora Press, 1986.

Schumann, Walter. *Gemstones of the World.* New York: Sterling, 1984.

Uyldert, Mellie. *The Magic of Precious Stones.* Northamptonshire, U.K.: Turnstone Press, 1984.

Genethliacal Astrology

Genethliacal (from Greek *genos,* birth, from which we also get words like genesis and genealogy) astrology is the traditional term for **natal astrology**, the branch of the science of the **stars** that interprets the significance of individual birth charts. Genethliacal astrology is distinguished from such other branches of astrology as **mundane astrology,** which interprets the significance of celestial events for nations, cultural trends, and world affairs.

Genetics and Astrology

Adherents as well as critics of astrology sometimes ask the question, How do astrological influences interact with the "forces" of genetic heritage to determine human nature? In the hands of critics, this issue becomes the assertion that genetics can explain any inborn traits. A subsequent assertion is then that contrary astrological influences cannot possibly overcome genetic factors, and hence astrology is false. However, this way of stating the problem does not do justice to the manner in which astrologers would actually approach the issue.

Instead of conceiving celestial influences as external forces that affect Earth like some kind of extraterrestrial radiation, most astrologers view the universe as an interconnected whole, and astrological "forces" as working in **synchronicity.** Synchronism refers to the occurences of events at one place simultaneously with those in another part of the universe, even though there is no causal link between them. Consider an analogy: Imagine the relationship between two clocks, both registering the same time. Their indicating the same time does not mean that one clock forces the other clock to read the same. Rather, they are both set to run parallel courses.

In a similar manner, astrological influences do not work by competing with and overcoming terrestrial forces, such as genetic inheritance. Instead, the universe runs in such a manner that events on the terrestrial sphere mirror events in the celestial sphere (the patterns of the **planets**). Thus, occasions do not arise in which genetics and astrology conflict with each other.

Geniture

Geniture is an older term for a personal **horoscope.**

Geocentric Astrology

Geocentric means Earth-centered, and geocentric astrology refers to any astrological system that uses Earth as the point of reference from which to record the positions of celestial bodies. All traditional systems were geocentric, but some astrologers have experimented with **heliocentric (Sun**-centered) systems, creating **heliocentric astrology.**

Geographical Astrology

Geographical astrology is a subdivision of **mundane astrology** that deals with the astrological associations between the **zodiac** and geographical locations.

George, Demetra

Demetra George is best known for her work with **asteroids** and goddess mythology. She was born July 25, 1946, in Chicago, Illinois, and was educated at Randolph-Macon Women's College and the State University of New York at New Paltz (B.A., philosophy). Her astrology teachers were Joanne Wickenburg, **Zipporah Dobyns**, Mark Robertson, and Virginia Dayan. George has been a counselor, teacher, writer, and researcher since 1972. She is a member of the Association for Astrological Networking and is president of the Asteroid Special Interest Group of the National Council for Geocosmic Research.

George's pioneering research synthesizes mythological archetypes and transpersonal healing therapies with contemporary astrology and theories of planetary evolution. One of the principles guiding her work is, "When a heavenly body is prominent in the sky at the time of your birth, the mythological story of the god or goddess who shares the same name with the **planet**, asteroid, or **star** becomes a major theme in your life." She has lectured throughout the United States, Canada, Mexico, Europe, Australia, and New Zealand and is coauthor of *Asteroid Goddesses* (1986), and *Astrology for Yourself* (1987) and author of *Mysteries of the Dark Goddess* (1992). She has two children and lives in a small town on the Oregon coast.

Selected Publications:

Mysteries of the Dark Moon: The Healing Power of the Dark Goddess. San Francisco, Calif.: Harper, 1992.
Asteroid Goddesses: The Mythology, Psychology and Astrology of the Reemerging Feminine (with Douglas Bloch). 2d ed. San Diego, Calif.: Astro Computing Services, 1990.
Astrology for Yourself: A Workbook for Personal Transformation (with Douglas Bloch). Berkeley, Calif.: Wingbow Press, 1987.

George, Llewellyn

Llewellyn George, born August 17, 1876, in Swansea, Wales, was a prominent astrologer and author and founder of Llewellyn Publications. His father died when he was young, and his mother remarried and moved to the United States. George's younger half-brother, Griff Abrams, was his partner in the astrological publishing field for many years.

George began studying astrology in Portland, Oregon, under L. H. Weston. Later he moved to Los Angeles, where his publishing business was highly successful. He began publishing the *Astrological Bulletin* in 1905 and *The Moon Sign Book* in 1906.

Throughout a busy lifetime, George supported astrologers, astrology, and astrological organizations. He seldom accepted office in these organizations, but did serve on committees. The American Federation of Astrologers (AFA) honored him by awarding him honorary life membership (1939), and the *Astrological Bulletin* of August 22, 1941, called him the "Dean of American Astrologers." In 1948, he contributed to the AFA building fund, and when the AFA library was being expanded, he contributed money for a bookcase dedicated to his brother, Griff Abrams, and filled it with copies of all available Llewellyn publications.

During a period of legal problems in California in the mid-forties, he cofounded and served as president of Educational Astrology, Inc., in Los Angeles. This organization was established to fight antiastrology legislation and ordinances. Toward the end of the 1940s, he established the Llewellyn Foundation for Astrological Research, with **Donald A. Bradley** as research director. He died on July 11, 1954, in Los Angeles.

Selected Publications:

(The New Improved) Planetary Hour Book. Portland, Oregon: Portland School of Astrology, [1907].
Practical Astrology for Everybody. Portland, Oregon: Bulletina Publishing Co., [1911].
Astrologer's Searchlight. 2d ed. rev. Los Angeles: Llewellyn Publications, 1933.
A to Z Horoscope Maker and Delineator. 8th ed. rev. Los Angeles: Llewellyn Publications, 1943.

Sources:

Holden, James H., and Robert A. Hughes *Astrological Pioneers of America.* Tempe, Ariz.: American Federation of Astrologers, 1988.

Georgium Sidus

Georgium Sidus (Latin for George's Star) was the name given to the newly discovered **Uranus** by **Sir William Herschel** in honor of his patron, George III. Needless to say, astronomers in the other countries of the world were not pleased with Herschel's choice of name, so that Georgium Sidus never became widely used.

Gilgamesh

Gilgamesh, **asteroid** 1,812 (1,812th asteroid to be discovered), is approximately 14 kilometers in diameter and has an **orbital** period of 5.2 years. It was named after the Sumerian hero of the *Gilgamesh* Epic. Gilgamesh was a king of Uruk who, after his best friend died, embarked on an unsuccessful quest for immortality. The asteroid represents an interest in death and physical immortality. The sign and **house** position of Gilgamesh in a **natal chart** indicates how this interest is manifested. If prominent in a chart (e.g., **conjunct** the **Sun** or the **ascendant**), it may show a person for whom this interest is a major life theme.

Sources:

Kowal, Charles T. *Asteroids: Their Nature and Utilization.* Chichester, West Sussex, U.K.: Ellis Horwood Limited, 1988.

Room, Adrian. *Dictionary of Astronomical Names.* London: Routledge, 1988.

Glyphs

Astrological glyphs are symbols that represent celestial bodies, signs, or other components of a **horoscope**. Glyphs constitute a kind of shorthand that allows astrologers to concentrate a large amount of information in a small space. To many new students of astrology, these symbols seem to constitute an unnecessary and difficult hurdle: Why not just write the names of the **planets** into the chart? But, once memorized, they are easy to use and are far preferable to drawing in other kinds of abbreviations. The increasing use of **asteroids** by astrologers has led to the proliferation of new, not particularly memorable, glyphs, as well as questions about who should have the final say on adopting new symbols. One proposal is that an interorganizational glyph committee, parallel to the International Astronomical Union nomenclature committee, be created to standardize new glyphs.

See pages xxv–xxvii, in the Introduction, for tables of astrological glyphs and abbreviations.

Sources:

Brau, Jean-Louis, Helen Weaver, and Allan Edmands. *Larousse Encyclopedia of Astrology.* New York: New American Library, 1980.

Foreman, Patricia. *Computers and Astrology: A Universal User's Guide and Reference.* Burlington, Vt.: Good Earth Publications, 1992.

Goat

The Goat is a popular name for the sign **Capricorn**. The original Mesopotamian creature associated with this sign was half goat and half fish.

In this engraving from an 18th century German fantasy novel, Mercury, Venus, Mars, Jupiter, and Saturn are represented by their glyphs. · Bettmann Archive

Grand Cross (Cosmic Cross)

The **configuration** of a cross formed in a **horoscope** by four or more **planets** is referred to as a grand cross. Each planet successively makes a **square** (an **aspect** of 90°) to the preceding planet, and the planets directly across the chart from each other are involved in **oppositions** (180° aspects). Because astrological signs at 90° angles to each other belong to the same **quality** (cardinal, mutable, or fixed), grand crosses tend to involve planets in all four signs of one quality. Thus, grand crosses can be classified as cardinal crosses, mutable crosses, or fixed crosses (grand crosses that involve planets in signs of different qualities are referred to as mixed crosses).

Because all the aspects contained in a grand cross are **hard** aspects, an individual with such a configuration in her or his **natal chart** is presented with more challenges than the average person, and these **natives** sometimes feel "crucified" by life. On the other hand, once the challenges proffered by a grand cross have been adequately met, the individual becomes an unusually well integrated person, with the power to accomplish great tasks.

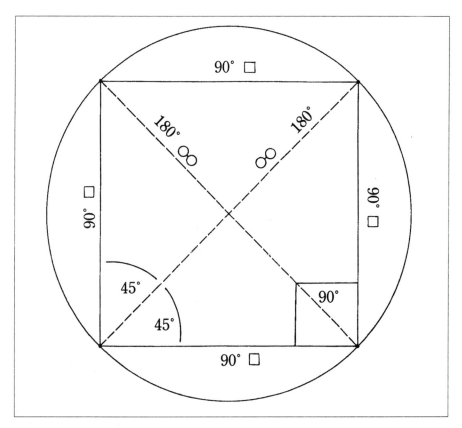

◄
Grand cross.

Grand Trine

A **trine aspect** is a 120° angle between two **planets** in an astrological chart. When a third planet on the other side of the chart makes trine aspects to the two planets forming the first trine, the resulting **configuration** is called a grand trine. Because astrological **signs** at 120° angles to each other belong to the same **element** (earth, air, fire, or water), grand trines tend to involve planets in all three signs of one element. Thus, grand trines can be classified as grand earth trines, grand air trines, grand fire trines, or grand water trines (grand trines that involve planets in signs of different elements are referred to as mixed grand trines). Because trines are **soft aspects**, a person with a grand trine in her or his **natal chart** tends to be unusually lucky, particularly in matters related to the **houses** and signs affected by this configuration. However, unless there are also some **hard aspects** in the chart, such individuals are often not presented with enough challenges to develop strong wills. Thus, this seemingly beneficial configuration can actually handicap the **native.** A more ideal configuration is a **kite**, which is a grand trine plus a fourth planet that makes an **opposition** to one of the other three planets.

▶
Grand trine.

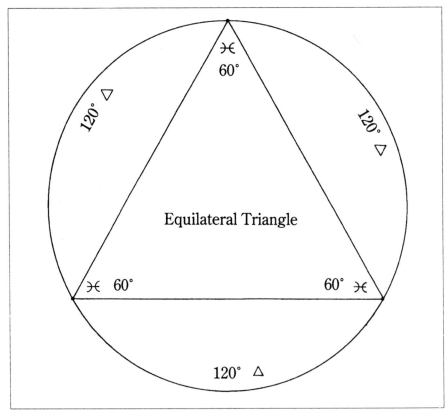

Grant, Ernest A.

Ernest A. Grant, one of the founders of the American Federation of Astrologers, was born on June 4, 1893, in Detroit, Michigan. Around 1906, he moved to the nation's capital. He initially worked as a stenographer and court reporter for the Norfolk Navy Yard and was later employed by different members of the U.S. Congress and by lobby groups. He worked, for example, for the Methodist Board of Temperance Promotion and Public Morals, for Sen. Harold Burton of Ohio, for the Securities and Exchange Commission, and so forth.

Grant's wife, Catherine, taught him astrology, and soon after their marriage he became an astrologer, lecturer, and teacher. In 1938, he was one of the 3 incorporators of the American Federation of Astrologers (AFA), one of the oldest astrology organizations in America. He was AFA's first president (1938–1941) as well as its first executive secretary (1941–1959). Federation work was centered in his home from 1938 to 1951, until it was moved to a small building in Library Court, adjacent to the Library of Congress, in 1951. This building served as its headquarters until the early 1970s, when the AFA moved to Arizona.

Grant and his wife also founded the National Astrological Library, a book publishing organization that was later acquired by the AFA. Despite his heavy organizational involvement, he found time to teach and write about astrology. Grant was an ardent student of political astrology. He researched the astrological history of the United States and, with Ralph Kraum, wrote *Astrological Americana*. Grant died on March 6, 1968, in Washington, D.C.

Selected Publications:

Astrological Americana. 1949. Reprint. Tempe, Ariz.: American Federation of Astrologers, n.d.
Tables of Diurnal Planetary Motion. Washington, D.C.: National Astrology Library, 1948.

Sources:

Holden, James H., and Robert A. Hughes. *Astrological Pioneers of America*. Tempe, Ariz.: American Federation of Astrologers, 1988.

Gratia

Gratia, **asteroid** 424 (the 424th asteroid to be discovered), is approximately 44 kilometers in diameter and has an **orbital** period of 4.6 years. It was named after the three Graces of Greek mythology. Like its mythological namesake, the asteroid confers "grace" upon **natives** in whose **natal chart** it is prominent. The **house** and sign position of Gratia indicate where and how one expresses gracefulness.

Sources:

Kowal, Charles T. *Asteroids: Their Nature and Utilization.* Chichester, West Sussex, U.K.: Ellis Horwood Limited, 1988.

Room, Adrian. *Dictionary of Astronomical Names.* London: Routledge, 1988.

Great Circle

A great circle is any circle drawn on a sphere, the plane of which also passes through the inside of the sphere. Great circles are the basis of various systems for locating terrestrial and celestial bodies in terms of sets of coordinates expressed in **degrees** of a circle. **Longitude** and **latitude** are the most familiar of these coordinates. Astrology utilizes several systems of celestial coordinates. Parallel to the manner in which terrestrial coordinates are great circles drawn on the surface of Earth, **celestial coordinates** are great circles drawn on the inside of the **celestial sphere.** The **ecliptic,** the **celestial equator,** and the **prime vertical** are examples of some of the great circles used in astrology.

▶
This illustration of the Grand Orrery by Rowley shows a number of different reference points on the celestial sphere. Note that because their centers are not co-extensive with the center of the earth, the Arctic Circle and the Tropic of Cancer are not great circles.
· Bettmann Archive

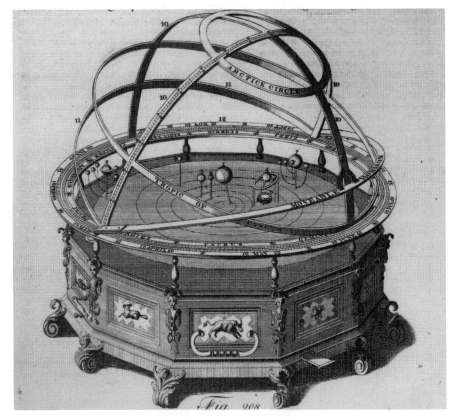

Greek Astrology

See: History of Western Astrology

Green, Jeffrey

Jeffrey Green was born on December 2, 1946, in Hollywood, California. He is best known for his pioneering work on the evolutionary journey of the soul as expressed in his best-selling book *Pluto: The Evolutionary Journey of the Soul,* which has been translated into Dutch, German, Spanish, Portuguese, and Slavic and is currently being translated into Hebrew and French. Green also wrote *Uranus: Freedom from the Known,* which details the archetype of liberation from all learned conditioning patterns necessary to actualize one's essential nature.

He has lectured throughout the world and been a faculty member at all major astrology conferences, including the United Astrology Conference, the American Federation of Astrologers, the Third World Astrological Conference in Zurich, etc. Green has been a full-time professional astrologer in Seattle, Washington, since 1976. His formal training is in psychology and philosophy, and he spent 2 years in a Vedantic monastery. He currently resides on San Juan Island, Washington.

Greenwich Time

Because of the variation in time caused by various time changes as one moves east or west across Earth, astrologers have found it convenient to construct tables such as **ephemerides** (tables of planetary positions) with the time at Greenwich, England, as a benchmark. Greenwich lies exactly on the 0° **longitude** line, which makes it relatively easy to determine the number of hours to add or subtract to local time in order to obtain Greenwich time (15° = 1 hour).

Sources:

Brau, Jean-Louis, Helen Weaver, and Allan Edmands. *Larousse Encyclopedia of Astrology.* New York: New American Library, 1980.

Filbey, John, and Peter Filbey. *The Astrologer's Companion.* Wellingborough, Northamptonshire, U.K.: Aquarian Press, 1986.

H

Hades

Hades is one of the eight **hypothetical planets** (sometimes referred to as the trans-Neptunian points or planets, TNPs) utilized in **Uranian astrology**. It is associated with such negative conditions and substances as poverty, ugliness, garbage, dirt, sickness, bacteria, loneliness, debasement, vulgarity, and crime. Hades is also connected with "past lifetimes," the ancient past, and secrets, and in certain combinations can even represent ancient wisdom and the older sciences. This hypothetical planet can have positive meanings, particularly when found in the **horoscopes** of individuals who deal with such Hades matters as the healing of disease.

Sources:

Lang-Wescott, Martha. *Mechanics of the Future: Asteroids.* Rev. ed. Conway, Mass.: Treehouse Mountain, 1991.

Simms, Maria Kay. *Dial Detective: Investigation with the 90 Degree Dial.* San Diego, Calif.: Astro Computing Services, 1989.

Hagar

Hagar, **asteroid** 682 (the 682d asteroid to be discovered), is approximately 12 kilometers in diameter and has an **orbital** period of 4.3 years. It is named after the biblical Hagar, Sarah's maid who fathered Ishmael through Abraham and was later driven away and left to die in the desert. Muslims trace their lineage to Ishmael. When prominent in a **natal chart**, the asteroid Hagar can show an individual who creates for another person but is later rejected out of jealousy of her or his work and creativity. Like the biblical Hagar, this person can later become an independent creator.

Sources:

Kowal, Charles T. *Asteroids: Their Nature and Utilization*. Chichester, West Sussex, U.K.: Ellis Horwood Limited, 1988.

Room, Adrian. *Dictionary of Astronomical Names*. London: Routledge, 1988.

Hall, Manly Palmer

Manly Palmer Hall, a modern occult writer and founder of the Philosophical Research Society, was born on March 18, 1901, in Peterborough, Canada, to William S. and Louise Palmer Hall, who moved to the United States in 1904. The family moved frequently, and part of Hall's youth was spent in Sioux Falls, South Dakota. He had especially fond memories of his paternal grandmother, who was the first person to take him to California.

Hall became interested in occult matters when he was young and joined, among other groups, the Theosophical Society, the Freemasons, the Societas Resecruciana in Civitatibus Folderatis (a Rosicrucian fellowship whose membership is limited to Masons), and the American Federation of Astrologers. Ordained in 1923, he became the leader of the Church of the People, Los Angeles, an occult–metaphysical group. The church, situated in the Trinity Auditorium building, grew into the center of his publishing concern, the Hall Publishing Company, and a magazine, *The All Seeing Eye* (initiated in 1923). (*The All Seeing Eye,* superseded by *Horizon,* is now published as the *PRS Journal.*) Hall's occult texts include *The Initiates of the Flame* (1922), *Shadow Forms* (1925), *Man, the Grand Symbol of the Mysteries* (1932), and *The Story of Astrology* (1933). His writing, particularly *An Encyclopedic Outline of Masonic, Hermetic, Qabbalistic, and Rosicrucian Symbolical Philosophy* (1928), established him as a major figure in occult thought.

In 1934, Hall established a philosophical–religious institution modeled on the ancient school of **Pythagoras.** This school, The Philosophical Research Society, became a vehicle for propagating occult wisdom throughout the West. Hall donated to the society an extensive library of more than 50,000 volumes, including many rare works, on religion, the occult, Eastern mysticism, parapsychology, and related topics.

Hall devoted most of his life to lecturing and writing. In addition to 50 books, he also wrote hundreds of shorter works that include transcripts of his lectures. His most important books include *Reincarnation: The Cycle of Necessity* (1939), *First Principles of Philosophy* (1942), *Self-Unfoldment by Disciplines of Realization* (1942), *Very Sincerely Yours* (1948), *The Mystical Christ* (1951), *The Secret Destiny of America* (1958), and, most recently, *The Rosicrucians and Magister Christoph Schlegel: Hermetic Roots of America* (1986). Hall also developed correspondence courses on the Wisdom of the Ages, Studies in Consciousness, and Lectures on Ancient Philosophy.

He died March 29, 1990.

Selected Publications:

Reincarnation: The Cycle Necessity. Los Angeles: Philosophical Research Society, 1942.
The Secret Destiny of America. Los Angeles: Philosophical Research Society, 1952.
The Little World of PRS. Los Angeles: Philosophical Research Society, 1982.
The Mystical Christ. Los Angeles: Philosophical Research Society, 1982.

Sources:

Contemporary Authors. vol. 132. Detroit, Mich.: Gale Research, 1991.
Melton, J. Gordon. *Religious Leaders of America.* Detroit: Gale Research, 1991.
Shepard, Leslie. *Encyclopedia of Occultism & Parapsychology.* 2d ed. Detroit: Gale Research, 1984–85.

Hamburg School

The Hamburg school is another name for **Uranian astrology**.

Hand, Robert S.

Robert S. Hand, a well-known contemporary astrologer, was born on December 5, 1942, in Plainfield, New Jersey. He was raised in Orleans, Massachusetts, on Cape Cod. He graduated magna cum laude with a bachelor of arts degree from Brandeis University in 1965 and attended the University of California at Berkeley. He later attended Princeton University, where he studied the history and philosophy of science at the graduate level.

His interest in astrology came from his father, Wilfred C. Hand, who discovered the usefulness of astrological methods in forecasting stock market price moves, at which he was quite successful. Hand first became interested in astrology in his teens and actively began studying it on his own and with the assistance of his father in 1960. He became a practicing astrologer in 1972, working in New York and Boston. He now practices on Cape Cod.

Hand's first book, *Planets in Composite,* was published in 1975, followed by *Planets in Transit* (1976), *Planets in Youth* (1977), *Horoscope Symbols* (1981), and *Essays on Astrology* (1982). These books have been translated into several foreign languages, including Dutch, German, French, Swedish, and Italian. Articles by Hand have appeared in the *Journal of the National Council for Geocosmic Research,* the *Journal of the Astrological Association of Great Britain,* and several other magazines and periodicals.

Since 1973, Hand has been on the board of directors of the National Council for Geocosmic Research, having served as publications chairman and research director. Since 1990, he has served as its national chairman. He also served for several years as a patron of the Faculty of Astrological Studies of Great Britain and is a member of the Astrological Association of Great Britain.

Hand is known chiefly, outside his books, for his work on the scientific aspects and implications of astrology and astrological research, as well as the application of astrology to financial and economic cycles. For this work he received the Regulus Award in research and development from the United Astrology Congress in 1989 and the Global Research Forum's Neil F. Michelsen award for research in the application of astrology to financial cycles in 1992.

In 1977, Hand was also one of the first to program microcomputers to do much of the tedious work of astrological calculations. This led in 1979 to the foundation of Astro-Graphics Services, later Astrolabe Software, of which he is still part owner and principal programmer.

More recently, Hand returned to his academic roots and began to do extensive work on the history of astrology, with a focus on methods, philosophical concepts, and modes of consciousness to be found in ancient astrology and the relevance these may have for the contemporary practice of astrology.

Other current projects include continuing work in financial and economic studies using astrology and astrological programming projects for both research and practical astrological applications.

Selected Publications:

Planets in Composite. Rockport Mass.: Para Research, 1975.
Planets in Transit. Rockport Mass.: Para Research, 1976.
Planets in Youth. Rockport Mass.: Para Research, 1977.
Horoscope Symbols. Rockport Mass.: Para Research, 1981.
Essays on Astrology. Rockport Mass.: Para Research, 1982

Hansa

Hansa, **asteroid** 480 (the 480th asteroid to be discovered), is approximately 64 kilometers in diameter and has an **orbital** period of 4.3 years. This asteroid was named after the merchant guild that gave its name to the Hanseatic League. Hansa shows mercantile ability, particularly in associations with others.

Sources:

Kowal, Charles T. *Asteroids: Their Nature and Utilization.* Chichester, West Sussex, U.K.: Ellis Horwood Limited, 1988.
Room, Adrian. *Dictionary of Astronomical Names.* London: Routledge, 1988.

Hard Aspects

Hard aspects are **aspects** that present a **native** with challenges—**squares, oppositions, semisquares,** and the like. Hard aspects is the preferred contemporary term for the aspects that were traditionally termed **malefic aspects** (malefic dropping out of usage because of its negative connotations).

Harmonia

Harmonia, **asteroid** 40 (the 40th asteroid to be discovered), is approximately 116 kilometers in diameter and has an **orbital** period of 3.4 years. Harmonia was named after the Greek daughter of Aries (**Mars**) and **Aphrodite** (**Venus**). Lehman associates this asteroid with musical as well as social harmony.

Sources:

Kowal, Charles T. *Asteroids: Their Nature and Utilization.* Chichester, West Sussex, U.K.: Ellis Horwood Limited, 1988.

Lehman, J. Lee. *The Ultimate Asteroid Book.* West Chester, Penn.: Whitford Press, 1988.

Room, Adrian. *Dictionary of Astronomical Names.* London: Routledge, 1988. 282pp.

Harmonic Chart

A harmonic chart is a secondary chart constructed by multiplying all of the various factors in the **radix** (initial) chart by the harmonic number under consideration. Although there exists much interesting research on **harmonic** theory, harmonic charts are rarely used in day-to-day astrological practice, except in **Hindu astrology.**

Harmonics

Harmonics is the study of the various integral divisions of a circle (e.g., fifths, sixths, and sevenths of 360°) and how these relate to the wheel of an astrological chart. It is, in a sense, a logical extension of the notion of **aspects** (specific angles between **planets** and other points in a **horoscope**), which divide a circle into halves (**oppositions**, which are 180° aspects), thirds (**trines**, which are 120° aspects), and so forth.

Many harmonic notions are very ancient (originating in **Hindu astrology** and in the work of older astronomers such as **Kepler**), but contemporary harmonics as a field of astrological research was founded by the British astrologer **John Addey** in the mid-twentieth century. This creative innovator stimulated many other astrologers to become involved in harmonics, and for several decades the field flourished.

A technique that lent itself well to large-scale research, harmonics was less useful for the practical task of interpretating individual **natal charts**. Thus, as new topics arose to attract the attention of researchers, interest in harmonics waned. At present, there are few books in print that do more than mention the field. Eleanor Bach's recent astrological reference book, *Astrology from A to Z,* does not even include an entry on it. Despite the current lack of interest, the general availability of computers (which eliminate the difficulty of calculating complex harmonics) and the increasing popularity of Hindu astrology (which, as stated earlier, provides one of the foundation stones for the field) could easily lead to a revival of harmonic studies.

Sources:

Bach, Eleanor. *Astrology from A to Z: An Illustrated Source Book.* New York: Philosophical Library, 1990.

Brau, Jean-Louis, Helen Weaver, and Allan Edmands. *Larousse Encyclopedia of Astrology.* New York: New American Library, 1980.

Harvey, Charles, and Michael Harding. *Working with Astrology: The Psychology of Harmonics, Midpoints and Astro*Carto*Graphy.* New York: Arkana, 1990.

Heavy Planets

The heavy planets are the outer **planets**, which take longer to travel through the **zodiac** and which thus seem to be "heavier" than the others. The heavy planets are **Jupiter, Saturn, Uranus, Neptune,** and **Pluto.** *Heavy planets* is infrequently used; the more common expression is outer planets.

Hebe

Hebe, **asteroid** 6 (the 6th asteroid to be discovered—in 1847, by the German amateur astronomer Karl Ludwig Hencke), is approximately 204 kilometers in diameter and has an **orbital** period of 3.8 years. Hebe was named after the Greek goddess of youth who took ambrosia to the Olympian deities. According to Lang-Wescott (1990, p. 78), Hebe "deals with co-dependency—the ways that one 'enables' the egocentricity and emotional immaturity of others." This asteroid's key word is *serving.*

Sources:

Lang-Wescott, Martha. *Asteroids-Mechanics: Ephemerides II.* Conway, Mass.: Treehouse Mountain, 1990.

———. *Mechanics of the Future: Asteroids.* Rev. ed. Conway, Mass.: Treehouse Mountain, 1991.

Hebrew Astrology

See: History of Western Astrology

Heindel, Max

Max Heindel, founder of the Rosicrucian Fellowship, was born Carl Louis von Grasshof. The oldest son in an aristocratic German family, he was born July 23, 1865. He went to Glasgow, Scotland, to study maritime engineering at age 16 and eventually became chief engineer on an oceanliner. He moved to New York City in 1895, worked as a consulting engineer, and married. He moved to Los Angeles 8 years later. There he began occult studies, soon joining the Theosophical Society in America, led by Katherine Tingley. Heindel served as vice-president of the Los Angeles branch in 1904–1905. He became interested in astrology and began lecturing on it in various cities on the West Coast.

In Germany in 1907, according to Heindel, a spiritual being later identified as an elder brother of the Rosicrucian order appeared in his room, informing him that he had passed a test. He subsequently traveled to the Temple of the Rosy Cross near the border of Germany and Bohemia and remained for a month. There he received information that became *The Rosicrucian Cosmo-Conception*. He then returned to the United States, and in Columbus, Ohio, established the first center of the Rosicrucian Fellowship in 1908.

Heindel's teachings differ from the Theosophical Society's in their greater emphasis on astrology, Christianity, Christian symbols, and a Rosicrucian heritage. His ideas reflect those of Rudolf Steiner.

Following the Ohio center, Heindel soon established centers in Seattle, Washington; North Yakima, Washington; Portland, Oregon; and Los Angeles, California. He had a heart problem and was hospitalized in March 1910. While there, he had an out-of-body experience that showed him plans for future work. In August 1910, he married Augusta Foss, a woman he had known before his first wife died in 1905. Part of his hospital vision was fulfilled when Rosicrucian headquarters were established at Mt. Ecclesia near Oceanside, California, in 1911. Mt. Ecclesia was complete with a sanctuary, offices, a woman's dormitory, cottages, and a vegetarian cafeteria.

Heindel's final years were productive ones in which he wrote several volumes and a regular column in the Rosicrucian Fellowship's monthly, *Rays from the Rosy Cross*. The fellowship was a major force in the spread and popularization of astrology. Astrologers not connected with the fellowship nevertheless use the annual **ephemeris** and **table of houses,** both published at Oceanside. Heindel's wife assumed leadership of the fellowship after he passed away in 1919.

Selected Publications:

The Rosicrucian Cosmo-Conception. Seattle, Wash.: Rosicrucian Fellowship, 1909.
Simplified Scientific Astrology. Oceanside, Calif.: The Rosicrucian Fellowship, 1928.
The Message of the Stars. Oceanside, Calif.: Rosicrucian Fellowship, 1963.

Sources:

Melton, J. Gordon. *Religious Leaders of America.* Detroit: Gale Research, 1991.

Hekate

Hekate, **asteroid** 100 (the 100th asteroid to be discovered), is approximately 84 kilometers in diameter and has an **orbital** period of 5.4 years. Hekate was named after a Greek goddess of the underworld. Lehman (p. 86) asserts that people with this asteroid strongly positioned in their **natal charts** "tend to break down other people's images of themselves, as well as their own."

Sources:

Kowal, Charles T. *Asteroids: Their Nature and Utilization.* Chichester, West Sussex, U.K.: Ellis Horwood Limited, 1988.
Lehman, J. Lee. *The Ultimate Asteroid Book.* West Chester, Penn.: Whitford Press, 1988.
Room, Adrian. *Dictionary of Astronomical Names.* London: Routledge, 1988.

Heliacal

Heliacal means associated with the **Sun** (from Greek *helios,* sun). The heliacal rising of a **star** is its first appearance following a period of invisibility due to its **conjunction** with the Sun. Similarly, the heliacal setting of a star refers to its last appearance before entering into a conjunction with the Sun.

Helio

Helio, **asteroid** 895 (the 895th asteroid to be discovered), is approximately 68 kilometers in diameter and has an **orbital** period of 5.7 years. Helio was named after the Greek god of the **Sun.** Lehman (p. 98) asserts that the person with this asteroid prominent in her or his **natal chart** "does her/his job, and expects to shine as a result of it."

Sources:

Kowal, Charles T. *Asteroids: Their Nature and Utilization.* Chichester, West Sussex, U.K.: Ellis Horwood Limited, 1988.
Lehman, J. Lee. *The Ultimate Asteroid Book.* West Chester, Penn.: Whitford Press, 1988.
Room, Adrian. *Dictionary of Astronomical Names.* London: Routledge, 1988.

Heliocentric Astrology

Although traditional astrology is **geocentric** (Earth-centered), some astrologers have undoubtedly considered using a heliocentric (**Sun**-centered) system ever since the Copernican revolution. The argument against heliocentric astrology is that, since we are situated on Earth, we need to focus on Earth's relationship to the other celestial bodies—a Sun-centered astrology would make sense only if we were born on the Sun. This argument was persuasive enough to prevent the emergence of a true heliocentric astrology until relatively recently. The two factors behind this emergence were (1) the discovery that scientists had found a correlation between sunspot activity and angles between the **planets** (the same basic **aspects** that are used in geocentric astrology) and (2) the personal computer revolution, which made casting heliocentric **horoscopes** quite easy. Use by NASA scientists of a form of heliocentric astrology—under the rubric *gravitational vectoring*—to predict high sunspot activity was not just an important verification of astrological principles; it also, because of the well-known effects of such activity on weather conditions, on radio wave propagation, and on other terrestrial events, alerted astrologers to the possibility that astrological forces impacting the solar sphere had an influence on Earth's astrological "atmosphere."

The early solar charts presented a barren appearance: There were no **house** divisions, no **ascendant**, no Sun, and, sometimes, no **zodiac** (because for the **tropical zodiac**, the first **sign** always begins at the spring equinox, a notion that has no meaning from a heliocentric viewpoint). Earth, which is always 180° away from where the Sun would be in a geocentric chart, is drawn in as a cross surrounded by a circle (like the symbol for the **Part of Fortune**, only shifted 45°). Because the Sun in traditional astrology represents one's deepest "soul" self, some heliocentric astrologers have proposed that solar horoscopes chart the astrology of the soul.

Heliocentric astrologers began with the principle that the heliocentric perspective would supplement rather than supplant the geocentric perspective. This principle paved the way for a newer approach to heliocentric astrology that represents the heliocentric and the geocentric positions in the same horoscope. These are technically "geo-helio" charts. Astrologers who use this system claim that including the heliocentric positions is like "finding the missing half of the horoscope." The heliocentric planets have the same meaning as when used geocentrically, although they are said to manifest their influence in a different manner. This newer approach did not entirely overturn the older heliocentric system, so there are now at least two distinct heliocentric approaches, one purely heliocentric (but which does not reject the validity of a geocentric chart, using it only in an entirely separate phase of the operation), and the other a mixed geo-helio approach in which the two charts are merged.

Most contemporary astrologers, although not actually opposed to heliocentric astrology, have not integrated it into their practice, primarily because there are so many new techniques that no one astrologer can possibly master them all. The heliocentric perspective is just one tool among a multitude available to the astrological practitioner. Many astrologers have adopted the attitude that really good astrologers are rare enough, so why not just stick to mastering the basics? This argument has more than a little merit. And, after all, if we adopt a Sun-centered astrology, why not also make use of the many insights that are probably waiting to be discoved in a **Moon**-centered or a **Mars**-centered or even a **Ceres**-centered astrology? If a heliocentric chart cast for one's birth time gives valid insights for a native of Earth, then it should be possible to apply the same principles to any planet or planetoid in the **solar system**.

Such considerations have caused many astrologers to greet heliocentric methods with indifference. At the same time, the widespread availability of chart-casting programs that include heliocentric positions as a standard option makes it almost inevitable that the astrologers who buy them will experiment with these positions, resulting in more and more astrologers who use heliocentric or geo-helio charts. Thus, the future of heliocentric astrology as a continuing presence within the astrological community seems ensured.

Sources:

Brau, Jean-Louis, Helen Weaver, and Allan Edmands. *Larousse Encyclopedia of Astrology.* New York: New American Library, 1980.

Davis, T. Patrick. *Revolutionizing Astrology with Heliocentric.* Windermere, Fla.: Davis Research Reports, 1980.

Sedgwick, Philip. *The Sun at the Center: A Primer of Heliocentric Astrology.* Saint Paul, Minn.: Llewellyn Publications, 1990.

Hemisphere

Hemisphere literally means a half sphere. In geography, hemisphere refers to the division of Earth into northern and southern and eastern and western hemispheres. In astrology, hemisphere usually refers to the division of a **horoscope** into upper and lower halves (using the **ascendant-descendant** axis as the dividing line) or into left and right halves (using the **midheaven–imum coeli** axis as the dividing line). The upper and lower hemispheres of a chart are technically termed the **diurnal** (day, because above the **horizon**) arc and the **nocturnal** (night, because below the horizon) arc, respectively. The left and right hemispheres are termed the oriental (eastern) arc and the occidental (western) arc. These technical terms are rarely used by contemporary astrologers.

In the interpretation of a **natal chart**, the occurence of many **planets** above the horizon is said to indicate extroversion; many planets below the horizon indicates introversion. Also, a chart with a preponderance of planets in the left hemisphere is said to indicate an individual who shapes her or his environment, and a preponderance in the right hemisphere indicates an individual who adapts to the environment. These interpretations are tentative, "first impression" **delineations** and can be quickly abandoned if other factors in a birth chart give contrary indications.

Sources:

Brau, Jean-Louis, Helen Weaver, and Allan Edmands. *Larousse Encyclopedia of Astrology.* New York: New American Library, 1980.

Gettings, Fred. *Dictionary of Astrology.* London: Routledge & Kegan Paul, 1985.

Hera

Hera, **asteroid** 103 (the 103d asteroid to be discovered), is approximately 96 kilometers in diameter and has an **orbital** period of 4.4 years. Hera was named after the Greek goddess of women and childbirth. She was the sister and wife of **Zeus**, king of the Olympian deities. Hera was the most jealous wife in ancient mythology, and she persecuted both her husband's lovers and the children of Zeus's many love affairs. According to Lang-Wescott, (1991, p. 78) Hera "illustrates the relationship model of the parents as perceived by the individual—and the way that model is acted out in present roles through assumptions about equality, fidelity and commitment in relationship." This asteroid's key phrase is *keeping accounts.*

Sources:

Lang-Wescott, Martha. *Asteroids-Mechanics: Ephemerides II.* Conway, Mass.: Treehouse Mountain, 1990.

———. *Mechanics of the Future: Asteroids.* Rev. ed. Conway, Mass.: Treehouse Mountain, 1991.

Herschel

Herschel was the original designation of **Uranus**. It was named after Sir William Herschel, the astronomer who discovered Uranus. British astrologers persisted in using the name long after the rest of the world had switched to Uranus.

William Herschel was born Friedrich Wilhelm Herschel in Hanover, Germany, on November 15, 1738, and anglicized his name after he moved to England. His original profession was music, and music students were said to have flocked to him because of his talent, amiability, and teaching ability. He became interested in **astronomy** and took it up as a hobby; in time, it consumed him. He taught himself calculus and optics and, dissatisfied with the quality of existing telescopes, designed and built his own (later declared to be far better than any other in existence). He was creative and resourceful. Concerned about the welfare of his sister Caroline, whose brilliance was being wasted by parents who held very traditional ideas about the proper place of women, William arranged for her to move to England and become his partner in the music (and later astronomy) business.

A modest individual, he brought Uranus to the attention of other astonomers with the announcement that he had discovered a new "comet." When, after he had become famous, the king wished to honor him with an official appointment, he made certain that his sister also received a royal subsidy—making her the first woman in history to become a professional astronomer. Sir William also went into the telescope-manufacturing business: It was through a Herschel telescope that the first **asteroid, Ceres,** was discovered.

While there is much more we could say about this remarkable man, enough has been said to perceive typically Uranian themes in Sir William's life and character: He was a brilliant man, with a natural aptitude for science, and with the creative originality to design and build the best telescopes around. In his own small way, he was also a social reformer, bringing a woman in as his partner during a period when females did not pursue professional careers. And last but not least, his discovery of Uranus revolutionized astronomy.

In fact, a study of William Herschel would have given astrologers of previous generations far more clues into the nature of Uranus than any study of Uranian mythology. About the only thing we can say about the classical god Uranus, other than that he was the only Greek god to give his name to a major **planet** (the rest were all Romans), is that he was an oppressive tyrant who was castrated and overthrown by his own son. As a starting point for astrological meaning, this myth pictures Uranus as embodying the principle of oppressive tyranny (the same may be said about yet another name for the first trans-**Saturn**ian planet, **Georgium Sidus**, a designation derived from the king against whom the American colonies revolted). Otherwise, the name Uranus is barren of astrological significance.

Sources:

Littmann, Mark. *Planets Beyond: Discovering the Outer Solar System.* 2d ed. New York: John Wiley & Sons, 1990.

Paul, Haydn. *Revolutionary Spirit: Exploring the Astrological Uranus.* Shaftesbury, Dorset, U.K.: Element Books, 1989.

Room, Adrian. *Dictionary of Astronomical Names.* London: Routledge, 1988.

Hesperus

Hesperus is the name given to the **planet Venus** when it appears as the Evening Star.

Hestia

Hestia, **asteroid** 46 (the 46th asteroid to be discovered), is approximately 164 kilometers in diameter and has an **orbital** period of 4 years. It was named after the Greek virgin goddess of the hearth and symbol of the home (parallel to the Roman **Vesta**). Hestia was the oldest and most sacred of the 12 Olympian dieties. As with the asteroid Vesta, the natal location of Hestia by sign and **house** indicates something about the **native**'s domestic inclinations. When prominent in a **natal chart** (e.g., **conjunct** the **Sun** or the **ascendant**), it can indicate a homebody.

Sources:

Kowal, Charles T. *Asteroids: Their Nature and Utilization.* Chichester, West Sussex, U.K.: Ellis Horwood Limited, 1988.

Room, Adrian. *Dictionary of Astronomical Names.* London: Routledge, 1988.

Hidalgo

Hidalgo, **asteroid** 944 (the 944th asteroid to be discovered—in 1920) was named after the revolutionary priest who attempted to overthrow Spanish rule in Mexico. It is about 28 1/2 kilometers in diameter and has an eccentric **orbit** that is the longest (14 years) of any asteroid. Hidalgo is one of the more recent asteroids to be investigated by astrologers. Preliminary material on Hidalgo can be found in **Demetra George** and Douglas Bloch's *Astrology for Yourself,* and an **ephemeris** (table of celestial locations) for Hidalgo can be found in the back of the second edition of George and Bloch's *Asteroid Goddesses.* Unlike the **planets,** which are associated with a wide range of phenomena, the smaller asteroids are said to represent a single principle. George and Bloch (1987) give Hidalgo's principle as "protecting and fighting for one's beliefs"; their tentative key phrase for Hidalgo is *My capacity for self-assertion in defense of my principles.* Zipporah Dobyns associates Hidalgo with **Saturn,** finding that it often **aspects** that planet in the charts of women who reach positions of success and power. J. Lee Lehman (p. 29) finds that Hidalgo represents "an assertion of will *over* others." This influence can be used in fighting for other people's rights, but "Hidalgo *expects* to be in control, to be the general in all situations" (Lehman, p. 29). Lehman describes Hidalgo as a "macho" asteroid.

Sources:

Dobyns, Zipporah. *Expanding Astrology's Universe.* San Diego, Calif.: Astro Computing Services, 1983.

George, Demetra, with Douglas Bloch. *Asteroid Goddesses: The Mythology, Psychology and Astrology of the Reemerging Feminine.* 2d ed. rev. and enl. San Diego, Calif.: Astro Computing Services, 1990.

————. *Astrology for Yourself: A Workbook for Personal Transformation.* Berkeley, Calif.: Wingbow Press, 1987.

Lehman, J. Lee. *The Ultimate Asteroid Book.* West Chester, Pa.: Whitford Press, 1988.

Hindu Astrology (Vedic Astrology)

Hindu, or as it is more commonly referred to by practitioners, *Vedic* astrology has made important inroads into the Western astrological community. The origins of Vedic astrology are primarily in India. According to modern Vedic scholars, a continuous record of astrological knowledge can be traced back to 4500 B.C.

The father of Vedic astrology was Parashara Muni. He was reported to have lived around 1500 B.C. and was one of the first astrologers to actually cast **natal charts** for individuals. It is recorded that he made a specialized study of **medical astrology** that reflected health, disease, and longevity issues. Copies of his manuscripts are still in existence in India. His greatest work was titled *The Brihat Parashara Hora Shastra.* In addition, he wrote beautiful esoteric hymns in the Rig Veda that were mantras to the planetary deities. Another important astrologer who lived during the same era was the seer Ranavira. He specialized in relationship compatibility, female horoscopy, and other psychological aspects of astrology. (In modern astrological practice in India, chart comparisons for marriage compatibility are still commonly utilized).

Vedic astrology is also called Joytisha, which means luminous, brilliant, celestial, shining, belonging to the world of light. It is truly the science of light. Vedic astrology attempts to shine the cosmic light on an individual's true life path. It is the key to understanding the soul's intention or divine plan for this incarnation. Similar to the function of a true guru, the Vedic astrologer attempts to be the "dispeller of darkness." She or he is a priest, counselor, teacher, and sage.

As in Western astrology, the **natal chart** is based on the date, place, and exact time of birth. The exact time of birth is usually considered to be the time of the first cry of the newborn. Planetary calculations are based on the **sidereal zodiac**, which is based on the fixed positions of the **stars**. Western astrology is based on the **tropical** (seasonal) **zodiac**, and there is an approximate difference of 22° to 24° between the tropical and sidereal zodiacs, depending upon which part of this century one was born in. To calculate the Vedic natal chart by hand, subtract approximately 23° from the tropical positions of the subject's natal planets and ascendant. For example, a 3° **Virgo** sun in Western astrology would be around 10° **Leo** in the Vedic natal chart.

According to Vedic philosophy, the natal chart represents an individual's past karmic patterns. In Varaha Mihara's *Brihat Jataka,* the natal chart reflects "the results of the good and bad deeds done by men in their previous births" (p. 12). Thus, this system is based on the theory of reincarnation and the laws of karma. It is important not to confuse the theory of astrology with fatalism.

According to Vedic astrologer Chakrapani Ullal, the Hindu system of astrology emphasizes that "the planets are only the indicative forces and they do not determine the events of life in a fatalistic way. It is for the person concerned, to make use of the indications available, to change the course of one's life by using one's willpower, self-effort and by gaining the grace of God" (personal communication).

The basis for understanding astrology is to learn the significations of the **planets**. The Vedic term for planet is *graha,* which means demon or what possesses a person. The planets represent the maya, or illusions that veil one's divine nature. One must learn to befriend all planets and make them allies. The positions of the planets in an individual's birth chart reflect the person's strengths as well as areas that may need to be healed. Each planet signifies certain aspects of life. Following is a list of planets and their *karakas,* or what they indicate in the person's life:

> *Sun (Surya)* Physical appearance, health and vitality, soul *(atman)* nature, father, leadership or status. Heart and head.

> *Moon (Chandra)* Emotions and perceptual mind, mother, early childhood, influence on the public. Breasts and womb.

> *Mercury (Budha)* Rational mind, speech, writing, intelligence, discrimination, education. Nervous system, lungs, skin.

> *Venus (Shukra)* Wife, beauty, art, music, happiness, marriage, love. Reproductive system, face.

> *Mars (Mangal)* Courage, energy, brothers, properties, war, enemies, accidents. Muscles and blood.

> *Saturn (Sani)* Structure, organization, discipline, diseases, delay, loss, father or authority figures. Bones, nerves.

The monumental observatory in ancient Delhi attests to the Indian fascination with celestial events. · Bettmann Archive

Jupiter (Guru) Religion, higher education, wealth, children, husband, good fortune, law. Liver and fat.

North Node (Rahu) Worldly power and desires, foreign lands, travel, the occult and psychology, crime, drugs. Mental illness.

South Node (Ketu) Mystical experiences, liberation, psychic or spiritual insights, accidents, injury, death.

Uranus, Neptune and **Pluto** are not usually utilized in traditional Vedic astrology. Vedic astrologers believe that the nodes of the moon reflect the energies of the trans-Saturnian planets adequately. Some modern Vedic astrologers utilize these planets in their natal chart analysis. They believe the planets reflect our divine birthright and our potential soul destiny. The planets operate as relay stations for the transmission and reception of stellar wisdom. It is our duty to begin to understand the star language and its divine messages being sent to planet Earth.

The Vedic natal chart is divided into 12 **houses** called *bhavas*. These houses represent different fields of action or activity. Following are significators for the 12 houses, which are somewhat similar to those in Western astrology:

First house Bodily appearance, character, early childhood, health and vitality, personality, fame, longevity. Dharma house (right action). Head or face.

Second house Money, family life, domestic harmony, food or diet, intellect, powers of speech and writing, jewelry, dress. Artha house (wealth). Mouth, nose, right eye.

Third house Brothers, younger siblings, fine arts (music, dance, drama), courage and adventure, skill with hands, short journeys, inquisitive mind, ambition, will. Kama house (desire). Hands, arms, throat.

Fourth house Mother, happiness and contentment, property and real estate, formal education, subconscious mind, close of life. Moksha house (liberation). Chest, lungs, heart.

Fifth house Children, love affairs and romance, creative intelligence, *poorvapunya* (past life credit), wisdom. Dharma house. Stomach (sometimes heart).

Sixth house Service, detail work, medicine, catering, pets, enemies, disease, effort and hard work, debts. Artha house. Navel, intestines.

Seventh house Marriage partner, quality of married life, love and passion, social nature, business partnerships. Kama house. Below navel, kidneys, veins.

Eighth house Death, longevity, inheritance, mysticism and psychic ability, delays, fears, misfortune. Moksha house. Reproductive systems, chronic illness.

Ninth house Wisdom, guru, father, religion, philosophy, long journeys, law teachers, good fortune. Dharma house. Thighs and hips.

Tenth house Career or vocation (also first house), status, power, house of action, achievement, good deeds. Artha house. Knees.

Eleventh house Friends, groups, profits and gains, sisters and older siblings, goals, hopes, dreams, aspirations. Kama house. Legs and ankles, calves.

Twelfth house Enlightenment, bed pleasures, sleep, expenditures, cofusion, sorrow, confinement, seclusion, the next life. Moksha house. Feet, left eye, hearing.

To illustrate how the planets and houses are combined, consider former President George Bush's natal chart. In viewing his Vedic natal chart, one can see that the houses/signs advance in clockwise fashion. The *rasi,* or natal chart, is set up so that each house contains a whole sign. As in Western astrology, there are 12 signs as well as 12 houses. The sign interpretations of Western and Vedic astrology are quite similar. The **ascendant** (rising sign) is of extreme importance in Vedic astrology. In Bush's Vedic chart, the **ascendant**, or *lagna (LG),* is at 17° **Leo**, and the entire first house is therefore Leo. Thus, any planets that fall in the sign Leo (e.g., his north node at 2° Leo) would be considered to be in the first house.

Bush's second house is the entire sign of **Virgo**, where its moon is placed at 25° Virgo. The third house is **Libra**, with Saturn retrograde at 3°, the fourth house is **Scorpio**, with Jupiter retrograde at 21°, and so on through the **zodiac**. Thus, each house equals 30 degrees or one sign. The *bhava* chart is also used to fine-tune planetary house positions. It calculates approximately 15° before and after the ascendant as the first house and then uses an equal-house method.

In Vedic astrology the ascendant determines the harmonic pattern of house rulerships as well as how the person acts upon and perceives the world. It is also a reflection of the individual's physical appearance and vitality. As mentioned earlier, in Bush's Vedic chart the Leo ascendant is shown. The ruler of the ascendant is the Sun and is located in the tenth house, indicating career and status. When the ruler of the first house is located in the tenth house, a combination exists that produces fame, leadership, recognition by society, and life in the public eye. In the sidereal zodiac, the Leo ascendant is found in the charts of many political leaders, including Franklin Roosevelt, Richard Nixon, and Bill Clinton.

George Bush's sun is located at 28° Taurus in the *dik bala,* or directional strength placement. According to Vedic astrology, the tenth house is the best house position for the Sun to be natally placed. Bush's Sun is also favorably **aspected** by two of its friends (Jupiter and Mars), and its **dispositor**, Venus, is located in the house of friends, groups, and profits and gains (the tenth house). This would indicate that George's career is greatly influenced by friends in high places (the ruler of the tenth house is located in the eleventh house) and by his wife (indicated by Venus). Throughout his political career, Bush has been placed in positions of power through his friends and often with little previous experience (e.g., director of the CIA). His wife, Barbara, has been a loyal companion and supporter also.

Bush also has the planet Mercury residing in the tenth house. This is an excellent placement for speech, writing, intelligence, and communication that will affect the masses. Mercury is in a friendly sign of Taurus's (Venus, ruler of Taurus, and Mercury are considered best friends in Vedic astrology), indicating good communication skills.

Like the Sun, Mercury also receives aspects from Mars (the square) and Jupiter (the opposition). The **square** of Mars to Mercury indicates Bush's tendency to put the proverbial foot in the mouth, as well as engage in harsh, critical speech. It also gives power to his words, as well as indicates a tendency to lie. In politicians' charts, there is a high percentage of Mercury/Mars natal squares or conjunctions (e.g., Richard Nixon, John F. Kennedy, Lyndon Johnson, John Glenn), and a strong Mercury is often seen.

In Vedic astrology, it is important to have a strong first and tenth house for positions of political power. Second in importance are the ninth and fifth houses. The Sun, Jupiter, and Mercury are the most important planets connected to politics. A strong Saturn is helpful as well.

A unique feature of Vedic astrology is what is called planetary periods. The planetary periods (*dasa* is the major period, *bhukti* the subperiod) can clearly reveal future trends and development cycles in life. They form the basis of a very powerful Vedic technique of dividing life into specific periods of emphasis. Predictions are made based on the strength or affliction of the planetary-period ruler, aspects to it, as well as the houses it rules. It is as if the planet ruling the dasa period becomes the president of one's life during its rulership, and the bhukti (subperiod) ruler becomes the vice-president during its sway. In examining the charts of famous personalities, one can see periods of introversion during weak planetary periods followed by speeches before thousands during a strong period.

How to Calculate the Planetary Period You Were Born In

The *dasas* (major periods) are based on a predetermined number of years for each planet or node of the Moon (excluding Uranus, Neptune, and Pluto). The order is based on the rulership of the 27 *nakshatras* or lunar mansions *(see table)*. Each sign of the zodiac contains 3 nakshatras of varying degrees. From 0° Aries to 13° 20′ Aries Aswini, which is ruled by the south node of the Moon (Ketu).

The order of the planetary periods is that of the rulerships of the nakshatras, starting with the first nakshatra of the first sign (Aries), which is ruled by Ketu (south node) and lasts for 7 years. The next nakshatra of Aries is ruled by Venus and lasts 20 years; the next by the Sun, 6 years; the Moon, 10 years; Mars, 7 years; Rahu (north node), 18 years; Jupiter, 16 years; Saturn, 19 years; and finally, Mercury, 17 years. The sequence repeats over and over through all the signs of the zodiac.

The total of the planetary periods is 120 years, which according to the Vedas would be the potential life cycle for a balanced, healthy person.

The beginning planetary period of an individual's life is determined by the nakshatra ruler of the natal Moon. For example, a person born with the

Moon at 15° Taurus, in the nakshatra Rohini, which is ruled by the Moon itself (located from 10° Taurus to 23° 20′ Taurus), was born in the 10-year planetary period of the Moon.

The task is to calculate how far along the 10-year period is at the time of the person's birth. If the natal moon was at exactly 15° Taurus, then it would be 5° into the 13° 20′ nakshatra of Rohini (see table). Therefore, the planetary period needs to be reduced in proportion. First, divide 5° by 13.33° (20/60 = .330), which equals approximately .375. Then multiply .375 by the total number of years of the planetary period: .375 x 10 = 3.75 years. Finally, subtract 3.75 from 10 years, which equals 6.25 years, the number of remaining years the person has left in the Moon dasa, at the time of birth. This person would have been in the Moon dasa for the first 6.25 years of life, followed by 7 years of Mars, 28 years of Rahu (north node) and so forth. (Matrix Software [1-800-PLANETS] offers products that will do these calculations.)

The native's experience of each planetary period is primarily based on the stature of that planet in the natal chart (bhava and navamsa charts should also be utilized). As an example, consider again the chart of George Bush. Bush has been under the influence of the planetary period of Mercury since July 1983. The Mercury dasa is a 17-year cycle and will end in July 2000. As previously stated, Bush has both Mercury and the Sun in the sign of Taurus, in the tenth house of career and fame. Mercury (representing intellect), placed with the Sun in the tenth house gives strong leadership ability, connections in the world of business and commerce, and a high position in society during the Mercury planetary period. It was during this Mercury dasa and the Venus bhukti (ruler of his tenth house) that he was elected president. The entire period of time since 1983 has reflected Bush's ascent to power, leadership, and career success. Also, the Mercury dasa's ruling the second and eleventh houses and placed in the powerful tenth house has also brought him increased income and success through friends, social groups, and organizations (eleventh house). The ruler of his tenth house (Venus) is located in the eleventh house, which is further indication of powerful friends helping his career.

Bush was in the minor period of Mars until January 1993. His Mars is his *yoga karaka,* or planet of power. Placed in the seventh house, it indicates the ability to defeat others as well as conflict with others. It also aspects his first house of health, by opposition. The Mars bhukti started in January 1992, about the time of his illness in Japan. This period could continue to be stressful and unhealthy for him. Bush was also born with the Mars/Ketu (south node) conjunction, which reflects possible past-life (south node) skill in the military (Mars). (President Ulysses S. Grant had this aspect as well.)

This conjunction is troubling. According to the Vedic system, Ketu acts like Mars, but it also can create confusion and doubt, leading to a critical, narrow vision of life. Both Mars and Ketu are in the nakshatra of Dhanistha, which is ruled by Mars, further empowering the troubling aspect. In fact, 5 of Bush's 9 planets are located in nakshatras ruled by *warlike* Mars. His Mars subperiod is followed by Rahu (north node), which began in January 1993. Bush's north node

The Nakshatras (Lunar Mansions)

	Extent	Ruler
1 Ashwini	00°00′ to 13°20′ Aries	Ketu
2 Bharani	13°20′ to 26°40′ Aries	Venus
3 Krittika	26°40′ Aries to 10°00′ Taurus	Sun
4 Rohini	10°00′ to 23°20 Taurus	Moon
5 Mrigahsira	23°20′ Taurus to 6°40′ Gemini	Mars
6 Ardra	6°40′ to 20°00′ Gemini	Rahu
7 Punarvasu	20°00′ Gemini to 3°20′ Cancer	Jupiter
8 Pushya	3°20′ to 16°40′ Cancer	Saturn
9 Ashlesha	16°40′ to 29°59′ Cancer	Mercury
10 Magha	00°00′ to 13°20′ Leo	Ketu
11 Purava Phalaguni	13°20′ to 26°30′ Leo	Venus
12 Uttara Phalguni	26°40′ Leo to 10°00′ Virgo	Sun
13 Hasta	10°00′ to 23°20 Virgo	Moon
14 Chitra	23°20′ Virgo to 6°40′ Libra	Mars
15 Swati	6°40′ to 20°00′ Libra	Rahu
16 Vishakha	20°00′ Libra to 3°20′ Scorpio	Jupiter
17 Anuradha	3°20′ to 16°40′ Scorpio	Saturn
18 Jyeshta	16°40′ to 29°59′ Scorpio	Mercury
19 Mula	00°00′ to 13°20′ Sagittarius	Ketu
20 Purvashadha	13°20′ to 26°30′ Sagittarius	Venus
21 Uttarashadha	26°40′ Sagittarius to 10°00′ Capricorn	Sun
22 Shravana	10°00′ to 23°20′ Capricorn	Moon
23 Dhanishta	23°20′ Capricorn to 6°40′ Aquarius	Mars
24 Shatabhisak	6°40′ to 20°00′ Aquarius	Rahu
25 Purvabhadra	20°00′ Aquarius to 3°20′ Pisces	Jupiter
26 Uttarabhadra	3°20′ to 16°40′ Pisces	Saturn
27 Reveati	16°40′ to 29°59′ Pisces	Mercury

is thus placed in an enemy's sign of Leo (recall that Leo is ascendant in Bush's chart), because the Sun and Rahu are adversaries in Vedic astrology. This period could be marked by great personal upheaval due to its placement in the first house.

Vedic or Hindu astrology is a predictive system of esoteric knowledge and is becoming more popular in Western culture. As many have embraced the wisdom of the East in other fields of study, such as philosophy and psychology, it is imperative to cultivate this exploration in astrology as well.

—*Dennis M. Harness*

Sources:

Braha, James T. *Ancient Hindu Astrology for the Modern Western Astrology.* Hollywood, Fla.: Hermetician Press, 1986.

Cameron, Barbara. *Predictive Planetary Periods: The Hindu Dasas.* Tempe, Ariz.: American Federation of Astrologers, 1984.

DeLuce, Robert. *Constellational Astrology: According to the Hindu System.* Los Angeles: DeLuce Publishing, 1963.

Parashara Muni. *The Brihat Parashara Hora Shastra.* Translated by R. P. Santhanam. New Delhi: Ranjan Publications, 1989.

Varaha Mihara. *Brihat Jataka.* Translated by J. R. Satyacharya. New Delhi: Ranjan Publications, 1987.

Hipparchus

Hipparchus, the preeminent ancient Greek astronomer, lived from approximately 190 B.C. to 120 B.C. He developed trigonometry, recorded the location of more than a thousand stars, and originated the idea of latitude and longitude. He is said to have discovered the phenomenon known as the **precession of the equinoxes**. Hipparchus was also a practicing astrologer.

History of Astrology in America

Astrology came to America during the colonial era along with the entire body of occult teachings available in Europe in the seventeenth century. The first American astrologers, the Rosicrucians under the leadership of Johannes Kelpius (1673–1708), established an astrological library and conservatory on Wissahickon Creek in what is now the Germantown section of Philadelphia, Pennsylvania. Among other activities, they helped upgrade the **almanac** already being published by Daniel Leeds, and in 1698 one of their better astrologers, Johann Seelig, was commissioned to cast the **horoscope** for the Swedish Lutheran church at Wisaco, Pennsylvania, in order to determine the best date to commence the new building. After the demise of Kelpius's group, which was known as the Chapter of Perfection, surviving members became the first hexmeisters, the well-known folk magicians of eastern Pennsylvania.

Through the eighteenth and nineteenth centuries, Americans interested in astrology derived their interest from a flow of materials from Europe, though several almanacs, which provided astrological data for farming and doctoring, were published in America. After reaching a low point in the eighteenth century, a distinct new era for astrology began in England in the early nineteenth century. This new era can be marked by the 1816 publication of James Wilson's *A Complete Dictionary of Astrology,* which for the first time gave its readers the basic kind of information they needed to construct and interpret astrological charts. A decade later, **Robert C. Smith** (1795–1832), writing under the pen name Raphael, launched the first successful astrological publishing house. His first book, *Manual of Astrology,* was an immediate success, but more importantly, he produced an **ephemeris**, a book of charts showing the position of the **planets** in the sky day-by-day. The annual *Raphael's Ephemeris* remains a standard astrological textbook. After Smith's death, a succession of individuals carried on his publishing work. Wilson, the various Raphaels, and the two men who wrote under the pseudonym Zadkiel (Richard James Morrison and Alfred J. Pearce) produced the initial library of books that circulated in the United States and through which Americans rediscovered astrology.

At the end of the century, astrology received additional support from the Theosophical Society. The first important Theosophical astrologer, **Walter Gorn Old**, also assumed a pen name, Sepherial. As popular as he became, and his books are still in print, his work was eclipsed by that of a man he introduced into the society of astrology, William Frederick Allen (1860–1917), better known by his pseudonym, **Alan Leo.** Allen launched the very successful *Astrologer's Magazine* (later renamed *Modern Astrology*), and in 1896, along with Old, he organized the first modern astrological society. The group was later reconstituted as the Society for Astrological Research and survives today as the Astrological Lodge of the Theosophical Society. Among its outstanding members were Allen's wife (whose pen name was Bessie Leo), and one of the first British astrologers not to use a pseudonym, **Charles E. O. Carter.**

New Beginnings in America

Through the colonial era, America had never been without astrology, but, as with Europe, astrology had been pushed to the hinterland and for many years survived only in the annual farmers' almanacs. It experienced a revival in 1840 when Thomas Hayes began the *Hayes United States Horoscope and Scientific and Literary Messenger,* which lasted eight years, and was followed by Mark Broughton's *Monthly Horoscope.* However, not until the 1880s, with the emergence of **Luke Dennis Broughton** (1828–1898), Mark's younger brother, did astrology experience a taste of its present success.

Broughton came from a family of astrologers. His grandfather, a physician, had become an enthusiastic student of astrology after reading **Nicholas**

Culpepper's *Herbal,* which provided astrological information about the medicinal plants then in use by physicians. The grandfather passed along this interest to Luke's father, who, in turn, passed it to Luke and his brothers. Mark had begun publishing an almanac and an ephemeris while still living in England, and after coming to the United States, began his magazine when Hayes's initial effort ceased. In 1860, Luke began issuing *Broughton's Monthly Planet Reader and Astrological Journal* from his Philadelphia home. Three years later he moved the magazine and himself to New York City, where he became the major American distributor of British astrological books and the teacher of the next generation of American astrologers.

Broughton also authored several astrology books. His *Elements of Astrology,* issued the year of his death, summarized the astrological knowledge of the day—providing a history of astrology, a survey of astrological theory, information on horoscope interpretation, and, in response to its critics, a lengthy apology for astrology.

The four decades of Broughton's career saw the movement of astrology from an almost non-existent state to the point where practitioners could be found in all major U.S. cities. In 1860 Broughton claimed that he knew "nearly every man in the United States who had any knowledge of the subject, and probably at that time there were not twenty persons that knew enough of Astrology to be able to erect a horoscope, and they were all either French, English, or German." But 40 years later, Broughton could say, "At present day [1898] there are many thousands American people who are studying Astrology, and some have become quite proficient in the science" (Broughton, xiii).

The growth of astrology in the 1880s and 1890s did not go unnoticed, and attacks on it were frequent. Broughton assigned himself the role of defender and at every opportunity made the case for the fledgling science. He went on the offensive against laws that prevented astrologers from freely doing their work. In 1886 he came to the defense of a Mr. Romaine, who had been sentenced to 18 months imprisonment for practicing astrology. Accusing Romaine's attackers of ignorance, he asked why "astrology [is] the only science or art in existence concerning which expert testimony is entirely discarded, and in regard to which only the opinions of men who are the most ignorant of the subject are entertained" (Broughton, 383). Broughton went on to do battle with other debunkers of astrology, such as Charles A. Dana, editor of the *New York Sun,* astronomer Richard A. Proctor, and popular encyclopedists Thomas Dick and William and Robert Chambers.

Broughton was, of course, neither the only astrologer nor the only astrology teacher in the late nineteenth century. Boston had developed its own astrological establishment, which included astronomer Joseph G. Dalton, who in 1898 published an American ephemeris. Also at least three astrological religions had emerged, the first of which dates to 1876 when Emma Harding Britten published her book *Art Magic.* The book included teachings of an occult order, the Brotherhood of Light, which she claimed dated from ancient Egypt.

During the early years of the Brotherhood of Light, the young lumberjack Hiram Butler, forced out of business by an accident that cost him several fingers, retired to a hermit's life in rural California. He began having visions, which he shared with others. A group of 12 formed around him and, pooling their resources, they moved to Applegate, California, where they formed the Esoteric Fraternity. Butler taught them what he called Esoteric Christianity, a form of Christian occultism. Butler called his astrological teachings Solar Biology. It differed from Broughton's more orthodox astrology in that Butler adjusted his system to include the Copernican insights on the position of the sun. The practical effect of Butler's alterations was to reverse the signs so that a **Libran** in solar biology would have all the characteristics of a person born under **Aries** in the more traditional system.

A third astrological religion, The Order of the Magi (magi being equated with astrologer) was founded in 1889 in Chicago. Its founder, Olney H. Richmond, had begun his occult career as a soldier during the Civil War. Eventually, Richmond became a teacher to a group of 30 men and women and in 1889 opened a temple in Chicago on South Division Street. The following year a second temple opened in Lansing, Michigan. The emergence of the Order of the Magi and other astrological religions merely underscores the genuine revival of astrology and the occult in general that was occurring in America during the last half of the nineteenth century.

The Astrological Universe

In trying to present itself anew to the culture that had previously banished it and therefore to a public that was largely ignorant of it, astrology aligned itself with the increasingly influential world of science. The single affirmation common to all of the nineteenth century astrologers was that "astrology is a science." As F. M. Lupton asserted, "Astrology is an exact science, and. . . as a science, is pure mathematics, and there is no guesswork about it" (Lupton, p. 5). This affirmation was made in the opening paragraph of almost every book published on astrology in the nineteenth century.

Like other new "sciences" of the era, such as psychology, astrology had a specific realm of knowledge assigned to it. Astrology described the nature of planetary influences on human life, and thus, the astrologer's task was to know and describe the **zodiac**al forces and the laws that govern them. Most astrology books would systematically take the reader through each of the **signs** of the zodiac and the planets, and minutely describe the influences exerted by each.

Astrologers claimed that as a science, astrology was not really new—that it was thousands of years old, dating to ancient Chaldea and Egypt. Its influence in Biblical times was obvious from the many Old Testament references, and more than one astrologer reminded readers that the New Testament opens with the account of Chaldean astrologers following the star to the Christ child. Astrology as it was practiced in the nineteenth century, and as we in the 1990s still know it, is ancient. It was derived from Ptolemy, the second-century Greek author of the *Tetrabiblos*. Rather than developing a new body of "scientific" knowledge, nineteenth century astrologers merely copied Ptolemy's system, taking their information on the significance of the signs and planets from his book.

While affirming astrology as a science, astrologers had to admit that it was a science with a difference—it was an "occult" science, meaning that it described the hidden (and some would say "spiritual") forces of the universe. Astrologers claimed that centuries of observations had demonstrated the truth of their assertions that the planetary movements through the zodiac affected human life. They were, however, at a loss to pinpoint the exact nature of the forces or connections between the stars and the earth. So, astrologers had to fall back on an esoteric—or occult—connection.

Most astrologers postulated a universe of heavenly correspondences to earthly conditions. Thomas Burgoyne of the Brotherhood of Light described it succinctly:

> Astrology, per se, is a combination of two sciences, viz.: astronomy and correspondences. These two are related to each other as hand and glove; the former deals with suns, moons, planets and stars, and the motion, while the latter deals with the spiritual and physical influences of the same bodies; first upon each other, then upon the earth, and lastly upon the organism of man. (Burgoyne, I, p. 199)

This law of correspondences had been a major building block of Emanuel Swedenborg's thought in the previous century and ultimately derived from the hermetic principle, "As above, so below." Hermetics assume that the individual is a microcosm of the universe, the macrocosm. For astrology, the movement of the planets through the zodiac activated correspondences. Only in the twentieth century could some astrologers move away from the hermetic approach, though, even today, many rely on it.

As an occult science, astrology tried to have the best of both worlds. As a science, it was as new and modern as the latest scientific journal and aligned to the wave of the future. As an occult body of thought, it was allowed to make "religious" affirmations about the place of individuals in a universe of meaning, purpose, and morals. At the very least, these affirmations might be little more than reflections about the nature of life, but, taken to its natural conclusion, astrology led directly to the religion of the stars.

Astrologers, even the most secular, were quite aware that they were offering a "religious" alternative to Christianity. Olney Richmond decried the traditional Creator Deity as unscientific—a mere convenience for those who pretended to give people the directives of the Almighty (Richmond, *Evolutionism*, pp. 5–6). "A far off God and a remote heaven," said Eleanor Kirk, "are no longer attractive. The quickening spirit has breathed a thought to those who have ears and hearts to feel, of the Eternal Now, and a God and a heaven in every human soul" (Kirk, pp. 10–11). The astrologer's God was an impersonal but immanent

force or a principle of order and causation. Butler described God as the Cause
World (Butler, p. 20).

The astrological universe, which replaced the traditional Christian one,
pictured God and nature and humanity as intimately connected in a matrix of
correlates. God was not someone or something apart from human beings. Each
individual, affirmed F. M. Lupton, was a soul that comes from God and "is part of
It—a part of the Great One" (Lupton, p. 6).

Astrology and Religion

The twofold nature of the occult science gives us the major clue as to astrology's
place in the developing culture of the West. Beginning with Deism in the
eighteenth century and continuing through Free Thought in the next, religious
skeptics conducted an intense attack on the essential "supernatural" elements
in Christianity. In the name of science, critics questioned the existence of a
personal Creator God, the viability of prayer, revelation, moral law, and the
legitimacy of the church. In the face of a new understanding of the world, the
spiritual world of traditional religion was seen like astrology—simply worthless
superstition.

Astrology, as occultism in general, however, aligned itself with this
critique of the supernatural in general and Christianity in particular, and
throughout the nineteenth century, Free Thought and the occult made common
cause. Yet Free Thought had a problem: Few could live with its cold hard
universe. The new occultism offered free thinkers a way both to accept the very
compelling critique of supernaturalism and yet to retain a "spiritual" vision that
offered many of the benefits of traditional religion without its ecclesiastical
trappings. Astrology replaced the controversy between science and religion
with a complete capitulation to science—an approach that has allowed it to
accept and feed off of new scientific insight. Most especially, astrology rejoiced
in scientific descriptions of the subtle and invisible forces of our universe, from
radio waves to gamma rays, as welcome confirmation of its previous insights.
More recently, new trends in psychology have been integrated into the astrological universe. Astrology tied itself to the rising wave of science and has ridden
that wave to new heights of success and acceptance.

Astrology in Twentieth-Century America, 1900–1920

For astrology the twentieth century began a year early in a fiery explosion as a
new astrological light appeared in the person of **Evangeline Adams** (1868–
1932). From a Massachusetts family that had given the country two presidents,
Evangeline was reared in the conservative atmosphere of Andover, Massachusetts. Although not in Boston, she was close enough to the city to be a part of the
large psychic community developing there. This community included former
president of the Society for Psychical Research, a Mr. Williams, and several of

his academic colleagues, including J. Hebert Smith, a professor of medicine at Boston University who introduced Adams to the practice of astrology and to Eastern religion.

In 1899, having already chosen astrology as her life's work, Adams moved to New York City and took up residence in the Windsor Hotel. The proprietor, Mr. Leland, was her first client. Since the following day, Friday, March 17, 1899, would be, in his opinion, a bad luck day, Leland went to her for advice. Adams cast his chart, only to find him under the "worst possible combination of planets" (*The Bowl of Heaven,* p. 37). Danger and disaster were imminent. Friday, following an equally ominous reading, Leland walked out of Adams's hotel room to find his fashionable hotel on fire.

Saturday morning, New Yorkers awoke to read of the fire and of the new celebrity in their midst. In bold type on the front page of newspapers was Leland's statement that Adams had predicted the fire. Adams became an instant astrological celebrity, America's first. Thus began her career as an astrologer to the rich, famous, and powerful. Adams gave astrology a respectability. By 1914, she had gained enough leverage to challenge and have overturned New York's statute against "fortune-telling," at least as it applied to astrologers.

While astrology continued a powerful force in the East, Chicago, the major occult center of the era, developed its astrological community. At its hub was Professor Alfred F. Seward, who for many years published astrology books, taught astrology by mail, and claimed to be America's largest dealer in astrology and occult books. Such proliferation in the East and Midwest set the stage for the emergence of three new astrology giants on the West Coast—Elbert Benjamine, Max Heindel, and Llewellyn George.

Elbert Benjamine had been a member of the Brotherhood of Light for nine years when in 1909 he was summoned to the home of Mrs. Anderson, one of the governing three, and informed that they wanted him as the Order's astrologer. They also wanted him to undertake that task of authoring a complete set of lessons on the 21 branches of occult science. The next year he agreed to take the position and assume the task. After 5 years of preparation, in 1915 Benjamine began conducting classes to Brotherhood members and in 1918 to the public at large. Work on the 21 volumes began in 1914 and took the next two decades. For this task Benjamine wrote under the pen name C. C. Zain, a name he assumed to separate his official Brotherhood of Light lessons from his other writings, which were numerous. He wrote a series of 12 reference books on astrology, several booklets and pamphlets, and many articles that were published in astrological and occult periodicals. Under Benjamine's leadership the Brotherhood of Light developed into a large occult body with centers across the United States and international centers in England, Mexico, Canada, and Chile. As a whole, the brotherhood became one of the major centers of learning for astrologers.

Max Heindel migrated to the United States from his native Germany in 1903. He had been a Theosophist, serving as head of the Los Angeles Lodge in

1904–05. He was also a student of German theosophist Rudolf Steiner. On a trip to Germany in 1907, he claimed that a being, described as an elder brother of the Rosicrucian Order, appeared to him. The Rosicrucian led Heindel to a secret temple near the border between Germany and Bohemia and there taught him the material later published in *The Rosicrucian Cosmo-Conception,* Heindel's major book.

In 1908, Heindel formed the Rosicrucian Fellowship, with its first chapter in Columbus, Ohio. Within two years chapters were established in Los Angeles, Seattle, Portland (Oregon), and North Yakima (Washington). In 1911, head-quarters were moved to Oceanside, California, where they remain to this day.

While teaching the whole range of occultism, astrology was one of Heindel's several main interests. He wrote popular astrology texts, which are still in print and are used far beyond the fellowship's borders. The fellowship began the publication of the annual *Ephemeris* and the *Table of Houses,* the two books of tables used by astrologers. Like the Brotherhood of Light, the fellowship became a national and international organization during its first decades of existence.

But as outstanding as Benjamine and Heindel were, neither approached the accomplishments of **Llewellyn George** (1876–1954). Welsh by birth, George grew up in Chicago. At the turn of the century he moved to Portland, Oregon, and in 1901 established the Llewellyn Publishing Company and the Portland School of Astrology. In 1906, he began publishing the annual *Moon Sign Book* and two years later the *Astrological Bulletina.*

A main thrust of George's career was his lifelong attempt to separate astrology from occultism. (Such an attempt was a natural outcome of the articulation of astrology as a science and the growing status that science was gaining in society in general.) To that end, his publishing house, school, and magazine dealt solely with astrology to the exclusion of such occult topics as card reading, tarot, palmistry, and numerology. He was able to drop much of the traditional language of astrology, but he ultimately failed in separating the occult from astrology, which relies on the occult to explain its operation. George did try to move away from the magical (i.e., hermetic) explanation of astrology. Instead of talking about correspondences between individual and universal phenomena, he spoke of planetary vibrations. Some of these cosmic vibrations were plainly physical, such as gravity and radiation. "A radio broadcasting station," asserted George, "vibrates all those receiving sets within range which are attuned to it. . . Each station sends out its own particular program. . . In astrology every planet is a broadcasting station; the nervous system of every person is a 'receiving set'" (George, *Astrology,* p. 27).

George also effectively associated astrology with findings in the natural sciences rather than with the ongoing development of occult thought. He lauded experiments in astrology that demonstrated the truth of particular astrological propositions, while denouncing the misuse of astrology for fortune-telling. But George's success could only be relative.

Astrology was, and still is, intimately linked to the occult, and physical "vibrations" or influences were never located to account for all the astrological effects. Also, most people attracted to astrology are also attracted to the occult in general. Both offer a religious worldview to those attracted to science, but not to those drawn to various secular philosophies, such as rational humanism. In the end Llewellyn Publications circulated their catalogue offering "hundreds of books on progressive subjects, including psychism, hypnotism, prophecy, spiritualism, character reading, magic, personality, prayer, yogi, personal-development, careers, diet and health, employment, business success, etc." (George, *Chats,* p. 124).

Expansion between the Wars: 1920–1940

By the roaring twenties astrology was well established across the United States and its clientele was growing. But it still had not broken into the mass market.

Prior to 1920, most astrology books were privately published. Only two received the imprint of a major American publisher—Katherine Taylor Craig's *Stars of Destiny* (E. P. Dutton, 1916), and Yarmo Vedra's (a pseudonym) *Heliocentric Astrology* (David McKay, 1910). When Dodd, Mead and Company published the first of four major volumes by Evangeline Adams, *The Bowl of Heaven,* in 1924, other major publishers took notice. Within the decade, both J. P. Lippincott and Doubleday had published a line of astrological titles and opened a new audience to the wonders of astrological speculations.

Astrology grew in popularity during the 1920s, with the public supporting several periodicals on the subject. Prior to World War I, a number of periodicals had begun and had attained some degree of success within the astrological community, but as a whole they had been unable to break into the mass market or the newsstands. That situation changed in 1923, when Paul G. Clancy began publishing *American Astrology,* the longest-running astrological periodical. His effort was followed the next year by that of **Sidney K. Bennett,** better known by his pen name, Wynn. *Wynn's Magazine* quickly joined *American Astrology* on the newsstands, and Wynn's books flooded the popular astrology market.

Though several astrological societies had been formed before 1920, the first organizations to claim widespread membership were formed after World War I. In 1923 Llewellyn George and A. Z. Stevenson founded the American Astrological Society and George helped found the National Astrological Society four years later. That same year a group of New York astrologers founded the Astrologers' Guild of America. The various national and regional organizations spurred the formation of many local groups such as the Oakland (Calif.) Astrological Society, founded in 1925, and the Friends of Astrology, founded in Chicago in 1938. They also led to the formation of the American Federation of Astrologers (AFA) in 1938. The AFA, the most prestigious of the several astrological organizations, has been the most effective in bringing professionalism to the field and creating a favorable public image for its members.

The massive growth of astrology in the 1920s and 1930s set the stage for another spurt after World War II. Only one step—the spread of the sun sign columns now carried in most daily newspapers and many monthly magazines—remained to create the popularity so evident today. Since the turn of the century, astrologers had tried to break into the popular press. Sepharial briefly had a column, but his forecasting ended in disaster both for him and the cause of astrology. Not until 1930 did a successful column, written by P. I. H. Naylor, appear in England. It was suppressed, however, in 1942, as England began to use astrology in its intelligence efforts against Hitler. After the war, newspapers on both sides of the Atlantic began to publish astrology columns and quickly recognized their popularity with the public.

Since World War II

The spectacular spread of astrology in the last generation was made possible by several developments, the most important being the gradual movement from a base in the hard sciences to one in psychology. The most significant thinker in that transition was **Dane Rudhyar** (1895–1985). Rudhyar developed what he initially called harmonic astrology, now called humanistic astrology. Deeply moved by Eastern metaphysics, theosophy and the teachings of Alice Bailey, and the occult speculations of psychiatrist Carl Jung, he was at the same time disturbed by the problems of the older astrology with its psychologically questionable analysis of good and bad points in individual horoscopes, not to mention the irresponsible predictions of some practitioners of traditional astrology. In the 1960s Rudhyar founded the International Committee for a Humanistic Astrology, which would attempt to orient astrology to the fulfillment of the individual and to undergird astrological practice with a sound philosophical and psychological experience.

The transformation of astrological thinking by Rudhyar and his students has been the most significant intellectual development of the discipline, and the least understood by astrology's critics. Using Jung's category of synchronicity, Rudhyar suggested that stellar and planetary bodies did not directly effect humans, merely that the astrological chart has a coincidental relationship to the individual's psychological makeup. (Students of astrology will recognize this argument as a sophisticated recasting of the correspondences theory.) By this means, Rudhyar removed the need to find specific physical forces that operated on humans, causing the behavioral consequences predicted by astrology. Rudhyar went beyond his predecessors, however, in his suggestion that astrology dealt in possibilities and potentialities inherent within the individual rather than in forces operating on him/her from outside—either from physical or occult forces. Thus Rudhyar completely discarded any need for empirical verification for astrological insight while at the same time distancing it from its albatross—determinism. (*See:* **Fate**.) According to Rudhyar, astrological forces do not determine but merely suggest a future with which the individual might cooperate.

Rudhyar's insights finally stripped astrology of the remnant of its "fortune-telling" image and recast it as a psychology helping profession. Contemporary astrologers have little problem with stepping into the role of counselors, assisting their clients.

Meanwhile, those astrologers who still operate from a base of hard science have continued to look for specific scientific findings to support their faith in the direct influence if the planetary bodies on human life. Some spectacular underpinnings come from the study of biological rhythms. The work of biologist Frank A. Brown at Northwestern University, demonstrated celestial influences on plant and animal life, and brought the results of the other scientists' studies of natural rhythms to the attention of the astrological community. What is more, **Michel Gauquelin** continued to demonstrate the coincidence of astrological delineations in large samples of various occupational groups. He found that particular planets were prominent in the **ascendant** and **midheaven** of those who were leaders in the fields that were tested—science, military, sports, medicine, and music. While Gauquelin presented much data against traditional astrology, only the positive results drew attention.

In the end, however, the scientific work has had little influence on the developing practice of astrology.

Astrology Today

The new wave of astrological thought set in motion by Dane Rudhyar, recent attempts to create a neo-astrology based on science, the continuing allegiance to more traditional astrological schools, and some new forms of astrology practice have combined to create the many schools that exist today. They are all heirs to the efforts of astrologers of the nineteenth and early twentieth centuries.

The advent of the computer has been a boon to the mathematics of astrology. Software programs have facilitated chart casting (*see* Appendix A)—the drawing of the basic horoscope—the running of progressions and mid-points, the placement of asteroids, and other calculations.

Sources:

Adams, Evangeline. *The Bowl of Heaven*. New York: Dodd, Mead & Co., 1924.
Blavatsky, H. P. *Isis Unveiled*. Wheaton, Ill.: Theosophical Publishing House, 1972.
———. *The Secret Doctrine*. Pasadena, Calif.: Theosophical Publishing House, 1963.
Broughton, Luke. *The Elements of Astrology*. New York: Privately printed, 1893.
Burgoyne, Thomas H. *The Light of Egypt*. 2 vols. San Francisco: Religio-Philosophical Publishing House, 1884.
Butler, Hiram E. *Solar Biology*. 25th ed. Applegate, Calif.: Esoteric Publishing Co., 1887.
George, Llewellyn. *Astrological Chats*. Los Angeles: Llewellyn Publications, 1941.
———. *Astrology/What It Is/What It Is Not*. Los Angeles: Llewellyn Publications, 1931.
Heindel, Augusta Foss. *The Birth of the Rosicrucian Fellowship*. Oceanside, Calif.: The Rosicrucian Fellowship, n.d.
Kirk, Eleanor. *The Influence of the Zodiac upon the Human Life*. New Life: Privately printed, 1894.

Lupton, F. M. *Astrology Made Easy.* Baltimore: I. & M. Ottenheimer, 1897.
Melton, J. Gordon. *A Bibliography of Astrology in America, 1840–1940.* Santa Barbara, Calif.: Institute for the Study of American Religion, 1987.
———. *Biographical Dictionary of Cult and Sect Leaders.* New York: Garland Publishing, 1986.
Richmond, Olney H. *Evolutionism.* Chicago: Temple Publishing Co., 1896.
———. *Temple Lectures.* Chicago: Privately published, 1891.

History of Western Astrology

Investigation of the heavenly bodies, in the forms that we now distinguish as astrology and **astronomy**, began in the European world at the beginning of Greek civilization (the word *astrology* comes from the Greek *astron,* star, and *logos,* study). The study of the **stars** had both scientific and religious purposes. The rhythms of the stars provided the basis for calculating **calendars**. The stars also represented a kind of natural watch in a clockless age and provided spatial reference points, important for such practical matters as navigation.

Berosus, a Chaldean priest from Belus who settled in Cos to teach, probably in the early fourth century B.C., is traditionally regarded as having introduced astrology to Greece. The Greeks were interested in the study of the stars much earlier, however. The pre-Socratic philosopher Thales (ca. 625–ca. 547 B.C.), who founded the Ionian school (a philosophy theorizing on the origin of the universe from one single principle), and Pythagoras of Samos (ca. 580–500 B.C.), founder of Pythagoreanism (a syncretistic philosophical system that combines medicine, astronomy, musical scales, and mathematics to describe reality in terms of numbers), had already devoted attention to the stars and speculated about the nature and constitution of the heavenly bodies. The fourth century B.C. was particularly fertile for the proliferation of astrology. **Plato** and Aristotle had a unified view of the universe (Aristotle even spoke of connections between the heavenly bodies and the sublunar world), reflecting Greek culture's Eastern heritage. Astrology also influenced the study of medicine, as is evident in the work of Hippocrates (ca. 460–ca. 377 B.C.), who lived on the island of Cos. Hippocrates defined the four humors, which are based on the status of blood (warm and moist), yellow bile (warm and dry), black bile (cold and dry), and phlegm (cold and wet), and set forth a correspondence of the humors with the **planets**. In 140 B.C., Hipparchus (190–120 B.C.) of Bythnia catalogued 1,081 stars, while a few decades later the Syrian Posidonius of Apamea spread his knowledge of **magic and astrology** in the school he founded in Rhodes, where both Romans and Greeks studied. Marcus Manilius was probably influenced by Posidonius of Apamea when he wrote his verses entitled "Astronomica."

The Romans, who had an indigenous form of divination traditionally practiced by augurs, received astrology in the second century B.C. from Greeks living in the colonies of southern Italy. The Romans adopted the Greek system of the **zodiac**, naming the planets after Roman-Latin deities (names which are still in use) and naming the seven days of the week after the corresponding planets and deities. This tradition also influenced the English names of the days of the week, which still reflect the ancient connection (e.g., "Saturn-day," "Sun-day," and "Moon-day"). In about 270 B.C., **judicial astrology** and **medical astrology** were mentioned in the poem *Diosemeia* by the Greek Aratus of Soli. Aratus's poem was translated into Latin and influenced the Romans.

In ancient Rome judicial astrology survived the years of the Republic despite anti-astrology efforts by such famous intellectuals as Cato and Cicero (*De divinatione*). In 139 B.C., after the unrest of the slaves and the lower class in Rome, astrologers were expelled from the city and from the Roman borders of Italy. Despite this opposition, astrology gradually came to be accepted among intellectuals toward the end of the first century B.C., largely as a result of the spread of Stoicism (which had adopted astrology as part of its system). Although during the imperial age astrology was several times forbidden as a private practice, astrologers continued to be consulted by the court. As the empire became Christianized, the Christian church began to officially oppose certain kinds of astrology in the fourth century A.D. (for example, in the writings of the Council of Laodicea).

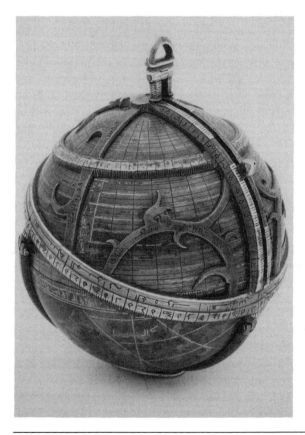

◄
**A 15th-century spherical
astrolabe from the eastern
Islamic world. · Bettmann
Archive**

During Hellenistic times astrology began to bloom in Egypt through the Alexandrian school, where Babylonian and Egyptian astrological lore mingled with Greek philosophy. The earliest Greek Hermetic literature, in the second century B.C., focused on astrology. Fragments of these texts, among which are the Salmeschiniaka and the textbook of Nechepso and Petosiris, have survived in the *Catalogus codicum astrologorum Graecorum,* as quotations in some Arabic works of the ninth century, and in later Latin writings. Within the Hermetic tradition, iatromathematics, or medical astrology (through which the various anatomical parts are associated with planets, herbs, and minerals), also developed, deriving its name from the Greek *iatromathematikos.* A poem on astrology, *Astronomica,* of which five books still exist, was composed in the early first century A.D. by Manilius. Manilius compiled contemporary knowledge of this science, often in contradictory forms and under the influence of the Stoicist vision of cosmic sympathy and correlation between macrocosm and microcosm. In the second century A.D., Vettius Valens, an Antiochian intellectual operating in Alexandria, Egypt, compiled the *Anthology,* a work on astrology that shows the new concept of this field as a secret art learned through initiation.

Ptolemy , one of the most influential intellectuals in the history of Western astrology, also lived in Alexandria in the second century. His main works were the *Almagest* (Greek, for the greatest) and the *Tetrabiblos* (*Quadripartitum* in Latin). The *Almagest* was an astronomy work that taught how to predict celestial phenomena, mostly through the use of mathematics. The *Tetrabiblos* became a major text for astrologers and occultists in the western world for several centuries. Ptolemy gathered the knowledge of Egyptian and Chaldean astrology and interpreted it in the light of Greek philosophy, Stoicism in particular. The Stoic idea that all matter is bound together in a cosmic sympathy became a rational explanation for the relationship between the changes in the universe (macrocosm) and in man (microcosm). Magic and such traditions as number symbolism, chiromancy, and geomancy became attached to astrological divination, although these did not change the basic principles of astrology.

Ptolemy's work was authoritative for centuries, particularly in Constantinople (Byzantium), the capital of the eastern part of the empire, where Greek remained the spoken language. In A.D. 500, Rhetorius introduced, among other new elements, the division of the **signs** of the zodiac into **triplicities**, corresponding to the four classical **elements** (still used in modern astrology). Although some theological schools in Byzantium accepted astrology, several Christian emperors (such as Constantius, Theodosius, and Valerianus) began to proscribe astrology and threatened astrologers with exile. Earlier, in the fifth century, in the Platonic Academy of Athens, the last bulwark of the Greek pre-Christian culture, Proclo (410–485) had commented on the *Tetrabiblos* with regard to the stars as a "secondary cause of earthly events." But in 529, the emperor Justinian (527–565) closed the academy, claiming it was a center of pagan thinking, and many of the scholars from Athens fled to Persia and Syria.

The *Catalogus Codicum Astrologorum Graecorum* shows the large amount of astrology literature that had been produced in Byzantium, although most of the extant manuscripts belong to the twelfth century. In this same century, despite the opposition of the church, there was interest in astrology—sometimes even within the church itself—although the stars were now considered to be signs rather than causes of events.

In the western world the study of the stars, called astronomy, was one of the seven *artes liberales* comprising the education curriculum of the time (along with grammar, rhetoric, dialectic, arithmetic, geometry, and music). The fathers of the Latin church condemned astrology as magic and as pagan. Augustine, referring to astrology in *De civitate Dei* (*The City of God,* 411), asserted that it was mere superstition. The fundamental astrology text, the *Tetrabiblos* was not yet known to the Latins, who had only a few sources on astronomy (such as a chapter on astronomy in *The Marriage of Mercury and Phylologiae* by Martianus Capella, the *Commentary* by Macrobius in the fourth century, and the works of Isidore and Bede during the seventh century).

In the sixth century, astronomy was defined by Cassiodoro (490–583), secretary at the court of Theodoricus, the Ostrogoth king of Italy, as the science that examines the heavenly bodies and their relation to one another and to Earth. It was not until the early seventh century that an effort was made to distinguish between astronomy and astrology—in the *Etymologiae* of Isidore, bishop of Seville. The definitions in the *Etymologiae* show how in antiquity it was impossible to consider as independent two arts considered as complementary as these. The study of the stars and the *computus* (the art of computing the calendar) were also part of monastic education, as a tool for calendrical reference to the course of time through the year.

A reawakened interest in astrology in the Western world began in the eleventh century under the influence of the Arabs, who had been settled in Spain and Sicily since the eighth century. The Arabs were the heirs of the philosophy and culture of Hellenistic Greece—a heritage they blended with Syrian, Indian, and Persian cultures—and this knowledge began to spread to the schools of northwestern Europe. Although in Islamic culture astrology was generally opposed for much the same reasons as in Christianity, scientific and intellectual interest in the movements of the stars persisted in the work of such Muslim astrologers as Masha'allah, al-Kindi, Abu Ma'shar, and al-Battani. The works of these scholars were eventually translated into Latin. Al-Kindi and Abu Ma'shar (ninth century) especially provided philosophical underpinnings for astrology, under the influence of Aristotelianism, Neoplatonism, Neopythagoreanism, and Stoicism.

In the early 1100s Ptolemy's *Tetrabiblos* was translated, possibly by Plato of Tivoli, from an Arabic edition that also contained information on Persian and Indian astrology. It became attractive for Western Latin intellectuals to study the astrological system of the Arabs, with its new terminology and complexity, alongside Ptolemy's *Tetrabiblos* and *Almagest.* Also, the discovery of Aristotle's *Physics,* among other works, was instrumental in the following centuries in supporting the validity of astrology in understanding natural science (medicine, alchemy, and meteorology). The intellectual milieu in which this new literature was accepted—the only intellectual milieu of the time before the first universities were founded in the thirteenth century—was that created by the Church. In Europe, paganism had disappeared and the superstitious aspect of astrology, which had been such a cause of concern for Saint Augustine, was now no longer an issue. The scientific aspect of astrology (its relation to alchemy, medicine, and meteorology) was still of interest in this environment.

With the founding of Oxford University (in 1249), astronomy was included in the liberal arts curriculum for its contribution in understanding medicine, meteorology, and alchemy. Judicial astrology, however, was explicitly opposed in the writings of Robert Grosseteste, bishop of Lincoln and chancellor of Oxford University, on the basis of Augustine's position (that astrology denies the will of God). The opposition of the Church to astrology also surfaced in 1277 in the list of statements of condemnation by the bishop of Paris, Stephen of Tempier, who condemned astrology and authors who connected astrology with the sublunar world. Some Scholastic theologians (who were influenced by Saint Augustine and later by Aristotelianism), including Albertus Magnus of Cologne (Albert the Great, 1200–1280), accepted the influence of the planets on the lower world. Nevertheless, they denied planetary influence over the human will, because they believed the soul is the image of God. Albertus Magnus recommended the *Almagest* for the study of astronomy and the *Tetrabiblos* for astrology (in their Latin translations). **Thomas Aquinas** (1225–1274), Magnus's pupil and one of the greatest Scholastic theologians, declared, in *Summa theologica* that heavenly bodies indirectly influence the human intellect and thus astrologers can make true predictions. In *De sortibus* and *De judiciis astrorum,* however, he expressed his opposition to **horoscopes** and election of propitious days.

Although Church intellectuals of the thirteenth century were opposed to the superstitious aspects of astrology, Roger Bacon (1214?–1294), the greatest scientist of his time, fully accepted medical astrology. In the following century also, intellectual churchmen were using astrology as an instrument for further understanding science (and for interpreting the Scriptures). Judicial astrology, however, is not even mentioned by such authors as Thomas Bradwardine (archbishop of Canterbury) and Henry of Langestein. The "scientific" application of astrology is reflected in the efforts of the University of Paris to explain the Black Death epidemic that ravaged Europe from 1347 to 1350; contemporary intellectuals were more inclined to attribute the plague to **conjunctions** of the stars rather than to conduct physical and medical investigations. At the University of Bologna, founded in 1119 for the education of a lay public and less influenced by the Church (though still under its control), students of medicine were required to undertake a four-year program in astrology, which culminated with the *Tetrabiblos* and the *Almagest*. Guidi Bonati, one of the most famous astrologers of the 13th century, was professor at this university and author of *De Astronomia*.

There were a number of other famous astrologers in this period. Michael Scot was court astrologer for Frederick II in Sicily and wrote the *Liber introductorius* as a student manual. Campanus of Novara, one of the few good mathematicians of the time, according to Bacon, wrote the *Sphaera* and the *Theorica planetarum*. In 1327, during the Inquisition, Cecco d'Ascoli was burned at the stake as a heretic. He was an astrologer and magician who had lectured at the University of Bologna and applied astrology to the birth and death of Christ. Although there were undoubtedly political factors behind Cecco's execution, the charge of heresy nevertheless reflected the concern of the Church over astrological matters.

Following the discovery of Arabic texts, the Church absorbed astrology and disapproved of it only when it seemed to imply fatalistic determinism (as in the case of Cecco d'Ascoli), which contradicted man's free will and God's omnipotence. Also, the writings of intellectuals in the fourteenth and fifteenth centuries, such as Oresme, Peter d'Ailly, and Jean Gerson, show that astrology was still part of contemporary science, and few doubts about its validity appear.

In the early Renaissance, various cultural and historical factors contributed to the development of interest in astrology. First, the technological improvement of printing techniques favored the production of **ephemerides, almanacs,** charts and calendars, and so on. In 1474, the first ephemeris, *Ephemeris ad XXXII annos futuros,* by **Regiomontanus** (Johann Müller, 1436–1476), eminent mathematician and astronomer, was printed in Nuremberg, and a second edition in Venice in 1484. In 1489, the *Introductorium in astronomia* by Abu Ma'shar was translated into Latin from Arabic.

Another important factor in the new interest in astrology was increased appreciation of the rediscovered classical authors of antiquity, beginning with the first humanists at the end of the fourteenth century. One reason for the new interest in the ancients was the siege of the city of Constantinople by the Turks in 1453, which forced Greek scholars to flee from the city (taking with them their literature) to Italy, a country which had already shown a renewed interest in the classics of the ancient world. Some Greek scholars were already settled in Italy before the siege of Constantinople. Manuel Chrysoloras, whose nephew Marsilio Ficino was one of the most important figures in the history of **occultism** during the Renaissance, went to teach Greek in Florence in 1396. The Florentine court of Cosimo de' Medici was also one of the first cultural centers to offer refuge to the Greeks and, as a consequence, to develop an interest in astrology.

At the Medici court, Giordano Bruno (1548–1600) and Marsilio Ficino (1433–1499) worked as the translators of Plato's writings (thus rediscovering Neoplatonism). Ficino also wrote the *Pimander,* a hermetic work full of astrological elements. A physician as well as an intellectual, Ficino also wrote *De vita libri tres,* a medical treatise on the health of the intellectual; in the third part of the book, "De vita coelitus comparanda," he describes his vision of astrology and planetary influences on one's health.

The intellectuals of the early fifteenth century could read the *Picatrix,* an Arab compilation translated into Spanish (in 1256), which dealt largely with astrological magic and influenced Ficino and his student Pico della Mirandola (1463–1494). The application of astrology to medicine, iatromathematics, received attention from Paracelsus (Bombast von Hohenheim, 1493–1541), who considered astrology a means of understanding one's innate physical disposition and allowing better control of one's life. Medical astrology was also the focus of the *Amicus medicorum,* written in 1431 by Jean Ganivet and in use for the following two centuries throughout the Western world.

Although court astrologers continued to enjoy their position as consultants to kings and princes throughout the fifteenth century, their way of doing

During the western Middle Ages, astrology and astronomy were preserved and developed within Arabic civilization. The science of the stars was reappropriated from Arabs by Europeans during the Renaissance. This woodcut, which contrasts the Arab astrolabe with the more advanced Renaissance sextant, implicitly acknowledges European indebtedness to Arab culture.
· Bettmann Archive

astrology was the object of an ongoing intellectual debate. The astrology of **natal charts** and forecasting the future, called judicial astrology, was considered superstitious by the intellectuals of the period. This kind of astrology was contrasted with medical astrology (iatromathematics), the study of the influence of the planets on the physical body. Ficino always disapproved of the use of judicial astrology for divinatory purposes, but devoted the entire third chapter of *De vita* to medical astrology. According to Ficino, however, the planets have an influence only at the moment of birth, while the balance of one's life is determined by one's own will.

The debate over judicial and medical astrology was especially animated after the publication in the 1490s of Pico della Mirandola's *Disputationes adversus astrologiam divinatricem*. In this work the author attacked judicial astrology, demonstrated it to be fallible and arbitrary, lacking consensus on its basic principles, and ruled by a materialistic determinism. He argued that astrology cannot be true because it requires an accuracy that is impossible to obtain in interpreting the movements of the stars. But the accusation he leveled against astrologers concerned their use of unclear and contradictory Latin sources in place of Ptolemy, whose work on astrology Pico did consider to be accurate. He was thus not attacking astrology itself. His *Disputationes* became an important work for its influence on the debate over astrology.

A response soon came from Pico's contemporary Pietro Pomponazzi (1462–1524), teacher in various Italian universities, who found Pico's observations unscientific and took apart his arguments against astrology. In 1508, Luca Gaurico, author of *Tractatus astrologicus,* published the *Oratio de inventoribus et astrologiae laudibus* to defend astrology. About the same time, the German occultist Cornelius Agrippa (1486–1535), in his *De occulta philosophia,* connected astrology with other magic arts, such as palmistry and alchemy, and laid the groundwork for the future development of astrology in the occultist milieu that arose during the Enlightenment (discussed later).

One of the most prominent astrologers from Italy in the sixteenth century, the Dominican Tommaso Campanella (1568–1639), wrote six books on astrology free of the superstitious aspects caused by Arabic and Jewish influence and concordant with the teachings of Church theologians. (The study of Arabic and Jewish astrology introduced a deterministic approach, in contradiction to the basic Christian principles of divine providence and free will.) He also wrote a defense of Galileo, *Apologia pro Galilaeo* (1616). He was twice imprisoned on charges of heresy.

The debate over astrology became intense during the sixteenth century, fueled by Copernicus's (1473–1543) postulation of heliocentrism (and continued into the next century as a result of Galileo's advocacy of that theory). The sixteenth century was also the time of the Reformation and the counter-Reformation, when the Church was particularly sensitive to heresies. In 1545, at the Council of Trent, the Church condemned judicial astrology, and at the end of the century the Church officially disassociated itself from it. Galileo was denounced for his *Letters on the Solar Spots* (1613) and was condemned by the Church in 1632 for his heliocentrism.

In the same period the English scientist Francis Bacon (1561–1626) demonstrated the invalidity of astrology as commonly practiced, and suggested a system purified of all superstitious elements and in agreement with basic scientific principles. According to Bacon, astrology cannot be applied to the individual but can help to predict mass changes and movements of heavenly bodies or people. Although Bacon attacked all superstition, as a scientist of the seventeenth century he still accepted astrology as a divinatory system.

Astrology still survived in the academic milieu as iatromathematics in the seventeenth century. But with the progress of medicine as an empirical science, medicine ultimately became a distinct field of investigation. At the same time, the slow process of evolution of astronomy as a descriptive science, had which begun with the new Copernican tables (1551), gradually widened the gap between divinatory astrology and scientific astronomy.

Astrology continued to be practiced throughout the sixteenth century in various parts of western Europe. In France, another member of the Medici family, Catherine, previously in contact with the astrologer Luca Gaurico, contributed to the spread of astrology in that country. She married Henry II and, after many years without children, consulted astrologers. The birth of her first child strengthened her faith in astrology. Among the astrologers invited to work at her court was **Nostradamus** (Michel de Nostredame, 1503–1566), an astrologer who became notorious for his prophecies written in quatrain in the poem called *Centuries* (1555). Working at Henry II's court, Nostradamus became known throughout the whole country, publishing almanacs and medical works that advocated the use of astrology for medical purposes.

While Copernicus's heliocentrism was gradually introduced into England by the early seventeenth century through the works of Thomas Digges and Thomas Bretnor, lay societies of professionals, not necessarily tied to the universities or to the Church, began to organize to discuss the new science. In England the Royal Society of London was chartered in 1662 by Charles II. At the time, England and Holland were the only two countries in Europe to offer freedom of thought during a period of strict censorship by both the Catholic and Protestant churches in all the other European countries. Astrology was not included among the principal subjects discussed by the Royal Society, but some of its members were practicing it.

Astrology was no longer debated in European universities. Also, there is not much in the historical record regarding astrologers in the 1700s and 1800s. Astrology did not die during this period; it was merely neglected in academic and scientific debate. Modern thought, which began with the Enlightenment, excluded astrology as an empirical science. It was not included, nor even mentioned, in the entry on astronomy in Diderot and D'Alembert's extensive *Encyclopedia* in 1781.

Astrology and its symbolism survived the Enlightenment, however, in esoteric circles. Various occultists revived the magic writings of the *Picatrix* and the *Corpus hermeticum* of the Renaissance and cabbala to give a new, more esoteric interpretation of the movements of the stars. Precursors of this "modern" vision of astrology were Emanuel Swedenborg (1688–1772) and Franz Anton Mesmer (1733–1815). The European astrological revival in the nineteenth century began in England. Francis Barrett, who wrote *The Magus* (1801), an important synthesis of magical lore, and **Nicolas Culpepper** (1616–1654), an astrologer, had already devoted their time to the study of occultism. But interest in astrology reawakened with the publication of certain books on the subject. In 1816, James Wilson wrote *A Complete Dictionary of Astrology,* and a few years later Robert C. Smith (1795–1832), whose pen name was Raphael, wrote the *Manual of Astrology* and compiled his *Ephemeris.* New works on astrology followed, such as Ely Star's *Les mystères de l'horoscope* in 1887. Also important was Eliphas Lévi (1810–1875), the modern magician, who synthe-

◄

An 18th-century academy. Note the celestial sphere (on the right) and the illustrations of eclipses in the center of the floor.
· Bettmann Archive

sized ancient esotericism and developed a new form of magic. An important work on astrology was written in 1915 by **Aleister Crowley** (1875–1947), a famous English occultist. He was a member of the Hermetic Order of the Golden Dawn, a magical society founded by S. L. MacGregor Mathers, who was learned in cabbala and magic. Crowley wrote *Astrology* in 1915, in which he taught a scientific astrology that reinterpreted the science of the stars in the light of the discovery of the last two planets, **Neptune** (1846) and **Uranus** (1781).

A revival of astrology also took place within the Theosophical movement, started by Madam Blavatsky in 1875 in the United States. Astrology became the focus of the Astrological Lodge of the Theosophical Society (which publishes *Astrology Quarterly*), founded in 1915 by **Alan Leo** (1860–1917), an important author in the British revival of astrology. Leo was initiated into theosophy by his friend **W. Gorn Old** (1864–1929), whose pen name was Sepharial, a man learned in astrology and cabbala. From the theosophical movement and the Astrological Lodge—where another famous astrologer, **Charles Carter** (1887–1968), was trained in astrology—the Faculty of Astrology and the Astrological Association were founded in England a few decades later. Leo's work also influenced the German Uranian system (Hamburg Astrology School, founded by Alfred Witte and Friedrich Sieggrün in the 1930s), cosmobiology (a scientific school of astrology founded by **Reinhold Ebertin** (1901–1988) in the 1930s that averred the existence of a physical connection between the movements of the stars and human behavior), and the Dutch Ram School. Within the theosophical milieu, **Alice Bailey** (1880–1949), founder of the Arcane School, devoted the third volume of the trilogy *A Treatise on the Seven Rays* to astrology. According to D.K., the Tibetan master channeled by Alice Bailey, astrology was the most occult science. Bailey's work contributed to the revival of astrology in the twentieth century.

Astrology also developed in France through the symbolist school. It drew upon the depth psychology of famous psychologist and psychiatrist **Carl Jung** (1875–1961), who explained astrology via his notion of **synchronicity**. For Jung, astrology embodied some of the archetypes that play an important role in the development of the human mind. The French symbolist school, in the same way, aimed at freeing astrology from its rigid mechanistic structure to enable a more descriptive approach to personality through the understanding of astrological symbols.

Under Jung's influence, astrology was also revived for application to psychology in **humanistic astrology** as the North American counterpart of the French symbolist school. As such, astrology's focus is not centered on events but on the person. Humanistic astrology was initially formulated by **Dane Rudhyar**, whose benchmark work in the field was *The Astrology of Personality: A Reformulation of Astrological Concepts and Ideals in Terms of Contemporary Psychology and Philosophy* (1936). Rudhyar was particularly influenced by the humanistic psychology of Abraham Maslow.

An effort to use a scientific approach, based on the application of statistical methodology, to astrology was carried out in the early twentieth century by Paul Choisnard and Karl Krafft. Their studies convinced them that "astrology exists." In 1950, **Michel** and **Françoise Gauquelin** again applied statistics to the study of astrology, testing a large number of individuals (approximately 25,000) according to profession. They found a correlation different from the traditional astrological one. The resulting controversy polarized modern astrology into humanistic astrology (which opposes the mechanical determinism of the scientific school) and scientific astrology (which claims to be empirical).

André Barbault, a French astrologer, wrote *De la psychanalyse a l'astrologie* (1961), in which he demonstrates the similarity between the psychological determinism of certain contemporary trends of psychoanalysis and the cosmic determinism of ancient astrology. Barbault was also the first to design a computer program that enabled astrologers to cast horoscopes. While Barbault's work continued the tradition of scientific astrology, a British astrologer, Sybil Leek (1923–1983), strengthened the occultist aspect of this ancient art. Leek moved to the United States later in her life, and through her several books, many of them on astrology, she contributed to the spread of witchcraft (she was a "white" witch) and astrology.

More recently, a revival of astrology has occurred within the subculture referred to as the New Age movement. The New Age began in the late 1960s in the United States and arrived in Europe soon afterward. The New Age, which was originally called the Age of Aquarius, is conceived of in terms of astrological symbolism. The New Age movement also draws upon a holistic vision of reality that is reminiscent of the unified vision of the cosmos of the ancients. The unity and correspondence of micro- and macro-cosmo legitimizes the use of an ancient art that, for the scientific milieu and for mainstream religion, is mere superstition. Nowadays, astrological horoscopes are included in a great majority of popular magazines and other "checkout counter" literature. Periodical publications specializing in astrology are published all over Europe and in the United States for all kinds of audiences, from the most popular to the most sophisticated. Although astrological charts are no longer cast for princes and kings, and astrology is no longer used to interpret major historical and natural phenomena, it still plays a large role in modern society. Today, astrology is the tool of individuals for the interpretation of their everyday life, from business to love affairs. In this form, astrology seems certain to survive into the future.

—*Isotta Poggi*

Sources:

Brau, Jean-Louis, Helen Weaver, and Allan Edmands. *Larousse Encyclopedia of Astrology.* New York: New American Library, 1980.

Cumont, Franz, ed. *Catalogus Codicum Astrologorum Graecorum.* 12 vols. Brussels: 1898–1953.

Diderot, Denis, and Jean D'Alembert. *Encyclopédie ou Dictionnaire raisonné des sciences, des artes et des metiers par une societe des gens de lettres.* Lausanne Societe Typographiques, 1781–82.

Filbey, John, and Peter Filbey. *The Astrologer's Companion.* Wellingborough, Northamptonshire,
U.K.: Aquarian Press, 1986.

Gettings, Fred. *Dictionary of Astrology.* London: Routledge & Kegan Paul, 1985.

Isidore of Seville, Saint. *Etymologies.* Paris: Les Belles Lettres, 1981.

Kitson, Annabella, ed. *History and Astrology: Clio and Urania Confer.* London: Mandala, 1989.

Ptolemy. *Tetrabiblos.* Translated by F. R. Robbins. London: Loeb Classical Library, 1940.

Rudhyar, Dane. *The Astrology of Personality: A Reformulation of Astrological Concepts and Ideas in
Terms of Contemporary Psychology and Philosophy.* Hague: Servire/Wasserman, 1963.

Tester, Jim. *A History of Western Astrology.* New York: Ballantine, 1987.

Homosexuality and Astrology

The treatment of homosexuality in **astrology** has tended to reflect the social conditions and the attitude toward homosexuals at the time. **Ptolemy,** the father of Western astrology, very matter-of-factly mentions patterns that distinguish homosexuals from heterosexuals in his classic work *Tetrabiblos:* If **Venus** (the **ruler** of romantic relationships) and **Jupiter** precede the **Sun** in a man's chart, and if the former two **planets** also **aspect Mars** (the ruler of passion), then he will be sexually interested only in other males. If, on the other hand, Mars and Venus are in **masculine signs** in a woman's chart, she will be inclined to lesbianism. In another place, Ptolemy notes that links between **Mercury** (corresponding to the Greek Hermes) and Venus (Greek Aphrodite) indicates an attraction to young men. This interpretation may have been suggested by the joining of the Greek names of these two planets, which results in *Hermaphroditos.*

By way of contrast, **astrologers** who matured during a period of time when society viewed homosexuality as a behavior disorder tend to attribute interest in the same sex to certain **afflictions** in a **horoscope. Charles Carter,** an important astrologer of the early twentieth century, discussed homosexuality under the heading "Immorality (Sexual)" in his *Encyclopedia of Psychological Astrology.* Carter saw the key to homosexuality in **Uranus** (ruler of, among other traits, eccentricity) and **Neptune** (ruler of, among other characteristics, secrets, deception, and hidden things). A **native** with a poorly aspected Uranus, particularly when Venus was involved, was thought to be a prime candidate.

As homosexuality has acquired a more acceptable position on the sexual landscape, astrological speculations that attributed same-sex preference to difficult aspects and unfavorable placements have been quietly put aside. The contemporary astrological community is highly tolerant of unconventional sexual orientations, and there now exist **sun sign** guides to love and romance expressly for homosexuals (e.g., Michael Jay's *Gay Love Signs).* There is no general agreement, however, on the process of determining sexual orientation from a birth chart. For a quick overview of astrological ideas on this subject, as well as original, research-based ninth **harmonic** charts (referred to as *navamsa* charts in **Hindu astrology),** consult van Dam's *Astrology and Homosexuality.*

Sources:

Carter, Charles E. O. *An Encyclopedia of Psychological Astrology.* 1924. Reprint. London: Theosophical
   Publishing House, 1963.
Dynes, Wayne R. *Encyclopedia of Homosexuality.* 2 vols. New York: Garland, 1990.
van Dam, Wim. *Astrology and Homosexuality.* 1983. Reprint. York Beach, Maine: Samuel Weiser, 1985.

Honoria

Honoria, **asteroid** 236 (the 236th asteroid to be discovered), is approximately
68 kilometers in diameter and has an **orbital** period of 2.3 years. Honoria is a
concept asteriod, the name being a personification of the word honor. In a **natal
chart,** this celestial body's location by sign and **house** indicates where one
gives or receives honor. When **afflicted** by inharmonious **aspects,** Honoria
may show dishonor or where one receives false honor.

Sources:

Kowal, Charles T. *Asteroids: Their Nature and Utilization.* Chichester, West Sussex, U.K.: Ellis
   Horwood Limited, 1988.
Room, Adrian. *Dictionary of Astronomical Names.* London: Routledge, 1988.

Hopi

Hopi, **asteroid** 2,938 (the 2,938th asteroid to be discovered), is approximately
25.4 kilometers in diameter and has an **orbital** period of 5.6 years. Hopi was
named after the Hopi tribe of North American Indians. According to Lang-
Wescott, Hopi represents awareness of oppression and prejudice. This asteroid
also represents the principle of "ambush," including psychological ambush.
This asteroid's key words are *prejudice* and *ambush.*

Sources:

Lang-Wescott, Martha. *Asteroids-Mechanics: Ephemerides II.* Conway, Mass.: Treehouse Mountain, 1990.
———. *Mechanics of the Future: Asteroids.* Rev. ed. Conway, Mass.: Treehouse Mountain, 1991.

Horary Astrology

The underlying theory of horary astrology is that, whenever one asks a
question, the conditions of—as well as the answer to—the question are
reflected in the patterns formed by the **Sun, Moon,** and **planets** at the moment
the question is asked (i.e., in the astrology chart cast for that moment).

One of horary astrology's late greats was **Evangeline Adams,** astrologer to J. P. Morgan among others. Adams took horary astrology a step beyond tradition by using it whenever she did a reading. Her assistant cast a chart for the time the client was scheduled. From their charts, Adams could tell clients the true issues of their lives at the time, even when they did not consciously know these issues themselves. As told in her book, *Bowl of Heaven,* she was taken to court in conservative Boston twice. Both times the case was thrown out of court. After a demonstration of her skill, one judge said she had raised astrology to the level of an exact science.

In current times, another heroine of horary astrology, the late Ivy Goldstein-Jacobsen, was reputedly the astrologer behind Joan Quigley, former President Reagan's astrologer. Ivy's principle work, *Simplified Horary Astrology,* belies its title with extensive detail.

The flip side of horary astrology is **electional astrology.** While horary asks the question after the event, electional astrology chooses or "elects" a time beforehand; an example choosing a wedding date. When scanning future positions of the planets, one can select the types of combinations that would

▶
Horary astrology.

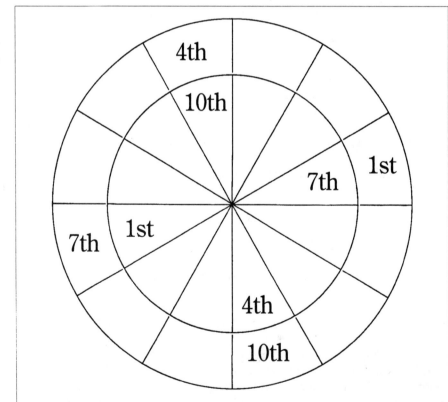

indicate favorable outcomes if the chart of that moment were to become the answer to a question that may occur in the future.

Even if a client is unhappy with the answer to a question, the horary astrologer must not cast a new chart to get a different answer unless conditions have changed significantly. In the case of a missing person, when new evidence is found, another chart is cast. Another technique used with ongoing timely questions is to cast a chart at the beginning of each day to check progress. For example, an abducted child may be moved from location to location, with each chart reflecting that change.

The appeal of horary astrology is its efficiency. It can be used for immediate information without lengthy examination of trend sheets. It can also be used without one's birth chart, eliminating the problem of birth chart inaccuracy due to inaccurate birth time data.

The accuracy of horary astrology has caused some astrologers to use it the assist the police. Often the answers supplied to investigators are not pleasant. One Southern horary astrologer is given police protection, false identities, and is moved frequently from city to city as she works on different cases. She often works on location as the case unfolds and new evidence is found.

Common questions asked of horary astrologers are, Should I buy this property? Should I take this job? Where is my lost ring; can it be found? Is the missing person alive, where is she, when will she be found? What is the description of the thief? Does my mate have a lover? Who will win in the election?

Marc Edmund Jones wrote a book on spiritual interpretation and right brain "soft" answers to horary questions entitled *Horary Astrology.* There are factors that the more traditional, linear, left brain yes/no horary astrology would ignore, but that spiritual horary would interpret symbolically and include more peripheral information about. For example, there is a period of time when the Moon makes no contact with other planets until it enters the next sign. This is called **void of course.** Traditional horary might interpret it time as having no significance. Spiritual astrology might interpret it as a time of rest.

Horary astrology is better learned after a person is well grounded in basic astrology, as its different set of rules can be confusing. The **ascendant** (rising sign) of the chart is considered to rule the querent. All the **houses** refer to the items or persons one can ask about. If there are the traditional favorable **aspects** formed between the **ruler** of the ascendant and the ruler of the house of the item or person asked about, the answer is favorable. Otherwise, the answer may be negative, conditional, or mixed, or some parts may be favorable and others not. Some astrologers simplify this yes/no reply by considering only the ascendant or only the aspects of the rulers of the first and the seventh houses, nothing more specific.

In horary astrology, there are always two rulers of the ascendant, the Moon being the primary ruler and the planet ruling the sign of the ascendant being the secondary ruler. The Moon, having the fastest motion of all the "planets," is granted all of its aspects through whatever sign it is in, whether they are in **orb** or not. This sequence of aspects represents the unfoldment of the answer. If the Moon makes no aspects until it enters the next sign, and if a project being asked about is already under way, the answer is that there is nothing to stop it. If the question is a "Shall I do it?" or "Shall I start it?" the answer is "Nothing will come of it."

The old-fashioned caveat "strictures against judgment" means "Don't read that chart!" Two circumstances require the ethical astrologer to inform the client that the chart might not be readable or should not be read. One is when **Saturn** is in or ruling the first house. The question itself is considered to be "damaged" in some way—not understandable, misinterpreted, not timely somehow. The second circumstance is when Saturn is in or ruling the seventh house. Then the astrologer is considered at fault—perhaps not skilled enough to know the answer, not confident enough, or did not understood the question.

Some other basic strictures apply when the **degrees** on the ascendant (out of the 30° possible for each sign of the zodiac) are the first three or last three. It is considered either too early to tell the answer (first 3°) or the issue has already been decided and will be as it is (last 3°). If the Moon makes no further aspects in the sign it is in, the answer to a question may be that nothing will come of the issue. If the question concerns fear of an illness, this answer may be a great relief. Another part of the chart may indicate the client's extreme worry.

There are other strictures that astrologers disagree about, but spiritual horary astrology definitely takes a turn here and says everything can be read, everything means something.

Correct rulership is a crucial issue in horary astrology. For example, what house in a chart would rule one's keys? If three different books are consulted, three different answers will likely be found. The rulership bible of horary astrology is Rex Bills's *Rulership Book*. Many years' experience is an asset when a specific rulership is not found in any of the books on the subject. As modern life unfolds, new rulerships are required—e.g., for AIDS, CD players, and stepchildren.

In addition to experience, choosing the right derivative house is also important in selecting correct rulerships. An example is when a question applies to a spouse's employer. The spouse is the seventh house. The tenth of the seventh, starting with the seventh as house one, is the fourth house of the chart equals the spouse's employer. As for siblings, the first *pregnancy* is the fifth house, the next pregnancy is the third of the fifth, the seventh house of the chart. A miscarriage is represented by whichever pregnancy it was. Stepchildren are the children of the spouse (seventh), the eldest stepchild is then the eleventh house (fifth of the seventh) the second eldest is the first house (third of the fifth of the seventh) and so on.

Anne Ungar and Lillian Huber give an excellent discussion with references about derivative houses and disputed rulerships in *The Horary Reference Book,* which also has listings of more modern rulerships than Rex Bills's *Rulership Book.* Anthony Louis's *Horary Astrology* also has a modern listing of rulerships, but better yet, a fabulous glossary of terms, many archaic and baffling to the beginner.

Adding to the complexity of selecting the correct derivative house, often a combination of houses is required to tell the whole story. In Derek Appleby's, *Horary Astrology* the author gives examples of the combination of houses used to read relationships. Signs, houses, **elements, angularity** (placement in an angular house), and many other factors are indicators of description, direction, and timing. Descriptions are often uncanny in their accuracy. Direction and timing are the weak spots of horary astrology, as discussed by Anthony Louis in his comparative study of different astrologers' systems.

In horary astrology, the outcome of a question is based on a combination of factors, for example, the Moon's last aspect before **transiting** out of a sign, the planets ruling and being located in the fourth house (end of the matter), and the planets' aspects to the Moon and the ruler of the ascendant. The Moon and the Sun making a major **soft aspect** may override any of the **hard aspects** the Moon might make as it goes through the sign it is in. If a **stellium** of positive planets, perhaps including **Jupiter** or **Venus**, are angular (at the ascendant, or, especially, at the **midheaven**, and with the querent's ruler), the stellium may indicate a positive response regardless of the sequence of aspects the Moon may make.

Tidbits and downright important learning can be had simply by checking back to find out what did happen after the original horary work has been done. Writing down one's estimate of the outcome allows an accurate comparison to be made later. Anthony Louis points out that where one misses the mark is often where something is amiss personally, but the learning is a rich reward.

Matrix Software of Big Rapids, Michigan, and perhaps others have horary computer programs available. One Matrix program produces a chart with the specific data horary astrologers need, including a time line of aspects, all on a convenient single page. This information would take a lot of time to look up and calculate by hand. The program is accurate and gives more information than most astrologers would take the time to gather. This wealth of information cannot help but result in greater insight.

The art is still in the interpretation, that profound synthesis of sight and spirit. Inspiration comes from the great souls: the old master William Lilly; Evangeline Adams, who simply practiced the art; contemporary artist Ivy Goldstein-Jacobsen, who added voluminous details; and Anthony Louis, who has dared to compare them and find their flaws.

—*Cerena*

Sources:

Adams, Evangeline. *The Bowl of Heaven.* 1926. Reprint. New York: Dodd, Mead & Co., 1970.
Appleby, Derek. *Horary Astrology.* Wellingborough, Northamptonshire, U.K.: Aquarian Press, 1985.
Bills, Rex E. *The Rulership Book.* Richmond, Va.: Macoy Publishing and Masonic Supply Company, 1971.
Goldstein-Jacobsen, Ivy M. *Simplified Horary Astrology.* Alhambra, Calif.: Frank Severy Publishing, 1960.
Jones, Marc Edmund. *Horary Astrology.* Berkeley, Calif.: Shambhala Publications, 1971.
Louis, Anthony. *Horary Astrology.* Saint Paul, Minn.: Llewellyn Publications, 1991.
Ungar, Anne, and Lillian Huber. *The Horary Reference Book.* San Diego, Calif.: Astro Computing Services, 1984.

Horary Time

Horary time is measured by dividing either the length of the day between sunrise and sunset, or the length of the night between sunset and sunrise, by 12.

Horizon

The term horizon has the same meaning in astrology as in other contexts, although in astrological practice it usually refers only to the eastern and western horizons. Extended out into space and projected against the background of the **stars,** the eastern horizon is referred to as the **ascendant,** which is the same as the **cusp** of the first house. Similarly, the western horizon projected against the background of the **stars** is the **descendant,** which is also the **cusp** of the seventh house. A distinction can be made between the tropocentric horizon, which is the horizon from a particular spot on the surface of Earth, and the geocentric horizon, which is a "horizon" created by drawing through the middle of Earth an imaginary line (or **great circle**) that is parallel to the tropocentric horizon. When extended out into space, the geocentric horizon is called the rational horizon. For most astrological work, the difference between the tropocentric horizon and the geocentric horizon is insignificant.

Sources:

Brau, Jean-Louis, Helen Weaver, and Allan Edmands. *Larousse Encyclopedia of Astrology.* New York: New American Library, 1980.
Filbey, John, and Peter Filbey. *The Astrologer's Companion.* Wellingborough, Northamptonshire, U.K.: Aquarian Press, 1986.

Horizon System

The horizon system is a system of **house** division in which the **horizon** is split into 12 arcs of 30°.

Horoscope (Astrological Chart)

Among contemporary astrologers, the term horoscope (from Greek *hora,* hour, plus *skopos,* watcher) is used to refer to any astrological chart. Because of the popularity of **newspaper astrology**, which often presents itself as a "horoscope," the word has become synonymous with "daily prediction" in the mind of the general public. Prior to the eighteenth century, however, *horoscope* was applied only to the **ascendant**, which is the sign on the eastern horizon at the moment for which the chart is constructed.

Horus

Horus, **asteroid** 1,924 (the 1,924th asteroid to be discovered), is approximately 8.2 kilometers in diameter and has an **orbital** period of 3.6 years. Horus was named after an Egyptian sky-god who in later mythology became the son of Osiris. Lehman associates Horus with "far-sightedness and avenging nature."

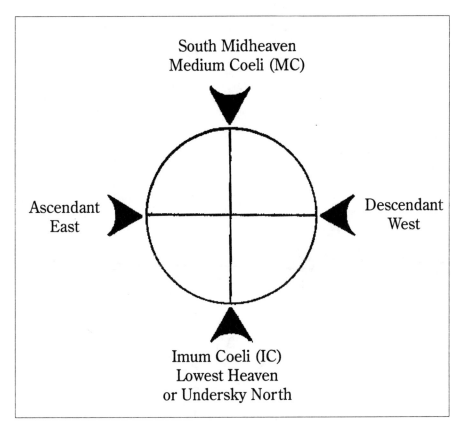

◀
Horoscope chart.

The Astrology Encyclopedia

Sources:

Kowal, Charles T. *Asteroids: Their Nature and Utilization.* Chichester, West Sussex, U.K.: Ellis Horwood Limited, 1988.
Lehman, J. Lee. *The Ultimate Asteroid Book.* West Chester, Penn.: Whitford Press, 1988.

Hot

The signs are numbered from 1 to 12 according to their order in the **zodiac** (e.g., from **Aries**, 1, to **Pisces**, 12). Hot and cold was one of the sets of categories utilized in premodern physics, and the ancients classified all odd-numbered signs (all **fire** and **air signs**) as hot. Traditionally, the **Sun** and **Mars** were also considered to be hot, while **Jupiter** and **Venus** were regarded as warm (an intermediate category). The terms hot and cold are rarely used in modern astrology.

► A horoscope drawn by German astronomer Johannes Kepler (1571–1630). The boxed triangles design was the traditional way of drawing astrological charts, and is still used by Hindu astrologers.
· Bettmann Archive

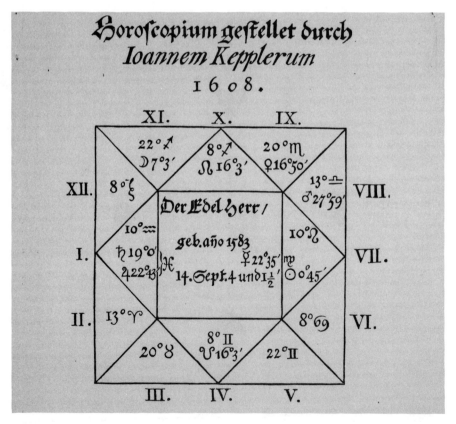

Hours

In traditional astrology, the period between sunrise and sunset was subdivided into 12 hours, each ruled by a different **planet**. The tradition, to which there have been no serious modifications since the discovery of planets beyond **Saturn**, stipulates that the day should be divided into 12 equal segments between sunrise and sunset, which will thus vary in length according to the season. On a particular day, the first of these hours is ruled by the planet **ruling** that day of the week. In other words, on Saturday, the first hour would be ruled by Saturn; on Sunday, the first hour would be ruled by the **Sun**; and so forth. The succeeding hours are ruled by the next planet in the following order: Saturn, **Jupiter, Mars**, the Sun, **Venus**, and the **Moon**. After reaching the Moon, one begins again with Saturn and repeats the same order. Ancient astrologers were careful to carry out certain activities during appropriate hours. It was said, for example, that Paracelsus (a sixteenth-century German alchemist and physician) always chose to prepare chemical compounds on days and during hours when the ruling planet matched the therapeutic intent behind his compounds. Despite the importance given this subject by the ancients, modern astrologers have largely ignored the planetary hours.

Sources:

deVore, Nicholas. *Encyclopedia of Astrology.* New York: Philosophical Library, 1947.

Hall, Manly P. *Astrological Keywords.* 1958. Reprint. Savage, Md.: Littlefield Adams, 1975.

Houses

Houses, sometimes termed mundane houses, are one of the basic building blocks of astrological meaning. Astrological influences manifest themselves primarily through the **planets** (for astrological purposes, the **Sun** and **Moon** are both regarded as planets). These basic influences are modified according to (1) the signs of the **zodiac** (i.e., the familiar 12 astrological signs—**Aries, Taurus, Gemini**, etc.) in which the planets are placed, (2) the **aspects** (geometric angles) between them, and (3) the houses in which they are placed. An oversimplified but nonetheless useful rule of thumb is that planetary sign positions indicate personality tendencies, aspects between planets reflect how various components of one's personality interact with one another, and house positions show how the personality manifests in the world.

As an illustration of these relationships, consider an individual with natal **Mars** in Virgo, who is also **square** to **Saturn** and in the eleventh house. As to personality, Mars represents outgoing, assertive, aggressive energies; this is what might be considered the *basic* nature of Mars.

---

1 Sign Individuals born when Mars was in Virgo need to organize to get anything done. They tend to be very patient with detailed work. (Organization and patience with detail are both Virgo traits.)

2 Aspect In contrast to Mars, Saturn is the cautious, security-seeking side of the personality. Square aspects often indicate conflicts, so, in this case, Mars square Saturn shows, among other things, an individual who vacillates between assertiveness and caution, between excitement-seeking and security-seeking.

3 House The eleventh house indicates things about friends, group associations, and ideals. Mars here shows someone who has a lot of energy for friendships and ideals; such a person expresses that energy best in the context of group activities. In over-aggressive individuals, Mars placed here shows a person whose assertiveness causes conflict with friends, as well as conficts related to that person's ideals.

Visually in an astrological chart, houses are the 12 "pie pieces" that together form the basic framework of the **horoscope.** Sign divisions (where signs begin and end) are not represented in a conventional chart. If they were, one would have to draw in another 12 lines, making a total of 24 (which would result in a cluttered, aesthetically unappealing appearance). The numbers and symbols that appear around the outside of the wheel indicate where houses begin and end with respect to the signs of the **zodiac.** Starting at the 9:00 position (which in most systems of house division corresponds with the eastern horizon) and moving counterclockwise, the houses are numbered from 1 to 12. Thus, the first house begins at the 9:00 position and ends at the 8:00 position; the second house begins at 8:00 and ends at 7:00, and so forth.

The zodiac is traditionally thought of as beginning with Aries. The subsequent order of the signs is then counterclockwise around the **ecliptic.** Because the signs and houses both contain 12 members, **astrologers** have often noted a special relationship between sequentially corresponding signs and houses; in other words, they have often noted certain parallels of meaning between Aries and the first house, Taurus and the second house, Gemini and the third house, etc. The following list, which is by no means exhaustive, outlines some of the principal meanings of corresponding signs and houses. It is taken from Ralph William Holden's *The Elements of House Division* (pp. 36–38). Note how sign traits indicate internal, psychological characteristics, while house traits tend to indicate external factors, as well as how personality traits manifest themselves in the world (houses tend to represent "signs in action," in Holden's words).

First Sector

Aries: Energy, drive, force, heat, initiative, courage, pugnacious, selfish

First House: The appearance, disposition, and manner of the native, outlook on life, carriage, capacity for self development, vitality, health, inherent strength and physical condition, mental and emotional qualities

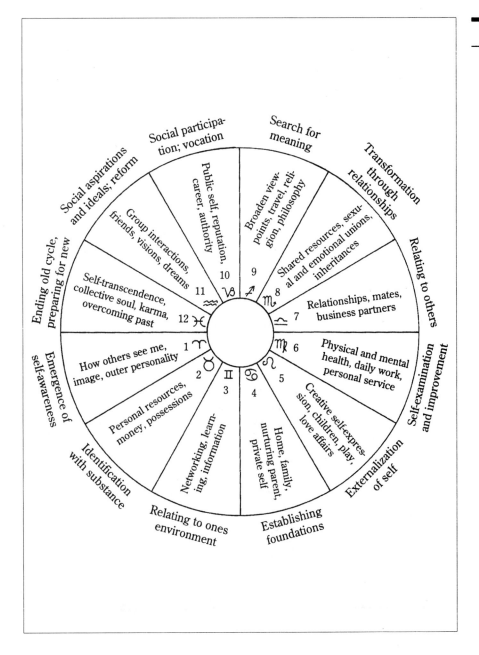

Astrological houses.

Second Sector

Taurus: Reliable, careful, trustworthy, hospitable, possessive, conservative, affectionate, greedy, grasping, obstinate

Second House: Hereditary and social background, financial standing, money, movable possessions and property, gain and loss of income, earning and spending capacity, personal debts, manner in which money is acquired and in which obligations are met

Third Sector

Gemini: Intelligent, lively, quick, versatile, inquisitive, communicative, restless, unstable, not dependable, erratic, oversmart

Third House: Power of mind, dexterity, cleverness, education, short journey, near relatives, neighbours, writing, communications, recording, lecturing

Fourth Sector

Cancer: Emotional, instinctive, protective, sensitive, maternal, domestic, moody, sullen

Fourth House: The home and domestic affairs, recollections, residence, base, end of life, private affairs, old age, early home life, lands, houses, estates, mines, things stored up, the hidden or unconscious, social care and concern, the sea

Fifth Sector

Leo: Proud, dignified, commanding, generous, reliable, strong-willed, confident, leadership, creative, sincere, wholehearted, reckless, power concious, conceited, domineering

Fifth House: Offspring, creative and procreative urges, recreation, games, pleasures, artistic efforts, romantic affairs, gaming, speculation, risks, acting, theatre

Sixth Sector

Virgo: Worker, servant, neatness, carefulness, precision, detail, sensible, critical, retiring, fault-finding, fussy, pinpricking, hygienic, clean

Sixth House: Food, clothing, pets, capacity to serve, employees, health, diseases, employment, daily work, servants, diet, hygiene

Seventh Sector

Libra: Companionable, harmonious, evenly balanced, diplomatic, indecisive, vacillating

Seventh House: Partnership, cooperation, marriage, war, legal contracts, lawsuits, divorce, treaties, enemies

Eighth Sector

Scorpio: Passionate, secretive, sexual, sensual, penetrating, resentful, mystical, unfathomable

Eighth House: Birth, death, regeneration, sexual instincts, occultism, legacies, others' property, investigation, afterlife

Ninth Sector

Sagittarius: Intellectual, exploration, research, wide-ranging, far-reaching, freedom loving, sporty, traveler, religious, moral

Ninth House: Philosophy, religion, law, travel, exploration, research, foreign lands or people, higher education, publishing

Tenth Sector

Capricorn: Cautious, practical, prudent, ambitious, grave, stern, restrained, disciplined, authoritarian

Tenth House: The personal image, authority, honour, prestige, career, ambition, father, organizations, rulers, employers

Eleventh Sector

Aquarius: Original, independent, detached, scientific, cool, humane, freedom loving, congenial, social, reformer, eccentric

Eleventh House: Friends, contacts, clubs, social groups, humanitarian enterprises, altruism, hopes and wishes

Twelfth Sector

Pisces: Intuitive, expansive, sensitive, sympathetic, intangible, mystical, artistic, occult, sacrificial, confused, deceived, escapist, sentimental

Twelfth House: Sacrifical service, repressions, neurosis, hidden enemies, prisons, asylums, institutions, occultism, mysticism, secrets

According to Holden, the notion of a belt of zodiacal signs that modify planetary influences according to the sign in which planets are placed originated over 2,500 years ago in the ancient Near East. At least 300 more years passed before the notion of houses was developed, probably by the Egyptian astrologer Petosiris in the mid-second century B.C. The earliest house system, which was the system put forward by **Ptolemy,** was an **equal house system.**

An equal house system, as the name implies, draws all houses equal in width with respect to the **ecliptic** (the **great circle** at the center of the belt of the zodiac). Most systems of equal houses, including the earliest, begin the first house on the eastern **horizon.** Thus, someone born when the eastern horizon was intersecting Virgo at 26° would have her or his first house begins at 26° Virgo, a second house that began at 26° **Libra,** a third house that begins at 26° **Scorpio,** and so forth. It is an ancient system of house division that is still used in **Hindu astrology.** For the most part, it had passed out of circulation among Western astrologers until fairly recently. Several popular books, particularly Derek and Julia Parker's *The Compleat Astrologer* have propagated the equal house system because it is the easiest system to use. The increasing popularity of Hindu astrology in the West has also helped the equal house system make a comeback. Most contemporary astrologers who do not use the system are severely critical of it.

The other house systems that enjoy widespread acceptance begin the tenth house at the degree of the zodiac that is highest in the heavens (termed the midheaven or **medium coeli**—the latter often abbreviated MC), and the fourth house exactly 180° away from the **cusp** (beginning) of the tenth house (termed the **nadir**). Because of the tilt of Earth's axis and the resulting inclination of the belt of the zodiac at a 23 1/2° angle (the angle of obliquity) away from the plane of the Earth's rotation, the highest degree of the zodiac for any given point on Earth is often not 90° along the ecliptic from the zodiacal **degree** on the eastern horizon, even though the **zenith** and the horizon do, of course, lie at a 90° angle to each other. Why this is so is difficult to understand unless one is familiar with spherical geometry. Suffice it to say that the substantial angle between the zodiacal belt and the plane of Earth's rotation results in either lengthening or shortening zodiacal degrees when the zodiac is superimposed on the plane of the horizon and the zenith.

Other than the equal house system, the systems of house division in popular use now all take the axis of the eastern and western horizon as demarcating the cusps of the first house (east) and the seventh house (west), and the axis of the medium coeli and the nadir as demarcating the beginnings of the tenth house (MC) and the fourth house (nadir). These systems differ in the various approaches they take to determining the other eight house cusps. Precisely how they differ is hard to explain unless one has thoroughly grasped all the notions related to the **celestial sphere** and celestial coordinates. The following brief summaries are provided in lieu of elaborately detailed explanations:

Porphyry Houses: The second-oldest house system was devised by the third-century astrologer Porphyry. The positions of the house cusps for the second, third, fifth, sixth, eighth, ninth, eleventh, and twelfth house are determined by dividing the arcs of the ecliptic contained in the four **quadrants** of a chart into even divisions of three. Few contemporary astrologers use this system.

Campanus Houses: Devised by Johannes Campanus, a thirteenth-century mathematician who was also chaplain to Pope Urban IV. Roughly similar to the Porphyry system, except that Campanus trisected the **prime vertical** in each quadrant, rather than the ecliptic. This system has enjoyed a modest revival because it was the system favored by the influential modern astrologer **Dane Rudhyar.**

Regiomontanus Houses: In the century after Campanus, Johannes Muller (who wrote under the name Regiomontanus), a professor of **astronomy** at Vienna, developed a similar system that trisected the **celestial equator.** Few contemporary astrologers use this system.

Placidian Houses: A seventeenth-century Italian monk and professor of mathematics named Placidus de Tito developed this system by trisecting the time it takes a degree of the zodiac to rise from the eastern horizon to the midheaven. Due to the widespread availability of Placidian **tables of houses**, this was the most popular house system in the early twentieth century, and it still enjoys widespread use.

Koch Houses: This is a very recent system, put forward in 1971 by Walter Koch, that also works by trisecting time. Although Holden characterizes it as possibly the least acceptable of all the time systems, it has enjoyed a surge of popularity over the past decade or so.

Although this overabundance of competing house systems may seem overwhelming, there are numerous other systems, of both ancient and modern origin, that have not been mentioned. These include, among others, Albategnian houses, Alcabitian houses, horizontal houses, meridian houses, morinus houses, and topocentric houses. At this point, the obvious question is, Which system is best? Astrologers who have not become strong advocates of any particular system usually just shrug their shoulders and say, "Use the one that works for you"—not a very satisfying answer. One school of modern astrology, namely, the cosmobiology of **Reinhold Ebertin,** has responded to this problem by eliminating houses altogether. This approach is not, however, the one favored by most astrologers.

Because the differences between the various systems that share the midheaven-nadir axis as the cusps of the tenth and fourth houses are comparatively small, the most significant disagreement between competing popular house systems lies in the divergence between these midheaven-nadir systems and the equal house system. Thus, any attempt to find the "best" system should begin with an examination of this disagreement.

The chief argument in favor of midheaven-nadir approaches is that much informal astrological research has found that the midheaven is a sensitive point in a **natal chart** for career matters, whereas the nadir is sensitive to matters having to do with house and home. Because these correspond with the traditional meanings of the tenth and fourth houses, it seems inescapable that the midheaven and the nadir should be utilized as the cusps of these houses.

One encounters problems with midheaven–nadir houses, however, when attempting to construct charts for high **latitudes**. Using of any of these systems at high latitudes can result in exaggeratedly large houses (encompassing arcs of over 60°) as well as extremely tiny ones (less than 10°). Thus, in a location like Fairbanks, Alaska, for example, it is unlikely that one would find professional astrologers using anything other than the equal house system as their primary system. Any serious consideration of the problem of high-latitude chart casting seems to present an incontrovertible argument in favor of some kind of equal house approach.

These competing considerations suggest that any house system capable of becoming universally accepted among astrologers must somehow integrate the long-standing astrological experience that stands behind the use of the midheaven-nadir axis for the tenth- and fourth-house cusps with the need to produce houses of reasonable width for individuals born in high latitudes. The basic incompatibility of these two requirements makes the likelihood of resolving the problem of competing house systems highly unlikely in the foreseeable future.

Sources:

Holden, Ralph William. *The Elements of House Division.* Essex, U.K.: L. N. Fowler (1977), 36–38.
McEvers, Joan. *The Houses: Power Places of the Horoscope.* Saint Paul, Minn.: Llewellyn Publications, 1991.
Parker, Derek, and Julia Parker. *The Compleat Astrologer.* 1971. Reprint. New York: Bantam, 1975.
Rudhyar, Dane. *The Astrological Houses: The Spectrum of Individual Experience.* Garden City, N.Y.: Doubleday, 1972.

Huberta

Huberta, **asteroid** 260 (the 260th asteroid to be discovered), is approximately 98 kilometers in diameter and has an **orbital** period of 6.3 years. This asteroid was named after Hubert, patron saint of hunters. When Huberta is prominent in a **natal chart**, it indicates someone for whom hunting, searching, researching, or investigating is a life theme. The sign and **house** position of Huberta indicate how and where this searching drive manifests itself.

Sources:

Kowal, Charles T. *Asteroids: Their Nature and Utilization.* Chichester, West Sussex, U.K.: Ellis Horwood Limited, 1988.
Room, Adrian. *Dictionary of Astronomical Names.* London: Routledge, 1988.

Human Signs

The human signs are the signs of the **zodiac** represented by human figures. The signs classified as human vary, but always include **Gemini** the Twins, **Virgo** the Virgin, and **Aquarius** the Water Bearer. Although the symbol for **Libra** the Scales is a nonliving artifact, Libra is usually considered a human sign because the older symbol of Libra was a woman holding scales. **Sagittarius** the Archer is often represented as a centaur—half human and half horse. When represented as an archer, Sagittarius is classified as human; when represented as a centaur, non-human. The signs not represented by human figures are referred to as **bestial**. The human/bestial contrast does not carry practical consequences for interpretation (e.g., persons born under human signs are not more humane or less "beastly" than others). For this reason, as well as the negative connotations of the term beast, this distinction has dropped out of general usage in modern **astrology**.

Sources:

Bach, Eleanor. *Astrology from A to Z: An Illustrated Source Book.* New York: Philosophical Library, 1990.
Lee, Dal. *Dictionary of Astrology.* New York: Paperback Library, 1969.

Humanistic Astrology

Humanistic astrology was created in the 1930s by **Dane Rudhyar**, who followed the lead of **Marc Edmund Jones** in reinterpreting traditional astrology in terms of modern psychology. Rudhyar combined the Theosophical approach to astrology that he had learned at the Krotona Institute with the insights of **Carl Jung**'s depth psychology, whose works he read during the summer of 1933.

By the 1940s, Rudhyar was trying to create an astrology based on a philosophy "freed not only from the materialistic biases of our Western tradition, but also from the glamour surrounding so much of what today passes for esoteric revelations and unprovable occult claims" (Rudhyar 1972, 9–10). By this time the letters he was receiving about his regular columns in *American Astrology* had alerted him to "the psychological danger involved in careless astrological statements about birth-charts. I therefore tried to stress the psychological responsibility of the practitioner, and to develop theoretically a consistent approach to those astrological factors which were more particularly related to the individuality and the potentiality of growth of the person whose chart was being studied. I increasingly emphasized the need to take a holistic approach to the birth-chart" (Rudhyar 1972, 9). In this approach, Rudhyar reinterpreted factors in the birth chart that had traditionally been called malefic or evil as being instead weaknesses in personality structure; and these he saw, not as tragic flaws, but as opportunities for learning and growth.

He went on to emphasize that "astrology is a *symbolic language* . . . attempting to formulate, by means of symbols based on the common experience of men facing the all-surrounding sky, an immensely complex structure of relationships between the universe and man" (Rudhyar 1972, 16). He proposed, for example, that the signs of the **zodiac** refer not to the vastly distant constellations they were named for, but to 12 zones in Earth's magnetic aura through which Earth turns every day.

He stresses the concept that astrology should be "person-centered," that the individual birth chart is intended as a guide for telling a person how best to actualize as fully as possible her or his birth potential. If the chart is to do this, then those elements in it that apply to mankind as a whole should not be emphasized; instead, those that reveal a person's unique individuality should be stressed. Behind this lies the concept common to all modern astrology, psychology, and therapy: The individual personality is not fixed and unchangeable; it can be revised, rewritten, reprogrammed, restructured; and any means that gives the individual some insights into her or his internal patterns can be used for such work on oneself. Rudhyar's belief—which goes back to his youthful reading of Nietzsche—is that the goal of the fully actualized individual is to become totally free "from the Collective and from an unconscious, compulsive bondage to the values of one's particular culture—values which a person takes for granted because they have been stamped during childhood upon his sensitive mind by the teachings and even more the example of his elders, and also by the ambience of his society" (Rudhyar 1972, 22) and to develop one's own unique qualities as fully as possible.

Rudhyar says that the birth chart is "a set of instructions . . . showing you how in your particular case the ten basic energies of human nature should be used to the best advantage. . . . In modern astrology, these basic energies are represented by the ten **planets** (the **Sun** and the **Moon** included). Where these planets are located indicates where (by zodiacal signs, and especially by houses) they can be used by you to produce the most valuable results" (Rudhyar 1972, 24).

Rudhyar also believed that humanistic astrology needed to be founded on certain basic principles that would guide the astrologer in deciding how to interpret a chart, that would function as a code of ethics in helping the astrologer decide what to tell a client, just as a therapist would choose not to state "facts" that would merely damage a patient's perhaps already eroded self-esteem. The central principle is that every individual has a right "to stand, erect and open, at the center of the universe around him" (Rudhyar 1972, 27).

Finally, Rudhyar says, "It is evident that many astrologers . . . mainly think of astrology in terms of conformism—if not to the goal of financial profit, at least to popular expectations and the wishes of their clients' egos. I believe instead in an astrology of transformation. . . . I hope to awaken the sleeping god in every person. By sounding the 'true name' of an individual one may arouse to life the divine within him. Every person is a 'celestial,' if only he gains the strength and has the courage to stand by the truth of his being and to fulfill his place and function on this earth by following the 'celestial set of instruction' revealed by the sky" (Rudhyar 1972, 30–31).

In *From Humanistic to Transpersonal Psychology,* Rudhyar expands on *My Stand on Astrology* to discuss astrology as a spiritual discipline whose highest goal is to assist the individual to manifest his or her own special relationship to divinity. From this viewpoint, he argues against the use of statistics and other research to provide a "scientific" basis for astrology, on the grounds that, were astrology to be socially sanctioned, licensed, and regulated, it would become a force for conformity, not for actualization of individual potentials. He thought that the situation would be as ridiculous as looking to the American Medical Association for spiritual guidance. Rudhyar specifically allied himself with the Eleusinian Mysteries against Aristotle, with the Gnostics against the fathers of the Church, with the Albigensians against the pope and the king, with the alchemists against the chemists, with the Romantics against the scientific materialism and bourgeois boredom and mediocrity of the Victorian Age. Consequently, his popularity with the young during the 1970s and 1980s is not at all difficult to understand.

—*Aidan A. Kelly*

Sources:

Rudhyar, Dane. *My Stand on Astrology.* Palo Alto, Calif.: The Seed Center, 1972.
———. *From Humanistic to Transpersonal Astrology.* Palo Alto, Calif.: The Seed Center, 1975.

Humors

One of the cornerstones of traditional medicine (dating back to Galen, the famous Greek physician) was a concept of physiology based on differing proportions of four fluids—phlegm, blood, melancholy (black bile), and choler (yellow bile). According to ancient medical theory, deficiencies or excesses in the humors lead to illnesses. The four humors also form the basis for a classification of personality temperaments, namely, phlegmatic, sanguine, melancholic, and choleric. The connection between *humoralism* and **astrology** is the result of the further correlation of these four categories with the four classical **elements**—water, air, earth, and fire. In traditional **medical astrology**, for example, dominances or deficiencies of particular elements in a **natal chart** could be taken to indicate an over- or underabundance of particular humors in the individual's physiological makeup.

Hurtful Signs

Hurtful signs is an older designation for the signs **Aries, Taurus, Cancer, Scorpio,** and **Capricorn**. They are so called because the animal symbols of these **zodiacal** signs appear capable of "hurting" human beings.

Hygiea

Hygiea, **asteroid** 10 (the 10th asteroid to be discovered—in 1849 by the Italian astronomer Annibale de Gasparis), is approximately 430 kilometers in diameter and has an **orbital** period of 5.5 years. Hygiea was the daughter of Aesculapius and the goddess of health and hygiene. According to Lang-Wescott, the position of Hygiea and the aspects to it provide some indications of the native's health. This asteroid's key words are *health* and *hygiene*.

Sources:

Lang-Wescott, Martha. *Asteroids-Mechanics: Ephemerides II.* Conway, Mass.: Treehouse Mountain, 1990.
———. *Mechanics of the Future: Asteroids.* Rev. ed. Conway, Mass.: Treehouse Mountain, 1991.

Hyleg

Hyleg, from a Persian term for the physical body, is a traditional term for a **planet** used to determine an individual's life span. It has also been called the giver of life, the apheta, and the prorogator. The various rules for determining which planet should be regarded as hyleg are highly complex. This complexity, combined with the dubious ethics of predicting the length of another person's life, has caused this practice, as well as this set of terms, to be dropped from modern astrological practice.

Hypothetical Planets

Hypothetical planets are **planets** presumed to exist but not yet verified by astronomers. The most well known of these is **Transpluto**, a planet thought to be orbiting the **Sun** beyond **Pluto**. For a long time, astronomers also thought there existed an intramercurial planet, **Vulcan**, following an orbital path between **Mercury** and the Sun. The notion of Vulcan has been abandoned by astronomers, but not by all astrologers. The expression *hypothetical planets* is particularly associated with the eight hypothetical planets of **Uranian astrology**: Cupido, Hades, Zeus, Kronos, Apollon, Admetos, Vulcanus, and Poseidon.

I

Iatromathematics

Iatromathematics is a traditional term for **medical astrology.**

Icarus

Icarus, **asteroid** 1566 (the 1566th asteroid to be discovered—in 1949), was named after the character from Greek mythology who died because he flew so close to the **Sun** that his wings (which were made of feathers and wax) melted. At the time, Icarus and his father were flying away from imprisonment on the island of Crete. The name is appropriate, in that Icarus's eccentric **orbit** (which takes a little more than a terrestrial year) carries it closer to the Sun than to **Mercury.** The asteroid is less than 1 1/2 kilometers in diameter and is one of the more recent asteroids to be investigated by astrologers. Preliminary material on Icarus can be found in **Demetra George** and Douglas Bloch's *Astrology for Yourself,* and an **ephemeris** (table of celestial locations) for Icarus can be found in the back of the second edition of George and Bloch's *Asteroid Goddesses.* Unlike the **planets,** which are associated with a wide range of phenomena, the smaller asteroids are said to represent a single principle. George and Bloch (1987) give Icarus's principle as "liberation"; their tentative key phrase for Icarus is *My capacity for liberation and risk-taking.* Zipporah Dobyns regards the occurrence of Icarus in a prominent **house,** sign, or **aspect** related to the **element** fire as indicating the danger of overreaching oneself or acting prematurely. J. Lee Lehman relates Icarus to shamanistic power, the power one gains from reconstituting oneself after the experience of "death" (in one form or another). In a more exoteric vein, Lehman also associates Icarus with flight, risk-taking, and accidents.

Sources:

Dobyns, Zipporah. *Expanding Astrology's Universe.* San Diego, Calif.: Astro Computing Services, 1983.

George, Demetra, with Douglas Bloch. *Asteroid Goddesses: The Mythology, Psychology and Astrology of the Reemerging Feminine.* 2d ed. rev. and enl. San Diego, Calif.: Astro Computing Services, 1990.

———. *Astrology for Yourself: A Workbook for Personal Transformation.* Berkeley, Calif.: Wingbow Press, 1987.

Lehman, J. Lee. *The Ultimate Asteroid Book.* West Chester, Pa.: Whitford Press, 1988.

Immersion

Immersion is a term used to describe the **Sun** or the **Moon** as it enters an **eclipse**. Sometimes the term is applied to **occultations**.

Impeded

A celestial body was traditionally said to be impeded or impedited when poorly **aspected**.

Imum Coeli

Imum coeli (IC) is the point directly opposite the **midheaven** (which is the most elevated **degree** of the **zodiac**). In many systems of **house** division, it is also the **cusp** (beginning) of the fourth house. The term imum coeli means bottom of the sky in Latin. Imum coeli is often used interchangeably with **nadir,** although this usage is technically incorrect: The nadir is the point directly opposite the **zenith,** not the point opposite the midheaven. The IC is occasionally referred to as the antimidheaven.

Inception

Inceptional astrology is the branch of astrology dealing with the beginnings of things, and an inception chart is a **horoscope** calculated for the beginning of a given enterprise. The term was originally coined by **C. E. O. Carter** to encompass **electional astrology** (consciously choosing the most astrologically propitious times to begin projects) as well as the retrospective study of starting points (e.g., **casting a horoscope** for the launch date of the *Titanic* to determine if its sinking could have been predicted).

Inclination

An inclination is the angle at which two planes cross. In astrology, it is used to refer to the movement of a celestial body to a position other than the one occupied at birth.

Industria

Industria, **asteroid** 389 (the 389th asteroid to be discovered), is approximately 70 kilometers in diameter and has an **orbital** period of 4.2 years. This asteroid's name is a personified form of *industry*. In a **natal chart**, Industria's location by sign and **house** position indicates where and how one is most likely to be industrious, as well as where one has skill and ability. When **afflicted** by inharmonious **aspects**, Industria may show either laziness or workaholism. If prominent in a natal chart (e.g., **conjunct** the **Sun** or the **ascendant**), it can show an exceptionally able, industrious person.

Sources:

Kowal, Charles T. *Asteroids: Their Nature and Utilization.* Chichester, West Sussex, U.K.: Ellis Horwood Limited, 1988.
Room, Adrian. *Dictionary of Astronomical Names.* London: Routledge, 1988.

Inferior Conjuntions

Inferior conjunctions are **conjunctions** between the **Sun** and the **inferior planets** in which **Mercury** or **Venus** lies between the Sun and Earth. The antonymous expression **superior conjunction** refers to conjunctions in which Mercury or Venus is located behind the Sun. None of the other planets are capable of inferior conjunctions, because their **orbits** never carry them between the Sun and Earth.

Inferior Planets

The original meaning of *inferior* was below. In the concept of the universe that was prevalent prior to the Copernican revolution, when Earth was thought to be the stable center around which every other celestial body revolved, the **orbits** of **Mercury** and **Venus** were considered to be closer to the Earth and thus "below" the orbit of the **Sun**. These two **planets** were thus referred to as the inferior planets. The current negative connotations of the term *inferior* have caused this expression to be dropped in favor of the term inner planets.

Influence

Astrologers often speak of the correlation between planetary positions and earthly events in terms of influence, as if the **planets** actually exert forces—analogous to gravity or magnetism—that cause a particular incident. If pressed for an explanation, however, the majority of professional astrologers would probably offer a different type of explanation, such as the **Jungian** notion of **synchronicity.**

Infortunes

Traditionally, the planets most likely to lead to difficulties in life—namely, **Mars** and **Saturn**—were referred to as the infortunes (unfortunates). Mars was further designated as the infortune minor, and Saturn as the infortune major. This older terminology has been abandoned by contemporary astrologers.

Ingress

The term ingress refers to the entry of a **planet**, one of the **luminaries** (the **Sun** or the **Moon**), or some other celestial body such as an **asteroid** into a sign of the **zodiac**. Modern **ephemerides** (tables of planetary positions) often include information on the exact time one of the planets or one of the luminaries enters a new sign. The term has also been used to refer to the entry of a **transit**ing planet or luminary into a new **house**.

▶
The Sun's ingress into the four cardinal signs— Aries, Cancer, Libra, and Capricorn—signals the beginning of one of the seasons. In actuality of course, it is the Earth's movement around the sun rather than Solar movement that is responsible for seasonal changes.
· Bettmann Archive

Intercepted

With the exception of the **equal house system**, most systems of **house** division utilize houses of varied sizes. One result of this variability is that sometimes a wide house will begin in the latter part of one sign, encompass the next sign, and end in a third sign. The middle sign is said to be intercepted. Because houses that are directly opposite each other are the same size, the sign opposite the intercepted sign will also be intercepted. For example, say that in a given **natal chart** the second house begins at 25° **Gemini** and ends at 3° **Leo**. The intervening sign, which is **Cancer**, is thus intercepted in the second house. Correspondingly, the opposite house, which is the eighth house, will begin at 25° **Sagittarius** and end at 3° **Aquarius**. Cancer's opposite sign, **Capricorn** ,will be intercepted in the eighth house. Astrologers are divided as to the influence of interception, some asserting that there is a weakening effect on **planets** placed in an intercepted sign, others asserting just the opposite. At the very least, it is safe to say that the affairs of an intercepted house are usually more complex than those of other houses. When giving a general, introductory interpretation of a natal chart, the majority of astrologers ignore interceptions.

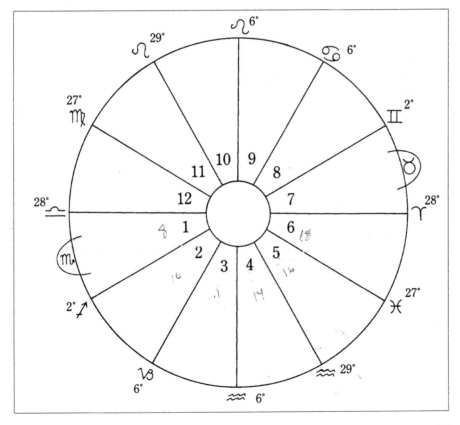

◄
Scorpio intercepted in 1st house; Taurus intercepted in 7th house.

In charts where signs are intercepted, there are other, narrower houses that begin and end in the same sign. This results in two successive houses with the same sign on their **cusps** (the same sign at the beginning of both houses), which are thus both **ruled** by the same planet. Some contemporary astrologers interpret this situation as indicating that the affairs of these two houses are linked. Thus, for example, in a natal chart in which the second and third houses are so linked, the **native** might earn her or his living (second house) through communication, publishing, or travel (third house).

Sources:

Filbey, John, and Peter Filbey. *The Astrologer's Companion.* Wellingborough, Northamptonshire, U.K.: Aquarian Press, 1986.

McEvers, Joan. "Insight on Interceptions." In *Astrology: Old Theme, New Thoughts* (pp. 41–50). Edited by Marion D. March and Joan McEvers. San Diego, Calif.: ACS Publications, 1984.

Isis

Isis, **asteroid** 42 (the 42d asteroid to be discovered), is approximately 94 kilometers in diameter and has an **orbital** period of 3.8 years. It was named after a major Egyptian goddess. Initially a divinity of fertility, in later mystery religions Isis became a goddess of wisdom. Her chief myth concerns the dismemberment of her husband Osiris, whom she reconstructed. According to Lang-Wescott, Isis may represent sibling relationships, efforts to get or put things or people "together," fragmentation or scattered locations. This asteroid's key word is *collate.* According to Lehman (p. 142), Isis, as well as the asteroid Osiris, indicates "something about the masculine-feminine or left-brain–right-brain balance of a person." For people in whose charts either of these asteroids is prominent, androgyny will be an issue.

Sources:

Lang-Wescott, Martha. *Asteroids-Mechanics: Ephemerides II.* Conway, Mass.: Treehouse Mountain, 1990.
———. *Mechanics of the Future: Asteroids.* Rev. ed. Conway, Mass.: Treehouse Mountain, 1991.
Lehman, J. Lee. *The Ultimate Asteroid Book.* West Chester, Penn.: Whitford Press, 1988.

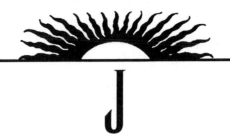

J

Jawer, Jeff

Jeff Jawer, born May 16, 1946, in New York City, is one of the pioneers of experiential astrology and a leader in astrological organizations. He began his astrological studies in 1973 in Amherst, Massachusetts, where he earned a B.A. degree in The History and Science of Astrology through a special program at the University of Massachusetts. He established OMetrics Astrology Services there with Barry Lynes, his first teacher. Jawer also presented for 2 years a daily astrological radio program called "High Tides," which continued 2 more years in Atlanta, Georgia.

In Atlanta, Jawer became corporate astrologer for International Horizons, Inc., and coinvented Astro, the first hand-held astrological calculator. He passed the professional-level examination of the American Federation of Astrologers and the professional examination of the City of Atlanta's Board of Astrology Examiners. He served as chairman of the board of the Metro Atlanta Astrological Society in 1983 after serving two terms as president. He also completed Zip Dobyns's 16-day intensive course, is a certified Astro*Carto*Graphy (A*C*G) interpreter, and taught at the first A*C*G seminar, which he organized with Jim Lewis.

Jawer coined the now widely used term *astrodrama* in an article for *Astrology Now* magazine and has had numerous articles published on a variety of subjects in journals and in three books. He has led workshops on experiential and other aspects of astrology at over 30 conventions. Jawer has taught astrology throughout the United States and in Canada, Brazil, France, England, Holland, Belgium, Spain, and Switzerland. He lived and worked in France for 2 years with Alexander Ruperti's Network for Humanistic Astrology.

In 1982, Lawer was one of the founders of the Association for Astrological Networking (AFAN) and served on its steering committee for 4 years. In 1986, he helped organize the first United Astrology Congress and currently serves on its board of directors. He has received the Mars Award from the Fraternity for Canadian Astrologers and has been a nominee for the Regulus Award. At present he lives with his wife and two daughters in a suburb of Atlanta.

Selected Publications:

Spiritual, Metaphysical & New Trends in Modern Astrology. By Jawer and others. Saint Paul, Minn.: Llewellyn Publications, 1988.
Intimate Relationships, The Astrology of Attraction. By Jawer and others. Saint Paul, Minn.: Llewellyn Publications, 1991.
How to Personalize the Other Planets, The Astrology of Uranus, Neptune and Pluto. By Jawer and others. Saint Paul, Minn.: Llewellyn Publications, 1992.

Jayne, Charles A., Jr.

Charles A. Jayne, Jr., born October 9, 1911, in Jenkintown, Pennsylvania, was an eminent astrologer, writer, teacher, and lecturer who stressed the importance of mathematics and **astronomy**. He began studying astrology in the mid-thirties. After serving in the U.S. Army during the Second World War, he became deeply involved in astrological work. During the 1946 fall semester, he served on the astrological faculty of the American Foundation for Metaphysical Arts & Sciences in New York City. He contributed technical material such as data on eclipses, to Nicholas DeVore's *Encyclopedia of Astrology* and wrote frequently for such astrological periodicals as *Horoscope* magazine.

Jayne joined many astrological organizations and formed several of his own, most notably Astrological Research Associates in 1958, which published the periodical *In Search.* He was one of the founders of the National Council For Geocosmic Research (NCGR), an officer in deVore's Astrologic Research Society, and president of the Astrologers Guild (1958–1960). He joined the American Federation of Astrologers in May 1956 and was chairman of the Resolutions Committee at the 1972 convention. He died on December 31, 1985, in Goshen, New York.

Selected Publications:

Horoscope Interpretation Outlined. New York: Astrological Bureau, 1970.
The Technique of Rectification. 2d ed. New York: Astrological Bureau, 1972.
The Unknown Planets. New York: Astrological Bureau, 1974.
A New Dimension in Astrology. . . . New York: Astrological Bureau, 1975.

Sources:

Holden, James H., and Robert A. Hughes. *Astrological Pioneers of America.* Tempe, Ariz.: American Federation of Astrologers, 1988.

Johndro, L. Edward

Lorne Edward Johndro was born in Quebec January 30, 1882, the same day that Franklin D. Roosevelt was born. While still a young man, he moved south to the

United States, settling in Lockport, New York. He became friends with Ernest Wykes, a superintendent of a children's home in Lockport who frequently discussed astrology with him.

Johndro worked as an electrical engineer from 1914 to 1917. He afterward studied radio and graduated from the National Radio Institute in the twenties. He perceived parallels between radio/electromagnetism and astrology, and this was reflected in his books and articles, which contain frequent references to radio and electromagnetism. Johndro's writing style is difficult, and his references to electricity only compound these difficulties.

He published two books on the **fixed stars** in 1919. Their purpose was to assist astrologers in locating terrestrial locations where certain celestial configurations might be anticipated to manifest. Because of their mathematical complexity, these techniques have been infrequently used.

Johndro also introduced the **vertex** as an important point in the astrological chart, described a technique for constructing a "locality chart" from terrestrial latitude and longitude, and theorized a complex schema of planetary **rulership.** He continued to write and experiment for the rest of his life. Johndro has a well-deserved reputation as a highly technical astrological writer. He died in the late afternoon of November 11, 1951, in San Diego, California.

Selected Publications:

Astrological Dictionary and Self-Reading Horoscope. 2d ed. Washington, D.C.: American Federation of Astrologers, n.d.
A New Conception of Sign Rulership. Washington, D.C.: American Federation of Astrologers, n.d.
The Earth in the Heavens. 1929. Reprint. New York: Weiser, 1970.
The Stars: How and Where They Influence. 1929. Reprint. New York: Weiser, 1970.

Sources:

Holden, James H., and Robert A. Hughes. *Astrological Pioneers of America.* Tempe, Ariz.: American Federation of Astrologers, 1988.

Jones, Marc Edmund

Marc Edmund Jones, born October 1, 1888, in St. Louis, Missouri, was a well-known occultist and astrologer. He was educated at the Theological Seminary of the United Presbyterian Church and Columbia University (Ph.D. in education, 1948). A long-lived individual, he pursued such diverse careers as astrologer, editorial consultant, Protestant minister, and motion-picture scenarist.

Jones became interested in astrology in 1913 and founded the Sabian Assembly in 1923. He served as president of the American Foundation for Metaphysical Arts and Sciences in New York City some 20 years later. He was an early member of the American Federation of Astrology (AFA) and a member of the Astrologers' Guild of America, serving as the latter's vice-president (1941–42). Late in life he was one of the best-known astrologers in America. He died March 5, 1980, in Stanwood, Washington.

Jones's approach to **delineation** utilizing **horoscope** patterns (in *Guide to Horoscope Interpretation*) has proved to be highly popular with astrologers, as has his approach to **degree** interpretations (in *The Sabian Symbols*). These methods were especially popularized by **Dane Rudhyar,** who built upon Jones's work.

Selected Publications:

Guide to Horoscope Interpretation. Philadelphia: David McKay Co., 1941.
How to Learn Astrology. Philadelphia: David McKay Co., 1941.
Astrology, How and Why It Works. Philadelphia: David McKay Co., 1945.
The Sabian Symbols. New York: Sabian Publishing Society, 1953.
How to Live with the Stars. Wheaton, Ill.: Theosophical Publishing House, 1975.

Sources:

Holden, James H., and Robert A. Hughes. *Astrological Pioneers of America.* Tempe, Ariz.: American Federation of Astrologers, 1988.

Jones Patterns

The Jones patterns are the planetary arrangements first described by the astrologer **Marc Edmund Jones,** such as the **locomotive pattern**, the **bucket pattern**, and so forth.

Jubilatrix

Jubilatrix, **asteroid** 652 (the 652d asteroid to be discovered), is approximately 15 kilometers in diameter and has an **orbital** period of 4.1 years. Its Latin name means woman who rejoices. In a **natal chart,** Jubilatrix's location by sign and **house** indicates where and how one is most likely to "rejoice." When **afflicted** by inharmonious **aspects,** Jubilatrix may indicate either the opposite of rejoicing or rejoicing for the wrong reasons. If prominent in a natal chart (e.g., **conjunct** the **Sun** or the **ascendant**), it may show an exceptionally joyful person.

Sources:

Kowal, Charles T. *Asteroids: Their Nature and Utilization.* Chichester, West Sussex, U.K.: Ellis Horwood Limited, 1988.
Room, Adrian. *Dictionary of Astronomical Names.* London: Routledge, 1988.

Judicial Astrology

Judicial astrology is an older name for **mundane astrology**, which is the study of celestial influences on nations, cultural movements, world affairs, etc.

Julian Day

For simplifying certain kinds of calculations, it was found to be helpful to delete references to months and years, and simply number all days consecutively. Each such numbered day is referred to as a Julian Day (JD).

Jung, Carl

Carl Jung was a turn-of-the-century psychoanalyst whose formulation of psychology had a major impact on modern astrology. Jung was born in Basel, Switzerland, on July 26, 1875. After completing medical school, he went on to study psychoanalysis with Sigmund Freud, but later struck off to formulate his own distinctive brand of psychology. Jung utilized astrology in his counseling work, and it was his work with myths and symbols that most influenced modern astrology.

Among other achievements, Jung took the ancient approach to symbolic interpretation and recast it in a form acceptable to the modern world. While astrology has utilized symbolic methods since ancient times, the appeal of the Jungian system has been such that many contemporary astrologers have adopted the language as well as some of the methodology of this school of psychology. The study and integration of Jung's approach by such influential figures of modern astrology as **Dane Rudhyar** has also had the effect of "psychologizing" contemporary astrology, meaning that the **planets** and signs are now viewed as representing primarily aspects of one's psychological makeup, as well as psychological types. By way of contrast, traditional astrology was more focused on the prediction of events and on helping clients choose the most auspicious moments to carry out certain actions.

Although many astrologers have attempted to reformulate astrology in terms of Jung (making Jungian psychology the primary component of the mixture), more astrologers have adopted Jungian language to explain what astrologers have always done—interpreted symbols. Three Jungian terms—**collective unconscious**, archetype, and **synchronicity**—are almost universally familiar to contemporary astrologers. Practitioners with deeper interests in Jungian psychology have gone so far as to correlate Jung's system of classifying people into psychological types (feeling, thinking, sensate, and intuitive), with the four classical **elements**.

Sources:

Bach, Eleanor. *Astrology from A to Z: An Illustrated Source Book*. New York: Philosophical Library, 1990.

Brau, Jean-Louis, Helen Weaver, and Allan Edmands. *Larousse Encyclopedia of Astrology*. New York: New American Library, 1980.

The Journal of Geocosmic Research (Autumn 1975): vol. 1. no. 3.

Lewis, James R. *Martian Astrology*. Goleta, Calif.: Jupiter's Ink, 1992.

Juno

Juno was one of the first four **asteroids**, along with **Ceres, Vesta**, and **Pallas**, to be investigated by astrologers. It was named after the Roman goddess of marriage (the equivalent of the Greek Hera). Juno was the third asteroid to be discovered (in 1804 by the German astronomer Karl Ludwig Harding). It has a diameter of 248 kilometers and **orbits** the **Sun** in slightly more than 4 1/3 terrestrial years. Because it was one of the earliest asteroids to be researched, there is a fair amount of material on Juno. Juno represents the principle of marriage and indicates traits of one's marriage partner, as well as features of one's marriage(s).

Sources:

Dobyns, Zipporah. *Expanding Astrology's Universe*. San Diego, Calif.: Astro Computing Services, 1983.

Donath, Emma Belle. *Asteroids in the Birth Chart*. Tempe, Ariz.: American Federation of Astrologers, 1979.

George, Demetra, with Douglas Bloch. *Asteroid Goddesses: The Mythology, Psychology and Astrology of the Reemerging Feminine*. 2d ed. rev. and enl. San Diego, Calif.: Astro Computing Services Publications, 1990.

———. *Astrology for Yourself: A Workbook for Personal Transformation*. Berkeley, Calif.: Wingbow Press, 1987.

Lehman, J. Lee. *The Ultimate Asteroid Book*. West Chester, Pa.: Whitford Press, 1988.

Jupiter

Jupiter, named after the ruler of the Roman pantheon (also called Jove, the Roman equivalent of the Greek Zeus), is the largest **planet** in the **solar system**. The mythological Jupiter was a sky-god associated with storms, victory, and justice. In **Mesopotamian astrology**, Jupiter was linked to Marduk, ruler of the gods. Marduk was associated with wisdom, justice, water, and vegetation.

Jupiter has an **orbital** period of 11.86 years, and as a consequence it stays in each sign of the **zodiac** approximately 1 year. Jupiter's cycles appear to be the cornerstone of the Chinese **zodiac**: The 12 signs of the Chinese zodiac take 12 years to complete (1 sign for each year), which is approximately the time it takes Jupiter to complete one circuit of the **ecliptic**. Traditionally, Jupiter was said to rule both **Pisces** and **Sagittarius.** Sometime after **Neptune** was discovered, astrologers began to perceive a correlation between Neptune's characteristic influence in a chart and the traits of the sign Pisces. Eventually the **rulership** of Pisces was reassigned to Neptune, leaving Sagittarius with Jupiter.

The links between the astrological influence of Jupiter and the characteristics of the planet's mythological namesake are less extensive than is the case with many of the other planets. The primary characteristics of Jupiter are expansiveness and good fortune. The trait of expansiveness is represented better by the planet's physical size—it is the largest planet in the **solar system**—than by its mythological associations. The added characteristic of good fortune, which earns this planet the title the Greater Benefic, also does not appear to be directly linked to its mythology. However, some of Jupiter's less central characteristics, such as its association with justice and generosity, are clearly linked to the ancient king of the gods. Jupiter is also related to religion (especially of the conventional kind), philosophy, wealth, and success.

The area in which Jupiter is placed in a birth chart shows multiplicity or largeness, as well as good luck. In the fifth **house,** for example, it might indicate many children as well as good luck with children. While the various planets are connected with a wide range of activities and objects, they also, when found in a **natal chart**, represent different parts of the psyche. Jupiter represents the expansive, optimistic, generous side of the self. Thus, its placement in a natal chart shows much about where one's more generous, optimistic side manifests.

Jeff Mayo's *The Planets and Human Behavior,* provides useful lists of traits and associations for the planets. For Jupiter, under the rubric *characteristic desire trends,* Mayo lists "self-expansion, opportunism, conscientiousness, generosity, justice, exploration, progressiveness, studiousness, philosophizing, protectiveness (towards others)" (p. 91). Under the heading *traditional associations* are listed "religion and the clergy, philosophy, higher education, study, the Law and legalities, guardianship, professions generally, dignitaries, sport—especially horse-racing and hunting and athletics, gambling, speculative ventures, banking and the Stock Market, abundance, development, growth, supply, surplus, wealth, financial dealings, affluence, luxury, profit, prosperity, good fortune, good favor, honors, prestige, opportunity, success, optimism, happiness, protection, philanthrophy, luck, physicians, foreign affairs, distant travel, gluttony, obesity, wholesomeness, inflation, insurance, judgement, fulfilment, devotion, prodigality" (p. 92).

Sources:

Campion, Nicholas. *The Practical Astrologer.* New York: Harry N. Abrams, 1987.

George, Llewellyn. *The New A to Z Horoscope Maker and Delineator.* Saint Paul, Minn.: Llewellyn Publications. 1910. rev. and enl. 1987.

McEvers, Joan. *Planets: The Astrological Tools.* Saint Paul, Minn.: Llewellyn Publications, 1989.

Mayo, Jeff. *The Planets and Human Behavior.* 1972. Reprint. Reno, Nev.: CRCS Publications, 1985.

Valentine, Christine. *Images of the Psyche: Exploring the Planets through Psychology and Myth.* Shaftesbury, Dorset, U.K.: Element Books, 1991.

Justitia

Justitia, **asteroid** 269 (the 269th asteroid to be discovered), is approximately 35 kilometers in diameter and has an **orbital** period of 4.2 years. Justitia is a "concept" asteriod. Its name is a personified form of justice. In a **natal chart**, Justitia's location by sign and **house** position indicates where one gives or receives justice. When **afflicted** by inharmonious **aspects**, Justitia can show injustice or rigid, legalistic justice. If prominent in a natal chart (e.g., **conjunct** the **Sun** or the **ascendant**), it may show an exceptionally fair person or someone for whom justice is a dominant life theme.

Sources:

Kowal, Charles T. *Asteroids: Their Nature and Utilization.* Chichester, West Sussex, U.K.: Ellis Horwood Limited, 1988.

Room, Adrian. *Dictionary of Astronomical Names.* London: Routledge, 1988.

K

Kassandra

Kassandra (or Cassandra), **asteroid** 114 (the 114th asteroid to be discovered), is approximately 132 kilometers in diameter and has an **orbital** period of 4.4 years. Kassandra was the most beautiful of the 12 daughters of Priam and Hecuba of Troy. She was granted the gift of prophecy by Apollo, but, because she refused to honor her promise to make love to the sun-god, Apollo pronounced a curse that her prophecies would never be believed. According to Lang-Wescott, Kassandra represents the giving (or receiving) of advice. This asteroid also represents the broadcasting of ideas, but there is usually an issue of whether or not one is believed. Kassandra's key word is *hearing*. Lehman's interpretation of Kassandra is essentially the same as Lang-Wescott's.

Sources:

Lang-Wescott, Martha. *Asteroids-Mechanics: Ephemerides II.* Conway, Mass.: Treehouse Mountain, 1990.
———. *Mechanics of the Future: Asteroids.* Rev. ed. Conway, MA: Treehouse Mountain, 1991.
Lehman, J. Lee. *The Ultimate Asteroid Book.* West Chester, Penn.: Whitford Press, 1988.

Katababazon

Katababazon (also spelled Catahibazon or Katahibazon) is an antiquated but once widely used Arabic term for the south **lunar node**.

Katharsis

Katharsis, a now-defunct spiritual community, was begun in 1971 by a group of people attempting to set up a community that would focus on spiritual growth and harmony. Land was obtained near Nevada City, California, in 1974. Katharsis emphasized (1) spiritual growth and self-realization through the study of yoga and related sciences, (2) the development of a natural life-style based on diet,

(3) cooperative living, and (4) promotion of the practice of **astrology** as an aid to a fuller life.

Katharsis published the Solar Lunar Calendar every year and sold a line of astrology products.

Kepler, Johannes

Johannes Kepler, the last Western astronomer of note to believe in astrology, was born on January 6, 1571, in Weil, Württemberg, Germany. He studied the elliptical **orbits** of the **planets** and discovered the three laws of planetary motion that were to lead to Newton's law of universal gravitation. In 1600, Kepler became assistant to **Tycho Brahe**, succeeding him as court astronomer to Rudolf II. Kepler was deeply mystical, and many of his astronomical discoveries were motivated by a desire to demonstrate that a Neoplatonic/Pythagorean mathematical order governed the heavens.

The son of peasants, Kepler erected **horoscopes** and published **almanacs** to supplement his income as court astronomer. On the title page of *De fundamentis,* Kepler inscribed, "Discover the force of Heavens O Men: once recognized it can be put to use." He asserted that astrological influence "is so convincing that it can be denied only by those who have not examined it." He also said, "We cannot deny the influence of the stars, without disbelieving in the wisdom of God" (*Larousse Encyclopedia of Astrology,* 165).

In much the same way as **Saint Thomas Aquinas**, Kepler felt that human beings could rise above planetary influences. He thus, much as do contemporary astrologers, cast his predictions in terms of tendencies and probabilities rather than in terms of absolute fate. Kepler's contribution to astrology was his general theory of **aspects,** and he also invented the **quintile**, the **biquintile**, and the **sesquiquadrate**. Kepler died November 15, 1630.

Sources:

Brau, Jean-Louis, Helen Weaver, and Allan Edmands. *Larousse Encyclopedia of Astrology.* New York: New American Library, 1980.

Field, J.V. "A Lutheran Astrologer: Johannes Kepler," in *Archive for History of Exact Sciences,* vol. 31, 1984.

Kitson, Annabella, ed. *History and Astrology: Clio and Urania Confer.* London: Mandala, 1989.

Kite

A kite is a **configuration** in which one of the **planets** in a **grand trine** opposes a fourth planet that simultaneously forms **sextile aspects** (60° angles) with the remaining two planets. This is considered a fortunate configuration in a **natal chart**: Depending on the indications of the balance of the chart, a grand trine can be *too* fortunate, bringing the **native** good luck but not challenging the person to develop character. The inclusion of an opposed fourth planet adds an element of challenge and tension that stimulates the native to release the energies of the grand trine in a dynamic manner. The **house** position of the fourth planet usually indicates the area of life in which this release will occur.

Koch House System

When the casual observer looks at an astrological chart for the first time, it is easy to make the incorrect assumption that the 12 "pie pieces" are the 12 signs of the **zodiac**. These lines indicate the **house** divisions (sign divisions are usually not represented), which can begin or end at different places in different signs. Astrologers disagree about how to draw the houses, although most agree that the first house should begin on the eastern horizon and the seventh house (180° away) should begin on the western horizon. Also, the great majority of systems begin the tenth house at the **degree** of the zodiac that is highest in the heavens and the fourth house at exactly 180° away from the **cusp** of the tenth house.

◄
Kite.

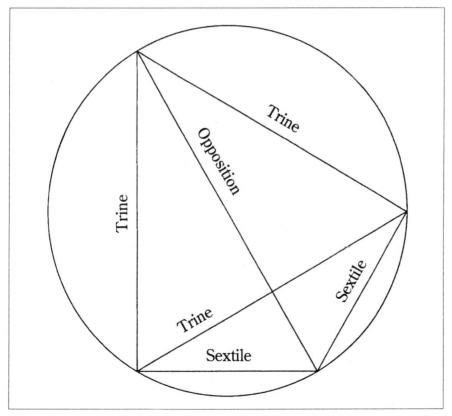

The Koch house system, also called the birthplace house system, is a very recent one (though not significantly different from the ancient system of Alcabitus) that was put forward in 1971 by Walter Koch. Although a relative newcomer, it has quickly become popular. Like the also popular **Placidean house system**, the Koch system finds the house cusps intervening between the **ascendant** and the **medium coeli** by trisecting the time, in this case the time it takes to rise from the horizon to the **ecliptic**. In actual practice, Koch house cusps do not vary significantly from Placidean cusps.

Koch, Walter A.

Walter Koch, German schoolteacher and astrologer, was born in Esslingen, Germany, on September 18, 1895. His father was a manufacturer. During the First World War, Koch was severely wounded in his right leg. He studied classics and history at the Universities of Strasbourg and Tübingen and entered a career of civil service after graduation.

In 1924, he began publishing in the astrology periodicals. During the Nazi era, he (and most other astrologers) was arrested and spent several years in jail before being transferred to the Dachau concentration camp, where he was held until the end of the Second World War. After the war, he was an instructor in the Hohenstaufen Classical High School in Göppingen and spent his spare time on astrological research and writing.

Koch was critical of charlatanism and new systems of astrology (as someone trained in classical studies, he was inclined to be a traditionalist). He was especially antagonistic toward fatalism in astrology. He was especially interested in colors and in systems of **house** division, and it is his work in the latter field that made him known in North America. The Koch system is based on the older Regiomontanus system and is discussed in his book *Regiomontanus and the Birthplace House System* (1960). Koch died on February 25, 1970.

Selected Publications:

Astrologische Farbenlehre. By Koch and O. von Bressendorf. Munich: O. W. Barth Verlag, 1930.
Psychologische Farbenlehre.. By Koch and O. von Bressendorf. Halle, Germany: Carl Marhold Verlagsbuchhandlung, 1931.
Regiomontanus und das Häusersystem des Geburtsortes. Göppingen, Germany: Siriusverlag, 1960.

Sources:

Holden, James H., and Robert A. Hughes. *Astrological Pioneers of America.* Tempe, Ariz.: American Federation of Astrologers, 1988.

Kochunas, Bradley Wayne

Bradley Wayne Kochunas was born July 29, 1950, in Hartford, Connecticut. He is a graduate of Baldwin Wallace College in Berea, Ohio (B.A., religion, 1975), and Miami University, Oxford, Ohio (M.A., religion, 1985). He first became interested in astrology in college after reading Grant Lewi's introduction to astrology, *Heaven Knows What*.

Kochunas majored in religion in graduate school with the express purpose of researching astrology to help it gain academic legitimacy. His thesis focused upon the religious and therapeutic dimensions within contemporary astrology, applying the methods of religion historian, Mircea Eliade (one of the modern founders of religious studies as an academic discipline), to the field of astrology to establish that it could be regarded as a cosmological discipline evidencing structures of sacred space and sacred time as elaborated by Eliade's work in the phenomenology of religions.

Kochunas views his contribution to astrology as promoting it as a discipline of the imaginal rather than the literal: "The whole enterprise to concretize astrology, to insist that it is a science, and to pour time and money into research to prove this is simply misdirected, albeit entertaining. My viewpoint is that astrology is more closely related to religion, mythology, and poetry than to science or mathematics" (personal communication, 1992).

Kochunas is a member of the Association for Astrology Psychology and a member of the Association for Astrological Networking. He also holds membership in the American Counseling Association and the American Mental Health Counselor Association.

Sources:

Lewi, Grant. *Heaven Knows What*. New York: Doubleday, 1935.

Kolisko Effect (Kolisko Experiments)

The Kolisko effect refers to modifications in the behavior of metallic solutions during certain **aspects**—particularly during **conjunctions**—involving the **planet** traditionally said to **rule** the **metal** involved. Rudolf Steiner, the founder of anthroposophy (an offshoot of Theosophy), taught astrology in many of his lectures, including the astrological principle that the **Sun**, **Moon**, and planets rule certain metals. Traditionally, the Sun has been thought to rule gold; the Moon, silver; **Mercury**, mercury; **Venus**, copper; **Mars**, iron; **Jupiter**, tin; and **Saturn**, lead. Steiner claimed, among other things, that "so long as substances are in a solid state, they are subject to the forces of the **Earth**, but as soon as they enter the liquid state, the planetary forces come into play" (as quoted in Gettings, p. 175.).

In the early twentieth century one of Steiner's students, Lilly Kolisko, began a series of experiments designed to demonstrate this link empirically. While her experiments were diverse, Kolisko's basic technique was to prepare solutions in which particular metallic salts had been dissolved and then record the pattern that these solutions made when they crystallized onto filter paper. Her hypothesis was that major aspects involving the traditional seven planets (which included the Sun and Moon) would affect the corresponding metal and thus modify the resulting patterns. Kolisko reported marked success. Particularly memorable are experiments during which Saturn was occulted (eclipsed) by the Sun or the Moon. During these **occultations**, the crystallization of lead salts was either delayed or completely obstructed. These experiments and others are recorded in Kolisko's *Workings of the Stars in Earthly Substance, Das Silber und der Mond,* and *Saturn und Blei.*

While some researchers have reported negative or mixed results in attempts to replicate Kolisko's experiments, others have reported success. Theodore Schwenck, in a laboratory of the Swiss Weleda Company, found that the crystallization pattern of a relevant solution was markedly influenced by the Mars-Saturn conjunction of 1949, an experiment that was replicated by Karl Voss in 1964. In 1967, another anthroposophist, Agnes Fyfe, published a paper in which she reported that the precipitation of carefully prepared iron-silver solutions was delayed during the half hour following exact conjunctions between Mars (ruler of iron) and the Moon (ruler of silver). Beginning in 1972, Nicholas Kollerstrom began a series of experiments involving conjunctions and other aspects between Mars and Saturn, the Moon and Saturn, and the Moon and Mars. He "met with success in experiments where the metals used corresponded to the planets involved in the conjunction" (Kollerstrom, p. 41). He also found that Mars–Saturn conjunctions (which are less fleeting than aspects involving the **transiting** Moon) produced especially marked effects that typically lasted several days. He also found that the peak influence of conjunctions involving planets other than the Moon always occurred *after* the conjunctions were exact, as if the effect of the disturbance in the Mars–Saturn "energies" was delayed in reaching Earth.

These studies do not exhaust the list of researchers who have successfully replicated Kolisko's experiments. Needless to say, the Kolisko effect stands out as an interesting phenomenon that merits close examination by anyone attempting to either support or debunk astrology from an empirical perspective.

Sources:

Davidson, Alison. *Metal Power: The Soul Life of the Planets.* Garberville, Calif.: Borderland Sciences Research Foundation, 1991.

Fyfe, Agnes. "Uber die Variabilitat von Silver-Eisen-Steigbildern." *Elemente der Naturwissenschaft* 6 (1967): 35–43.

Gettings, Fred. *Dictionary of Astrology.* London: Routledge & Kegan Paul, 1985.

Kolisko, Lilly. *Das Silber und der Mond.* Stuttgart: Orient-Occident Verlag, 1929.

———. *Saturn und Blei.* Stroud: Privately published, 1952.

———. *Workings of the Stars in Earthly Substance.* Stuttgart: Orient-Occident Verlag, 1928.

Kollerstrom, Nicholas. "Planetary Influences on Metal Ion Activity." *Correlation* 3, no. 1 (1983): 38–50.

Krafft, Karl Ernst

Karl Ernst Krafft, a Swiss **astrologer**, was born in Basel on May 10, 1900. He studied at the Universities of Basel and Geneva. He began to investigate astrology with statistical methods, constructing birth charts from data available from public records. He replicated **Choisnard's** studies and conducted others of his own.

From 1924 to 1937, Krafft pursued various employments and practiced astrology and astrological research in his spare time. He moved to Germany not long after his marriage in 1937, where he devoted his time to writing and lecturing on his favorite subject. His major work, *Le premier traité d'astrobiologie,* was published in 1939.

Despite work that he performed for the Propaganda Ministry of the German government, Krafft was in and out of jail, eventually dying during a transfer between detention centers. His importance for astrologers lies in his large-scale statistical work, which began with Choisnard and led to the work of **Michel** and **Françoise Gauquelin**. Krafft died in Germany on January 8, 1945.

Selected Publications:

Le premier traité d'astrobiologie. By Krafft and E. Budai, and Ad. Ferrière. Paris: Wyckmans, 1939.

Sources:

Holden, James H., and Robert A. Hughes. *Astrological Pioneers of America.* Tempe, Ariz.: American Federation of Astrologers, 1988.

Kronos

Kronos is one of the eight **hypothetical planets** (sometimes referred to as the trans-Neptunian points or planets, TNPs) utilized in Uranian astrology. It indicates elevated matters, both literally and figuratively. Thus, Kronos may represent, on one hand, mountains and airships and, on the other, leaders, executives, and government authorities. It may symbolize authority and expert status as well as the questioning of authority and expertise.

Sources:

Lang-Wescott, Martha. *Mechanics of the Future: Asteroids*. Rev. ed. Conway, Mass.: Treehouse Mountain, 1991.

Simms, Maria Kay. *Dial Detective: Investigation with the 90 Degree Dial*. San Diego, Calif.: Astro Computing Services, 1989.

L

Lacrimosa

Lacrimosa, **asteroid** 208 (the 208th asteroid to be discovered), is approximately 48 kilometers in diameter and has an **orbital** period of 4.9 years. Lacrimosa is Latin for weeping. The location of this tiny planetoid by sign and **house** indicates a source of tears. Crying is not necessarily a negative experience; one can also have "tears of joy." Lacrimosa generally shows where a person's emotions are so deeply invested that the individual experiences extremes of happiness or sadness.

Sources:

Kowal, Charles T. *Asteroids: Their Nature and Utilization*. Chichester, U.K.: Ellis Horwood Limited, 1988.
Room, Adrian. *Dictionary of Astronomical Names*. London: Routledge, 1988.

Laetitia

Laetitia, **asteroid** 39 (the 39th asteroid to be discovered), is approximately 156 kilometers in diameter and has an **orbital** period of 4.6 years. It was named after the Latin word for gladness. When prominent in a **natal chart,** Laetitia indicates a person with a generally positive attitude. Its location by sign and **house** indicates potential sources of happiness. When involved in many inharmonious **aspects**, Laetitia may show a person who is glad about the wrong things or unwisely optimistic.

Sources:

Kowal, Charles T. *Asteroids: Their Nature and Utilization*. Chichester, West Sussex, U.K.: Ellis Horwood Limited, 1988.
Room, Adrian. *Dictionary of Astronomical Names*. London: Routledge, 1988.

Lamb

The Lamb was an older, alternate name for the sign **Aries**. The animal that came to replace the Lamb in contemporary astrology is the **Ram**.

Lancelot

Lancelot, **asteroid** 2,041 (the 2,041st asteroid to be discovered), is approximately 19 kilometers in diameter and has an orbital period of 5.6 years. Lancelot was named after the knight of the Round Table. According to Lehman (p. 121), this asteroid "represents 'glory' thrust on the individual, not due to any personal qualities or actions, but simply from being in the right place at the right time."

Sources:

Kowal, Charles T. *Asteroids: Their Nature and Utilization.* Chichester, West Sussex, U.K.: Ellis Horwood Limited, 1988.

Lehman, J. Lee. *The Ultimate Asteroid Book.* West Chester, Penn.: Whitford Press, 1988.

Latitude

Latitude (properly called terrestrial latitude) refers to a location's distance from the **equator**. Celestial latitude refers to the **angular distance** (distance measured in **degrees** [°] and minutes ['] of an arc) that a **planet** or other celestial body is located above or below the **ecliptic**. One can also talk about galactic latitude, which is the distance above or below a plane drawn through the center of the Milky Way, as well as heliographic latitude, which is the distance north or south of the **Sun's** equator. Clearly, the notion of latitude can be extended to any celestial body.

Sources:

deVore, Nicholas. *Encyclopedia of Astrology.* New York: Philosophical Library, 1947.

Filbey, John, and Peter Filbey. *The Astrologer's Companion.* Wellingborough, Northamptonshire, U.K.: Aquarian Press, 1986.

Law and Astrology

As a practice carried on, for the most part, outside the bounds of mainstream society, astrology "slips through the cracks" of most state regulatory agencies. Many communities have laws against "fortune-telling" (a rubric under which astrology is grouped, although most astrologers do not regard themselves as "fortune-tellers"), but they are rarely enforced. Some of twentieth-century astrology's most important figures, such as **Evangeline Adams** and **Alan Leo**, were arrested on fortune-telling charges (a charge that does not usually carry more than a modest fine as punishment).

Astrology is an anathema to two different groups of people, conservative Christians and crusading secularists. From time to time, one or both of these groups have influenced local governments to enact or to enforce anti-fortune-telling codes. To oppose anti-astrology legislation, among other purposes, astrologers formed the Association for Astrological Networking (AFAN). AFAN is a networking organization, but the association also lobbies to have anti-astrology codes removed from the books, lobbies against new anti-astrology legislation, and provides astrologers with legal advice.

Sources:

AFAN Newsletter 8, no.4 (July 1990). (Available From the Association For Astrology Networking.)
Brau, Jean-Louis, Helen Weaver, and Allan Edmands. *Larousse Encyclopedia of Astrology.* New York: New American Library, 1980.

Leo

Leo, the fifth sign of the **zodiac**, is a **fixed fire sign**. It is a positive, **masculine** sign, and is **ruled** by the **Sun**. Its symbol is the Lion, and its **glyph** is said to be a modified version of the initial letter of its Greek name (although this is not universally accepted). It takes its name from the Latin word for lion. Leo is associated with the back and, especially, the heart, and individuals with a Leo **sun sign** are prone to heart and back problems. The association of Leo with the heart is the astrological background for the common expression lionhearted. The key phrase for Leo is *I will.*

Like many of the other signs of the zodiac, Leo lacks a developed mythology. It is said to be the Nemean lion slain by Hercules and placed as a **constellation** in the heavens by Zeus to commemorate the event. Turning to lion symbolism more broadly, we find the lion often regarded as king of beasts, known more for its kindness and mercy than its ferocity. Aesop's fables include a number of lion tales, such as *The Lion and the Mouse,* in which the merciful King of Beasts releases the mouse, who later nibbles through the lion's bonds to rescue him; *The Lion in Love,* in which the lion allowes himself to be declawed and detoothed in order to be allowed to marry a woodsman's daughter, only to be driven away after he has rendered himself powerless; and *The Lion's Share,* in which the King of Beasts invites other beasts to hunt with him, but then keeps all of the spoils (moral: Many may share in the labors but not in the spoils).

Like the lions and kings of mythology (the sign is associated with royalty), Leos can embody some of the best as well as some of the worst of human traits. On the positive side, they can be brave and noble to a fault. Associated with the heart, they can give everything for love. On the other hand, they can be ferocious and brutal. Leos have big egos, but these egos are peculiarly sensitive:

Whereas ego signs like **Scorpio** neither need nor seek compliments, Leos require constant acknowledgment. In a group, they often seek to be the center of attention. The need for acknowledgment by others is so great that, like the lion of *The Lion's Share,* they can take credit for the labors of others. Like all fire signs, they are fond of physical and social activity.

There is a wealth of information available on the characteristics of the zodiacal signs, so much so that one book would not be able to contain it all. One traditional way in which astrologers condense information is by summarizing sign and **planet** traits in lists of words and short phrases called keywords or key phrases. The following Leo key words are drawn from Manly P. Hall's *Astrological Keywords:*

> *Emotional key words:* "Faithful, rich in emotional life, affectionate, idealistic, proud, sympathetic, merciful, chivalrous, domestic, excitable, foreseeing, vain, subject to illusions" (p.18).

> *Mental key words:* "Commanding, generous, ambitious, self- sacrificing, optimistic, fixed in opinion yet magnanimous, opposed to secrecy, oblivious to enmity, challenging, bold, domineering, autocratic" (p.21).

Most popular works on astrology contain data on the signs, and these can be consulted for more detailed information.

Sources:

Evans, Colin. *The New Waite's Compendium of Natal Astrology.* Revised by Brian E. F. Gardener. York Beach, Maine: Samuel Weiser, 1971. (Originally published 1917).

Green, Landis Knight. *The Astrologer's Manual: Modern Insights into an Ancient Art.* Sebastopol, Calif.: CRCS Publications, 1975.

Hall, Manly P. *Astrological Keywords.* 1958. Reprint. Savage, Md.: Littlefield Adams (1975), 18, 21.

Leo, Alan

Alan Leo, an important turn-of-the-century English astrologer, was born in Westminster, London, on August 7, 1860. He was brought up by his mother in difficult circumstances and had no formal education beyond grade school. His given name was William Frederick Alan. He pursued various employments but found nothing satisfactory until he became a traveling salesman for a vending machine company. He stayed in that work until 1898.

He taught himself astrology and in 1888 became acquainted with another astrologer, F. W. Lacey. Through Lacey he met **W. Gorn Old**, who belonged to the inner circle of the Theosophical Society. Leo joined the society in 1890 and formed a partnership with Lacey to publish *Astrologer's Magazine.* For years the magazine advertised a free chart reading for new subscribers. (Leo met his wife through such an advertisement.) Although the offer and consequently the magazine proved popular, Lacey withdrew in 1894 to pursue other interests, which left Leo as sole proprietor. He renamed the magazine *Modern Astrology* in 1895.

By 1898, the prosperity of his magazine was such that Leo was able to abandon his sales job and give his full energies to astrology. His Modern Astrology Publishing Company grew steadily and built up a big business in astrological materials. In the early 1900s, he wrote seven substantial books as well as a number of short works on astrology. The former were so popular that they were repeatedly reprinted, and after almost a century they are still in print.

Leo founded the Astrological Lodge of the Theosophical Society in 1915. The lodge thrived and became a permanent part of the society. His success in creating popular interest in astrology was such that he was prosecuted for "fortune-telling" twice. In the first case, in May 1914, he was acquitted on a technicality. In the second case, in July 1917, he was fined 25 pounds (equivalent to thousands of dollars in today's money). These cases were not much different from religious persecution. Some of Leo's friends thought these prosecutions contributed to his death (from cerebral hemorrhage) in 1917.

Selected Publications:

Esoteric Astrology. London: L. N. Fowler, 1967.
The Art of Synthesis. 9th ed. London: L. N. Fowler, 1968. (Originally published 1912.)
Astrology for All. London: L. N. Fowler, 1969.
Casting the Horoscope. 11th ed. London: L. N. Fowler, 1969. (Originally published 1904.)
How to Judge a Nativity. 1903. Reprint. London: L. N. Fowler, 1969.
The Key to Your Own Nativity. 10th ed. London: L. N. Fowler, 1969. (Originally published 1910.)
The Progressed Horoscope. 1905. Reprint. London: L. N. Fowler, 1969.

Sources:

Holden, James H., and Robert A. Hughes. *Astrological Pioneers of America.* Tempe, Ariz.: American Federation of Astrologers, 1988.

Lewi, William Grant II

Grant Lewi was born June 8, 1902, in Albany, New York. He was educated at Hamilton College and Columbia University. After graduating from Columbia, Lewi taught English at Dartmouth, at the University of North Dakota, and at the University of Delaware. He was married to Carolyn Wallace, daughter of astrologer Athene Gayle Wallace, in 1926. He began to study astrology with his mother-in-law.

His first career choice was writing, but the economic pressures of the times were difficult, and in 1934 he began working as a professional astrologer. Under the pseudonym Oscar, he provided a short outline of his life in *Astrology for the Millions.* In the late thirties and forties, Lewi edited *Horoscope Magazine.*

In 1950, he resigned in order to initiate his own magazine, *The Astrologer.* He moved to Arizona in the same period and passed away July 14, 1951.

Lewi devised a unique approach to astrological interpretation based upon equating **house** and sign indications. He also utilized certain psychological considerations at a time when astrology was more event-oriented. He used **transits** exclusively for predictive purposes. This approach was developed in his *Astrology for the Millions* and certain of his magazine articles. Lewi's two major works, *Astrology for the Millions* and *Heaven Knows What,* remain popular to the present day and have introduced countless numbers of people to astrology.

Selected Publications:

Heaven Knows What. New York: Doubleday, 1935.
Astrology for the Millions. New York: Doubleday, 1940.

Sources:

Holden, James H., and Robert A. Hughes. *Astrological Pioneers of America.* Tempe, Ariz.: American Federation of Astrologers, 1988.

Lewis, Jim

Jim Lewis (not to be confused with the author of this volume) is an internationally recognized authority on relocation astrology, who is best known for his groundbreaking work on ASTRO*CARTO*GRAPHY (*see* **locational astrology**). Lewis is a noted author and lecturer, and was the recipient of the Marc Edmund Jones Award for outstanding contribution to astrology (1978)—National Astrological Society, and the Regulus Award for Research and Innovation (1992)—United Astrology Congress.

In 1982, he co-founded the Association for Astrological Networking (AFAN), an activist organization that works to ensure astrologers' rights and public image. He has served 7 years on its steering committee and 5 as its newsletter editor.

Selected Publications:

*ASTRO*CARTO*GRAPHY Sourcebook of Mundane Maps.* San Francisco: ASTRO*CARTO*GRAPHY, 1979–1994.
*CYCLO*CARTO*GRAPHY.* San Francisco: ASTRO*CARTO*GRAPHY, 1982.
*ASTRO*CARTO*GRAPHY Explained.* San Francisco: ASTRO*CARTO*GRAPHY, 1986.
*ASTRO*CARTO*GRAPHY Book of Maps.* St. Paul, Minn.: Llewellyn Publications, 1989.

Sources:

Harding, Michael, and Charles Harvey, eds. *Working with Astrology: The Psychology of Harmonics, Midpoints, and Astro*Carto*Graphy.* London: Arcana, 1990.

Liberatrix

Liberatrix, **asteroid** 125 (the 125th asteroid to be discovered), is approximately 63 kilometers in diameter and has an **orbital** period of 4.5 years. Liberatrix is Latin for *liberator woman*. When prominent in a **natal chart**, it may indicate a "rescuer," in either the positive or negative manifestation of this personality type. A prominent Liberatrix may also indicate a "liberated woman," again in either the positive or negative sense.

Sources:

Kowal, Charles T. *Asteroids: Their Nature and Utilization*. Chichester, West Sussex, U.K.: Ellis Horwood Limited, 1988.

Room, Adrian. *Dictionary of Astronomical Names*. London: Routledge, 1988.

Libra

Libra, the seventh sign of the **zodiac**, is a **cardinal air sign**. It is a positive, **masculine** sign, **ruled** by the **planet Venus** (some contemporary astrologers want to transfer **rulership** to several of the **asteroids**; others assert that an as-yet-undiscovered planet beyond **Pluto** will rule Libra). Its symbol is the Scales, which its **glyph** is said to represent. It takes its name from the Latin word for pound weight, or scales. Libra is associated with the lower back, buttocks, and kidneys, and individuals with a Libra **sun sign** are susceptible to lower back and kidney problems. The key phrase for Libra is *I balance*.

Although many classical accounts say that the goddess **Astraea** was transformed into the **constellation Virgo**, Astraea is more properly associated with Libra, which is the next constellation in the zodiac. Older images of Libra represented the sign as a set of scales being held by a young woman, but the actual constellation is constituted by a handful of **stars** that form only the scales. To make the figure complete, the tendency was to imagine Virgo holding the scales—thus, the mistaken association of Virgo with Astraea. Although her image was widespread, the classical mythology about Astraea is scanty. The daughter of Zeus and Themis, she spread justice and virtue among humankind during the Golden Age and was the last divinity to leave Earth after humanity became wicked. The association of scales with justice is very old (e.g., in ancient Egyptian mythology souls were judged by weighing their hearts on scales), and our modern image of the scales of justice is derived from Astraea's image.

Like their patron goddess, Libras enjoy human company; they find themselves through their relationships with others. While people born under Libra are said to be stubborn, they are more often just sticklers for fairness. They can easily become upset with social injustices. The image of the scales resting at balance conveys a false sense of Libran nature: Even though Libras constantly strive for harmony, the scales can easily become a see-saw, especially when Libras are forced to decide between two alternatives: In many cases, they would rather not choose but let the circumstances dictate choices for them. Libras are also known for their charm, as well as their attraction to visual beauty. They are natural diplomats.

There is a wealth of information available on the characteristics of the zodiacal signs, so much that one book would not be able to contain it all. One traditional way in which astrologers condense information is by summarizing sign and planet traits in lists of words and short phrases called key words or key phrases. The following Libra key words are drawn from Manly P. Hall's *Astrological Keywords:*

> *Emotional key words:* "Suave, aesthetic, romantic, enthusiastic, changeable, artistic, easily thrown off emotional balance, secretive in matters of the heart, amorous but fickle" (p.18).

> *Mental key words:* "Persuasive, imitative, judicial, tactful, undecided, inclined to be a dilettante, fond of show and approbation, intriguing, materialistic, liable to pout, and enjoy feeling abused" (p.21).

Most popular works on astrology contain data on the signs, and these can be consulted for more detailed information.

Sources:

Evans, Colin. *The New Waite's Compendium of Natal Astrology.* Revised by Brian E. F. Gardener. York Beach, Maine: Samuel Weiser, 1971. (Originally published 1917).

Green, Landis Knight. *The Astrologer's Manual: Modern Insights into an Ancient Art.* Sebastopol, Calif.: CRCS Publications, 1975.

Hall, Manly P. *Astrological Keywords.* 1958. Reprint. Savage, Md.: Littlefield Adams (1975), 18, 21.

Lilith

In astrology, Lilith refers to either an **asteroid** or a cloud of small dust particles that **orbit** Earth like a second moon. Lilith, asteroid 1,181 (the 1,181st asteroid to be discovered), was named after the legendary first wife of Adam, who was expelled from Eden for not acknowledging Adam's superiority. It has an orbital period of 4 1/3 years and is 18 kilometers in diameter. Lilith is one of the more recent asteroids to be investigated by astrologers. Preliminary material on Lilith can be found in **Demetra George** and Douglas Bloch's *Astrology for Yourself* and an **ephemeris** (table of celestial locations) for Lilith can be found in the back of the second edition of George and Bloch's *Asteroid Goddesses.* Unlike the **planets,** which are associated with a wide range of phenomena, the smaller asteroids are said to represent a single principle. George and Bloch give Lilith's principle as personal power and conflict resolution; their tentative key phrase for Lilith is *My capacity to constructively release my anger and resolve conflict.* **Zipporah Dobyns** views Lilith as related to many **Pluto** concerns, namely, a strong will, interest in the occult and the unconscious, and power and control issues. J. Lee Lehman relates Lilith to the "wild women" in each of us (in men, the anima of female shadow self). This aspect of ourselves is often repressed, leading to misogyny in men and self-hatred in women.

Lilith the dust cloud, Earth's "dark moon," received much attention from a handful of important early twentieth century astrologers, such as Ivy **Goldstein-Jacobson** and **W. Gorn Old** (Sepharial). While the very existence of Lilith has been questioned, some astrologers have taken the claimed observations of a dust cloud obscuring—or being illumined by—the **Sun** and constructed ephemerides for this body. Early investigators regarded the influence of Lilith as **malefic,** believing the dust cloud to be involved in such unpleasant matters as betrayal and stillbirth. However, the feminist movement—which has strongly influenced the astrological community, if for no other reason than that the majority of practitioners are women—has caused reevaluation of mythological figures like Lilith: Perhaps the rejection of Adam's authority should be seen as commendable, as the first time in history (even though it is a mythological history) that a woman refused to be ordered around by a man. Thus, more recent interpreters have tended to give Lilith a richer range of meanings, including many positive ones.

The majority of contemporary astrologers reject the notion of astrological influence from an obscure dust cloud, and fewer actually use "the dark moon Lilith" in their work. (One measure of its rejection is its absence from such standard twentieth-century reference works as the *Larousse Encyclopedia of Astrology*.) Attributing influence to Lilith persists, nevertheless, particularly among astrologers in the lineage of Goldstein-Jacobson and Sepharial. An important modern treatment of Lilith by Delphine Jay (*Interpreting Lilith*) and her very usable *Lilith Ephemeris* were published in the early 1980s. In 1988 and 1991, respectively, these two books went through their third printing. Thus, like her namesake, Earth's dark moon continues to refuse to submit to the astrological mainstream, which would prefer to deal with more manageable celestial bodies.

Sources:

Dobyns, Zipporah. *Expanding Astrology's Universe.* San Diego, Calif.: Astro Computing Services, 1983.

George, Demetra, with Douglas Bloch. *Asteroid Goddesses: The Mythology, Psychology and Astrology of the Reemerging Feminine.* 2d ed. rev. and enl. San Diego, Calif.: ACS, 1990.

———. *Astrology for Yourself: A Workbook for Personal Transformation.* Berkeley, Calif.: Wingbow Press, 1987.

Jay, Delphine. *Interpreting Lilith.* Tempe, Ariz.: American Federation of Astrologers, 1981.

———. *The Lilith Ephemeris 1900–2000 A.D.* Tempe, Ariz.: American Federation of Astrologers, 1983.

Lehman, J. Lee. *The Ultimate Asteroid Book.* West Chester, Pa.: Whitford Press, 1988.

Lilly, William

William Lilly, the famous English astrologer, was born in Diseworth, Leicester, England, on May 1, 1602. He was a master of **horary astrology**, and his classic

Christian Astrology was the (often unacknowledged) point of reference for most subsequent English-language books on that subdivision of the science of the stars. He was a colorful figure, and his autobiography makes interesting reading.

He was on a career track to become a Church of England minister until his father became impoverished and was unable to fund Lilly's further education. In 1620, he moved to London, taking a job as a secretary to a wealthy but unlettered merchant. After his employer's death, he married the widow. Consequently, the year 1627 found him financially independent. After six years of marriage, his wife died. He was to marry three times.

In 1632, Lilly began his study of astrology. He had been educated in the classics and was able to bring together a personal library encompassing most astrology books then available (most were in Latin). His celebrated classic, *Christian Astrology,* summarized the older authors in light of his own work. Lilly was a good writer and teacher, and his text is easy to follow. Contemporary astrologers still find reading *Christian Astrology* profitable.

Like many of his contemporaries, Lilly published a prophetic **almanac,** beginning in 1644. His dramatic prophecies brought him into the public eye, and one was interpreted as a prediction of a plague (one hit London in 1665), and another of a fire (large sections of the city burned in 1666). Later in life he acquired a license to practice medicine and moved to Hersham, Surrey. He appears to have had a stroke, and he died in 1681. Sir Elias purchased his library, and in time it was incorporated into the Ashmolean Museum at Oxford. Sir Elias persuaded Lilly to write his autobiography not long befored he died. This work provides a fascinating account of the world of astrology in seventeenth- century England.

Selected Publications:

Merlinus Anglicus Junior. London: Privately printed, 1644. [Lilly's prophetic almanac.]
Anima Astrologiae, or a Guide for Astrologers. Washington, D.C.: National Astrology Library, 1956. [Reprint of the 1676 edition with notes and a preface by Wm. C. Eldon Sarjeant of the Theosophical Society.]
Christian Astrology. Exeter, U.K.: Regulus Publishing Co., 1985. [Facsimile reprint of the 1647 edition with color portrait and supplementary comments by Patrick Curry and Geoffrey Cornelius.]

Sources:

Holden, James H., and Robert A. Hughes. *Astrological Pioneers of America.* Tempe, Ariz: American Federation of Astrologers, 1988.

Lion

The Lion is a popular name for the sign **Leo.**

Local Mean Time

Before the advent of rapid travel and modern means of long distance communication, particular localities kept time according to the noontime position of the **Sun**. Because this varied east or west of any given location, the local time also varied as one traveled east or west. The imposition of what we know as **standard time** zones, in which one must set her or his watch forward or backward as an imaginary line is crossed, is a comparatively recent innovation. Time zones are fine and good for many purposes, but, to properly **cast a horoscope**, astrologers must find the true local time that a **native** was born. In other words, they must convert a birth time expressed in standard time back into local "Sun time." The more common designation for Sun time is local mean time.

Traditionally, astrologers made this conversion by making certain calculations based on the longitude where a native was born. In more recent years, tables of time conversion (astrologers' atlases, such as *Longitudes and Latitudes in the U.S.*) have been published by people who have made the necessary calculations for most large and medium-size cities, thus saving the astrologer a

◄
An 18th-century illustration of sun dials, the chief means of determining time (local mean time) before the advent of clocks.
· **Bettmann Archive**

step in the calculations necessary to set up a chart. The personal computer revolution has largely eliminated the need for such tables, as such calculations have been incorporated into chart-casting programs.

Sources:

Dernay, Eugene. *Longitudes and Latitudes in the U. S.* Washington, D.C.: American Federation of
    Astrologers, 1945.
deVore, Nicholas. *Encyclopedia of Astrology.* New York: Philosophical Library, 1947.
Filbey, John, and Peter Filbey. *The Astrologer's Companion.* Wellingborough, Northamptonshire,
    U.K.: Aquarian Press, 1986.

Locational Astrology

Astro*Carto*Graphy™ (A*C*G) is one of many methodologies used in locational astrology, that branch of astrology which ascribes specific astrological effects to different localities. It is an elaboration of the "relocation chart," wherein the **horoscope** is recalculated as if the individual had been born in the new place of residence instead of the actual place of birth. In this, A*C*G differs from much older locational techniques, most of which relate geography directly to parts of the **celestial sphere.** The best-known classical example of these older, "geodetic" techniques is **Manilius's** first century A.D. ascription of areas of the ancient world to signs of the **zodiac.**

In contrast, A*C*G works by determining where on **Earth** the ten astrological **planets** were angular at the moment of an individual's birth, that is, where any one of them was rising, setting, straight overhead, or anticulminating (straight underneath). For example, even though it may have been nighttime at the actual place of birth, at the moment of birth the **Sun** was rising someplace else on Earth. All the various localities where the Sun was rising at that moment can be displayed as a line drawn across a map of the world. Such a line is labeled SU ASC (SUn on the **ASCendant**) on an A*C*G map; with 10 astrological planets and four angular positions, the map will be crossed by 40 lines in all.

Interpreting an A*C*G map is easy: Since being angular enhances the expression of a planet's nature in the personality, affairs symbolized by the planet can be expected to be more prominent in the life of an individual who travels through or resides under an SU ASC line on such a map. By moving to a locality under an SU ASC line on one's A*C*G map, an individual can expect more self-confidence, theatricality, creativity, and leadership to manifest.

Although the idea of preparing such a map for applications in mundane astrology occurred to other (for the most part **sidereal**) astrologers in the early part of the twentieth century, it was only the development of modern **computers** that made maps easily enough attainable for their value to be recognized in individual astrology. Astro*Carto*Graphy pioneered the provision and interpretation of maps to tens of thousands of individuals who, by comparing their life experiences to the angular planets identified by the map, have confirmed A*C*G to be among the most reliable natal astrological techniques. It works so well because it uses only the relevant planet and **angles**, the two most tangible and indisputable of **astrological data**.

Since most people have resided at several locations during their lifetime, an A*C*G map can confirm impressions of earlier residences as well as forecast outcomes of future moves. Moreover, a location's planetary identity seems consistent even when dealt with remotely, as, for example, through people who at one time lived at a particular place or have investments or other indirect involvement there. Many people have reported that love mates were born near a place where **Venus** was angular, or that they met in such a zone.

In A*C*G, planet angularities are calculated by oblique **ascension**, that is, when the planet is bodily on the **meridian** or horizon, rather than when its zodiacal **degree** rises or culminates. Where two lines on an A*C*G map cross they identify a place at which two planets were simultaneously angular at the moment of birth (e.g., one rising while the other occupied the midheaven). In addition to collocating a place-specific interoperation of the two planets' energies, this **paran** (line crossing) also establishes a latitude at which the two planets' energies are related anywhere on Earth; that is, a crossing of any two lines on an A*C*G map creates a special latitude line completely circling Earth, and on which the energies of the two planets are blended in the life of the individual. However, this "crossing" energy is far weaker than that of the planet-angle lines.

On pages 336 and 337 is the natal A*C*G for Paramahansa Yogananda, among the first of many east Indian sages to travel to the United States to transmit the highly sophisticated religious knowledge of the subcontinent. Over his native India is found the **Moon** ascendant (MO ASC) line, meaning that at his birth the Moon was actually rising there. Since the Moon defines the student, the child, the listener, and the "taker-in" of information, this connotes a sensitive individual, receptive, emotional, and responsive to his surroundings.

Near the Moon line is the **Uranus imum coeli** (UR IC) line. The IC is perhaps the most personal and mysterious of the astrological angles, because it symbolizes what one comes into the world equipped with: one's family heritage, social class, ethnic background (and the social status it bestows), religion, etc. Uranus, the planet of individualism, at this angle suggests that Yogananda was to transform his natal social standing by developing his spiritual individuality and, coupled with the Moon line, indicates that this could be accomplished by attention to external forces and devotion. He was to transcend his social identity by discipleship to his spiritual master; he would find his true individuality by giving it up.

But the most meaningful manifestation of Yogananda's potential was to occur in Los Angeles, where he arrived in the 1930s, complete with flowing robes and long hair—unheard of in that era. In Los Angeles he has the Sun on the ascendant (SU ASC), connoting the expression of life energy, opposite to the

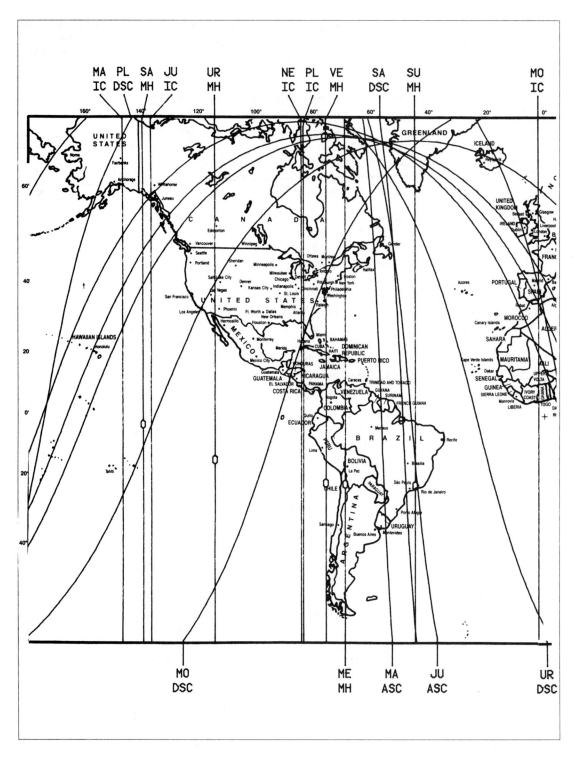

Locational Astrology: Yogananda, January 5, 1893, 8:38 P.M. Time Zone—5:33

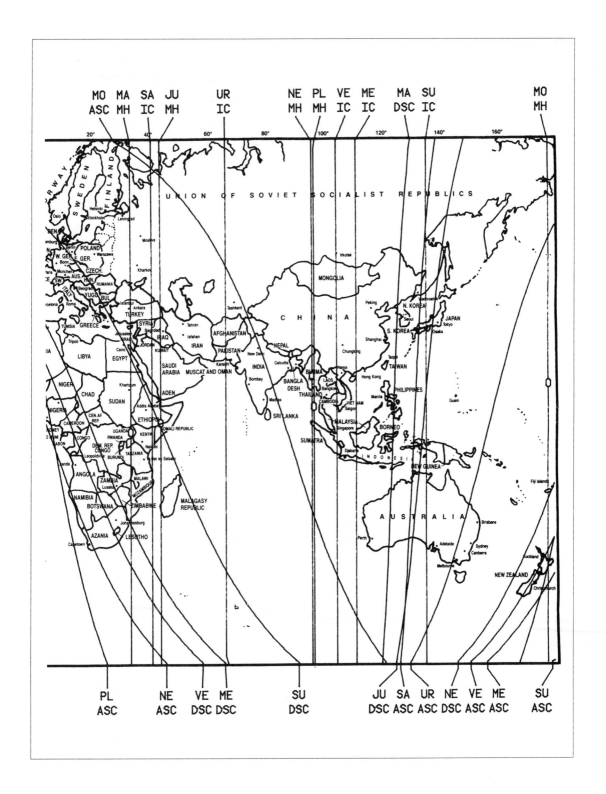

Moon's absorption. Moreover, the UR IC line from India to Los Angeles becomes the UR MH (midheaven) line, showing that the transcendence of Yogananda's individual cultural and family limitations is here transformed into the capacity to act out that role publicly for others—to become an exemplar of the human potential to grow beyond one's natal limitations. This coupled with the charismatic Sun line ensured a large following for Yogananda, who packed lecture halls in California, a state where such separation from tradition and individual self-expression have always been encouraged.

This example, while briefly delineated, makes clear how important it is to look at the whole map—not just small subsections of Earth. The reciprocal nature of the Sun and Moon lines should be obvious, as well as the interesting inversion of the Uranus line's angles, accomplished by plotting Yogananda's move half a world away. Since an individual at best is going to exemplify only one or two planetary archetypes in her or his life, knowing which parts of the world hold these lines can be vitally important in recognizing and implementing the potential of the planets they identify.

Perhaps the most powerful argument in favor of A*C*G's validity is that every modern American president whose time of birth is known has initiated armed conflict in a zone marked by **Mars** on his map, with the sole exception of Nixon, who took over a war begun by his predecessors. In addition to using A*C*G in this fashion to forecast world events, some astrologers use national charts, which can be quite revealing, and any map can be projected forward in time through standard techniques of progression, transits, and solunar returns.

A*C*G is unique among astrological techniques in offering the individual something that she or he can do to alter the astrological indications under which she or he is laboring. Many have, upon discovering that they have been struggling under a **Saturn** line, relocated to a less oppressive zone and noted dramatic changes immediately. But residence in such difficult zones has its purpose also, as life cannot be all social gatherings and pleasures. In any case, knowing the astrological influence brought about by relocating—or by choosing a favorable location in advance from the A*C*G map—has proved to be an important adjunct to standard birth chart delineation; Astro*Carto*Graphy is now used universally by modern astrologers serving clients for whom travel or relocation is an option.

—*Jim Lewis*

Sources:

Lewis, Jim. *ASTRO*CARTO*GRAPHY.* San Francisco: ASTRO*CARTO*GRAPHY, 1976.
———. *ASTRO*CARTO*GRAPHY Explained.* San Francisco: ASTRO*CARTO*GRAPHY, 1986.
———. *The ASTRO*CARTO*GRAPHY Sourcebook of Mundane Maps.* San Francisco: ASTRO*CARTO*GRAPHY, 1979–1994.
———. *CYCLO*CARTO*GRAPHY.* San Francisco: ASTRO*CARTO*GRAPHY, 1982.
Lewis, Jim, and Guttman, Ariel. *The ASTRO*CARTO*GRAPHY Book of Maps.* Saint Paul, Minn.: Llewellyn Publications, 1989.

Harding, Michael, and Charles Harvey. *Working with Astrology, the Psychology of Harmonics, Midpoints, and ASTRO*CARTO*GRAPHY.* London: Arcana, 1990.

Hathaway, Edith. *Navigating by the Stars.* Saint Paul, Minn.: Llewellyn Publications, 1991.

Locomotive Pattern

In astrology, a locomotive, (or open-angle) pattern is a **horoscope** arrangement in which all **planets** occupy two-thirds of a chart, leaving one-third empty. Ideally, most of the planets in such a pattern are spread across the occupied 240° arc.

Logarithms

Logarithms, which most schoolchildren are taught but promptly forget, were invented in 1614 to assist in astrological calculations. They constitute the most tedious part of traditional astrological mathematics and have been superseded by the computer.

Longitude

Longitude (properly called terrestrial longitude) refers to the distance of a given location east or west of 0° longitude (which runs through Greenwich, England, where the system of **latitudes** and longitudes was worked out in its present form). The expression celestial longitude refers to the **angular distance** (distance measured in degrees [°] and minutes ['] of an arc) that a **planet** or other celestial body is located east of 0° **Aries**. The numbers beside planets in a **horoscope**, which express their position in terms of a certain number of degrees and minutes of a particular sign, are celestial longitudes.

Lord

Lord is an older term for **ruler**, as in "**Mars** is the lord (ruler) of **Aries**." In the case of the **Moon** and **Venus**, traditionally regarded as feminine, the proper term was *lady.* Many astrologers want to retain this term but reserve its use for the ruler of a **house**. Thus, for example, in a **horoscope** in which Aries is on the **cusp** (beginning) of the third house, Mars would be the *ruler* of Aries and the lord of the third house. Most contemporary astrologers have dropped the term lord and use the term ruler for both relationships.

Lucifer

Lucifer, **asteroid** 1,930 (the 1,930th asteroid to be discovered), is approximately 21 kilometers in diameter and has an **orbital** period of 4.9 years. Lucifer was named after the fallen angel of light who became the Devil in Western religions. Lehman associates this aspect with "torch bearers."

Lucifer also means light-bearer and is sometimes applied to **Venus.**

Sources:

Kowal, Charles T. *Asteroids: Their Nature and Utilization.* Chichester, West Sussex, U.K.: Ellis Horwood Limited, 1988.
Lehman, J. Lee. *The Ultimate Asteroid Book.* West Chester, Penn.: Whitford Press, 1988.

Lucina

Lucina, **asteroid** 146 (the 146th asteroid to be discovered), is approximately 140 kilometers in diameter and has an **orbital** period of 4.4 years. It was named after the Roman goddess of childbirth and the travails of women, who was the daughter of Jupiter and Juno. In addition to indicating something about one's children, Lucina's position by sign and **house** shows where one "gives birth" to various activities or ideas.

Sources:

Kowal, Charles T. *Asteroids: Their Nature and Utilization.* Chichester, West Sussex, U.K.: Ellis Horwood Limited, 1988.
Room, Adrian. *Dictionary of Astronomical Names.* London: Routledge, 1988.

Luminaries

Traditionally, the **Sun** and the **Moon** were referred to as the luminaries because, in contrast to the **planets,** they "lit up" Earth. The majority of contemporary astrologers have ceased to use the term, in spite of its pleasant connotations.

Luna

Luna is the Roman name for the **Moon,** and the root of the adjective lunar. Due to the increasingly eccentric behavior that insane people exhibit during the full moon, the Moon became linked with insanity–hence the terms lunatic and lunacy.

Lunar Mansion

The lunar mansions are a kind of lunar **zodiac,** constituted by dividing the **Moon's** orbital path into 28 segments. Twenty-eight roughly corresponds to the number of days the Moon takes to complete its **orbit** (28 is a day short of a **synodic period** and a day longer than a **sidereal month**). The Arabs, the Hindus, and the Chinese all devised systems of lunar mansions, termed, respectively, the *manzils* (from which we probably derive lunar *mansion),* *nakshatras,* and *sieu.* Traditionally, these included interpretations of the man-

	Manzil (Arabic)	Nakshatra (Hindu)	Sieu (Chinese)
1	Al Thurayya	Krittika	Mao
2	Al Dabaran	Rohini	Pi
3	Al Hak'ah	Mrigasiras	Tsee
4	Al Han'ah	Ardra	Shen
5	Al Dhira	Punarvarsu	Tsing
6	Al Nathrah	Pushya	Kwei
7	Al Tarf	Aslesha	Lieu
8	Al Jabhah	Magha	Sing
9	Al Zubrah	Purva Phalguni	Chang
10	Al Sarfah	Uttara Phalguni	Yen
11	Al Awwa	Hasta	Tchin
12	Al Simak	Citra	Kio
13	Al Ghafr	Svati	Kang
14	Al Jubana	Visakha	Ti
15	Iklil al Jabhah	Anuradha	Fang
16	Al Kalb	Jyestha	Sin
17	Al Shaulah	Mula	Wei
18	Al Na'am	Purva Ashadha	Ki
19	Al Baldah	Uttara Ashadha	Tow
20	Al Sa'd al Dhabih	Abhijit	Nieu
21	Al Sa'd al Bula	Sravana	Mo
22	Al Sa'd al Su'ud	Sravishta	Heu
23	Al Sa'd al Ahbiyah	Catabhishaj	Shih
24	Al Fargh al Mukdim	Purva Bhadra-Pada	Shih
25	Al Fargh al Thani	Uttara Bhadra-Pada	Peih
26	Al Batn al Hut	Revati	Goei
27	Al Sharatain	Asvini	Leu
28	Al Butain	Bharani	Oei

sions that approached them in approximately the same way Western astrologers use the signs of the zodiac. The mansions in each system are given in the table that follows.

Traditional cultures attributed great significance to the phases of the Moon, particularly to the **waxing and waning** cycle. Our 7-day week is derived from the ancient custom of further dividing up the lunar month according to new moon, first quarter, full moon, and last quarter. The lunar mansions represent a refinement of this tendency, subdividing the Moon's phases according to its day-to-day increase or decrease in apparent size.

Sources:

Brau, Jean-Louis, Helen Weaver, and Allan Edmands. *Larousse Encyclopedia of Astrology.* New York: New American Library, 1980.
Gettings, Fred. *Dictionary of Astrology.* London: Routledge & Kegan Paul, 1985.

Lunar Nodes

The north and south nodes of the **Moon** are not "planets." They are imaginary points that mark off a sort of **celestial equator** and are used by astronomers to calculate distances, **eclipses**, and so on. When the **Sun** and Moon are in exact **conjunction** with each other and also conjunct one of the nodes, a solar eclipse occurs. When the Sun and Moon are in exact **opposition** to each another and each is conjunct one of the nodes, a lunar eclipse occurs. The north node, which is the one listed in **ephemerides**, denotes the point on the **ecliptic** where a planet passes from south latitude to north latitude. The south node is always exactly opposite the north node.

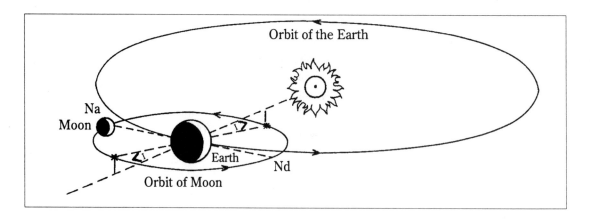

Orbit of moon seen edge-on.

Like the **ascendant–descendant** axis, and as with other axes in the astrological chart, the nodal axis symbolizes a relationship between time and space. The nodes, therefore, need to be interpreted as a continuum rather than as individual points.

In **Hindu astrology**, the north node has been referred to as the Dragon's Head (Rahu) and the south as the Dragon's Tail (Ketu). They are generally judged as karmic points, with the north node roughly the nature of **Jupiter** and the south node roughly the nature of **Saturn**. Some Western astrologers have adopted this theory, including the concept of the nodes as karmic points. Others consider the north node to be somewhat solar and the south node somewhat lunar; they see the north node as symbolic of an area where growth or development is needed, with the south node symbolizing talents already developed through karma, early conditioning, or some combination thereof. Most astrologers agree that there is often a subconscious or unconscious dynamic at work where the nodal axis is involved by sign, **house**, and **aspect**; this can often be seen especially in connection with **transits** to the nodal axis. There is additionally almost universal agreement that the nodes give an indication of how one relates to one's environment, the people in it, and sociocultural trends.

Conjunctions to the nodal axis by secondary **progression** or solar arc direction frequently seem to correspond with important beginnings, endings, or turning points in life. Should the natal angles, their **rulers**, or the **Sun** be involved, these can be quite dramatic. Transits to the nodal axis often symbolize new people entering one's life; they also sometimes symbolize "last straw" types of events involving others, things that change the nature of a relationship and occasionally cause an actual breakup.

The Moon's nodes move roughly 3 minutes a day on average, taking a bit more than 18 1/2 years to transit the complete **zodiac** as a rule. **Retrograde**

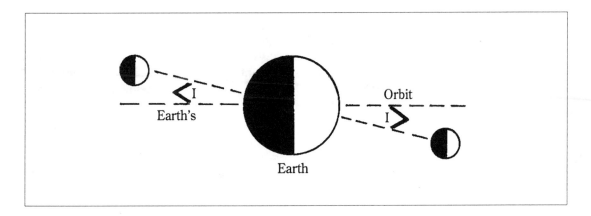

Orbit of earth seen edge-on.

rather than direct motion is the norm, although the nodes do go "direct" for brief periods.

—Donna Van Toen

Sources:

Ebertin, Reinhold. *The Combination of Stellar Influences.* Tempe, Ariz.: American Federation of Astrologers, 1972.
Hickey, Isabel M. *Astrology: A Cosmic Science.* Sebastopol, Calif.: CRCS Publications, 1992.
Sivapriyananda, Swami. *Astrology and Religion in Indian Art.* New Delhi: Abhinav Publications, 1990.
Van Toen, Donna. *The Astrologer's Node Book.* York Beach, Maine: Samuel Weiser, 1989.

Lunar Year

A lunar year is a year of 12 lunar months (12 **synodic periods**), or 354.367 days. There are 34 such lunar years for every 33 solar years. The traditional Muslim year is a lunar year. Many civilizations have utilized soli-lunar years, which retain the **Moon's** synodic period for months but also insert an intercalary month to keep the years aligned with the period of Earth's revolution around the **Sun**.

Lunation

A lunation is a complete cycle between two new moons, also referred to as a synodic month. Lunations average 29 days 12 hours 44 minutes and 2.7 seconds. The term lunation can also be used interchangeably with new moon.

Lysistrata

Lysistrata, **asteroid** 897 (the 897th asteroid to be discovered), is approximately 46 kilometers in diameter and has an **orbital** period of 4.1 years. It was named after the heroine of the Greek comedy *Lysistrata*. Lysistrata led a revolt of women across Greece, who as a group withheld sexual favors until the men agreed to stop war. Lysistrata represents the healing as well as the manipulative power of sex. The sign and **house** position of this planetoid in a **natal chart** indicates how and where this power manifests for each individual.

Sources:

Kowal, Charles T. *Asteroids: Their Nature and Utilization.* Chichester, West Sussex, U.K.: Ellis Horwood Limited, 1988.
Room, Adrian. *Dictionary of Astronomical Names.* London: Routledge, 1988.

M

McEvers, Joan

Author of *12 Times 12* and coauthor with Marian March of the highly acclaimed series The Only Way to Learn Astrology, Joan McEvers is an internationally known professional astrologer based in Coeur d'Alene, Idaho. She has achieved a worldwide reputation as a teacher and lecturer, speaking for many groups in the United States and Canada.

In 1975, McEvers and March founded Aquarius Workshops, Inc. McEvers also helped establish its quarterly publication, *Aspects,* which is widely recognized for its wealth of astrological information. She continues to contribute to this periodical.

As an offshoot of their interest in astrology and vocational choice, McEvers and March are currently conducting a "vocational probe," seeking to establish a computer program that can be given to schools to assist students in selecting career fields.

A member of several professional astrology associations, she has had articles published in many national and international astrology magazines. She is the author of *Astro-Analytics Newsletter* and editor of the New World Series of Astrological Anthologies by Lewellyn Publications. Cowinner with Marion March of the Regulus Award for contribution to astrological education, McEvers has also received a special award from the Astrological Monthly Review for the excellence of her published works. She also received an award in 1989 from Professional Astrologers Incorporated for her outstanding contribution to the art and science of astrology.

Magic and Astrology

Magic is the art of controlling events by **occult** (hidden) means. Astrology is not, in the proper sense of the term, magical, but such techniques as **electional astrology**—determining the best times to perform certain actions—border on magic. Traditional Western magic views astrology as providing insight into the occult forces that are playing on **Earth** at any given time, and a specialized form of electional astrology is utilized by magicians to determine the best times for performing particular rituals.

Much of the astrological lore associated with magic is focused on the **days of the week**, the planetary **hours**, and the **gems** and **metals** connected with the **planets**. Each of the traditional seven "planets"—the **Sun**, the **Moon, Mars, Mercury, Jupiter, Venus**, and **Saturn—rules**, in sequence, the seven days of the week. A similar relationship exists between the planets and the hours of the day. Magicians utilize these relationships and other traditional associations with the planets by, for example, performing rituals to gain love on Friday (Venusday) during an hour ruled by Venus (the planet of love), performing rituals to gain money on Thursday (Jupiterday) during an hour ruled by Jupiter (the planet of wealth), and so forth.

Amulets, which are fabricated objects used as charms, are also constructed during days and hours associated with the task the amulet is intended to perform. Additionally, such objects are constructed from materials ruled by the relevant planet. In the above examples, for instance, an amulet designed to attract love might be constructed from copper (the metal traditionally associat-

▶
Beyond the traditional use of the science of the stars by magicians, magic and astrology have often been associated with each other in the popular imagination. In this magician's poster from the 1840s, the signs of the zodiac are prominently displayed. · Bettmann Archive

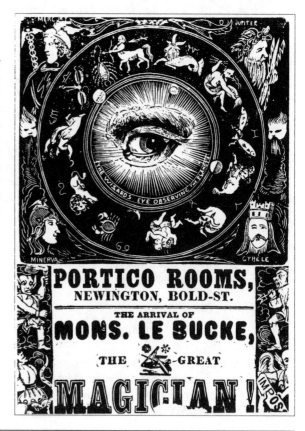

ed with Venus), and an amulet intended to attract prosperity might be made from tin (associated with Jupiter).

Magicians who are competent astrologers also pay attention to the sign in which the relevant planet is placed, as well as the **aspects** the planet is making at the time of the ceremony. Thus, to once again take Venus as an example, a magician would wait until Venus was in a favorable sign (which, for Venus, would be **Libra**, **Taurus**, or **Pisces**) and favorably aspected (making harmonious aspects with other planets) before performing a love ritual or constructing a love amulet.

Sources:

Cavendish, Richard. *The Black Arts*. New York: Capricorn Books, 1967.
Denning, Melita, and Osborne Phillips. *Planetary Magick: The Heart of Western Magick*. Saint Paul, Minn.: Llewellyn Publications, 1989.

Malefic (Malefic Aspects; Malefic Planets)

Malefic is a traditional term found in older astrological works. It refers to **aspects** and **planets** regarded as having an unfortunate, inharmonious influence. Malefic aspects are angles like **squares** and **oppositions** (called **hard aspects** by modern astrologers) and planets like **Mars** (the Lesser Malefic) and **Saturn** (the Greater Malefic). The antonym of malefic is **benefic**. Contemporary astrologers have largely abandoned these older terms, if for no other reason than to avoid frightening clients with medieval terminology. There are, however, other good reasons for dropping such language, the primary one being that the "benefics" do not always indicate unmitigated benefits, nor do "malefics" always indicate unmitigated difficulties.

Manilius

Manilius was a Roman poet who compiled the astrological knowledge of his day into an important verse treatise, the *Astronomica,* five books of which are still extant. Details of his life are unknown, except that he composed his treatise during the first few decades of the first century.

Mann, A. T.

A. T. "Tad" Mann was born August 18, 1943, in Auburn, New York. He graduated from Cornell University in 1966 with an architecture degree and worked as a professional architect for a time. He is a member of the Association for Astrological Networking (AFAN) and the Association of Scandinavian Professional Astrologers (SAFA). He lives and works in Copenhagen, Denmark, and is married to the astrologer Lise-Lotte Mann. He has one daughter, Ptolemy.

Mann applied the concept of biological time and the philosophical system of George Gurdjieff, Pyotr Ouspensky, and Rodney Collin to astrology. The resultant logarithmic time scale grades the periphery of the **horoscope** from the ninth **house cusp** (conception point) to the **ascendant** (birth) to the ninth cusp (symbolic death point). During the three periods of gestation, childhood, and maturity, the physical, emotional, and mental bodies are created. There is a fourth period, the transcendent octave, which represents the higher level of gestation influences.

Mann's life time astrology system is used by astrologers, psychologists, and healers in Europe, the United States, Australia, and the Far East. It is unique as a synthesis of biology, physics, psychology, and astrology. This combination has led to the development of a unique method of treatment at a distance through the horoscope, called Astro*Radionics as described in *Astrology and the Art of Healing* (1987). Mann applied the principle of logarithmic time scales to the historical process and mechanism of **reincarnation** in *The Divine Plot: Astrology and Reincarnation* (1986) and *The Eternal Return: A Thinking Human's Guide to Reincarnation* (1993). Astrology is used as an organizing device for understanding the universe, from the subatomic level to the astronomical.

The application of astrology to **tarot** led to the development and painting of the Mandala Astrological Tarot in 1987. Each card is related to a **planet**, sign, **element**, or **decanate** and is composed of a circular mandala with Eastern, medieval, and symbolic images. As the work of a former practicing architect in New York City and Rome, Mann's *Sacred Architecture* (1992) describes the importance of astronomical/astrological, elemental, mythic, and symbolic organizational structures and images in architecture, from megalithic times to the Renaissance, and includes a critique of modern architecture.

Selected Publications:

The Future of Astrology. London: Unwin Hyman, 1987.
The Round Art: The Astrology of Time and Space. New York: Mayflower, 1979.
The Divine Plot: Astrology and Reincarnation. Rockport, Mass.: Element, 1991 (rpt. of 1986).
Life Time Astrology. London: Allen & Unwin, 1984.

Manto

Manto, **asteroid** 870 (the 870th asteroid to be discovered), is approximately 16 kilometers in diameter and has an **orbital** period of 3.5 years. It is named after a Greek prophetess. If prominent in a **natal chart** (e.g., **conjunct** the **Sun** or the **ascendant**), Manto may show a person able to intuit the future or someone who is always seeking information about the future. Manto's location by sign and **house** may indicate how and where one best intuits the future.

Sources:

Kowal, Charles T. *Asteroids: Their Nature and Utilization.* Chichester, West Sussex, U.K.: Ellis Horwood Limited, 1988.

Room, Adrian. *Dictionary of Astronomical Names.* London: Routledge, 1988.

Manzil

Manzil is the Arabic term for the **lunar mansions**.

March, Marion D.

Marion D. March was born February 10, 1923, in Nürnberg, Germany. She was raised in Switzerland, where she received most of her schooling. Her father was a banker; her mother's family was in the book publishing business. In 1941, after a year's stay in Chile, she moved to the United States, where she pursued an acting career for 6 years, both in Hollywood and New York. After that she worked for the American Foreign Service in Zürich, Switzerland, where she met her future husband, Nico, who was then studying law and economics. After their marriage they moved to the Los Angeles area and still live there. Her husband is a vice-president of Merrill Lynch, and they have two children.

March began to study astrology seriously in 1965, and she turned professional in 1970. She has a large clientele in Los Angeles as well as other parts of the United States and in some European countries, since she speaks five languages. She has lectured all over the United States, England, Australia, New Zealand, Ireland, France, Denmark, Norway, Germany, and Switzerland and has been on the faculties of the American Federation of Astrologers (AFA), the International Society for Astrological Research (ISAR), and the Southwest Astrology Council (SWAC) since 1976. She has also been active in the European International Congress, the San Diego Astrological Conference, and the United Astrology Conference. She is also one of the founders of the Association for Astrological Networking (AFAN).

In 1975, March and **Joan McEvers** founded Aquarius Workshops, a school of astrology with headquarters in Los Angeles. Their magazine *Aspects* has a worldwide circulation. Aquarius Workshops is very active locally as a school and a forum for astrology speakers. With McEvers, March wrote a series of best-selling books called *The Only Way to . . . Learn Astrology.*

In 1972, March received the prestigious Regulus Award given by the United Astrology Congress for community service. In 1989, she and McEvers won a Regulus for their contribution in the field of education. She has also received many other awards. Many of March's articles have been published in the popular *American Astrology* and about 10 other trade magazines. She has given numerous radio and TV interviews in foreign countries and in the United States.

Selected Publications:

The Only Way to . . . Learn about Tomorrow By March and Joan McEvers. San Diego, Calif.: Astro Computing Services, 1988.

The Only Way to . . . Learn about Relationships. By March and Joan McEvers. San Diego, Calif.: Astro Computing Services, 1992.

The Only Way to . . . Learn about Horary and Electional Astrology. By March and Joan McEvers. San Diego, Calif.: Astro Computing Services, Forthcoming.

Mars

Mars, named after the Roman god of war (the Roman equivalent of the Greek Aries), is one of our closest neighbors, the next **planet** from the **Sun** after Earth. Whereas the Greek Ares (the source of the name **Aries**) was an impulsive youth, the Roman Mars was a mature god who was originally invoked to protect crops. In **Mesopotamian astrology**, Mars was associated with Nergal (who became identified with the god Erra), the god of war, who was also associated with forest fires, fevers, and plagues. He had a passionate affair with the goddess Ereskigal, whom he later married.

Mars has an orbital period of 686.98 days, which is somewhat less than 2 terrestrial years. Traditionally, Mars was said to rule both Aries and **Scorpio.** Sometime after **Pluto** was discovered, astrologers began to percieve a correlation between Pluto's characteristic influence in a chart and the traits of the sign Scorpio. Eventually the rulership of Scorpio was reassigned to Pluto, leaving Aries with Mars.

Like its mythological namesake, Mars is associated with aggression, emotional passion, and conflict. Mars has further connotations of mechanical work, physical skills, fire, and the like. Even though associated with aggression, Mars was primarily a defender whose aggressive energies were originally associated with protection and defense. Additionally, Mars is associated with spontaneity, impulsiveness, and ambition.

The various planets are connected with a wide range of activities and objects, and when found in a **natal chart**, they represent different parts of the psyche. Mars represents outgoing, aggressive energy—the part of the self that gets up and does things. Thus, its placement in a natal chart shows much about how and where a person can best express her or his energy, as well as how and where that person is likely to experience conflict.

Jeff Mayo's *The Planets and Human Behavior* provides useful lists of traits and associations for the planets. For Mars, under the rubric *characteristic desire trends,* Mayo lists "energetic activity, initiative, self-assertion, enterprise, combativeness, aggressiveness, ambition, independence, forcefulness" (p. 88). Under the heading *traditional associations* are listed "energy, activity, passion, fire, fevers, burns, cuts, scalds, war, strife, heat, bloodshed, violence, accidents, murder, arson, the Armed Services, masculinity, munitions, slaughter-houses; all engineering and constructional industries; industries dependent upon machinery, iron, steel, or furnace-heating; pungent odors, hot acids, burning astringents; manual skill and technical ability—able to use tools and instruments of all types for the utilization of energy; sexual desire; dispersion" (p. 88–9).

Sources:

Campion, Nicholas. *The Practical Astrologer.* New York: Harry N. Abrams, 1987.

George, Llewellyn. *The New A to Z Horoscope Maker and Delineator.* Saint Paul, Minn.: Llewellyn Publications, 1910. Rev. and enl. 1987.

McEvers, Joan. *Planets: The Astrological Tools.* Saint Paul, Minn.: Llewellyn Publications, 1989.

Mayo, Jeff. *The Planets and Human Behavior.* 1972. Reprint. Reno, Nev.: CRCS Publications, 1985.

Valentine, Christine. *Images of the Psyche: Exploring the Planets through Psychology and Myth.* Shaftesbury, Dorset, U.K.: Element Books, 1991.

Van Toen, Donna. *The Mars Book: A Guide to Your Personal Energy and Motivation.* York Beach, Maine: Samuel Weiser, 1988.

Mars Effect

Of the various attempts to demonstrate astrological influence by statistical means, the most successful have been the large-scale studies by **Michel Gauquelin and Françoise Gauquelin**. The Gauquelins uncovered correlations between vocation and the position of certain specific **planets**. The most significant of these was the so-called Mars effect, a correlation between athletic achievement and the position of the planet **Mars**—a planet traditionally associated with physical energy and therefore with athletic achievement—in certain influential sectors of the sky (e.g., close to the eastern **horizon** and near the **zenith**) at the time of birth.

Sources:

Curry, Patrick. "Research on the Mars Effect." *Zetetic Scholar* 9 (March 1982): 34–53.

Gauquelin, Michel and Françoise. *Psychological Mongraphs. Series C: The Mars Temperament and Sports.* Vol. II. Paris: Laboratoire d'Etudes des Relations entre Rythmes Cosmiques et Psycholphysiologiques, 1973.

Melton, J. Gordon, Jerome Clark, and Aidan A. Kelly. *New Age Encyclopedia.* Detroit, Mich.: Gale Research, 1990.

Masculine Signs (Positive Signs)

The 12 signs of the **zodiac** are classified in several different ways, including a division into positive, masculine signs and negative, **feminine** signs (using negative and positive in the neutral sense of opposite poles rather than as value judgments). The masculine signs are all of the **fire signs (Aries, Leo, Sagittarius)** and all of the **air signs (Gemini, Libra, Aquarius)**. The gender of the signs was originally determined by the Pythagorean notion that odd numbers were male and even numbers female. This caused the signs that came first (Aries), third (Gemini), fifth (Leo), etc., in the zodiac to be classified as masculine. By comparison with the feminine signs, the masculine signs tend to be more active and extroverted.

Sources:

Leo, Alan. *Dictionary of Astrology*. Reprint. New York: Astrologer's Library, 1983.
Tester, Jim. *A History of Western Astrology*. New York: Ballantine, 1987.

Mathematicians (Mathematicals)

Prior to the advent of modern astrology tables and, especially, the computer revolution, extensive mathematical calculations characterized the practice of astrology. For this reason, the ancients often referred to astrologers as mathematicians or mathematicals.

▶
Masculine signs.

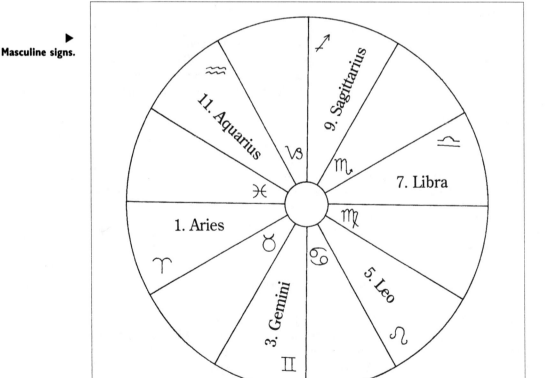

Mathesis

Mathesis, **asteroid** 454 (the 454th asteroid to be discovered), is approximately 88 kilometers in diameter and has an **orbital** period of 4.3 years. Its name represents the desire for learning and the power of knowledge. In a **natal chart**, Mathesis's location by sign and **house** indicates where and how the desire for learning is most likely to manifest. When **afflicted** by inharmonious **aspects**, Mathesis may show aversion to learning or attraction to unhelpful subjects of learning. If prominent in a chart (e.g., **conjunct** the **Sun** or the **ascendant**), it may indicate an exceptionally studious person, or an individual for whom learning is a major life theme.

Sources:

Kowal, Charles T. *Asteroids: Their Nature and Utilization*. Chichester, West Sussex, U.K.: Ellis Horwood Limited, 1988.

Room, Adrian. *Dictionary of Astronomical Names*. London: Routledge, 1988.

Matutine (Matutinal)

Stars that rise in the early morning before the **Sun** are referred to as matutine. The **planets**, particularly the **Moon, Mercury**, and **Venus**, can be matutinal.

Mean Motion

Because celestial bodies move in elliptical **orbits**, their speed varies depending upon their location. Mean motion refers to their average speed.

Medea

Medea, **asteroid** 212 (the 212th asteroid to be discovered), is approximately 132 kilometers in diameter and has an **orbital** period of 5.5 years. Medea was named after the princess who helped Jason obtain the Golden Fleece. Lehman associates this asteroid with planning strategy, as well as with bringing together seemingly opposed emotions.

Sources:

Kowal, Charles T. *Asteroids: Their Nature and Utilization*. Chichester, West Sussex, U.K.: Ellis Horwood Limited, 1988.

Lehman, J. Lee. *The Ultimate Asteroid Book*. West Chester, Penn.: Whitford Press, 1988.

Room, Adrian. *Dictionary of Astronomical Names*. London: Routledge, 1988.

Medical Astrology

Medical astrology, as the name suggests, is the subdivision of astrology dealing with correlations between celestial patterns and health. The foundation of this ancient branch of the science of the stars is a system of correspondence between the signs (and their **ruling planets**) of the **zodiac** and various parts of the human body. The great Greek physician Hippocrates is said to have required his students to learn astrology. While the basic anatomical correlations were developed by earlier cultures, it was systematized in **Arabic astrology**.

These anatomical and zodiacal correspondences begin with Aries (associated with the head and face) and follow the order of the zodiac down the body to Pisces (associated with the feet). The **sun sign**—and, to a lesser extent, the Moon sign and the rising sign (**ascendant**)—people are born under usually indicates an area of the body with which they are likely to have trouble. Aries **natives,** for instance, tend to experience a disproportionate number of blows to the head or frequent headaches. Pisces people, on the other hand, tend to have accidents involving the feet (and easily contract such diseases as athlete's foot).

▶
Medical astrology associates different illnesses with the various signs of the zodiac. This 16th-century woodcut is from an astrological tract by Paracelsus. · Bettmann Archive

As outlined in Manly P. Hall's *Astrological Keywords* (pp. 23–24), the anatomical correspondences of the 12 signs of the zodiac are as follows:

Aries: Head and face with their bones and muscles; eyes, cerebrum; upper jaw

Taurus: Neck; cerebellum; upper cervical vertebrae; ears; throat; pharynx; larynx; eustachian tubes; uvula; tonsils; upper part of esophagus; palate; thyroid gland; vocal cords; lower jaw

Gemini: Arms; shoulders; muscles and bones of arms and shoulders; lungs, including trachea and bronchi; thymus gland; upper ribs; capillaries; hands

Cancer: Stomach; armpits; breasts; lacteals; chest cavity; solar plexus; pancreas; epigastric region; diaphragm and upper lobes of liver; thoracic duct; to some extent the womb

Leo: Heart; spinal column with its marrow, especially dorsal region; and spinal cord

Virgo: Intestines; alimentary canal; abdominal cavity and its membranes; spleen; lower lobe of liver; duodenum

Libra: Kidneys; ovaries; adrenals; loins; appendix; ureters; lumbar vertebrae and contiguous areas; skin in general

Scorpio: Generative organs; nasal bone; bladder; gall; pubic bone; lower lumbar vertebrae; prostate gland; testicles; colon; rectum

Sagittarius: Hips; thighs; coccygeal vertebrae; sacral region; sciatic nerves

Capricorn: Knees; kneecaps; hair; outer epidermis; various joints of the body; bones in general

Aquarius: Lower leg, including the calves and ankles; teeth; blood circulation in general

Pisces: Feet; toes; especially their bones and muscles; matrix; generative organs; the lungs

While there is general agreement on these correspondences, minor variations are often found from one astrologer to the next. The rectum, for example, which Hall assosciates with Scorpio, is more often associated with Virgo.

The signs are also associated with the body's various physiological systems—Gemini with respiration, Cancer with digestion, Leo with circulation, and so forth. The planets are correlated with the part of the body corresponding to the sign(s) they rule and are further correlated with certain other conditions. **Mars,** for example, is associated with fevers, **Jupiter** with conditions resulting from overindulgence, such as excess weight, the **Sun** with general vitality, etc.

In a **natal chart,** the sixth-**house** indicates health matters. The sign on the sixth-house **cusp** (i.e., at beginning of the sixth house) often indicates an area of potential health problems, particularly if that sign's ruling planet is involved in **hard aspects** with other planets. Other problems can be indicated by the planets placed in the sixth house. For example, an **afflicted** Mars in the sixth house can show a proneness to fevers and accidents, an afflicted **Moon**

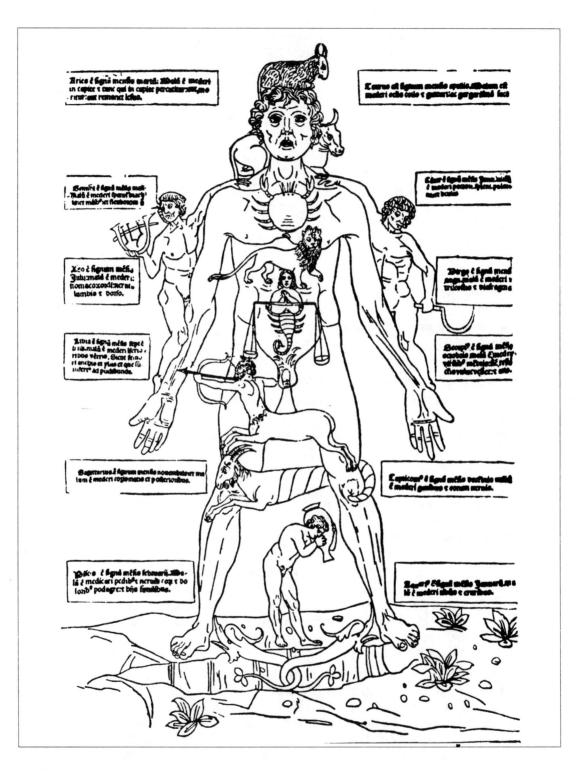

A 15th-century Italian illustration showing the associations between the signs of the zodiac and parts of the anatomy.
· **Bettmann Archive**

indicates digestive problems, and so forth. Medical astrology, the full extent of which is far more complex than suggested here, is also able to help diagnose illnesses, as well as predict future health conditions.

Sources:

Brau, Jean-Louis, Helen Weaver, and Allan Edmands. *Larousse Encyclopedia of Astrology*. New York: New American Library, 1980.

Corneel, Howard Leslie. *Encyclopedia of Medical Astrology*. 3d ed. New York: Samuel Weiser, 1979.

Hall, Manly P. *Astrological Keywords*. 1958. Reprint. Savage, Md.: Littlefield Adams (1975), 22–24.

Raphael's Medical Astrology; or the effects of the Planets and Signs upon the Human Body. 1924. Reprint. Santa Fe, N. Mex.: Sun Books, 1991.

Ridder-Patrick, Jane. *A Handbook of Medical Astrology*. London: Arkana, 1990.

Medium Coeli

Medium coeli is another term for midheaven, which is the most elevated **degree** of the **zodiac** in an astrological chart. In many systems of **house** division, it is also the **cusp** (beginning) of the tenth House. Medium coeli, (frequently abbreviated MC) means middle of the sky in Latin. Medium coeli is often used interchangeably with **zenith**, although this usage is incorrect.

Medusa

Medusa, **asteroid** 149 (the 149th asteroid to be discovered), is approximately 26 kilometers in diameter and has an **orbital** period of 3.2 years. Medusa was named after the famous Greek woman whose visage could turn men into stone. Lehman associates this asteroid with "volcanic" temperaments, although she adds that in small doses, it may add spice to one's character.

Sources:

Kowal, Charles T. *Asteroids: Their Nature and Utilization*. Chichester, West Sussex, U.K.: Ellis Horwood Limited, 1988.

Lehman, J. Lee. *The Ultimate Asteroid Book*. West Chester, Penn.: Whitford Press, 1988.

Room, Adrian. *Dictionary of Astronomical Names*. London: Routledge, 1988.

Melancholic

Melancholic is the traditional name for the personality temperament indicated by an excess of the **element** earth.

Melete

Melete, **asteroid** 56 (the 56th asteroid to be discovered), is approximately 144 kilometers in diameter and has an **orbital** period of 4.2 years. Its name is derived from the Greek word for care or anxiety. The location of Melete by sign and **house** indicates a source of anxiety. When prominent in a **natal chart**, Melete may indicate a **native** overburdened by cares.

Sources:

Kowal, Charles T. *Asteroids: Their Nature and Utilization.* Chichester, West Sussex, U.K.: Ellis Horwood Limited, 1988.
Room, Adrian. *Dictionary of Astronomical Names.* London: Routledge, 1988.

Melothesic Man

The melothesic man or **zodiacal** man is the image, often found in medieval astrology works, of a human being with the signs superimposed on the parts of the anatomy they are traditionally said to rule (e.g., **Aries** on the head, **Taurus** on the throat, and so on to **Pisces** on the feet). *See also:* **Medical Astrology**.

Mercury

Mercury, named after the Roman god who carried messages between the gods and humanity (the Roman equivalent of the Greek Hermes), is the **planet** nearest the **Sun**. In **Mesopotamian astrology**, Mercury was associated with Nabu (biblical Nebo), the divine scribe of destiny who presided over learning, writing, and science. He was referred to as the administrator of heaven and earth, and had further associations with irrigation and agriculture.

Mercury has a short orbital period of only 88 days. Because its **orbit** lies between Earth and the Sun, it does not appear, from our terrestrial perspective, ever to be very far from the Sun. For astrology, one practical implication of this is that Mercury is never more than one sign away from the sign the Sun is in. Thus, for example, if the Sun is in **Leo**, Mercury can only be in Leo, **Cancer**, or **Virgo**. Mercury **rules** both **Gemini** and Virgo, although many contemporary astrologers anticipate that a new planet will be discovered and come to be viewed as the ruler of Virgo.

Like its mythological namesake, Mercury is associated with travel and communication. The Roman Mercury was also the god of commerce and trade, which, because such activity involves travel and communication, is also naturally connected with this planet. Additionally, Mercury is associated with relatives, writing, teaching, and learning. While the various planets are connected with a wide range of activities and objects, they also, when found in a **natal chart**, represent different parts of the psyche. Mercury represents the mind, particularly that part of the mind that interfaces with the outer world—perception, reason, and communication. Thus, its placement in a natal chart will show much about how one thinks and communicates.

Individuals with their natal Mercury in the sign **Libra**, for example, regard ideas in a balanced manner, although their ability to see both sides of an issue can make them indecisive. In communication, the harmonizing and refining effect of this **Venus**-ruled sign gives them the ability to communicate in a pleasant, tactful manner. The **house** placement shows less about a planet's basic nature than it does about the **native's** environment. Thus, when Mercury is placed in the tenth house (the house of profession), for instance, individuals are usually able to communicate well in business or undertake a career in a Mercury-related profession, such as teaching or mass communications. When Mercury **aspects** another planet in a natal chart, the native's thinking and communication will be modified according to the planet and aspect involved. Thus, for example, a **soft aspect** like a **trine** between Mercury and **Saturn** would give the individual mental discipline, as well as business and management ability (both positive traits of Saturn). A **hard aspect** between these two planets, on the other hand, might still give the individual discipline and business ability, but the person would also be prone to over seriousness and even depression—seeing the cloud but not the silver lining. An individual with such an aspect may further experience times when it is difficult to communicate.

Jeff Mayo's *The Planets and Human Behavior* provides useful lists of traits and associations for the planets. For Mercury, under the rubric *characteristic desire trends,* Mayo lists "adaptability, mental exercise, versatility, communicativeness, coordination, information exchange, volatility" (p. 80). Under the heading *traditional associations* are listed "literary works, publishing, printing, correspondence, the Press, advertising, messengers, teaching and education, study, the intelligentsia, communications generally, the postal services, transport generally, commerce, trading, merchandise, agents, changes, travel, markets, mathematics, libraries" (p. 80).

Sources:

Campion, Nicholas. *The Practical Astrologer.* New York: Harry N. Abrams, 1987.

George, Llewellyn. *The New A to Z Horoscope Maker and Delineator.* Saint Paul, Minn.: Llewellyn Publications, 1910., Rev. and enl. 1987.

McEvers, Joan. *Planets: The Astrological Tools.* Saint Paul, Minn.: Llewellyn Publications, 1989.

Mayo, Jeff. *The Planets and Human Behavior.* 1972. Reprint. Reno, Nev.: CRCS Publications, 1985.

Valentine, Christine. *Images of the Psyche: Exploring the Planets through Psychology and Myth.* Shaftesbury, Dorset, U.K.: Element Books, 1991.

Meridian

A meridian (from the Latin for midday) is formed by taking a line of **longitude** and projecting it outward from **Earth** onto the **celestial sphere**. Another way of imagining a meridian is to picture the circle that would be formed by drawing a line connecting the north pole, the **zenith** (the point in the sky directly overhead), the south pole, and the **nadir** (the point directly opposite the zenith).

Merlin

Merlin, **asteroid** 2598 (the 2,598th asteroid to be discovered), is approximately 16 kilometers in diameter and has an **orbital** period of 4.6 years. It is named after Merlin the magician. If prominent in a **natal chart**, Merlin may signify a person for whom things seem to come together "magically" or, in rare instances, someone who is actually interested in magic. The sign and **house** position of Merlin in a natal chart indicates how and where this "magic" manifests.

Sources:

Kowal, Charles T. *Asteroids: Their Nature and Utilization.* Chichester, West Sussex, U.K.: Ellis Horwood Limited, 1988.
Room, Adrian. *Dictionary of Astronomical Names.* London: Routledge, 1988.

Mesoamerican Astrology

As in the ancient Near East, astrology and the birth of civilization coincided in Mesoamerica, today's Mexico and northern Central America. During the Pre-Classic period, around 600 B.C., stone carvings made by Olmec artists are evidence that Mesoamerican astrology's key signs were in use then. During the Classic period, the time of the rise and fall of Mayan civilization (from about 300 to 900 A.D.), astrology became a guide to religion, war, and daily life. Ancient Mayan astrologers had both power and status within society and they were able to devise many sophisticated methods for computing planetary and calendric positions. During the Post-Classic, a time during which the Maya were in decline and the Toltec, and later the Aztec, dominated the Mexican highlands, the astrological tradition continued to flourish, though it did not evolve beyond its high-water mark of the Classic period. The Spaniards arrived in Mesoamerica in the early 16th century and quickly brought an end to more than 2,000 years of the native culture.

While the Spanish conquistadors and friars were very thorough in their burning of books and destruction of stone inscriptions, the astrological tradition survived. From the conquest to the present, an oral tradition has kept alive some of the most basic principles of the astrological system. In their attempts to learn about indigenous practices so as to better eliminate them, friars left writings about the ancient astrology. Today's archaeo-astronomers have examined ancient ruins with precise instruments and have found numerous astronomical alignments that indicate the importance of celestial phenomena to these ancient peoples. The astrological tradition in Mesoamerica was a central pillar shared by the several civilizations that arose there and today we are able to piece together enough of it to appreciate its high level of sophistication.

Mesoamerican astrology gives blocks of *time* the same importance as Western astrology gives blocks of *space*. The Western **zodiac**, the **aspects**, and the **houses** are all spatial elements. In the Mesoamerican system, blocks of time, with the day being the fundamental unit, serve the same purpose. There are twenty key signs that move in a consistent order, ruling blocks of time that are 1 day or 13 days in length. Western astrology's twelve signs of the zodiac correspond to the Mesoamerican **decans**, a set of **signs** within the signs. Like

◀
Mesoamerican
astrological
symbols.

the zodiac, the twenty key signs of Mesoamerican astrology depict an archetypal evolutionary sequence. Celestial events and births were interpreted according to the symbolism of the block of time in which events occurred.

The twenty signs of Mesoamerican astrology are grouped in five sets of four. Like the **elements** in Western astrology, the directions are important considerations in the evaluation of a Mesoamerican sign. The signs and their directional compliments are as follows:

EAST	NORTH	WEST	SOUTH
(1) Crocodile	(2) Wind	(3) House	(4) Lizard
(5) Serpent	(6) Death	(7) Deer	(8) Rabbit
(9) Water	(10) Dog	(11) Monkey	(12) Grass
(13) Reed	(1) Ocelot	(2) Eagle	(3) Vulture
(4) Motion	(5) Knife	(6) Rain	(7) Flower

Each of the signs, called *tonalli* by the Aztec, rules a single day in the order shown above from left to right. After twenty days the cycle begins again. Along with these twenty signs run thirteen numbers as follows: 1-Crocodile, 2-Wind, 3-House, 4-Lizard, 5-Serpent, etc., to 13-Reed. After that comes 1-Ocelot, 2-Eagle, 3-Vulture, etc. There are twenty cycles of the thirteen numbers in exactly the same number of days as thirteen cycles of the twenty signs. This full cycle is called the 260-day astrological calendar; the *tzolkin* of the Maya and the *tonalpouhalli* of the Aztec. Each sign rules a day and so, is called a day-sign. Signs that are attached to the number 1 rule the next 13 days and, since there are 20 of these in the 260-day period, they operate like signs themselves, though in a different order than the days. In other words, any given day in the cycle of 260 days is both a day-sign and a part of a 13-day sign. Day-sign and 13-day sign are two of the fundamental building blocks of Mesoamerican astrology and provide a key to personality and the analysis of celestial events.

While for the most part the Maya correspondences have been lost, we know that for the Aztec, each of the twenty signs was said to be ruled by a specific deity in the pantheon. Knowledge of the Aztec gods and goddesses is crucial in understanding what the signs stand for, just as an understanding of zodiac signs requires a knowledge of planetary rulers. The few books that survived the Spanish conquest hint at a complex body of symbolic knowledge that was used by priests and astrologers. From these books eclipses and conjunctions could be predicted as well as which signs they would occur in. Predictions of the effects of the various combinations may be drawn along with the relevant mathematical detail.

Mesoamerican astrology is a complex subject. There was a **mundane astrology** that utilized blocks of time of 7,200 days, a period close to the length of the Jupiter/Saturn cycle, called a *katun*. The katun was regarded by the Maya as the fundamental unit of time for political and cultural matters. Katuns were grouped in bunches of 13 and 20, and 260 of them made up a creation epoch. Because the Maya were excellent mathematicians and left behind many dates in stone, we are fairly certain that the current epoch began 8.11.3113 B.C. and we know that it will end 12.21.2112 A.D. The 5,125 year span of 260 katuns is almost exactly one-fifth of a precession cycle. In Mesoamerican astrology the passage of the ages is not measured in twelfths and indicated by signs (as in age of Pisces, Aquarius, etc.); instead it is divided into fifths that are in turn divided up the same way as the 260-day astrological calendar, into 20 units of 13 and 13 units of 20. The Harmonic Convergence of 1987 signalled that we entered the last katun of the entire creation epoch, which according to most researchers began April 6, 1993.

The rehabilitation of Mesoamerican astrology is far from complete. In Mexico today there are a number of practitioners who utilize the system in what they believe to be a pure form. In many cases they reject the work of the academic researchers and there are discrepancies over the exact correlation between the ancient pre-Colombian calendar and that of the Christian calendar. However, after much research and painstaking comparisons with colonial documents, oral traditions, and ancient inscriptions, the consensus seems to be

◄
An ancient Aztec
calendar.
· Bettmann Archive

that the Goodman-Martinez-Thompson correlation that places the beginning of the present creation epoch (the Long Count) at 8.11.3113 B.C. is the correct correlation. The tradition of Mesoamerican astrology is the world's most sophisticated time-based astrological system and it may eventually be a major contributor to a world-class astrology of the future.

—Bruce Scofield

Sources:

Arguelles, Jose. *The Mayan Factor.* Santa Fe: Bear and Company, 1987.

Aveni, Anthony F. *Skywatchers of Ancient Mexico.* Austin: University of Texas Press, 1980.

Burland, C. A. *The Gods of Mexico.* New York: G. P. Putnam's Sons, 1967.

Duran, Fray Diego. *The Book of the Gods, the Rites and the Ancient Calendar.* Translated and edited by F. Horcasitas and D. Heyden. Norman: University of Oklahoma Press, 1971.

Sahagun, Fray Bernardino de. *Florentine Codex: General History of the Things of New Spain, Books 4 and 5.* Translated by C. E. Dibble and A. J. O. Anderson. Ogden: University of Utah Press, 1957.

Scofield, Bruce. *Day-Signs: Native American Astrology from Ancient Mexico.* Amherst, Mass.: One Reed Publications, 1991.

—— and Angela Cordova. *The Aztec Circle of Destiny.* St. Paul: Llewellyn Publications, 1988.

—— and Barry Orr. "Aztec Astro-Report" (computer program). Brewster, Mass.: Astrolabe, 1991.

Tedlock, Barbara. *Time and the Highland Maya.* Albuquerque: University of New Mexico Press, 1982.

Thompson, J. Eric S. *Maya Hieroglyphic Writing: An Introduction.* Norman: University of Oklahoma Press, 1985.

Mesopotamian Astrology (Babylonian Astrology; Chaldean Astrology)

Mesopotamia, the ancient name for the plains and highlands that lie between the Tigris and Euphrates rivers, is one of the areas of the world where humankind made the transition from simple modes of living to so-called civilization. (The other areas were Egypt, India, and China.) Several successive peoples controlled this area, from the ancient Sumerians to the Abbasid caliphs. This cradle of civilization was the birthplace of both Western astrology and **Hindu astrology. Chinese astrology** is the only major system of astrology to develop independently of Mesopotamian influence.

Astrologers tend to refer to Mesopotamian astrology as Chaldean astrology. The word Chaldean is somewhat confusing, however, sometimes being used for a group of people who lived in ancient Mesopotamia and at other times for a group of priests. From late classical times, *Chaldean* became synonymous with *astrologer.* One of the peoples to control Mesopotamia were the ancient Babylonians. Because of negative biblical associations with this group, people who wish to deprecate the science of the stars sometimes emphasize astrology's Babylonian associations and refer to it as Babylonian astrology.

Older generations of scholars tended to view the Mesopotamians as star-worshipers, as if the ancients actually regarded the **stars** and **planets** as gods. Astrology could then be explained as a more or less natural outgrowth of star-worship. Contemporary scholarship has overthrown this view, demonstrating that the Mesopotamians *associated* the gods with celestial bodies, rather than *identified* the bodies as gods. If anything, recent studies have gone to the opposite extreme of ignoring the role of astrology in Mesopotamian religion. For instance, Thorkild Jacobsen's important work on the religion of the ancient Tigris-Euphrates river valley, *The Treasures of Darkness,* fails even to mention astrology.

If celestial bodies were not venerated as gods, what, then, was the motivation for the development of astrology? Mesopotamian astrology developed first as a form of divination—foretelling events like famines or plagues on the basis of such ominous portents as **eclipses**. There was no personal, individual astrology (a later innovation by the Greeks) as we know it today; the most ancient astrologers were, rather, priests in the employ of the king who divined the fortunes of the country. This oldest of astrological systems did not view the stars and planets as exerting quasi-naturalistic "forces" that determined future events in the way that the force of gravity determines the rate of acceleration of falling objects. Instead, the signs in the skies were seen as clues to the intentions of the gods.

Our familiar 12-sign **zodiac** was devised in Mesopotamia, although the Mesopotamians used the signs to help them locate celestial bodies along the **ecliptic**, rather than as indicators of sets of personality traits. The original zodiac actually seems to have been composed of 18 rather than 12 signs. By 1000 B.C., these 18 **constellations** were:

The Hired Man (corresponding to **Aries**)

The Stars (the Pleiades)

The Bull of Heaven (**Taurus**)

The True Shepherd of Anu (Orion)

The Old Man (Perseus)

The Crook (Auriga)

The Great Twins (**Gemini**)

The Crab (**Cancer**)

The Lion (**Leo**)

The Furrow (**Virgo**)

The Scales (**Libra**)

The Scorpion (**Scorpio**)

Pabilsag (**Sagittarius**; Pabilsag is a deity)

The Goat-Fish (**Capricorn**)

The Great One (**Aquarius**)

The Tail (first part of **Pisces**)

The Swallow (middle of Pisces)

Anunitu (last part of Pisces)

At a later date, the Field (Pegasus) was added. By the middle of the first century B.C. certain pairs of these constellations were being grouped together so that the constellations corresponded with the 12 months (with the 12 yearly cycles of the **Moon**). By 400 B.C., the signs of the zodiac had been reduced to the now familiar 12.

The five planets observable with the naked eye—**Mercury, Venus, Mars, Jupiter**, and **Saturn**—were recognized as composing a distinct group of celestial bodies, clearly different from the **fixed stars**. Some of the associations between the planets and the gods foreshadowed associations in Greek and Roman astrology. For instance, Ishtar, the Mesopotamian goddess of love, was associated with the planet Venus; Venus was the name of the Roman god of love. Nergal, the god of war, was associated with Mars, the planet the Romans also associated with war. And Marduk, the king of the gods, was associated with Jupiter; Jupiter was the king of the gods in the Roman pantheon.

Contemporary astrologers seeking to shed light on the signs and planets by exploring their mythological associations always seem to stop short in classical mythology. For reasons that are difficult to fathom, the mythology of astrology's birthplace—in which the associations between myths, planets, and signs were originally forged—is ignored. Thus, a potentially fruitful field for astrological research is Mesopotamian mythology.

Sources:

Black, Jeremy, and Anthony Green. *Gods, Demons and Symbols of Ancient Mesopotamia*. Austin: University of Texas Press, 1992.

Dalley, Stephanie, ed. and trans. *Myths from Mesopotamia*. 1989. Reprint. Oxford: Oxford University Press, 1991.

Jacobsen, Thorkild. *The Treasures of Darkness: A History of Mesopotamian Religion*. New Haven: Yale University Press, 1976.

Spence, Lewis. *Myths and Legends of Babylonia and Assyria*. London: George G. Harrap, 1916.

Metals

At least 4,000 years ago, various metals began to be associated with the different **planets** (including the **Sun** and the **Moon** which in classical astrology were also classified as planets). By the seventh century, the following set of associations had come to be generally agreed upon: the Sun and gold, the Moon and silver, **Mercury** and mercury, **Venus** and copper, **Mars** and iron, **Jupiter** and tin, and **Saturn** and lead.

By extension, the signs were also associated with the metals ruled by their ruling planet (e.g., **Leo**, ruled by the Sun, was associated with gold, the metal ruled by the Sun; **Cancer**, ruled by the Moon, was associated with silver, the Moon's metal, etc.). The analogical relationship between many metals and their rulers is fairly straightforward: It was natural, for instance, that the most important heavenly body, the "golden" Sun, should be associated with the most precious metal, gold; Saturn, the slowest of the planets known to antiquity, was naturally associated with the heaviest metal, lead; Mars, god of war, had a natural connection with iron, the metal of weapons; and so forth for the other planet–metal associations. Prior to the emergence of the modern world, these planet–metal connections were taken quite seriously as real links (not merely as symbolic analogies). Medieval alchemists, for example, paid attention to the positions of the planets when working with metals, avoiding the use of certain metals when the corresponding planets were involved in **hard aspects**.

When the "new" planets were discovered, **astrologers** experienced difficulty expanding the old system of **rulerships**. Certain associations seemed obvious, such as **Uranus's** rulership of "uranium" and **Pluto's** rulership of "plutonium," but no astrologer has really been interested in exploring these new rulerships in any depth, largely because contemporary astrology is focused on individual human beings, with the result that almost all contemporary astrologers are primarily counselors, interested more in the psychological effects of the outer planets. If a significant number of astrologers were also metallurgists, pharmacists, and chemists, the question of the metals ruled by Uranus, **Neptune**, and Pluto would have been resolved long ago. The testing would be relatively easy: Assuming, as did the ancients, that there is a subtle yet tangible link between metals and planets, then some variation on the **Kolisko** experiments should determine precisely which metals are ruled by the planets beyond Saturn.

Sources:

Bach, Eleanor. *Astrology from A to Z: An Illustrated Source Book.* New York: Philosophical Library, 1990.

Davidson, Alison. *Metal Power: The Soul Life of the Planets.* Garberville, Calif.: Borderland Sciences Research Foundation, 1991.

Kollerstrom, Nicholas. "Planetary Influences on Metal Ion Activity." *Correlation* 3, no. 1 (1983): 38–50.

Meteorites

See: Comets

Meteorological Astrology (Astrometeorology)

Correlations between celestial events and the weather have been a long-standing concern in astrology. The very name given to weather study—meteorology—harkens back to a time when the appearance of meteors was associated with changes in the weather. Even contemporary scientific meteorology, which does not generally look kindly on astrological methods, has noted a relationship between long-term weather patterns and sunspot activity.

Ptolemy, whose classic work on astrology exercised a powerful influence on **astrologers** for centuries, discussed the influence of the **planets** on weather as far back as the second century B.C. Even prior to Ptolemy, the ancient Mesopotamians viewed changes in the weather as being linked to the **Moon.** According to Hungarian Egyptologist Barna Balogh (Ostrander & Schroeder, pp. 92–3), the Mesopotamian rule of thumb (which Balogh originally came across in Egyptian sources) is that weather pulsates in 2-week cycles. The prevailing weather can only change significantly on the fifth day after a new or full moon, and the weather on the fifth day gives an indication of what the weather will be like for the next 2-weeks. This rule does not predict the nature of the change, only that there will be a change.

Contemporary astrometeorologists pay attention to the daily positions of the planets, their positions at the times of the new and full moons, and planetary patterns at the beginning of each season. A useful summary of meteorological astrology containing guidelines for predicting the weather can be found in Nancy Soller's "Weather Watching with an Ephemeris." Soller notes, for example, that the prominence of particular planets in a seasonal **ingress** chart (an astrological chart constructed for the exact moment of the **Sun's** entry into one of the **cardinal signs**) will indicate seasonal patterns (p. 237):

> **Mercury** prominent on an Ingress chart signifies strong winds and atypical cooler or colder weather. **Venus** prominent on an Ingress chart indicates a season with more than the average precipitation. **Mars** prominent indicates weather that will be hotter and drier than normal. **Jupiter** brings good weather. Jupiter prominent in a Capricorn Ingress chart indicates a mild winter. A prominent **Saturn** indicates cold, wet weather. A prominent **Uranus** signifies a dry, windy drought, unless Uranus happens to be in a **Water sign. Neptune** prominent signifies precipitation and mild temperatures, and **Pluto** operates in much the same way as Mars, bringing higher temperatures and little precipitation.

A good ephemeris (table of planetary positions), such as Neil F. Michelsen's *American Ephemeris for the 20th Century,* contains the exact times of ingresses as well as the exact times of the full and new moons.

Sources:

Brau, Jean-Louis, Helen Weaver, and Allan Edmans. *Larousse Encyclopedia of Astrology.* New York: New American Library, 1980.

Michelsen, Neil F. *The American Ephemeris for the 20th Century.* San Diego, Calif.: ACS Publications, 1980.

Ostrander, Sheila, and Lynn Schroeder. *Astrological Birth Control.* Englewood Cliffs, N.J.: Prentice-Hall, 1972.

Soller, Nancy. "Weather Watching with an Ephemeris." In Joan McEvers, ed., *The Astrology of the Macrocosm.* Saint Paul, Minn.: Llewellyn Publications, 1990.

Metonic Cycle

The ancient Greek Meton discovered that the **Moon** has a cycle of 19 years, after which a new moon occurs on the same day of the year.

Michelsen, Neil Franklin

Neil Franklin Michelsen, born May 11, 1931, in Chicago, was the founder and inspiration behind Astro Computing Services (ACS) and ACS Publications. He was a well-known figure in the astrological community for his contributions to contemporary astrology. He was a generous person who gave money, computer time, personal time, technical expertise, and encouragement to many different astrologers, holistic healers, and practitioners of occult arts.

Michelsen graduated magna cum laude from the University of Miami and was for 17 years a systems engineer for IBM. He founded Astro Computing Services in 1973. ACS grew from a one-man business run out of Michelsen's home in Pelham, New York, to the current San Diego corporation staffed by almost two dozen people. A creative individual with solid programming skills, Michelsen became one of the greatest of contemporary astrological technicians. His work in the form of continually refined **ephemerides** and books of tables was the standard of accuracy by which other astrological calculations were judged. He has written or contributed to more than 20 reference books, including *The American Ephemeris* (1901–1930, then every decade up to the year 2000); *The American Sidereal Ephemeris, 1976–2000; The American Heliocentric Ephemeris, 1901–2000; Uranian Transneptune Ephemeris, 1850–2050; The American Book of Tables; The Koch Book of Tables; The American Ephemeris for the 20th Century 1900 to 2000, Midnight; The American Ephemeris for the 20th Century 1900 to 2000, Noon; The American Ephemeris for the 21st Century 2001 to 2050, Midnight; The American Midpoint Ephemeris 1986–1990; The Comet Halley Ephemeris 1901–1996; Tables of Planetary Phenomena* (July 1990); and with Maria Kay Simms, *Search for the Christmas Star.*

Neil F. Michelsen was chairman of the National Council for Geocosmic Research (NCGR), and through the NCGR he contributed to projects beneficial to the astrological community. After his death on May 15, 1990, an NCGR Neil F. Michelsen Memorial Fund was set up to continue such projects.

Middle Ages, Astrology in

See: History of Western Astrology

Midheaven

The midheaven is the most elevated degree of the **zodiac** in an astrological chart. In most systems of **house** division, it is also the **cusp** (beginning) of the tenth house. Midheaven is often used interchangeably with **zenith**, but this usage is inaccurate.

Midpoint

A midpoint, as the name implies, is a point halfway between two other points. For example, the midpoint between a **planet** located at 1° **Cancer** and a planet located at 29° Cancer would be 15° Cancer. Certain schools of contemporary astrology regard midpoints as significant, sensitive points in an astrological chart.

A midpoint between two planets is said to indicate where their combined energies is strongest, and **transits** to midpoints are particularly important. A third planet located near—or in close **aspect** with—a midpoint is particularly significant. In **hard aspects** such as a **square**, for instance, a third planet located near the midpoint provides the key to resolving the conflict indicated by the square.

Employed by early schools of astrology, midpoints fell into disuse until revived by Alfred Witte, the founder of Uranian astrology. Witte in turn influenced Reinhold Ebertin, the founder of cosmobiology, who further developed the use of midpoints.

Sources:

Brau, Jean-Louis, Helen Weaver, and Allan Edmands. *Larousse Encyclopedia of Astrology.* New York: New American Library, 1980.
Hand, Robert. *Horoscope Symbols.* Rockport, Mass.: Para Research, 1981.

Minerva

Minerva, **asteroid** 93 (the 93rd asteroid to be discovered), is approximately 168 kilometers in diameter and has an **orbital** period of 4.6 years. Minerva was the Roman goddess of wisdom, the Roman equivalent of the Greek Athena. Minerva was also the patroness of arts and crafts. According to Lang-Wescott, Minerva represents the principle of analyzing demands in order to alter behavior to please others and get their approval. This asteroid's key word is *calculations.* According to Lehman, the three asteroids Pallas, Athene, and Minerva all represent the application of skill. In contrast with one another, however, "Pallas people are concerned with being right, Athene people are more interested in being competent, and Minerva people with being accomplished" (Lehman, p. 25).

Sources:

Lang-Wescott, Martha. *Asteroids-Mechanics: Ephemerides II.* Conway, Mass.: Treehouse Mountain, 1990.

———. *Mechanics of the Future: Asteroids.* Rev. ed. Conway, Mass.: Treehouse Mountain, 1991.

Lehman, J. Lee. *The Ultimate Asteroid Book.* West Chester, Penn.: Whitford, 1988.

Mithraism and Astrology

Mithraism was an enigmatic Hellenistic mystery religion that drew heavily on astrology and astrological symbolism. It was Christianity's last great competitor during the period immediately prior to official conversion of the Roman Empire to the religion of Jesus. As such, Mithraism left its mark on Christianity. For example, the Romans celebrated Mithras's birthday (Mithras was the central deity of Mithraism) on December 25, the time of year when the daylight hours—which had gradually been shortening over the course of the previous 6 months—begin to lengthen (thus symbolically representing the victory of the forces of light over the forces of darkness). Christ's birthday began to be celebrated on the same date so that Christianity could compete more effectively with Mithraism.

Although Mithraism left a rich heritage of temple art and architecture for archaeologists to uncover, the actual doctrines of Mithraism were not preserved. In the late nineteenth century, the Belgian scholar Franz Cumont put forward a convincing hypothesis about these doctrines that held sway in Mithraic studies for the next 70 years. Beginning with the similarity in name between Mithras and the Persian god Mithra, Cumont developed an explanation that portrayed Mithraism as a form of Zoroastrianism that had branched off and transformed into a mystery religion. If this initial premise is granted, it is

The bull-slaying scene—tauroctony—is the central motif in Mithraism.

then possible to find other Persian myths (often quite obscure) that seem to apply to most of the sculpted forms found in Mithraic sanctuaries (Mithraeum). There were certain problems, however, with Cumont's interpretation—problems that came to a head in 1971 at the First International Conference of Mithraic Studies. At this meeting, devastating critiques were leveled against Cumont's Iranian (Persian) hypothesis. These critiques opened the door for entirely new interpretive approaches.

Freed from the "conventional wisdom" about the meaning of Mithraic statuary, scholars were able to look at Mithras imagery with fresh eyes, and one of the first things they noted was that many of the figures surrounding the tauroctony (the bull-slaying scene that is the central motif in every Mithraeum) seemed to compose a star map of certain **constellations**. This impression was reinforced by the **zodiacal** wheels found in many sanctuaries. With these clues as a starting point, contemporary scholars gradually pieced together a picture of a mystery cult that arose out of the religious speculations of a group of astrologically inclined Stoic philosophers in Tarsus (the birthplace of Saint Paul).

David Ulansey, in his *Origins of the Mithraic Mysteries,* has convincingly proposed that this group of philosophers responded to the discovery of the **precession of equinoxes** by postulating that a previously unknown god was responsible for the gradual movement of Earth's axis (the **stars** and **planets**, which were now relegated to positions of lesser importance, had earlier been identified by the Stoics as gods who controlled human fate). This new god, who was clearly more powerful than all the other gods in the heavens because he controlled the very axis of the universe, was linked by these Stoics with the chief local deity, Sandan, who had earlier been identified with the Greek hero Perseus, as well as with the Persian Mithra (hence the name Mithras).

The link between Sandan/Mithras and Perseus is an important key to unlocking the meaning of the tauroctony. In his constellation, Perseus is pictured with an upheld knife and is located immediately above the constellation **Taurus**. It is thus not difficult to imagine the scene in the star-map as leading to the scene in the tauroctony, in which the knife is plunged into the bull. What, however, is the significance of this sacrifice?

Several thousand years ago—during the period when Mithraism emerged—the **Sun** was positioned at the beginning of the constellation **Aries** during the spring **equinox**. Because of the precession of equinoxes, the spring equinox moves slowly backward through the constellations of the zodiac, so that approximately every 2,000 years the equinox begins taking place in an earlier constellation. It has been occurring in **Pisces** for the past 2,000 years and will begin to occur in the constellation **Aquarius** in the near future (which is the background for current speculations about the so-called **Age of Aquarius**). This also means that the spring equinox occurred in the sign Taurus several thousand years prior to the Hellenistic period. Ulansey takes this information and postulates that the tauroctony represented Mithras's destruction of the earlier Age of Taurus.

Ulansey's theory is far more intricate, and his argument far more nuanced, than can be developed here. The theory also leaves some questions unanswered: How did a religion originally devised by a group of intellectuals in Tarsus become one of the most popular religions of the Roman Empire? What did the rituals and other concrete practices of Mithraism actually involve? How did Mithraism change over time? Even though these questions are not addressed, and although many particulars of Ulansey's analysis are open to criticism, the starting place of his discussion—that much of Mithraism's core symbolism is astrological and related to the precession of equinoxes—can be regarded as firmly established.

Sources:

Cumont, Franz. *The Mysteries of Mithra.* 1903. Reprint. New York: Dover, 1956.
Ulansey, David. *The Origins of the Mithraic Mysteries: Cosmology and Salvation in the Ancient World.* New York: Oxford, 1989.

Mixed Application

Mixed application (**applying**) is when two **planets** are moving into an **aspect** with each other while one is in **retrograde** motion.

Mnemosyne

Mnemosyne, **asteroid** 57 (the 57th asteroid to be discovered), is approximately 116 kilometers in diameter and has an **orbital** period of 5.5 years. It is named after the Greek goddess of memory, who was mother of the Muses. The location of Mnemosyne by sign and **house** indicates something about how one remembers. When involved in inharmonious **aspects**, this celestial body may indicate a poor memory or unpleasant memories.

Sources:

Kowal, Charles T. *Asteroids: Their Nature and Utilization.* Chichester, West Sussex, U.K.: Ellis Horwood Limited, 1988.
Room, Adrian. *Dictionary of Astronomical Names.* London: Routledge, 1988.

Modern Planets

The expression modern planets refers to the **planets** beyond **Saturn** that were not discovered until the development of modern telescopes, namely, **Uranus,**

Neptune, and **Pluto.** Although technically not "planets," some contemporary astrologers classify the **asteroids** and **Chiron** as modern planets because they were not discovered until the development of astronomical telescopes.

Modestia

Modestia, **asteroid** 370 (the 370th asteroid to be discovered), is approximately 44 kilometers in diameter and has an **orbital** period of 3.5 years. Its name is a personified form of the Latin word for modesty. In a **natal chart**, Modestia's location by sign and **house** indicates where one is most likely to be modest or experience modesty. When **afflicted** by inharmonious **aspects**, Modestia may show immodesty or false modesty. If prominent in a chart (e.g., **conjunct** the **Sun** or the **ascendant**), it may show an exceptionally modest person, or someone for whom the seeking of modesty and humility is a dominant life theme.

Sources:

Kowal, Charles T. *Asteroids: Their Nature and Utilization.* Chichester, West Sussex, U.K.: Ellis Horwood Limited, 1988.
Room, Adrian. *Dictionary of Astronomical Names.* London: Routledge, 1988.

Modus Equalis

Modus equalis is the older term for what is now called the **equal house system.**

Moira

Moira, **asteroid** 638 (the 638th asteroid to be discovered), is approximately 41 kilometers in diameter and has an **orbital** period of 4.5 years. Its name is derived from the Greek word for the Fates. In an astrological chart, Moira's location by sign and **house** indicates an area of life that is governed by "fate" or **karma.** When **afflicted** by inharmonious **aspects**, Moira may show "negative karma." When prominent in a chart, it shows an individual whose whole life is "fated."

Sources:

Kowal, Charles T. *Asteroids: Their Nature and Utilization.* Chichester, West Sussex, U.K.: Ellis Horwood Limited, 1988.
Room, Adrian. *Dictionary of Astronomical Names.* London: Routledge, 1988.

Moon

As Earth's **satellite**, the Moon is the only one of the **planetary moons** regarded as having astrological influence. Moon and month are cognate words that can be traced to the same etymological root as the English word measure, the Moon being the heavenly body by which traditional peoples measured time. The Moon, as the second-most prominent body in the terrestrial sky, became associated with many different divinities and thus has a complex mythology. The most prominent deity in ancient Greece was Artemis (later identified with the Roman Diana), goddess of childbirth, wild animals, and hunting. We get the word *lunar* from the Roman goddess Luna, who was also identified with the Moon. The correlation between the length of a menstrual cycle and the length of a lunar month has influenced cultures all over the world to associate the Moon with women and fertility. Mesopotamia, the area of the world in which both Western and **Hindu astrology** has its roots, was an exception to this general rule. The Mesopotamian Moon deity was the male divinity Nanna (also called Suen or Sin). Interestingly, Nanna was the father of the Sun-god and considered to be superior to him.

The Moon completes an **orbit** of Earth every 27.32 days (a **sidereal month**). Because of the constantly changing relationships between the **Sun**, Earth, and the Moon, it takes somewhat longer (29.53 days) for the Moon to go from one new moon to the next new moon (a *synodic month)*. The Moon is said to **rule** the sign **Cancer**, a relationship indicating similarity between the characteristics of the Moon and the traits of Cancer.

Like its mythological namesake, the astrological Moon is associated with women and childbirth. It also represents the principle of creativity, in the sense of giving birth to ideas. With respect to Artemis as a huntress, the Moon and Cancer are not so much associated with the passion of the hunt as they are with nourishment, which is the purpose behind hunting. The Moon's placement in a birth chart can show where and how we nurture, as well as where and how we seek nurturance. Rather than being an outgoing planet like the Sun or **Mars**, the Moon is responsive and adaptable.

While the various planets are connected with a wide range of activities and objects, they also, when found in a **natal chart**, represent different parts of the psyche. The Moon represents the sensitive, emotional side of the self that responds to the world. It also represents the subconscious mind, embodying the unconscious patterns from our past. Thus, its placement in a natal chart by sign and house shows much about such patterns, as well as the area of life where we express them. The **house** position of the Moon shows us an area of life where we can create ("give birth") as well as experience fluctuation.

Jeff Mayo's *The Planets and Human Behavior* provides useful lists of traits and associations for the planets. For the Moon, under the rubric *characteristic* desire trends, Mayo lists: "creativeness, protectiveness, productiveness, adaptation, tenacity, animation, spontaneity" (p. 74). Under the heading *traditional associations* are listed "liquids—especially water and milk, the seas and marine life, rain, humidity, moisture, swamps, floods, rivers, oils, shipping, travel generally but especially voyages, females generally but especially the mother, family and home, menstruation, gestation, maternal instincts, midwives, fertilization fruitfulness, mediumship, nursing, fermentation, vessels in general–as receptacles, brewing and baking, property and place of residence, the land and crops, the general public, public commodities, changes and fluctuations, rhythm" (p. 75).

Sources:

Campion, Nicholas. *The Practical Astrologer.* New York: Harry N. Abrams, 1987.

George, Llewellyn. *The New A to Z Horoscope Maker and Delineator.* Saint Paul, Minn.: Llewellyn Publications, 1910. Rev. and enl. 1987

McEvers, Joan. *Planets: The Astrological Tools.* Saint Paul, Minn.: Llewellyn Publications, 1989.

Mayo, Jeff. *The Planets and Human Behavior.* 1972. Reprint. Reno, Nev.: CRCS Publications, 1985.

Valentine, Christine. *Images of the Psyche: Exploring the Planets through Psychology and Myth.* Shaftesbury, Dorset, U.K.: Element Books, 1991.

Moore, Marcia M.

Marcia M. Moore, astrologer and occultist was born May 22, 1928, in Cambridge, Massachusetts. Her father was Robert L. Moore, the founder of Sheraton Hotels. Her sister was Robin Moore (who used the pen name Robert L. Moore, Jr.), a novelist. She was a graduate of Radcliffe College, where she wrote a B.A. thesis on the subject of astrology. The thesis was later published in book form by the Lucis Trust. Moore became an active astrologer and a well-known figure in the American astrological community.

Moore's second husband, Mark Douglas, collaborated with her on several of her books. She was married on the third occasion to Howard Alltounian, Jr. In her final years she was experimenting with mind-altering drugs, which contributed to her death on January 15, 1979, in Bothwell, Washington.

Selected Publications:

Astrology Today—A Socio-Psychological Survey. New York: Lucas Publishing Co., 1960.

Astrology in Action. By Moore and Mark Douglas. York Harbor, Maine: Arcane Publications, 1970.
Astrology, The Divine Science. 2d ed. rev. York Harbor, Maine: Arcane Publications, 1978.

Sources:

Holden, James H., and Robert A. Hughes. *Astrological Pioneers of America.* Tempe, Ariz.: American Federation of Astrologers, 1988.

Morin, Jean-Baptiste

Jean-Baptiste Morin, a French physician and astrologer, was born in Villefranche, Rhone, on February 23, 1583, and died in Paris on November 6, 1656. Morin studied at Aix and Avignon, where in 1613 he received his medical degree. His initial career was as a physician. In 1630, he was appointed professor of mathematics at the Collège de France. He was also an accomplished astronomer and wrote an important paper on determining **longitude** by making observations of the **Moon** (the method of lunar distances). In the 1620s, Morin began to study astrology and soon became a well-known court astrologer. His reputation was such that he was present at the birth of Louis XIV in 1638. He was astrologer–physician to such notables as the bishop of Boulogne, the duke of Luxembourg, the duke of Effiat, Cardinal Richelieu, and Cardinal Mazarin.

Morin described himself as having a quarrelsome and boastful character, which tended to annoy close associates. Cardinal Richelieu, for example, respected his knowledge but disliked him. Philosopher-mathematician Pierre Gassendi of the Collège Royal issued regular attacks on astrology, and Morin responded with countercriticisms.

Morin worked for the last 30 years of his life on his magnum opus, *Astrologia Gallica,* which was published posthumously, partially with the patronage of Queen Marie of Poland. It departed from the techniques of **Ptolemy** by relying on "analogy," "determinations," and house **rulerships**. This important work was not influential at the time, partially because astrology was in decline in France and also because it was written in Latin. Morin also wrote a commentary on Ptolemy's *Centiloquy.* In 1897, Henri Selva published a translation of Book 21 of *Astrologia Gallica* and Morin's theories were launched. The translation attracted attention in France and later in Germany.

There exists a system of **house** division that bears Morin's name, although his sample charts are cast in the **Regiomontanus system**.

Selected Publications:

Astrologia Gallica. The Hague, 1661.

Remarques Astrologiques sur le Commentaire du Centilogue de Ptolomee mis en lumière par Nicolas de Bourdin, etc. [Astrological Notes on the Commentary on Ptolemy's *Centiloquy* elucidated by Nicolas de Bourdin, etc.] Paris: Pierre Ménard, 1657.

Sources:

Holden, James H., and Robert A. Hughes. *Astrological Pioneers of America.* Tempe, Ariz.: American Federation of Astrologers, 1988.

Morinus (Morinean) System

The Morinus system of **house** division, proposed by the seventeenth-century astrologer Morin de Villefranche, is based on equal divisions of the equator, which are then projected onto the **ecliptic.**

Morrison, R. J.

Richard James Morrison (Zadkiel), an English astrologer, was born in Enfield, London, on June 15, 1795. He enlisted in the navy at age of 11, became a lieutenant in 1815, and retired in 1817, although he later served in the coast guard from 1827 to 1829. In 1828, he rescued four men and a boy from a wrecked vessel and later received a medal for this act of bravery.

Morrison became interested in astrology before he was 30. He was acquainted with the astrologer R. C. Smith, and, inspired by Smith's **almanac,** *The Prophetic Messenger,* Morrison started his own in 1830. *The Herald of Astrology,* which was renamed *Zadkiel's Almanac* in 1836, was quite successful and was published for the next hundred years. Morrison also had interests in spiritualism, phrenology, and crystal gazing.

In the 1861 issue of his almanac, Morrison predicted an "evil year" for Queen Victoria's husband. As it turned out, Prince Albert died suddenly and unexpectedly of typhoid fever in December 1861. As often happens in the wake of an accurate astrological prediction, some individuals were outraged at the triumph of "medieval superstition." In this case, Edward Belcher, a writer for the London *Daily Telegraph,* attacked Morrison, who responded by suing for libel. The jury found in favor of Morrison, but he was awarded only 20 shillings. He was rewarded, however, by the substantial increase in sales of his almanac that the publicity brought him. Beyond his almanac, Morrison is best known for the abridged edition of **Lilly's** *Christian Astrology,* which he published. Morrison died on February 8, 1874.

Holden, James H., and Robert A. Hughes. *Astrological Pioneers of America.* Tempe, Ariz.: American Federation of Astrologers, 1988.

Morrison, R. J. *An Introduction to Astrology by William Lilly, being the whole of that celebrated Author's Rules for the Practice of Horary Astrology, divested of the Superstitions of the 17th Century; to which are added numerous Emendations.*... [An abridgment of Parts 1 & 2 of William Lilly's *Christian Astrology* with various alterations and additions by Morrison.] 2d ed. Hollywood, Calif.: Newcastle Publishing Co., 1972. (Originally published 1835.)

Movable Signs

Movable signs is an alternative expression for the **cardinal signs**, which are **Aries, Cancer, Libra**, and **Capricorn**. Movable signs should not be confused with **mutable signs**, which sound alike but refer to four entirely different signs.

Muise, Roxana

Roxana Muise, a contemporary, second-generation astrologer, was born October 1, 1935, in Chicago. She graduated from St. Catherine's Academy in Lomita, California, and was ordained on February 14, 1974, in the Abundant Life Church of Jesus Christ, a spiritualist, metaphysical church based in Mira Loma, California She graduated summa cum laude from California State University, Dominguez Hills, in 1981 with a degree in health science.

Muise began astrological studies in 1968 with her mother, Patricia Crossley, and graduated from the Scorpio School of Astrology in 1970. Her teachers were **Zipporah Dobyns**, Gina Cegglio, **Dane Rudhyar**, Virginia Wilson Fabre, Constance G. Mayer, Robert Jansky, Sabrinah Millstein, Al H. Morrison, James Eshelman, **Lois Rodden**, Edwin Steinbrecher, Buz Meyers, Tony Joseph, Charles Emerson, **Robert Hand**, Diana Stone, Arlene Kramer, and **Manly Palmer Hall**.

Muise cofounded South Western Astrology Conference (SWAC) and was its director from 1974 to 1985. She is a past president of International Society for Astrological Research (ISAR) and has served as its membership director. She has been a member of the board of directors of the United Astrology Congress (UAC) since its beginning in 1986. She has also served as secretary of Syn-Siq, the Synastry Special Interest Group of the National Council for Geocosmic Research (NCGR), as vice-president of the Washington State Astrological Association (WSAA), and on the board of directors of Kepler College of Astrological Arts and Sciences in Seattle, Washington.

Muise is the author of *A-Year-At-Glance: The 45 Degree Graphic Ephemeris for 101 Years,* which presents her method of creating an overlay of one's natal **planets** on a yearly graph that shows all hard **transiting aspects** for an entire year and provides a worksheet that instantly shows dynamic aspects between charts. She is also the author of *The Fourth Sign,* which is based on her research of historical references that give the cat, instead of the crab, as a symbol for the sign Cancer. She lectured in many cities in the United States and in Singapore. She married in 1957 and lives with her husband, Ralph Muise, in Bellevue, Washington. They have two sons. Muise teaches astrology and metaphysics and has a private counseling practice. She is working on a book on soul connections.

Selected Publications:

A-Year-At-Glance: The 45 Degree Graphic Ephemeris for 101 Years. South Western Astrology Conference Press, 1986; distributed by ACS, San Diego.
The Fourth Sign. South Western Astology Conference Press, 1990.

Mundane Aspect

A mundane aspect is an **aspect** (an astrological **angle**) between two points in space—for example, between two **planets**—that is measured along the **celestial equator.** This distinguishes mundane aspects from the aspects relied upon by most astrologers, who usually consider only angles that are measured along the **ecliptic** (the circle of the **zodiac**). Mundane aspects are rarely used by contemporary astrologers.

Mundane Astrology

Traditionally, mundane (from Latin *mundus,* world) astrology was a comprehensive category encompassing everything not covered by **genethliacal astrology** and **horary astrology.** Thus, the astrology of the weather, earthquakes, business, agriculture, and so forth all fell within the domain of mundane astrology. In contemporary practice, the term *mundane astrology* is used in a more restricted manner to refer to what is sometimes called political astrology—the astrology of nations and political events.

In mundane astrology, charts are drawn for nations, for events (such as wars), for national leaders, for political parties, etc. The **horoscopes** of nations are read much as one would read the horoscopes of individuals. For example, the second **house** of a nation indicates national resources, banks, general prosperity, and so forth, much as the second house in an individual natal chart represents personal possessions and finances. Similarly, the various **planets** are taken to represent groups and functions traditionally associated with each celestial body. Thus, **Mercury** would indicate academics and the press, **Mars** military leaders and wars, **Jupiter** clergy and the courts, and so forth.

As the astrology of the state, mundane astrology is one of the oldest, if not *the* oldest, form of astrology. In ancient **Mesopotamia**, the birth place of the science of the stars, astrologers were not independent counselors who interpreted individual natal charts. They were, rather, government officials who studied the heavens for the king, predicting plagues, wars, and future economic conditions. It was only later, after the Greeks adopted and developed celestial science, that astrology changed its focus from the nation to the individual.

As one of the oldest branches of astrology, mundane astrology has developed many different techniques for studying the fate of nations and broader social trends. The earliest state astrologers paid particular attention to unusual celestial events, such as **eclipses** and **comets**. Later, mundane astrologers watched these phenomena, as well as planetary positions at the time of

◄

Major planetary configurations—particularly major conjunctions—are regarded as especially significant in mundane astrology. This illustration accompanied a description of the mass conjunction of planets that occurred in Cancer in 1504 · Bettmann Archive

ingresses, equinoxes, **lunations**, and major **conjunctions** (separate charts are cast for these events). The emphasis on these latter techniques represents a marked departure from **natal astrology**.

Sources:

Baigent, Michael, Nicholas Campion, and Charles Harvey. *Mundane Astrology*. 2d ed. London: Aquarian Press, 1992.

Kitson, Annabella, ed. *History and Astrology: Clio and Urania Confer*. London: Mandala, 1989.

McEvers, Joan. *The Astrology of the Macrocosm: New Directions in Mundane Astrology*. Saint Paul, Minn.: Llewellyn Publications, 1990.

Mutable Signs

The 12 signs of the **zodiac** are subdivided according to three **qualities**: cardinal, mutable, and fixed. The four mutable signs (the *mutable quadruplicity*

▶
Mutable signs.

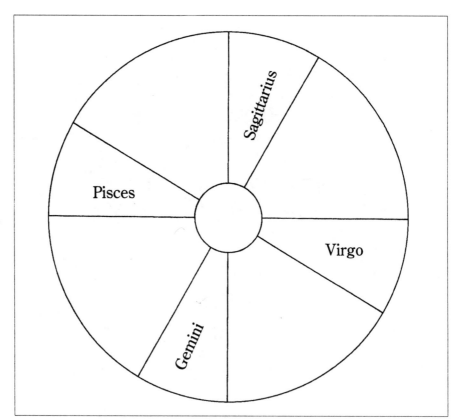

or *mutable cross*) are **Gemini**, **Virgo**, **Sagittarius**, and **Pisces**. The exit of the **Sun** from each of these four signs indicates the end of a new season: Gemini, the end of spring; Virgo, the end of summer; Sagittarius, the end of fall; and Pisces, the end of winter. The identifying trait of the mutable signs (sometimes referred to as common signs) is adaptability or flexibility. Mutable signs tend to react to new situations by adapting to them. Negatively, mutable signs can be too malleable or changeable. (*See* illustration, p. 382.)

Mute Signs

The mute signs are the **water signs**, **Scorpio**, **Cancer**, and **Pisces**. It is said that when **Mercury** is **afflicted** in one of these signs, it results in quietness, difficulty in speaking, or even a speech impediment. The designation mute probably was given because these three creatures are "mute."

Mutual Application

A mutual application (**applying**) occurs when two **planets** are moving toward each other—one in **direct** motion and the other in **retrograde** motion—to form an **aspect**.

Mutual Reception

Two **planets** are in mutual reception when they are in each other's signs. If in a given **horoscope**, for example **Mercury** is in **Aries** (which is **ruled** by **Mars**) and Mars is in **Gemini** (which is ruled by Mercury), then Mercury and Mars are in mutual reception. **Astrologers** interpret mutual reception as being equivalent to a **conjunction** between the two planets involved.

Mystic Rectangle

Mystic rectangle is a modern term for a planetary **configuration** composed of two **trines** that are connected by two **sextiles.** To qualify as a mystic rectangle, the pairs of **planets** on opposite sides of the **horoscope** from each other must form **oppositions** (see illustration). Despite the name, individuals with mystic rectangles in their **natal charts** need not be mystically inclined. The name seems to have originated with Madam Blavatsky, one of the founders of the Theosophical Society, who had this configuration in her chart.

Mythology and Astrology

In everyday language, the term myth often connotes false or untrue. In academic circles, however, myths are regarded as narratives that express a traditional culture's understanding about the way the world works, normative values, and the meaning of human life. The recent popularity of Joseph Campbell's work has helped to disseminate this latter point of view to the larger society. The new evaluation of myths as valuable—and even, according to some thinkers, necessary—for human life flows ultimately out of the psychologization of mythology that was carried out by **Carl Jung** and his followers at the turn of the century.

Much of traditional Jungian analysis focuses on the interpretation of dreams. Jung found that the dreams of his clients frequently contained images

Mystic rectangle.

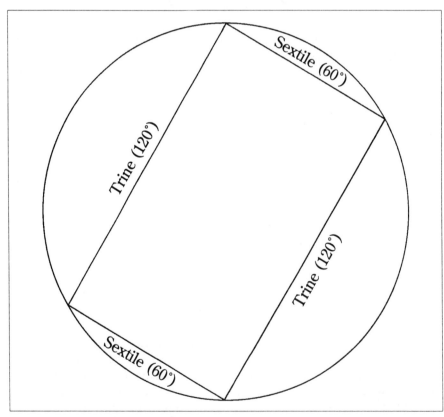

with which they were completely unfamiliar but which seemed to reflect symbols that could be found somewhere in the mythological systems of world culture. The notion of the **collective unconscious** was used to explain this phenomenon. Jung further found that he could often interpret his patients' dreams if he studied and reflected upon the particular myth or symbol to which the dream image seemed to allude. In certain cases, deeper and more complete significance for the dream image could be uncovered by locating similar images in more than one cultural system. Researching such images in the quest for deeper meanings is referred to as amplification.

The discovery of connections between psychological and mythological patterns was the starting point for the modern world's reevaluation of the significance of myths. It is easy to see how **astrology** could be incorporated into this new understanding of the relationship between psychology and mythology: On the one hand, astrology was already a psychological system that attributed personality traits to celestial patterns; on the other hand, the signs of the **zodiac** were traditionally associated with classical myths and symbols, and the **planets** were named after the gods and goddesses of the ancient Mediterranean world. It should thus come as no surprise that modern astrology has been reshaped by the psychological mythology/mythological psychology (psychology utilizing myth as a therapeutic tool) of the twentieth century.

Mythologically informed astrologers have often utilized amplification to uncover new or obscure meanings of the traditional signs and planets. The technique of amplification has really seen its most extensive application, however, in the field of newly discovered—or, as in the case of **asteroids**, newly utilized—celestial bodies. For example, within recent years astrologers have begun to explore the influence of the asteroid **Eros**. Using the accepted astrological principle that the influence of a celestial body is related to its name, one would begin by assuming that Eros—from whose name we derive the English word erotic—is somehow related to romantic love or sexual passion. In addition to placing this tiny planetoid in various people's charts and attempting to perceive correlations between its placement and certain personality tendencies, one could also further amplify the possible meanings of Eros by carefully studying as many myths as possible in which Eros was a figure, from the older Greek myths to the discussion of Eros in Plato's *Symposium*. One could also try to explore the symbolism of parallel mythological figures in other cultures, for example, Hindu myths about the god Kama.

However, contemporary astrologers seeking deeper meanings—or, even, more meanings—for traditional or nontraditional celestial bodies all too often begin and end their quests within classical, Mediterranean mythology (or, frequently, within only Greek mythology). The problem with this way of proceeding is that, to cast the issue in Jungian terms, *archetypes* (the univeral patterns of myths and symbols) express themselves somewhat differently in different cultures. Consequently, some aspect of a particular archetype might be expressed inadequately or not at all in one culture's mythology but be fully articulated in another. It would be reasonable to assert that the amplification of meaning resulting from careful reflection on comparable mythological figures in other cultures would uncover new astrological meanings in the traditional elements of astrological science.

Sources:

Bach, Eleanor. *Astrology from A to Z.* New York: Philosophical Library, 1990.

Burt, Kathleen. *Archetypes of the Zodiac.* Saint Paul, Minn.: Llewellyn Publications, 1990.

Hamaker-Zondag, Karen. *Psychological Astrology: A Synthesis of Jungian Psychology and Astrology.* York Beach, Maine: Samuel Weiser, 1990.

Mayo, Jeff. *The Planets and Human Behavior.* 1972. Reprint. Reno, Nev.: CRCS Publications, 1985.

N

Nadir

The nadir is the point in the heavens directly opposite the **zenith,** which means that it is the point in the heavens on the other side of Earth directly underneath one's feet. It should be carefully distinguished from the **imum coeli,** which is the point directly opposite the **midheaven.**

Natal Astrology

Natal astrology is the branch of astrology that deals with the astrological forces that influence individuals at the moment of birth. It is the more contemporary term for what traditional astrologers called **genethliacal astrology.** Natal astrology is to be distinguished from such other branches of astrology as **mundane astrology,** which interprets the significance of celestial events for cultural trends and national world affairs.

Natal Chart (Birth Chart; Nativity)

When most people talk about their "astrological chart," they are usually referring to their natal (from Latin *natus,* born) chart. A natal or birth chart is a map of the **solar system,** with respect to **Earth** (in traditional, **geocentric astrology**) at the moment an individual was born. Because the **planets,** signs, and so forth are usually represented by symbols (referred to by astrologers as **glyphs**) rather than by words, a natal chart appears confusing to anyone unfamiliar with astrological codes. To the experienced astrologer, however, a natal chart reveals a wealth of information about the person for whom it was constructed.

The expression natal chart is used exclusively to refer to the birth chart of an individual. It is thus distinguished from such terms as **horoscope** and **radix,** which can refer to the chart of an event or to other nonpersonal phenomena. The natal chart is also distinguished from such secondary charts as **progressed** charts.

Nations, Astrology of

See: Mundane Astrology

Native

A native is a person born in a particular place. In astrology, this term refers to the person for whom a **natal chart** was cast. In the latter sense, it is a useful, concise term that, in any extended discussion, is preferable to "person for whom this chart was cast" or some such other unwieldy expression. The term native can also refer to someone born under a particular sign, as when one says that she or he is a native of **Cancer**.

Nativity

Nativity is another term for **natal chart,** which is a **horoscope** set up for time, date, and place of birth. Other kinds of horoscopes include **progressed** charts and **electional** charts.

Natural Astrology

Natural astrology is the branch of astrology dealing with the motions of the heavenly bodies and with the effects of the **planets** on such natural phenomena as the weather. The former is now called **astronomy**, the latter **meterological astrology** or astrometeorology.

Natural House (Natural Chart; Natural Ruler)

The signs of the **zodiac** refer to a person's nature, and astrological **houses** refer to a person's environment, and there is a natural association between each of the 12 signs and each of the 12 houses (e.g., **Aries** is associated with the first house, **Taurus** with the second house, **Gemini,** with the third house, and so forth.). Thus, for example, the fourth sign of the zodiac, **Cancer**, is associated with the home, while the fourth astrological house is also identified with the home and with property. To take another example, the third sign, Gemini, is a sign of communication, and the third house is associated with, among other things, communication. Such correspondences hold between all the signs and houses.

This correspondence is what is referred to, for example, when it is said that a person with Aries on the **ascendant** (with the first sign on the beginning or **cusp** of the first house), and with each succeeding sign on the cusp of each succeeding house, has a natural chart: The signs and houses with "natural" links are found together in the chart. Similarly, when a planet is located in the house associated with the sign it **rules**, it is said to be in its natural house—a placement in which the planet is said to be in **accidental dignity**. For example, when **Jupiter** is found in the ninth house, it is in its natural house (and is accidentally dignified), because Jupiter rules the ninth sign, **Sagittarius**. To complete this series of related terms, the planets are sometimes said to be the natural rulers of the houses associated with the signs they rule.

Sources:

Brau, Jean-Louis, Helen Weaver, and Allan Edmands. *Larousse Encyclopedia of Astrology*. New York: New American Library, 1980.
Fleming-Mitchell, Leslie. *Running Press Glossary of Astrology Terms*. Philadelphia: Running Press, 1977.

Nelson, John

John Nelson was an American radio engineer who specialized in the analysis of shortwave radio propagation. In the fifties and sixties, he was an employee of RCA Communications and worked on the problem of how to predict fluctuations in Earth's magnetic field that disrupted radio communication. It was well known that these fluctuations were affected by, among other things, sunspot activity. Using this clue as a starting point, Nelson began investigating correlations between the **heliocentric configurations** of the **planets** and radio wave disturbances. His findings were so remarkable that he was eventually able to predict such disturbances with a better than 93% accuracy.

His discoveries verified certain elements of traditional astrology to a remarkable extent. For instance, he found that when two or more planets either lined up with the **Sun** (thus forming an **opposition aspect** of 180°) or formed a 90° angle (a **square** aspect) with the Sun, there would be a disturbance. He also found, again consistent with the principles of traditional astrology, that if yet another planet formed an exact **trine** (120° angle) to either of these configurations, the disturbance rapidly abated. Because Nelson could further predict the areas of the world where disturbances would be most severely felt, RCA could reroute transmissions without loss of service.

The astronomical and academic communities greeted his discoveries with a thundering silence. But Richard Head of NASA's Electronics Research Center investigated Nelson's studies and found them to be accurate. NASA was interested in the implications of his research for predicting sunspot activity, so that they would be able to avoid the risk of exposing astronauts to excessive solar radiation. NASA thus came to adopt Nelson's methods, under the name gravitational vectoring.

The Astrology Encyclopedia

Sources:

Brau, Jean-Louis, Helen Weaver, and Allan Edmands. *Larousse Encyclopedia of Astrology.* New York: New American Library, 1980.
Ostrander, Sheila, and Lynn Schroeder. *Astrological Birth Control.* Englewood Cliffs, N.J.: Prentice-Hall, 1972.

Nemesis

Nemesis, **asteroid** 128 (the 128th asteroid to be discovered), is approximately 116 kilometers in diameter and has an **orbital** period of 4.6 years. Nemesis was the ancient goddess of vengeance. According to Lang-Wescott, the position of Nemesis indicates one's Achilles' heel. She also views this asteroid as indicating one's tendency to attribute fault or blame. Nemesis's key phrase is *source of blame.*

Sources:

Lang-Wescott, Martha. *Asteroids-Mechanics: Ephemerides II.* Conway, Mass.: Treehouse Mountain, 1990.
———. *Mechanics of the Future: Asteroids.* Rev. ed. Conway, Mass.: Treehouse Mountain, 1991.

Neptune

Neptune, named after the Roman god of the sea (the Roman equivalent of the Greek Poseidon), is the **planet** that **orbits** between **Uranus** and **Pluto** (although Pluto's eliptical orbit occasionally brings it inside Neptune's orbit). Poseidon was also the god of fresh water, especially as it sprang out of the ground at the sources of streams and rivers. This connects him with the Mesopotamian divinity Enki, who was, as god of subterranean fresh waters, one of the principal deities of ancient Mesopotamia. Enki was especially associated with wisdom and magical incantations, as well as the arts and crafts of civilization. In some of his images, two streams of water in which fish swim flow from his upper arms.

Neptune completes an orbit of the **Sun** every 164.79 years, meaning that it stays almost 14 years in each sign of the **zodiac.** Neptune's sign influence is thus more generational than individual. Neptune is said to **rule** the sign **Pisces,** a relationship indicating a similarity between the characteristics of Neptune and the traits of Pisces.

The mythology of Neptune seems less connected with the astrological characteristics of the planet Neptune than is the case for most other planetary myths. The clearest link is through the symbology of water, the element ruled by Poseidon and associated with sensitivity. Neptune represents the subtle, intangible side of human existence and tends to embody artistic sensitivity, especially as expressed through music. Neptune is also mysticism and mystical love. The negative expressions of this planet are escapism (including alcohol and drug addiction), deception (including self-deception), confusion, and vagueness.

While the various planets are connected with a wide range of activities and objects, they also, when found in a **natal chart**, represent different parts of the psyche. Neptune represents the sensitive imagination, as well as the idealistic dreamer and mystic in all of us. Thus, its placement in a natal chart will show much about how and where a person expresses imagination. The position of Neptune also indicates the area of life where it is easiest for us to delude ourselves.

Jeff Mayo's *The Planets and Human Behavior* provides useful lists of traits and associations for the planets. For Venus, under the rubric *characteristic desire trends,* Mayo lists "creativeness, sensitivity, imagination, aesthetic appreciation, humanitarianism, subtlety, idealism, romance, tenderness, religious devotion or a "universal love" embraced by mysticism, perfectionism" (p. 105). Under the heading *traditional associations* are listed "aetheticism, inspiration, mysticism, spiritualism, trance conditions, visions, secret societies, the hypnotist and the hypnotized, the sea and marine life generally, submarines, fishing, divers, ether, intoxicating beverages, drugs, anaesthetics, gases, chaos, disorganization, confusion, misrepresentation, disappearances, mysteries, drowning, hospitals and charitable institutions, glamor, idealism, self-deception, deceit, disguises, seduction, day-dreaming, dreams, coma, hallucinations, vagueness, fog and cloud, asylums, prisons, obsession, enchantment, scandal, plots, religious devotion and conversion, the highest form of "spiritual" experience" (p. 106).

Sources:

Campion, Nicholas. *The Practical Astrologer.* New York: Harry N. Abrams, 1987.
George, Llewellyn. *The New A to Z Horoscope Maker and Delineator.* Saint Paul, Minn.: Llewellyn Publications, 1910. Rev. and enl. 1987.
McEvers, Joan. *Planets: The Astrological Tools.* Saint Paul, Minn.: Llewellyn Publications, 1989.
Mayo, Jeff. *The Planets and Human Behavior.* 1972. Reprint. Reno, Nev.: CRCS Publications, 1985.
Valentine, Christine. *Images of the Psyche: Exploring the Planets through Psychology and Myth.* Shaftesbury, Dorset, U.K.: Element Books, 1991.

Nerthus

Nerthus, **asteroid** 601 (the 601st asteroid to be discovered), is approximately 43 kilometers in diameter and has an **orbital** period of 5.5 years. It is named after a Scandinavian goddess of fertility. When prominent in a **natal chart**, Nerthus may show an exceptionally productive, "fertile" individual. By sign and **house**, it may show an area of great potential that need only be "cultivated" a little to produce results.

Sources:

Kowal, Charles T. *Asteroids: Their Nature and Utilization.* Chichester, West Sussex, U.K.: Ellis Horwood Limited, 1988.
Room, Adrian. *Dictionary of Atronomical Names.* London: Routledge, 1988.

New Planets

New planets are **Uranus, Neptune,** and **Pluto**, which were not part of traditional astrology.

Newspaper Astrology

The simplified astrology found in newspapers, women's magazines, and other popular publications emphasizes **sun signs** as well as a rudimentary form of solar astrology. While there are many different influences in every individual's **natal chart,** the single most important astrological influence on personality is usually the sign of the **zodiac** the **Sun** was in at birth. Sun sign astrology has the advantage of simplicity—a person's birthday is all that must be known to figure out her or his sign—but this simplicity is purchased at the price of ignoring all other astrological influences, and hence is rarely 100% accurate.

Solar astrology is a system that is often used when an individual's birth time cannot be determined. Rather than beginning the chart's **houses** from the **ascendant** (which cannot be calculated when the birth time is unavailable), a **solar chart** uses the position of the Sun on the day of birth as the place to begin the first house and then calculates succeeding houses in equal arcs of 30°. Newspaper astrology further simplifies this system by using the 30° arc of the sun sign as the first house, the next sign in order of the zodiac as the second house, and so forth. In other words, for a **Scorpio** (i.e., a Scorpio sun sign), all 30° of the sign is regarded as the first house, all 30° of **Sagittarius** (the next sign of the Zodiac after Scorpio) as the second house, all 30° of **Capricorn** as the third house, etc.

These highly simplified houses are used to determine the influences of the **transiting planets** that are generic to each sun sign. As a concrete example, take the planet **Jupiter,** which embodies a principle that expresses itself variously as multiplicity, expansion, joviality, and good luck. When transiting Jupiter is in Capricorn, it is in the solar third house of all Scorpios. The third house represents travel, relatives, communication, and related matters, so the presence of transiting Jupiter in this area indicates a period of time during which one experiences more trips, as well as more communications, than usual. Relations with relatives also tend to improve. Capricorn is the solar *second* house for all Sagittarians. The second house has to do with money and possessions, and the presence of transiting Jupiter here usually corresponds with a period of comparative financial abundance. Capricorn is the solar *first* house for all

Capricorns. The first house is the basic self and the physical body, and transiting Jupiter here tends to make one happier and also corresponds with a period during which Capricorns put on weight. These basic principles can be extended to every sign of the zodiac, which is precisely what newspaper astrologers do.

The exact origin of newspaper astrology is difficult to determine, though it probably originated in popular **almanacs**. Astrology columns have been abundant in the English-speaking world since at least the early twentieth century. Because newspaper astrology ignores all other astrological influences and is thus a hit-or-miss system that works only occasionally, professional astrologers tend to dislike it inasmuch as its inaccuracy can lead nonastrologers to reject astrology as untrue.

Sources:

Bach, Eleanor. *Astrology from A to Z: An Illustrated Source Book.* New York: Philosophical Library, 1990.

Gettings, Fred. *Dictionary of Astrology.* London: Routledge & Kegan Paul, 1985.

Newton, Sir Isaac

Sir Isaac Newton, the scientist famous for formulating the law of universal gravitation, was born January 5, 1642, in Woolsthorpe, Lincolnshire, England, and died on March 31, 1727, in Kensington, England. He was highly regarded in his time, much as Albert Einstein later was. Newton's study of Kepler's third law of motion led him to theorize that the gravitational attraction between Earth and the **Moon**–and, by extension, the gravitational attraction between all bodies— is inversely proportional to the square of the distance between them. This law of universal gravitation was put forth in his *Principia Mathematica* (1687). Newton is credited with many other achievements, such as the invention of calculus.

As a young man studying mathematics, Newton also studied astrology. An often-repeated though probably apocryphal tale is that the astronomer Halley kidded Newton about his interest in astrology. Newton, it is said, defended himself by asserting, "I have studied the subject, Mr. Halley, and you have not." In any event, Newton never recanted his belief in astrology, nor did he ever imply that the new science he and his contemporaries were creating invalidated astrology in any way.

Night Horoscope

A night horoscope is a **horoscope** in which the **Sun** is below the horizon.

Nike

Nike, **asteroid** 307 (the 307th asteroid to be discovered), is approximately 58 kilometers in diameter and has an **orbital** period of 5 years. It is was named after the Greek goddess of victory. Nike indicates a fortunate outcome to activities undertaken in matters associated with its sign and **house** position.

Sources:

Kowal, Charles T. *Asteroids: Their Nature and Utilization.* Chichester, West Sussex, U.K.: Ellis Horwood Limited, 1988.

Room, Adrian. *Dictionary of Astronomical Names.* London: Routledge, 1988.

Niobe

Niobe, **asteroid** 71 (the 71st asteroid to be discovered), is approximately 106 kilometers in diameter and has an **orbital** period of 4.6 years. There were two mythological Niobes. One was the first mortal woman loved by Zeus. The other was a woman who was inordinately proud of her many children and ridiculed the goddess Leto about her children. In revenge, Leto had all of Niobe's children slain, upon which witnessing, Niobe turned to stone. According to Lang-Wescott, the asteroid Niobe indicates inordinate pride in children, creativity, fertility, or virility, which leads to humbling experiences or sorrow. Niobe's key words are *humility* and *fertility*.

Sources:

Lang-Wescott, Martha. *Asteroids-Mechanics: Ephemerides II.* Conway, Mass.: Treehouse Mountain, 1990.

———. *Mechanics of the Future: Asteroids.* Rev. ed. Conway, Mass.: Treehouse Mountain, 1991.

Nocturnal

Nocturnal means of or belonging to the night. In classical astrology, particular **planets** were classified as nocturnal or **diurnal**, no matter where they were in a **horoscope**. In contemporary astrology, planets are nocturnal if they are located below the **horizon** (in **houses** one through six). Many astrologers believe that planets above the horizon line show their influence more in the public sphere whereas planets below the horizon are more private, but this distinction clearly breaks down when considering planets in such locations as the twelfth house (a largely private house situated above the horizon). The expression nocturnal arc refers to the distance, expressed in degrees (°) and minutes (′) of a circle, that a planet traverses between its setting in the west and its rising in the east. Classical astrology also classified signs as diurnal (the **masculine signs**) and nocturnal (the **feminine signs**). Contemporary astrologers no longer use the expression nocturnal sign.

Sources:

Bach, Eleanor. *Astrology from A to Z: An Illustrated Source Book.* New York: Philosophical Library, 1990.
Brau, Jean-Louis, Helen Weaver, and Allan Edmands. *Larousse Encyclopedia of Astrology.* New York: New American Library, 1980.

Nodes of the Planets

Take the **orbit** of Earth around the **Sun**, imagine it as a flat plane, and project it outward against the backdrop of the **stars**. This projection is the **ecliptic.** Although all the principal **planets** in the **solar system** orbit the Sun in *approximately* the same plane, none of their orbital paths lies in *exactly* the same plane. The geocentric (earth-centered) nodes are the points at which the planets cross the ecliptic. The point at which a planet moves northward—with respect to our terrestrial perspective—as it crosses the ecliptic is its north node; correspondingly, the point at which it moves southward is the south node. Traditionally, the only nodes regarded as important were the **lunar nodes** because these were the points where **eclipses** occurred.

In **heliocentric** (Sun-centered) **astrology,** the nodes are located where the orbits of any two planets cross. While only the lunar nodes are significant in traditional, **geocentric astrology**, the planetary nodes are major points of reference in heliocentric systems. Some astrologers have also tried to develop interpretations of the geocentric planetary nodes, but these have not caught on, partly because the basic astrological tool required to place these points in a chart—an adequate **ephemeris** (table of positions)—is not generally available. Even computer programs, which could include such information quite easily, lack ephemerides for the nodes. Until such time as these become available, the planetary nodes will remain an esoteric research topic for geocentric astrologers.

Sources:

Fitzwalter, Bernard, and Raymond Henry. *Dark Stars: Invisible Focal Points in Astrology.* Wellingborough, Northamptonshire, U.K.: Aquarian Press, 1988.
Gettings, Fred. *Dictionary of Astrology.* London: Routledge & Kegan Paul, 1985.

Nonplanets

Nonplanets are everything placed in a **horoscope** that is not the **Sun, Moon,** or one of the eight **planets** (e.g., the **part of Fortune**, the **lunar nodes**, etc.).

Northern Signs

The northern signs are the zodiacal signs from **Aries** to **Virgo**.

Nostradamus

Nostradamus (Latin name of Michel de Nostredame), the famous doctor and astrologer, was born on December 14, 1503 in St. Remy, France. He prophesied the manner of death of Henry II, was a favorite of Catherine de Médici, and served as physician to Charles IX. His fame derives from the *Centuries,* a book of prophecies set to rhyme that was published in 1555. This book has often been reprinted, and is still being reprinted today. The fame of Nostradamus is such that many people have at least heard of "the prophecies of Nostradamus." He died on July 12, 1566, in Salon, France.

Novile

A novile (also called a nonagon or a nonagen) is a minor **aspect** of 40°, created by subdividing a circle (360°) into nine equal parts. According to Emma Belle Donath, noviles refer to the activity of "brooding," both physical and mental. Noviles are given an **orb of influence** of 1° to 2°.

Sources:

Donath, Emma Belle. *Minor Aspects Between Natal Planets.* Tempe, Ariz.: AFA, 1981.

Numerology and Astrology

Like astrology, numerology interprets character and predicts future conditions. Following the Cabbala (also spelled Kabalah, Kabbala, Qabbalah, and other variations), which is a system of Jewish mysticism popular in occult circles, the letters of the alphabet are assigned numerical values. When the letters of a person's name are added together, the resulting number indicates her or his basic character—the numerological equivalent of an astrological **sun sign**. The numbers making up one's birth date are also added together, providing a second number, which is interpreted in like manner.

Although modern numerology has been mediated to the contemporary world through the cabbalistic tradition, it is rooted in the number mysticism of **Pythagoras** (ca. 580–500 B.C.), the ancient Greek philosopher and mathematician. The gender of the signs originated with the Pythagorean notion that odd numbers were male and even numbers female. This caused the first (**Aries**), third (**Gemini**), fifth (**Leo**), seventh (**Libra**), ninth (**Sagittarius**), and eleventh (**Aquarius**) signs in the **zodiac** to be classified as **masculine**, and the signs that came second (**Taurus**), fourth (**Cancer**), sixth (**Virgo**), eighth (**Scorpio**), tenth (**Capricorn**), and twelfth (**Pisces**) as **feminine**.

In numerology, the **planets**, including the **luminaries** (the **Sun** and the **Moon**) are used to represent the principles of the different numbers. Different systems of numerology utilize different correlations. In the cabbalistic system, the associations were traditionally as follows: the Sun, 1 or 4; the Moon, 2 or 7; **Jupiter**, 3; **Mercury**, 5; **Venus**, 6; **Saturn**, 8; and **Mars**, 9. When the "new" planets were discovered, Cheiro (Count Louis Hamon) popularized a modified version of this system that assigned the extra numbers associated with the luminaries to **Uranus** (4) and **Neptune** (7).

Sources:

Cheiro Hamon, Count Louis. "Astrology and Numbers." In *The Best of the Illustrated National Astrological Journal.* (pp. 18, 93). N.p.:Richard Wagner, 1978.

Gettings, Fred. *Dictionary of Astrology.* London: Routledge & Kegan Paul, 1985.

Westcott, W. Wynn. *The Occult Power of Numbers.* North Hollywood, Calif.: Newcastle, 1984. (Originally published 1890.)

Nymphe

Nymphe, **asteroid** 875 (the 875th asteroid to be discovered), is approximately 13 kilometers in diameter and has an **orbital** period of 4.1 years. It is named after the mythological spirits of nature, the nymphs. Nymphe represents an exuberance for the natural world. If prominent in a **natal chart** (e.g., **conjunct** the **Sun** or the **ascendant**), it may show a person somehow deeply involved with nature.

Sources:

Kowal, Charles T. *Asteroids: Their Nature and Utilization.* Chichester, West Sussex, U.K.: Ellis Horwood Limited, 1988.

Room, Adrian. *Dictionary of Astronomical Names.* London: Routledge, 1988.

O

Occultation

An occultation (from Latin *occultus,* to hide) is an **eclipse** of a **star** or **planet** by another heavenly body, particularly by the **Moon**. Despite its seemingly "exotic" connotation, it is a commonly used term in **astronomy** as well as in astrology. The astrological importance, if any, of occultations has been hotly debated. Part of what is at issue in this debate is competing theories of celestial influence. If, as one school of thought asserts, astrology works via the mechanism of acausal **synchronicity**, then occultations should have no influence beyond what one would expect from a simple **conjunction**. If, however, the celestial bodies influence events on Earth through forces analogous to gravity or electromagnetism, then an occultation should have a measurable effect on the star or planet that has been "occulted," especially when it is being eclipsed by a large body like the **Sun**. Certain experiments, such as those in which the **Kolisko effect** have been observed, seem to corroborate the latter view.

Sources:

Jansky, Robert Carl. *Interpreting the Eclipses.* San Diego, Calif.: Astro Computing Services, 1979.
Robinson, J. Hedley, and James Muirden. *Astronomy Data Book.* 2d ed. New York: John Wiley & Sons, 1979.

Occultism and Astrology

In the same way that the media seized upon the expression New Age in the late 1980s and transformed it into a term of derision, an earlier wave of media interest in the early 1970s seized upon the word occult and succeeded in connecting it with such negative phenomena as black magic. Ever since the media sensationalized the "occult explosion" of the 1970s, the word occult has come to be associated with images of robed figures conducting arcane rituals for less than socially desirable purposes.

Occult comes from a root word meaning hidden, and it was originally interpreted as denoting a body of esoteric beliefs and practices that were in some sense "hidden" from the average person on the street (e.g., practices and knowledge that remain inaccessible until after an initiation). Alternately, it was sometimes said that practices were occult if they dealt with forces that operated by means that were hidden from ordinary perception (e.g., **magic, tarot** cards, astrology, etc.). Modern astrology is not occult in the sense of secret initiations, but it is occult in the sense that it deals with "hidden" forces.

In earlier times, when there was a widespread knowledge of the science of the **stars** beyond **sun signs**, astrology was a universal symbolic code that contained widely recognized archetypes of general principles, types of humanity, and aspects of the personality. Given the completeness of this code, it was natural that astrological language and symbols would be adopted by the other occult sciences, such as tarot and **palmistry**. In palmistry, for example, the fingers were named after the **planets—Mercury** finger, **Saturn** finger, **Jupiter** finger, etc.

Sources:

Cavendish, Richard. *The Black Arts.* New York: Capricorn Books, 1967.
Lewis, James R., and J. Gordon Melton. "The New Age." *Syzygy: Journal of Alternative Religion and Culture,* vol. 1, no. 3 (1992): 247–258.

Occursions

Celestial events, from **conjunctions** to **ingresses**, are referred to as occursions.

Odysseus

Odysseus, **asteroid** 1,143 (the 1,143d asteroid to be discovered), is approximately 174 kilometers in diameter and has an **orbital** period of 12 years. Odysseus was named after the hero of Homer's *Odyssey.* Lehman associates this asteroid with the ability to view a situation from a fresh perspective, without projecting past experiences on to each new moment.

Sources:

Kowal, Charles T. *Asteroids: Their Nature and Utilization.* Chichester, West Sussex, U.K.: Ellis Horwood Limited, 1988.
Lehman, J. Lee. *The Ultimate Asteroid Book.* West Chester, Penn.: Whitford Press, 1988.

Old, Walter Gorn (Sepharial)

Walter Richard Old, a well-known astrologer under his pseudonym Sepharial, was born March 20, 1864, in Handsworth, Warwick, England. He attended King Edward's School at Birmingham. He studied astrology and the Cabbala from an early age, and for some years studied medicine and psychology along with occultism. He later studied such Oriental languages as Coptic, Assyrian, Sanskrit, and Chinese.

Sepharial moved to London in 1889. Soon thereafter he was admitted into Madame Blavatsky's "inner group." Sepharial introduced **Alan Leo** to Theosophy, and Leo remained within the Theosophical fold for the balance of his life. Sepharial, on the other hand, left formal Theosophy at some point between Blavatsky's passing in 1891 and Annie Besant's ascension to presidency of the society in 1907. In contrast with Leo, Sepharial was interested in astrology as a practical science rather than as some esoteric art produced by marrying it to theosophy.

Sepharial retained a strong interest in cabala and numerology along with his astrological interests. He was a significant, widely influential astrologer. His reflections on prenatal astrology inspired **E. H. Bailey's** theorizing on the prenatal epoch. He died on December 23, 1919, in Hove, East Sussex.

Selected Publications:

The New Manual of Astrology. London, 1898.
Prognostic Astronomy. London: L. N. Fowler, 1901.
Eclipses. London: L. N. Fowler, 1915.

Sources:

Holden, James H., and Robert A. Hughes. *Astrological Pioneers of America.* Tempe, Ariz.: American Federation of Astrologers, 1988.

Opposition

An opposition is an **aspect** of 180° between two points—e.g., between two **planets**—in an astrological chart. An opposition is a major aspect, regarded as challenging and inharmonious. It is sometimes referred to as the aspect of separation. It is difficult, but not as difficult as a **square**, partially because a 180° angle carries overtones of a polar relationship. By way of contrast to a square, which tends more to signify inner conflicts, an opposition indicates conflicts between internal and external factors. People with a **Mars–Saturn** opposition, for example, might regularly attract people into their lives whose impulsive, aggressive behavior (Mars) disrupts their sense of security (Saturn).

Sources:

Gettings, Fred. *Dictionary of Astrology.* London: Routledge & Kegan Paul, 1985.
Hand, Robert. *Horoscope Symbols.* Rockport, Mass.: Para Research, 1981.

Orb of Influence

Few **aspects** are ever exact (exact aspects are referred to as **partile** aspects). For this reason, astrologers speak of the orb—or the orb of influence—within which specific aspects are effective. For a **sextile**, or 60° angle, for example, many astrologers use a 6° degree orb in a **natal chart**, which means that if any two **planets** are making an angle (with respect to Earth as the vertex) anywhere in the 54°–66° range, then they are are regarded as making a sextile aspect with each other. The closer an aspect is to being exact, the stronger it is. Major aspects (e.g., **conjunctions** and **squares**) are given larger orbs than minor aspects (e.g., **quintiles** and **semisextiles**), and the more important heavenly bodies, such as the **Sun** and the **Moon**, are thought to have larger orbs of influence than the smaller and more distant celestial bodies. Beyond these general principles, there is much disagreement among astrologers as to specifically how large orbs should be. Some allow, for instance, as much as a 12° orb for major aspects, while others allow only a 6° orb for the same aspects.

Sources:

deVore, Nicholas. *Encyclopedia of Astrology.* New York: Philosophical Library, 1947.
Hand, Robert. *Horoscope Symbols.* Rockport, Mass.: Para Research, 1981.

Orbit

An orbit is the path in space that one heavenly body makes in its movement around another heavenly body. The **Moon**, for example, makes an orbit around Earth, while Earth and the other planets make orbits around the **Sun**. The technical name for the orbiting body is **satellite**. The orbited body is called a primary. Because primaries are also in motion, the orbits described by satellites are elliptical rather than circular.

Satellites form stable orbits by counterbalancing two forces—their movement away from the primary and the force of gravity drawing them back toward the primary. In other words, in the absence of gravity a satellite would move in a straight line, which would soon take it away from its primary; in the absence of satellite motion, gravity would draw a satellite and its primary together until they collided.

Sources:

Robinson, J. Hedley, and James Muirden. *Astronomy Data Book.* 2d ed. New York: John Wiley & Sons, 1979.

Smoluchowski, Roman. *The Solar System: The Sun, Planets, and Life.* New York: Scientific American Books, 1983.

Orpheus

Orpheus, **asteroid** 3,361 (the 3,361st asteroid to be discovered), is approximately 12.2 kilometers in diameter and has an **orbital** period of 5.3 years. Orpheus was named after a masterful player of the lyre who is best remembered for his attempt to rescue his wife Eurydice from the underworld. According to Lang-Wescott, Orpheus represents haunting, lyrical music, mourning or grief, or a sense of loss or longing for what is past. This asteroid's key words are *loss, grief,* and *sad songs.*

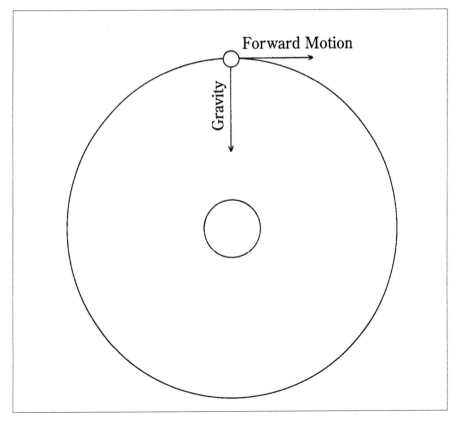

◀
Orbit.

Sources:

Lang-Wescott, Martha. *Asteroids-Mechanics: Ephemerides II.* Conway, Mass.: Treehouse Mountain, 1990.

———. *Mechanics of the Future: Asteroids.* Rev. ed. Conway, Mass.: Treehouse Mountain, 1991.

Osiris

Osiris, **asteroid** 1,923 (the 1,923th asteroid to be discovered), is approximately 7.6 kilometers in diameter and has an **orbital** period of 3.8 years. Osiris was named after the Egyptian god of death and resurrection. Lehman associates this asteroid with androgyny.

Sources:

Kowal, Charles T. *Asteroids: Their Nature and Utilization.* Chichester, West Sussex, U.K.: Ellis Horwood Limited, 1988.

Lehman, J. Lee. *The Ultimate Asteroid Book.* West Chester, Penn.: Whitford Press, 1988.

P

Pales

Pales, **asteroid** 49 (the 49th asteroid to be discovered), is approximately 176 kilometers in diameter and has an **orbital** period of 5.4 years. It is named after the Roman god of flocks, pastures, and shepherds. When prominent in a **natal chart**, Pales may indicate a **native** with an interest in these matters. More often, it indicates more of a metaphorical shepherding; someone with a strong Pales may be involved in some kind of guarding activity, shepherding a congregration, and so on.

Sources:

Kowal, Charles T. *Asteroids: Their Nature and Utilization.* Chichester, West Sussex, U.K.: Ellis Horwood Limited, 1988.
Room, Adrian. *Dictionary of Astronomical Names.* London: Routledge, 1988.

Pallas

Pallas was one of the first four **asteroids**, along with **Ceres, Vesta**, and **Juno**, to be investigated by astrologers. It was named after the goddess Athena, although, at the time, astronomers thought that all asteroids should receive Roman names (little knowing the full extent of the asteroid population, which quickly exhausted Roman goddess names). Pallas was the second asteroid to be discovered, in 1802 by the German doctor and astronomer Heinrich Olbers. It has a diameter of 588 kilometers, and **orbits** the **Sun** in slightly less than 4 2/3 terrestrial years. Because it was one of the earlier asteroids to be researched, a fair amount of material on Pallas is available. It is believed to represent the principle of creative wisdom.

Sources:

Dobyns, Zipporah. *Expanding Astrology's Universe.* San Diego, Calif.: Astro Computing Services, 1983.

Donath, Emma Belle. *Asteroids in the Birth Chart.* Tempe, Ariz.: American Federation of Astrologers, 1979.

George, Demetra, with Douglas Bloch. *Asteroid Goddesses: The Mythology, Psychology and Astrology of the Reemerging Feminine.* 2d ed. rev. and enl. San Diego, Calif.: Astro Computing Services, 1990.

————. *Astrology for Yourself: A Workbook for Personal Transformation.* Berkeley, Calif.: Wingbow Press, 1987.

Lehman, J. Lee. *The Ultimate Asteroid Book.* West Chester, Pa.: Whitford Press, 1988.

Palmistry and Astrology (Astropalmistry)

In earlier times when the general populace's knowledge of astrology extended beyond newspaper predictions and **sun signs**, astrology was more than just the science of the **stars**. Properly understood, astrology was a universal language or symbolic code that contained widely recognized archetypes of general principles, types of humanity, and aspects of personality. Given the usefulness of this symbolic code, it was natural that astrological language and symbols would be adopted by other occult arts, such as the **tarot** and palmistry.

In palmistry, the **planets** including the **luminaries** (the **Sun** and the **Moon**), were used to name as well as to represent the principles of certain parts of the hand: **Mercury,** the little finger; the Sun, the ring finger; **Saturn,** the middle finger; **Jupiter,** the index finger; **Mars,** the center of the palm; **Venus,** the root of the thumb; and the Moon, the lower mound of the hand. Various other lines and areas also bore the names of planets. The classical **elements** were utilized in certain systems of hand classification, so some palmistry books contain the expressions water hand, earth hand, fire hand, and air hand. As a student of astrology might anticipate, a water hand indicates a sensitive disposition, an air hand indicates an intellectual nature, and so forth. Despite palmistry's wholesale borrowing of astrological terminology, modern astrologers have shown little or no interest in studying correlations between patterns in palms and patterns in astrological charts.

Sources:

The Cheiro Book of Fate and Fortune: Palmistry, Numerology and Astrology. New York: Arco Publishing Co., 1971.

Gettings, Fred. *The Book of Palmistry.* London: Triune Books, 1974.

Pandora

Pandora is the name of two distinct celestial bodies: A moon of **Saturn** and an **asteroid**. Pandora, the recently discovered (1980) moon in the Saturnian

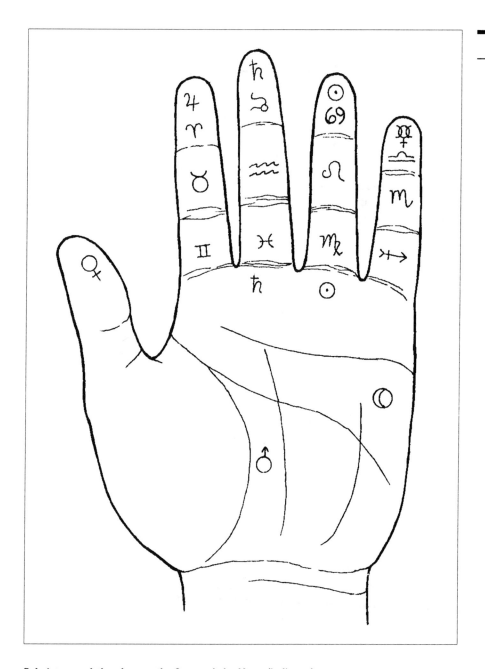

Palmistry used the planets, the Sun, and the Moon (indicated here by their glyphs) to represent parts of the hand.

system, is about 55 miles in diameter and **orbits** Saturn in less then 2/3 of a terrestrial day at an average distance of 88,200 miles. Pandora, asteroid 55 (the 55th asteroid to be discovered), has an orbital period a bit longer than 4 1/2 years, and it is almost 113 kilometers in diameter. Both celestial bodies were named after the mythological Greek woman who released the ills of humanity by opening a box that the gods had sent her but had forbidden her from unsealing. Only the asteriod has been investigated by astrologers.

Pandora is one of the more recent asteroids to be investigated by astrologers. Preliminary material on Pandora can be found in **Demetra George** and Douglas Bloch's *Astrology for Yourself,* and an **ephemeris** (table of celestial locations) for Pandora can be found in the back of the second edition of George and Bloch's *Asteroid Goddesses.* Unlike the **planets**, which are associated with a wide range of phenomena, the smaller asteroids are said to represent a single principle. George and Bloch give Pandora's principle as "curiosity that initiates change." Zipporah Dobyns also associates Pandora with curiosity and has found it prominent in the charts of many astrologers. J. Lee Lehman sees the effect of Pandora as twofold: "to stir a person into doing something, and to produce unintended options of the person" (p. 45).

Sources:

Dobyns, Zipporah. *Expanding Astrology's Universe.* San Diego, Calif.: Astro Computing Services, 1983.

George, Demetra, with Douglas Bloch. *Asteroid Goddesses: The Mythology, Psychology and Astrology of the Reemerging Feminine.* 2d. ed. rev. and enl. San Diego, Calif.: Astro Computing Services, 1990.

———. *Astrology for Yourself: A Workbook for Personal Transformation.* Berkeley, Calif.: Wingbow Press, 1987.

Lehman, J. Lee. *The Ultimate Asteroid Book.* West Chester, Pa.: Whitford Press, 1988.

Paradise

Paradise, **asteroid** 2,791 (the 2,791st asteroid to be discovered), is approximately 20 kilometers in diameter and has an **orbital** period of 3.7 years. Paradise is a concept asteroid, named after the Garden of Eden. Lehman (p. 66) asserts that if this asteroid is well-**aspected** in a **natal chart**, the **native** believes paradise can be found in this existence. If, however, "the asteroid is poorly aspect, then the person is less than optimistic that Paradise exists outside of the movies."

Sources:

Kowal, Charles T. *Asteroids: Their Nature and Utilization.* Chichester, West Sussex, U.K.: Ellis Horwood Limited, 1988.

Lehman, J. Lee. *The Ultimate Asteroid Book.* West Chester, Penn.: Whitford Press, 1988.

Parallel

The **orbits** of most of the **planets** in the **solar system** lie in approximately the same geometric plane, which is why we are able to draw an astrological chart using only a two-dimensional representation rather than one with three dimensions. There is, nevertheless, a variation in the tilt or angle of these orbits, so at any given time most of the planets are either north or south of the **celestial equator** (the plane described by projecting Earth's equator against the background of the **stars**). This variation is measured in degrees of **declination**. Two planets are **parallel** when they are on the same side of the celestial equator and have the same degree of declination. Planets with the same declination are said to have a relationship similar to a **conjunction**.

Paran (Paranatellon)

A paran (from the same family of words as parallel) is said to occur when two **planets** cross an **angle** (whether the same or different angles) at the same time. The notion of parantellon goes back to **Ptolemy**; it was revived by **Robert Hand**, who abbreviated its designation to paran. The concept is infrequently employed in modern astrology,, although contemporary chart-casting programs can usually calculate it.

Parsifal

Parsifal, **asteroid** 2,095 (the 2,095th asteroid to be discovered), is approximately 10 kilometers in diameter and has an **orbital** period of 4.3 years. Parsifal was named after the hero of Chrétien de Troyes's novel *Perceval*. Lehman associates this asteroid with the quest for knighthood, as well as with compassion.

Sources:

Kowal, Charles T. *Asteroids: Their Nature and Utilization.* Chichester, West Sussex, U.K.: Ellis Horwood Limited, 1988.
Lehman, J. Lee. *The Ultimate Asteroid Book.* West Chester, Penn.: Whitford Press, 1988.

Part of Fortune

The Part of Fortune is a point in an astrological chart that is calculated by measuring the **angular distance** between the **Sun** and the **Moon**, and then finding the point in the chart where the Moon would fall if—keeping the angular distance constant—the Sun were to be moved to the **ascendant** (the sign and degree of the **zodiac** on the eastern **horizon** at the moment of birth). The point where the Moon would then fall is the part of fortune. To clarify this with a concrete example, if in a given **natal chart** the Sun is at 10° **Aries** and the Moon at 20° **Taurus** (Aries and Taurus are successive signs), then the Sun-Moon angle (i.e., the angular distance between the Sun and Moon) is 40°. Let us say further that in this same chart the ascendant is located at 15° **Libra**. If the chart is then imaginarily rotated until the Sun is at 15° Libra, the Moon would be at 25° **Scorpio** (40° away from 15° Libra). Thus, the Part of Fortune would be located at 25° Scorpio. The **house** and sign placement of the Part of Fortune indicate, as the name intimates, good fortune. The placements also indicates areas and activities in which the native finds enjoyment.

The Part of Fortune is but one member of a system of points referred to as the **Arabian Parts**, but which in fact antedates the flowering of Arabic astrology (the Part of Fortune as well as the other parts were utilized in the pre-Islamic Mediterranean world). Western astrologers, impressed by the compendium of parts written by the great Muslim scholar **Al-Biruni**, called them the Arabic Parts, and the name stuck. The many other parts discussed by Al-Biruni— death, children, commerce, and so forth, which are calculated by measuring the

▶
Part of Fortune.

angular distance between various **planets** and placing one planet or the other on the ascendant or on another house **cusp**—are rarely used by contemporary astrologers. The Part of Fortune, however, is utilized by most modern astrologers. Many chart-casting programs can calculate the other parts in an instant, making experimentation with them relatively easy. Thus, we may see a revival of the whole system in the not-too-distant future.

Sources:

deVore, Nicholas. *Encyclopedia of Astrology.* New York: Philosophical Library, 1947.
Granite, Robert Hurzt. *The Fortunes of Astrology.* San Diego, Calif.: Astro Computing Services, 1980.

Partile

The astrological **aspects**—the angles between the **planets**, such as **squares** and **trines**—do not have to be exact (e.g., exactly 90° (square) or exactly 120° (trine) to be counted as having an influence. (On the basis of the particular aspect and planets involved, astrologers allow aspects a larger or smaller orb of **influence**, within which they are regarded as having an effect.) Exact aspects are referred to as partile aspects and are considered to have a stronger influence than **platic** (nonexact) aspects.

Partridge, John

John Partridge, born January 18, 1643, in East Sheen, London, was an influential astrologer and producer of **almanacs**. Apprenticed to a shoemaker, he acquired enough books to teach himself Greek, Latin, and Hebrew. He may have studied with the astrologer **John Gadbury** and seems to have given up making shoes when his first publication was issued about 1678. Partridge's first major work, *Mikropanastron,* was published the next year. In 1680, he started turning out an almanac entitled *Merlinus Liberatus.* He left England for political reasons in 1685 and studied medicine in Leyden, Holland, for the next four years. Partridge returned to his native country after receiving his M.D. degree and married a well-to-do widow. He also resumed his astrological publishing activities.

Partridge came to prefer the **Placidian house system,** a choice evident in his final major works, such as the *Opus Reformatum* (1693) and the *Defectio Geniturarum* (1697), both highly technical analyses of primary directions in sample **horoscopes.** By 1700, he was the most prominent astrologer in Britain. His almanac was so popular that other people began to publish almanacs in Partridge's name.

Partridge is best remembered for his role in promoting the Placidian system and for an incident involving the famous author and social critic Jonathan Swift (1667–1745). Under the pseudonym Isaac Bickerstaff, Swift published a bogus almanac containing a prediction of Partridge's death on March 29, 1708. Swift issued another small tract on March 30, 1708, in which he, as Bickerstaff, claimed that his prediction was correct and gave the particulars of Partridge's supposed death. The trick was believed, and Partridge had difficulty convincing others that he was still alive. He curtailed his almanac for the next four years. When it was reissued, he included some pointed reflections on Swift's character. Partridge died on June 24, 1715, in Mortlake, London.

Selected Publications:

Mikropanastron, or an Astrological Vade Mecum. . . . London, 1679.
Nebulo Anglicanus, or the First Part of the Black Life of John Gadbury. . . . London, 1693.
Opus Reformatum, or a Treatise of Astrology in which the Common Errors of that Art are modestly exposed and rejected. . . . London, 1693.
Defectio Geniturarum. . . . London, 1697.

Sources:

Holden, James H., and Robert A. Hughes. *Astrological Pioneers of America.* Tempe, Ariz.: American Federation of Astrologers, 1988.

Patientia

Patientia, **asteroid** 451 (the 451st asteroid to be discovered), is approximately 280 kilometers in diameter and has an **orbital** period of 5.4 years. Its name is a personified form of the word patience. In a **natal chart**, Patientia's location by sign and **house** indicates where and how one is most likely to be patient. When **afflicted** by inharmonious **aspects**, Patientia may show impatience or a pattern of being forced to wait for results. If prominent in a chart (e.g., **conjunct** the **Sun** or the **ascendant**), it may signify an exceptionally patient person or an individual for whom the cultivation of patience is a life goal.

Sources:

Kowal, Charles T. *Asteroids: Their Nature and Utilization.* Chichester, West Sussex, U.K.: Ellis Horwood Limited, 1988.
Room, Adrian. *Dictionary of Astronomical Names.* London: Routledge, 1988.

Pax

Pax, **asteroid** 679 (the 679th asteroid to be discovered), is approximately 72 kilometers in diameter and has an **orbital** period of 4 years. Its name means peace. In a **natal chart**, Pax's location by sign and **house** indicates where and how one is most likely to experience or seek peace, especially in the sense of outward tranquility. When **afflicted** by inharmonious **aspects**, Pax may show conflict or the seeking of peace in situations where a tranquil response is inappropriate. If prominent in a chart (e.g., **conjunct** the **Sun** or the **ascendant**), it may indicate an exceptionally tranquil person or an individual who seeks to create peaceful circumstances.

Sources:

Kowal, Charles T. *Asteroids: Their Nature and Utilization*. Chichester, West Sussex, U.K.: Ellis Horwood Limited, 1988.
Room, Adrian. *Dictionary of Astronomical Names*. London: Routledge, 1988.

Pecker

Pecker, **asteroid** 1,629 (the 1,629th asteroid to be discovered), is approximately 7.6 kilometers in diameter and has on **orbital** period of 3.3 years. Lehman associates Pecker with sex-murder victims and perpetrators.

Sources:

Kowal, Charles T. *Asteroids: Their Nature and Utilization*. Chichester, West Sussex, U.K.: Ellis Horwood Limited, 1988.
Lehman, J. Lee. *The Ultimate Asteroid Book*. West Chester, Penn.: Whitford Press, 1988.

Peregrine

A peregrine (foreign) **planet** is one so situated as to be neither **dignified** nor **exalted**, and simultaneously not in **aspect** with any other planet. A planet so situated in a **natal chart** indicates a part of the psyche that seems to operate independently from the rest of the **native**'s personality, and that the native must therefore make a special effort to integrate. The term is seldom used today, except in **horary astrology**.

Perigee

Every **orbit** is elliptical. When a **satellite** is closest to Earth, it is at its perigee (from Greek *peri,* near, and *gaia,* earth).

Perihelion

Although they approximate circles, every **orbit** is elliptical. The point in a **satellite**'s orbit when it is nearest the **Sun** is called its perihelion (from Greek *peri,* near and *helios,* sun).

Periodical Lunation

Periodical lunation refers to the chart cast for the moment the **Moon** returns to the exact **degree** it occupied at birth. It is used for monthly forecasts.

Perry, Glenn A.

Glenn A. Perry is a contemporary astrologer who started working professionally in 1974. After a brief stint giving traditional "readings," he felt that he was not sufficiently trained as a counselor to provide the kind of help many of his clients needed. So, in 1975 he began graduate work in psychology at Lone Mountain College in San Francisco. During the next 5 years, he studied under Richard Idemon, who was well known for his integration of astrology and **Jungian** psychology. He graduated from Lone Mountain College with an M.A. degree in clinical psychology in 1978. His masters thesis was titled *"Inside Astrology: A Psychological Perspective,"* a substantial portion of which was devoted to correlat-

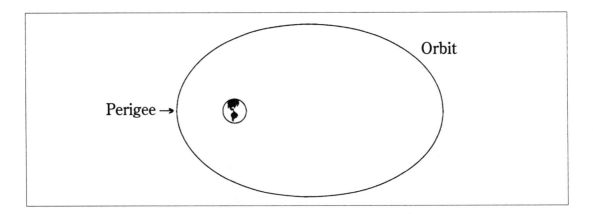

Perigee (not drawn to scale).

ing Jungian/humanistic ideas and astrology. After some years as a teacher and therapist, he went back to school in 1981 at Saybrook Institute in San Francisco and graduated with a Ph.D. degree in psychology in 1991.

In addition to teaching, giving lectures, and appearing on talk shows, Perry has also published several articles integrating astrology and psychology in *Aspects* and *Dell Horoscope* magazines, *NCGR Memberletter, NCGR Journal, Mountain Astrologer,* and *Astrotherapy Newsletter.* He has also worked for Antioch College and Goddard College as clinical evaluator and supervisor for graduate students attempting to integrate astrology and psychology in their course work.

In 1987, Perry founded the Association for Astrological Psychology (AAP), a professional organization for psychologists and counselors who are interested in using astrology as a diagnostic tool in ongoing psychotherapeutic work with clients. In addition to serving as the president of AAP, he is also the editor–publisher of its official publication, *The Astrotherapy Newsletter.*

Persephone

Persephone is one of the names given to the hypothetical **planet** orbiting the **Sun** beyond **Pluto.** Peresephone, asteroid 399 (the 399th asteroid to be discovered), is approximately 55 kilometers in diameter and has an **orbital** period of 5.3 years. Persephone was named after the daughter of Demeter, who was kidnapped by Hades and taken to the underworld to become his queen. According to Lang-Wescott (1991, p. 78), Persephone represents "separation anxiety; attitudes toward making transitions (that take one away from familiar people and circumstances); experience of feeling separate from family/others." This asteroid's key word is *separation.* Lehman notes that the location of Persephone may indicate an area where skills are undeveloped. The less

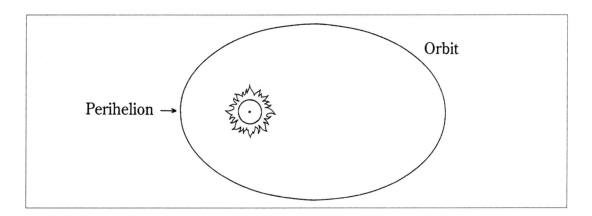

Perihelion (not drawn to scale).

pleasant side of this asteroid is that it may indicate where one is an innocent yet willing victim.

Sources:

Lang-Wescott, Martha. *Asteroids-Mechanics: Ephemerides II.* Conway, Mass.: Treehouse Mountain, 1990.
———. *Mechanics of the Future: Asteroids.* Rev. ed. Conway, Mass.: Treehouse Mountain, 1991.
Lehman, J. Lee. *The Ultimate Asteroid Book.* West Chester, Penn.: Whitford Press, 1988.

Perseverantia

Perseverantia, **asteroid** 975 (the 975th asteroid to be discovered), is approximately 24 kilometers in diameter and has an **orbital** period of 4.8 years. Its name is a personification of perseverance. In an **natal chart**, Perseverantia's location by sign and **house** indicates where and how one is most likely to be persevering. When **afflicted** by inharmonious **aspects**, Perseverantia can show lack of perseverance or a pattern of persevering in situations one should abandon. If prominent in a chart (e.g., **conjunct** the **Sun** or the **ascendant**), it may suggest an exceptionally persevering person or an individual for whom cultivating perseverance is a life goal.

Sources:

Kowal, Charles T. *Asteroids: Their Nature and Utilization.* Chichester, West Sussex, U.K.: Ellis Horwood Limited, 1988.
Room, Adrian. *Dictionary of Astronomical Names.* London: Routledge, 1988.

Personal Name Asteroids

An **asteroid** is one of thousands of small planets, 95% of whose **orbits** lie between the orbits of **Mars** and **Jupiter**. Initially these were given mythological names, but as telescopes increased in strength and more and more asteroids were discovered, astronomers began naming them after places and people. The various astrologers who have studied the influence of asteroids have reached a consensus, which is, to quote from J. Lee Lehman's *The Ultimate Asteroid Book* (p. 10), that "asteroids have astrological effects which may be studied," and the "name of an asteroid has astrological significance."

The essential clue with which one begins this type of research is the name of the asteroid, which gives preliminary insight into the asteroid's astrological "temperament." The early asteroids studied by astrologers were named after mythological figures, and an exploration of the relevant myths provided a preliminary clue to the nature of these tiny planets' influence. When researchers began shifting from explicitly mythological asteroids and started examining asteroids with common names like Barry and Patricia, they continued to follow their previous line of exploration by finding initial clues in certain specialized reference works that provided etymologies for common names. Patricia, for example, is derived from the Latin *patricius,* meaning noble one, which provides "nobility" as an initial clue to the influence of the asteroid.

Astrologers also found that individuals have a special relationship with the asteroid bearing their name. Thus, the natal location of the appropriate personal name asteroid will show something about the character of the individual, and the transits of the same asteroid will give indications about current influences.

Sources:

Lehman, J. Lee. *The Ultimate Asteroid Book.* West Chester, Penn.: Whitford Press, 1988.
Press, Nona Gwynn. *Personal Name Asteroids.* San Diego, Calif.: Astro Computing Services, 1987.

Philagoria

Philagoria, **asteroid** 274 (the 274th asteroid to be discovered), is approximately 36 kilometers in diameter and has an **orbital** period of 5.3 years. Its name means fond of assembly in Greek. When prominent in an **astrological chart**, it may indicate, as the name suggests, an individual who is fond of gatherings of all sorts. The sign and **house** position offer greater specificity as to where and how the **native** enjoys assemblies.

Sources:

Kowal, Charles T. *Asteroids: Their Nature and Utilization.* Chichester, West Sussex, U.K.: Ellis Horwood Limited, 1988.
Room, Adrian. *Dictionary of Astronomical Names.* London: Routledge, 1988.

Philia

Philia, **asteroid** 280 (the 280th asteroid to be discovered), is approximately 26 kilometers in diameter and has an **orbital** period of 5.0 years. Its name is a personification of a Greek word for love. The Greeks distinguished Philia love from Eros love, identifying Philia more with friendship than romance. When prominent in an **natal chart**, this asteroid indicates a friendly personality. The sign and **house** position indicates both how one interacts with friends as well as what the friends are like.

Sources:

Kowal, Charles T. *Asteroids: Their Nature and Utilization.* Chichester, West Sussex, U.K.: Ellis Horwood Limited, 1988.
Room, Adrian. *Dictionary of Astronomical Names.* London: Routledge, 1988.

Philosophia

Philosophia, **asteroid** 227 (the 227th asteroid to be discovered), is approximately 60 kilometers in diameter and has an **orbital** period of 5.6 years. Philosophia is named after *philosophy* (literally, the "love of wisdom"). If other elements of a **natal chart** concur, this asteroid indicates wisdom or a "philosophical attitude" with respect to the matters indicated by Philosophia's sign and **house** position.

Sources:

Kowal, Charles T. *Asteroids: Their Nature and Utilization.* Chichester, West Sussex, U.K.: Ellis Horwood Limited, 1988.
Room, Adrian. *Dictionary of Astronomical Names.* London: Routledge, 1988.

Phlegmatic

Phlegmatic is the traditional name for the personality temperament indicated by an excess of the **element** water.

Phobos and Deimos (Moons of Mars)

The **planet Mars** is circled by two small, irregularly shaped moons, Phobos and Deimos. Phobos, with dimensions of 17 x 14 x 13 miles, **orbits** Mars every 7.7 hours in a circular path that never carries it more than 3,720 miles away from its *primary* (the celestial body around which a satellite orbits). Deimos, which is 10 x 7 x 6 miles, orbits Mars every 30.3 hours, traveling approximately 12,470 miles above the surface. These distances represent the inner and outer extremes for bodies orbiting a planet the size of Mars (i.e., if Phobos were a little closer, it would crash into its primary; if Deimos were a little more distant, it would escape the Martian field of gravity altogether). As in most planetary moon systems, the orbital paths of the Martian moons align with their parent body's equator.

Astronomers speculate that Phobos and Deimos may once have been **asteroids** (perhaps one asteroid that later split apart into two) that wandered close to Mars and were captured by the planet's gravitational field. Whether or not these satellites are former asteroids, the asteroid connection provides the link between current astrological research and **planetary moon** studies: Given the growing astrological acceptance of asteroids, many of which are smaller and farther away than the Martian moons, it is only natural that astrologers begin considering the influence of Phobos and Deimos (not to mention the influence of the moons of the other planets).

The moons of Mars constitute a useful starting place for planetary moon studies for three reasons:

1. Mars is the closest planet with moons.

2. The principle indicated by *phobos* (fear; the source of our term *phobia*) and *deimos* (panic or terror) is comparatively straightforward and clearly represents the polar opposite principle of Martian assertiveness or courage (other planet-moon relationships are more complex).

3. The moons of Mars have attracted the imagination of human beings more than the moons of the other planets (with the exception, of course, of our home planet's moon), indicating that their astrological significance should be more easily retrieved from the **collective unconscious**.

With respect to the last reason, it is interesting to note that, a century and a half prior to Asaph Hall's discovery of Phobos and Deimos in 1877, Jonathan Swift's fictional hero Lemuel Gulliver found the Laputans had discovered two Martian moons. Also, later in the eighteenth century, Voltaire wrote about a visitor from Sirius who mentioned the two as-yet-undiscovered moons of Mars. Both Swift and Voltaire based their speculations on the work of Kepler, who as early as 1610 hypothesized that Mars was circled by two moons. Mars itself has also figured prominently in imaginative literature, having often served as the backdrop for stories of "martial" bravery (e.g., Edgar Rice Burroughs's series of Martian novels featuring the brave and noble John Carter), as well as the home world of "fearful," "terrifying" monsters who invaded **Earth** (the most well known of which are the Martians in H. G. Wells's *The War of the Worlds*). Although both these subgenres draw on the Mars archetype (war), the latter also draws on what we might refer to as the Phobos-Deimos archetype (fear-panic).

Hall named the Martian moons after the sons of Ares (**Aries**), who was the Greek equivalent of Mars, the Roman god of war. Phobos and Deimos have no mythological tales of their own. Rather, they are simply mentioned in the context of other myths, where they serve as their father's chariot drivers. Developed myths are not necessary, however, for us to decipher the meaning of these "brother" moons; unlike the names of many other celestial bodies, Fear and Panic are self-explanatory. Similarly, it does not take much reflection to see why they should be associated with Mars: As a psychological principle, Mars represents outgoing energy, assertiveness, courage, and aggression. This planet's placement in a **natal chart** indicates how, and in what area of life, we express this principle most readily. What is not usually mentioned, however, is that where we most tend to express ourselves in acts of courage and aggression is also where we experience the most fear. Courage, especially, makes no sense by itself; courage is always courage that overcomes fears, and acts in spite of them.

The significance of Phobos and Deimos for astrology is that astrologers have traditionally associated fears with **Saturn** (sometimes with **Neptune**) and cast that planet in a role that belongs to Mars's sons. Psychologically, Saturn represents the principle of security-seeking, and its polar opposite principle, which manifests in the sign and **house** occupied by Saturn, is insecurity—not fear. Although these two emotions (insecurity and fear) are clearly related, it should also be evident that they are not identical. With this distinction in mind, psychologically inclined astrologers (and astrologically inclined psychologists) can more precisely analyze their clients' anxieties.

This utilization of the Martian moons—**delineating** fears in terms of the sign and house position of Mars (the position where Phobos and Deimos will also be found)—is fairly straightforward. However, Phobos and Deimos are in constant motion around their parent body, and the constantly changing dynamic of their orbits introduces variations that merit further research. For example, with respect to our **geocentric** (Earth-centered) perspective, it appears that Phobos and Deimos move forward with Mars half the time and in the opposite (**retrograde**) direction the other half. Recent astronomical **ephemerides** include information from which this alternation can be calculated. It should thus be possible to research the variation that retrograde motion introduces into the astrological influence of the Martian moons.

Also, following the lead of practitioners of **heliocentric astrology** (the branch of astrology that casts **Sun**-centered charts, even for individuals born on Earth), investigators should be able to cast areocentric (Mars-centered) charts for the positions of Phobos and Deimos and obtain a more complex delineation of our fears. Perhaps these areocentric positions can even be placed in a geocentric natal chart, as the geo-helio approach does with heliocentric planets. These are just a few of the research directions opening up in the emerging field of planetary moon studies.

Sources:

Lewis, James R. *Martian Astrology.* Goleta, Calif.: Jupiter's Ink, 1992.
McEvers, Joan, ed. *Planets: The Astrological Tools.* Saint Paul, Minn,: Llewellyn Publications, 1989.
Room, Adrian. *Dictionary of Astronomical Names.* London: Routledge, 1988.
Wilford, John Nobel. *Mars Beckons: The Mysteries, the Challenges, the Expectations of Our Next Great Adventure in Space.* New York: Vintage, 1991.

Photographica

Photographica, **asteroid** 443 (the 443d asteroid to be discovered), is approximately 32 kilometers in diameter and has an **orbital** period of 3.3 years. The name derives from a new approach to discovering asteroids with a camera. When prominent in a **natal chart**, Photographica may indicate interest or skill in photographic representation as well as in other media of visual representation.

Sources:

Kowal, Charles T. *Asteroids: Their Nature and Utilization.* Chichester, West Sussex, U.K.: Ellis Horwood Limited, 1988.
Room, Adrian. *Dictionary of Astronomical Names.* London: Routledge, 1988.

Pisces

Pisces, the twelfth and last sign of the **zodiac**, is a **mutable water** sign. It is a negative (in the value-neutral sense of being negatively *charged)*, **feminine** sign, **ruled** by the **planet Neptune** (in traditional astrology it was ruled by **Jupiter**). Its symbol is the Fish (two fish moving in opposite directions, tied together by a rope or, in other versions, by their tails); its **glyph** is said to be a stylized representation of this symbol. It takes its name from the plural of the Latin word for fish. Pisces is associated with the feet, and individuals with a Pisces **sun sign** are susceptible to athlete's foot and other foot problems. The key phrase for Pisces is *I believe.*

The mythology of Pisces is complex. The image is usually said to represent **Aphrodite** (goddess of love) and her son **Eros** (god of erotic attraction), who held hands and turned themselves into fishes as they jumped into the water to escape a conflict. Both these divinities are the subjects of lengthy mythologies. The fish symbol is similarly complex, with rich associations in Hindu, Buddhist, Christian, Norse, and Sumerian mythologies; it is often a goddess symbol. In classical mythology, fish were sacred to **Venus** (Aphrodite) and **Neptune (Poseidon)**.

The symbols for the other two water signs are associated with water, but are in a certain sense only "part" watery: **Cancer** is a crab, sticking close to the shoreline, while one of **Scorpio**'s symbols is the snake, a creature having earth as well as water associations. A fish, however, is a purely marine creature, indicating that Pisceans are more at home in the subtle dimension beyond this realm than they are in everyday life. Unless other factors in a **natal chart** indicate otherwise, Pisceans have a difficult time coping. They attempt to transcend life through an ethereal art form like music (Aphrodite was patron divinity of the arts) or through some form of mysticism. Negatively, this same tendency can manifest as escapism through daydreaming, drugs, alcohol, or the like. Pisces natives can also be highly intuitive or psychic. Like the divinities of love who became fish, Pisceans can be loving, compassionate people; alternatively, they can be so trapped in the swamp of their emotional insecurities that they become obsessed with themselves.

There is a wealth of information available on the characteristics of the zodiacal signs, so much that one book would not be able to contain it all. One traditional way in which astrologers condense information is by summarizing sign and planet traits in lists of words and short phrases called key words and/or *key phrases.* The following Pisces key words are drawn from Manly P. Hall's *Astrological Keywords:*

Emotional key words: "The emotions are inhibited, native is sensitive and impressionable, psychic, devoted, melancholy, lacks ability to resist environment, secretive, misunderstood" (p. 19).

Mental key words: "Abstract, intuitive, compassionate, introspective, quick in understanding, executive, philosophical, religious, clairvoyant, versatile, synthetical, loquacious, impractical, procrastinating, lack confidence." (p. 22).

Most popular works on astrology contain data on the signs, and these can be consulted for more detailed information.

Sources:

Evans, Colin. *The New Waite's Compendium of Natal Astrology.* Revised by Brian E. F. Gardener. York Beach, Maine: Samuel Weiser, 1971. (Originally published 1917.)

Green, Landis Knight. *The Astrologer's Manual: Modern Insights into an Ancient Art.* Sebastopol, Calif.: CRCS Publications, 1975.

Hall, Manly P. *Astrological Keywords.* 1958. Reprint. Savage, Md.: Littlefield Adams (1975), 19, 22.

Pittsburghia

Pittsburghia, **asteroid** 484 (the 484th asteroid to be discovered), is approximately 32 kilometers in diameter and has an **orbital** period of 4.4 years. Pittsburghia is named after the city of Pittsburgh. The unusual name of this planetoid (who would name an asteroid after a city with a name like Pittsburgh?) led to its inclusion in *The Asteroid Ephemeris: Dudu, Dembowska, Pittsburgh, Frigga,* Batya Stark and Mark Pottenger's tour de force of astrological humor.

Sources:

Kowal, Charles T. *Asteroids: Their Nature and Utilization.* Chichester, West Sussex, U.K.: Ellis Horwood Limited, 1988.

Room, Adrian. *Dictionary of Astronomical Names.* London: Routledge, 1988.

Stark, Batya and Mark Pottenger. *The Asteroid Ephemeris: Dudu, Dembowska, Pittsburgh, Frigga.* San Diego, Calif.: Astro Computing Services, 1982.

Placidean House System

It is easy for a person looking at an astrological chart for the first time to make the incorrect assumption that the 12 "pie pieces" are the 12 **signs** of the **zodiac.** These lines indicate the **house** divisions (sign divisions are usually not represented), which can begin or end at different places in different signs. Astrologers disagree about how to draw the houses, although most agree that the first house should begin on the eastern **horizon** and the seventh house (180° away) should begin on the western horizon. Also, the great majority of systems begin the tenth house at the **degree** of the zodiac that is highest in the heavens and the fourth house at exactly 180° from the **cusp** of the tenth house.

The Placidean house system was developed by a seventeenth-century Italian monk and professor of mathematics named Placidus de Tito. In this system, the house cusps between the **ascendant** and the midheaven are obtained by trisecting the time it takes a degree of the zodiac to rise from the eastern horizon to the midheaven. Owing to the widespread availability of Placidean **tables of houses**, this was the most popular house system in the early twentieth century, and it still enjoys widespread use.

Placidus

Placidus de Tito (1603–1668) was an Italian mathematician and astrologer best known for the **house** system that bears his name. He joined the Olivetan Order when he was 21. He was a reader of mathematics and physics at the University of Padua for some years, and he was appointed professor of mathematics at the Milanese University in Pavia in 1657, a position he held for the rest of his life. He was also astrologer to some prominent religious and political figures of the time.

Placidus attributes the initial inspiration for his system of division to a remark made by **Ptolemy** in *Tetrabiblos*. Ptolemy equates different semidiurnal arcs because they are equivalent to the same number of temporary hours. Analogically, Placidus reasoned, the twelfth-house **cusp** should begin at 1/3 of the semidiurnal arc above the **horizon**, the eleventh-house cusp at 2/3 of the semidiurnal arc above the horizon, and so forth.

Although mistaken, Placidus was convinced he had discovered Ptolemy's lost method of determining houses, and he began to write books in which he described the new system. This system was adopted by **John Partridge** but rejected by most other English astrologers. At the beginning of the revival of astrology in England in the late eighteenth century, Manoah Sibly published English translations of Placidus's *Primum Mobile*. The system of Placidus became the dominant system in England, and later the Placidian system was passed to France and Germany. Beyond his house system, Placidus was the inventor of secondary and tertiary directions. He also promoted the use of **transits** to both the natal and the **progressed** positions of the **planets**.

Selected Publications:

Physiomathematica sive Coelestis Philosophia Naturalibus hucusque desideratis ostensa principiis. . . . [Physico-mathematical (questions) or Celestial Philosophy set forth by means of natural principles hitherto lacking. . . .] 2d ed. [Revised by his pupils Brunaccio and Onorati from the 1650 edition.] Milan: Fran. Vigoni, 1675.

Tabulae Primi Mobilis cum. . . Triginta clariss. natalium Thematibus. [Tables of the Primum Mobile with thirty horoscopes of famous births.] 2d ed. Milano: Fran. Vigoni, 1675. (Originally published 1657.)

Sources:

Holden, James H., and Robert A. Hughes. *Astrological Pioneers of America.* Tempe, Ariz.: American Federation of Astrologers, 1988.

Planet X

In anticipation of discovering a **planet** beyond the **orbit** of **Neptune**, astronomers referred to the celestial body as Planet X. This planet, now called **Pluto**, was finally discovered in 1930. A common astrological practice is to assign a newly discovered body a tentative meaning that can be derived from associations with its name. (In the present case, the mythology of Pluto, the ancient Roman god of the underworld, was explored for initial clues about the planet's astrological influence.) Astrologers then study the influence of the body in charts in which it is prominent (i.e., charts in which it is in very close **conjunction** with another **planet** or with an **angle**). After further study of these charts, the preliminary meanings are revised so that they align with the empirical effects of the new body. This astrological principle is based on the well-established observation that the names astronomers give to newly discovered celestial bodies are not coincidental—that by virtue of some kind of nonapparent, **synchronicity,** non-astrologically inclined astronomers give astrologically significant names to things.

Astrologers have not generally considered, however, how alternative names—or, especially, older, abandoned ones—might shed light on the meaning of a celestial body. Pluto, for example, is associated with X rays, sex (which, in contemporary society, is "X-rated"), and the unearthing of what is hidden (as in the "X marks the spot" of treasure maps). These are all meanings of Pluto that could easily have been derived from reflection on the significance of the X in the designation Planet X. X is also the symbol for multiplication (the Pluto principle of sex "multiplies"). In Roman numerals, X is the number 10. If the **asteroid** belt is considered to be the remains of a planet, Pluto is the tenth-outermost planet in the **solar system**. It was also the tenth celestial body to be included in the **delineation** of astrological charts (after the **Sun**, the **Moon**, **Mercury, Venus, Mars, Jupiter, Saturn, Uranus**, and Neptune). Additionally, X is a common designation for Christ (as in Xmas), which links Pluto with the redemptive drama central to Christianity: Christ's death on the cross (another X), followed by his resurrection (death and rebirth are both ruled by Pluto).

These are all commonly understood associations with the planet Pluto. There are, however, other, less explored associations with X that can also be connected with Pluto. X is, for example, the biological designation for the female chromosome that everyone carries—females carry two (XX); males carry one (X plus the male chromosome Y). Pluto is thus linked with our primordial female nature. X is also used to cross out errors (as in the expression, "to X out an error"), indicating a correcting principle not commonly noted in delineations of Pluto. More associations are possible when entries for *cross, crossroads,* etc., are explored in a good symbolism dictionary, as well as when such X-words as expose and exorcise are examined in a standard dictionary.

Sources:

Lewis, James R. *Martian Astrology.* Goleta, Calif.: Jupiter's Ink, 1992.
Littmann, Mark. *Planets Beyond: Discovering the Outer Solar System.* 2d ed. New York: John Wiley & Sons, 1990.
Room, Adrian. *Dictionary of Astronomical Names.* London: Routledge, 1988.

Planetary Moons

The planetary moons are the focus of a branch of astrology devoted to the **satellites** of **Mars, Jupiter, Saturn, Uranus, Neptune,** and **Pluto.** In the past, the principal objection to planetary moon astrology was that, even if these satellites had distinct astrological meanings, such meanings were so blended with their *primaries* (an astronomical term for the **planets** around which moons **orbit**) that their separate influences could not be distinguished—the implication being that the meanings of the moons had already been integrated into existing interpretations of the planets. This objection made good logical sense and prevented the emergence of planetary moon studies until relatively recently; however, recent studies have demostrated that this traditional objection is empirically untrue. (*See* **Phobos and Deimos** and **Galilean Moons.**)

Planetary moon studies was significantly influenced by **asteroid** studies: For several decades, astrologers have been exploring the astrological meaning of the asteroids, and at this stage the idea that asteroids have astrological significance is accepted by the majority of mainstream astrologers. The notion advanced by astronomers that some of the planetary moons may be "captured asteroids" prompted astrologers with asteroid interests to begin investigating the possible independent influence of the planetary satellites. Such research was further prompted by consideration of the mass of some of the moons. Four of the 16 satellites of Jupiter, for example, are larger than the planet Pluto (which is 1,457 miles in diameter, at latest estimate). The Big Four Jovian moons are Ganymede (3,270 miles in diameter), Callisto (2,980 miles), Io (2,260 miles), and Europa (1,950 miles). Europa, the smallest of these four, has a diameter more than three times the diameter of Ceres, the largest asteroid. Thus, four significant celestial bodies larger than Pluto are in **conjunction** with Jupiter. Jupiter, in other words, constitutes a sort of de facto **stellium** (multiple conjunction) wherever it is placed in a horoscope.

The importance of the planetary moons has already been convincingly demonstrated. At this stage in the development of the field, planetary moon studies has shown how consideration of the satellites provides insight into the complementary principles of the planet involved (e.g., Mars, the planet of courage, is orbited by Phobos and Deimos, moons whose names mean, respectively, fear and panic). Other lines of research are being explored, such as

---

the constantly alternating direction of the moons (which are **retrograde** with respect to Earth half the time), as well as use of planet-centered positions of the moons in a **geocentric** chart.

Sources:

Davis, T. Patrick. *Revolutionizing Astrology with Heliocentric.* Windermere, Fla.: David Research Reports, 1980.
Lewis, James R. *Martian Astrology.* Goleta, Calif.: Jupiter's Ink, 1992.

Planets

Planets (from Greek *planasthai,* to wander) are the familiar celestial bodies **orbiting** the **Sun.** They were regarded as **stars** by the ancients, who referred to them as wanderers because, unlike the so-called **fixed stars**, the planets were always changing their positions with respect to the background of the **celestial sphere.** The Sun and the **Moon** (the **luminaries**) are also wanderers, and in traditional astrology were referred to as "planets." Although they are no longer classified as such by astronomers, many contemporary astrologers still call the two luminaries planets.

Astrological influences manifest themselves primarily through the planets. These basic influences are modified by (1) the signs of the **zodiac** (i.e., the familiar 12 astrological signs of **Aries, Taurus, Gemini**, etc.) in which the planets are placed, (2) the **aspects** (geometric **angles**) between the planets, and (3) the **houses** in which the planets are placed. An oversimplified but nonetheless useful rule of thumb is that planetary sign positions indicate personality tendencies, aspects between planets reflect how various components of one's personality interact, and house positions show how the personality manifests in the world.

As an example, consider an individual with natal **Mercury** (i.e., Mercury's position at birth) in **Libra** in the second house, with Mercury also **trine** (at a 120° angle) to **Mars.** In regard to personality, Mercury represents the mind, particularly the aspect of the thinking mind that deals with day-to-day affairs; this is what we might think of as the *basic* nature of Mercury.

> *1. Sign.* Individuals born when Mercury was in **Libra** usually communicate in a refined way and have the ability to be highly diplomatic. It is also easy for them to see both sides of an issue, which can make them indecisive, swaying back and forth between the two alternatives.
>
> *2. Aspect.* Mars represents the outgoing, assertive, aggressive energies. It also rules mechanical and other kinds of physical skills. Trine aspects often indicate where two influences blend together harmoniously. In this case, Mercury trine Mars shows, among other things, an individual who can tap her or his assertive energies in a positive manner and express them through powerful communications. This person also has a mind that can easily understand mechanical skills, or any other subject associated with Mars.

3. House. The second house is the house of earned income and personal possessions. Mercury here shows someone who can earn money with her or his communication skills. She or he also acquires possessions related to Mercury, such as books and other forms of communication media.

The planets have a special relationship with the signs of the zodiac whereby each planet is said to "rule" a certain sign (or signs). The relationship between the planets and the signs is one of kinship in their basic traits and associations. Prior to the discovery of **Uranus**, a general consensus about these relationships had endured since the time of **Ptolemy**. The traditional system held that the Sun ruled **Leo**, the Moon ruled **Cancer,** Mercury ruled **Virgo** and Gemini, **Venus** ruled Taurus and Libra, Mars ruled Aries and **Scorpio, Jupiter** ruled **Sagittarius** and **Pisces**, and **Saturn** ruled **Capricorn** and **Aquarius.** This is still the primary **rulership** system used in **Hindu astrology.** After the more recently discovered planets were studied, astrologers gradually came to assign Uranus to Aquarius, **Neptune** to Pisces, and **Pluto** to Scorpio, leaving Saturn, Jupiter, and Mars as the rulers of Capricorn, Sagittarius, and Aries. Only Mercury and Venus are still viewed as ruling two signs each.

The planets are classified in various ways, such as according to whether they are **inferior** (circle the Sun within Earth's **orbit**) or superior (circle outside the terrestrial orbit), exert **benefic** ("good") or **malefic** ("bad") astrological influences, and so forth. See the individual entries on the planets for more information.

Sources:

Campion, Nicholas. *The Practical Astrologer.* New York: Harry N. Abrams, 1987.
deVore, Nicholas. *Encyclopedia of Astrology.* New York: Philosophical Library, 1949.
McEvers, Joan. *Planets: The Astrological Tools.* Saint Paul, Minn.: Llewellyn Publications, 1989.

Platic

Astrologers allow individual **aspects** a particular **orb of influence** within which they are regarded as having an effect. Nonexact aspects are referred to as platic aspects and are considered to have a weaker influence than **partile** (exact) aspects.

Plato

Plato, the most famous of all Greek philosophers, lived in Athens from approximately 427 B.C. to 347 B.C. Although some sources have claimed that Plato lived for a period in Egypt and studied astrology, this is not reflected in his writings. Plato's significance for astrology is that directly through his own surviving works and indirectly through the Neoplatonic tradition, he was the most influential advocate of the idea that the human being is a miniature version (microcosm) of the larger universe (macrocosm). The microcosm and the macrocosm are linked by—and affect each other through—certain correlations. This notion is basic to ancient astrology.

Plotinus

Plotinus, the greatest Roman Neoplatonist, lived from approximately 205 to 270 A.D. He studied in Alexandria, Egypt, one of the centers of learning that preserved classical astrology, **magic,** and medicine (Alexandrian Neoplatonists were responsible for the survival of astrological science in the West). Plotinus accepted astrology but was opposed to a deterministic view of planetary influence. Like **Plato** (from whom the term Neoplatonism is derived), Plotinus is not important for any direct contribution to astrology but for the elaboration and propagation of the Pythagorean view that the individual human being is linked to the greater cosmos through a system of correlations—a view that is a foundation stone of ancient astrological theory.

Pluto

Pluto, named after the Roman god of the underworld and death (the Roman equivalent of the Greek Hades), is the **planet** farthest from the **Sun.** Although a grim deity, Pluto was not—in contrast with the ruler of the underworld in the Christian tradition—a totally evil character. Pluto was not discovered until 1930, but the existence of a subterranean deity is widespread in world mythology. In ancient Mesopotamia, the ruler of the dead and the underworld was the goddess Ereskigal, the Queen of the Great Below. Unlike her Roman and Greek counterparts, Ereskigal was an unhappy figure who resented her exclusion from the divinities of the upper world and agonized over the fate of those souls unlucky enough to die in early childhood. In one story she sexually seduced Nergal, the Mesopotamian **Mars,** whom she eventually married. She was also associated with irrigation canals.

Pluto completes an **orbit** of the Sun every 247.69 years, meaning that it spends more than 20 years in each sign of the **zodiac.** Thus, an entire generation is born while Pluto is **transiting** each sign. Pluto is said to **rule** the sign **Scorpio,** a relationship indicating a similarity between the characteristics of Pluto and Scorpio.

Like its mythological namesake, Pluto is associated with death and hidden ("underworld") matters. Like Ereskigal, Pluto is also associated with sexuality and sexual seduction, aggression, emotional passion, and conflict. The most basic principle characterizing Pluto is transformation (e.g., the process of changing from a worm into a butterfly). This is why death is associated with Pluto: One must die to the old to be transformed into the new. Like the sign Scorpio, Pluto also represents intensity and extremes.

Although the various planets are connected with a wide range of activities and objects, they also, when found in a **natal chart**, represent different parts of the psyche. Pluto represents the will (as in a person's inclination or disposition) in the sense of the basic life drives of sex and aggression—the part of the self that cuts through externals and gets down to life-and-death matters. Thus, its placement in a natal chart shows much about how the person expresses these drives. Pluto can also indicate a will to control and dominate.

Jeff Mayo's *The Planets and Human Behavior* provides useful lists of traits and associations for the planets. For Pluto, Mayo lists "transformation, elimination, purgation, exposure, drastic measures, an attitude of inevitability, regeneration" (p. 110). Under the heading *traditional associations* Mayo also lists "the underworld, mob violence and war, terrorist activities; abysses, sewers, mines; transformation, transmutation, transfiguration, renewal, resurrection, regeneration, the ending of a chapter of experience and the beginning of a new chapter; cataclysms, atomic energy, subterranean activities, fumigation; group activity; dictatorship; psychoanalysis; the sexual act, death; the "orgasm" of the sexual act" (p. 110–111).

Sources:

Campion, Nicholas. *The Practical Astrologer*. New York: Harry N. Abrams, 1987.
George, Llewelyn. *The New A to Z Horoscope Maker and Delineator*. Saint Paul, Minn.: Llewellyn Publications, 1910. Rev. and enl. 1987
McEvers, Joan. *Planets: The Astrological Tools*. Saint Paul, Minn.: Llewellyn Publications, 1989.
Mayo, Jeff. *The Planets and Human Behavior*. 1972. Reprint. Reno, Nev. CRCS Publications, 1985.
Valentine, Christine. *Images of the Psyche: Exploring the Planets through Psychology and Myth*. Shaftesbury, Dorset, U.K.: Element Books, 1991.

Poesia

Poesia, **asteroid** 946 (the 946th asteroid to be discovered), is approximately 40 kilometers in diameter and has an **orbital** period of 5.5 years. Its name is a personification of the word poetry. In a **natal chart**, Poesia's location by sign and **house** indicates one's poetic sensitivity, or where and how one is most likely to experience poetry. If prominent in a chart (e.g., **conjunct** the **Sun** or the **ascendant**), it may show a poetically talented individual.

Sources:

Kowal, Charles T. *Asteroids: Their Nature and Utilization*. Chichester, West Sussex, U.K.: Ellis Horwood Limited, 1988.
Room, Adrian. *Dictionary of Astronomical Names*. London: Routledge, 1988.

Polyhymnia

Polyhymnia, **asteroid** 33 (the 33d asteroid to be discovered), is approximately 62 kilometers in diameter and has an **orbital** period of 4.8 years. Polyhymnia is named after the Greek muse of singing, mime, rhetoric, and sacred dance, who was a daughter of Zeus and Mnemosyne and whose symbol is the veil. Like its mythological namesake, the asteroid Polyhymnia confers talent in singing, dance, mime, and rhetoric to **natives** in whose chart it is prominent.

Sources:

Kowal, Charles T. *Asteroids: Their Nature and Utilization.* Chichester, West Sussex, U.K.: Ellis Horwood Limited, 1988.

Room, Adrian. *Dictionary of Astronomical Names.* London: Routledge, 1988.

Porphyry System

The Porphyry, or Porphyrian, system is one of the older systems of **house** division, obtained by evenly trisecting the **ecliptic** in each of the four **quadrants**. It was named after the Neoplatonic philosopher Porphyry, who is said to have devised it.

Poseidon

Poseidon is one of the eight **hypothetical planets** (sometimes referred to as the trans-Neptunian points or planets, TNPs) utilized in Uranian astrology. On the one hand, it is mind, spirit, and ideas; on the other, it is enlightenment, inspiration, spirituality, and "vision." Thus, for example, a **Mercury**–Poseidon connection may indicate spiritual perception; **Venus**–Poseidon connection, pure love or religious faith.

Sources:

Lang-Wescott, Martha. *Mechanics of the Future: Asteroids.* Rev. ed. Conway, Mass.: Treehouse Mountain, 1991.

Simms, Maria Kay. *Dial Detective: Investigation with the 90 Degree Dial.* San Diego, Calif.: Astro Computing Services Services, 1989.

Posited

Posited (from the Latin for placed) is where a **planet** is located or placed in an astrological chart.

Pottenger, Maritha

Maritha Pottenger, was born on May 21, 1952, in Tucson, Arizona. She received a B.A. degree in psychology from University of California, Berkeley, in 1974 and an M.A. degree in clinical psychology from the California School of Professional Psychology in 1976. She studied astrology with **Zipporah Dobyns** from 1964 onward. Pottenger is the author of *Encounter Astrology, Healing with the Horoscope, Complete Horoscope Interpretation, Astro Essentials,* and several booklets and articles as well. She is also the author of numerous computerized interpretive reports sold through Astro Communications Services, such as "Planetary Profile," "Compatibility Profile," "Astro Map Analysis," "Relocation Profile," and "Your Astro Analysis."

She is a member of the National Council for GeoCosmic Research and the International Society for Astrological Research. Pottenger has taught astrology and led workshops all over the United States, Canada, and western Europe. Her focus is on using the **horoscope** as a map of the psyche to illuminate choices and options, to help turn weaknesses into strengths.

Selected Publications:

Encounter Astrology. Los Angeles: Tia Publications, 1978.
Healing with the Horoscope. San Diego: ACS, 1982.
Complete Horoscope Interpretation. San Diego: ACS, 1986.
Astro Essentials. San Diego: ACS, 1991

Precession of Equinoxes

The phenomenon known as the precession of equinoxes was said to have been discovered by Hipparchus in the second century B.C., but there is evidence that some groups of people were aware of the phenomenon much earlier. To recall some basic science, the seasons are the result of the slant of Earth's axis: When the hemisphere in which we live is inclined away from the **Sun,** we experience winter; when the hemisphere is inclined toward the Sun, we experience summer. The spin of Earth makes it behave like a gyroscope (always tending to maintain the same angle), but, because our planet is not perfectly round, it tends to "wobble" a little. One result of this wobble is that each year the Sun appears to have moved ever so slightly backward (against the backdrop of the relatively unmoving **stars**) from where it was at the same point (e.g. at a **solstice** or an **equinox** point) the preceding year (at the rate of 1° every 71.5 years).

This precession is the reason that the **tropical zodiac,** which most Western astrologers use, is a "moving" zodiac: Following the admonitions of **Ptolemy,** the great astrologer- astronomer of antiquity, the beginning of the **Zodiac**—0° **Aries**—is located where the Sun is positioned during the spring (vernal) equinox. Thus, each year the zodiac is moved very slightly. This movement keeps the zodiac aligned with the seasons, but it is always slipping backward with reference to the stars. This is disconcerting to anyone who feels that sign influence emanates from the **constellations** after which the signs of the zodiac take their names. However, if one switches over to one of the **sidereal zodiacs** (which align the zodiac with the stars), then the zodiac—which contains much seasonal symbolism—slips out of alignment with the seasons. The upshot of this is that it is possible to make a good argument for either system.

Sources:

Bach, Eleanor. *Astrology from A to Z: An Illustrated Source Book.* New York: Philosophical Library, 1990.

Filbey, John, and Peter Filbey. *The Astrologer's Companion.* Wellingborough, Northamptonshire, U.K.: Aquarian Press, 1986.

Predicting the Future

See: Prognostication

▶
**Precession of
equinoxes: the
earth like a
spinning top.**

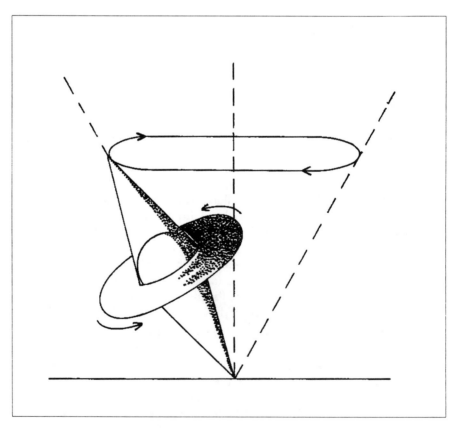

Primary Directions

See: Progressions and Directions

Prime Vertical

The prime vertical is the **great circle** that intersects the east point, the west point, the **nadir**, and the **zenith** at any given point on Earth. It is perpendicular to both the **meridian** and the **horizon**. Some systems of **house** division utilize this great circle as their primary point of reference, deriving the house **cusps** by dividing the prime vertical in to 12 equal subdivisons.

Prison

Prison is an obsolete term for **fall** (when a **planet** is in a sign opposite the sign of its **exaltation**).

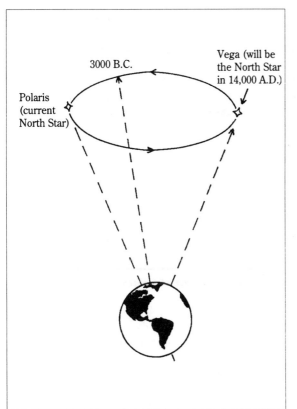

North star orientation in the precession of equinoxes: The slow but continuous change in orientation of the earth's rotational; axis resembles the spinning motion of a top, each revolution (wobble) taking about 25,800 years.

Probitas

Probitas, **asteroid** 902 (the 902d asteroid to be discovered), is approximately 12 kilometers in diameter and has an **orbital** period of 3.8 years. Its name is a personification of the Latin for probity or uprightness. In a **natal chart**, Probitas's location by sign and **house** indicates where and how one is most likely to be honest and upright. When **afflicted** by inharmonious **aspects**, Probitas may show improbity or projecting a false image of integrity. If prominent in a chart (e.g., **conjunct** the **Sun** or the **ascendant**), it can show a person of exceptional integrity, or an individual for whom integrity is a major life theme.

Sources:

Kowal, Charles T. *Asteroids: Their Nature and Utilization.* Chichester, West Sussex, U.K.: Ellis Horwood Limited, 1988.

Room, Adrian. *Dictionary of Astronomical Names.* London: Routledge, 1988.

Prognostication (Prognosis)

Astrological prognostication refers to astrological prediction, although the term prognosis is more accurate for what astrologers actually do. If the future were rigidly fated, then, no matter what we did, only one future would be possible. Given this assumption, we should be able to predict the future. The term *prognostication,* however, does not imply a rigidly fated future. Instead, the term seems to suggest that human willpower can, within certain limits, change the future. Like a weatherman, an astrologer can only predict upcoming *conditions.* Whether or not one chooses to go for a picnic on a day a meteorologist predicts rain—or on a day an astrologer advises staying at home—is a matter of personal will.

Progressed Horoscope

See: Progressions and Directions

Progressions and Directions

Progressions and directions are two related astrological methods for predicting future conditions and developments. Prediction is the oldest element of the astrologer's craft: Whereas contemporary astrologers tend to be more concerned with understanding individuals and their potential, traditional astrology tended to focus on **prognostication** (predicting the future). The most ancient and still the most important astrological tool for prognostication is **transits**, current and forthcoming movements of the planets that are transiting the sky.

Progressions and directions are other ways of examining a **natal chart** for prediction purposes.

Secondary progressions (sometimes called secondary directions), the most popular method of prognostication other than transits, uses the forumula "a day for a year" to predict the future. This method's underlying notion is that there is a relationship between the first day of life and the first year of life, between the second day of life and the second year of life, and so forth. The actual technique involves finding a person's current age and moving the **planets** and **house cusps** of the **natal chart** to the positions they occupied at the same number of days after birth as the individual's current age in years. These positions are then examined and tell the astrologer about the client's life for the current year..

An oversimplified but nevertheless useful generalization of the transit/ progression distinction is that transits indicate external conditions, whereas progressions indicate inner development (in the sense of changes in one's personality and personal interests). Thus, transits are used to predict future *environments,* whereas progressions are used to predict *inner changes* (although, because there is always a relationship between inner and outer influences, these two cannot be so neatly separated in actual practice). For readings, astrologers often erect a chart consisting of three concentric circles. The inner circle contains the natal chart, the intermediate circle contains the progressed positions (in what is referred to as the progressed chart), and the outer circle records the positions of the transiting planets, usually calculated for the time of the reading. This tripartite chart allows the astrologer to view the interactions between the various levels at a glance.

The method of secondary progressions examines changes in the progressed chart, as well as how planets in a progressed chart interact with the natal chart. For example, John Smith was born when the **Sun** was at four° in the **sign Sagittarius.** The Sun (which in astrological parlance is one of the "planets") represents John's basic self, so the sign Sagittarius colors his entire personality. Unless this **sun sign** is counterbalanced by other factors in the chart, John is probably a fun-loving guy who does not like to be tied down by obligations to anybody. Around age 26, his *progressed Sun* will enter the sign **Capricorn.** This sign tends to be focused on business and duty—very different from John's sun sign. The progressed Sun's change of sign does not indicate that John will suddenly drop his Sagittarian traits and be transformed overnight into a Capricorn. Rather, his personality will acquire an "overlay" of the latter sign's orientation, becoming somewhat more serious and mature. Business matters may become more important, and the commitments entailed by such relationships as business partnerships and marriage will seem less unappealing.

Another method of progression, termed tertiary progressions, could be referred to as "a day for a month" system. In a manner parallel to secondary progressions, this approach takes each day after birth as representing a month (a lunar month, which is shorter than a calendar month) of life. This method,

---

The Astrology Encyclopedia

devised by the twentieth-century astrologer Edward Troinski, is used far less frequently than secondary progressions. Another infrequently used method, converse secondary progressions, entails using each day *before* birth as equivalent to a year of life.

Primary directions (also termed Placidean arcs, primary arcs, and equitorial arcs) is the name for another method of astrological prognostication—"a degree for a year" system. As one might anticipate, this method involves predicting events according to the movement of a planet through **degrees**, although primary directions uses degrees of **right ascension** (measured along the **celestial equator**) rather than degrees of the **zodiac** (measured along the **ecliptic**). Prior to the advent of computer chart-casting programs, primary directions was a comparatively difficult method to use, and thus fell into disuse.

Other degree-for-year systems are solar arc directions, which measures movement in degrees of celestial **longitude** (along the ecliptic), and solar declination arc directions, which measures movement in terms of degrees of **declination.** Yet other systems of directions are ascendant arc directions, vertical arc directions, radix directions, and symbolic directions. The very overabundance of these approaches is a principal (if not *the* principal) reason most astrologers stick with transits and secondary progressions. Nonetheless, the best contemporary chart-casting programs allow one to calculate all of them, a provision which vastly simplifies experimentation and research. Many if not all of these methods are thus likely to be the subjects of renewed interest to computer-equipped astrologers.

Sources:

Brau, Jean-Louis, Helen Weaver, and Allan Edmands. *Larousse Encyclopedia of Astrology.* New York: New American Library, 1980.
deVore, Nicholas. *Encyclopedia of Astrology.* New York: Philosophical Library, 1947.

Prometheus

Prometheus, the rebellious Titan from Greek mythology, has given his name to **asteroid** 1,809, as well as to one of the moons of **Saturn**. In contemporary astrological circles, however, Prometheus is most familiar through the work of Richard Tarnas as the mythological figure best expressing the astrological nature of the **planet Uranus**. Astrologers have long noted, though few expressed the observation, that the traits attributed to the astrological Uranus appear to have no association whatsoever with the mythological Uranus. Using this discrepancy as his starting point, Tarnas took the further step of observing that the mythological figure best expressing the character traits of the astrological Uranus was Prometheus. He says, "The more I examined the matter the more I realized that every quality astrologers associate with the planet Uranus was reflected in the myth of Prometheus: the initiation of radical change, the passion for freedom, the defiance of authority, the act of cosmic rebellion against a universal structure to free humanity of limitation, the intellectual brilliance and genius, the element of excitement and risk" (Tarnas 1989, 189).

Tarnas's ideas have received widespread acceptance in the astrological community. Astrologers who hesitate accepting an exception to the widely held principle that the name given to a celestial body by an astronomer **synchronistically** corresponds with its archetypal meaning might note that the mythological Uranus is related to the astrological Uranus as its complementary polarity: The Greek Uranus was a tyrant who opposed change, which represents characteristics that must be in place before Prometheus can express his rebellious, freedom-seeking, change-at-any-cost nature.

Other planets embody such polar characteristics. Thus, the astrological **Saturn**, for example, expresses both security-seeking and insecurity. And **Mars**, (as discussed in the entry on **Phobos and Deimos** indicates both courage and fear, although traditionally astrologers noted only the courageous, assertive nature of Mars and not the corresponding Martian anxiety. In eccentric Uranus, it is the polar opposite principle that is expressed by the planet's namesake. Thus, to acknowledge both Tarnas and the tradition of synchronistic meanings, one could assert that the area of the **natal chart** where a **native** feels rebellious (as indicated by the placement of natal Uranus) is also the area where she or he feels most oppressed.

Sources:

Tarnas, Richard. "Uranus and Prometheus." *Journal of the British Astrological Association* (July–August 1989): 187–196.
———. "The Western Mind at the Threshold." *The Astrotherapy Newsletter 3, no. 4* (November 1990): 2–5.

Promitter

Promitter (from Latin *promittere,* to promise) is an older term that refers to the things "promised" by the sign, **house**, and **aspects** of a particular **planet**. The related term **significator** refers to another planet or important point that, by **transit** or **progression**, activates the first planet's "promise." These terms are rarely used in modern **natal astrology**, although they are common in **horary astrology**.

Proper Motion

Proper motion refers to the motion of a **planet** or other celestial body in space as opposed to **apparent motion** caused by such factors as the **axial rotation** of Earth.

Proserpina

Proserpina, **asteroid** 26 (the 26th asteroid to be discovered), is approximately 88 kilometers in diameter and has an **orbital** period of 4.3 years. Proserpina was the Roman name for the Greek Persephone, who was kidnapped by Hades and taken to the underworld to become his queen. According to Lang-Wescott, Proserpina represents rites of passage—infant awareness of separateness, adolescent crisis, leaving home for school, marriage, job change, or personal growth. This asteroid's key word is *transition*.

Sources:

Lang-Wescott, Martha. *Asteroids-Mechanics: Ephemerides II*. Conway, Mass.: Treehouse Mountain, 1990.
———. *Mechanics of the Future: Asteroids*. Rev. ed Conway, Mass.: Treehouse Mountain, 1991.

Prudentia

Prudentia, **asteroid** 474 (the 474th asteroid to be discovered), is approximately 26 kilometers in diameter and has an **orbital** period of 3.8 years. Its name is a personification of the word prudence. In a **natal chart**, Purdentia's location by **sign** and **house** indicates where and how one is most likely to be prudent. When **afflicted** by inharmonious **aspects**, Prudentia may show imprudence. If prominent in a chart (e.g., **conjunct** the **Sun** or the **ascendant**), it may signal an exceptionally prudent person.

Sources:

Kowal, Charles T. *Asteroids: Their Nature and Utilization*. Chichester, West Sussex, U.K.: Ellis Horwood Limited, 1988.
Room, Adrian. *Dictionary of Astronomical Names*. London: Routledge, 1988.

Psyche

Psyche is the name of an **asteroid** as well as the soul or mind. Psyche, asteroid 16 (the 16th asteroid to be discovered), was named after a beautiful woman in a Greek myth, said to represent the soul. It has an **orbital** period of 5 years and is 248 kilometers in diameter (making it the same size as **Juno**). Psyche is one of the more recent asteroids to be investigated by astrologers. Preliminary material on Psyche can be found in **Demetra George** and Douglas Bloch's *Astrology for Yourself,* and an **ephemeris** (table of celestial locations) for Psyche can be found in the back of the second edition of their *Asteroid Goddesses*. Unlike the **planets**, which are associated with a wide range of phenomena, the smaller asteroids are said to represent a single principle. George and Bloch (1987) give Psyche's principle as "psychic sensitivity"; their tentative key phrase for Psyche is *my capacity to be psychically sensitive to another person*. **Zipporah Dobyns** views Psyche as either the capacity to understand and care for others or the incapacity to do so if one is self-centered or insecure. J. Lee Lehman regards Psyche as representing the unconscious aspect of the mind, particularly our unconscious mental habits.

Sources:

Dobyns, Zipporah. *Expanding Astrology's Universe*. San Diego, Calif.: Astro Computing Services, 1983.

George, Demetra, with Douglas Bloch. *Astrology for Yourself: A Workbook for Personal Transformation*. Berkeley, Calif.: Wingbow Press, 1987.

———. *Asteroid Goddesses: The Mythology, Psychology and Astrology of the Reemerging Feminine*. 2d ed. rev. and enl. San Diego, Calif.: Astro Computing Services Publications, 1990.

Lehman, J. Lee. *The Ultimate Asteroid Book*. West Chester, Pa: Whitford Press, 1988.

Psychology and Astrology

Because so much of astrology—at least as it is currently practiced—is psychological, the relationship between psychology and astrology is complex. Various aspects of this interface are dealt with elsewhere in this encyclopedia (*see* **Carl Jung**, **Astrotherapy**, and **Research, Astrological**). This essay examines some of the issues that psychological researchers have addressed when questioning the validity of astrology.

Femininity

In September 1973, the *Journal of Psychology* published an article by Robert J. Pellegrini, "The astrological 'theory' of personality: An unbiased test by a biased observer," which found significant correlations between people's **sun sign** and their score on the California Psychological Inventory's Femininity scale. In March 1975, the same journal published another article by Pellegrini in which he noted that the highest Femininity scores in the 1973 study corresponded with the consecutive **signs** from **Leo** through **Capricorn**, a correlation that does not correspond with the traditional astrological characterization of *every other* sign as **feminine**. Later studies failed to confirm Pellegrini's original findings.

Introversion/Extroversion

In 1978, the *Journal of Social Psychology* published an article by Jeff Mayo et al., "An empirical study of the relation between astrological factors and personality," which found correlations between people's **sun sign** and their score on a measure of introversion and extroversion. This study found that, congruent with what one might anticipate from astrological tradition, even-numbered signs

(Aries, Gemini, etc.) were more extroverted than odd-numbered signs (Taurus, Cancer, etc.). Most later studies failed to confirm Mayo's study, with the exception of one by Jan J. Van Rooij et al., "Introversion-extroversion and sun-sign," which successfully replicated Mayo et al.

Occupation

The various studies by the **Gauquelin's**, dealt with in the essay on **vocational astrology**, have successfully demonstrated significant correlations between occupation and the positions of certain **planets** at birth. Most studies of sun signs have failed to find statistically significant correlations between sun signs and professions, although there was a series that appeared in *The Guardian,* a British newspaper, in 1984 that showed correlations from census data. A disingenuous critique published in the *Skeptical Inquirer* the next year attempted to explain away *The Guardian* study as resulting from the imputed tendency of people to pick professions based on a prior knowledge of the professions associated with their sun signs.

Belief in Astrology

An interesting line of research that several different researchers have pursued is the correlation between belief in astrology and certain other personality traits, although most such studies are undertaken to demonstrate that "believers" in the science of the stars are weak or defective in some way. Thus, for example, in February 1980, the *Journal of Social Psychology* published an article by Ruth H. Sosis et al., "Perceived locus of control and beliefs about astrology," that found a belief in fate was correlated with belief in astrology. It was also found that females were more likely to believe in astrology than males. In 1982, the journal *Personality and Individual Difference* published an article by G. A. Tyson that hypothesized a correlation between astrological clients and stressful social roles. And in 1983, the same journal published an article reporting a study by Michael Startup, "Belief in astrology: A system of maladjustment?" that found no signs of neuroticism in astrology students, although it did find correlations between astrology students and psychology students.

Miscellaneous Studies

Other interesting studies have appeared both within and outside mainstream academic psychology. For example, in April 1988, the journal *Perceptual and Motor Skills* published a study by Steven Stack and David Lester, "Born under a bad sign? Astrological sign and suicide ideation," which found a correlation between suicide ideation and people born under the sign **Pisces** (a correlation that one would have anticipated from traditional astrology). Another interesting piece was a 1973 study by John Newmeyer and Steven Anderson, "Astrology and addiction: An empirical probe," that found Geminis, Virgos, and Aquarians most likely to be heroin abusers, and Scorpios and Capricorns least likely.

Vernon Clark Administers Psychological Tests

The studies conducted by the American psychologist **Vernon Clark** belong in a class by themselves. In 1959, he designed three tests that were given to 50 astrologers. In the first, astrologers were asked to match the **natal charts** of 10 people with 10 short biographies that highlighted career, marriage, medical history, and hobbies. All subjects were well established in their chosen profession.

In the second, astrologers were asked, in 10 instances, to match one of two charts with a brief case history. They were not informed that one of each pair was an actual **horoscope** and the other a chart cast for a random place and time. In the third, astrologers were asked to distinguish natal charts for high-IQ people from charts of victims of brain damage. As a control group, the same tests were given to psychologists and social workers with no background in astrology.

In all three tests, the accuracy of the astrologers was statistically significant. In comparison, the accuracy of the control groups was never more than what would be expected from random chance. Clark's first and second tests, with some variations, were also successfully conducted by both **Zipporah Dobyns** and Joseph Ernest Vidmar in the 1970s.

Clark's work was important for providing a suggestive model from which to design other experiments. This model has been referred to as holistic because of the way in which it is able to bring the entire astrological chart into the test. Other approaches, such as the studies discussed at the beginning of this entry, isolate one factor, such as the sun sign, and ignore other influences.

Sources:

Brau, Jean-Louis, Helen Weaver, and Allan Edmands. *Larousse Encyclopedia of Astrology.* New York: New American Library, 1980.

Mayo, Jeff, O. White, and Hans Eysenck. "An empirical study of the relation between astrological factors and personality." *Journal of Social Psychology* 105 (1978): 229-36.

Miller, Neil Z. *Astrology (Newsletter).* Santa Fe, N. Mex.: UniSearch, 1991.

Newmeyer, John, and Steven Anderson. "Astrology and addiction: An empirical probe." *Drug Forum* (Spring 1973): 271-78.

Pellegrini, Robert J. "The astrological 'theory' of personality: An unbiased test by a biased observer." *Journal of Psychology* (Sept. 1973): 21-28.

———. "Birthdate psychology: A new look at some old data." *Journal of Psychology* (March 1975): 261-65.

Sosis, Ruth H., et al. "Perceived locus of control and beliefs about astrology." *Journal of Social Psychology* (Feb. 1980): 65-71.

Stack, Steven, and David Lester. "Born under a bad sign? Astrological sign and suicide ideation." *Perceptual and Motor Skills* (April 1988): 461-62.

Startup, Michael. "Belief in astrology: A system of maladjustment?" *Personality and Individual Difference* 4: no. 3 (1983): 343-45.

Tyson, G. A. "People who consult astrologers: A profile." *Personality and Individual Difference* v.3, iss. 2 (1982): 119-126.

Van Rooij, Jan J., et al. "Introversion-extroversion and sunsign." *Journal of Psychology* (May 1988): 275-78.

Ptolemy, Claudius

Claudius Ptolemy (100 to 178 A.D.), sometimes called the father of Western astrology, was a Greek astronomer and astrologer who lived in Alexandria, Egypt. Ptolemy was a highly learned individual, with a broad grasp of geography, mathematics, **astronomy**, and music. His account of the motions of the **planets**, which placed Earth as the stable center around which the **Sun, stars**, and planets revolved, was generally accepted until the time of the Copernican revolution.

In his classic astrological work, the *Tetrabiblos,* Ptolemy attempted to compile the astrological knowledge of his predecessors and systematize it into a unified discipline. He also offered a theory of astrological influence in terms of the science of his day. Despite the shortcomings of his work, Ptolemy's organization of the body of diverse information into a coherent whole made him the most influential single astrologer in Western history.

Sources:

Brau, Jean-Louis, Helen Weaver, and Allan Edmands. *Larousse Encyclopedia of Astrology.* New York: New American Library, 1980.

deVore, Nicholas. *Encyclopedia of Astrology.* New York: Philosophical Library, 1948.

Pythagoras

Pythagoras, a Greek philosopher, mathematician, and astronomer, lived from approximately B.C. 580 to 500 Pythagoras was the first to conceive of the **heliocentric** theory of the universe (the notion that Earth and the **planets** revolve around the **Sun**), a notion that did not catch on until **Copernicus**. Pythagoras and his followers also developed basic mathematical notions, such as the concepts of equation and proportion.

Pythagoras is said to have searched widely for wisdom and is believed to have introduced the idea of **reincarnation** to the Western world. One of his teachings regards the "music of the spheres," the notion that the intervals between the planets correspond to musical tones and that the movements of the planets produce an ethereal music. Pythagoras's significance for astrology is that he clearly formulated the notion that the human being is a miniature version (microcosm) of the larger universe (macrocosm). The microcosm and the macrocosm are linked by—and affect each other through—certain correlations. This notion is basic to ancient astrology.

Q

Quadrant

The quadrants of a **horoscope** refer to four sets of three **houses**: Houses one, two, and three (first quadrant), houses four, five, and six (second quadrant), houses seven, eight, and nine (third quadrant), and houses ten, eleven, and twelve (fourth quadrant).

◄
A quadrant from the mid-16th century.
· **Bettmann Archive**

A quadrant is also an instrument used to calculate the position of celestial bodies. In Europe, quadrants superseded the use of **astrolabes** during the Renaissance.

Quadrupedal

The quadrupedal signs are the so-called **four-footed signs**, namely, **Aries, Taurus, Leo, Sagittarius**, and **Capricorn**.

Qualities (Quadruplicities)

The primary categories by which the signs are classified are the four **elements**—earth, air, fire, and water—and the three **qualities**—cardinal, mutable, and fixed. Each of the 12 signs of the **zodiac** is a unique combination of an element and a quality (e.g., **Aries** is a cardinal fire sign, **Taurus** is fixed earth, **Gemini** is mutable air, and so forth). The elemental nature of a sign is said to

▶
The quadrants.

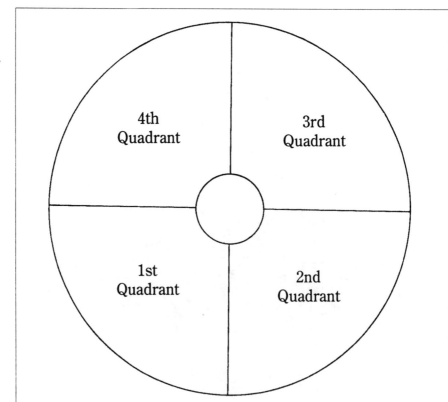

refer to its basic temperament, whereas its quality refers to its mode of expression.

Cardinal signs are said to be outgoing signs that initiate new activities; fixed signs, by way of contrast, persist with their established activities; mutable signs adapt to changing circumstances. Some modern astrologers use an analogy to certain notions in physics to contrast the nature of the three qualities: **cardinal signs** are said to represent centrifugal force, **fixed signs** centripetal force, and **mutable signs** wave (back and forth) motion.

Although the qualities are on par with the elements as categories for classifying the zodiac, they tend to be treated less fully in most astrological textbooks, partly because the symbols for the elements are more concrete and thus more intuitively obvious, but also because the traits said to characterize each of the qualities do not seem to apply (or, at least, do not seem to apply fully) to certain signs. Thus, for example, individuals born under the cardinal sign **Cancer** do not typically tend to be outgoing people who initiate new activities (a cardinal trait); rather, Cancers tend to adapt (a mutable trait) or to resist (a fixed trait) changing circumstances. **Capricorn**, another cardinal sign, is good at initiating new business activities but is also one of the more stubborn signs (a fixed trait).

Although the confusion introduced by these exceptions might lead one to abandon this system of classification altogether, there are certain other sign characteristics that the qualities explain quite well. Fixed signs, for example, are said to manifest the characteristic of stubbornness, and when the fixed quadruplicity is examined, this characterization—with predictable variations introduced by the different elements—works out quite well: Although all the fixed signs are stubborn, Taurus is most stubborn about practical matters (earth), **Leo** is most stubborn about certain ways of doing things (fire), **Scorpio** is most stubborn about feelings (water), and **Aquarius** is most stubborn about ideals (air). Thus, the usefulness of the qualities when they are truly applicable (which is the majority of the time) counterbalances the confusion introduced by a few exceptions.

Sources:

Hand, Robert. *Horoscope Symbols.* Rockport, Mass.: Para Research, 1981.
Sakoian, Frances, and Louis S. Acker. *The Astrologer's Handbook.* New York: Harper & Row, 1989.

Querent

In **horary astrology**, the individual asking the question is referred to as the querent.

Quesited

In **horary astrology**, the quesited is the person, thing, or event, that is the subject of the question.

Quetzalcoatl

Quetzalcoatl, **asteroid** 1,915 (the 1,915th asteroid to be discovered), is approximately .4 kilometer in diameter and has an **orbital** period of 4 years. Quetzalcoatl was named after a god who was simultaneously a creator and a millennialist figure in Aztec mythology and for whom Cortez was mistaken. Lehman views this asteroid as a blend of **Mars** and **Sun** characteristics, a "Hero-God: more active than the Sun, more creative than Mars" (p. 100).

Sources:

Kowal, Charles T. *Asteroids: Their Nature and Utilization*. Chichester, West Sussex, U.K.: Ellis Horwood Limited, 1988.

Lehman, J. Lee. *The Ultimate Asteroid Book*. West Chester, Penn.: Whitford Press, 1988.

Quincunx

A quincunx (also called an inconjunct) is a minor **aspect** of 150°. The effect of a a quincunx is comparatively weak. With the exception of double quincunx (**yod**) **configurations**, quincunxes received little attention until relatively recently. Their influence was usually regarded as being mildly favorable, like a **semisextile**, but more recent interpreters regard them as a source of stress, requiring change and adjustment in the areas of the chart that they affect.

Quindecile

A quindecile is a minor **aspect** of 24° created when a circle is divided into 15 equal parts. As a third part of a **quintile**, a quindecile is a very weak but favorable influence that is studied in the branch of astrology referred to as **harmonics**. It is given a very narrow **orb of influence** of 1° or less.

Quintile

A quintile is a minor **aspect** of 72° created by subdividing a circle into five parts. The great astronomer **Johannes Kepler** devised quintiles and biquintiles (144°) for his astrological work. Quintiles refer to the aptitudes or talents related to the **planets** involved in the aspect. It is given an **orb of influence** of 1° to 3°, depending on the astrologer.

R

Radical

Radical is an adjective form of the noun **radix**, as in the "radical" position of the **planets**, meaning their original position in a **horoscope** chart.

Radix

Radix (Latin for root) refers to the original **horoscope**. It is used to distinguish the radix from such secondary charts as **progressed horoscopes**. In **genethliacal astrology** it is equivalent to the **natal chart**. Radix, however, may also refer to the original chart of a horoscope cast for an event (as opposed to a person). It hence has a wider application than natal chart.

Ram

The Ram is a popular alternate name for the sign **Aries**.

The Reagans and Astrology

In May 1988, *For the Record,* Donald Regan's account of his years as chief of staff of the Reagan White House, was published. Regan's description of the role Joan Quigley (Nancy Reagan's astrologer) played in the Reagan presidency became an occasion for the press to ridicule both astrology and the president. The *New York Post,* for instance, ran the headline "Astrologer Runs the White House." According to Regan, astrology was a daily, sometimes an hourly, factor in Ronald Reagan's schedule. In his book, he made it appear that this control over scheduling amounted to placing the president's life—and consequently the American nation—under the control of Quigley.

Nancy Reagan's memoir *My Turn* was published the following year. Chapter 3 of this book is devoted to a defense of her reliance on the science of the **stars**. The former First Lady defended herself by portraying astrology as a kind of emotional "pacifier." She says, for example, that "each person has his own way of coping with trauma and grief, with the pain of life, and astrology was one of mine." She also downplayed the role astrology had in the Reagan presidency, asserting that Quigley did nothing more than time events.

For her part, Joan Quigley claims that, in deference to the Reagans, she was reticent to talk about her relationship with the Reagan White House until *My Turn* appeared. Asserting that what Nancy Reagan had "left out about the way she used astrology and my ideas would fill a book," she decided to write her own. *"What Does Joan Say?"* was published the next year. If *My Turn* underestimated the role the science of the stars played in the Reagan presidency, *"What Does Joan Say?"* seems to overstate astrology's—or, at least, Quigley's—role. Her book makes it appear not only that her advice was an essential ingredient in most of Reagan's sucesses but also that she was responsible for such important advice as persuading the president to stop viewing USSR as the Evil Empire. Quigley, in other words, portrays herself as the pivotal influence behind the rapprochement between the United States and the Soviet block and, by implication, as responsible for the subsequent collapse of the iron curtain.

For astrologers, *"What Does Joan Say?"* raises broader issues. In the first place, the relationship between Quigley and the Reagans reminds astrologers that their science was founded by people who studied the stars for the benefit of powerful political figures. Thus, while some contemporary astrologers might condemn Quigley's advice to Ronald Reagan (a president views as too right-wing by the generally liberal astrology community), she clearly falls into the tradition of court astrologers of former eras—a tradition that nurtured and even gave birth to astrology as we know it today. What are the ethical ramifications of providing as astrological information for political leaders? As astrology acquires greater acceptance in the larger society, these issues will become increasingly important to future generations of astrologers.

Another issue raised by the Quigley case concerns the way the practice of astrology is portrayed in *"What Does Joan Say?"* which emphasizes **electional astrology** (determining or "electing" the appropriate times to initiate certain actions) almost to the exclusion of other branches of astrological science. Contemporary astrology has tended to go to the opposite extreme, downplaying the importance of such "elections" and focusing instead on the interpretation of clients' personality and personality potentials. Thus, part of the importance of *"What Does Joan Say?"* is to remind astrologers of a powerful technique that has been relegated to a back seat for far too long.

Sources:

Quigley, Joan. *"What Does Joan Say?"* New York: Birch Lane Press, 1990.
Reagan, Nancy. *My Turn: The Memoirs of Nancy Reagan.* New York: Random House, 1989.

Reception

Reception is an older term for a relationship between two **planets** in which one is located in a sign **ruled** by the other. For example, **Mars** in **Taurus** is said to be "received by" **Venus** (the ruler of Taurus). Contemporary astrologers rarely use this term, except in the expression **mutual reception** (which occurs when two planets are in each other's sign).

Rectification

Rectification is the process of adjusting the birth chart to the precise birth time in cases where the birthday is known but the birth moment is inexact or completely unknown. Rectification is accomplished by working backward from the **native**'s personality traits and from important events in the person's life. In other words, an astrologer rectifying a **natal chart** asks the question, Given such and such traits and such and such events, what should this person's birth chart look like?

For example, suppose someone the astrologer knows was born around sunrise. Further assume that before 7:15 A.M. on the day of birth the **planet Uranus** would have been in the native's eighth **house** and after 7:15 it would have been in the seventh house. Uranus represents, among other things, sudden, unexpected changes. The eighth house indicates inheritance, other people's money, and the like. The seventh house is partnership and marriage. Thus, if the individual had experienced many sudden beginnings and endings of relationships, the astrologer would infer that the person was born when Uranus was in the seventh house; if, by contrast, the individual had regularly received money from other people in sudden, unexpected ways, the astrologer would infer that the person was born when Uranus was in the eighth house. Through a reasoning process like this, applied to as many different factors as possible, the astrologer could eventually determine precisely when the native was born.

Sources:

Foreman, Patricia. *Computers and Astrology: A Universal User's Guide and Reference.* Burlington, Vt.: Good Earth Publications, 1992.
Gettings, Fred. *Dictionary of Astrology.* London: Routledge & Kegan Paul, 1985.

Reformation, Astrology during

See: History of Western Astrology

Refranation

Refranation is a technical term used in **horary astrology** referring to a situation in which a **planet** turns **retrograde** (reverses its **apparent motion**) before it completes an **aspect** to which it has been **applying**. In such a situation, the matter for which the horary chart was cast will not result in a successful conclusion.

Regiomontanus (Johann Müller)

Regiomontanus (born Johann Müller), a German astronomer and astrologer, was born on June 6, 1436, in Königsberg. He established an observatory at Nuremberg, where he observed Halley's comet. Regiomontanus also published **ephemerides** (tables of planetary positions) that were used by, among other people, Columbus. He was brought to Rome by Pope Sixtus IV to help devise the **calendar**. Regiomontanus was also the translator of **Ptolemy's** *Almagest.* He died in Rome on July 6, 1476. He is best remembered by astrologers for the system of **house** division that bears his name.

Regiomontanus System

The Regiomontanus (Regiomontanean) system is a system of **house** division devised by Johann Müller (Regiomontanus was his pseudonym) in the fifteenth century. At one time it was the most popular sysem in Europe.

Reincarnation, Karma, and Astrology

Reincarnation is the theory that each individual soul progressively incarnates in a succession of different bodies. Belief in reincarnation usually carries with it certain other, related notions, such as the idea that one is learning from one lifetime to another and that, in time, every soul will become perfected and consequently no longer need to return to corporeal form. Another idea often associated with reincarnation is the notion of karma, which is the moral law of cause and effect formulated by Hindu and Buddhist thinkers. For example, if one steals money from another person, the thief will eventually have money stolen from her or him, either later in this life or in a future lifetime.

The notions of reincarnation and karma together explain why some people are born into lucky circumstances while other people are born into unfortunate conditions. For astrologers concerned with the issue of why some people come into this life with hardship written large across their **natal charts** and other people seem to be born under a lucky star, reincarnation and karma provide an important explanatory tool. Reincarnation also provides a framework for explaining why a person should have certain personality traits—they are carryovers from "past lifetimes."

There are different approaches for determining which factors in a chart indicate information about the **native's** karma and past lifetimes. **Planets** in **intercepted signs** and in the twelfth **house**, for example, are often said to provide insight into one's past lives. The branch of astrology especially concerned with these issues is **esoteric astrology**.

Sources:

Brau, Jean-Louis, Helen Weaver, and Allan Edmands. *Larousse Encyclopedia of Astrology.* New York: New American Library, 1980.
Gettings, Fred. *Dictionary of Astrology.* London: Routledge & Kegan Paul, 1987.

Renaissance, Astrology during

See: History of Western Astrology

Research, Astrological

Astrology has grown and changed considerably in recent decades in response to new ideas that have been researched and perfected by various members of the astrological community. Certain organizations, such as the International Society for Astrological Research (ISAR) and the National Council for Geocosmic Research (NCGR), have been involved for many years with the task of creating networks of astrologers with similar research interests. While astrological research may take many different forms, most avenues of research boil down to two basic approaches: statistical and "clinical."

> *1. Statistical.* Following the model of the social sciences, astrologers can test certain astrological correlations with statistical methods. The research of the **Gauquelins**, which demonstrated significant statistical correlations between professions and the prominence of certain planets, is the best-known example employing this model. Such methods, however, are not very accessible to the majority of astrologers, who do not usually have the resources to collect large pools of data.

> *2. Clinical.* Following the model of psychiatry, astrologers can also intensively investigate a smaller number of cases, using more informal methods to determine correlations. When new **planets** were discovered, for example, astrologers placed them in **horoscopes** and then attempted to perceive patterns in the people who came to them as clients. After many years of such observations, the astrological community reached a consensus on the general influence of the new celestial bodies.

The clinical approach, which is easily the most widespread of the two, can be carried out fairly systematically by studying people who have charts in which the new celestial body is prominent. The essential clue with which one begins is the name of the new body, which gives preliminary insight into its astrological "temperament."

This preliminary clue derives from what may be thought of as a third research methodology, *amplification,* a term rooted in **Carl Jung's** psychology. Much of traditional Jungian analysis focused on the interpretation of dreams, and Jung found that the dreams of his clients frequently contained images with which they were completely unfamiliar but which seemed to reflect symbols that could be found somewhere in the mythological systems of world culture. The notion of the **collective unconscious** was used to explain this phenomenon. Jung further found that he could often interpret his patients' dreams if he studied and reflected upon the particular myth or symbol to which the dream image seemed to allude. In certain cases, deeper and more complete significance for the dream image could be uncovered by locating similar images in more than one cultural system. Researching such images in the quest for deeper meanings is referred to as amplification.

To use amplification for research purposes, astrologers must further embrace the Jungian principle of **synchronicity.** For example, for a newly discovered celestial body, a common astrological practice is to assign it a tentative meaning that can be derived from associations with its name. Take, for instance, the **asteroid Eros.** Beginning with a preliminary clue, such as the idea that this small celestial body is somehow related to passion (the English word erotic comes from the Greek *eros*), an astrologer would place Eros in the **natal charts** of acquaintances as well as in the charts of famous people whose lives are open to public scrutiny. The astrologer would then study the influence of the body in charts in which it is prominent—charts in which it is in very close **aspect** (especially a **conjunction**) with an important planet or with an **angle.** As these charts are studied, the astrologer then revises the preliminary meanings so that they align with the empirical effects of the new body. The initial step in this approach to astrological research is based on the well-established observation that the designations astronomers assign to newly discovered celestial bodies are not coincidental, that by virtue of some sort of nonapparent, synchronistic process, non-astrologically inclined astronomers give them astrologically significant names.

If an astrologer wished to further amplify the possible meanings of Eros, she or he would carefully study as many myths as possible in which Eros was a figure, from the older Greek myths to the discussion of Eros in Plato's *Symposium.* The astrologer would also try to explore the symbolism of parallel mythological figures in other cultures. In the case of Eros, for example, she or he might research myths on Kama, the Hindu god of love.

Sources:

Brau, Jean-Louis, Helen Weaver, and Allan Edmands. *Larousse Encyclopedia of Astrology.* New York: New American Library, 1980.
Lewis, James R. *Martian Astrology.* Goleta, Calif.: Jupiter's Ink, 1992.

Retrograde

Retrograde (from Latin, to step backwards) refers to the apparent backward motion of a **planet** in its **orbit**. Because all the planets in the **solar system** are moving in orbits of different sizes at different rates of speed, there will be periods in the orbit of **Earth** when each of the other planets seems to reverse direction for a period of time. The effect can be compared with that of a jet as it passes a slower-moving airplane that is flying in the same direction at a lower altitude: As the pass is made, the slower craft appears—particularly when viewed against the backdrop of Earth—to be moving in the opposite direction. Similarly, retrograde planets appear to move in reverse direction when viewed against the backdrop of the **fixed stars**.

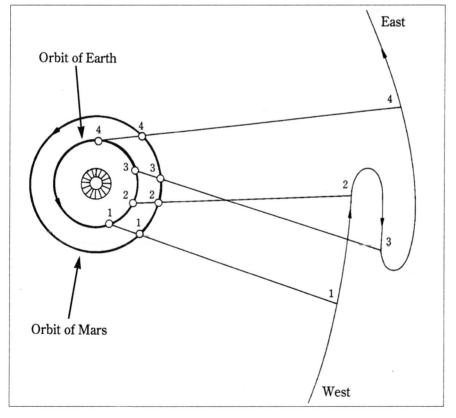

◄

Retrograde motion.

In an astrological chart, retrograde planets are usually indicated by a small capital R, which appears at the lower right of the planet symbol. Traditional astrology regarded retrograde planets in a birth chart as suffering from a **debility** (a weakening of influence). Modern astrologers have largely dropped this interpretation and tend instead to characterize retrograde planets found in **natal charts** as having a delayed influence. Following the suggestion of **Dane Rudhyar**, other contemporary astrologers interpret retrograde planets as influencing the **native**'s subconscious mind more than the person's conscious mind. For the most part, however, astrologers do not regard retrograde motion as a major influence: Unless an astrologer is delving into the more subtle aspects of a natal chart, the effect of a planet's retrogradation is rarely mentioned.

This situation changes when astrologers are interpreting **transits**. The usual advice in this area is to refrain from the activities associated with a transiting planet when it is retrograde. Astrologers tend to pay particularly close attention to the retrograde periods of **Mercury**, ruler of the mind, communication, travel, and related matters. The period of Mercury's retrogradation may be fortunate for introverted activities like reflection and meditation but it is considered unfortunate for traveling and for making important decisions (e.g., signing contracts). Travel is sometimes delayed while Mercury is retrograde, and decisions made during such periods are often reversed after Mercury goes **direct**.

Sources:

Adams, Helen J. *Understanding Retrogrades.* Tempe, Ariz.: American Federation of Astrologers, 1980.
Brau, Jean-Louis, Helen Weaver, and Allan Edmands. *Larousse Encyclopedia of Astrology.* New York: New American Library, 1980.
Krupp, Edwin C. *Beyond the Blue Horizon.* New York: HarperCollins, 1991.

Retrograde Application

Retrograde application (**applying**) is when two **planets** are moving into an **aspect** with each another while both are in **retrograde** motion.

Return

A return is when a **planet**—or, by extension, any other celestial body—makes a complete circuit of the **zodiac** and returns to a particular place, usually the position it occupied at birth. Returns are particularly significant for certain methods of **prognostication,** such as for **solar returns** and lunar returns. The solar returns method is based on **casting a chart** for the moment the **Sun** or the **Moon** returns to the exact position it occupied at the moment of birth. From this chart, astrologers are able to describe conditions for the upcoming year (in the case of a solar return) or for the upcoming month (lunar return).

A special kind of return that astrologers watch carefully is the so-called **Saturn** return. A Saturn return, as the name implies, refers to the period when the planet Saturn returns to its natal position. However, rather than casting a chart for the moment this return becomes exact as a way of predicting the next 28 years or so, astrologers are interested in what occurs *during* the return. A slow-moving planet, Saturn often crosses over its natal place, **retrogrades** back over the same position, and then goes forward, completing a total of three contacts with its natal point. Depending on whether Saturn contacts this position once or thrice, the effects of a Saturn return can make themselves felt for as few as 2, or as many as 8 months.

During these periods, Saturn forces us to examine our lives truthfully: If we have been striving with integrity and growing the best we know how, a Saturn return can bring the fulfillment of many years of hard work (because this planet represents the principle of manifestation or "concretization"). If, however, we have been drifting along with the strongest wind, having built our lives on foundations of sand, Saturn tends to pull the rug out from under us.

Most people experience at least two Saturn returns in their life: The first one, around age 28 or 29, often corresponds to the shocking realization that we are no longer young. If we have not gotten down to the serious business of being adults, this **transit** will force upon us the realization that we are growing old. The second Saturn return, around age 56 or 57, frequently brings with it the unpleasant realization that we are growing older: Middle age is past, and the crippling effects of old age—not to mention death—are just around the corner. At their best, Saturn returns are maturing experiences that prepare us for the next stage of life. Even at their best, however, Saturn returns are rarely pleasant.

Sources:

Brau, Jean-Louis, Helen Weaver, and Allan Edmands. *Larousse Encyclopedia of Astrology.* New York: New American Library, 1980.
Lewi, Grant. *Astrology for the Millions.* 4th rev. ed. Saint Paul, Minn.: Llewellyn Publications, 1971.

Revolution

While revolution may be used to refer to **orbital** revolution, it is most often used to refer to the return of a celestial body to the place it occupied in the **radical** chart.

Richter, Haloli Q.

Haloli Q. Richter, a native of Austria, is a contemporary astrologer with a practice in Washington, D.C. She was educated in Vermont and holds a B.A. degree in psychology from Goddard College. She has been an astrological counselor since 1970 and has translated several books on astrology and psychology from German into English.

In addition to an extensive private practice, she has been a book reviewer (1975–1980) and associate editor (1977–1980) for *Astrology Now* magazine and currently reviews books for *The Astro-Therapy Newsletter* and writes a column for *Washington Entertainment* magazine. She has also spoken at numerous astrology conferences over the past two decades.

Right Ascension

Right ascension and **declination** together comprise a pair of celestial coordinates for locating **planets** and other celestial objects. Right ascension is the **angular distance** (distance expressed in terms of **degrees** [°], minutes ['], and seconds ["]) along the **celestial equator** (which is the terrestrial equator extended out into space and projected against the background of the **stars**). Right ascension is measured from the **vernal point** (the point in the sky where the **Sun** was at the spring **equinox**).

Rodden, Lois Mae

Lois Mae Rodden, a contemporary astrologer, was born May 22, 1928, in Land, Saskatchewan, Canada. She was raised in a small prairie community. On October 17, 1940, her father was found on the street with several skull fractures; the case was never solved. In December 1940, she moved to Los Angeles with her mother, who remarried the following September. After 17 moves in the next 8 years, she became a high school dropout at age 16.

On February 13, 1949, she married George F. Rodden, with whom she had several children. Her husband worked as an aircraft mechanic, car salesman, factory representative, and then executive. In 1964, he began conducting youth symphonies as an avocation, which he continues to do. On September 1, 1961, they moved to Los Angeles, California, and Lois Rodden began astrology classes at the **Church of Light** within the month. She divorced in 1966.

Lois Rodden was a charter member of PAI (Professional Astrologers, Inc.). She is a professional astrological counselor and writes books and articles, including articles on **sun sign** astrology. She is best known for her work on **astrological data** especially her classification of such data.

Roman Astrology

See: History of Western Astrology

Rosicrucian Fellowship

The Rosicrucian Fellowship was established in 1907 by the well-known astrologer **Max Heindel**. Heindel moved to the United States from his native Germany and settled in Los Angeles in 1903. He joined Katherine Tingley's branch of the Theosophical Society, lecturing and serving as president of the local lodge in 1904 and 1905. He was also acquainted with Rudolf Steiner, who broke away from the Theosophical Society following the promotion of Jeddu Krishnamurti as the new world teacher.

In 1907, Heindel traveled to Germany and there claimed to have encountered an elder brother of the Rosicrucian order who led him to the Temple of the Rosy Cross, where he "received" his first book, *The Rosicrucian Cosmo-Conception*. After his return to America, he established the first center of his new order in Columbus, Ohio, in 1908. Centers were soon established in Los Angeles, North Yakima (Washington), Portland (Oregon), and Seattle.

The Rosicrucian Cosmo-Conception is a variation of theosophy, differing principally in its more extensive reliance upon Christianity and Christian symbols (reflecting the influence of Rudolf Steiner). Heindel also placed a greater emphasis upon astrology. The Rosicrucian Fellowship was a major factor in the expansion of astrology in the the early part of century. Until relatively recently, most astrologers, even those not connected with the fellowship used the ephemerides and table of houses published by the fellowship.

Sources:

Heindel, Max. *Rosicrucian Philosophy in Questions and Answers*. Oceanside, Calif.: Rosicrucian Fellowship, 1922.
——. *The Rosicrucian Cosmo-Conception*. Oceanside, Calif.: Rosicrucian Fellowship, 1937.
——. *Simplified Scientific Astrology*. Oceanside, Calif.: Rosicrucian Fellowship, 1928.
Heindel, Mrs. Max [Augusta Foss]. *The Birth of the Rosicrucian Fellowship*. Oceanside, Calif.: Rosicrucian Fellowship, n.d.

Royal Stars (Watchers of the Heavens)

The ancients referred to the **stars** through which the **Sun** passed during the **equinoxes** and the **solstices** as the Royal Stars. In the third millennium B.C., these were Aldebaran (the Watcher of the East, spring), Regulus (the Watcher of the North, summer), Antares (the Watcher of the West, fall), and Formalhaut (the Watcher of the South, winter). Because of the **precession of equinoxes**, these four stars no longer mark the beginning of the seasons.

Rudhyar, Dane

Dane Rudhyar was the leading figure in the movement that reoriented twentieth-century astrology from the prediction of events to its present emphasis on the analysis of personality. Born Daniel Chennevierre on March 23, 1895, in Paris, to a middle-class family of Norman and Celtic stock, he spent his first 20 years in Paris. A serious illness and surgery at age 12 led him to begin developing his mind; he passed his baccalaureate at the Sorbonne at age 16, majoring in philosophy. He began meeting people who introduced him to the artistic and musical world of Paris, then in a great ferment, and to the thought of Friedrich Nietzsche, who freed him from what remained of his past conditioning and sowed in his mind the seed of the concept that all existence is cyclic in character. At this time he wrote *Claude Debussy* and the *Cycle of Musical Civilization,* in which he saw Western civilization as having reached an autumnal state.

He then refocused his attention on music and the piano and was able to meet M. Durand, the music publisher, who read his book on Debussy, commissioned another booklet on him, and published three of Rudhyar's piano pieces. Rudhyar began studying with Pessard at the Paris Conservatoire but broke off his studies when World War I began. He was exempted from military service for health reasons and in 1916 left for New York with two friends to prepare for a performance of their dance-drama *Metachory,* for which he had written some music. His pieces *Poemes Ironique* and *Vision Vegetale* were performed at the Metropolitan Opera under the baton of Pierre Monteux in April 1917 and were the first polytonal music heard in America.

Having met Sasaki Roshi, who later became a Zen teacher, Rudhyar spent the summer of 1917 in the New York Public Library, reading about Oriental music and philosophy and Western occultism. In December, he parted ways with his former friends and moved to Toronto, where he stayed with Sigfried Herz, and later to Montreal, where he stayed with Alfred Laliberté, a pupil of Scriabin. He gave lectures in French and recited some of his recent poetry, published in 1918 under the title *Rhapsodies.* After a summer in Seal Harbor, Maine, where he met Leopold Stokowski, he moved to Philadelphia. There he wrote an orchestral work, *Soul Fire,* which won him a $1000 prize from the newly formed Los Angeles Philharmonic. He also wrote *Mosaics,* a cycle of piano pieces; *Ravishments,* a series of short preludes; and *Tres Poemes Tragique,* for contralto. He also wrote French poems, essays on the Baha'i movement and social organization, and plans for a world city (anticipating those for Auroville, the international community founded by Indian Saint, Sri Aurobindo). During the winter of 1918–19, he had free access to the Philadelphia orchestra's rehearsals; at one of them Stokowski introduced him to Christine Wetherill Stevenson, founder of the Philadelphia Art Alliance and initiator of the Little Theatre Movement, who had been producing a play about the life of the Buddha, on the Hollywood grounds of Krotona, then the headquarters of the American branch of the Theosophical Society. She asked Rudhyar to compose scenic music for a play about the life of Christ; it was produced in the summer of 1920 in an amphitheater close to what would become the Hollywood Bowl.

Living among Theosophists and studying astrology, music, and philosophy at Krotona in 1920–21 further deepened Rudhyar's interest in Oriental philosophy, in which he found confirmation of his beliefs about the cyclic nature of civilization and inspiration to dedicate his life to building a new civilization on a non-European basis. Working as an extra in the movies, he met a Dutchwoman from Java, Aryel Vreedenburgh Darma, and with her founded a store importing artifacts from Indonesia. Unfortunately, the store was destroyed by a fire. In other film work, he was cast as Christ in a long-running theatrical prologue at Grauman's Egyptian Theater and also worked with John Barrymore and Alla Nazimova.

After leaving motion picture work in 1927, Rudhyar eked out a living giving lecture-recitals and composing a new type of music, mostly for the piano. He also wrote many articles on music and philosophy, had his *Rebirth of Hindu Music* (1928) published in Madras, India, and published a volume of poems, *Towards Man* (1928). He was a charter member of the International Composers Guild, founded in New York in 1922 by Edgar Varese and Carlos Salzedo, and of the New Music Society of California, begun by Henry Cowell, who featured Rudhyar's orchestral *Surge of Fire* at the society's first concert (in the fall of 1925) in Los Angeles and published several of his compositions with financial backing from Charles Ives.

Living in Carmel, California, in 1929, Rudhyar composed music, including a piano piece, *Granites,* a poetic novel, *Rania,* and *Art as Release of Power.* (Except for two works for string quartet written in 1950 and revisions of earlier work, all of Rudhyar's music was written before 1930.) In 1930, he wrote a booklet entitled *Education, Instruction, Initiation.* After moving back and forth between California and New York, on June 9, 1930, Rudhyar married Malya Contento, then secretary to the writer Will Levington Comfort. Through her he met **Marc Edmund Jones**, then living and teaching in Hollywood, in September 1930; Rudhyar then returned to New York, where Jones sent him his mimeographed courses for the Sabian Assembly, in which he presented astrology in terms of what was then an unprecedented philosophical approach. These courses and a growing acquaintance with the depth psychology of **Carl Jung** awoke Rudhyar to the possibility of marrying astrology and depth psychology into a new kind of synthesis. In the winter of 1931–32 in Boston, he wrote a series of seven pamphlets under the general title *Harmonic Astrology;* he later renamed his concept "humanistic astrology."

In 1931, Rudhyar started a small magazine, *Hamsa,* but the Depression, ill health, and lack of support led him to drop it in 1934. By then he had met Paul Clancy, founder in 1932 of the first successful popular magazine in astrology, *American Astrology,* who was willing to publish anything Rudhyar wanted to write on his new kind of astrology. Month after month, Rudhyar was able to write two to five articles for one, then several, astrological magazines with national circulations of several million readers. During the summer of 1933, while staying at Mary Tudor Garland's ranch in New Mexico, he was able to read through all of Jung's works that had been translated at that time, and realized that he could "develop a series of connections between Jung's concepts and a reformulated type of astrology." Rudhyar used his new approach to write on many topics—politics, philosophy, psychology, esoteric traditions—that no other magazine would have printed, simply by centering the discussion on the birth chart of a person important in one of these fields. **Alice Bailey** encouraged him to develop these articles into a unified treatise, which he wrote during his summers in New Mexico in 1934 and 1935 and which Bailey proceeded to publish under the title *The Astrology of Personality* (1936); Rudhyar dedicated the book to her, in gratitude for her support and for the influence her earlier works had had on him in the 1920s. His next book, *New Mansions for New Man* (1938), was also published under her auspices. Rudhyar was also writing poetry during these years, gathered in a volume entitled *White Thunder* (1938). After 1939, he began developing a style of nonrepresentational painting and composed music during two summers in New Mexico.

Crises of personal development in his 40s, plus marriage difficulties led Rudhyar to question many things he had accepted on faith, and he wrote two more (unpublished) books, "Man, Maker of Universes" (1940) and "The Age of Plenitude" (1942). His circumstances worsened during the war, and the marriage broke down completely. Rudhyar was sustained during this period by his friendship with D. J. Bussell, head of a small, liberal esoteric Christian church.

The crisis over, on June 27, 1945, Rudhyar married Eya Fechin, daughter of a famous Russian painter, Nicolai Fechin (who died in Santa Monica, California, in 1955). They left for Colorado and New Mexico, where Rudhyar did most of his paintings and wrote *The Moon: The Cycles and Fortunes of Life* (1946; reprinted as *The Lunation Cycle,* 1967) and *Modern Man's Conflicts* (1946; rewritten and published as *Fire Out of the Stone,* 1959). He also continued writing his monthly articles for astrology magazines. All of Rudhyar's colored paintings were done between 1938 and 1949, although he continued doing works in black and white during the 1950s.

In 1948, the pianist Bill Masselos discovered and performed Rudhyar's piano piece *Granites,* thus setting off a new period of interest in Rudhyar's music among a small group of musicians. Rudhyar and Eya moved to New York, where some performances took place; the rendition of a string quartet by the New Music Quartet at the McMillan Theater of Columbia University was particularly memorable.

After several years of apprenticeship to Jacob Moreno, the founder of Psychodrama, financial pressure forced Eya to accept the task of starting a psychodrama department in a mental health institute in Independence, Iowa, where she and her husband lived for two exceedingly difficult years. During this period, Rudhyar turned to science fiction, writing short stories, novellas, and a novel, *Return from No-Return* (1954). When Rudhyar's second marriage collapsed, he returned to California, accepted being divorced (in 1954) philo-sophically, and began rebuilding his life at age 60.

After a few months at the Huntington Hartford Art Colony in the Santa Monica hills, where he completed his orchestral work Thresholds, Rudhyar began a series of lectures on astrology while still writing his articles, mainly for *Horoscope* and *American Astrology*. With secretarial assistance from a friend, Virginia Seith, he began publishing monthly mimeographed booklets under the series title Seeds for Greater Living. These came out regularly for 7 years, until 1962. Despite the maturity of his philosophy, he could find no publisher for any of his later works, astrological, musical, or literary.

After years of isolation in a small Hollywood apartment and another painful crisis in 1957–58, Rudhyar accepted an invitation to visit Switzerland from a Madame Honegger, whom he had aided with astrological advice. During this trip, he stopped in Boston, where Marcia Moore arranged lectures for him, in New York, where he lectured under the sponsorship of the astrologer Charles Jayne, and in London, where he was honored at an official dinner arranged by Brigadier Firebrace, at which the major British astrologers paid tribute to the effect that his early book *The Astrology of Personality* had had on them. In Switzerland, Madame Honegger having become ill, he found himself alone in a renovated 16th-century tower overlooking the Rhone Valley. There he complet-ed and translated into French *Fire Out of the Stone*.

After a few months of lecturing in Paris, Rudhyar returned to the United States, but after a dismal year in Redlands, California, he returned to Europe for a longer stay. At a lecture in Holland, he met the Dutch publisher Carolus Verhulst, who offered to reprint *The Pulse of Life,* a Dutch translation of *The Astrology of Personality,* which had been circulated in 1946–47. At last the logjam blocking Rudhyar's career was broken; a gradual stream of his other books was brought out by Verhulst's Servire Press.

In 1963, Rudhyar, while in Italy on a third journey to Europe, received a letter from a young woman named Gale Tana Whitall, then living in Edmonton, Alberta, where she had heard about his work from a music teacher. Returning to America on the day President Kennedy was assassinated, Rudhyar met Tana about a month later at Palm Springs, California, during her Christmas vacation. They were married on May 27, 1964, and after a lecture tour to Saint Paul, Minnesota, and Boston, they settled in San Jacinto, California, where they lived for the next 10 years. Tana soon became a proficient typist, editor, and organizer of Rudhyar's work and sustained him as he learned to cope with his growing popularity among the young. As often happens to creative innovators who live on into their 70s and 80s, Rudhyar finally received the recognition and respect he had worked so hard for during the last decade and a half of his life.

The far-seeing initiative of Samuel Bercholtz, founder of Shambhala Bookstore and Publications in Berkeley, California, allowed Rudhyar's books to become acceptable to such New York publishers as Penguin, Doubleday, and Harper & Row. From 1965 on, life became very full for Rudhyar and his wife, as she diligently typed manuscripts for offset printing in Holland. The volume of correspondence mounted, as did the number of lectures from coast to coast. His books during these years included *The Practice of Astrology* (1966), *Astrological Study of Psychological Complexes and Emotional Problems* (1966), *The Rhythm of Human Fulfillment* (1966), *Of Vibrancy and Peace* (1967; poems) *Astrological Triptych* (1968), and *Astrological Timing: The Transition to the New Age* (1968). In March 1969, feeling the need to promote his approach to astropsychology more vigorously, Rudhyar founded the International Committee for Humanistic Astrology but refused to build an official organization that could lay claim to this new field. About this time, thanks in part to Claudio Naranjo's interest in him, Rudhyar was invited to speak at Esalen, a human potentials institute, and to similar groups.

More books followed: *Birth Patterns for a New Humanity* (1969), *A Seed and Directives for New Life* (1970), *Astrological Themes for Meditation* (1971), *The Astrological Houses* (1972), *The Magic of Tone and Relationship* (1972), *Person-Centered Astrology* (1973), *An Astrological Mandala* (1974), and *The Astrology of America's Destiny* (1975). The number of his books in print grew from zero in 1960 to 25 in 1975, and most of them were either entirely new or thorough revisions of older works. Of these, Rudhyar considered *The Planetarization of Consciousness* (1970) to be his most basic work, condensing all his thought into a single integrated statement. It was followed by *We Can Begin Again—Together* (1970), *My Stand on Astrology* (1972), *Occult Preparations for a New Age* (1975), *The Sun Is Also a Star: The Galactic Dimension in Astrology* (1974), *From Humanistic to Transpersonal Psychology* (1975), and *Culture, Crisis, and Creativity* (1977).

Rudhyar's marriage to Tana ended in 1976, and he married Leyla Rasle in 1977. The last years of his life were especially rich. He wrote *Astrology and the Modern Psyche* (1977), *Astrological Triptych* (1978), *Beyond Individualism* (1979), *Astrological Insights* (1979), *Astrology of Transformation* (1980), and *Rhythm of Wholeness* (1983). Rudhyar died in California on September 13, 1985.

—*Aidan A. Kelly*

Selected Publications:

The Astrological Houses. Garden City, NY: Doubleday, 1972.
The Astrology of Personality. New York: Lucis Publishing, 1936.
The Lunation Cycle. The Hague: Servire, 1967.
The Planetarization of Consciousness. New York: Harper, 1972.
The Pulse of Life. Philadelphia: David McKay, 1943.

Sources:

Brau, Jean-Louis, Helen Weaver, and Allan Edmands. *Larousse Encyclopedia of Astrology.* New York: New American Library, 1980.

Melton, Gordon, Jerome Clark, and Aidan A. Kelly. *New Age Encyclopedia.* Detroit, Mich.: Gale Research, 1990.

"Seed Man: Dane Rudhyar," *Human Dimensions* 4, no. 3, (1975).

Rulership (Ruler)

In astrology, rulership is an association of the **planets** with the signs of the **zodiac** whereby each planet is said to "rule" a certain sign (or signs) and, secondarily, certain sets of objects and activities. Since the discovery of **Uranus** and the other newly detected planets, the question of which planets rule which signs has been a subject of hot debate among astrologers. However, prior to the advent of Uranus, a general consensus about these relationships had endured since the time of **Ptolemy.** The traditional system held that the **Sun** and the **Moon** (the two **luminaries**) ruled 1 sign apiece, **Leo** and **Cancer,** respectively. The known planets each ruled 2 signs: **Mercury** ruled **Virgo** and **Gemini, Venus** ruled **Taurus** and **Libra, Mars** ruled **Aries** and **Scorpio, Jupiter** ruled **Sagittarius** and **Pisces,** and **Saturn** ruled **Capricorn** and **Aquarius.** This is still the rulership system held by the great majority practicing **Hindu astrology.**

The relationship between the planets and the signs is one of kinship in their basic traits and associations. Thus, when the new planets were discovered, astrologers placed them in **horoscopes** and attempted to determine precisely what the nature of their influence was. From these observations, it was determined that Uranus ruled Aquarius, **Neptune** ruled Pisces, and **Pluto** ruled Scorpio, leaving Saturn, Jupiter, and Mars as the rulers of Capricorn, Sagittarius, and Aries. (There often appears in late nineteenth and early twentieth century transitional astrological works the expression coruler, an appellation that allowed astrologers to keep the old schema while introducing new rulerships— e.g., Saturn and Uranus were at one time said to be the corulers of Aquarius.) Only Mercury and Venus are still viewed as ruling 2 signs each.

Because of the attractiveness of a balanced system in which 12 heavenly bodies rule 12 signs, twentieth-century astrologers have often speculated that two new planets would eventually be discovered that would come to be accepted as the rulers of Virgo and Libra. For example, the hypothetical planet **Vulcan,** which some astronomers said might be found between the Sun and Mercury, was thought to be the ruler of Virgo, while an as-yet-undiscovered planet lying beyond Pluto was thought to rule Libra. Some current astrologers speculate that the planetoid **Chiron** and/or some of the larger **asteroids** rule these these signs.

The ruler of the sign on the **cusp** (i.e., the beginning) of a particular **house** is said to rule that house, and the ruler of the sign on the **ascendant** is said to rule the chart. Astrologers who feel that the term ruler should be reserved for the planet-sign relationship sometimes prefer to use the traditional term lord for the planet-house relationship; hence, the relevance of the expression lord of a house; ruler of a sign. Lord and such related expressions as has dominion over are generally not employed by modern astrologers, who tend to use ruler to cover all such associations between planets, signs, houses, etc. Finally, the planets are said to rule the matters associated with their signs. Thus, for example, Pluto rules death, the sexual organs, the principle of regeneration, and all of the other matters associated with the sign Scorpio. Neptune rules mysticism, music, the feet, and all Piscean matters. And so forth for all of the other planets and signs.

Sources:

deVore, Nicholas. *Encyclopedia of Astrology.* New York: Philosophical Library, 1947.
Hand, Robert. *Horoscope Symbols.* Rockport, Mass.: Para Research, 1981.

Ruth

Ruth, **asteroid** 798 (the 798th asteroid to be discovered), is approximately 54 kilometers in diameter and has an **orbital** period of 5.2 years. It was named after the biblical Ruth and represents loyalty. In a **natal chart**, Ruth's location by sign and **house** indicates where and how one is most likely to be loyal or to experience loyal devotion from others. When **afflicted** by inharmonious **aspects**, Ruth may show disloyalty or overt displays of loyalty that are not felt. If prominent in a chart (e.g., **conjunct** the **Sun** or the **ascendant**), it may signal an exceptionally loyal person or someone for whom loyalty and devotion are important life themes.

Sources:

Kowal, Charles T. *Asteroids: Their Nature and Utilization.* Chichester, West Sussex, U.K.: Ellis Horwood Limited, 1988.
Room, Adrian. *Dictionary of Astronomical Names.* London: Routledge, 1988.

§

Sabian Symbols

See: Degrees, Meanings of

Sabine

Sabine, **asteroid** 665 (the 665th asteroid to be discovered), is approximately 72 kilometers in diameter and has an **orbital** period of 5.6 years. It is named after a group of people to the east of Rome whose women were abducted by the Romans. They fought the Romans but finally joined with them to become one people. In a **natal chart**, Sabine's location by sign and **house** may indicate where and how one is most able to negotiate conflicts. When **afflicted** by inharmonious **aspects**, Sabine may indicate where one is taken advantage of.

Sources:

Kowal, Charles T. *Asteroids: Their Nature and Utilization.* Chichester, West Sussex, U.K.: Ellis Horwood Limited, 1988.
Room, Adrian. *Dictionary of Astronomical Names.* London: Routledge, 1988.

Sagittarius

Sagittarius, the ninth sign of the **zodiac**, is a **mutable fire sign**. It is a positive, **masculine** sign, **ruled** by the **planet Jupiter** (although some astrologers would say that it is ruled or coruled by the planetoid **Chiron**). Its symbol is the Centaur (sometimes, the Archer) and its **glyph** is an arrow, denoting the arrow in the bow that the centaur is holding. It takes its name from the Latin word for arrow, *sagitta*. Sagittarius is associated with the hips, the thighs, and the liver, and individuals with a Sagittarius **sun sign** are susceptible to hepatitis and other liver problems. The key phrase for Sagittarius is *I see*.

Unlike many other members of the **zodiac**, Sagittarius has a complex mythology. Symbolically half human and half animal, the alternative mythical figures for this sign also tend to place Sagittarius between the poles of animal brutality and high refinement. Chiron, the son of Philyra and Chronos, was a highly learned and refined centaur. A wise teacher who tutored Aesculapius, Jason, Achilles, and Hercules, Chiron's vast knowledge encompassed hunting, ethics, music, medicine, and the martial arts. Wounded by a poison arrow, he was unable to heal himself. He gave his immortality to Prometheus so that he could die and put an end to his misery. Out of pity, Zeus is said to have transformed Chiron into a **constellation**. The figure of the kindly Chiron, however, is somewhat at odds with the image in the constellation Sagittarius, which points its drawn bow menacingly at **Scorpio**. Thus, an alternative image for Sagittarius is as an average, nondivine centaur with all the impulsive, savage brutality normally attributed to this mythical species.

Like the worst centaurs, Sagittarians can be crude, wild wanderers, always seeking adventure and freedom from all restraint. They can be reckless, irresponsible, and excessively blunt. Positively, **natives** of the sign are humorous, entertaining, and optimistic. Like Chiron, they prize wisdom and make inspiring teachers. All Sagittarians strive upward. For the less evolved, this may mean social climbing; for the more evolved, a striving toward higher wisdom and spiritual insight. Like all fire signs, they are fond of physical and social activity.

There is a wealth of information available on the characteristics of the zodiacal signs, so much that one book would not be able to contain it all. One traditional way in which astrologers condense information is by summarizing sign and planet traits in lists of words and short phrases called key words or key phrases. The following Sagittarian key words are drawn from Manly P. Hall's *Astrological Keywords:*

> *Emotional key words:* "Proud, zealous, energetic, hail-fellow-well-met, buoyant, openhearted, amiable, tender, idealistic, sincere, speculative, daring, impatient, not domestic, self-indulgent" (p. 18).

> *Mental key words:* "Jovial, progressive, philosophic, intellectual, eclectic, frank, just, good-tempered, intrepid, punctilious, oratorical, prophetic, curious, altruistic, extremely ambitious, financially inclined" (p. 21).

Most popular works on astrology contain data on the signs, and these can be consulted for more detailed information.

Sources:

Evans, Colin. *The New Waite's Compendium of Natal Astrology.* Revised by Brian E. F. Gardener. York Beach, Maine: Samuel Weiser, 1971. (Originally published 1917.)

Green, Landis Knight. *The Astrologer's Manual: Modern Insights into an Ancient Art.* Sebastopol, Calif.: CRCS Publications, 1975.

Hall, Manly P. *Astrological Keywords.* 1958. Reprint. Savage, Md.: Littlefield Adams (1975), 18, 21.

Sanguine

Sanguine is the traditional name for the personality temperament indicated by an excess of the **element** air.

Sapientia

Sapientia, **asteroid** 275 (the 275th asteroid to be discovered), is approximately 108 kilometers in diameter and has an **orbital** period of 4.6 years. Its name is a personification of a Latin word for wisdom. If other elements of an **natal chart** concur, Sapientia shows wisdom with respect to the matters indicated by its sign and **house** position. When **afflicted**, it may suggest false wisdom. When prominent in a chart (e.g., **conjunct** the **Sun** or the **ascendant**), it may show a wise person or an individual who seeks wisdom.

Sources:

Kowal, Charles T. *Asteroids: Their Nature and Utilization.* Chichester, West Sussex, U.K.: Ellis Horwood Limited, 1988.
Room, Adrian. *Dictionary of Astronomical Names.* London: Routledge, 1988.

Sappho

Sappho, **asteroid** 80 (the 80th asteroid to be discovered), was named after a legendary Greek love poetess of the sixth century B.C. who lived on the island of Lesbos (from which the term lesbian derives). Its **orbital** period is about 3 1/2 years, and it is approximately 84 kilometers in diameter. Sappho is one of the more recent asteroids to be investigated by astrologers. Preliminary material on Sappho can be found in **Demetra George** and Douglas Bloch's *Astrology for Yourself,* and an **ephemeris** (table of celestial locations) for Sappho can be found in the back of the second edition of their *Asteroid Goddesses.* Unlike the **planets,** which are associated with a wide range of phenomena, the smaller asteroids are said to represent a single principle. George and Bloch give Sappho's principle as "romantic and artistic sensitivity." **Zipporah Dobyns** has found it prominent in the chart of people involved with poetry and the other arts, as well as in the charts of people involved in nurturing others (the semilegendary Sappho was devoted to nurturing young women). Contrary to the connotations of its name, Sappho does not appear to be associated with homosexuality. J. Lee Lehman associates Sappho with impersonal sexual drive, although the libido represented by this asteroid may be channeled into other endeavors, particularly work.

Sources:

Dobyns, Zipporah. *Expanding Astrology's Universe.* San Diego, Calif.: Astro Computing Services, 1983.

George, Demetra, with Douglas Bloch. *Asteroid Goddesses: The Mythology, Psychology and Astrology of the Reemerging Feminine*. 2d ed. San Diego, Calif.: 1990.

———. *Astrology for Yourself: A Workbook for Personal Transformation*. Berkeley, Calif.: Wingbow Press, 1987.

Lehman, J. Lee. *The Ultimate Asteroid Book*. West Chester, Pa.: Whitford Press, 1988.

Sasportas, Howard

Howard Sasportas, a contemporary astrologer, was born April 12, 1948 in Hartford, Connecticut. He was educated at Antioch University, New York, and earned an M.A. degree in humanistic psychology. He moved to England in 1973 and became involved in astrology. He was particularly associated with the independent Faculty of Astrological Studies (FAS), which had been founded in London in 1948 by Edmund Casselli, Charles Carter, Margaret Hone, and Lorenz von Sommaruga. Sasportas was awarded the Gold Medal for FAS's diploma exam in 1979 and that same year became a tutor for FAS. He continued to study both psychology and astrology. He also graduated from Psychosynthesis and Education Trust.

In 1983, Sasportas linked up with astrologer and **Jungian** analyst Liz Greene to found the Centre for Psychological Astrology in London. This center provides students with a curriculum built around the principal modern psychological ideas and mythology. These are all presented in the context of the astrological model, so that everything is related to the cycles of the planets. Sasportas was also a writer, and his *The Gods of Change* (1989) is already a classic. The series editor for Viking-Penguin's Arkana Contemporary Astrology Series from 1987 to 1991, he was responsible for organizing an important collection of books by some of the world's leading astrologers. He died in London on May 12, 1992.

Selected Publications:

The Twelve Houses. Wellingborough, Northamptonshire, U.K.: Aquarian Press, 1985

The Gods of Change: Pain, Crisis and the Transits of Uranus, Neptune and Pluto. New York: Arkana, 1989

The Development of Personality. By Sasportas and Liz Greene. Seminars in Psychological Astrology, vol. 1. York Beach, Maine: Samuel Weiser, 1987.

The Dynamics of the Unconscious. By Sasportas and Liz Greene. Seminars in Psychological Astrology, vol. 2. York Beach, Maine: Samuel Weiser, 1989.

The Luminaries, Sun and Moon By Sasportas and Liz Greene. Seminars in Psychological Astrology, vol. 3, York Beach, Maine: Samuel Weiser, 1992.

Satellite

A satellite is any body that **orbits** another body. The body being orbited is referred to as the primary. The most familiar examples of satellites are the **Moon**, a satellite of Earth, and Earth, a satellite of the **Sun.** This term was originally used to refer to attendants of important people. It was first applied to

Saturn

Saturn, named after a mythological king of Italy (Saturnus), and identified by
the Romans with the Greek Chronos (Kronos; Cronus), is the farthest **planet**
from the **Sun** that can be seen with the unaided eye. As the most distant and
slowest-moving planet known to the ancients, it was attributed with age and
wisdom. The Roman Saturnus was a god of agriculture who founded civilization
and the social order. The Greek Chronos was god of time and originally a
harvest deity. Unlike the Roman Saturnus, Chronos was a tyrant who was
overthrown by his son, Zeus. In ancient Mesopotamia, Saturn was associated
with Ninib (Ninip), god of strife.

It takes Saturn 29.46 years to complete an **orbit** of the Sun. Traditionally,
Saturn was said to rule both **Aquarius** and **Capricorn.** Sometime after **Uranus**
was discovered, astrologers began to perceive a correlation between Uranus's
characteristic influence in a chart and the traits of the sign Aquarius. Eventually
the **rulership** of Aquarius was reassigned to Uranus, leaving Capricorn with
Saturn.

Like its mythological namesake, Saturn is associated with time, age, and
the social order. It is an embodiment of the principle of stability, and the
opposite of upheaval. The harvest connection comes through in Saturn's
association with work (Saturn is not, in itself, a "fertile" planet, but is more of a
"harvester"); the kingly connection comes through in Saturn's association with
administration (especially, but not exclusively, with the adminstration of big
businesses). Saturn also represents the principle of contraction and the related
process of bringing what is vague and unformed into manifestation. While the
various matters associated with the planet are clearly important, Saturn is also
the taskmaster, a characteristic that earned it the title the Greater Malefic in
traditional astrology.

While the various planets are connected with a wide range of activities and
objects, they also, when found in a **natal chart**, represent different parts of the
psyche. Saturn represents the conservative, self-controlled, security-seeking
part of the self that resists change. Thus, its placement in a natal chart shows
much about how we seek security and where we resist change. The **house**
position of Saturn shows an area of life where we seek security, as well as where
we are likely to experience "insecurities."

Jeff Mayo's *The Planets and Human Behavior* provides useful lists of traits
and associations for the planets. For Saturn, under the rubric *characteristic
desire trends,* Mayo lists "self-consciousness, self-control, self-reliance and
discipline, practicality, resourcefulness, caution and restraint, conservation,
self-protection" (p. 95). Under the heading *traditional associations* are listed
"coldness, frigidness, limitation, frustration, obstruction, delays, coagulation,

crystallization, confinement, coherence, fixation, consolidation, weightiness, atrophy, decay, death, deficiency, losses, famine, burial grounds, chronic ailments, suffering, filtering processes, millstones, economy, habits, old age, time, weights and measure, framework, structure, form, routine, monotony, hard work, sorrow, adversity, fatalism, depression, failure, poverty, demotion, retributive justice, defects, budgeting, debts, responsbility, bruises, broken bones, fear, dark things and places, property, mining coal, the past, lead" (p. 96).

Sources:

Campion, Nicholas. *The Practical Astrologer.* New York: Harry N. Abrams, 1987.
George, Llewellyn. *The New A to Z Horoscope Maker and Delineator.* Saint Paul, Minn.: Llewellyn Publications, 1910. Rev. and enl. 1987.
McEvers, Joan. *Planets: The Astrological Tools.* Saint Paul, Minn.: Llewellyn Publications, 1989.
Mayo, Jeff. *The Planets and Human Behavior.* 1972. Reprint. Reno, Nev.: CRCS Publications, 1985.
Valentine, Christine. *Images of the Psyche: Exploring the Planets through Psychology and Myth.* Shaftesbury, Dorset, UK: Element Books, 1991.

Saturn Return

See: Return

Saturnine

There are many common terms and expressions that originate in the science of the stars. **Saturn rules**, among other matters, sour and depressed dispositions. Hence, someone with a dour, melancholy temperament is sometimes called saturnine.

Scales

The Scales is a popular alternate term for the sign **Libra**.

Schema

Schema (scheme) is an older, medieval term for a **horoscope**.

Scofield, Bruce

Bruce Scofield, a contemporary astrologer, was born July 21, 1948, in New Brunswick, New Jersey. The focus of his work is psychological dynamics, choice, and timing. He holds a B.A. degree in history from Rutgers University and an M.A. degree in social sciences (concentration in history) from Montclair College. He also holds a Professional Certificate from the American Federation of Astrologers (AFA), and a Level IV (professional consulting astrologer) certification from the National Council for Geocosmic Research (NCGR).

Scofield is a member of the Boston chapter of the NCGR and the Astrological Society of Princeton. His publications include *The Timing of Events: Electional Astrology, Daily Astro-Report* (four computer texts), *The Aztec Circle of Destiny,* Aztec Astro-Report (a computer program) *Day-Signs: Native American Astrology,* and *A Reconstruction of Mesoamerican Astrology* (forthcoming). His articles on astrology have appeared in *Aspects, Considerations, NCGR Journal, NCGR Newsletter, American Astrology, Llewellyn's Astrological Calendar, Llewellyn's Sun Sign Book, Fate, Dell Horoscope, The Mountain Astrologer, The Journal of the Astrological Society of Princeton, Welcome to Planet Earth,* and others.

Selected Publications:

The Aztec Circle of Destiny. By Scofield and Angela Cordova. St. Paul, Minn.: Llewellyn Publications, 1988.
Days-Signs: Native American Astrology from Mexico. Amherst, Mass.: One Reed Publications, 1991.

Scorpio

Scorpio, the eighth sign of the **zodiac**, is a **fixed water** sign. It is a negative (in the value-neutral sense of being negatively *charged),* **feminine sign ruled** by the **planet Pluto** (in traditional astrology it was ruled by **Mars**). The only sign with three symbols—the Scorpion, the Snake and the Eagle—its symbology is complex. Its **glyph** is said to represent a serpent (some astrologers say a male member). It takes its name from the Latin word for scorpion. Scorpio is associated with the sexual organs, and individuals with a Scorpio **sun sign** are susceptible to kidney infections and venereal disease. Male Scorpios are prone to prostate problems; female Scorpios to female problems. The key phrase for Scorpio is *I desire.*

Scorpio is associated with the myth of the goddess Artemis's calling an enormous scorpion out of the ground to slay Orion. The reasons given for this attack vary in different versions of the tale—some say jealousy, others that she was defending herself from rape, and yet others say that she feared Orion would kill all animals on Earth. In any event, she rewarded the scorpion by transforming it into a **constellation**. In ancient Mesopotamian mythology, scorpion men guarded the gates of the underworld, which is the original reason Scorpio became associated with death. In European folklore, both scorpions and snakes were associated with evil and treachery, but, outside the Jewish and Christian traditions, snakes were more usually associated with wisdom (they were believed to know the secret of immortality, because when they shed their skins, it appears that they are discarding an old body for a young one). Scorpio's eagle, symbolizing an evolved soul that can soar aloft above earthly concerns, may also represent the Phoenix, a mythological bird that died only to be reborn from its own ashes. On a star map, two alternative symbols can be seen in two constellations above Scorpio: Aesculapius, who is pictured holding a serpent, and Aquila the Eagle, a constellation near the serpent's tail.

All these various mythological associations enter into the sign Scorpio. Scorpio can be viewed as a form of Artemis herself, and the various versions of Artemis's attack reflect the various ways in which the sign's violent passion can manifest—as intense jealousy, as enraged self-defense, or in defense of others. Scorpios can be debauched, evil, treacherous people who always remember a slight and seek vengeance. They can also be healers and social reformers, manifesting the best traits of humanity. Scorpios are best known for their sexual intensity, although this intense drive can be channeled into other activities. They are also associated with death and, more than any other sign, have within themselves the capacity to "die" to their old selves and be transformed into new beings.

There is a wealth of information available on the characteristics of the zodiacal signs, so much that one book would not be able to contain it all. One traditional way in which astrologers condense information is by summarizing sign and planet traits in lists of words and short phrases called key words or key phrases. The following Scorpio key words are drawn from Manly P. Hall's *Astrological Keywords:*

> *Emotional key words:* "Extremes of emotions; when highly evolved, the native is impersonal, unselfish, imaginative; when not highly evolved, is revengeful, secretive, quick-tempered, and self-indulgent; not domestic; suspicious" (p. 18).

> *Mental key words:* "Scientific, altruistic, executive, penetrating, intellectual, prone to investigate the secret forces of nature, temperamental, sarcastic, vindictive" (p. 21).

Most popular works on astrology contain data on the signs, and these can be consulted for more detailed information.

Sources:

Evans, Colin. *The New Waite's Compendium of Natal Astrology.* Revised by Brian E. F. Gardener. York Beach, Maine: Samuel Weiser, 1971. (Originally published 1917.)

Green, Landis Knight. *The Astrologer's Manual: Modern Insights into an Ancient Art.* Sebastopol, Calif.: CRCS Publications, 1975.

Hall, Manly P. *Astrological Keywords.* 1958. Reprint. Savage, Md.: Littlefield Adams (1975), 18, 21.

Second Station

When, from the perspective of Earth, a **planet** that has been moving **retrograde** (i.e., appeared to go backward in its **orbit**) pauses and resumes forward motion, the point at which it pauses is called the second station.

Secondary Progression

See: Progressions and Directions

Seesaw Pattern

In astrology, a seesaw pattern is a **horoscope** arrangement in which all of the **planets** fall into one of two identifiable clusters that face each other across opposite ends of the chart.

Selene

Selene, **asteroid** 580 (the 580th asteroid to be discovered), is approximately 41 kilometers in diameter and has an **orbital** period of 5.8 years. It is named after the goddess of the **Moon**. She granted a boon to the handsome, vain king Endymion, who chose to sleep forever without aging. Selene was also seduced with a gift of a golden fleece from Pan. The placement of this planetoid in a **natal chart** shows where and how vanity opens one up to seduction, as well as where and how one is willing to seduce others.

Sources:

Kowal, Charles T. *Asteroids: Their Nature and Utilization.* Chichester, West Sussex, U.K.: Ellis Horwood Limited, 1988.
Room, Adrian. *Dictionary of Astronomical Names.* London: Routledge, 1988.

Semioctile

A semioctile (also known as a semi-**semi square**) is a minor **aspect** of 22 1/2° that is created by subdividing a circle into 16 equal parts. It exerts a very weak, inharmonious influence and, according to contemporary researchers, is involved in health concerns. It is rarely utilized outside cosmobiology and Uranian astrology.

Semisextile

A semisextile (also called a dodecile) is a minor **aspect** of 30° created by subdividing a circle into 12 equal parts. Semisextiles exert a weak though helpful influence. Unlike **sextiles**, which indicate opportunities, semisextiles often refer to inherited characteristics. The **orb of influence** is very small, no more than 1° or 2°.

Semisquare

A semisquare is a minor **aspect** of 45° created by dividing a circle into eight equal segments. A semisquare, as the name implies, is half a **square**, and a semisquare acts as a weak square. Though weak, it is perhaps the strongest of the minor aspects, and astrologers give it an **orb of influence** of 2° to 3°.

Separating Aspect

When a **transiting planet** has completed making an **aspect** with another planet or a **house cusp** and is beginning to pull away, it is said to be separating. Before the aspect became exact—as the transiting planet was approaching—the aspect was **applying**. To illustrate, let us say that **Neptune** is located at 25° in the sign **Leo**. As transiting **Venus** passes Neptune (e.g., moves past 25° and reaches 26°, 27°, and 28°Leo) we say that Venus is separating from a **conjunction** with Neptune. Prior to reaching 25° (prior to becoming exact), the aspect was applying.

A doubly separating aspect occurs when both planets are moving away from an aspect. In other words, if in the preceding example Neptune was moving **retrograde** (backward through the **zodiac**) as Venus was moving **direct** (forward through the zodiac) after Venus had passed 25° Leo, the aspect would be doubly separating. For the purpose of interpretation, applying aspects are regarded as being stronger than separating aspects.

Sources:

Gettings, Fred. *Dictionary of Astrology.* London: Routledge & Kegan Paul, 1985.
Lee, Dal. *Dictionary of Astrology.* New York: Paperback Library, 1969.

Septile

A septile is an unusual minor **aspect** of 51 3/7° created by dividing a circle into seven equal parts. Because of the **numerological** association of the number seven with **Neptune**, it has been regarded as having a mystical or a "beclouding" influence. Such eminent astrologers as **John Addey** have researched this aspect, and material on septiles can be found in astrology books dealing with **harmonics**.

Sesquisquare

A sesquisquare (also called a sesquiquadrate or a sesquare) is a minor **aspect** of 135°. Like the **semisquare**, a sesquisquare's influence is like that of a weak **square**. Though weak, it is, like the semisquare, relatively strong for a minor aspect, and astrologers give it an **orb of influence** of 2° to 3°.

Sextile

A sextile is an **aspect** of 60° between two points—e.g., between two **planets**—in an astrological chart. This aspect is traditionally regarded as beneficial, although, unlike the **trine** aspect, the potential contained in a sextile has to be developed. For this reason, it is sometimes referred to as the aspect of opportunity.

Shea, Mary E.

Mary E. Shea, a contemporary astrologer, was born April 8, 1947, in New Haven, Connecticut. She holds an M.A. degree in counseling psychology from Loyola College (1984), studied with Olivia Barclay, and is in a partnership with Gilbert Navarro. She is the writer–coeditor of a yearly **electional astrology** datebook, *Good Days Action Planning Guide,* which can be understood by the general public yet has the technical information professional astrologers need. This guide helps one plan activities for a desired outcome, which Shea calls "masterminding the world." She also wrote *Planets in Solar Returns: Yearly Cycles of Growth and Transformation* (1992). This book about yearly birthday horoscopes was written specifically for astrologers.

Shea does astrological counseling for clients across the country via phone and tape. Her readings are psychospiritual as well as practical. She is an international speaker and a favorite lecturer at many astrological conventions. She is on the faculty of the Princeton Astrological Society and is a teacher with the Gilbert Navarro Correspondence School of Horary Astrology. Besides teaching astrology, Shea also runs workshops on experiencing and balancing the *chakras* (psychic energy centers) and opening the spiritual paths to consciousness.

Selected Publications:

Good Days Action Planning Guide. [Annual datebook. Published by the author: 14185 Day Farm Rd., Glenelg, Md. 21737]
Planets in Solar Returns: Yearly Cycles of Growth and Transformation. San Diego, Calif.: 1992.

Sidereal Day

A sidereal day is the period of time it takes for Earth to complete one rotation on its axis with respect to a fixed point in space. Specifically, a sidereal day begins and ends when the local **meridian** for any given location on Earth passes through 0° **Aries** (the **vernal point**). Because of the motion of Earth around the **Sun,** sidereal days are slightly shorter than ordinary solar days. A sidereal day is 23 hours 56 minutes and 4.09 seconds in length; a sidereal hour is 1/24 the length of a sidereal day.

Sidereal Hour

See: Sidereal Day

Sidereal Month

A sidereal month is the period of time it takes the **Moon** to complete an **orbit** of Earth with respect to a fixed point in space, specifically, with respect to a fixed star (hence the designation sidereal, from Greek *sidus,* star). Because of the motion of Earth around the **Sun,** sidereal months are shorter than months measured from one new moon to the next. A sidereal month is 27 days 7 hours 43 minutes and 11.5 seconds in length.

Sidereal Period

A sidereal period is the time it takes a celestial body such as a **planet** to complete an **orbit**, as measured against the background of the **fixed stars**. **Sidereal months** (the time it takes the **Moon** to complete an orbit) and **sidereal years** (the time it takes Earth to complete an orbit) are examples of sidereal periods.

Sidereal Time

Sidereal (from Greek *sidus,* star) time, like most ordinary measurements of time, is based on the rotational and **orbital** motion of Earth. However, unlike other ways of measuring the passing of time, sidereal time uses a fixed point in space (usually one of the **fixed stars**; hence the name *sidereal)* as a point of reference for the beginning and ending of a day, a month, or a year. By way of contrast, ordinary days and years, as well as lunar months (from one new moon to the next), use the constantly changing, relative positions of the Sun, the Moon, and Earth. As a result, there are slight differences in length between sidereal days, months, and years and ordinary days, months, and years. Sidereal time, which is also employed by astronomers, is used in tables of planetary positions (**ephemerides**) as well as **tables of houses.** The first step in casting a **natal chart** is to convert birth time to sidereal time.

Sidereal Year

A sidereal year is the time it takes Earth to complete an orbit of the **Sun** relative to the **fixed stars**. The length of a sidereal year is 365 days 6 hours 9 minutes and 9.54 seconds, which is slightly longer than a solar year.

Sidereal Zodiac (Fixed Zodiac)

The **zodiac** is the belt constituted by the 12 **signs—Aries, Taurus, Gemini, Cancer, Leo, Virgo, Libra, Scorpio, Sagittarius, Capricorn, Aquarius,** and **Pisces**. The names of the signs correspond with a belt of 12 **constellations** ringing our solar system that, several thousand years ago, gave their names to the zodiac. The sidereal zodiac, also referred to as the fixed zodiac, is located where these constellations are actually positioned. Practitioners of **Hindu astrology** are the most notable users of the sidereal system. The other zodiac originated with **Ptolemy**, the great astrologer–astronomer of antiquity, who was very careful to assert that the zodiac should begin at (i.e., 0° Aries should be positioned at) the point where the **Sun** is located during the spring **equinox**. Because of the phenomenon known as the **precession of equinoxes**, this point very gradually moves backward every year; currently, 0° Aries is located near the beginning of the constellation Pisces. Astrologers who adhere to the Ptolemaic directive—the great majority of modern Western astrologers—use the **tropical zodiac** (also called the moving zodiac, for obvious reasons). The sidereal zodiac, however, has become increasingly popular in the West over the last decade or so.

The question of which zodiac to use is more involved than might be initially imagined. When the astrological novice first encounters this issue, the initial tendency is to think that the zodiac should correspond with the constellations; why, after all, should one keep shifting the zodiac just because Ptolemy said to? There is more at stake, however, than the authority of Ptolemy. For example, much seasonal symbolism is associated with the signs: Ever-youthful, pioneering Aries is the sign of spring; cold, restrictive Capricorn is the sign of winter; and so forth. In the tropical zodiac the signs are congruent with the seasons; in the sidereal zodiac these associations are lost. A siderealist, on the other hand, could make the observation that in the **Southern Hemisphere**, where the seasons are reversed, these associations are meaningless anyway (unless the zodiac is shifted 180° in southern latitudes—a highly problematic but nevertheless logically possible response). There is thus no decisive argument favoring one system over the other.

Some attempts to resolve this problem have been made by assigning different significances to the two zodiacs: The tropical zodiac, some have argued, provides a "map" of the personality (the outer self), whereas the sidereal zodiac provides a chart of the soul (the inner self). Other astrologers, most notably James T. Braha in his *Ancient Hindu Astrology for the Modern Western Astrologer,* have argued that Western, tropical astrology has better tools for analyzing the psyche, but Hindu astrology (the principal form of sidereal astrology) works better in the area of predicting future conditions. Neither of these attempts at reconciliation is likely to become widely accepted. Nor does it seem likely that either zodiac will supplant the other, at least not in the foreseeable future.

Sources:

Braha, James T. *Ancient Hindu Astrology for the Modern Western Astrologer.* Hollywood, Fla.: Hermetician Press, 1986.

Brau, Jean-Louis, Helen Weaver, and Allan Edmands. *Larousse Encyclopedia of Astrology.* New York: New American Library, 1980.

Significator

In general, every **planet** is a significator (one who signifies) of the matters associated with the **house** in which it is located, or with the house it **rules**. **Mars**, for example, is a significator of marriage and partnerships if it is located in the seventh house (the house of marriage and partnerships), or if **Aries**, the sign Mars rules, is on the **cusp** (at the beginning) of the seventh house. This term is infrequently used outside **horary astrology.**

Signorella, Frank

Frank Signorella, a contemporary astrologer and numerologist, was born February 5, 1947, in southern Italy. He holds a B.A. degree in political science from Hunter College, State University of New York. Having a special interest in philosophy and religion, Signorella's quest for deeper meaning led him to astrology. After considerable research, he developed a comprehensive view of **locational astrology** from **Ptolemy** to the present, with all of the various rules for gaining or realizing power in a new locality. In addition, his work on marriage charts (selecting the best time to marry) is notable. Other astrologers have particularly expressed their respect for his expertise in correlating **numerology and astrology**, specifically in regard to **Chaldean numerology.**

Signorella has published numerous articles. Of particular note are "Why Reagan Won" and "Power Stations," which correlates the AIDS crisis and the entrance of **Pluto** and **Saturn** into **Scorpio.**

Signorella served for six years as publicity chairman of the New York chapter of the National Council for Geocosmic Research and is on its teaching faculty. He lectures widely, is a consultant to private and corporate clients, and often appears on radio and television. At present, his work with clients focuses on **natal chart** analysis, relationships, forecasting, relocation, and numerology.

Selected Publications:

"Power Stations." *Geocosmic News* (summer, 1985).
"Why Reagan Won." *The Astrological Journal (U.K.)* (winter, 1985).

Simms, Mary Kay

Mary Kay Simms, a contemporary **astrologer,** was born in Princeton, Illinois, on November 18, 1940, to Anne and Frank Simms. She received a B.F.A. degree with a major in painting from Illinois Wesleyan University in 1962. She taught public school art for 5 years and later was a gallery painter and commercial artist for many years. She began studying astrology in 1973 while living in San Francisco. In 1976, in New Milford, Connecticut, she combined interests in art and astrology by opening Mystic Arts, a metaphysical bookshop and arts and crafts gallery.

Simms started the local chapter of the National Council for Geocosmic Research (NCGR) and was president for the first 3 years. She worked primarily as a consulting astrologer until 1985, when she left Connecticut, divorced, worked for a year doing art production and publicity for a professional dinner theater in Florida, and then began working as a free-lance cover designer for

Astro Computing Services (ACS) Publications. She moved to San Diego and became art director of ACS in June 1987. She married Neil Michelson, the founder of ACS, and took over as CEO after Michelson's death.

Simms was elected to the national board of directors of the NCGR in 1982 and is currently serving her fourth elected 3-year term. She is also director of publications and editor of *NCGR Journal.*

Selected Publications:

Twelve Wings of the Eagle. San Diego, Calif.: ACS, 1988.
Dial Detective. San Diego, Calif.: ACS, 1989.
Search for the Christmas Star. By Simms and Neil F. Michelsen. San Diego, Calif.: ACS, 1989.

Singleton

In a **bucket** (or funnel) chart, all of the **planets** but one are on one side of an astrological chart. The isolated planet is called the handle or singleton.

Sinister

Sinister, from a Latin term meaning left (not "evil"), refers to one of the many ways of classifying the astrological **aspects.** The antonym is **dexter** (right). A sinister aspect occurs when a faster-moving **planet** makes an aspect with a slower-moving one that is located counterclockwise from it (to its left) in the **zodiac.** Even though astrologers from **Ptolemy** onward have regarded sinister and dexter aspects as having somewhat different influences, the differences are comparatively minor. In most general chart readings, this distinction is ignored.

Sisyphus

Sisyphus, **asteroid** 1,866 (the 1,866th asteroid to be discovered), is approximately 7.6 kilometers in diameter and has an **orbital** period of 2.6 years. Sisyphus was a mythological figure whose punishment in the underworld was to roll a stone up a hill, only to have it roll back to the bottom, and then have to push it up the hill, over and over again for eternity. According to Lang-Wescott, Sisyphus represents "determination; dogged persistence; to start over (again or anew); to repeat effort" (Lang-Wescott 1990, 78). This asteroid's key phrase is *start over.*

Sources:

Lang-Wescott, Martha. *Asteroids-Mechanics: Ephemerides II.* Conway, Mass.: Treehouse Mountain, 1990.
———. *Mechanics of the Future: Asteroids.* Rev. ed. Conway, Mass.: Treehouse Mountain, 1991.

Siva

Siva, **asteroid** 140 (the 140th asteroid to be discovered), is approximately 104 kilometers in diameter and has an **orbital** period of 4.5 years. Siva was named after one of the principal Hindu divinities, a complex deity who was, among other things, a god of destruction. According to Lang-Wescott, Siva represents "entrenched beliefs and expectations that are 'wiped out' to enable a liberation...; interest in India or oriental culture, objects and influences" (Lang-Wescott 1990, 78). This asteroid's key words are *insight* and *episodic*.

Sources:

Lang-Wescott, Martha. *Asteroids-Mechanics: Ephemerides II.* Conway, Mass.: Treehouse Mountain, 1990.
———. *Mechanics of the Future: Asteroids.* Rev. ed. Conway, Mass.: Treehouse Mountain, 1991.

Smith, R. C. (Raphael)

At the beginning of the nineteenth century, R. C. Smith (1795–1832) published an **ephemeris** (table of planetary positions) that became one of the best known in the field. The astrological information was initially bound together with a more diverse **almanac**, and was only later published independently as *Raphael's Ephemeris*. It is still put out every year and includes everything from planetary positions to a **table of houses**. The popularity of the Placidean system of house division has even been attributed to its inclusion in *Raphael's Ephemeris*.

Soft Aspects

Soft aspects refer to **aspects** that present a **native** with opportunities—namely, **trines, sextiles**, and the like. Soft aspects is the preferred, contemporary term for what were traditionally termed **benefic aspects** (the word benefic has dropped out of general usage because soft aspects are not always "good" ones).

Sol

Sol is the Latin word for **Sun** and the root of such words as solar and **solstice**.

Solar Chart (Solar Astrology)

Solar astrology is a system often used when an exact birth time cannot be determined. Rather than begin the **natal chart**'s **house cusps** at the **ascendant** (which cannot be calculated when the birth time is unavailable), a solar chart uses the location of the **Sun** on the day of birth as the position to begin the first house and then calculates succeeding houses in equal arcs of 30°. For example, if someone was born during a day when the Sun was at, say, 12° in the sign **Capricorn**, the first solar house would begin at 12° Capricorn, the second at 12° **Aquarius,** the third at 12° **Pisces,** and so forth through the remaining signs of the **zodiac**. This solar chart is interpreted exactly the same way as a standard natal chart.

Solar Return

A solar return is one of many astrological methods for forecasting conditions. The basic technique is to **cast the horoscope** for the moment the **transiting Sun** returns to the exact position it occupied at the time of birth. This solar return occurs on or around one's birthday. From the solar return chart, astrologers are able to predict conditions for the upcoming year (or, rather, for the year-length span between birthdays). Astrologers pay special attention to the **house** position of the Sun in a solar return chart, as it indicates an area of life that will become a major focus of activity during the upcoming year. For month-to-month forecasts, astrologers may use a lunar return chart. This method works in precisely the same manner but uses the moment of the **Moon's** return to its natal place rather than the Sun's return.

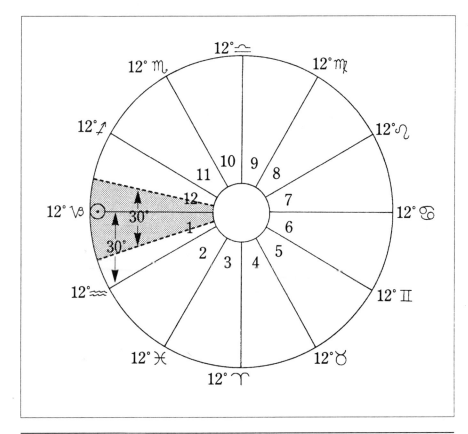

◄

Solar chart for someone born when the Sun was at 12° Capricorn (♑): the first solar house begins at 12° ♑ , the second at 12° Aquarius (♒), the third at 12° Pisces (♓), and so forth through the signs of the Zodiac, ending with the 12th house (which begins at 12° Sagittarius [♐]). In this illustration, the shaded area shows the 30° angle occupied by Capricorn.

Solar return is a fairly old method of astrological **prognostication** that fell into disfavor until relatively recently. It has been enjoying a revival for the past several decades. One indication of a technique's widespread acceptance is its inclusion in the options of computer chart-casting programs; solar returns are commonly included in such programs. A good recent book on the subject is Mary Shea's *Planets in Solar Returns*.

Sources:

Eschelman, James A. *Interpreting Solar Returns*. San Diego, Calif.: Astro-Computing Services, 1985.

Shea, Mary. *Planets in Solar Returns: A Yearly Guide for Transformation and Growth*. San Diego, Calif.: Astro-Computing Services, 1992.

Solar System

The solar system is formed by the **Sun** and all of the various heavenly bodies held within its gravitational field, namely, the **planets**, their **moons**, and the **asteroids**. The **orbits** of the planets and the asteroids all lie within roughly the same geometric plane, and all move in the same direction around the Sun (all clockwise or all counterclockwise, depending on the position from which they are viewed from outside the system). If the various elements of the solar system were not all within the same plane, it would be difficult to represent astrological influences on a two-dimensional chart. With the exception of some of the **fixed stars**, all of the influences taken into account by contemporary astrology are confined to our solar system.

Sources:

Robinson, J. Hedley, and James Muirden. *Astronomy Data Book*. 2d ed. New York: John Wiley & Sons, 1979.

Smoluchowski, Roman. *The Solar System: The Sun, Planets, and Life*. New York: Scientific American Books, 1983.

Solstice

The solstices (from Latin *sol,* sun, plus *sistere,* to stand still) are the longest and the shortest days of the year. In the Northern Hemisphere, from the summer solstice to the winter solstice the sunrise occurs a little farther north each day. On the day of the winter solstice, the **Sun** pauses ("stands still") in its gradual northward movement and begins to move south. This continues until the next summer solstice, when the Sun once again pauses and reverses direction. In the

tropical zodiac, the solstices correspond with the moment the Sun enters 0° **Cancer** (summer solstice) and 0° **Capricorn** (winter solstice).

Sophia

Sophia, **asteroid** 251 (the 251st asteroid to be discovered), is approximately 35 kilometers in diameter and has an **orbital** period of 5.4 years. The name Sophia means wisdom or cleverness in Greek. If other elements of a **natal chart** concur, Sophia shows wisdom or cleverness with respect to the matters indicated by its sign and **house** position. When **afflicted**, it may indicate false wisdom or sly cleverness.

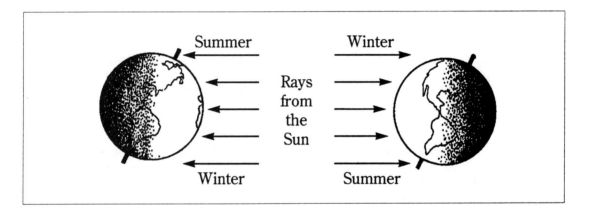

Solstices.

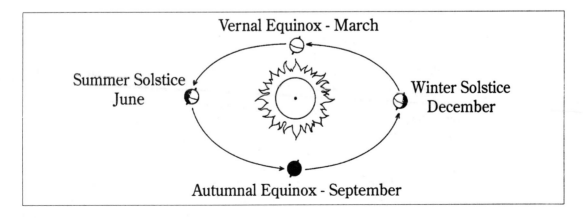

Solstices: Northern hemisphere.

Sources:

Kowal, Charles T. *Asteroids: Their Nature and Utilization.* Chichester, West Sussex, U.K.: Ellis Horwood Limited, 1988.
Room, Adrian. *Dictionary of Astronomical Names.* London: Routledge, 1988.

Sophrosyne

Sophrosyne, **asteroid** 134 (the 134th asteroid to be discovered), is approximately 116 kilometers in diameter and has an **orbital** period of 4.1 years. The name Sophrosyne is Greek for prudence, one of the four virtues in Plato's philosophy. When prominent in a **natal chart,** Sophrosyne indicates a person with a prudent approach to life. Its location by sign and **house** position indicates how and where one expresses prudence. When involved in many inharmonious **aspects,** Sophrosyne may show a person who is imprudent or someone who is inappropriately prudent.

Sources:

Kowal, Charles T. *Asteroids: Their Nature and Utilization.* Chichester, West Susses, U.K.: Ellis Horwood Limited, 1988.
Room, Adrian. *Dictionary of Astronomical Names.* London: Routledge, 1988.

Southern Hemisphere

The Southern Hemisphere is the half of Earth located below the equator. Because most **tables of houses** are developed for the Northern Hemisphere, **casting horoscopes** for the Southern Hemisphere involves an extra set of calculations. To construct a southern chart with a northern table, an extra 12 hours must be added to the sidereal time for which it is being cast (for the moment of birth in the case of a **natal chart**), calculate the house **cusps** and then the signs on the cusps exchanged for their opposite signs (i.e., for the sign 180° away). Most computer chart-casting programs do these extra calculations automatically.

The reversal of seasons that occurs in the Southern Hemisphere has raised certain questions about how the standard, **tropical zodiac** should be applied below the equator. In particular, there is much seasonal symbolism associated with the signs: Ever-youthful, pioneering Aries is the sign of spring; cold, restrictive **Capricorn** is the sign of winter; and so forth. In southern latitudes, these associations become meaningless. Some astrologers have proposed shifting the **zodiac** 180° in the Southern Hemisphere. Thus, someone born on November 2 in Buenos Aires, for example, would be a **Taurus** rather than a **Scorpio**; someone born on September 2 in Capetown, South Africa, would be a **Pisces** rather than a **Virgo**; and so forth. Despite the apparent logic of this argument, few southern astrologers have found a 180° shift in the zodiac useful in the practice of their craft. It thus does not appear that this proposal will be adopted in the foreseeable future.

Brau, Jean-Louis, Helen Weaver, and Allan Edmands. *Larousse Encyclopedia of Astrology.* New York: New American Library, 1980.
deVore, Nicholas. *Encyclopedia of Astrology.* New York: Philosophical Library, 1947.

Southern Signs

The southern signs are the zodiacal signs from **Libra** to **Pisces**.

Spartacus

Spartacus, **asteroid** 2579 (the 2,579th asteroid to be discovered), is approximately 8 kilometers in diameter and has an **orbital** period of 3.3 years. It is named after the leader of a slave revolt in ancient Rome and represents the breaking of bonds and revolt against oppressive authority. The sign and **house** position of Spartacus in a **natal chart** indicates how this tendency manifests. If prominent in a chart (e.g., **conjunct** the **Sun** or the **ascendant**), it can show a person for whom this tendency is a major life theme.

Sources:

Kowal, Charles T. *Asteroids: Their Nature and Utilization.* Chichester, West Sussex, U.K.: Ellis Horwood Limited, 1988.
Room, Adrian. *Dictionary of Astronomical Names.* London: Routledge, 1988.

Speculum

A speculum is a table constructed in tandem with an astrological chart that records such information as the **planets' declination, right ascension, latitude**, etc.

Splash Pattern

A splash pattern is a **horoscope** arrangement in which the **planets** do not appear to organize themselves into any identifiable pattern, but rather seem to have just been "splashed" across the chart.

Splay Pattern

A splay pattern is a **horoscope** arrangement in which all or most of the **planets** group themselves into a number of different identifiable clusters.

Square

A square is an **aspect** of 90° between two points—such as two **planets**—in an astrological chart. A square is a major aspect, regarded as challenging and inharmonious. It is the most difficult of all the **hard aspects**, though much depends on the nature of the planets involved. A square involving planets like **Jupiter** and **Venus**, for instance, will usually bring fewer hardships into a **native**'s life than squares involving planets like **Saturn** and **Pluto**. In a **natal chart**, the planets represent, among other things, various aspects of an individual's psyche. For example, **Mars** represents the forceful, outgoing, aggressive aspect of self, whereas Saturn represents the security-seeking, self-disciplined aspect of self. Although everyone experiences some tension between these two principles, an individual with a Mars-Saturn square in her or his chart experiences this conflict in an exaggerated manner, often overrepressing outgoing, aggressive urges and at other times exploding with impulsive actions or words.

Many modern astrologers, in an effort to overcome the sometimes frightening **delineations** of traditional astrology, have tended to go to the opposite extreme. In the case at hand, the square is sometimes presented to clients as a source of "creative tension" or given some other such interpretation. Accurate though such delineations may be, clients ultimately are not served well by calling attention to the silver lining while ignoring the cloud. Squares—and almost everybody has a few—are the most challenging, destabilizing aspects in a natal chart. They demand attention and inner work if they are ever to manifest positively.

Sources:

Hand, Robert. *Horoscope Symbols.* Rockport, Mass.: Para Research, 1981.
Sakoian, Frances, and Louis S. Acker. *The Astrologer's Handbook.* New York: Harper & Row, 1989.

Standard Time

Before the advent of rapid travel and modern means of long distance communication, particular localities kept time according to the noontime position of the **Sun**. Because this varied east or west of any given location, the local time also varied as one traveled east or west. The imposition of what we know as **standard time** zones, in which one must set her or his watch forward or backward as an imaginary line is crossed, is a comparatively recent innovation. To properly **cast a horoscope**, astrologers must find the "true" local time that a **native** was born. In other words, a birth time expressed in standard time must be converted back into local "Sun time." The more common designation for Sun time is **local mean time**.

Star

A star is a self-luminous celestial body. Although we do not usually think of it in these terms, the **Sun** is a star. Self-luminosity distinguishes stars from **planets**, which shine by virtue of reflected light. The ancients did not make this distinction but instead referred to the planets as wandering (the etymological meaning of the word planet) stars, and to the stars proper as **fixed stars**.

Star of Bethlehem

One of the few biblical accounts in which the practice of astrology can be unambiguously perceived is the story of the three wise men. The Magi were clearly astrologers, and the Star of Bethlehem, as scholars have long pointed out, was actually a major planetary **conjunction** involving **Jupiter** and **Saturn**. The ancients referred to these two celestial bodies as chronocrators—literally, the "rulers of time." Before the discovery of **Uranus,** Jupiter and Saturn were the slowest-moving of the known **planets**. As a consequence, their interacting cycles—particularly their conjunctions every 20 years—were taken to mark off longer epochs of time. Around the time of Jesus birth, this 20-year conjunction occurred in the sign **Pisces**, which was the sign of the "age" Earth was believed to be entering (by reason of the phenomenon known as the **precession of equinoxes**). The Magi believed, as do many people today, that Earth was on the verge of entering a "new age," and this particular conjunction was taken to indicate the birth of a new world teacher for the age of Pisces.

Sources:

Jacobs, Don. *Astrology's Pew in the Church*. San Francisco: The Joshua Foundation, 1979.
Simms, Maria Kay. *Twelve Wings of the Eagle: Our Spiritual Evolution Through the Ages of the Zodiac.* San Diego, Calif.: Astro Computing Services, 1988.

Star Pattern

A star pattern is a **horoscope** arrangement in which the **planets** are organized into four, five, or six clusters that form symmetrical angles with one another.

sTARBABY

The "sTARBABY" incident was a scandal in which the Committee for the Scientific Investigation of Claims of the Paranormal (CSICOP) inserted nonrandom, biased **astrological data** into a statistical test of astrological influence. The effect of the extra data was to transform test results that verified a particular astrological relationship into test results that appeared to negate the relationship. The unusual name sTARBABY, which was the title of the principal article exposing the fraud, alludes to the Uncle Remus tale in which Br'er Rabbit tries to force the Tarbaby to release him—only to become more deeply entrapped.

In the mid-1970s, Paul Kurtz, a professor of philosophy at the State University of New York at Buffalo, collected 186 scientists' signatures in support of an anti-astrology statement. This document, "Objections to Astrology," was published in the September-October 1975 issue of *The Humanist* magazine, of which Kurtz was the editor. The tone of the statement was harsh: It portrayed astrology as irrational superstition and called astrologers charlatans. "Objections to Astrology" was also released to the press, and it received widespread publicity. This unexpected publicity encouraged Kurtz and others to found CSICOP, an organization dedicated to debunking "pseudoscience."

"Objections to Astrology" was published in the same issue of *The Humanist* in which Lawrence E. Jerome's "Astrology: Magic or Science?" appeared. This article attacked, among others, the highly respected French scientists **Michel and Françoise Gauquelin**. The Gauquelins had undertaken sophisticated statistical tests of astrological claims. These tests largely failed to support traditional astrology, but they also uncovered a few statistically significant correlations. These correlations formed the basis for further studies, and eventually the Gauquelins concluded that they had discovered certain astrological relationships. Michel Gauquelin refuted Jerome's article, and intimated possible legal action against *The Humanist* for misrepresenting his views. The Gauquelins's response in combination with the publicity generated by "Objections to Astrology" prompted CSICOP to undertake an empirical refutation of astrology—a refutation that focused on the work of the Gauquelins.

Of the various correlations uncovered by the Gauquelins, the strongest was the so-called **Mars effect**, correlation between athletic achievement and the position of the planet **Mars**—a planet traditionally associated with physical energy—in certain influential sectors of the sky (e.g., close to the eastern **horizon** and near the **zenith**) at the time of birth. Confident that any genuine test of astrological influence would disconfirm such correlations, *The Humanist* issued a challenge to the Gauquelins to subject their original findings on the Mars effect to an empirical test. The original research had compared the birth data of athletes against statistical probabilities; *The Humanist* challenged them to test their findings against the actual birth data of nonathletes. Contrary to the expectations of skeptical critics, as the **Zelen Test** (after Marvin Zelen, the person who carried out the test) confirmed the Gauquelins' original findings. Reluctant to admit defeat, Zelen, Kurtz, and their colleagues quickly changed tack and began questioning the validity of the Gauquelins's original sample of athletes. This disagreement eventually led the Gauquelins to agree to a new test of the Mars effect, which was to be conducted by CSICOP with a sample of American athletes.

Dennis Rawlins, one of the founders of CSICOP and a planetary motion specialist, oversaw the calculations. Anxious to have a "sneak peak" at the preliminary findings of the new test, Kurtz called Rawlins, only to be told that the early results seemed to confirm the Mars effect. According to Rawlins (p. 72), Kurtz responded to the news with a groan and spoke "in a pained voice, as someone cursed with a demon that would not go away." Kurtz then supplied Rawlins with additional samples of athletes. The last sample supplied to Rawlins contained athletes with an extremely low Mars effect—so low as to effectively cancel the Mars effect of the original sample. Rawlins became convinced that the last group of athletes was not a random sample (i.e., that the sample had been intentionally designed to negate the Mars effect).

Rawlins initially attempted to correct what he saw as a coverup by appealing to other people within CSICOP. CSICOP's leadership responded by ejecting him from the organization. Meanwhile, Kurtz published the results of the "test," claiming that the Mars effect had been decisively disproved. Rawlins, however, soon published his "sTARBABY" exposé in *Fate,* a popular paranormal magazine. Rawlins's accusations were reinforced by Patrick Curry's article "Research on the Mars Effect" which appeared in the *Zetetic Scholar* soon after the publication of "sTARBABY." The ensuing uproar eventually forced Kurtz and the other CSICOP personnel involved with the test to issue a partial confession. This "reappraisal" acknowledged many weaknesses in the test without admitting either that the data had been manipulated or that the Mars effect might possibly be the result of astrological influences.

To most astrologers, the "sTARBABY" incident has come to epitomize the attitude of would-be debunkers. While many skeptics are far more reasonable than CSICOP, the individuals behind the "sTARBABY" coverup were clearly more interested in defending a rather narrow interpretation of scientific orthodoxy than in empirical truth. Its image tarnished by the incident, CSICOP has since avoided active experimentation.

Sources:

Abell, George O., Paul Kurtz, and Marvin Zelen. "The Abell-Kurtz-Zelen 'Mars Effect' Experiments: A Reappraisal." *The Skeptical Inquirer* 7, no. 3 (Spring 1983): 77–82.

Bok, Bart J., Lawrence E. Jerome, and Paul Kurtz. "Objections to Astrology: A Statement by 186 Leading Scientists." *The Humanist* 35, no. 5 (September/October 1975): 4–6.

Curry, Patrick. "Research on the Mars Effect." *Zetetic Scholar* 9 (March 1982): 34–53.

Forrest, Steven. "Exploring the Fear of Astrology Among the Educated." Paper delivered at the Cycles and Symbols conference, San Francisco, California, July 26–29, 1990.

Jerome, Lawrence E. "Astrology: Magic or Science?" *The Humanist* 35, no. 5 (September/October 1975): 10–16.

Melton, J. Gordon, Jerome Clark, and Aidan A. Kelly. *New Age Encyclopedia.* Detroit, Mich.: Gale Research, 1990.

Pinch, T. J., and H. M. Collins. "Private Science and Public Knowledge: The Committee for the Scientific Investigation of the Claims of the Paranormal and Its Use of the Literature." *Social Studies of Science* 14 (1984): 521–546.

Rawlins, Dennis. "sTARBABY." *Fate* 34, no. 10 (October 1981): 67–98.

Starck, Marcia R.

Marcia R. Starck is a contemporary astrologer best known for her work in the area of astrology and healing. She was born December 24, 1939, in Paterson, New Jersey, and was educated at Douglass College, Rutgers University (B.A., English literature, 1961, *Phi Beta Kappa*), San Francisco State College (drama), and North American College (physiology and nutrition). She became interested in astrology as a tool for healing in the winter of 1969–70; a year later she began teaching and consulting work. Four years later she began studying herbs, nutrition, and medical astrology. In 1977, she began lecturing and traveling throughout the United States and Canada.

Starck is the author of *Astrology, Key to Holistic Health* (1982), *Earth Mother Astrology* (1989), *The Complete Handbook of Natural Healing* (1991), *Women's Medicine Ways—Cross Cultural Rites of Passage* (1993), and *Dancing with the Shadow Side—the Dark Goddess in Each of Us* (1993). She also contributes articles on astrology and ritual to *The Mountain Astrologer.* She lives in Santa Fe, New Mexico, where she teaches classes on earth mother and medical astrology and conducts women's rites of passage classes and a goddess circle.

Selected Publications:

Earth Mother Astrology. Saint Paul, Minn.: Llewellyn Publications, 1989.
The Complete Handbook of Natural Healing. Saint Paul, Minn.: Llewellyn Publications, 1991.
Astrology, Key to Holistic Health. 2d ed. Birmingham, Mich.: Seek-It Publications, 1992.
Dancing with the Shadow Side—the Dark Goddess in Each of Us. Freedom, Calif.: Crossing Press, 1993.
Women's Medicine Ways—Cross Cultural Rites of Passage. Forthcoming.

Stathis, Georgia

Georgia Stathis has been a professional astrologer for over 15 years. Throughout the years her experience as a realtor, real estate investor, and advertising saleswoman has placed her on a path of working with individuals helping them time or choose their career directions. She also works with companies, analyzing their company charts as well as those of their employees, to help determine the best placement for employees within the working structure of the company.

A well-loved speaker, Strathis has clients all over the world and has been lecturing for 15 years; she is a member of the National Speakers Association. She has been interviewed on radio shows throughout the country and was recently interviewed by a well-known London magazine.

Stathis is coauthor of *Financial Astrology for the 1990's,* now in its second printing. Recently released is her excellent studio-produced series of tapes *Myths and Signs of the Zodiac.*

"Delineating the Corporation." In *Financial Astrology for the 1990s,* edited by Joan McEvers, 264–305. Saint Paul, Minn.: Llewellyn Publications, 1989.

"The Real Estate Process." In *Financial Astrology for the 1990s,* edited by Joan McEvers, 118-149. Saint Paul, Minn.: Llewellyn Publications, 1989.

Myths and Signs of the Zodiac. Pleasant Hill, Calif.: Starcycles, 1993. (Tape series)

Stationary

Because of the **planets'** differing speeds and differing **orbits**, they all appear at times to reverse their usual direction and go **retrograde**. On the day a planet reverses direction, as well as on the day it resumes its **direct** motion, it is said to be stationary because, against the background of the **fixed stars**, it appears to have paused in space. A planet that has paused before going retrograde is said to be stationary retrograde, while a planet pausing before going direct is said to be stationary direct. When a planet becomes stationary, it is said to take its station. The stationary period for each planet is regarded as being inversely proportional to the speed of its motion. Thus, for example, the period of **Mercury's** station would be 1 day; **Venus's**, 2 days; **Mars's**, 3 days, and so forth (i.e., the slower a planet moves, the longer it tends to remain stationary).

In an astrological chart, stationary planets are usually indicated by a small "*S*" that appears at the lower right of the planet symbol. (Many astrologers use *SR* and *SD* to distinguish stationary retrograde from stationary direct.) Someone born when a planet was stationary will have that planet's particular characteristics deeply engraved in her or his nature. For example, someone born when **Mercury** was stationary will mature into a highly mental person. With respect to **transiting**, the days that a planet is stationary are considered to be fortunate for the matters associated with the particular planet, although the interpretation varies according to whether the planet is going direct or retrograde. Thus, for example, the day Mercury is stationary direct would be good for embarking on a journey, while the day it is stationary retrograde would be good for beginning a meditative retreat. Some contemporary astrologers regard the points in a chart where planets take their stations as highly sensitive areas that should be watched when other planets transit them.

Sources:

Brau, Jean-Louis, Helen Weaver, and Allan Edmands. *Larousse Encyclopedia of Astrology.* New York: New American Library, 1980.

Bach, Eleanor. *Astrology from A to Z: An Illustrated Source Book.* New York: Philosophical Library, 1990.

Stellium (Satellitium)

A stellium (also called a satellitium) is a multiple **conjunction** involving three or more **planets** in one **house** and/or one **sign** in an astrological chart. As might be anticipated, this **configuration** indicates an emphasis on the matters associated with the house and/or sign in which the stellium occurs.

Strong Signs

In traditional astrology, **Scorpio** and **Aquarius** were referred to as the strong signs, presumably because of their fixed natures.

Sublunar

The ancient **geocentric** concept of the universe arranged the **Sun, Moon,** and **planets** in concentric, moving, crystalline spheres around a stable Earth at the center of the **solar system**. Because the Moon is closest to Earth, it is the last *celestial* body. Everything that is sublunar—meaning below the Moon— belongs to this *terrestrial,* earthly realm. In classical astrology, astrological forces were viewed as having an influence in the sublunar realm, but not in the celestial realm.

Succedent Houses

The **houses** of an astrological chart are classified into three groups of four: **angular houses** (the first, fourth, seventh, and tenth), succedent houses (the second, fifth, eighth, and eleventh), and **cadent houses** (the third, sixth, ninth, and twelfth). Traditionally, the succedent houses have been referred to as the resource houses, although this ascription applies best to the second house and the eighth house (the houses of personal resources that we ourselves earn and of the resources that come our way through inheritance and partnership). In classical astrology, **planets** positioned in succedent houses are said to exercise a stabilizing effect.

Sources:

Brau, Jean-Louis, Helen Weaver, and Allan Edmands. *Larousse Encyclopedia of Astrology.* New York: New American Library, 1980.
Hand, Robert. *Horoscope Symbols.* Rockport, Mass.: Para Research, 1981.

Sullivan, Erin

Erin Sullivan, a contemporary astrologer, was born November 9, 1947, in Vancouver, British Columbia, Canada. She has been a full-time practicing astrologer for more than 20 years, having taken up the study in 1965. She has lectured throughout North America, in Europe, and Australia. Her articles have appeared in all of the astrological trade journals in North America and Holland, and some have been translated into German. She wrote features for the *Daily*

Planet Almanac in the late 1970s and for the Llewellyn *Sun Sign Book and Calendar* for three years running.

Sullivan has been involved in the founding and activities of many astrological groups, including the Association for Astrological Networking (AFAN), the United Astrology Conference, and the Cross Canada Council for the Fraternity for Canadian Astrologers. She has received numerous astrology awards and is one of the "Who's Who" in matrix astrology.

Sullivan is the series editor for the Arkana Contemporary Astrology Series. She is the author of *Saturn in Transit: Boundaries of the Mind, Body and Soul* (1990) and *Retrograde Planets: Traversing the Inner Landscape* (1992). She has appeared on many television programs in Canada and the United States and had a regular radio spot in Victoria, British Columbia, where she resided from 1979 to 1989.

Sullivan moved to London in the fall of 1989 and set up a private practice in counseling astrology. She lectures and teaches classes for the Centre for Psychological Astrology in both London and Zurich. She also goes to Sydney and Melbourne, Australia, once a year to teach. She has two grown daughters.

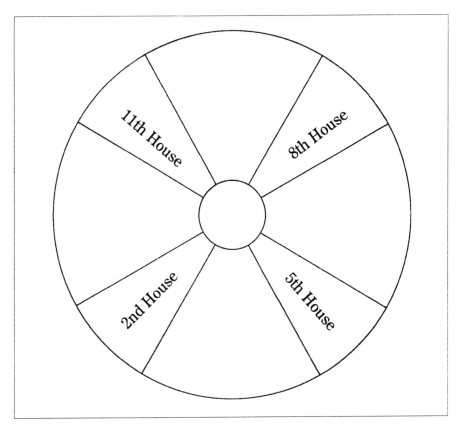

◀
Succedent houses.

Selected Publications:

Saturn in Transit: Boundaries of the Mind, Body and Soul. Arkana Contemporaty Astrology Series, New York: Arkana, 1990.
Retrograde Planets: Traversing the Inner Landscape. Arkana Contemporary Astrology Series, New York: Arkana, 1992.

Sun

The Sun is the **star** around which Earth and the rest of the **planets orbit**. Because it is the most prominent heavenly body, it is surprising that in many mythologies the sun-god is a comparatively unimportant figure (in contrast to **Jupiter,** for example, who is king of the gods). The Greek Helios, whom the Romans later identified with Sol (from which we get *solar),* drove his fiery chariot across the sky daily and was said to hear and see everything. He was characterized as loyal to his children, even though some of them were notoriously unpleasant characters. In **Mesopotamian astrology,** the sun-god was Shamash (Utu), who represented the life-giving rays of the Sun. Like Helios, he was an all-seeing god, but he was also the god of justice, who protected the good and destroyed evil. He was the special protector of heroic kings, such as the famous Gilgamesh.

The Sun is said to **rule** the sign **Leo**, a relationship indicating a similarity between the characteristics of the Sun and the traits of Leo. Leo is the sign of the king, the central personality of a country and the person responsible for overseeing the kingdom, coordinating its activities, and administering justice. The astrological Sun, particularly in a birth chart, is very much the "king" of a chart. The **native**'s basic self–the "soul self," if you will—is represented by the Sun, making this the most important celestial body in the **horoscope.** For this reason, the sign position of the Sun (the **sun sign**) is usually the single most important sign influence in the chart; the sign that the Sun is in colors the whole orientation of the personality. The **house** position of Helios, as well as the **aspects** made to the Sun by the planets, also tend to be more significant than other house placements and aspects.

Like its mythological namesake, the Sun is associated with life-giving vitality, and its placement can be an important indicator of physical vitality. The Sun can also represent important personages and people in authority. On the other side of the coin, the Sun can show where we have an urge for power or an urge to express our leadership potential. The characteristics of the Sun's expression in the signs of the **zodiac** are dealt with in the entries on those signs.

Jeff Mayo's *The Planets and Human Behavior* provides useful lists of traits and associations for the planets. For the Sun, under the rubric *characteristic desire trends,* Mayo lists "ambition, urge for power, leadership, creativeness, constructiveness, self-reliance, organization and administration, masculinity, individuality" (p. 69). Under the heading *traditional associations* are listed "generating power, procreation, bringing into being, the monarchy or other supreme authority in the State, positions of rank or title, Government or public officials, celebrities, the father, judges, superiors generally, powerful or influential friends, the source of "heart-felt" desires" (p. 70).

Sources:

Campion, Nicholas. *The Practical Astrologer.* New York: Harry N. Abrams, 1987.
George, Llewellyn. *The New A to Z Horoscope Maker and Delineator.* St. Paul, Minn.: Llewellyn Publications, 1910. Rev. and enl. 1987.
McEvers, Joan. *Planets: The Astrological Tools.* Saint Paul, Minn.: Llewellyn Publications, 1989.
Mayo, Jeff. *The Planets and Human Behavior.* 1972. Reprint. Reno, Nev.: CRCS Publications, 1985.
Valentine, Christine. *Images of the Psyche: Exploring the Planets through Psychology and Myth.* Shaftesbury, Dorset, U.K.: Element Books, 1991.

Sun Sign

The sign of the **Zodiac** the **Sun** is in, particularly in a **natal chart**, is the sun sign (sometimes also called the birth sign). The Sun, as the most important celestial body for Earth dwellers, is the most important influence in a **horoscope**. Consequently, the sign that the Sun is in at birth is usually the single most important influence on a **native**'s personality. Thus, when people say that they are such and such a sign, they are almost always referring to their sun sign. Interestingly, the ancient Romans regarded the **Moon** as the most influential astrological body, so when they said they were such and such a sign, they were referring to the sign the Moon was in when they were born.

Sun sign astrology, which is the kind of astrology found in newspapers and women's magazines, has the advantage of simplicity—a person's birthday is all that must be known to figure out the person's sign—but this simplicity is purchased at the price of ignoring all other astrological influences. These other influences make sun sign astrology a hit-or-miss system that works sometimes but fails miserably at others. Professional astrologers tend to dislike sun sign astrology because it creates a misconception of the science of the stars (i.e., the misconception that astrology is entirely about sun signs) and because its inaccuracy leads nonastrologers to reject all astrology as untrue.

Sources:

Bach, Eleanor. *Astrology from A to Z: An Illustrated Source Book.* New York: Philosophical Library, 1990.
Gettings, Fred. *Dictionary of Astrology.* London: Routledge & Kegan Paul, 1985.

Superior Conjunctions

Superior conjunctions are **conjunctions** between the **Sun** and the two inner **planets** in which **Mercury** or **Venus** lies on the other side of the Sun from Earth. The antonym, **inferior conjunction**, refers to conjunctions in which Mercury or Venus is located in front of the Sun.

Superior Planets

The original meaning of the word superior was above. In the concept of the universe that was prevelant prior to the Copernican revolution, when Earth was thought to be the stable center around which every other celestial body revolved, the **orbits** of **Mars**, **Jupiter**, and **Saturn** were considered to be "above" the orbit of the **Sun**. These three **planets** were thus referred to as the superior planets. The evaluative connotations of the term have caused this expression to be dropped in favor of outer planets.

Sweet Signs

Sweet Sign is an archaic term applied to the **air signs**, which were said to be sweet (in contrast to the **bitter signs**).

Swift

A **planet** is said to be swift when it appears to be moving faster than average. Because of its elliptical **orbit**, the **Moon**, especially, can move noticeably more slowly or more rapidly than its average of 13° 10′ per 24-hour period.

Synastry (Chart Comparison)

Synastry, or chart comparison, is the practice of superimposing two or more **horoscopes** and examining their interactions. Synastry is an especially popular technique for evaluating romantic relationships, but it can also be used for illuminating business partnerships, parent-child interactions, and so forth. The basic idea of chart comparison is very old. In **Hindu astrology**, for example, the practice of comparing charts to determine marital compatibility is quite ancient. In the Western tradition, **Ptolemy** mentions synastry in his *Tetrabiblos,* the single most influential astrological treatise in European history. Even the famous Swiss psychiatrist **Carl Jung** used chart comparison in his work with married couples.

Traditional chart comparison focuses on the **aspects** between key **planets**. Thus, if the natal **Mercury** (planet of communication) of one individual is **conjunct** the Mercury of the other, the relationship will be characterized by easy communication between the two. Mentally, they will see eye to eye on many issues. In romantic relationships, it is especially interesting to note how **Venus** (the planet of relating) and **Mars** (the planet of passion) are aspected. A close conjunction between one person's Mars and the other person's Venus, for instance, is traditionally viewed as a powerful romantic-sexual aspect.

Among astrologers who accept the notion of reincarnation, **Saturn** is viewed as the planetary **ruler** of karma (one's ledger of debts and dues from previous lifetimes). Where the Saturn of a person with whom we are in a close relationship falls in our **natal chart** indicates something about the nature of our karmic tie. For example, if a close relative's Saturn is located in one's second **house** (the house of money and possessions) when the charts are superimposed, there is some sort of financial karma from past lifetimes. If neither person's Saturn is strongly aspected in a comparison, there is no significant karmic tie, and the relationship will usually be transitory.

Sources:

Brau, Jean-Louis, Helen Weaver, and Allan Edmans. *Larousse Encyclopedia of Astrology.* New York: New American Library, 1980.

Sakoian, Frances, and Louis S. Acker. *The Astrology of Human Relationships.* New York: Harper & Row, 1976.

Synchronicity

Synchronicity (from Greek *syn,* together, plus *chronos,* time) is a term popularized by **Carl Jung** to explain what might be called "meaningful" coincidences. The great Swiss psychologist defined synchronicity as an "acausal (i.e., noncausal) connecting principle." Jung used synchronicity to refer to connections between events that had no discernible connection. Under normal circumstances, a correlation between two events often indicates that some sort of causal link exists between them. For example, at the time of the first cold snap every year certain birds migrate south. If the same pattern recurs year after year, it can be concluded that event A (cold snap) causes event B (bird migration).

There are correlations, however, with no obvious "causes," which are normally referred to as coincidences, for example, a person humming a particular song that suddenly begins to play on the radio.

Where Jung departed most radically from mainstream psychology was to assert that quite often these coincidences are not coincidences; rather, the universe is structured so that such correlations occur all the time, and, further, that while there is no causal connection, these correlations are meaningful. A useful example for understanding "noncausal connections" is the correlation between the time on two clocks: just because they both show the same time, should it be concluded that one exerts some kind of "force" on the other, *causing* it to read the same? Obviously not. Similarly, Jung postulated that the universe, for reasons and by processes that we do not yet understand, is set up like clocks that have been set in motion so as to infinitely reflect the same "time."

Although not always explicitly stated, synchronicity is assumed in certain forms of **astrological research**. For example, an accepted astrological practice is to assign newly discovered celestial bodies a tentative meaning that can be derived from associations with their name. This initial step is based on the well-established observation that the designations astronomers assign to newly discovered celestial bodies are not coincidental—that by virtue of some sort of nonapparent, *synchronistic* process, non-astrologically inclined astronomers give astrologically significant names to things.

Some astrologers also adopt synchronicity to explain astrological influence more generally; rather than limit the scope of synchronicity to the exploration of the meaning of new celestial bodies, they view the relationship between the stars and human life as two clocks that read the same time. This contrasts with the view that astrological influence is a "force" exerted by the **planets** and other celestial bodies that is radiated to Earth like the forces of gravity or electromagnetism.

Sources:

Brau, Jean-Louis, Helen Weaver, and Allan Edmands. *Larousse Encyclopedia of Astrology.* New York: New American Library, 1980.
Lewis, James R. *Martian Astrology.* Goleta, Calif.: Jupiter's Ink, 1992.

Synodic Period

A synodic period (from the Greek, meaning to meet or travel together) is the period a heavenly body takes to move from one **conjunction** with the **Sun** to the next. A synodic month, for example, is the period of time between successive **new moons** (which is 29 days 12 hours 44 minutes). Because Earth is always moving forward in its **orbit**, the time it takes the **Moon** to complete a synodic month differs from the time it takes the Moon to return to its original position relative to the backdrop of the comparatively stationary **stars**. Synodic *cycle* refers to the time between the conjunctions of two **planets** (not to the time between the conjunctions of a planet and the Sun).

Synthesis

Synthesis refers to the final stage in **horoscope** interpretation, when the astrologer weaves the many particular influences into a coherent whole. The ability to meaningfully synthesize astrological information rather than to simply list the interpretations of each individual component of a chart is the mark of an experienced astrologer.

Syzygy

Syzygy traditionally referred to a **conjunction** of the **Sun** and the **Moon**, such as occurs during a solar **eclipse**. By extension, it is currently applied to the alignment of any three celestial bodies in a straight line (such as occurs during eclipses and **occultations**). The etymology of the term is interesting: The *sy[n]*, which is related to the prefix of such words as synchronic, means together, like; *-zygy* derives from the Greek *zugón* (yoke), so syzygy literally means to yoke together. This makes syzygy appear to be a macrocosmic parallel to certain yoga practices in which the internal, symbolic (microcosmic) Sun and Moon are joined together—as in alternate nostril breathing, a technique said to join the Sun (right nostril) and Moon (left nostril) energies. What makes this parallel all the more striking is that both *zugón* and *yoga* ultimately derive from the same Indo-European root word *yug* (yoke).

Sources:

deVore, Nicholas. *Encyclopedia of Astrology*. New York: Philosophical Library, 1947.

Gettings, Fred. *Dictionary of Astrology*. London: Routledge & Kegan Paul, 1985.

T square

Three or more **planets** that together form a **configuration** of a *T*—two directly opposite each other and a third at right angles to each of the opposed planets—in a **horoscope** are referred to as a T square. To qualify as a T square, the planets directly across the chart from each other must be involved in an **opposition** (180° aspect) and the third planet must make a **square** (an **aspect** of 90°) to the first two. Because astrological signs at 90° angles to each other belong to the same **quality** (cardinal, mutable, or fixed), T squares tend to involve planets in three signs of one quality. Thus, T squares can be classified as cardinal T squares, mutable T squares, or fixed T squares (T squares that involve planets in signs of different qualities are referred to as mixed T squares).

Because all the aspects contained in a T square are **hard aspects**, an individual with such a configuration in her or his **natal chart** is presented with more challenges than the average person. At the same time, a T square is a powerfully dynamic configuration (it is considered to be the most dynamic of all configurations, particularly when the constituent planets are in cardinal signs). Once the challenges proffered by a T square have been adequately met, the individual has tremendous personal power.

In certain ways, a T square is like a **grand cross** (a configuration with four planets in all four corners of a chart) minus one of its "legs." Like a table with only three legs, the T square tends to draw attention to the house where a fourth leg would be required in order to produce a stable table. Imagine, for example, a natal chart in which the three component planets of a T square are in the second, eleventh, and eighth houses. One's attention is thus drawn to the fifth house. This indicates that if **natives** with this particular T square invested their energy in one or more of the matters associated with this house—children, creations, self-expression, entertainment, and so forth—their lives should become more stable. Simultaneously, this configuration indicates that the lessons learned in houses two, eleven, and eight could be brought to bear on whatever tasks were undertaken in the fifth house. (*See* illustration, p. 502.)

Sources:

Brau, Jean-Louis, Helen Weaver, and Allan Edmands. *Larousse Encyclopedia of Astrology.* New York: New American Library, 1980.

Marks, Tracy. *How to Handle Your T Square.* Arlington, Mass.: Sagittarius Rising, 1979.

Table of Houses

A table of houses is, as the name indicates, a table that allows astrologers to locate the position of the **houses** when **casting a horoscope**. Tables of houses are usually published in book form, with the house positions arranged according to **latitude** and **sidereal time**. This information is incorporated into chart-casting programs, so, with the increasing use of personal computers by astrologers, traditional tables of houses are becoming somewhat obsolete.

T square.

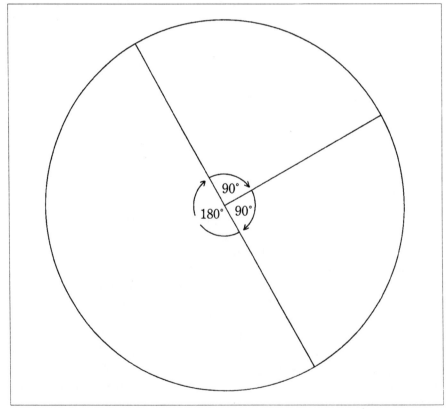

Tarnas, Richard Theodore

Richard Theodore Tarnas, Ph. D., is a contemporary intellectual historian, best known in astrological circles for his analysis of **Uranus** in terms of the mythology of **Prometheus**, for his recognition of the correlation between the four outer **planets** and the four basic perinatal matrices discovered by Stanislav Grof, and for his work in analyzing and setting forth the philosophical and historical implications of astrology in the larger context of the evolution of the Western mind. Outside of astrology, he is known for his work on psychedelic therapy at Esalen and for his book, *The Passion of the Western Mind*.

Tarnas was born on February 21, 1950, in Geneva Switzerland of American parents, Mary Louise and Richard Tarnas. His father was an attorney and professor of law. He grew up in Michigan where he received a classical education with the Jesuits. He graduated from the University of Detroit Jesuit Preparatory School in 1968, and attended Harvard College from 1968 to 1972 (A.B. *cum laude,* 1972). He received his Ph.D. from Saybrook Institute in 1976.

After several years of travel, Tarnas settled at Esalen Institute in Big Sur, California. At Esalen, which is well-known as the cutting edge of the human potentials movement, Tarnas studied with such leading thinkers as Gregory Bateson, Joseph Campbell, Stanislav Grof, Fritjof Capra, James Hillman, Huston Smith, David Steindl-Rast, R. D. Laing, and Rupert Sheldrake. Tarnas became Esalen's director of programs and education in 1979. He resigned from Esalen in 1983 to write and research full-time. He also has a part-time practice as a psychologist and counselor, and attends conferences and lectures on various topics. He married Heather Malcom of Toronto, Canada, in 1982, and has two children, Christopher and Rebecca.

Selected Publications:

The Passion of the Western Mind. New York: Harmony Books, Random House, 1991.
"Uranus and Prometheus." *Journal of the British Astrological Association* (July–August 1989).
"The Western Mind at the Threshold." *The Astrotherapy Newsletter* 3:4 (November 1990).

Tarot and Cabbala

The tarot is a set of cards related to contemporary playing cards that are used for divination. Tarot cards are often viewed as being an extension of Cabbala (or Cabala), a form of Jewish **occultism**. Cabbalistic mysticism is built around the Tree of Life, a widespread diagram of the cosmos consisting of 10 circles (spheres) that are connected by 22 paths (lines). Each of the principal 22 tarot cards (the Major Arcana) is associated with one of these lines.

One characteristic practice in traditional occult thought has been to connect the symbol system of a given occult art with other symbol systems. Because of the prestige enjoyed by astrology in past eras, practitioners of other occult systems were especially interested in drawing on astrological symbolism. **Palmistry**, for example, deploys the symbolism of astrology, particularly in the names given to the fingers and to certain mounds on the palms.

Over the centuries, astrology and astrological symbolism became associated with both the tarot and the Cabbala. However, as systems that grew to maturity independently of the science of the stars, this connection was never quite natural. The difficulty is easy enough to see from a purely mathematical standpoint: How does one appropriately associate 10 spheres or 22 cards with 7 **planets** (the number of significant heavenly bodies known to the ancients) or 12 signs? Such associations, while useful in some instances, are never really convincing as a complete system.

Sources:

Cavendish, Richard. *The Black Arts.* New York: Capricorn Books, 1967.
Gettings, Fred. *Dictionary of Astrology.* London: Routledge & Kegan Paul, 1985.

Taurus

Taurus, the second sign of the **zodiac**, is a **fixed earth sign**. It is a negative (in the value-neutral sense of being negatively *charged*), **feminine sign**, **ruled** by the **planet Venus**. Its symbol is the Bull, and its **glyph** is said to represent a bull's head and horns. It takes its name from the Greek word for bull. A sign known for its stubbornness, Taurus is the source of such expressions as bullheaded and stubborn as a bull. Taurus is associated with the throat and neck. People with a Taurus **sun sign**, while they often have beautiful voices, are also prone to sore throats, thyroid irregularities, and other neck problems. The key phrase for Taurus is *I have.*

Taurus, like many signs of the zodiac, does not have a developed mythology associated with it. Taurus is most often said to be the bull who kidnapped Europa. As the story goes, the god Zeus saw the princess Europa playing with female attendants on the beach and was filled with love for her great beauty. Zeus then transformed himself into a beautiful white bull, wandered into the group of females, and laid down among them. He presented such a peaceful appearance that they petted him, and Europa climbed onto his back. Zeus then unexpectedly took off swimming, eventually depositing Europa on the beach at Crete, where he made love to her. She bore him three sons and received three gifts from the king of the gods—an unerring spear, an inexorable hound, and a bronze man who drove away strangers.

Like Zeus, Taureans are fond of beauty and sensuality and like to place themselves in beautiful surroundings. They make a special effort to enjoy the good things of life. Similar to the bull of this tale, they are usually handsome and peaceful and are content to lie around and be "petted" (they enjoy receiving massages more than any other sign). They can remain calm when others panic but can explode into rage when pushed too far; though slow to anger, they have the worst temper in the zodiac when aroused. Like the unerring spear and the inexorable hound of the myth, Taureans are "doggedly" stubborn, pursuing a task in the face of all odds. And like the bronze man who chased away strangers, Taureans prefer the familiar over the new.

There is a wealth of information available on the characteristics of the zodiacal signs, so much that one book would not be able to contain it all. One traditional way in which astrologers condense information is by summarizing sign and planet traits in lists of words and short phrases called key words or key phrases. The following Taurus key words are drawn from Manly P. Hall's *Astrological Keywords*:

> *Emotional key words*: "Amorous, artistic, gentle, loyal, domestic, proud, quick-tempered, self-indulgent, sensual, moods make definite statements concerning emotions impossible" (p. 17).

> *Mental key words*: "Patient, persistent, thorough, steadfast, conservative, retentive, discriminating, determined, argumentative, stubborn, materialistic" (p. 20).

Most popular works on astrology contain data on the signs, and these can be consulted for more detailed information.

Sources:

Evans, Colin. *The New Waite's Compendium of Natal Astrology*. Revised by Brian E. F. Gardener. York Beach, Maine: Samuel Weiser, 1971. (Originally published 1917.)

Green, Landis Knight. *The Astrologer's Manual: Modern Insights into an Ancient Art*. Sebastopol, Calif.: CRCS Publications, 1975.

Hall, Manly P. *Astrological Keywords*. 1958. Reprint. Savage, Md.: Littlefield Adams (1975), 17, 20.

Terpsichore

Terpsichore, **asteroid** 81 (the 81st asteroid to be discovered), is approximately 122 kilometers in diameter and has an **orbital** period of 4.8 years. Terpsichore was named after the Greek muse of dance and choral song. According to Lang-Wescott, Terpsichore represents flexibility, agility, dance, body language and gestures, and movement. This asteroid's key words are *movement* and *body ego*.

Sources:

Lang-Wescott, Martha. *Asteroids-Mechanics: Ephemerides II*. Conway, Mass.: Treehouse Mountain, 1990.

———. *Mechanics of the Future: Asteroids*. Rev. ed. 1988; Conway, Mass.: Treehouse Mountain, 1991.

Tetrabiblos

The *Tetrabiblos* (literally, "four books") is the oldest existing systematic "text-book" of astrology. Its author, **Claudius Ptolemy**, is regarded as the father of Western astrology.

Tetragon

Tetragon is an alternate, though rarely used, term for **square**, an **aspect** of 90°.

Tezcatlipoca

Tezcatlipoca, **asteroid** 1,980 (the 1,980th asteroid to be discovered), is approximately 6.2 kilometers in diameter and has an **orbital** period of 2.2 years. Tezcatlipoca was named after the dark god of Aztec mythology. Lehman associates it with the dark side of life.

Sources:

Kowal, Charles T. *Asteroids: Their Nature and Utilization.* Chichester, West Sussex, U. K.: Ellis Horwood Limited, 1988.

Lehman, J. Lee. *The Ultimate Asteroid Book.* West Chester, Penn.: Whitford Press, 1988.

Thomas Aquinas, Saint

See: Aquinas, Saint Thomas

Toro

Toro, **asteroid** 1,685 (the 1,685th asteroid to be discovered), was named after the Spanish word for bull. Its **orbital** period is somewhat more than 1 1/2 years, and its diameter is 7 1/2 kilometers. Toro is one of the more recent asteroids to be investigated by astrologers. Preliminary material on Toro can be found in **Demetra George** and Douglas Bloch's *Astrology for Yourself,* and an **ephemeris** (table of celestial locations) for Toro can be found in the back of the second edition of George and Bloch's *Asteroid Goddesses.* Unlike the **planets**, which are associated with a wide range of phenomena, the smaller asteroids are said to represent a single principle. George and Bloch give Toro's principle as "the power of boundless strength"; their tentative key phrase for Toro is *my capacity to use and control power.* **Zipporah Dobyns** hypothesizes that Toro may resonate with the meaning of **Taurus**, attracted to comfort, beauty, and sensuality, and characterized by a strong will and potential power struggles.

Sources:

Dobyns, Zipporah. *Expanding Astrology's Universe*. San Diego, Calif.: Astro Computing Services, 1983.
George, Demetra, with Douglas Bloch. *Asteroid Goddesses: The Mythology, Psychology and Astrology of the Reemerging Feminine*. 2d. ed. rev. and enl. San Diego, Calif.: Astro Computing Services, 1990.
———. *Astrology for Yourself: A Workbook for Personal Transformation*. Berkeley, Calif.: Wingbow Press, 1987.
Lehman, J. Lee. *The Ultimate Asteroid Book*. West Chester, Pa.: Whitford Press, 1988.

Transit

Transit, from Latin *trans* (across, beyond, or over) plus *ire* (go), has two related astrological meanings. The first simply identifies **planets** that are moving across the sky, in contrast to planets positioned in a birth chart (or in other kinds of **horoscopes**). For example, a given individual's *natal* **Mercury** (Mercury's position at birth) is at 25° **Aquarius**, whereas *transiting* Mercury is moving through the early **degrees** of **Sagittarius.** One can also talk about a planet's **transit** (movement) through a given sign or **house.**

The second meaning of transit refers to a method of predicting conditions on the basis of the interaction between transiting planets and one's **natal chart** (birth chart). Secondary **progressions**, the other method of **prognostication** most in use among contemporary astrologers, entails finding a person's age—say, for example, 40 years—and moving the planets and house **cusps** of the natal chart to the positions they occupied the same number of days after birth as the individual's age in years—in this case, 40 days. An oversimplified but nevertheless useful generalization is that transits indicate external conditions, whereas progressions indicate inner development (in the sense of changes in one's personality). Thus, transits are used to predict future environments, and progressions are used to predict inner changes. For readings, astrologers often erect a chart that has three concentric circles; the inner circle contains the natal chart, the intermediate circle contains what is referred to as the progressed chart, and the outer circle records the positions of the transiting planets for the time of the reading. This tripartite chart allows the astrologer to view the interactions between the various levels at a glance.

The transiting planets exert generic influences that affect everybody. Thus, the period during which Mercury (which is associated with communication and concrete thinking) is **retrograde** *(appears* to move backward in its **orbit)**, for example, is not a good time for anyone to sign contracts. However, when astrologers discuss transits, they usually have in mind the interaction between the planets currently moving through the heavens and the planets in a particular person's natal chart. A natal chart is a bit like a two-way template that shows how a person views the universe as well as how the universe affects the individual. The positions that the planets occupied at the person's birth, in other words, remain sensitive spots that respond to the transiting celestial bodies making **aspects** to them. Say, for example, that an individual's natal Mercury (the position Mercury occupied at birth) is 10° in the sign **Capricorn.** Furthermore, transiting **Neptune** (a planet that is associated with, among many other things, delusion and foggy thinking) is moving over the person's Mercury, while simultaneously making inharmonious aspects with other planets. For the period this transit is in effect, this individual should refrain from signing contracts. In this situation, unlike the case of retrograde Mercury, the advice is particularized for one person rather than for everybody.

The transiting planets also affect a person according to the house through which they are moving. Thus, for example, a transit of **Jupiter** (which embodies the principle of expansion and good luck) through the tenth house (career and public standing) would be, unless other transits dictate the contrary, a good period for a businessperson to undertake a business expansion. The length of time a transit has an effect varies according to the relative speed of the planet. Jupiter, for example, usually takes about a year to cross through an average-sized house, giving the hypothetical businessperson in this example a year to take advantage of Jupiter's transit through her or his tenth house. By way of contrast, the **Moon** transits a house in 2 or 3 days, whereas **Pluto** takes 15 years. For further information, the best general handbook for interpreting transits is probably still Robert Hand's ambitious *Planets in Transit: Life Cycles for Living.*

Sources:

Hand, Robert. *Planets in Transit: Life Cycles for Living.* West Chester, Pa.: Whitford Press, 1976.
Lunstead, Betty. *Transits: The Time of Your Life.* York Beach, Maine: Samuel Weiser, 1980.
Sasportas, Howard. *The Gods of Change: Pain, Crisis and the Transits of Uranus, Neptune and Pluto.* London: Arkana, 1989.

Translation of Light (Borrowed Light)

A translation of light occurs when a **transiting planet** is **separating** from an **aspect** with one planet while simultaneously **applying** an aspect to another. The transiting planet briefly connects the two planets (which may otherwise not be in aspect with each another), imparting the influence (the "light") from the planet from which it is separating to the planet to which it is applying. For example, say that in an individual's **natal chart, Mars** is at 12° **Aquarius** and **Venus** is at 24° Aquarius. As the transiting **Moon** reaches 18° Aquarius, it is separating from a **conjunction** with Mars and applying a conjunction to Venus. While thus in between conjunctions, the Moon is said to be translating (imparting) the light (the energy) of Mars to Venus.

Sources:

Bach, Eleanor. *Astrology from A to Z: An Illustrated Source Book.* New York: Philosophical Library, 1990.
Lee, Dal. *Dictionary of Astrology.* New York: Paperback Library, 1969.

Transpluto (Persephone; Bacchus; Isis; Minerva)

Of the many **hypothetical planets** postulated by astrologers, the one most likely to have an empirical existence is Transpluto, so called because, if discovered, it would be found beyond the **orbit** of **Pluto**. This hypothetical planet has been called by many different names—Persephone, Isis, Minerva, and Bacchus, to name a few—but Transpluto is its most commonly accepted designation. Many astrologers have been attracted by the idea of one or more transplutonian planets, because their discovery would allow astrologers to complete the transferral of sign **rulerships** that has been in progress since the discovery of **Uranus**: In the premodern system of sign rulerships, each of the traditional **planets** ruled 2 signs apiece, while the **luminaries** (the **Sun** and the **Moon**) each ruled 1 sign. As the outer planets were discovered, the rulerships of **Aquarius**, **Pisces**, and **Scorpio** were gradually transferred to Uranus, **Neptune**, and **Pluto**, leaving **Saturn, Jupiter**, and **Mars** as the rulers of **Capricorn, Sagittarius**, and **Aries**. Only **Mercury** and **Venus** are still viewed as ruling 2 signs each.

Because of the attractiveness of a balanced system in which 12 heavenly bodies rule 12 signs, twentieth-century astrologers have often speculated that 2 new planets would eventually be discovered and come to be accepted as the rulers of **Virgo** and **Libra**. In particular, it has been speculated that the hypothetical planet **Vulcan**, which some astronomers said could be found between the Sun and Mercury, is the ruler of Virgo, while trans-Pluto has been thought to rule Libra. The abandonment of the notion of an intramercurial planet by astronomers has also tended to call into doubt the notion of an extra-Plutonian planet, and some contemporary astrologers have begun to put forward certain **asteroids** as candidates for the rulerships of Virgo and Libra.

Neptune was discovered by astronomers who used perturbations in the orbit of Uranus to calculate the position of a transuranian planet. Its position was determined mathematically by a Frenchman as well as an Englishman, and German astronomers were actually able to locate the new planet. In a similar manner, some astrologers believe they have enough data to plot the orbit of a transplutonian planet, and more than one **ephemeris** has been published (trans-Pluto has even been incorporated into chart-casting programs). The most significant astrological publication in this area is John Robert Hawkins's *Transpluto, Or Should We Call Him Bacchus, The Ruler of Taurus?*, which book includes an ephemeris as well as preliminary delineations for trans-Pluto's **house** positions, sign positions, and **aspects**. *Transpluto, Or Should We Call Him Bacchus* has generated enough interest to merit three printings, but the transplutonian planet is still outside the astrological mainstream and will undoubtedly remain so until astronomers definitively establish its existence.

Sources:

Corliss, William R. *The Sun and Solar System Debris: A Catalog of Astronomical Anomalies.* Glen Arm, Md.: The Sourcebook Project, 1986.
Hawkins, John Robert. *Transpluto, Or Should We Call Him Bacchus, The Ruler of Taurus?* 1976. Reprint. Tempe, Ariz.: American Federation of Astrologers, 1990.

Trecile

A trecile (also called a tresile) is a minor **aspect** of 108°. Some astrologers place it in the family of aspects created by subdividing a circle into 10 parts (36°, 72°, 108°, 144°, etc.). It could also be regarded as a quintile (72°) and a half and is thus related to that family of aspects. It is given an **orb of influence** of 1° to 2°.

Trine

A trine is an **aspect** of 120° between two points—such as two **planets**—in an astrological chart. This **soft aspect** is traditionally regarded as harmonious and beneficial, although too many **soft aspects** combined with too few **hard aspects** is regarded as unfortunate because people with this chart pattern do not usually experience enough of life's hard edges to develop strong character. It is sometimes referred to as the aspect of good fortune. Trines indicate an easy flow of energy between two planets. Thus, for example, an individual with a natal trine between **Mercury** (which represents the mind) and **Uranus** (which rules, among other sciences, astrology) would have a natural aptitude for undertanding astrology.

Sources:

Gettings, Fred. *Dictionary of Astrology.* London: Routledge & Kegan Paul, 1985.
Hand, Robert. *Horoscope Symbols.* Rockport, Mass.: Para Research, 1981.

Triplicity (Trigon)

Triplicity refers to a group of three, usually three signs of the same **element**—the *fire triplicity,* **Aries, Leo,** and **Sagittarius**; the *earth triplicity,* **Taurus, Virgo,** and **Capricorn**; the *air triplicity,* **Gemini, Libra,** and **Aquarius**; and the *water triplicity,* **Cancer, Scorpio,** and **Pisces**. Sometimes it is also used to refer to groups of three houses. The traditional term for triplicity is trigon, which comes from the Latin transliteration of the Greek word for triangle (when, on the wheel of the **zodiac**, lines are drawn so as to connect all the signs of the same element, the resulting figure is a triangle).

Tripod Pattern

A tripod pattern is a **horoscope** arrangement in which the **planets** are organized into three distinct clusters. Ideally, each cluster forms **trine aspects** with the other two clusters.

Tropical Signs

The tropical signs are **Capricorn** and **Cancer**. The term tropical comes from the Greek *tropos,* meaning to turn. As the **Sun** enters these signs during the summer and winter **solstices**, it appears to reverse its direction (to "turn" around) in its gradual movement north or south of the **equator**.

Tropical Year

The tropical year (also called the solar year, the seasonal year, the natural year, the equinoctial year, and the astronomical year) is the time that it takes the **Sun** to go from one spring equinox to the next—365 days 5 hours and 48 minutes. Because of the **precession of equinoxes**, the equinox point changes slightly (when looked at against the background of the **stars**), making a tropical year shorter than a **sidereal year** (a "star" year) by a little more than 20 minutes.

Tropical Zodiac (Moving Zodiac)

The tropical zodiac, also called the moving zodiac, is the familiar circle of 12 signs that begins at 0° Aries (the point where the **Sun** is located at the spring **equinox**). Because of the **precession of equinoxes**, the equinox point changes slightly so that each year it moves farther and farther back when looked at against the background of the **stars**. The net effect of this movement is that the signs no longer correspond with the **constellation** after which they are named, and at this time the tropical sign Aries begins near the beginning of the constellation **Pisces**. The antonym of tropical zodiac is **sidereal zodiac**, which refers to the **zodiac** constituted by the actual constellations. The sidereal zodiac is used in **Hindu astrology**, and also by a few Western astrologers.

Sources:

Bach, Eleanor. *Astrology from A to Z: An Illustrated Source Book.* New York: Philosophical Library, 1990.

Brau, Jean-Louis, Helen Weaver, and Allan Edmands. *Larousse Encyclopedia of Astrology.* New York: New American Library, 1980.

Tyche

Tyche, **asteroid** 258 (the 258th asteroid to be discovered), is approximately 68 kilometers in diameter and has an **orbital** period of 4.2 years. It is named after the Greek goddesss of fortune and personification of luck and indicates good luck and a fortunate outcome to activities undertaken in matters associated with its sign and **house** position. A prominent Tyche in a **natal chart** signals a lucky person.

Sources:

Kowal, Charles T. *Asteroids: Their Nature and Utilization.* Chichester, West Sussex, U.K.: Ellis Horwood Limited, 1988.
Room, Adrian. *Dictionary of Astronomical Names.* London: Routledge, 1988.

Tyl, Noel

Noel Tyl, a contemporary astrologer, was born on December 31, 1936, in West Chester, Pennsylvania. A Harvard University graduate with a degree in psychology, Tyl emerged on the American astrological stage in 1972 with dynamic ideas that linked psychological need theory and astrological symbolism. His 12-volume series *The Principles and Practice of Astrology* and his other textbooks, including *Holistic Astrology,* were astrological best-sellers.

Tyl founded and edited the magazine *Astrology Now* for 5 years. He was on the founding steering committee of the Association for Astrological Networking (AFAN), and is currently its presiding officer. Tyl has lectured throughout the United States and Europe. He was a keynote speaker at each of the first three conventions of the World Congress of Astrology. His latest book, *Prediction in Astrology,* is a comprehensive presentation of solar arc theory and practice.

Selected Publications:

The Principles and Practice of Astrology. 12 vols. St. Paul, Minn.: Llewellyn Publications, 1974–76.
Holistic Astrology. St. Paul, Minn.: Llewellyn Publications, 1980 (rpt.).
Prediction in Astrology. Saint Paul, Minn.: Llewellyn Publications, 1991.

U

Ultimate Dispositor

A **planet** is the **dispositor** of other planets when they are located in the sign **ruled** by the first planet. For instance, if both **Pluto** and **Venus** are in the sign **Leo**, then the **Sun**, the ruler of Leo, is the dispositor of Pluto and Venus. In some charts, a chain of dispositors (e.g., the Sun is the dispositor of Pluto and Venus, while Saturn is the dispositor of the Sun, and so on) can be traced all the way to a single planet that is the final or ultimate dispositor of every other planet in the chart. Such a planet is regarded as having an especially strong influence over the entire **horoscope**.

Urania

Urania, **asteroid** 30 (the 30th asteroid to be discovered—in 1854) was named after the Greek muse of **astronomy**. Its **orbital** period is 3 2/3 years, and its diameter is 94 kilometers. Urania is one of the more recent asteroids to be investigated. Preliminary material on Urania can be found in **Demetra George** and Douglas Bloch's *Astrology for Yourself,* and an **ephemeris** (table of celestial positions) for it can be found in the back of the second edition of George and Bloch's *Asteroid Goddesses.* Unlike the **planets**, which are associated with a wide range of phenomena, the smaller asteroids are said to represent a single principle. George and Bloch give Urania's principle as "inspired knowledge." **Zipporah Dobyns** speculates that the meanings of Urania are related to those of **Uranus**, namely, seeking of freedom, the need for variety, intellectual openness, etc. The late **John Addey** regarded Urania as the **ruler** of astrology (which Uranus is usually said to rule); he found it prominent in the charts of astrologers. J. Lee Lehman associates it with science (perhaps even "the muse of science"), particularly with the ability to take a range of data and translate them into intelligible form.

Sources:

Dobyns, Zipporah. *Expanding Astrology's Universe*. San Diego, Calif.: Astro Computing Services, 1983.

George, Demetra, with Douglas Bloch. *Astrology for Yourself: A Workbook for Personal Transformation*. Berkeley, Calif.: Wingbow Press, 1987.

————. *Asteroid Goddesses: The Mythology, Psychology and Astrology of the Reemerging Feminine*. 2d ed. rev. and enl. San Diego, Calif: Astro Computing Services, 1990.

Lehman, J. Lee. *The Ultimate Asteroid Book*. West Chester, Pa.: Whitford Press, 1988.

Uranian Astrology

The Uranian system, sometimes referred to as the Hamburg School of Astrology, was established by Friedrich Sieggrün (1877–1951) and Alfred Witte (1878–1943). It relies heavily on **hard aspects** and **midpoints,** and utilizes eight **hypothetical planets** in its analyses. In decline for many decades, it has experienced a revival in recent years.

Uranus

Uranus was the first **planet** beyond **Saturn** to be discovered and as such caused something of an upheaveal in traditional **astronomy** and astrology. Uranus is the only planet to be named after a Greek rather than Roman god. This is because the Greek god Chronos, whom the Romans identified with Saturn, was the son of the oldest god, Uranus (the Roman Saturn's father was not named in existing myths). Astronomers of the time must have felt that they had discovered the "ancestor" of all the planets. This, of course, made a certain amount of sense, but the pattern was upset when **Neptune** was discovered in the next century.

Uranus was god of the sky. A tyrant who imprisoned his offspring, he was castrated by his son Chronos. Some modern astrologers believe that the more proper mythological association with this planet is **Prometheus**, the Greek creator and defender of humanity who stole fire from heaven and gave it to humankind. With respect to his relationship with the other gods, Prometheus was a trickster and rebel who was ultimately punished by Zeus.

It takes Uranus 84.01 years to complete an **orbit** of the **Sun**, which means that it stays in each sign of the **zodiac** for 7 years. Uranus is said to **rule** the sign **Aquarius,** a relationship indicating a similarity between the characteristics of Uranus and those of Aquarius. Like Aquarius, Uranus is associated with humanity, ideals, eccentricity, and rebelliousness. These traits clearly link the planet more to Promethean traits than to those of the *mythological* Uranus (who seems, if anything, to embody the polar opposite traits of the *astrological* Uranus). Astronomically, the planet is unusual and even eccentric: Rather than having an axis that is perpendicular to the plane of its orbit around the Sun, Uranus rolls around the Sun on its side. Also, unlike all other **planetary moon** systems, the moons of Uranus were named after Shakespearean characters rather than traditional mythological figures.

Uranus is especially associated with sudden, unexpected change. It is said to rule astrology, science, electricity, and occultism. Although the various planets are connected with a wide range of activities and objects, they also, when found in a **natal chart**, represent different parts of the psyche. Uranus represents the creative, innovative, freedom-seeking part of the self. Thus, its placement in a natal chart shows much about how a person best expresses creative genius. The **house** position of Uranus shows us an area of life where one can express originality as well as anticipate sudden, dramatic change.

Jeff Mayo's *The Planets and Human Behavior* provides useful lists of traits and associations for the planets. For Uranus, under the rubric *characteristic desire trends,* Mayo lists "independence, originality, inventiveness, curiosity, unconventionality, rebelliousness, idealism" (p. 102). Under the heading *traditional associations* are listed "the unusual, the unorthodox and unconventional; science and anything connected with electronics or electricity, radio and television, aeronautics; invention, originality, genius, curiosity, freaks, the unexpected and the unplanned, sudden and disruptive happenings, sudden changes, anarchism, revolution, the unpredictable, surprises, shocks; catastrophes such as earthquakes and volcanic eruptions; accidents, divorce, estrangement, sudden broken ties, ups and downs in life, sudden changes of fortune, liberty, freedom, independence, occultism, civic bodies, societies and associations" (p. 102).

Sources:

Campion, Nicholas. *The Practical Astrologer.* New York: Harry N. Abrams, 1987.

George, Llewellyn. *The New A to Z Horoscope Maker and Delineator.* Saint Paul, Minn.: Llewellyn Publications, 1910. rev. and enl. 1987.

McEvers, Joan. *Planets: The Astrological Tools.* Saint Paul, Minn.: Llewellyn Publications, 1989.

Mayo, Jeff. *The Planets and Human Behavior.* 1972. Reprint. Reno, Nev.: CRCS Publications, 1985.

Valentine, Christine. *Images of the Psyche: Exploring the Planets through Psychology and Myth.* Shaftesbury, Dorset, U.K.: Element Books, 1991.

Utopia

Utopia, **asteroid** 1,282 (the 1,282d asteroid to be discovered), is approximately 35 kilometers in diameter and has an **orbital** period of 5.5 years. Utopia (literally, "no place,") was named after the imaginary republic of Sir Thomas More. Lehman associates this asteroid with ideals and, more particularly, with people who act from a blueprint for a better society.

Sources:

Kowal, Charles T. *Asteroids: Their Nature and Utilization.* Chichester, West Sussex, U.K.: Ellis Horwood Limited, 1988.

Lehman, J. Lee. *The Ultimate Asteroid Book.* West Chester, Penn.: Whitford Press, 1988.

Van Toen, Donna

Donna Van Toen, was born on March 5, 1949, in Watertown, New York. Her formal education was at Plattsburgh State University. She originally got involved in astrology at age 16 in an attempt to disprove it to a friend. She is mostly self-taught, but she has also attended close to 150 lectures, 50 workshop/ intensives, and at least 20 conferences, including seminars with Frances Sakoian, Isabel Hickey, Richard Idemon, and others.

Van Toen's works include *The Astrologer's Node Book* (1981) and *The Mars Book* (1988), both of which have been translated into Portuguese. She has had more than 100 articles published in such magazines as Dell's *Horoscope, American Astrology,* and *The Mountain Astrologer.* She has been a full-time astrological consultant since 1975 and a teacher since 1977. Van Toen has lectured at numerous astrological conferences in the United States, Canada, and Australia. She is a book reviewer for *The Mountain Astrologer* and is also involved in several committees exploring educational standards and professional issues, with an interest in seeing astrology become a recognized, credentialed profession.

Selected Publications:

The Astrologer's Node Book. York Beach, Maine: Samuel Weiser, 1981.
The Mars Book. York Beach, Maine: Samuel Weiser, 1988.

Venus

Venus, named after the Roman goddess of fertility and beauty (the Roman equivalent of the Greek Aphrodite), is the second **planet** nearest the **Sun.** In **Mesopotamian astrology** Venus was associated with the goddess Ishtar (Istar; Inana; Astarte), a goddess of both love (particularly eroticism, rather than "romantic love") and war. This dual character was split between Venus's role as the Morning Star, in which she personified the war goddess, and her role as the

Evening Star, in which she personified the love goddess. Venus's combative associations were not retained in later astrology, in which she is represented exclusively as a goddess of love, harmony, and beauty.

The planet Venus has an orbital period of 244 days. Because its **orbit** lies between Earth and the Sun, Venus does not ever appear, from our terrestrial perspective, to be far from the Sun. For astrology, one practical implication of this is that Venus is never more than two signs away from the sign of the **zodiac** the **Sun** is in. Thus, for example, if the Sun is in **Leo**, Venus can only be in Leo, **Gemini, Cancer, Virgo**, or **Libra**. Venus **rules** both **Taurus** and Libra, although many contemporary astrologers anticipate that a new planet will be discovered and come to be viewed as the ruler of Libra.

Like its mythological namesake, Venus is associated with beauty and love. Additionally, Venus is associated with charm, aesthetic sense, pleasure, affection, partnership, harmony, money, possessions, sensuality, and romantic love. While the various planets are connected with a wide range of activities and objects, they also, when found in a **natal chart**, represent different parts of the psyche. Venus represents what may traditionally be thought of as the "heart"—a center of interpersonal and aesthetic feelings. Its placement in a natal chart shows much about how one relates and what one loves.

Individuals with their natal Venus in the sign **Cancer**, for example, love their home and mother. In financial matters, this sign represents the ability to make money through real estate and other Cancer-ruled matters. The **house** placement shows less about a planet's basic nature than it does about the **native's** environment. Thus, Venus in the sixth house, for instance, is favorable for health (a sixth-house matter), although such individuals can also overindulge. These people can also enjoy their work (another sixth house matter) or turn what they enjoy into their work.

When Venus **aspects** another planet in a natal chart, the native's manner of relating to other people will be modified according to the planet and aspect involved. Thus, for example, a **soft aspect** like a **trine** between Venus and **Uranus** will make the individual magnetic, attracting unusual people as well as being attracted by them. A **hard aspect** between these two planets, on the other hand, might still make the individual magnetic, but the "sudden change" influence of Uranus would introduce disruption into relationships, so that the person would be prone to drop associates—or be dropped by them—suddenly and unexpectedly. A hard aspect might also indicate a person who is erratic with money.

Jeff Mayo's *The Planets and Human Behavior* provides useful lists of traits and associations for the planets. For Venus, under the rubric *characteristic desire trends,* Mayo lists "co-operation, harmony, sympathy, compromise, creativeness, artistry, idealism, aestheticism" (p. 83). Under the heading *traditional associations* are listed "love and romance, marriage, sociability, love affairs, sensuality, sexual intercourse, beauty, pleasures, entertainment, social functions, festivities, the arts, dancing, rhythm, harmony, money, beautiful possessions, females generally, sugars and spices, the significator of victory in war, trades and industries catering mainly for women (such as cosmetics and jewellery)" (p. 84).

Sources:

Campion, Nicholas. *The Practical Astrologer.* New York: Harry N. Abrams, 1987.
George, Llewellyn. *The New A to Z Horoscope Maker and Delineator.* Saint Paul, Minn.: Llewellyn Publications, 1910. rev. and enl. 1987.
McEvers, Joan. *Planets: The Astrological Tools.* Saint Paul, Minn.: Llewellyn Publications, 1989.
Mayo, Jeff. *The Planets and Human Behavior.* 1972. Reprint. Reno, Nev.: CRCS Publications, 1985.
Valentine, Christine. *Images of the Psyche: Exploring the Planets through Psychology and Myth.* Shaftesbury, Dorset, U.K.: Element Books, 1991.

Vera

Vera, **asteroid** 245 (the 245th asteroid to be discovered), is approximately 84 kilometers in diameter and has an **orbital** period of 5.4 years. Its name is Latin for true. In a **natal chart**, Vera's **house** and sign position indicates where we are especially able to perceive the truth or where we search for the truth. When **afflicted**, Vera may suggest "false truth."

Sources:

Kowal, Charles T. *Asteroids: Their Nature and Utilization.* Chichester, West Sussex, U.K.: Ellis Horwood Limited, 1988.
Room, Adrian. *Dictionary of Astronomical Names.* London: Routledge, 1988.

Veritas

Veritas, **asteroid** 490 (the 490th asteroid to be discovered), is approximately 128 kilometers in diameter and has an **orbital** period of 5.6 years. Its name is a personification of the Latin word for truth. In a **natal chart**, Veritas's **house** and sign position indicates where one is especially able to perceive the truth or searches for the truth. When **afflicted**, Vera may suggest "false truth."

Sources:

Kowal, Charles T. *Asteroids: Their Nature and Utilization.* Chichester, West Sussex, U.K.: Ellis Horwood Limited, 1988.
Room, Adrian. *Dictionary of Astronomical Names.* London: Routledge, 1988.

Vernal Equinox (Spring Equinox)

Equinox, Latin for "equal night," refers to one of the two days of the year on which daytime and nighttime are equal in duration. The vernal equinox, which occurs on or around March 21, marks the beginning of both the sign **Aries** and the spring season. The vernal equinox is especially important for Western astrologers, who utilize the Sun's position against the backdrop of the **stars** at the spring equinox (the **vernal point**) as the place where the **zodiac** begins.

Vernal Point

The vernal (from the Latin, of the spring) point is the position of the **Sun** against the backdrop of the **stars** at the moment of the vernal **equinox** (i.e., the spring equinox). The vernal equinox is especially important for astrologers, who use the vernal point as the place to begin the **zodiac** (i.e., 0° **Aries**). Because of the phenomenon known as the **precession of equinoxes,** this point occurs at a slightly different place every year.

Vertex

In geometry, a vertex is the pivot point of an angle. In astrology, the vertex is the point in a **horoscope** where the **prime vertical** intersects the **ecliptic** in the west. The antivertex is the corresponding point in the east. The vertex was discovered/invented L. Edward Johndro and elaborated upon by Charles Jayne. The point where the vertex falls in a chart is said to be the most fated (least amenable to conscious choices) part of the horoscope. Few contemporary astrologers employ the vertex–antivertex axis.

Vespertine

Vespertine (from Latin *vesper,* evening) refers to the evening, especially the early evening, and in astrology was traditionally applied to a **planet** or **star** that dropped below the **horizon** soon after sunset. Vespertine is the opposite of **matutine** (which refers to planets and stars that rise above the horizon just before sunrise). Both terms are rarely used in modern astrology.

Vesta

Vesta was one of the first four **asteroids,** along with **Ceres, Juno,** and **Pallas,** to be investigated by astrologers. It was named after the Roman goddess of the hearth (the equivalent of the Greek Hestia) and represents the principle of dedicated work. Vesta was the fourth asteroid to be discovered (in 1807 by the German astronomer Heinrich Olbers). It has a diameter of 576 kilometers and orbits the **Sun** in slightly less than 3 2/3 terrestrial years. Because it was one of the earlier asteroids to be researched, a fair amount of material on Vesta is available.

Sources:

Bach, Eleanor. *Astrology from A to Z: An Illustrated Source Book.* New York: Philosophical Library, 1990.

Dobyns, Zipporah. *Expanding Astrology's Universe.* San Diego, Calif.: Astro Computing Services, 1983.

Donath, Emma Belle. *Asteroids in the Birth Chart.* Tempe, Ariz.: American Federation of Astrologers, 1979.

George, Demetra, with Douglas Bloch. *Astrology for Yourself: A Workbook for Personal Transformation.* Berkeley, Calif.: Wingbow Press, 1987.

———. *Asteroid Goddesses: The Mythology, Psychology and Astrology of the Reemerging Feminine.* 2d ed. rev. and enl. San Diego, Calif.: Astro Computing Services, 1990.

Lehman, J. Lee. *The Ultimate Asteroid Book.* West Chester, Penn.: Whitford Press, 1988.

Via Combusta

Via combusta is Latin for burning way, which usually refers to the first half of the sign **Scorpio**. The first 15° of that sign—and sometimes the last 15° of **Libra** through the full 30° arc of Scorpio—were taken by the ancients to exert an especially unfortunate influence, particularly for one's natal **Moon**. Some modern astrologers speculate that this negative ascription may have derived from the many **malefic fixed stars** that, in older times, were located in the first half of Scorpio (but which, because the Western, **tropical zodiac** is slowly moving, are no longer located in Scorpio). Although contemporary astrologers no longer use the *via combusta* to interpret **natal charts**, it is still utilized in **horary astrology**.

Sources:

Bach, Eleanor. *Astrology from A to Z: An Illustrated Source Book.* New York: Philosophical Library, 1990.

deVore, Nicholas. *Encyclopedia of Astrology.* New York: Philosophical Library, 1947.

Vibilia

Vibilia, **asteroid** 144 (the 144th asteroid to be discovered), is approximately 132 kilometers in diameter and has an **orbital** period of 4.3 years. It is named after the Roman goddess of journeys. When prominent in an **natal chart**, Vibilia may show someone who is involved in many journeys, either in the sense of travel or in a more figurative way. Vibilia's position by sign and **house** indicates how and where one journeys.

Sources:

Kowal, Charles T. *Asteroids: Their Nature and Utilization.* Chichester, West Sussex, U.K.: Ellis Horwood Limited, 1988.
Room, Adrian. *Dictionary of Astronomical Names.* London: Routledge, 1988.

Vigintile

A vigintile (also called a semi**decile**) is a minor **aspect** of 18° formed by dividing a circle into 20 equal subdivisions. The effect of a vigintile is subtle, so it is rarely used. The influence of this minor aspect is mildly favorable; Emma Belle Donath asserts that it represents innate understanding.

Virgin

The Virgin is a popular (but not particularly appropriate) name for the sign **Virgo**.

Virgo

Virgo, the sixth sign of the **zodiac**, is a mutable earth sign. It is a negative (in the value neutral sense of being negatively charged), **feminine** sign, **ruled** by the planet **Mercury**—though some modern astrologers dispute this rulership, claiming that it is ruled by several of the major **asteroids** or by the planetoid **Chiron**; an older generation of astrologers associated **Virgo** with the hypothetical planet **Vulcan**. Its symbol is a young woman, and its **glyph** is said to represent a serpent that was formerly linked to the serpent-like glyph of **Scorpio** since it is said that Virgo and Scorpio were once one sign. Virgo takes its name from the Latin word for virgin. Virgo is associated with the nervous system and, especially, with the bowels, and people with a Virgo **sun sign** are susceptible to bowel problems and ulcers. The key phrase for Virgo is *I analyze.*

This sign has either a very simple or a very complex mythology, depending upon which mythological figure is taken to represent Virgo. The constellation Virgo is pictured as a young woman holding an ear of corn, linking the sign to Demeter, the Greek goddess of the harvest (in the Northern Hemisphere, the **Sun** is in Virgo during harvest time). She taught humanity agriculture, and was the mother of **Plutus**, "wealth." Far from being a virgin, Demeter was a mature earth goddess, and the patroness of fertility. Virgo, however, is one of the traditional **barren** signs. Thus a better (or, perhaps, an alternative) representative of Virgo is Hygeia, goddess of health and hygiene. Hygeia was the unmarried daughter of Asklepios, the eminent physician, who, attended by his daughter, was often pictured with serpents (commonly associated with doctors; e.g., the serpents twisted around the medical caduceus).

Rather than embodying Demeter's fertility, Virgo represents Demeter's harvest aspect, and people born under this sign are good workers. This, perhaps, is the association with wealth, which is more often built on the foundation of steady labor than on sudden lucky windfalls. Virgos have fewer ego needs than many other signs of the Zodiac, and—similar to Demeter who served as a nursemaid, as well as Hygeia who served as her father's assistant—Virgos typically find happiness working under someone else. Like Demeter who taught both agriculture and the Eleusinian Mysteries, Virgos excel at teaching. Like Hygeia, they can also be good doctors and nurses. Virgos are especially concerned with good hygiene, which is derived from the name of the goddess Hygeia.

The following Virgo key words are drawn from Manly P. Hall's *Astrological Keywords*:

> *Emotional key words*: "Kindly, humane, a high evolved type, lives to serve mankind without thought of self, domestic, melancholy, somewhat petty, fussy, superficial in affairs of the heart" (p. 18).

> *Mental key words*: "Ingenious, witty, studious, dextrous, versatile, introspective, scientific, methodical, skeptical, critical, fears disease and poverty, ulterior in motive, self-centered, scheming" (p. 20).

Sources:

Evans, Colin. *The New Waite's Compendium of Natal Astrology*. Revised by Brian E. F. Gardener. York Beach, Maine: Samuel Weiser, 1971. (Originally published 1917.)

Green, Landis Knight. *The Astrologer's Manual: Modern Insights into an Ancient Art*. Sebastopol, Calif.: CRCS Publications, 1975.

Hall, Manly P. *Astrological Keywords*. 1958. Reprint. Savage, Maryland: Littlefield Adams, 1975. 18, 20.

Virtus

Virtus, **asteroid** 494 (the 494th asteroid to be discovered), is approximately 98 kilometers in diameter and has an **orbital** period of 5.2 years. Its name is a personification of the Latin for virtue. In a **natal chart**, Virtus's **house** and sign position indicates where in life one displays virtue in the original sense of power and excellence. When **afflicted**, Vera may signal false virtue.

Sources:

Kowal, Charles T. *Asteroids: Their Nature and Utilization*. Chichester, West Sussex, U.K.: Ellis Horwood Limited, 1988.

Room, Adrian. *Dictionary of Astronomical Names*. London: Routledge, 1988.

Vocational Astrology

Vocational astrology, as the name suggests, is the branch of astrology that studies a **native**'s career possibilities on the basis of her or his **natal chart**. In popular astrology, vocational aptitude is often discussed in terms of **sun sign** (e.g., **Leos** make good actors, **Virgos** make good nurses, etc.). Professional astrologers, however, are less concerned with sun signs than they are with the signs on the **cusps** of—and placement of **planets** in—the second **house** (earned income), the sixth house (work), and, especially, the tenth house (career). A favorably **aspected Neptune** in the tenth house, for instance, shows potential for a career related to music (or, perhaps, to shoes—another item associated with Neptune). A favorably aspected **Mercury** in the tenth house, on the other hand, shows potential for a career in teaching, travel, or communications (all traditionally associated with Mercury).

Vocational astrology is a vast subject about which entire books have been written. It is one of the older branches of the science of the stars. In contemporary times, the association of astrological temperament with career choice has been the basis of certain types of research designed to test the validity of astrology. The most famous of these was done by the **Gauquelins**, whose research has withstood the critical attacks of skeptics.

Voice, Signs of

The signs of voice are those signs of the **zodiac** said to indicate oratorial capacity—**Gemini, Virgo, Libra, Aquarius,** and the first half of **Sagittarius**.

Void of Course

A **planet** is void of course after it makes its last major **aspect** with another planet before **transiting** out of a given sign. It remains void of course until it enters a new sign (almost invariably the next sign) in which it will make another major aspect. This is an old notion, originating in **horary astrology**, that has begun to enjoy a new wave of popularity. Many contemporary astrologers pay special attention to transiting void-of-course Moons, regarding their influence as being on par with that of **retrograde** motion—meaning that these are poor periods during which to sign contracts, initiate new projects, or acquire new possessions. It is a good time, however, to reflect and "recharge."

To clarify the mechanics of void of course, imagine that the transiting **Moon** has just entered **Aquarius**. Over the course of several days, as the Moon moves from 0° to 26° Aquarius, it will make a half dozen or so major aspects (**conjunctions, sextiles, squares, trines,** and **oppositions**) with the **Sun** and the transiting planets. However, at 26° Aquarius, it will make its last aspect, say, a sextile (60°) aspect with **Jupiter**. As it sweeps across the next 4° (taking approximately 8 hours to do so), and until it makes its **ingress** (entry) into the sign **Pisces**, it is void of course. The length of a void of course varies from a few minutes to more than 24 hours, depending on where the planets are while the Moon transits each sign.

Al H. Morrison, the widely acknowledged expert on void-of-course moons, has observed that "actions taken while the Moon is void of course somehow always fail of their intended or planned results." Morrison studied law enforcement activities and found that whenever investigative actions were initiated during void-of-course moons, individuals violating the law failed to be convicted (although the investigation always managed to upset their criminal operation). Thus, although activities may not turn out as anticipated, the result need not be unfortunate. After 45 years of study, Morrison concluded that the Moon's last aspect has to be a true major aspect with the Sun or one of the planets (not **Chiron** or one of the **asteroids**). Minor aspects, such as the **semisextile**, the **quintile**, etc., do not save the Moon from being void of course. Morrison also noted a cyclic mood pattern peculiar to people born during void-of-course moons.

Another astrologer, Janis Huntley, studied 250 charts and found that approximately 1 out of every 12 people were born while the Moon was void of course. She also found a significantly higher percentage—1 out of every 8—among famous people. Thus, this placement does not appear to dampen achievement. Like Morrison, Huntley found that individuals born during void-of-course moons seemed to suffer somewhat from the turmoils of their emotions. They often experience loneliness, feeling "different and misunderstood."

Morrison has published a void-of-course moon **ephemeris** for many years. Also, some astrological magazines, such as *The Mountain Astrologer*, contain day-by-day accounts of transiting conditions that note when the Moon goes void of course (often abbreviated VOC) as well as when the Moon enters a new sign. Finally, certain of the major emphemerides, such as the *American Emphemeris,* published by Astro Computing, contain last-aspect and ingress information for the Moon. By all indications, the void-of-course moon has found a permanent niche in the mainstream of modern astrology.

Sources:

Huntley, Janis. *Astrological Voids: Exploring the Missing Components in the Birth Chart.* Rockport, Mass.: Element Books, 1991.

Michelsen, Neil F. *The American Ephemeris for the 20th Century.* San Diego, Calif.: Astro Computing Services, 1988.

Morrison, Al H. "Notes on the Void-of-Course' Moon." *The Mountain Astrologer* 889 (August/September 1989): 11, 29.

Vulcan

Vulcan (related to the word volcano) is a "hypothetical **planet**" that astronomers formerly speculated would be—and that a few astrologers still anticipate will be—found orbiting the **Sun** inside the **orbit** of **Mercury**. The nineteenth-century French astronomer Urbain Le Verrier was the first person to hypothesize its existence and, shortly after he made his theories known, people began to claim that they had observed Vulcan. It was named after the ancient Roman god of fire, who was also blacksmith to the gods. **Alice Bailey**'s system of **esoteric astrology** makes extensive use of Vulcan, and some esoteric astrologers still utilize it. Many astrologers anticipated that Vulcan, when discovered, would be assigned the **rulership** of **Virgo**. As astronomers gradually abandoned the notion of an intermercurial planet, Vulcan slowly faded from astrological discourse. There is, for example, no entry for Vulcan in such standard references as the *Larousse Encyclopedia of Astrology* or Eleanor Bach's *Astrology from A to Z*. Thanks to the "Star Trek" television series, the name is still alive, although Mr. Spock's home planet bears little resemblance to the hypothetical planet of astronomical history.

Sources:

Bach, Eleanor. *Astrology from A to Z: An Illustrated Source Book*. New York: Philosophical Library, 1990.
Brau, Jean-Louis, Helen Weaver, and Allan Edmands. *Larousse Encyclopedia of Astrology*. New York: New American Library, 1980.
Corliss, William R. *The Sun and Solar System Debris: A Catalog of Astronomical Anomalies*. Glen Arm, Md.: The Sourcebook Project, 1986.
deVore, Nicholas. *Encyclopedia of Astrology*. New York: Philosophical Library, 1947.
Gettings, Fred. *Dictionary of Astrology*. London: Routledge & Kegan Paul, 1985.

Vulcanus

Vulcanus is one of the eight **hypothetical planets** (sometimes referred to as the trans-Neptunian points or planets, TNPs) utilized in **Uranian astrology**. It represents powerful and even explosive energy and force, especially the urge that one cannot quite control, or the experience of charismatic coercion. Vulcanus can also symbolize a person's reservoir of energy and the depletion of that energy.

Sources:

Lang-Wescott, Martha. *Mechanics of the Future: Asteroids*. Rev. ed. Conway, Mass.: Treehouse Mountain, 1991.
Simms, Maria Kay. *Dial Detective: Investigation with the 90 Degree Dial*. San Diego, Calif.: Astro Computing Services, 1989.

W

Walkure

Walkure, **asteroid** 877 (the 877th asteroid to be discovered), is approximately 27 kilometers in diameter and has an **orbital** period of 3.9 years. Walkure was named after the maidens in Scandinavian mythology who conducted fallen warriors to Valhalla. Lehman asserts that the pattern represented by this asteroid is that of "enjoining the battle, without actually engaging in the fighting" (p. 79).

Sources:

Kowal, Charles T. *Asteroids: Their Nature and Utilization*. Chichester, West Sussex, U.K.: Ellis Horwood Limited, 1988.

Lehman, J. Lee. *The Ultimate Asteroid Book*. West Chester, Penn.: Whitford Press, 1988.

Room, Adrian. *Dictionary of Astronomical Names*. London: Routledge, 1988.

War Time

During World Wars I and II, many countries, including the United States, adopted daylight saving time on a year-round basis to provide a longer workday to meet the increased demands of wartime production. When **horoscopes** are cast for individuals born during war years, it is thus necessary to subtract 1 hour to obtain **standard time**. For natives of the United Kingdom born during WWII, during the war years the clocks were 2 hours ahead of standard time in the summer (this was termed double summer time).

Water Bearer

The Water Bearer is a popular name for the sign **Aquarius**.

Water Signs

The 12 signs of the **zodiac** are subdivided according to the 4 classical **elements** of earth, air, fire, and water. The 3 water signs (the *water triplicity* or *water trigon*) are **Cancer**, **Scorpio**, and **Pisces**. Astrologically, water refers to sensitivity, intuition, emotion, and fluidity. Water sign sensitivity can manifest as artistic sensitivity, psychic sensitivity, or as sensitivity to others. This element also embodies the traits of compassion, nurture, and protection.

The emotional sensitivity of the water element shows itself somewhat differently in each of the signs of the water **triplicity**. Cancer's watery nature typically manifests as feelings about home, security, and family. Scorpio's emerges as strong feelings about sex, death, and occult mysteries. Pisces' watery nature appears as mysticism, sensitivity to music, and impressionability.

Negative water people can be moody, depressed, emotionally grasping, and possessive. Unless counterbalanced by other factors, excess water in a chart indicates an individual who is hypersensitive and overemotional. Conversely, lack of water can indicate a person who is insensitive and unemotional.

▶
Water signs.

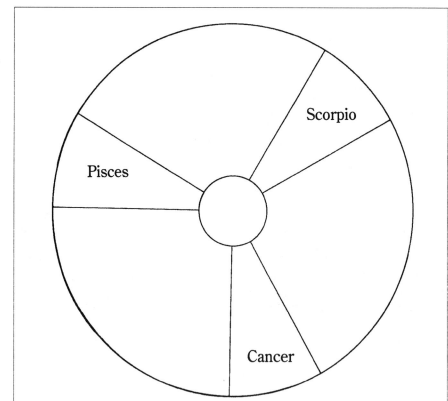

Sources:

Hand, Robert. *Horoscope Symbols.* Rockport, Mass.: Para Research, 1981.
Sakoian, Frances, and Louis S. Acker. *The Astrologer's Handbook.* New York: Harper & Row, 1989.

Waxing and Waning

The term *waxing* may be used to indicate the increasing strength of any given astrological influence. More commonly, waxing and waning refers to the **Moon**'s monthly cycle during which the portion of its surface lighted by the **Sun** increases (waxes) or decreases (wanes) in size. The increase or decrease in the Moon's size is especially important in **electional astrology.** The basic principle at work here is that activities hoped to quickly expand, such as a new business venture, should be initiated during a waxing (increasing) Moon. Activities hoped to stop or slow down, such as the growth of hair after a haircut, should be undertaken during a waning (decreasing) Moon. (*See* illustration, p. 530.)

Weak Signs

Traditionally, the weak signs were **Cancer**, **Capricorn**, and **Pisces**. Although one can perceive the rationale for regarding Cancer and Pisces as "weak," it is difficult to understand why strong, stubborn Capricorn was thus designated.

Weiss, J. Claude

J. Claude Weiss, born May 6, 1941, in Basel, Switzerland, is a Swiss astrologer who has specialized in psychological astrology (along the lines of transactional analysis), karmic astrology and **mundane astrology.** He is president of the Swiss Astrological Association, president of Astrodata, Ltd., and the editor of a bimonthly astrological magazine, *Astrologie Heute.*

After college, Weiss studied at the Swiss Institute of Technology (ETH) and completed an engineering degree in agronomy. During a 2-year stay in India, he came in touch with astrology in 1967, and it became his unique professional activity from 1977 onward. In 1978, he created Astrodata, a calculation and interpretation service for astrological delineations that soon became the largest in Europe. Methods were developed along the lines of transactional analysis and **Jungian** psychology, placing the accent on the free will and the potential found in the astrological **constellations**. Weiss was co-organizer of four Astrology World Congresses. He has lectured in Europe, the United States, and Australia, and has written many books. He lives in Wettswil, near Zurich.

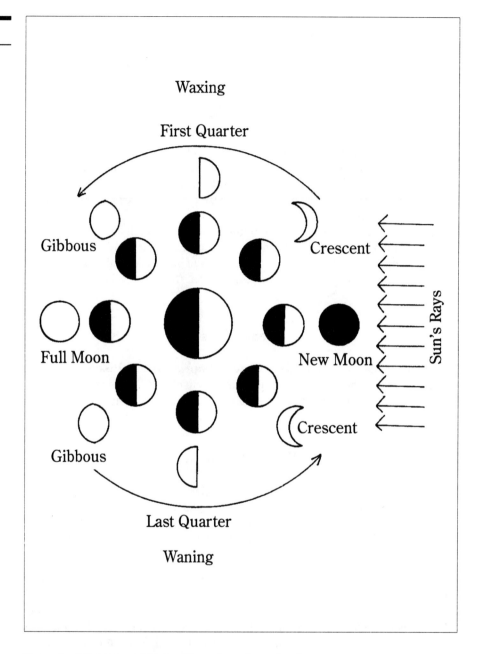

The cycle of the moon, which is said to wax as its surface is increasingly lighted by the Sun, and to wane as its surface is decreasingly lighted by the Sun.

Selected Publications:

Astrologie—Eine Wissenschaft von Raum und Zeit. Wettswil, Switzerland: 1987.

Horoskopanalyse Band I—Planeten in Häusern und Zeichen. 3d ed. Wettswil Switzerland: Edition Astrodata, 1992.

Horoskopanalyse Band II—Aspekte im Geburtsbild. 3d ed. Wettswil Switzerland: Edition Astrodata, 1992.

PLUTO—Das Erotische und Dämonische. 2d ed. By Weiss and Verena Bachmann. Wettswil, Switzerland: Edition Astrodata, 1991.

Whole Signs (Perfect Signs)

Whole signs (also called, in more recent works, perfect signs) is an archaic term referring to certain signs said to indicate strong, healthy bodies. The whole signs are variously listed, but usually include the three air *triplicity signs* (**Gemini, Libra,** and **Aquarius**). This classification has been abandoned by modern astrologers. The antonym is **broken signs** (imperfect signs).

XYZ

Yod (Double Quincunx; Finger of Destiny; Hand of God)

A yod is a **configuration** involving at least three **planets** in which two of them form a **sextile** (60°) **aspect** and both then form a **quincunx** (150°) aspect with a third planet; hence, double quincunx is one of the several alternative names for this configuration. If lines were drawn to the center of the **horoscope** from all three planets, the resulting pattern would look like a capital Y—thus the name yod, which is the name of the tenth letter of the Hebrew alphabet and the letter that corresponds with the English *Y* (though, sometimes, with *I* or *J*). The tenth Hebrew letter is an ideogram meaning hand or pointing finger, from which the other names for this configuration derive (finger of destiny, hand of God, etc.). The term yod, as well as the other, more dramatic names for the pattern, originated with Carl Leipert, a student of history and comparative religion. This configuration has been intensively studied by Thyrza Escobar and **Dane Rudyhar**.

A yod indicates a strange or unusual destiny. The interpretation often given to a natal yod is that it indicates a life that proceeds along in a certain pattern for a period of time until the established pattern is abruptly interrupted and the **native** is forced to proceed in a new direction. Often, though not always, the change has been prepared for, as in the case of an unknown understudy who on opening night must fill the shoes of the leading actor (owing to the latter's sudden illness or some other unforeseen event). A yod is not necessarily **benefic**, in the sense that the interruptions in the life pattern that it indicates are not always pleasant. The disruptive changes foretold by the configuration take place when a **transiting** or **progressed** planet makes a major aspect, particularly a **conjunction**, with the planet at the "fingertip" of the yod. This disruption will be most keenly felt in the affairs related to the **house** (and, to a lesser extent, the sign) position of this focal planet, though there will also be reactions in the house and sign directly across the chart from the focal planet. (*See* illustration, p. 534.)

Sources:

Brau, Jean-Louis, Helen Weaver, and Allan Edmands. *Larousse Encyclopedia of Astrology.* New York: New American Library, 1980.
Escobar, Thyrza. *Side Lights of Astrology.* 3d ed. Hollywood, Calif.: Golden Seal Research, 1971.

Zelen Test

Of the various attempts to demonstrate astrological influence by statistical means, the most successful have been the large-scale studies by **Michel and Françoise Gauquelin**. The Gauquelins uncovered correlations between vocation and the position of specific **planets**, the most significant of which were those between athletes and the position of **Mars**. The Zelen Test was part of an extended attempt to disprove this **Mars effect** by *The Humanist* magazine. The original study had compared the birth data of athletes against statistical probabilities. Confident that an empirical challenge would demolish astrology, *The Humanist* challenged the Gauquelins to test their findings against a control group of nonathletes. Contrary to the expectations of critics, this test, conducted

Yod.

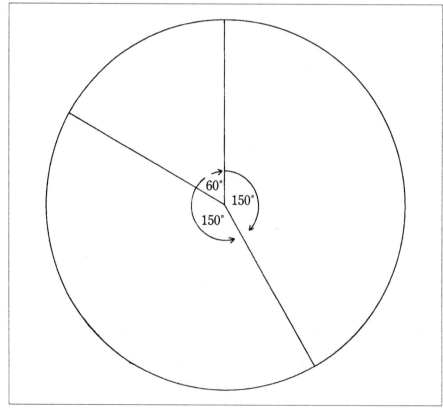

by Marvin Zelen (hence the name), confirmed the Gauquelins's original findings.

Sources:

Curry, Patrick. "Research on the Mars Effect." *Zetetic Scholar* 9 (March 1982) 34–53.
Melton, J. Gordon, Jerome Clark, and Aidan A. Kelly. *New Age Encyclopedia.* Detroit, Mich.: Gale Research, 1990.
Rawlins, Dennis. "sTARBABY." *Fate* 34, no. 10 (October 1981): 67–98.

Zenith

The zenith is the point in the heavens directly overhead at any given location on Earth. It should be carefully distinguished from the **midheaven** (with which it is often confused).

Zeus

Zeus is an **asteroid** and is also one of the eight **hypothetical planets** (sometimes referred to as the transNeptunian points or planets, TNPs) utilized in Uranian astrology. As a Uranian **planet**, Zeus represents the control of strong forces and powers—weapons, anger, willpower, machines, fuel, etc. Although Zeus represents control and restraint, adverse positions of Zeus can also indicate the loss of control.

Sources:

Lang-Wescott, Martha. *Mechanics of the Future: Asteroids.* Rev. ed. Conway, Mass.: Treehouse Mountain, 1991.
Simms, Maria Kay. *Dial Detective: Investigation with the 90 Degree Dial.* San Diego, Calif.: Astro Computing Services, 1989.

Zodiac

The zodiac (literally, "circle of animals," or, in its more primary meaning, the "circle of life" or "circle of living beings") is the "belt" constituted by the 12 signs—**Aries, Taurus, Gemini, Cancer, Leo, Virgo, Libra, Scorpio, Sagittarius, Capricorn, Aquarius,** and **Pisces**. This belt is said to extend 8° or 9° on either side of the **ecliptic** (the imaginary line drawn against the backdrop of the **stars** by the **orbit** of Earth). The orbits of the various **planets** in the **solar system** all lie within approximately the same geometric plane, so from a position within the system, all the heavenly bodies appear to move across the face of the same set of **constellations**. Several thousand years ago, the names of these constellations became the basis for the zodiac.

A distinction must be drawn between the **sidereal zodiac** and the **tropical zodiac**: The sidereal zodiac is located more or less where the constellations are positioned. The other zodiac originated with **Ptolemy**, the great astrologer– astronomer of antiquity, who was very careful to assert that the zodiac should begin at (i.e., 0° Aries should be placed at) the point where the **Sun** is positioned during the spring **equinox**. Because of the phenomenon known as the **precession of equinoxes**, this point very gradually moves backward every year, and currently 0° Aries is located near the beginning of the constellation Pisces. Astrologers who adhere to the Ptolemaic directive, the great majority of modern, Western astrologers, use the tropical zodiac (also called the moving zodiac, for obvious reasons). If the tropical zodiac is used, it should always be carefully distinguished from the circle of constellations (i.e., from the sidereal zodiac).

The notion of the zodiac is ancient, with roots in the early cultures of Mesopotamia; the first 12-sign zodiacs were named after the gods of these cultures. The Greeks adopted astrology from the Babylonians, and the Romans, in turn, adopted astrology from the Greeks. These peoples renamed the signs of the Babylonian zodiac in terms of their own mythologies, which is why the

▶

A representation of the zodiac from the early 16th century. A symbol for Pisces is seen in the middle.
· Bettmann Archive

familiar zodiac of the contemporary West bears names out of Mediterranean mythology. The notion of a 12-fold division derives from the lunar cycle (the orbital cycle of the **Moon** around Earth), which the Moon completes 12 times per year.

From a broad historical perspective, zodiacal symbolism can be found everywhere, and zodiacal expressions are still in use in modern English—e.g., *bullheaded* (an allusion to Taurus), *crabby* (an allusion to Cancer), etc. Throughout the centuries people have drawn parallels between the zodiac and many other 12-fold divisions—the Twelve Labors of Hercules, the Twelve Disciples, the Twelve Tribes of Israel, and so forth. The popularity of **sun sign** astrology (the kind found in the daily newspaper) has kept these ancient symbols alive in modern society, and even such prominent artifacts as automobiles have been named after some of the signs (e.g., the Taurus and the Scorpio). If you were born between

March 21 and April 19 your sun sign is **Aries** (the Ram);
April 20 and May 20 your sun sign is **Taurus** (the Bull);
May 21 and June 21 your sun sign is **Gemini** (the Twins);
June 22 and July 22 your sun sign is **Cancer** (the Crab);
July 23 and August 22 your sun sign is **Leo** (the Lion);
August 23 and September 22 your sun sign is **Virgo** (the Young Woman);
September 23 and October 23 your sun sign is **Libra** (the Scales);
October 24 and November 21 your sun sign is **Scorpio** (the Scorpion, the Snake, and the Eagle);
November 22 and December 21 your sun sign is **Sagittarius** (the Centaur or the Archer);
December 22 and January 19 your sun sign is **Capricorn** (the Goat);
January 20 and February 18 your sun sign is **Aquarius** (the Water Bearer);
February 19 and March 20 your sun sign is **Pisces** (the Fishes).

If you were born on any of the dates listed above, you are on the **cusp**, the dividing line separating a sign from its preceding sign. An individual born on a cusp is said to manifest traits of both signs (the preceding and the subsequent sign). So, for example, if you were born on April 20, you are on the cusp of Aries and Taurus, and it is thought that you would manifest traits of both those signs.

Sources:

Cirlot, J. E. *A Dictionary of Symbols.* 1971. Reprint. New York: Dorset Press, 1991.
Gettings, Fred. *Dictionary of Astrology.* London: Routledge & Kegan Paul, 1985.
Tester, Jim. *A History of Western Astrology.* New York: Ballantine, 1987.

Appendix A

Casting a Chart

Although the mathematics involved in erecting a **horoscope** is not basically difficult, people often have an emotional block against math, and many potentially good astrologers have been turned away from learning astrology because of the computational requirements of the astrological art. The personal computer revolution, however, has removed this roadblock: Professional-looking charts can now be turned out with the press of a button. For people who cannot afford to set themselves up with chart-casting software and computer hardware, there are mail-order computer chart-casting services. One of the more established firms that casts basic computer charts for a minimal amount ($6 at the time of this writing) is Astro Communication Services (P.O. Box 34487, San Diego, CA 92163-4487; 619-297-9203). Another is Great Bear Astrological Center (P.O. Box 5164, Eugene, Oregon 97405; 503-683-1760). Other such companies advertise in astrology magazines. However, for those readers who are brave enough to attempt the math, I have included enough information to enable them to cast their own **natal chart**.

A natal chart is a picture of the heavens with respect to the Earth at the moment of birth. There are at least two sets of calculations involved: Calculating the positions of the **planets** and calculating the positions of the **houses**. The basic information one needs to start with are date, time, and place of birth. Time of birth is the one essential item that most people do not immediately have at their fingertips. If the birthtime one is using is off by 2 hours or more, the **ascendant** (rising sign) will be incorrect and every planet will be in an incorrect house. One's birth certificate, obtainable from the county in which one was born, usually contains the birth time. The time zone in which one was born must also be determined, as well as whether or not daylight saving time (DST) was in effect. One should further note that daylight saving time was in effect all year long during the two world wars and for a period during and around 1974 when former President Nixon declared an energy crisis (the better computer programs will do all of this for you). Astrologers not plugged into the computer revolution have tables of time changes in which they can simply look up time zone and DST information.

Also required for chart casting is an **ephemeris** (table of planetary positions) for the year in which one was born (with exception of the Rosicrucian ephemerides for the most recent years, they are usually sold for 10-year, 50-year, and 100-year periods), as well as a table of houses. Ephemerides, and sometimes tables of houses, can often be found in larger public libraries. (There is a rough ephemeris as well as a partial table of houses at the end of Derek and Julia Parker's *The Compleat Astrologer.*) Finally, professionals also have an astrologer's atlas listing **longitudes** and **latitudes** of most cities—an atlas that conveniently provides the exact number of hours and minutes to add to or subtract from standard time to arrive at true Sun time, which astrologers refer to as **local mean time** (LMT). Although someone wishing to cast only her or his own chart needs just an ephemeris and a table of houses, anyone wanting to "set up shop" without a computer requires the following four references, most of which would still be useful even if one later switched to computer chart casting:

1. *An ephemeris.* A 100-year ephemeris for the 20th century is a good investment. The Michelsen ephemerides (published by Astro Communication Services) are the current standard, although no ephemerides are really bad. These can often be found in larger public libraries (particularly the Rosicrucian ephemerides).

2. *A table of houses.* Most systems of house division agree on the placement of the first/seventh house axis and the tenth/fourth house axis (with the exception of the **equal house system**, which agrees only with the former), so the differences are relatively minor. The older standard (and still popular) system is the **Placidean House System**; a current favorite is the **Koch House System**. Many current tables of houses allow one to calculate several systems, so that it should be possible to obtain a table with at least Placidus or Koch. (If the book is older and no particular system is mentioned, it is probably a Placidus table.) These can sometimes be found in public libraries.

3. *A table of time changes.* These are specialty volumes that are most easily obtained at (or ordered through) a "metaphysical" bookstore. There are also many astrological book retailers who do business through the mail. Two of these are Astro Communication Services (P.O. Box 34487, San Diego, CA 92163-4487) and the American Federation of Astrologers (AFA, P.O. Box 22040, Tempe AZ 85285).

4. *An astrologer's atlas.* These are again specialty books obtainable through specialty bookstores or through mail services.

It is usually helpful for a novice astrologer to pick up a calculation guide, such as Ivy M. Goldstein-Jacobson's classic *Foundation of the Astrological Chart.*

Using these references, let us cast the natal chart for a hypothetical person, Jane Smith, who, we will say, was born in San Diego, California, on August 30, 1965, at 11:00 A.M.

Looking in a table of time changes (the table on my book shelf is an old edition of Doris Chase Doane's *Time Changes in the USA),* we find that Jane was born during Daylight Saving Time. Subtracting an hour for DST gives her a birth time of 10:00 A.M., PST (Pacific Standard Time). With the date, place of birth, and corrected birth time in hand, we can now undertake two sets of calculations: (1) house **cusps** and (2) planetary positions.

I. House Cusps

House cusps involve finding the **sidereal time** (ST) of birth, and then looking up the positions of the cusps in a table of houses for the latitude at which one was born. The calculation of ST is basically not difficult, although the addition of two very tiny corrections—for the slight difference between sidereal time and clock time—make it appear complex. First, let us look up San Diego's longitude and latitude.

The table in my immediate reach is the older *Longitudes and Latitudes in the United States* by Eugene Dernay. San Diego, we find, is located at 117° W 10′ (117 degrees 10 minutes West longitude) and 32° N 43′ (32 degrees, 43 minutes North latitude). Since it is an astrologer's atlas, Dernay's notes that LMT for San Diego can be found by adding 11 minutes 20 seconds to standard time. Correcting Jane's birthtime from PST to LMT thus gives us 10:11:20 (10:00 A.M. PST + 11 min., 27 sec.).

Dernay also notes that San Diego's LMT is 7 hours 48 minutes and 40 seconds ahead of **Greenwich Time** (GMT), the time for which most ephemerides list planetary positions and sidereal time. Looking in my ephemeris, which is Neil F. Michelsen's *The American Ephemeris for the 20th Century, 1900-2000 at Noon,* I find that the sidereal time for noon (clock time) at Greenwich, England, on Jane Smith's birthday was 8:32 A.M. However, because Jane was born before noon, we use the sidereal time for the preceding day for our calculations. On August 29, 1965, sidereal time at noon at Greenwich was 8:27 (8:27:42, to be exact).

The first set of calculations one performs is to find the time that has elapsed between the prior noon and Jane's birthtime:

11:00 A.M. PDST (Jane's recorded birthtime)

– 1:00 (correction for DST)

_____

10:00 A.M. PST (standard time)

+11:20 (correction, at San Diego, for LMT)

_____

10:11:20 (Jane's birthtime, expressed as LMT)

+12:00:00 (the 12 hours between noon and midnight of the prior day)

22:11:20 (Time elapsed since previous noon)

Finding the sidereal time of Jane's birth requires adding 22:11:20 to the sidereal time at the prior noon at Greenwich, which we have already noted was 8:27:42. This gives us 30:39:02. When, as in this case, the resulting sum is more than 24 hours, we simply subtract 24, which leaves 6:39:02.

There is, however, one remaining problem. This is that—because of the slight difference in length between sidereal hours and clock hours—6:39:02 is not quite correct. To take this difference into account, it is necessary to divide the time elapsed since the previous noon (which we calculated 22:11:20) and the time difference between Greenwich and San Diego's LMT (which Dernay gave as 7:48:40), and divide them by 360. The result is 3 minutes 42 seconds for the first division, and 1 minute 8 seconds for the second. These are then added to our previously calculated sidereal time of birth (6:39:02) to give us a result of 6:43:52—the sidereal time at the moment of Jane Smith's birth. To repeat this in outline form:

22:11:20 (Time elapsed since previous noon)

3:42   (Correction for sidereal time)

1:08   (Correction for sidereal time)

+ 8:27:42 (Sidereal time at previous noon)

——————

30:43:52

–24:00:00

——————

6:43:52 (Sidereal time at Jane Smith's birth)

Next, to find the house cusps, we take this sidereal time and the latitude of Jane's birthplace to a table of houses. The twenty-year old copy I have of *Occidental Table of Houses* gives me the option of using several different house systems. Because the table that is most likely found at the library is Placidus, this is the one we will use for Jane.

The *Occidental Table of Houses* provides the house cusps (beginnings) for the first, second, third, tenth, eleventh, and twelfth houses. The cusps for the seventh, eighth, ninth, fourth, fifth, and sixth are not explicitly provided because astrologers know that they are exactly 180 degrees away from the respective cusps of the first, second, etc. houses (i.e., the positions of houses 7, 8, 9, 4, 5, and 6 can be directly derived from the positions of 1, 2, 3, 10, 11, and 12).

If one is doing the chart by hand, it is easier to round off numbers to the nearest degree. For Jane, this gives us the following:

1st - 8 degrees Libra

2nd - 5 degrees Scorpio

3rd - 6 degrees Sagittarius

10th - 10 degrees Cancer

11th - 14 degrees Leo

12th - 14 degrees Virgo

Knowing these cusps, we also know the cusps of the seventh, eighth, ninth, fourth, fifth, and sixth are as follows:

7th - 8 degrees Aries

8th - 5 degrees Taurus

9th - 6 degrees Gemini

4th - 10 degrees Capricorn

5th - 14 degrees Aquarius

6th - 14 degrees Pisces

With these cusps, we can erect the basic wheel. Next we need to calculate planetary positions, and place them within the wheel.

2. Planetary Positions

Earlier generations calculated planetary positions with the aid of logarithms—a tedious mathematical exercise. Now it is easy to use a simple hand calculator and basic proportional math to determine planetary positions.

The ephemeris I am using provides the daily positions of the planets for noon at Greenwich, England. There is a difference of 7 hours between GMT and PST; thus noon in England corresponds to 5:00 A.M. in California. Jane's 10:00 A.M. PST (corrected from 11:00 A.M. DST) birth time is thus 7 hours later than the positions in my ephemeris. How do we use that knowledge to calculate planetary positions? Let us use the planet Venus as an example.

At 3:00 A.M. PST (12:00 noon at Greenwich) on August 30, 1965, Venus was at 13 degrees 4 minutes (13:04) in the sign Libra. Because Jane was born after 3:00 A.M., we look at Venus's position the next day, August 31, again at 3:00 A.M. and find that its position was 14 degrees 15 minutes (14:15) Libra. To find the distance this planet has moved in 24 hours, we subtract the August 30 position from the August 31 position, which gives us 1 degree and 11 minutes (1:11). To simplify the next operation, it is necessary to convert any degrees to minutes. There are 60 minutes in each degree. Thus 1 degree 11 minutes, converted entirely to minutes, equals 71 minutes. This, again, is the distance Venus has moved in 24 hours. Now let us find the proportional distance.

Jane was born 7 hours after the first position of Venus for which we have a precise location. This can be expressed as a fraction of 24 hours, which is 7/24 (or, expressed as a decimal, 0.29). With this fraction, it is now quite easy to find the distance Venus has moved in 7 hours: 7/24 × 71 minutes = 20.7 minutes— or, rounded to the nearest whole minute, 21 minutes. To find Venus's position at the moment of Jane Smith's birth, now simply add 21 minutes to Venus's position at 3:00 A.M. on August 30: 13:04 Libra + 0:21 minutes = 13:25 Libra. Using the same fraction, 0.29, we perform a similar operation on each planet, and then place them all on the horoscope wheel. The basic birth chart is now complete.

Astrological Computer Programs

If the reader has learned nothing else from the above discussion, it is why the personal computing revolution has been such a boon to astrology. As long as the original data is entered correctly, an astrological computer program will do all of the above calculations and much more in a matter of minutes and at the touch of a button.

A good chart-casting program, which used to run $800 or more, can now be purchased for about $300 (either MacIntosh or IBM-compatible). Because the software industry is dynamic, the variety of astrology programs available is likely to change. With that caveat, at this writing the current leaders for chart-casting software are produced by Matrix Software and Astrolabe:

Matrix Software
315 Marion Avenue
Big Rapids, MI
800-PLANETS
800-843-6682

Astrolabe Software
Box 1750
350 Underpass Road
Brewster, MA 02631

The Blue*Star program and support services from Matrix has long been regarded as the "Rolls Royce" of astrology programs. Astrolabe is, however, a close competitor, and, in terms of its chart-casting ability, is in no way inferior to Matrix. Other excellent programs—and the following should not be viewed as an exhaustive listing—are available from:

AIR Software
115 Caya Avenue
W. Hartford, CT 06110
800-659-1AIR

Cosmic Patterns
P.O. Box 1460
Gainsville, FL 32604
904-373-1504

Time Cycles
527 Dimmock Road
Waterford, CT 06385
203-444-6641

Programs from any of these companies would serve an astrologer well. An unusual book designed to help astrologers evaluate programs is Patricia Foreman's *Computers & Astrology: A Universal User's Guide and Reference,* published in 1992 by Good Earth Publications.

Appendix B

Organizations

Astrological organizations range from large, serious research groups to small, informal study groups. Such organizations are regularly coming into and passing out of existence. The following list is taken from Susie Cox's *The International Directory of Astrologers*. It is arranged alphabetically, first by country and second by name of organization.

ARGENTINA

Centro Estudios Astrologicos
Arturo M. Bas
Depto 1 P A
5000 Cordoba, Argentina

Fundación Centro Astrológico
Jerry Brignone
Arenales 2432
Av. Rivadavía 3220
8V034 Buenos Aires, Argentina

Instituto Superior de Investig
Boedo 158
Buenos Aires, Argentina

Olmos Y Roca
Andrew Homer
Villa Carlos Paz
5152 Cordoba, Argentina

AUSTRALIA

ESCEF
23 Everard Terrace
Forestville
Adelaide, SA 5035 Australia

Federation of Australian Astrologers
Donna Ashley
13 Greig St.
Victoria Branch
Albert Park, VIC 3206 Australia

Federation of Australian Astrologers
Brian Clark
407 Johnston St.
Abbotsford, VIC 3067 Australia

Federation of Australian Astrologers
Tony Drew
P.O. Box 672
Campbelltown, NSW 2107 Australia

Federation of Australian Astrologers
Gail Kelly
25 Oxford St.
Kensington, WA 6151 Australia

Federation of Australian Astrologers
Noelle Raitray
113 Melbourne St.
North Adelaide, SA 5006 Australia

Federation of Australian Astrologers
Lyla Williams
23 Borrows St.
Virginia, QLD 4014 Australia

AUSTRIA

Ost. Astrol. Gesellschaft
Sandor Belcsak
Schubertring 8/Stiege 2/7
A 1010 Vienna, Austria

BELGIUM

Astrosophia
Jany Bessière
21 Plekkerstr.
9404 Aspelare, Belgium

Axe Holistique A.S.B.L.
Anne Guyot
7 rue du Château
B 6032 Mont-Sur Mar Chienne, Belgium

Federation Astrologique Belge
Astrid Fallon
69 Ave. Marechal Joffre
B-1190 Brussels, Belgium

L'Ecliptique
167 Av. Molière
1060 Bruxelles, Belgium

BRAZIL

ABA
Antonio Neto
Rua del Xavier de Toledo 114
Cons 205
São Paulo 22461, Brazil

Argos
Alameda Dr. Sebastiao Fleury
Setor Marista
Goiania, Brazil

ASAS
Aline A. Leite
Rua dos Dominicanos 512
Curitiba 82540, Brazil

Astrol. Society of Rio de Janeiro
Rua Jardim Botanico, 700
Room 523/524
Rio de Janeiro, Brazil

CANADA

Assn. Canadienne/Astrologues
CP 1715 Succ. B
Montréal, QUE H3B 3L3, Canada

Astrology Toronto, Inc.
P.O. Box 286 Station F
Toronto, ONT M4Y 2N7, Canada

Ottawa Astrological Society
Marguerite Day
31 McEwen Ave. #1002
Ottawa, ONT K2B 5K6, Canada

Société d'Astrologie de Montréal
P.O. Box 73
La Macaza, QUE J0P 140, Canada

Stariao Research Centre
Robin Armstrong
P.O. Box 5265 Sta. A
Toronto, ONT M5W 1N5, Canada

CZECHOSLOVAKIA

Czech Astrological Society
Jindriska Johanisova
Na Stahlvacve 1741/19
16000 Prague 6, Czechoslovakia

DENMARK

Ekliptika
Gammelmosevej 107 H, 1.TH
2800 Lyngby, Denmark

Institut for Astrologi
J M Morksgade 18
8000 Aarhus C, Denmark

SAFA
Blagardsgade 4
2200 Copenhagen N, Denmark

ENGLAND

Assn. Professional Astrologers
24 Birchington Court
West End Lane
London NW6, England

Astro-Helpline
Sylvie Weber
56 Genesta Rd. Plumbstead
London SE18 3EV, England

Astrological Association
396 Caledonian Rd.
London NI IDN, England

Astrological Lodge of London
BM Astrolodge
London WCIN 3XX, England

Astrological Psychology Inst.
P.O. Box 9
Totnes TQ9 5DZ, England

Astrological Twin Research
P.O. Box 21
Diss Norfolk IP22 1PJ, England

Centre for Psychosynthesis Studies
P.O. Box 9
Totnes TQ9 5YN, England

Faculty of Astrological Studies
BM 7470
London WCIN 3XX, England

Plymouth/Astrological Studies
Craig Roscall
8 Lake Dr.
Holly Park Tamerton Foliot
Plymouth PL20 6JN, England

Suffolk Astrological Society
Tina Cox
3 South Close
Bury St. Edmunds IP33 3JZ, England

Urania Trust
Charles Harvey
396 Caledonian Rd.
London NI 1DN, England

FINLAND

Astrological Assn. of Tampere
Niemi-Mattila, Marja-Liisa
Janislahdink. 7E84
33410 Tampere, Finland

FRANCE

AERA
5 rue de Port au Vin
44000 Nantes, France

Assn. La Vie Astrologique
Jacques Halbronn
Alva 8, rue de la Providence
75013 Paris, France

Astro-Group International
Georges Schepers
9 rue de la Merci
34000 Montepellier, France

CEDRA
Maurice Charvet
7 Place des Terreaux
69001 Lyon, France

Cercle Astrologique d'Auvergne
BP 86
63400 Chamalieres, France

Cercle Astrologique de Lyon
7 rue de Major Martin
69001 Lyon, France

Comac
Route de Parfondeval
61400 St. Denis Sur Huisne, France

Eveil et Tradition
4 rue de Parme
75009 Paris, France

Institut d'Etudes Astrologique
Alain de Chivre
29 rue de l'Heronnère
44000 Nantes, France

Institut Français d'Astrologie
7 rue de l'Avre
75015 Paris, France

Jupitair
8 rue Vasco da Gama
75015 Paris, France

Rah Humanistic Astrol. Network
Marief Cavaignac
9 rue Michel Peter
75013 Paris, France

Reseau d'Astrologie Humaniste
16 rue Chapon
75003 Paris, France

Société Française d'Astrologie
Colette Cholet
5 rue las Cases
75007 Paris, France

GERMANY

Astro-Med Forschungsinstitut
Tony & Isolde Bonin
Kemptener Str. 14A
FRG-8939 Bad Wörishofen, Germany

Astrolog Studiengesellschaft
Udo Rudolph
Olenland 24
D-2000 Hamburg 62, Germany

Astrolog Wassermannzeitalter
Ruth Nielsen
Hohenberg 3
2308 Rastorfer
Passau, Germany

Astrologic Kunst & Gesundheit
Gloria Moth
Schleissheimerstr. 1836
IV-Rudrgeb Vou 181
D-8000 Munich 40, Germany

Astrologie Zentrum Berlin
Vorbergstr. 9A
1000 Berlin 62, Germany

Astrologischer Arbeitskreis
Ingolstadter Str. 38
D-6000 Frankfurt Main 1, Germany

Astrologo
Postfach 48
DW-7347 Bad Uberkingen, Germany

Deutscher Astrologen-Verband
Ulrike Voltmer
Kufergasse 12
D-6600 Saarbrucken, Germany

Geistiges Schulungszentrum
Gunda Scholdt
Waldstr. 23
D-8031 Worthsee, Germany

Kaa-Kosmobiologische Akademie
Herbert Boss
Am Schattwald 37
D-7000 Stuttgart 80, Germany

Refugium
Irma Weber
IM Holzmoor 14C
3300 Braunschweig, Germany

Studiegroep Vanessa
Van Schijndel, A.H.M. Strack
Weiszenburgstr. 49
D-5000 Koln-1, Germany

HUNGARY

Astro Studio
Katalin Horani
PF 300
Budapest 1536, Hungary

ICELAND

Astrological Assoc. of Iceland
Gunnlaugur Gudmundsson
Asgardur 32
108 Reykjavíc, Iceland

INDIA

Hindu Astrology Research Center
Amu Maharshi
9 Sanskar Bharti, Ankur Rd.
Ahmedabad 380013, India

Institute of Astrological Studies
K. Aswathappa
P.O. Box 3717
Madras-2, India

Tibetan Med. and Astrology Inst.
Mackoidganj, HP, India

IRELAND

Astrological Federation of Ireland
Rina Condrat
New Haggard
Dublin, Ireland

Irish Astrological Association
Rose Deane
193 Lower Rathmines Road
Dublin 6, Ireland

ITALY

Cida
Maurizio Malagoli
Via Susano, 46
41100 Modena, Italy

Horos
Vasile Droj
Via L. Muratori, 15
00186 Rome, Italy

Ricerca '90
Viale Gramsci, 16
80122 Napoli, Italy

Synthesis
Louisa de Giuli
Via Tito Omboni, 49
00147 Rome, Italy

MEXICO

Centro Cultural Citaltepec
Norte 2 #812
Orizaba, Mexico

Esoteric Center
Juarez 409
Veracruz, Mexico

Eutimio Pinzón
David Rubio Zacarias
Paseo de los Olivos, 3
Col. Independencia Colomos
Guadalajara, Mexico

Investigaciones Astrológicas
Apartado Postal 2-588
Guadalajara 44280, Mexico

NCGR Mexican Chapter
Victoria Malo
Apto Postal #582
Cuernavaca 62000, Mexico

NCGR Mexican Chapter
Cynthia Rivenoll
Amsterdam #27 Dept. 301
Col. Condera
México DF, Mexico

Search Astrological New Moon
Laura & Emilio Pérez-Limón
P.O. Box 2-1011
Guadalajara 44280, Mexico

MOLDOVA

Astrologers Assn. of Moldavia
Inna G. Volchek
Lenin Prosp 6 #130
277001 Moldavia, Moldova

NETHERLANDS

A.S.T.
Martien Hermes
Dekkerdreef 15
5051 McGoirle, Netherlands

ACON
Mariastraat 41
2595 GL S Granvenhage, Netherlands

Academie Voor Astrol. Chiron
V Speijkstraat 108 HS
1057 HG Amsterdam, Netherlands

Ast. Vereniging Eindhoven
Jongemastate 45
5655 HN Eindhoven, Netherlands

Astro-Visier
Steenboerweg 4232
8042 AT Zwolle, Netherlands

Astrologie Docenten Werkgroep
Oosterkade 2-A4
9711 RS Groningen, Netherlands

Astrologisch Centrum
Mercatorsingel 68
2803 Gouda, Netherlands

Astrologisch Research Institut
Postbus 1078
1400 BB Bussum, Netherlands

Bosch
Korte Tuinstr. 12
5212 SL Hertogenbosch, Netherlands

Chiron
Louise Vandemeer
Spinner 36
1625 VC Hoorn, Netherlands

Cora
Rudolf H. Smit
Rietkreek 7
8032 JN Zwolle, Netherlands

Dirah Foundation
Roelandde Looff
Brunostraat 64B
5042 JA Tilburg, Netherlands

Ecliptica
Fazentenhamp 616
3607 DJ, Netherlands

Federation Astrol. Groeperingen
Neherlaan 4
5361 NH Eindhoven, Netherlands

H.C.C.
Vleutenseweg 215
3532 HC Utrecht, Netherlands

I.T.A.N.
Oude AA 4A
3621 LB Breukelen, Netherlands

N.G.P.A.
Bankaplein 9
3531 HK Utrecht, Netherlands

Perspectief
Fritz Johann
P.O. Box 1035
2001 BA Haarlem, Netherlands

Spirituoel Centrum Chiron
Spinnder 36
1625 VO Hoorn, Netherlands

Stichting Astrologisch Studie
Prinseneiland 155
1013 LP Amsterdam, Netherlands

Stichting Cabella
Armhoefstraat 31
5010 EH Tilburg, Netherlands

Stichting Harmonia Universalis
Waterlooplein 51
1011 PB Amsterdam, Netherlands

Stichting Inspiratie
Vijverlaan
2411 AJ Bodegraven 5, Netherlands

Stichting Mens
L. Vastenhout
Postbus 366
7300 AJ Apeldoorn, Netherlands

Stichting Natalis
Apeldoornseweg 68
6814 BM Arnhem, Netherlands

Stichting Olivijn
Mounlaan 57
6681 GX Bommel, Netherlands

Stichting Opleidingen Astrologie
Bever 9
1273 AZ Huizen, Netherlands

Stichting Osiris
Molenaarslaan 10
6093 GV Heythuysen, Netherlands

Stichting Vanessa
Postbus 13131
3507 LC Utrecht, Netherlands

Totaliteitsdiagnostiek
Mariastraat 41
2595 GL S Gravenhage, Netherlands

VMA
Paul Horsthuis
Singel 54
1015 AB Amsterdam, Netherlands

VVANN
Jacolstr. 13 51-D
9724 JN Groningen, Netherlands

NEW ZEALAND
Astrological Society of NZ
P.O. Box 5266, Wellesley St.
Auckland, New Zealand

Astrology Foundation, Inc.
Hamish D. Saunders
21 Mt. Eden Rd.
Auckland, New Zealand

Palmerston North Astrology
P.O. Box 522
Palmerston North, New Zealand

Personal Transformation Centre
Stephen Hill
P.O. Box 522
Palmerston North, New Zealand

Wellington Astrology Society
P.O. Box 11678
Wellington, New Zealand

NORWAY
Astrologisk Forum
Postboks 7667 Skillebekk
N-0205 Oslo 2, Norway

Norsk Astrolgisk Forening
Birgit Lauras
Grefsenkollvn 120-215
0490 Oslo, Norway

POLAND
Astrological Society of Poland
Cariusz Proskurnicki
Warzaqsk 28-11
81-317 Gdynia, Poland

ROMANIA
Assn. of Romanian Astrologers
Sorin Ripea
Str. Tutora 4
SC.C. Apt. 11
6600 Iasi, Romania

RUSSIA

All-Union Assn. of Astrology
Pavel P. Globa
Marshal Ustinov St. 5-3 #782
Moscow, Russia

Astral
Alexander Ilmov
L Bashrina St. 2
193024 St. Petersburg, Russia

Astro
Alexander Grebennikov
P.O. Box 58
129343 Moscow, Russia

Astrolog
Elena Kopylova
A/R 25
109432 Moscow, Russia

Astrology Association of Omsk
Svetlana Plotztaja
UL 24 Severnaja 208-6
644071 Omsk-71, Russia

Astrology Research Center
48 Birulevskaya Str. Apt. 171
115547 Moscow, Russia

Federation of Astrologers
Michael Levin
U1 Akademika Bargi 24 #115
117133 Moscow, Russia

IC AAC
Nataly Dodonova
Krestovsky Prosp 9
P.O. Box 934
197042 St. Petersburg, Russia

Moscow Assn. of Astrologers
St. Otradnaya 18-A #105
127273 Moscow, Russia

Moscow Assn. of Astrologers
Vitaly A. Vaisberg
12 Stavropolskaya Str. Apt. 21
109386 Moscow, Russia

Moscow Omega Center
Farida Asadullina
7th Street Tekstilschchiki
House 22, Apt. 2
109263 Moscow, Russia

Nijnegorodskaja Astrology Sect
Victoria J. Ermilova
UL Luganskaja 7-49
603009 Nizny Novgorod, Russia

SCOTLAND

Aberdeen Astrology Group
Susan Taylor
67 Friarsfield Road
Aberdeen, Scotland

Glasgow Astrology Circle
Joe Bonner
237 Langlands Rd.
Flat 3/3
Glasgow G51 3QB, Scotland

Glasgow Astrology Group
Lis Martin
23 Esmond Street
York Hill
Glasgow G3, Scotland

Matrix UK
Martin Davis
P.O. Box 9
Pitlochry PH9 0YD, Scotland

Pulsar Association
Caroline Gerard
6 Belford Mews
Dean Village
Edinburgh EH44 3BT, Scotland

Scottish Astrological Assn.
Theosophical Society
29 Great King St.
Edinburgh, Scotland

Sheila O'Hara
16 Napier Terrace
Glasgow G51 2LJ, Scotland

SOUTH AFRICA

ASC Astrology Centre
P.O. Box 81300
Parkhurst 2120, South Africa

Astro Group
P.O. Box 146288
Brackengardens 1452, South Africa

Astrological Soc. of S. Africa
P.O. Box 2968
Rivonia 2128, South Africa

Astrological Study Group
Carole Buck
341 Queen Elizabeth Ave.
Manor Gardens
Durban 4001, South Africa

Cape Astrology Society of S.A.
25 Silwood Rd.
Rondebosch 7700, South Africa

Labyrinth
Yvonne Taylor
P.O. Box 1435
Rivonia 2138
Johannesburg, South Africa

Natal Society of Astrology
11 Falcon Dr.
Yellowwook Park 4001, South Africa

Thorburn School of Astrology
Cynthia Thorburn
P.O. Box 146288
Brackengardens 1452, South Africa

SOUTH KOREA

Korean Astrological Society
Jung Dekin
c/o Advalue Products #779 15
Daerim 3 Dong, Yg Deungpo Ku
Seoul, South Korea

SPAIN

AEBHU
Antonio Arjona
Apartado 150.001
28080 Madrid, Spain

Centro Astrológico Ceres
Calle del Pez 27 1-1
28004 Madrid, Spain

Centro de Medicina Integral
Francisco Bedate
Marajalillo Alto 8-1 B
Motril, Spain

Falcultad Estudios Astrológico
Apartado 51.064
28080 Mardrid, Spain

SWEDEN

Malmo Forening
c/o Ulrich Aspegren
Flormansgatan 2B
22354 Lund, Sweden

SWITZERLAND

ASRA
Narcel Bianchi
Case Postale 27
1000 Lausanne 4, Switzerland

Sera
Nicole Krentz
Case Postale 408
1211 Genève 17, Switzerland

Société Astrologique Romande
19 Rue Fertinand Holder
1207 Genève, Switzerland

Société d'Astrologie Neuchatel
Patricia Bourpuin
Case Postale 1242
2000 Mahatel
Neuchatel, Switzerland

UKRAINE

Aura
P.O. Box 157
254025 Kiev, Ukraine

Mensch
Iwan Antonowitsch
Botscharow Str. 12 #115
270111 Odessa, Ukraine

Ukrainian Assn. of Astrologers
A/YA 65
254025 Kiev, Ukraine

UNITED STATES

ACA PF Astrological Studies
P.O. Box 419
Santa Ysabel, CA   92070

Academy of Astrology
1135 Clifton Ave.
Clifton, NJ   07013

AFA
Bob Cooper
P.O. Box 22040
Tempe, AZ   85285

AFAN
8306 Wilshire Blvd. 537
Beverly Hills, CA   90211

AISA
7248 Forest Blvd.
Ft. Lauderdale, FL   33068

Akron Astrol. Society
Kathryn Sheets
698 Congress Lake Rd.
Mogadore, OH   44260-9622

Akron Astrology
640 Firestone Blvd.
Akron, OH   44301

Aquarian Age Astrol. Workshop
25702 Byron Dr.
N. Olmstead, OH   44070

Aquarian Fellowship Foundation
295 Turnpike Rd. #020
Westborough, MA   01581

Aquarian Light Center
1249 Beverly Rd.
Warminster, PA   18974

Aquarian Org. of Astrologers
P.O. Box 36493
Kansas City, MO   64111

Aquarian Revelation Center
P.O. Box 250982
W. Bloomfield, MI   48325

Aquarian Voices
P.O. Box 2070
Arnold Hollow Rd.
Brandon, VT   05733

Aquarius Org. of Astrologers
15 E. 62nd Street
Kansas City, MO   64113

Assn. of Astrological Psychology
Glen Perry
360 Quietwood Dr.
San Rafael, CA   94903

Astro Awareness
P.O. Box 10185
Phoenix, AZ   85011

Astro Morsels
Edward Dearborn
310 Trites Ave.
Norwood, PA   19074-1631

Astrol. Assn. of N. Virginia
P.O. Box 6323
Falls Church, VA   22046

Astrol. Assn. of St. Louis
P.O. Box 16282
St. Louis, MO   03105

Astrol. Assn. of N. Virginia
P.O. Box 1521
Vienna, VA   22183

Astrol. Society of S. California
P.O. Box 642
Glendora, CA   91740

Astrol. Research Guild, Inc.
Carole Smelser
883 37th St.
Orlando, FL   32805

Astrol. Society of Ft. Worth
Sherry Lentz
5816 Steeplewood Dr.
N. Richland, TX   76180

Astrologers Corner
2137 S. Collins
Arlington, TX   76010

Astrologers of the North
P.O. Box 4-2189
Anchorage, AK   99509

Astrological Bureau
5 Old Quaker Hill Rd.
Monroe, NY   10950

Astrological Forum of Dayton
4309 Natchez Ave.
Dayton, OH   45416

Astrological Information
P.O. Box 9237
Naples, FL   33068

Astrological Society of Connecticut
P.O. Box 9346
Wethersfield, CT   06109

Astrologik
P.O. Box 45758
Seattle, WA   98145

Astrology & Spiritual Science
4535 Hohman
Hammond, IN   46327

Astrology Assn. of Colorado Springs
2209 W. Colorado Ave.
Colorado Springs, CO   60302

Astrology Assn. of St. Petersburg
Jan Walsek
P.O. Box 48171
St. Petersburg, FL   33743

Astrology Club
1253 Hazel Drive NE
Cedar Rapids, IA   52402

Astrology Forum
P.O. Box 22607
Santa Fe, NM   87502

Atlanta Astrological Society
P.O. Box 451123
Atlanta, GA   30345

Arizona Society of Astrologers
P.O. Box 1092
Scottsdale, AZ   85251

Aztec-Mayan Astrology
P.O. Box 39315
Ft. Lauderdale, FL   33339

California Astrology Assn.
P.O. Box 810
N. Hollywood, CA   91603

Cambridge Circle Ltd.
4463 Vande Hei Rd.
Green Bay, WI   54301

Capital Futures Associates, Ltd.
James Schildgen
P.O. Box 2618
Chicago, IL   60690

Celebration of the Signs
Carlin Diamond
P.O. Box 9355
San Rafael, CA   94912

Celestial Communication
P.O. Box 650
Broomfield, CO   80038

Center for Archaeoastronomy
P.O. Box X
College Park, MD   20740-1024

Cincinnati Astrology Society
3832 Woodford St.
Cincinnati, OH   45213

Colorado Fellowship of Astrology
Terry Matheny
7352 N. Washington
Denver, CO   80229

Cosmobiology Research
100 W. Undercliff St.
Pittsburgh, PA   15223

D.O.M.E. Center
Edwin C. Steinbrecher
P.O. Box 46146
Los Angeles, CA   90046

Daily Planets Astrol. Center
1168 Euclid Ave.
Atlanta, GA   30358

Delaware Interested in Astrology
19 Darlington Rd.
Newcastle, DE   19720

Earthfriends
P.O. Box 8468
Atlanta, GA   30306

El Paso Astrology Assn.
1508 Oakdale
El Paso, TX   77027

Energies, Trends, Cycles
P.O. Box 76691
Atlanta, GA   30358

Federation of Scientific Astrologers
2022 Ferrier Rd.
Eden, NY   14057

Federation of Astrologers
69 Center Avenue
Cheektowaga, NY   14227

First Temple of Astrology
P.O. Box 57282
Los Angeles, CA   90057

Florida Astrological Assn.
1712 Lake Downey Dr.
Union Park, FL   32807

Foundation/Study of Cycles
Jeffrey Harowitz
3333 Michelson Dr. #20
Irvine, CA   92715-1607

Friends of Astrology
133 S. Wall
Spokane, WA   99204

Golden Seal Research HQ
P.O. Box 27822
Hollwyood, CA   90027

Grand Trine
2094 Earl Dr.
Bay City, MI   48706

Greater Harrisburg Astrol. Society
3812 Hearthstone Rd.
Camp Hill, PA   17011

Houston Astrology Assn.
P.O. Box 90036
Houston, TX   72790

Indiana Federation of Astrologers
9439 Evergreen
Indianapolis, IN   46240

Inner Development Center
P.O. Box Drawer H
Miami, FL   33133

Institute of Astrology & Metaphysics
2700 Lincoln
Merrick, NY   11566

Institute of Astro-Psychology
2640 Greenwich St. #403
San Francisco, CA   94123

Institute of Transpersonal Activity
3635 Lupine Ave.
Palo Alto, CA   94530

Institute of Vedic Astrology
P.O. Box 2489
Mill Valley, CA   94942

Inteli-Quest
Jene Ripke
7337 College Ave.
Sutter, CA   95982

International School of Astrology
4047 N. Stratford Rd. NE
Atlanta, GA   30342

ISAR
P.O. Box 38613
Los Angeles, CA   90038

Life Research Center
P.O. Box 73284
Puyallup, WA   93873

Medina Astrol. Research Society
P.O. Box 1245
Medina, OH   44258

Metro Atlanta Astrol. Society
P.O. Box 451123
Atlanta, GA   30345

Michigan Academy of Astrology
416 W. Hillside St.
Lansing, MI   48917

Michigan Federation of Astrology
4907 Eastlawn Dr.
Lansing, MI   48910

Milwaukee Astrology Center
4556 N. 704th St.
Milwaukee, WI   53218

National Academy of Astrologers
918 F. St. NW
Washington, DC   20004

NCGR
5826 Greenspring Ave.
Baltimore, MD   21209

NCGR
105 Snyder Ave.
Ramsey, NJ   07446

NCGR
P.O. Box 14338
San Francisco, CA   94114

NCGR
Amarillo, TX Chapter
Bette Judd
Amarillo, TX

NCGR
Carolinas Chapter
Timothy Bost
Rt. 2, Box 412
Granite Falls, NC 28630

NCGR
Connecticut Berkshire Chapter
Box 1101
New Milford, CT   06776

NCGR
Florida Atlantic Chapter
Shirley Stephenson
2040 NE 163 St. #303
Miami, FL   33162

NCGR
Gulf Coast Chapter
Betty Ramsey
4200 Westheimer #260
Houston, TX   77027

NCGR
Rocky Mountain Chapter
Dee Davis
5823 Queen
Orvada, CO 80004

NCGR
SW Suburban Illinois Chapter
Cindy Rossa
12604 Kinvarra Dr.
Palos Park, IL 60464

NCGR
Virginia Beach Chapter
Carol Devine
3748 Lake Tahoe Trail
Virginia Beach, VA 32456

NCGR
West Texas Chapter
P.O. Box 2263
Amarillo, TX 79105

N. Florida Astrol. Society
P.O. Box 1741
Jacksonville, FL   32101

NORWAC
4518 University Way NE
Seattle, WA   98105

NW Florida Astrological Assn.
P.O. Box 997
Ft. Walton Beach, FL   32548

Ohio Astrology Assn.
14755 Drexmore Rd.
Shaker Heights, OH   44120

Philosophical Research Society
3910 Los Feliz Blvd.
Los Angeles, CA   90027

Pittsburgh Astrology Assn.
815 Copeland St.
Pittsburgh, PA   15232

Professional Astrologers, Inc.
1020 10th St.
Sacramento, CA   95814

Registry Sidereal Astrology
1317 Monterey
Monrovia, CA   91016

Riverside Astrologers
5548 Lyford St.
Memphis, TN   38117

RKM Consultant Co.
Robert "Buz" Myers
26241 Lakeshore Blvd.
Euclid, OH   44132

Rosicrucian Fellowship
P.O. Box 713
Oceanside, CA   92054

S.T.A.R.
334 Olney Dr.
San Antonio, TX   78209

S.T.A.R. Society
23136 N. Woodward
Ferndale, MI   48220

Sagittarius Rising
P.O. Box 252
Arlington, MA   02174

San Diego Astrological Society
P.O. Box 16430
San Diego, CA   92116

San Joaquin Astrology Assn.
P.O. Box 1136
Bakersfield, CA   93303

Scientific Astrology Research
45 Sherman Bridge Rd.
Wayland, MA   01775

Service Thru Awareness Astrol.
RT1-Studio House
Stratsburg, NY   12580

S. Florida Astrological Assn.
P.O. Box 330466
Miami, FL   33133

S. California Astrological Network
Laura De Jardins
18850 Douglas Drive
Irvine, CA   92664

Star Visions
Maryanne Hoffman
The Galleria
7537 Mentor Ave.
Mentor, OH   44060

Stellar Research Association
14 Eliot St.
Brattleboro, VT   05301

Sun In Aquarius, Inc.
Jane Semple
27340 Lorain Rd.
N. Olmsted, OH   44070

Sun Time Astrology
J. Bowles
P.O. Box 322
Live Oak, CA   95953

Tallahassee Astrology Group
P.O. Box 3825
Tallahassee, FL   32315

TAO
105 Serra Way
Milpitas, CA   95035

Texas Astrological Assn.
2202 West Main
Grand Prairie, TX   75050

Transpersonal Astrology
1827 Haight St. #10
San Francisco, CA   94117

Tucson Astrologers Guild
Leyla Elam
P.O. Box 44019
Tucson, AZ   85733

USA Latin Astrological Center
303 S. Cascade, Suite 200
Colorado Springs, CO   80903

Virginia Astrological Assn.
3504 Horseway
Virginia Beach, VA   23452

W. Michigan Assn. of Cosmic Astrologers
Kentwood Public Library
4700 Kalamazoo SE
Kentwood, MI   49508

Washington State Astrological Assn.
Bruce Hamerslough
P.O. Box 45386
Seattle, WA   98145

Washington Astrology Forum
Warren Kinsman
P.O. Box 6731
Washington, DC   20020

Western Astrology Group
7500 Derby Rd.
Derby, NY   14047

Western States Astrology
P.O. Box 1083
Newport Beach, CA   92663

World Conference of Astro-Economics
Grace Morris
4931 W. 95th St.
Oaklawn, IL   60453

Wright Institute Astrol. Study
2136 E. Sprague Rd.
Broadview Heights, OH   44147

Zodiac Society, S.T.A.R.
5200 Hilltop Dr. #W21
Brookhaven, PA   19015

WALES

South Wales Astrology Group
Bridie Kerslake
2 Handel Close
Penarth CF6 2QP, WALES

West Wales Astrology Group
Robin Holtom
Glan Helyg Healing Centre
Llechryd, WALES

Appendix C
Periodicals

Astrological periodicals run the gamut from mass circulation magazines to highly specialized newsletters. The smaller publications are often transitory. The following list is arranged alphabetically, and is taken from *The Mountain Astrologer*.

American Astrology
475 Park Ave.
New York, NY 10016.
(Renewals: P.O. Box 339
Mt. Morris, IL 61054-0339)

Designed for general readership and beginners with both tropical and some sidereal portions. Sun-sign forecasts, aspectarian, interesting articles and columns. Monthly. $17.95 per yr. in U.S.; elsewhere, $26.98 in U.S. funds. Special issues not covered in the subscription appear from time to time.

AFA Bulletin/Today's Astrologer
American Federation of Astrologers, Inc.
P.O. Box 22040
Tempe, AZ 85285-2040

Articles, announcements of lectures at affiliated groups and teachers' classes, people and some events. Issued each lunar month. Sent to members only; new membership for the first 2 years is $70 plus $10 enrollment fee; continuing membership is $35 annually.

AFAN Network Newsletter
Association for Astrological Networking, Inc.

8306 Wilshire Blvd., Ste. 537
Beverly Hills, CA 90211

Short articles, letters, announcements, and a media watch and image net. Quarterly. $20 per yr.; available through membership.

Alaska Metaphysical Council Newsletter
P.O. Box 93006
Anchorage, AK 99509-3006

Has an "Astrologers of the North" feature but is mainly a New Age periodical; announcements of over 30 local activities in Anchorage. Monthly. Donation of $12 for year's subscription, with check payable to Alaska Metaphysical Council.

The Amethyst
737 Easley St.
Silver Spring, MD 20910

Articles and materials on eastern European retrogrades; calendar with void-of-course moon data noted. Quarterly. $7.50 per yr.; $8 in Canada.

The ASCendant
Astrological Society of Connecticut

P.O. Box 9346
Wetherfield, CT 06109.
Laura Glaser, Editor

Articles, book reviews, local announcements. Quarterly. $11 per yr.

Aspects
Aquarian Workshops, Inc.
P.O. Box 260556
Encino, CA 91426

Articles, columns, book reviews, research findings, lunations (current), letters to the editor, and a "What's Happening" column. Quarterly. $25 per yr.; in Canada, $30.

Asteroid World
LCCRS
838 Fifth Ave.
Los Angeles, CA 90005

Loaded with asteroid information and delineations concerning our mundane affairs; each issue gives meanings of several asteroids. Quarterly. Included with The *Mutable Dilemma*, but $6 if alone; $8 in Canada.

Astralis
CEDRA
7, Place des Terreaux
69001 Lyon, France

Center for Documentation, Research, and Study about Astrology. The most important, non–mass market, French astrology magazine. CEDRA members have access to data base. Write for rates.

Astro-Analytics
P.O. Box 16440, Haynes St.
Van Nuys, CA 91406-5719

Contains chart data for famous persons, publicity for new books, and tapes with brief reviews. Bimonthly. Sent free of charge to members of the Book & Tape Club. Write for details.

Astro-Economic Newsletter
8535 N.E. Beech St.
Portland, OR 97220.

Current transits and financial market. Quarterly. $5 per yr.

Astroflash
Astro Communications Services, Inc.
P.O. Box 34487
San Diego, CA 92163-4487

Articles of merit; advertises ACS books and chart services. Quarterly. Free to customers.

The Astrologers' Newsletter
NCRG, Boston Chapter
42 Gayland Rd.
Needham, MA 02192

Articles, letters, data. Monthly, September through May; 9 issues per yr. $13 ($1.50 a single), with check payable to Lorraine Welsh/Newsletter.

The Astrologer's Point
Pittsburgh Astrology Assn.
815 Copeland St.
Pittsburgh, PA 15232

Articles, announcements. Ten issues per yr. New membership/subscription $25 per yr.; renewals $20; sample $2.

Astrology Today: A Feminist Newsletter for the Information Age
3839 Los Feliz Blvd.
Los Angeles, CA 90027

Astrology and current planetary patterns from a feminist perspective. $8 per year.

Astro News
5821 Cyrus St.
Baton Rouge, LA 70805

Data, transits, book reviews; newsy. Write for prices.

Astronotes
PAI
1500 W. El Camino #130
Sacramento, CA 95833-1945.

Available only to members of Professional Astrologers, Inc.

The Astrotherapy Newsletter
Association for Astrological Psychology
83 Porteous Way
Fairfax, CA 94930

Integration of astrology and psychology (theory and technique, case histories, book reviews). Articles by professional astrologers in mental health field. Quarterly. $20 per yr.; foreign subscribers $25.

The Atlanta Astrologer
Metropolitan Atlanta Astrological Society
P.O. Box 451123
Atlanta, GA 30345

Articles of merit, announcements, and speaker schedules. Monthly. Subscription sent to members; $36 per yr.

The Career Astrologer Quarterly
631 Central Ave. #2
Lexington, KY 40502

Articles by contributing members on issues of maintaining a professional practice—ethics, counseling, marketing, teaching, public relations. Quarterly. $60 per yr.

The Chiron Communiqué
Chiron Communications
P.O. Box 328
New Ipswich, NH 03071

Key insights into national and world affairs and local announcements. Quarterly. $10 per yr.

Church of Light Quarterly
Church of Light
2341 Coral St.
Los Angeles, CA 90031-2916

Church of Light organizational matters plus articles on natal, horary, and mundane astrology; also articles of interest on matters occult and metaphysical. Quarterly. $10 per yr.

Collection of Light
20801 Biscayne Blvd., Ste. 400
North Miami Beach, FL 33180

Horary articles with charts and interpretations, mundane items; horary astrology throughout history. Quarterly. $12 per yr. in U.S.; elsewhere, $15 in U.S. funds.

Considerations
Considerations, Inc.
P.O. Box 644
Mount Kisco, NY 10549

Scholarly articles mainly directed toward advanced astrologers. Quarterly. $25 per yr. ($45 for 2 yr.); Canada $30 per yr. ($55 for 2 yr.) in U.S. funds.

Cosmic Cycles
P.O. Box 32208
Raleigh, NC 27622

Articles on astrology, letters. MENSA publication. Quarterly. $10 per yr.; foreign $12 in U.S. funds; $3 sample copy.

Cycles
Foundation for the Study of Cycles
3333 Michelson Dr. #210
Irvine, CA 92715-1607

Scholarly work found in many college libraries; deals with many types of cycles. Although not strictly astrology (not mentioned in issues) the subject is a closely related area that researchers should not neglect. Bimonthly. $75 per yr.; (single issue $15); Canada $20 in U.S. funds; subscription also includes membership.

Data News
11736 Third St.
Yucaipa, CA 92399

Very reliable data about people and events; provides an adjunct to L. M. Rodden's 3 textbooks of data; noteworthy. Bimonthly. $14 per yr.; foreign, $16 per yr. in U.S. funds.

Diamond Fire
Malchitsedek Productions
3704 Lyme Ave.
Brooklyn, NY 11224

Astrology, meditation, metaphysics, and esoteric review. Quarterly. $20 per yr. in U.S. funds.

The Experience
Institute of Astrology
Metaphysics Ltd.
P.O. Box 288
Merrick, NY 11566

Articles about astrology; birth data and events; calendar with aspectarian. Write for rates.

Financial & Mundane Special Interest Group Newsletter
**78 Hubbard Ave.
Stamford, CT 06905**

Collection of information from members interested in either financial or mundane matters; not intended as a forum for scholarly articles but for information exchange. Irregular; plans are for quarterly. $8 per yr. in U.S. funds.

Firesign Astrological Express
**P.O. Box 370
Carmel, NY 10512**

A commercial venture offering "shareware," low-priced computer software on a wide range of programs. Information on current transits; humorous dialogue. Bimonthly. $9 per yr. in US funds; sample $2.

Friends of Astrology Bulletin
**535 Woodside Ave.
Hinsdale, IL 60521**

Monthly forecast, lunation, events in the news, lessons, book reviews, articles. Monthly. $15 per yr. in U.S.; foreign $20 in U.S. funds.

GAIA
**P.O. Box 405
Waldport, OR 97394**

Articles concerning asteroids; letters. (Asteroid resource guide available.) Quarterly. Write for rates.

Good Days Action Planning Guide
**14185 Day Farm Rd.
Glenelg, MD 21737**

Electional astrology; daily transits. Monthly. $25 per yr.

The Horary Practitioner
**JustUs & Associates
1420 N.W. Gilman, Ste. 2154
Issaquah, WA 98027-5327**

Traditional horary astrology, separate theme each issue; articles with example charts and explanations. Quarterly. $25 per yr.; Canada $30 in U.S. funds; single copy $7 U.S. or Canada; $8 other foreign.

Heliogram
**2240 Pimmit Run Ln. #203
Falls Church, VA 22043**

Articles concerning heliocentric astrology and blends of geocentric and helio; letters. Quarterly. NCGR member $12 per yr.; nonmember $16; Canada and Mexico add $1; others write for details.

The Ingress
**NCRG, New York Chapter
330 E. 46th St., #1E
New York, NY 10017**

Human interest items, "technical" astrology, occasional book reviews, and chapter announcements and news. Quarterly. $10 per yr.

Kósmos
**International Society for Astrological Research, Inc.
P.O. Box 38613
Los Angeles, CA 90038**

Articles, research findings, book reviews. Quarterly. $25 first yr. (includes membership); $20 for renewals.

The Llewellyn New Times
**Llewellyn Publications, Inc.
P.O. Box 64383-893
St. Paul, MN 55164-0383**

Articles cover a variety of subjects besides astrology, book reviews, classifieds, and publicity for books, tapes, and chart services. Bimonthly. $2 for 2 yrs. or sent at no charge to active mail order customers.

Matrix Journal
**Matrix Software
315 Marion Ave.
Big Rapids, MI 49307**

Articles emphasize computer technology. Semi-annual or annual. Write for details.

Asteroid data, including keywords and meanings; gives lesser-known asteroids listed by Nona Press. Bimonthly. Free but $2 donation is welcome to cover postage.

Mercury Hour
3509 Waterlick Rd. C-7
Lynchburg, VA 24502

Newsy exchange of letters from subscribers, some articles, and much more. Quarterly. Write for details and rates.

The Mutable Dilemma
LACCRS (Los Angeles Community Church of Religious Science, Inc.)
838 Fifth Avenue
Los Angeles, CA 90005

Psychological approach to astrology—articles involve asteroids, mundane affairs, gurus, famous or interesting persons, etc. Quarterly. $16 per yr. (includes *Asteroid World*); Canada $20.

Mini Examiner
P.O. Box 3893-APL
Chatsworth, CA 91313

Biorhythm character and compatibility analysis. $1 and SASE for a sample issue.

NCGR Chicago Journal
NCGR, Chicago Chapter
9125 S. Avers Ave.
Evergreen Park, IL 60642

Mainly articles on astrology and allied arts; letters to the editor; chapter news. Bimonthly. $12 payable to NCGR Chicago.

Moon Wobble
2973 Harbor Blvd. #236
Costa Mesa, CA 92626

Gives times of emotionally unstable periods (dates and graph) associated with the solar transits that conjunct and square the nodes of the Moon. Quarterly. Send four 29ò stamps for next 4 mailings.

NCGR Memberletter
NCGR Journal
Geocosmic News
National Council for Geocosmic Research, Inc.
5826 Greenspring Ave.
Baltimore, MD 21209

The Mountain Astrologer
P.O. Box 17275
Boulder, CO 80308

Articles, reviews, asteroids, transit forecasts, humor. Bimonthly. $22 in U.S. funds for 1st class and Canada; $16.75 per yr. bulk rate.

Articles, research results, letters, announcements, and more. Memberletter is monthly, the journal and *Geocosmic News* total 4 issues per yr. (all are included in members' annual dues). Membership $35; foreign $45 in U.S. funds.

Planet Watch
Planet Watch Publications
P.O. Box 515
Old Chelsea Station
New York, NY 10113

Moving Horizons
2808 School Dr.
Rolling Meadows, IL 60008

Asteroids, transits, planetary stations, and retrograde motion emphasized; roles of direct and retrograde degrees in personal and mundane highlighted; hidden aspects delineated. Monthly. $30 per yr.; Canada $33 in U.S. funds; overseas $36 in U.S. funds.

Pulsar: The Journal of Scottish Astrology
6 Belford Mews Dean Village
Edinburgh EH4 38T
Scotland

Write for details.

Rising Signs
Seacoast Astrological Association
P.O. Box 4683
Portsmouth, NH 03802

Timely articles, announcements. Monthly (9 issues per yr.). $8 for the 9 issues; free with $35 membership fee; foreign please write for rates.

Riverside Astrologers Transits and Directions
5401 Poplar, #7
Memphis, TN 38119

Articles, book reviews, announcements. Bimonthly. $5 per yr. for newsletter only; free with $15 membership; foreign please write for rates.

SCASA Newsletter
Southern California Assn. of Sidereal
  Astrologers
33424 Bodie St.
Yucaipa, CA 92399-2122

Articles on sidereal astrology; explains how to erect various sidereal charts and discusses controversial details; information about people and events; letters. Monthly. $25 per yr.; renewals $20.

Shooting Star
727 President St.
Brooklyn, N.Y. 11215

Explores the integration of astrology and flower remedies, each issue having themes related to one zodiac sign. Announces remedy-related events; cites sources for purchase of flower essences. Approximately quarterly. $15 for 4 issues, $4 single; $3 sample copy, foreign please write for rates.

Star Source
P.O. Box 1405
Warner Robins, GA 31099

Diverse astrological articles, advertisements. Bimonthly. $12 per year. in U.S. funds; single copy $2.

Tools of the Trade
Treehouse Mountain
Reeds Bridge Rd.
Conway, MA 01341-9713

Mainly asteroid interpretation, natal and event. Thirty-day ephemeris for trans-Neptunians and 5-day ephemeris for 39 asteroids. Monthly. $15 per year; foreign, $20.

URANIA
840 Eighth Ave. #5M
New York, NY 10019

Articles and letters about Uranian astrology and cosmobiology. Quarterly. Write for rates.

The Uranian
San Diego Astrological Society
P.O. Box 16430
San Diego, CA 92116

Write for details.

Uranian Forum
Penelope Publications
7671 N.W. 6th St.
Plantation, FL 33324

Uranian astrology magazine lesson plans. Bi-monthly. $20 per yr.; foreign $30 1st. class, $25 surface.

The Washington Astrology Forum Newsletter/ Astroturf
406 North Howard St., #403
Alexandria, VA 22304

Timely articles with charts, announcements, and local happenings. Quarterly. Membership $12 per yr.; newsletter $7 per yr.

Welcome To Planet Earth
The Great Bear
P.O. Box 5164
Eugene, OR 97405

Timely articles on national and international matters, daily transit insights with references to void-of-course moon and Chiron. Monthly. $30 per yr.; foreign please write for rates.

W.S.A. Astrological Newsletter
Western States Astrology Research Group
P.O. Box 1083
Newport Beach, CA 92663-0083

Book reviews, letters, financial/astronomy pages, announcements of astrological seminars and conferences worldwide, and other happenings of interest. Monthly with Nov./Dec. issue combined. Nonmember subscriptions $12 per yr.

Index

Index

Bold face page numbers denote primary references;
Italicized page numbers denote references to illustrations

A

AAP. *See* Association for Astrological Psychology (AAP)

ABA, 546

Aberdeen Astrology Group, 551

Abraham, 237

Abrams, Griff, 227, 228

Ab'l-Rayhan Muhammad ibn Ahmad Al-Biruni. *See* Al-Biruni

Abu'l'Abbas Ma'mun ibn Ma'mun, 11

Abu Ma'shar, 271; *Introductorium in astronomia,* 273

Abundantia, **1**

Academie Voor Astrol. Chiron, 549

Academy of Astrology, 552

ACA PF Astrological Studies, 552

Accidental ascendant, **1**

Accidental dignity, **1–2**

Achelous, 108

Achilles: asteroid, **2**; hero, 466

ACON, 549

Acronycal, **2**

ACS. *See* Astro Computing Services (ACS)

ACS Publications, 369

Adad, **3**

Adam: and Lilith, 330

Adams, Evangeline, **3–4**, 156, 262, 285, 324; *Astrology for Everyone,* 3; *Astrology: Your Place Among the Stars,* 3; *Astrology Your Place in the Sun,* 3; *The Bowl of Heaven,* 3, 265, 282; first client, 263; and horary astrology, 282; *Monthly Forecasts,* 3

Adams, George, 3

Adams, Harriette E. (Smith), 3

Adams, John Quincy, 3

Addey, John, **4**, 221, 241, 474, 513; *Astrology Reborn,* 4; *Harmonics Anthology,* 4; *Harmonics in Astrology,* 4 *Selected Writings,* 4

Adjusted calculation date, **5**

Admetos, **5**, 150, 300

Adonis, 48

Adorea, **5**

AEBHU, 552

Aegipan, 108

AERA (France), 547

Aesculapius, 466, 471

Aesop: *The Lion and the Mouse,* 325; *The Lion in Love,* 325; *The Lion's Share,* 325, 326

Aestival signs, **5**

Aeternitas, **6**

Aex, 108

AFA. *See* American Federation of Astrologers (AFA)

AFA Bulletin/Today's Astrologer, 559

AFAN. *See* Association for Astrological Networking (AFAN)

AFAN Network Newsletter, 559

Affinity, **6**

Affliction, **6**

Age of Aquarius, **7–8**, 279, 372. *See also* New Age

"Age of Aquarius: A Modern Myth, The," (Campion), 7

Age of Pisces: and ministry of Jesus, 7

Age of Plenitude (Rudhyar), 460

Age of Taurus, 372–373

Ages of Man, **8**

Agricultural astrology, **8–9**, 80, 184, 213

Agrippa, Cornelius: *De occulta philosophia,* 275

Ostrander, Sheila: *Astrological Birth Control,* 87, 88; *Psychic Discoveries Behind the Iron Curtain,* 87
Ottawa Astrological Society, 546
Ouspensky, Pyotr, 348
Ox (Chinese zodiac), 125, 126
Oxford University: founding of, 272

P

PAI. *See* Professional Astrologers, Inc.
Painswick Astrolabe, *51*
Pales, **405**
Pallas, 45, 46, 47, 48, 114, 312, **405**
Palmerston North Astrology, 550
Palmistry, 400, 406, *407,* 504
Pan, 473
Pandora: two celestial bodies with name of, **406,** 408
Paracelsus, 274, 289
Paradise, **408**
Parallel, **409**
Paran, 335, **409**
Paré, Ambroise, 139
Parker, Ann: *Astrology and Alcoholism,* 17
Parker, Derek and Julia: *The Compleat Astrologer,* 191, 294, 540
Pars Fortunae. *See* Part of Fortune
Parsifal, **409**
Part of Fortune, 29, 141, **409–411,** *410*
Partile, **411**
Partridge, John, **411–412,** 423; *The Black Life of John Gadbury,* 215; *Defectio Geniturarum,* 411; *Mikropanastron,* 411; *Opus Reformatum,* 411; and Placidian house system, 411, 423
Passion of the Western Mind, The (Tarnas), 503
Past-lives therapy, 67
Patientia, **412**
Paul, Saint: and Tarsus, 372
Pax, 142, **413**
Pearce, Alfred J. (Zadkiel), 258
Pecker, **413**
Pegasus Products, 209
Peking Observatory, *117*
Pellegrini, Robert J.: "The Astrological 'Theory' of personality: An unbiased test by a biased observer," 439
Pentateuch (Dorotheus), 14, 31
Perceval (De Troyes), 409
Peregrine, **413**

Perigee, 13, 22, **414,** *414*
Perihelions, 22, **414,** *415*
Periodical lunation, **414**
Peron, Evita, 52
Perry, Glenn A., **414–415**; "Inside Astrology: A Psychological Perspective," 414
Persephone, **415**
Perseus, 372
Perseverantia, **416**
Personal Transformation Centre, 550
Person-Centered Astrology (Rudhyar), 462
Personal name asteroids, **416–417**
Personal unconscious, 136
Perspectief, 550
Pessard, Emile (Louis Fortúne), 458
Petosiris: textbook of, 270, 294
Pharmacopea (Culpepper's translation), 158
Philagoria, **417**
Philia, **417**
Philosophia, **418**
Philosophical Research Society, 238, 556
Philyra, 466
Phlegmatic, **418**
Phobos, 218, **418,** 419, 420
Phobos-Deimos archetype, 419
Photographica, **420**
Physics (Aristotle), 272
Piazzi, Giuseppi, 114
Picatrix, 274, 277
Pickford, Mary, 3
Pig (Chinese zodiac), 125, 127
Pimander (Ficino), 274
Pioneer probe, 218
Pisces, 7, **421**; characteristics of, 421; colors correlated with, 137; gemstones correlated with, 137; key words for, 422; relation to Neptune, 17; short ascension and, 39; and water triplicity, 188
Pittsburgh Astrology Association, 556
Pittsburghis, **422**
Placidean house system, 318, 411, **422–423,** 540
Planetarization of Consciousness, The (Rudhyar), 462
"Planetary heredity," 222
Planetary Influence (Broughton), 93
Planetary moon studies, 218
Planetary moons, **425–426.** *See also* Jupiter, moons of; Mars, moons of
Planetary periods: in Hindu astrology, 254–255

and mythology, 385; and Vernon Clark tests for, 441. *See also* Astrotherapy; Jung, Carl; Humanistic astrology

Psychopathology: application of astrology to, 67, 68

Ptolemy, Claudius, 7, 16, 50, 184, 476–477, 506; *Almagest,* 12, 14, 18, 270, 272, 273, 450; on bicorporeal signs, 85; *Centiloquy,* 377; on Dexter, 167; equal house system of, 294; on Paran, 409; on planets and weather, 368; on prenatal events, 142; on synastry, 496; *Tetrabiblos,* 12, 14, 15, 261, 270, 271, 272, 280, 423, 442, 496; and tropical zodiac, 536

Pulsar: The Journal of Scottish Astrology, 564

Pulsar Association, 551

Pulsars, 217

Pulse of Life, The (Rudhyar), 461

Pythagoras, of Samos, 238, 268, **442**; and idea of reincarnation, 442; number mysticism of, 396

Pythagoreanism, 268

Pythagorean theorem: Euclidean, 12

Q

Quadrant, **443**, *443, 444. See also* Astrolabe

Quadrepedal, **444**

Qualities, 84, **444–445**. *See also* Cardinal quality; Fixed quality; Mutable quality

Quasars, 217

Querent, **445**

Quesited, **446**

Quetzalcoatl, **446**

Quigley, Joan, 282; *What Does Joan Say?,* 448

Quincunx, 42, 169, **446**

Quindecile, 42, **446**

Quintile, 42, 316, **446**

R

Rabbit (Chinese zodiac), 125, 126

Radical, **447**

Radix, **447**

Radix Vitae. *See* Root of Life

Rah Humanistic Astrological Network, 547

Ram, **447**. *See also* Aries

Ranavira, 250

Rania (Rudhyar), 459

Raphael. *See* Smith, Robert C.

Raphael's Ephemeris (Smith), 258, 277, 480

Rasi, 253. *See also* Natal chart

Rasle, Leyla, 462

Rat (Chinese zodiac), 125

Ravishments (Rudhyar), 458

Rawlins, Dennis, 488–489

Rays from the Rosy Cross, 243

Reagan, Ronald, 52, 448

Reagan, Nancy: *My Turn,* 447, 448

Reagans: and astrology, **447–448**

Rebirth of Hindu Music (Rudhyar), 459

Reception, **449**

Reconstruction of Mesoamerican Astrology (Scofield), 471

Rectification, 16, 52, **449**

Red Bird of Summer, 118, 124–125

Reformation. *See* History of Western astrology

Refranation, **450**

Refugium, 548

Regan, Donald: *For the Record,* 447

Regiomontanus, **450**; *Ephemeris ad XXXII Annos Futuros,* 273

Regiomontanus system, 377, **450**

Registry Sidereal Astrology, 556

Regulus, 457

Regulus Award, 36, 160, 240, 307, 345

Reincarnation: The Cycle of Necessity, 238

Reincarnation, **450–451**; ancient doctrines, of, 32; and esoteric astrology, 193; Hindu theory of, 250; karma and astrology, 450–451; Mann's principles and, 348; Pythagorean idea of, 442

Reinhardt, Melanie: *Chiron and the Healing Journey,* 129

"Relocation Profile" (Pottenger), 431

Remarks on Astrology and Astromedical Botany (Broughton), 93

Renaissance, astrology during the. *See* History of Western astrology

Research, astrological, **451–453**

Reseau d'Astrologie Humaniste, 547

Retrograde, 169, **453**

Retrograde application, **454**

Retrograde Planets: Transversing the Inner Landscape (Sullivan), 493

Return, **454–455**

Return from No-Return (Rudhyar), 460

Revolution, **455**

"Revolution of Years of the World," 13, 30. *See also* Ingresses

Ruperti, Alexander, 307
Ruth, **464**

S

Sabian Assembly: courses for, 459; founding of, 309
Sabian symbols, 165, **465**
Sabian Symbols, The (Jones), 310
Sabine, **465**
Sacred Architecture, 348
SAFA, 546. *See also* Association of Scandinavian Professional Astrologers
Sagittarius, 211, **465–466**; and the Archer, 33; characteristics of, 465; colors correlated with, 137; gemstones correlated with, 225; and fire triplicity, 188; key words for, 466; long ascension and, 39
Sagittarius Rising, 556
Sakoian, Frances, 36, 517
Salmeschiniaka, The, 270
Salzedo, Carlos, 459
Sandan, 372
San Diego Astrological Conference, 349
San Diego Astrological Society, 556
Sanguine, **467**
San Joaquin Astrology Association, 556
Sapientia, **467**
Sappho, 192, **467**
Sasportas, Howard, **468**; *The Gods of Change*, 468
Satellite, 24, **468**
Saturn, **469–470**; and affliction, 6; and Ages of Man, 8; as barren planet, 79; and chronocrators, 132; climacteric conjunction of, 134; and the Gauquelins' research, 220; gemstones correlated with, 225; and Jovian moons, 219; rulership of, 469; as taskmaster, 469
Saturnine, **470**
Saturn in Transit: Boundaries of the Mind, Body and Soul (Sullivan), 493
Saturn-Jupiter conjunctions, 14, 132. *See also* Star of Bethlehem
Saturn Return. *See* Return
Saturn und Blei (Kolisko), 320
Scales, 10, **470**. *See also* Libra
SCASA Newsletter, 564
Schema, **470**
School of Mythic Astrology, 40

Schroeder, Lynn: *Astrological Birth Control*, 87, 88; *Psychic Discoveries Behind the Iron Curtain*, 87
Schwenck, Theodore, 320
Scientific astrology, 279
Scientific Astrology Research, 556
Scientific Basis of Astrology, The (Gauquelin), 222
Scofield, Bruce, **470–471**; *Aztec Astro-Report*, 471; *Aztec Circle of Destiny*, 471; *Daily Astro-Report*, 471; *Day-Signs: Native American Astrology*, 471; *Reconstruction of Mesoamerican Astrology*, 471; *Timing of Events: Electional Astrology*, 471
Scorpio, **471–472**; characteristics of, 471; colors correlated with, 137; as fixed sign, 207; gemstones correlated with, 225; key words for, 471; long ascension and, 39; and Pluto, 1; and water triplicity, 188
Scorpio School of Astrology, 379
Scot, Michael, 273; *Liber introductorius*, 273
Scottish Astrological Association, 551
Scriabin, Alexander Nikolayevich, 458
Sea Bri, 89
Seafarer, 89
Search Astrological New Moon, 549
Search for the Christmas Star (Michelsen and Simms), 369
Secondary progression, **472**
Second Station, **472**
Secret Destiny of America, The, 238
Sedgwick, Philip, 55, 216; *Astrology of Deep Space*, 55
Seed and Directions for a New Humanity, A (Rudhyar), 462
Seeds for Greater Living (Rudhyar), 461
Seelig, Johann, 257
Seesaw pattern, **473**
Selected Writings (Addey), 4
Selene, **473**
Self-Unfoldment by Disciplines of Realization (Hall), 238
Selva, Henri, 377
Semioctile, 42, **473**
Semisextile, 42, **473**
Semisquare, 42, **473**
Separating aspect, **474**
Sepharial. *See* Old, W. Gorn
Septile, 42, **474**